The
Modern
Jewish Experience
in
World Cinema

The Modern Jewish Experience in World Cinema

Lawrence Baron, editor

Brandeis University Press
WALTHAM, MASSACHUSETTS

Brandeis University Press
An imprint of University Press of New England
www.upne.com
© 2011 Brandeis University
All rights reserved
Manufactured in the United States of America
Designed by Dean Bornstein
Typeset in Adobe Garamond by Keystone
Typesetting, Inc.

For permission to reproduce any of the material in
this book, contact Permissions, University Press of
New England, One Court Street, Suite 250, Lebanon NH 03766; or visit www.upne.com

Library of Congress Cataloging-in-Publication
Data
The modern Jewish experience in world cinema /
Lawrence Baron, editor.
p. cm.
Includes bibliographical references and index.
ISBN 978-1-61168-208-3 (cloth : alk. paper)
ISBN 978-1-61168-199-4 (pbk. : alk. paper)
1. Jews in motion pictures. 2. Holocaust, Jewish
(1939–1945), in motion pictures. 3. Israel—In
motion pictures. I. Baron, Lawrence.
PN 1995.9.J46M54 2011
791.43'652924—dc23
2011037717

This book was published with the generous support
of the Lucius N. Littauer Foundation.

5 4 3 2 1

*This book is dedicated
to the loving memory of
Gertrude Rubin (1921–2010):
mother-in-law, movie buddy,
poet, political activist,
and a real mensch.*

Contents

Preface

I began my sabbatical in 2008 determined to write the definitive survey of the depiction of Jews and Judaism in world cinema. I had been teaching a course on this topic for eighteen years. Each year when I designed the syllabus, I faced a growing problem: the existing books on Jewish film were either too narrowly focused or out of date. The cost of customized readers, consisting of copies of articles from journals or excerpts from books, became increasingly prohibitive as the legal victory of the publishing companies against Kinko's was enforced. Putting material online was another option, but it was time-consuming for me and often frustrating for students, as their older computers couldn't handle all the data, links broke, and the university's website sometimes went down. A book in the hand is worth two in cyberspace.

The more I read the existing scholarship on Jewish films and viewed as many of them as I could obtain on videotape or DVD, the more I had a gnawing feeling that the subject was too vast and varied for me to do an adequate job of teaching it. When I stumbled on Joel Rosenberg's marvelous overview of American Jewish film ("Jewish Experience on Film—An American Overview," *American Jewish Yearbook* [1996]), I realized what I was up against:

> *What* one needs to study is immense. The subject encompasses the world output of cinema. . . . It requires some familiarity with film theory, past and present. . . . It properly requires a knowledge of several languages, and of film scholarship in those languages. . . . It entails familiarity with particular Jewish film industries, such as Yiddish-language and Israeli film. . . . It involves examination and comparison of changing trends in fiction, film, documentary film, and political propaganda film. . . . It involves the concurrent histories of the film representation of other national, ethnic, and social groups. And, of course, it requires knowledge of modern Jewish and world history, of the history of anti-Semitism, of the rise and fall of Nazism, of the planning, enactment, and aftermath of the "Final Solution," of survivor experience, and the vast realm of postwar reflection and debate on the Holocaust and its representation. (5)

The response of Barack Obama, then a presidential candidate, to a question in a 2008 debate about when a fetus becomes endowed with human rights kept running through my mind: "That's above my pay grade."

The next step was the realization that I didn't need to reinvent the wheel. Brilliant analyses of key films produced over the course of the last hundred years were already in print. I approached their authors to see if they'd be willing to edit their pieces to be less technical, shorter, and more student-friendly, or if they'd let me perform that function. When a particular film had been overlooked or needed a more updated interpretation, I asked scholars with the expertise in the appropriate disciplines and subjects to write original essays. What began as my project quickly turned into a collaborative effort. I have enjoyed working with all the contributors to this anthology, even though I know most of them only through e-mail correspondence. I am indebted to them for their willingness to share their insights with a new generation of students enrolled in Jewish cinema courses.

Choosing which films to include in the anthology was the hardest decision. Many motion pictures stood out as classics, but other less distinguished ones covered significant aspects of the Jewish experience that merited inclusion as well. In 2009 *Moment* magazine asked twelve Jewish film critics and scholars to name the five greatest Jewish films. Only one film, *Fiddler on the Roof*, received three votes; five others got two (*Annie Hall*, *Blazing Saddles*, *The Frisco Kid*, *Green Fields*, and *The Pawnbroker*). As part of the review process of my book proposal, Brandeis University Press solicited the advice of professors who taught Jewish cinema courses. Once again there was a lack of consensus about which films should be included in my book. Although there were only a few objections to the majority of films on my initial list, there were far more recommendations of others I should add. Ultimately, I am responsible for the choices, a number of which were dictated by practical concerns about the size of the anthology.

As noted in the introduction, I felt strongly that any motion picture analyzed in the collection needed to be readily available in English dialogue or a subtitled version for purchase or rental by students and professors alike. One of my complaints about other surveys of Jewish cinema is that they devoted attention to motion pictures that were no longer accessible to the viewing public in any format. The acquisitions editors at Brandeis University Press dubbed this the "Netflix rule." Fortunately, within the past three years, the numbers of formerly hard-to-find films that have been released as DVDs and are now stocked by various Internet retailers and organizations that distribute and preserve films have increased exponentially.

This anthology provides instructors with the flexibility to select from a range of movies for courses taught on particular themes and national cinemas, and from a variety of disciplines. Its coverage of American, Holocaust, and Israeli cinema in particular should make it attractive to professors offering courses on these subjects. However, I hope that its global approach will prompt those who teach courses on Jewish cinema to internationalize the scope of their courses, and those who teach world or ethnic cinema courses to include the Jewish experience within them.

Now for the obligatory but heartfelt part of this preface: the acknowledgments. I could never have afforded to purchase my own copies of films, republish so many articles, and include so many stills without the financial assistance of the Littauer Foundation, San Diego State University, and the university's History Department, to which I belong.

I appreciate the wise advice given by the following people, even though I have unwisely not always heeded it: Alan Berger, David Brenner, Steven Alan Carr, Hasia Diner, Gordon Dueck, Sylvia Barack Fishman, Sylvia Fuks Fried, Kathryn Hellerstein, Marnie Hughes-Warrington, Yvonne Kozlovsky Golan, Giacomo Lichtner, Joanna Michlic, Pamela Nadell, Riv Ellen Prell, Catherine Portuges, Sharon Rivo, Alan Rosen, Joel Rosenberg, Robert Rosenstone, Jim Ross, Michael Rubinoff, Alyssa Goldstein Sepinwall, Susan Rubin Suleiman, Mary Wauchope, David Weinberg, Stephen Whitfield, Jennifer William, and Rochelle Wright.

Brandeis University Press was my first choice as a publisher because I had always been impressed both by the quality of their books and by their marketing of the works to the Jewish community and Jewish studies scholars. Another reason I wanted to have Brandeis University Press publish this book was that I had heard so many good things from Brandeis University Press authors about working with Phyllis Deutsch. Those comments have proved to be true. She gave me insightful feedback on the first and second versions of my book proposal and was an understanding, though tough, taskmaster after it was accepted. I appreciate her commitment to bringing this ambitious endeavor to fruition, particularly in a time when the printed page must compete fiercely with electronic venues for articles and books. I am grateful to all the people at Brandeis University Press who have assisted in various aspects of the publication of this book.

The National Center for Jewish Film provided me with screening copies of various films and a selection of stills from motion pictures that it distributes. The Photofest staff has been extremely helpful in obtaining the majority of stills used in the anthology.

When I was racing against a deadline, Claudia McMahon, a dear friend and my former administrative assistant, came to my rescue with her good humor and meticulous attention to the formatting and indexing of the manuscript. If it weren't for her, the publication of this book would have been much delayed.

Finally, I thank my family for their patience and support: my son, Ari, for watching movies with me; my sister, Bonnie; brother, Arnie; sister-in-law, Gail; and brother-in-law, Michael, for their enthusiasm about the project—and above all my wife, Bonnie, for putting up with my long hours at the computer and exhibiting compassion and love when I probably didn't deserve it.

Now get comfortable in your seat, darken the room, and enjoy the movies discussed in the book, not only for their entertainment value, but for what they can teach you about the modern Jewish experience.

Lawrence Baron
San Diego, California
February 2011

Abbreviations of DVD Rental and Purchase Sources

Abbreviations appear in brackets next to the director's name at the beginning of each essay.

- **A** Available from most online DVD distributors and wholesalers, like Amazon (http://www.amazon.com), Barnes and Noble (http://www.barnesandnoble .com), Blockbuster (http://www.block buster.com), Facets Multimedia (http:// facets.org), Half.com (http://www.half .ebay.com), and Netflix (http://movies .netflix.com).
- **EM** Available from Ergo Media (http:// www.jewishvideo.com).
- **NCJF** Available from National Center for Jewish Film (http://www.jewishfilm.org).

The
Modern
Jewish Experience
in
World Cinema

Introduction

The Modern Jewish Experience
in World Cinema

LAWRENCE BARON

Shortly before the end of the nineteenth century, inventors in England, France, Germany, and the United States simultaneously developed cameras and projectors to transform a series of sequential still photographs of a moving subject into the illusion of motion. Motion pictures rapidly emerged as a cheap and popular form of mass entertainment. Since they were originally silent, relying on images rather than spoken dialogue, films had an appeal that transcended national borders. Jewish characters showed up on theater screens when cinema attempted to mirror current events. The first movie image of a Jew appeared in 1899, in French short subjects reenacting key incidents from the Dreyfus Affair that had polarized French politics and world opinion during the last half of the 1890s. The pogroms—riots marked by vandalism and violence against Jewish communities—that swept the Jewish Pale of Settlement between 1903 and 1905 and the highly publicized 1911 arrest and 1913 trial of Mendel Beilis for ritual murder—both of which were instigated by the czarist regime in Russia, where the world's largest Jewish population lived—inspired films produced in France, Germany, the United States, and the Soviet Union, after the Russian Communists came to power in 1917. The escalation of anti-semitic discrimination and persecution in Eastern and Central Europe, and the lure of economic opportunity and civic equality in Argentina, Pal-

estine, the United States, and Western Europe served as the impetuses for massive demographic shifts that would radically change where Jews resided and how they defined themselves over the course of the twentieth century. Coinciding with the rise of the motion picture industry, these Jewish experiences of modernization provided plotlines for a considerable corpus of films.

Wherever they lived prior to 1700 CE, with the notable exception of Ethiopia, Jews read the same Bible and recited prayers in Hebrew. They ordered their lives according to 613 biblical commandments, which rabbinic scholars interpreted to apply them to the novel situations encountered in exile from Israel. Jews remembered a distant past when they had constituted a single holy nation and expected to return to their ancestral homeland, when a human leader would combine the messianic qualities prophesied in the Bible and lead them back there. They groomed and dressed themselves differently than the gentile majority, partly to maintain their own traditions and partly to obey state laws requiring them to wear badges, belts, colors, or hats that visibly identified them as Jews. Jews segregated themselves to practice their religion, even before they were required to reside in designated neighborhoods in predominantly Muslim societies or confined within ghetto walls in predominantly Christian ones. Although the Jews were subject to the authority of gentiles, who imposed additional taxes on them and relegated them to an inferior status, isolation afforded the Jews communal autonomy to adjudicate disputes among themselves in rabbinic courts, tax their fellow Jews to support Jewish religious and social services, and teach Jewish boys Hebrew to read sacred texts and perpetuate Judaism.

Recent surveys of Jewish history emphasize the diversity of the Jewish experience in the Diaspora. Jews wove the customs, cuisine, and languages of their host societies into the fabric of their lives. The Sephardim, descendants of the Jews expelled from Spain in 1492, spoke a version of Spanish called Ladino; the Ashkenazim, whose ancestors hailed from Central and Eastern Europe, communicated in Yiddish, a mixture of German, Hebrew, and Slavic languages; and the Mizrahim, who lived in North Africa and the Middle East, synthesized Arabic and Hebrew into Judeo-Arabic. All of these hybrid tongues employed Hebrew letters when they were transcribed onto the printed or written page. The degree to which the Jews' cuisine, folkways, and worship were influenced by the surrounding culture generally reflected the extent and cordiality of their relations with their gentile neighbors.

Jewish religious adaptation, secularization, and social integration began to accelerate sharply in the eighteenth century, when the revolutionary regimes in France and the United States granted the Jews equality. The liberalization of Western European governments and the concurrent commercialization and industrialization of their economies, the national unification of Germany and Italy in the second half of the nineteenth century, and the Russian Revolution of 1917 conferred legal equality on the Jews. As individuals, Jews disproportionately benefited from the development of the capitalist economies that replaced premodern modes of ownership, production, and trade. They often gravitated toward the businesses and professions that burgeoned under the new system or refashioned their traditional functions as moneylenders, pawnbrokers, and ped-

dlers into their modern counterparts as bankers, entrepreneurs, and retailers. In a process whose pace and timing varied according to how and when Jewish emancipation was granted in their respective countries, most Jews discarded traditional garb and grooming to make themselves visibly indistinguishable from the gentiles who were their fellow citizens. Moreover, by incorporating modern theories of history and science, they modified their religious beliefs and rituals to affirm their patriotism to the states that treated them as citizens.

Conversely, Christian clerics, trade and professional groups, and rulers whose power and status were eroded by the momentous transitions that had liberated the Jews accused them of collectively subverting the foundations of what had once been avowedly Christian societies. State-sponsored discrimination, official reluctance to respond to spontaneous pogroms, the subsequent fomentation of them in czarist Russia, the rise of populist political antisemitism in France and Germany in the late nineteenth century, and the Holocaust—which annihilated two-thirds of Europe's Jewish population—spurred massive Jewish immigration to North America, South America, and Palestine. In turn the growth of the Jewish Yishuv (settlement) in Palestine before and after Israeli independence in 1948 increased the antagonism of Arab nations in particular, and Muslim ones in general, toward the Jewish communities in the Middle East, ultimately inducing the latter to flee to the new Jewish state. Jews who immigrated to Palestine before 1948 and to Israel thereafter remained divided by their ethnic and religious origins while collectively exercising power over the Arab citizens, who were a minority in Israel and a Palestinian majority in the West Bank and Gaza after 1967.

The statistics attest to the dramatic shift in location of the main Jewish population centers. In 1880, 75 percent of the world's Jews resided in Eastern Europe, compared to 13.5 percent in the rest of Europe, 8 percent in the Middle East and North Africa, and 3.5 percent in North America. The estimated Jewish population in 2010 was 42 percent in North America, 42 percent in Israel, and 11 percent in Europe. Whereas Poland and Russia had the biggest Jewish communities in 1880, now Israel and the United States do. In Europe, France and the United Kingdom—whose Jewish populations were comparatively small in the nineteenth century—currently are home to the third and fifth largest Jewish populations in the world, respectively. Canada ranks fourth. The Soviet Union's formerly sizable Jewish population has dwindled to sixth as Jewish immigration, particularly to Israel and the United States, rose in the 1970s and 1980s and spiked with the collapse of communism in 1991. Argentina, which had beckoned as an attractive alternative to Palestine for Jewish agricultural settlement toward the end of the nineteenth century, now is the seventh largest Jewish community. The old European population centers have been supplanted by the new Jewish societies in the Americas and Israel.

These, however, are dry statistics about events and trends that drastically altered how people conceptualized what it meant to be Jewish. Although the history presented in feature films lacks the factual and interpretive complexity of historical scholarship, it provides viewers with a way to vicariously witness how seemingly abstract forces deeply affected the lives and deaths of characters whose stories they watch unfold. As Robert Rosenstone has remarked, "On the screen, several things occur simultaneously—image, sound, language, even text elements that support and work against each other to render a realm of meaning as different from written history as written was from oral history" (1995, 15).

The dramatization, personification, and visualization of how historical changes and individual choices were experienced fashion "prosthetic memories," to use Alison Landsberg's (2004, 20–21) term, which enable audiences to empathize with characters from backgrounds, eras, and places different from their own.

To be sure, historians and students need to identify discrepancies between the historical record and the film version of it. The first level of analyzing film as history requires identifying and explaining those discrepancies. As an entertainment medium that must rivet the audience's attention for usually 90 to 120 minutes, movies typically personify ethnic groups, political ideologies, religious beliefs, and social classes in the actions and dialogue of representative characters. They may collapse several historical personages into one, accelerate the passage of time, simplify causation, and impose morally edifying endings to satisfy the audience's need for closure. These devices, after all, derive from the economic concerns and previously successful formulas of filmmaking as a commercial enterprise.

Yet the re-envisioning of a historical event or trend also reveals the director's or screenwriter's interpretations of the subject matter and how they selectively recast the past to make it relevant to the present. To help readers separate the historical grain of truth—whether an accurate reproduction of a particular place and time, a poignant dramatization of the key dilemmas faced by those who inhabited that milieu, or their emotional responses and reasoning in coping with these dilemmas—from the chaff of pure fabrication and cinematic stylization, I have ended each chapter with bibliographies of pertinent articles, books, and websites that provide background information on the movie analyzed in it. If the movie is adapted from a work of fiction or based on a historical account, its source is listed separately to allow readers to compare the written and the filmed version.

Cinematic depictions of the transformation of Jewish identities in the twentieth century shed light on the opportunities afforded by acculturation and the psychological toll of adopting a different mind-set. They let viewers eavesdrop on what happens within the Jewish subculture when one of its members transgresses traditional Jewish beliefs, family structures, gender roles, and relations with gentiles. Motion pictures can convey a semblance of what it was like to face discrimination despite legal emancipation; persecution as an "alien" minority or potential ally caught in the crossfire between contending ideologies and nationalisms in Eastern Europe; or protection for a fortunate few and deprivation and death in ghettos and camps designed to dehumanize, enervate, and ultimately liquidate the majority of Jews confined in them during the Holocaust. Legitimizing the establishment of Israel, portraying its internecine conflicts, and chronicling the ongoing hostility of neighboring Arab states and the Palestinians who remained within its borders or became refugees have been central concerns of Israeli films. Recent films from the Diaspora have grappled with the negotiation and preservation of Jewish identity in societies where the pressure to assimilate contends with the multicultural paradigm of mutual respect for ethnic, racial, and religious diversity.

But, as Pierre Sorlin (1980) reminds us, movies about the past are always about the present, too. Although directors usually try to imbue their rec-

reations of the ambience, conversations, motivations, personages, and sounds of an era and event with historical authenticity, they inevitably focus on occurrences, issues, and personalities that will resonate with contemporary audiences and their immediate concerns. Period pieces about a bygone phase of Jewish life not only possess relevance to the current status of Jews, but also to broader themes of ethnicity, gender roles, politics, race, and religion. When analyzing films as representations of history, keep in mind that they are delving into the past to salvage what is relevant in the present. The credibility of characterizations and story lines is just as important as their accuracy.

Jewish cinema consists of films whose plots revolve around events or cultural, economic, gendered, political, personal, religious, or social complications that arise because their antagonists or protagonists are Jews. This does not necessarily mean that these motion pictures serve as vehicles through which Jewish filmmakers and producers champion Jewish causes. Although Jews were disproportionately represented in every aspect of the American film industry, some of the greatest Jewish movies—like *Gentleman's Agreement* and even *Fiddler on the Roof* (whose director, Norman Jewison, is a Protestant)—were either directed or produced by gentiles. The Jewish movie moguls who controlled most of Hollywood's major studios until the 1960s felt constrained from tackling Jewish issues. When a considerable portion of their audiences consisted of first-generation immigrants, they naturally turned their cameras to the immigrant experience shared by Irish, Italian, Jewish, and other newcomers from Europe. Not surprisingly, after restrictive quotas were adopted in the 1920s to reduce the flood of immigration to a trickle, movies became more Americanized— along with the composition of the viewing public.

Thereafter the Jewish moguls approached the portrayal of Jewish characters more gingerly, if at all, for several reasons: they pitched their productions to the broadest possible audience; they prided themselves on being fully Americanized and having effaced their immigrant origins; and they observed the industry's Production Code, promulgated in the early 1930s, in depicting ethnic minorities and religious denominations, anticipating resistance to any images of Jews and Judaism that could be misconstrued as special advocacy or negative stereotypes.

These inhibitions were not uniquely American. In his insightful essay on the evolution of American Jewish film, Joel Rosenberg asserts "that the presence of the Jew in film needs to be rethought in the context of cinema history as a whole" (1996, 4). Expressions of overt ethnic or religious identity were downplayed or suppressed in the films of other liberal countries like England and France, in deference to homogenizing concepts of citizenship. There were, however, notable exceptions like *The Grand Illusion*, in which the antifascist exigencies of the 1930s compelled Jean Renoir to combat antisemitism. In Austrian and German cinema prior to Hitler's accession to power in 1933 and the *Anschluss* of 1938, Jewish characters appeared in biblical and folkloric stories or in contemporary settings as salutary or sinister agents of modernization.

During its first two decades, the Soviet Union subsidized Yiddish-language films to contrast the oppression, poverty, and retrograde piety of the Jews in the *shtetls* of czarist Russia with the liberating horizons accessible to them in the atheistic, collectivist, and egalitarian utopia that the Bolsheviks were building. After World War II and the revelations of Germany's slaughter of Jews and people of other nationalities in Eastern Europe, the USSR and its satellite countries officially discouraged the production of, or withdrew from distribution, films that might stoke ethnic, national, and religious separatisms, which not only seethed under the surface in the Soviet bloc, but which Marxist ideology deemed reactionary identities that undermined the international solidarity of the working classes. Sporadic liberalization of Soviet rule briefly permitted filmmakers to introduce Jewish themes into their works, but only the eventual collapse of communism opened the field to more probing cinematic explorations of Jewish history in the region.

On the other hand, prewar Yiddish filmmakers outside the Soviet Union showcased a broader array of Jewish characters and perspectives because they marketed their pictures primarily to Jewish audiences. These films continued to be produced as long as a mass market of Yiddish speakers remained in Argentina, portions of Europe, and the United States. Though today this body of films is often looked back on nostalgically after the decimation of the old Jewish centers of Eastern Europe and the abandonment of the *Mame-Loshn* (mother tongue) by the descendants of Jewish immigrants in the Americas, earlier Yiddish films frequently satirized the backwardness, hardships, and repressiveness of the *shtetl* and subsequently romanticized its traditional Jewish culture in the 1930s to memorialize a lifestyle on the brink of extinction.

Israeli films have followed the opposite trajectory. To foster patriotism, they initially lionized the early Zionist pioneers and fighters in the War of Independence. The ethnic and social stratification between the European Ashkenazim, who formed the leadership of the dominant Zionist Labor Party prior to 1948, and the Mizrahim from Arab and Islamic lands, whose mass aliyah (immigration to Israel) occurred primarily after independence, was treated as the butt of benevolent humor or as a problem that would be resolved gradually through "absorption," intermarriage, and military service. For the most part, these films were aimed at Israeli audiences or at Jews in the Diaspora. The cinematic consensus unraveled starting in the late 1970s, as the resulting of a number of developments: (1) the eventual disposition of the territories and the large Palestinian population inhabiting them became an increasingly divisive issue in Israeli politics; (2) the right-wing Likud Party under Menachem Begin gained power for the first time in the 1977 elections, owing partly to a shift in the Mizrahi vote; (3) the nation started its first war of choice, in Lebanon in 1982—a war whose legacy remains a bitter bone of contention; (4) mass immigration from the Soviet Union and its successor states, along with the rescue and resettlement of Jews from Ethiopia, dramatically diversified the ethnic and racial composition of Israeli society; (5) the concomitant growing political influence and insularity of the *heredim* (ultra-Orthodox Jews) deepened the chasm between secular and religious Jews; and (6) multinational financing and distribution started to become more common for Israeli films.

Consequently, over the last thirty years, Israeli movies have become more critical of governmental policies, especially pertaining to its wars in Lebanon, the treatment of Palestinians in the West Bank and Gaza, and the building of Jewish settlements there. The influx of Russian and Ethiopian Jews rekindled cinematic interest in the ethnic and racial differences among the Jewish communities that constitute Israeli society. The heightened assertiveness of the heredim and their antiquated attitudes toward family and women have elicited the production of some films that have been highly critical of their brand of Judaism, and of others that have idealized its vir-

tues. Some Israeli filmmakers have been accused of pandering to foreign audiences, critics, and investors by presenting politically correct messages about controversial Israeli policies, in the hope of winning awards, funding, and box-office success abroad. The creators of such films contend that they are merely articulating the grievances harbored by many dovish and secular Israelis.

In the Diaspora widespread acceptance of the multicultural model for appreciating the differences among ethnic, racial, and religious groups has fostered the production of more distinctly Jewish films. Whereas mainstream American movies and their counterparts in Western and Central Europe previously muted the Jewish dimensions of their narratives and traits of their Jewish characters, there has been a recent trend to accentuate the ethnic, racial, and religious dimensions of their stories and traits of their characters. In the United States this can be attributed to the success of the African American civil rights movement and the ethnic, feminist, gay, racial, and religious identity politics it spawned. The making of more self-consciously ethnic films in Western and Central Europe was a response to the large-scale immigration of people from former colonies in Africa and Asia, or to the employment of guest workers from less economically developed parts of the world, respectively. In Germany and to a lesser extent in the countries of the former Soviet bloc, Jewish themes have been reintroduced into the plotlines of films to come to terms with the devastation of the Jewish communities that once resided there, and whose absence has generated a willingness among socially conscious filmmakers to reconsider the lingering impact of Jews in the prewar and wartime histories of their nations.

In addition to contextualizing films in terms of when and where they were produced, or gauging their historical verisimilitude or fidelity to the fictional works from which they were adapted, the authors in this anthology employ a variety of approaches to examine how films distort, interpret, and reflect the events and trends they purport to portray. These include close readings of the films that analyze the implicit and explicit messages conveyed by the acting, casting, cinematography, dialogue, direction, editing, genres, iconography, music, and soundtrack, all of which contribute to how audiences respond to and understand the narratives they watch. Some of the essays apply the insights of feminist, Marxist, postcolonial, postmodern, psychoanalytic, queer, and trauma theory to films, detecting alternative latent meanings in the films that might be perceived by audiences from different ethnic, national, racial, religious, political, and social backgrounds or sexual orientations. As should be expected, the convictions of the reviewers shape their approval or disapproval of how the Jewish themes in the films are presented. Even when I do not concur with their interpretations, I am impressed by the erudition and logic of their arguments.

I categorize the movies encompassed by this volume as world cinema. I realize that this term is commonly used as a synonym for non-English and non-Hollywood productions. It is difficult to dispute, however, that the modern Jewish experience has been global, including the acculturation and upward mobility of Jews in liberal societies, their sensitivity to the persistence of antisemitic biases even where they ostensibly have achieved acceptance, their vulnerability as political scapegoats under both Nazi and Soviet rule, the transnational repercussions of the Zionist movement and the establishment of the state of Israel, and the spectrum of religious and secular identities espoused by Jews to accommodate or resist the sweeping historical changes that have transpired since the invention of motion pictures. Of the

fifty-nine films studied in this book, thirty-one are foreign productions and twenty-eight are from the United States. Of course, Hollywood movies often have enlisted the talents of émigré and foreign filmmakers. Many of the films covered in the following pages are recognized as classics, but others are less well-known movies whose merit lies in their treatment of important but neglected aspects of the modern Jewish experience on screen.

As Laura Marks has remarked, "intercultural cinema operates at the intersection of two or more cultural regimes of knowledge" and "must deal with the issue of where meaningful knowledge is located, in the awareness that it is between cultures and can never be fully verified in the terms of one regime or the other" (2000, 24). Through much of its history, Jewish cinema has been positioned at this vantage point between cultures, and the critical distance that this dichotomy affords is still evident in the independent American, European, Israeli, and Latin American films explicated in the last three parts of this anthology. Yet one should not automatically discount Hollywood productions as unable to handle controversial Jewish subject matter. *Crossfire* and *Gentleman's Agreement*, for example, may now seem tame in their exposure of antisemitic discrimination and sentiment in the United States, but they broached issues that many Americans of the time, including some Jewish studio owners, preferred not to be aired in public.

An international perspective on these films emerges not only from their countries of origin, but also from the geographical dispersion of the authors who have written the essays. Eighteen of the articles were penned by scholars residing in seven countries outside the United States: Belgium, Canada, Ireland, Israel, Mexico, New Zealand, and the United Kingdom. Their nuanced readings attest to a pervasive sense of estrangement, moral responsibility, or vulnerability that feature films about Jewish subject matter embody in their characters and the dilemmas they confront, although that sense has been progressively attenuated as Jews enter the mainstream of society. Many of the articles have been published elsewhere. Others I solicited for this collection. In the case of the former, the notes can be found in the original versions.

Although Jews underwent the process of accepting or rejecting the demands of modernization and struggling for equality in the not too distant past, their experience as portrayed in film has continuing relevance to ethnic, racial, and religious groups facing the same kinds of challenges in the present. Since many of the students who take Jewish cinema courses are not Jewish, I recommend comparing films about the Jewish experience with those on other immigrants and minorities whose status in the past or present was analogous to that of the Jews as discussed in this book. For example, I fondly recall the perceptive paper written by one of my Mexican-American students on the similarities between *Hester Street* (1975) and *Real Women Have Curves* (2002).

The diversification of global film distribution has opened up opportunities for screening films about Jewish subject matter. The proliferation of Jewish film festivals modeled after the San Francisco Jewish Film Festival, which was founded in 1980, has multiplied the venues available for the screening of Jewish-themed pictures. The advent of premium movie channels like HBO in 1975, cable stations like the Independent Film Channel, pay-per-view services, and Jewish cable networks serve as outlets for more self-consciously Jewish films. These films have found their niche in the comprehensive inventories afforded by major DVD and book retailers and renters like Ama-

zon, Barnes and Noble, Blockbuster, Facets, and Netflix. They are the only kinds of films rented or sold by Jewish companies and institutions like Ergo Media and the National Jewish Film Center. One important criterion for including the films discussed in this book was their availability for rental or sale from these sources. Corresponding to the Abbreviations: DVD Rental and Purchase Sources in the front of this volume, the letter in brackets after the title and director of a film at the top of each essay—or at the end of each citation in the appendix of alternate films—indicates a confirmed source for that particular film. All of the foreign films can be found in versions with English subtitles. I have listed the English title first and placed the foreign title in brackets.

This anthology fills a vacuum that currently exists for texts to assign in courses on modern Jewish cinema. Previous books on the portrayal of Jews and Jewish themes in motion pictures have fallen into one of three categories: studies of national or linguistic cinemas; discussions of key events and issues in modern Jewish life; and works on individual directors, producers, or films. Most scholarly attention has been paid to Hollywood's depiction of Jews and Jewish issues. Yet the standard surveys by Patricia Erens (1984) and Lester Friedman (1987) of this subject are now over twenty years old and do not discuss films released after 1983 or 1985, respectively. Erens's book remains in print; Friedman's does not. Since the coverage of both volumes is encyclopedic, their discussions of most films are superficial. This superficiality is even more pronounced in popular works about Jewish cinema, like Kathryn Bernheimer's collection of reviews, *The 50 Greatest Jewish Movies* (1998), and Joel Samberg's *Reel Jewish* (2000). Neal Gabler's collective biography of Hollywood's Jewish movie moguls (1988), a member of the third category of books, overgeneralizes about how their immigrant backgrounds and personal success undergirded their cinematic vision of the United States as a land of boundless opportunity. In addition, Gabler's book stops in the 1950s, when the studio system that the moguls had built was already in decline.

The Yiddish films produced in Europe and the United States until shortly after the end of World War II have received considerable scholarly attention. J. Hoberman's *Bridge of Light* (2010), which recently was republished in a new edition, exemplifies how film history should be written. It is indispensable for courses on Yiddish cinema, but it is limited to that niche. I am pleased to include Hoberman's discussion of *The Return of Nathan* in this anthology. Eric Goldman's (2011) survey of Yiddish films also has been released in a new edition. The other overview of Yiddish cinema, by Judith Goldberg (1983), and the reader edited by Sylvia Paskin (1999) have gone out of print.

Three surveys of Israeli cinema are currently available, but they all have a particular thematic focus: Ella Shohat's book on the construction of Israeli nationhood around the binary oppositions between East and West, which recently has appeared in a second edition (2010); Yosefa Loshitzky's exploration of Israeli identity politics in film (2001); and Raz Yosef's study of "queer masculinities and nationalism" in Israeli films (2004). Loshitzky and Shohat employ a postcolonial critique of Israel and promote a dovish political agenda. Loshitzky's postcolonialist reading of *Exodus* appears in this anthology. Since some of the most internationally acclaimed Israeli films have been produced between 2000 and 2010, I have included quite a few of them in my book.

Most thematic books on Jewish film deal with the cinematic representation of the Holocaust and its lingering impact on postwar Jewish life.

Ilan Avisar (1988), Joshua Hirsch (2004), Annette Insdorf (2003), Giacomo Lichtner (2008), Libby Saxton (2008), and I (Baron 2005) each trace the evolution of Holocaust cinema in two or more countries. André Colombat (1993), Judith Doneson (2002), Anton Kaes (1989), Millicent Marcus (2007), and Eric Santner (1990) focus on the cinema of one country. Caroline Picart and David Frank (2006) demonstrate how Holocaust movies resemble the narrative and visual strategies of American horror films.

Omer Bartov's *The "Jew" in Cinema* (2005) is an exception in its treatment of Jewish cinema from an international perspective. It examines films produced in Europe, North America, and Israel, starting with silent films like *The Golem* (1920) and going through films produced in the past decade like *The Pianist*. But Bartov warns readers that his objective is quite circumscribed: "The present study, however, focuses on a single, albeit pervasive theme: The manner in which the cinematic 'Jew' reflects the popularization, transformation, resistance to, and reintroduction of anti-Semitic imagery" (ix). Hence, the vast majority of films he analyzes are about antisemitism, the Holocaust, or the inversion of the stereotype of Jewish passivity in films about Israel. He omits American and European films that don't broach these subjects.

By its very nature, the last category of books concerns itself with individual films like *The Jazz Singer* and *Schindler's List*, or prominent Jewish directors. David Desser and Lester Friedman's *American Jewish Filmmakers* (2004) devotes chapters to Woody Allen, Mel Brooks, Sidney Lumet, and Paul Mazursky and has brief sections on Barry Levinson, Bryan Singer, and Steven Spielberg. With the exception of Lumet, these filmmakers did not start their movie careers until the 1960s. Desser and Friedman include many movies that have little overt Jewish content and exclude those by important Jewish directors like the Coen brothers, Jeremy Kagan, Joan Micklin Silver, and Barbra Streisand, to name but a few.

The essays in this volume offer readers explications of films that span the modern Jewish experience. The book begins with Jewish emancipation in Western Europe, the mass immigration to the United States, and the ethnic and religious oppression in Eastern Europe. It moves on to the Communist solution of transcending Jewish parochialism through economic egalitarianism; the "final solution" of Nazi Germany, and the collaboration, indifference, or resistance that it provoked in the countries Nazi Germany occupied or influenced; and the Zionist dream of building a Jewish state, whose realization in 1948 altered the status of Jews around the world. And it concludes with the varied identities that Jews have assumed in the Americas, Europe, and Israel since the Holocaust and the tolerance accorded to most, but not all, of them in the postwar period. By probing more deeply into the cinematic composition and historical contexts of these films, the contributors to this volume hope to enrich the experience of viewers.

The periods and regions covered in each part conform to the standard divisions employed to study modern Jewish history. France was the first European country to emancipate the Jews during the first phase of the French Revolution between 1789 and 1792. The enfranchisement of Jews in England was a more gradual and protracted process. The movies in part 1 emphasize the breakthroughs of Jews into institutions from which they were previously excluded. Benjamin Disraeli's first (1868) and second stints (1874–80) as prime minister gained him the gratitude of those who agreed with his policies of domestic reform

and imperial expansion and exacerbated the suspicions of opponents who believed both served "Semitic" interests. Based on a successful play and a silent movie version, the Warner Brothers' production of *Disraeli* (1929) won George Arliss the Oscar for best actor.

The entry of Jews into the officer ranks of the French army was another milestone greeted by liberal acclaim or xenophobic distrust. The Dreyfus Affair galvanized French public opinion over whether one of the first Jewish captains on the general staff was a German spy or an unjustly framed scapegoat. The most famous film about the affair is *The Life of Emile Zola* (1937), which garnered the Oscar for best picture. It epitomized the Hollywood biographical film of the 1930s, pitting the great writer Emile Zola against the conspiring generals who framed Dreyfus. Made in a period where the Production Code Administration demanded that slanders against ethnic groups be excised from scripts and final cuts, the movie makes only one brief visual reference to Dreyfus's Jewish origins. Yet the public burnings of Zola's books and the mass hysteria surrounding the affair echo what was happening in Hitler's Germany. *The Life of Emile Zola*'s approach to reenacting the affair contrasts sharply with that of HBO's *Prisoner of Honor* (1991), from the British director Ken Russell, in which antisemitism is so pervasive in French society that even Picquart, the intelligence officer who defended Dreyfus against the charge of espionage, is infected with it. The flawed protagonist Piquart has replaced the noble crusader for truth embodied by Zola.

Jean Renoir's *The Grand Illusion* (1937), a nominee for the Oscar for best picture in 1939, served as a poignant rebuttal to those who questioned the loyalty of French Jews to the Third Republic in general and of French Jewish soldiers in particular. Renoir's effort to make the Jew a credible character with an immigrant background and retail occupation has in retrospect been condemned as corroborating common antisemitic stereotypes. Renoir aimed at supporting the Popular Front's opposition to antisemitism and racism in France and Nazi Germany.

Chariots of Fire (1981), the recipient of an Oscar, a Golden Globe, and the Cannes Film Festival award for best picture, casts the Jew as the social outsider at Cambridge University and at the 1924 Olympics. Harold Abrahams, his Arab-Italian trainer Sam Mussabini, and his evangelical Scottish rival Eric Liddell encounter resistance to their ethnic backgrounds and sports ethic in the case of the first two, and to piety in the case of the third. The film follows the formula for sports films in which athletic prowess ultimately triumphs over discrimination. The movie also glorifies the individualism promoted by the Conservative Party politician Margaret Thatcher, who was the prime minister of the United Kingdom when the movie was released.

Part 2 of this book moves the setting of films eastward to czarist Russia whose government in the late nineteenth century still limited where Jews could reside and the numbers of Jews admitted to certain professions. Pogroms initially were spontaneous uprisings, but after the late nineteenth century, they began to be fomented by secret police. As a response to these assaults, some Jews retreated into faith and tradition to buffer themselves culturally and socially from external threats. Other Jews, who had been allowed to attend university or live outside the Pale of Settlement, often embraced secular movements like socialism, which promised them equality. The movies on Eastern European Jews mirror the conflicts within the *shtetl* over changes in family structure

and gender roles, as well as the ubiquitous threat of a hostile state.

In the American Yiddish film *Tevye* (1939), the Ukrainian priest cannot contain his glee at Chava's marriage to a Christian, and the Ukrainian villagers exhibit no remorse for expelling Tevye and buying his belongings for a pittance. Indeed, Chava quickly realizes she has made a terrible mistake and divorces her husband to rejoin her father. This instance of family solidarity as a response to oppression resonated with Yiddish-speaking Jewish audiences, who witnessed the diminishing vitality of their culture among their American-born children and the precarious situation of their relatives in Europe as antisemitism in Europe escalated in the 1930s. *Fiddler on the Roof* (1971) toned down the animosity of its Russian characters and sympathized with Tevye's daughter's desire to marry for love, without minimizing his fears of the erosion of tradition, which he futilely tries to halt. Its representation of the conflicts between choice and custom and between secular and religious salvation, as well as the uneasy relationships between ethnic groups, struck a responsive chord with American gentile and Jewish audiences alike who were chronologically removed from their immigrant roots and just beginning to reclaim them in the ethnic revival of the 1970s.

Although both *Tevye* and *Fiddler* unabashedly presume the subordinate position of women in traditional Jewish culture, Barbra Streisand's *Yentl* (1983) evinces both reverence for the learning of the Torah and Talmud and outrage that women were barred from engaging in it. To be sure, the persecution that Jews endured in the *shtetl* receives little attention, but the intellectual sparring of the Yeshiva gets more screen time here than in *Fiddler*. The film testifies to Streisand's advocacy of second-generation feminism and its goal of educational and occupational equality for women. Concluding that the *shtetl is* too constrictive, Yentl immigrates to the United States to pursue her ambitions.

The Dybbuk (1937) has been praised as the greatest Yiddish movie ever made. On one level, this tale about broken pledges and spiritual possession taps into the rich folklore of Eastern European Hasidism. On another level, it continued the ethnographic project started by the Russian Jewish author S. An-Sky to preserve a culture that was being overwhelmed by modernization, Polish nationalism, and Soviet communism. When we watch it today with awareness that the Holocaust eradicated the villages where this kind of piety and superstition had existed, mourning and reverence overshadow the anthropological and critical intent of the author of the play and the director of the film.

The Commissar (1967) is one of the few philosemitic films produced in the USSR after the death of Stalin. Inspired by a Vassili Grossman short story, it tells the tale of a woman commissar who is placed on furlough and dispatched to live with a Jewish couple shortly before and after she gives birth to a child. The film contrasts Soviet ideological rigidity with the humanity of the Jewish family. The commissar learns to appreciate the fundamental decency of her hosts, who act as midwives for her and huddle with her in their cellar, entertaining their children, while anti-Communist soldiers ransack their village. Haunted by a premonition of the Holocaust killing her hosts, the commissar feels compelled to return to the Red Army to fight for a society that will protect the victims of prejudice. Since *Commissar* criticized Bolshevik ideology and openly sympathized with Jewish characters in the same

year that Egypt, a Soviet ally, was soundly defeated by Israel, the movie was banned for twenty years.

Both *Fiddler on the Roof* and *Yentl* end with their protagonists seeking freedom in the United States. The third part of this book looks at films set in the United States, the destination of over two million Jews fleeing Russia and Poland to escape persecution and take advantage of the opportunities offered by an expanding American economy between 1880 and 1932. Many stayed in the New York metropolitan area after arriving at Ellis Island and then congregating in the tenements of the Lower East Side of Manhattan. Anzia Yezierska was the daughter of one those immigrants. In her writings she documented the experiences of impoverished Jews rising above their humble beginnings through acculturation, education, and hard work. Her literary success caught the attention of Hollywood, which adapted her collection of short stories *Hungry Hearts* into a silent film released in 1922. Contradicting its happy ending, the movie retains some of Yezierska's ambivalence about the Americanization experience, in which economic exploitation, material success, and renunciation of religiosity were closely intertwined.

The low-budget *Hester Street* (1975), which received an Oscar nomination for best actress for Carol Kane's performance as Gitl, meticulously recreated the microcosm of the Lower East Side. It personalized the forces of assimilation in the character of Jake, who divorces his traditional Jewish wife, Gitl, to marry the worldly Mamie. While Gitl and Jake's co-worker Bernstein are committed to perpetuating the pattern of the husband who becomes a religious scholar while the wife runs the business to support him, the closing scene intimates that this won't last long, as Gitl is no longer wearing a traditional wig and dress, and Bernstein is interested in what they will sell at the grocery store she plans to open.

The Jazz Singer (1927) emblematized individual aspirations triumphing over custom and parental dictates in the United States. Though primarily a silent film, it did contain novel scenes in which some dialogue is heard, along with singing and musical instruments. In it, the prodigal son, Jakie, chooses a career as an entertainer and defies his father's expectation that he become a cantor and follow in the footsteps of generations of males in the family. Sympathizing with her son, the mother pleads his case but fails to dissuade her husband from disowning him. The rift is surmounted when the dying father forgives his son, and the son agrees to take the father's place to sing the Kol Nidre on the first night of Yom Kippur. The final scene, however, undercuts this pat resolution as Jakie, who has changed his name to Jack, performs on Broadway to the obvious delight of his now widowed mother. That he sings his last two songs in blackface—since this was what Al Jolson, who plays Jakie, was famous for—has raised questions of how the Jewish experience is related to the African American one: is this emulation a sincere homage to the authenticity of jazz as an American art form, or a racist caricature that enabled Jewish and other immigrant entertainers to prove their whiteness by demeaning blacks?

Woody Allen's mocumentary *Zelig* (1983) parodies *The Jazz Singer*. Whereas Jakie Rabinowitz morphs into the singer Jack Robin to climb the ladder of show business success, Leonard Zelig becomes so obsessed with blending in with whomever he consorts that he literally assumes their appearance and mannerisms. This plasticity earns him ephemeral fame, but then it gets out of control. Jack advanced himself; Zelig loses himself. Featuring doctored documentary footage and head shots of distinguished scholars commenting on the social significance of Zelig's "chameleonism," *Zelig* blurs the boundaries between reality and illusion in cinematic reenactments of history while critiquing how far members of minority groups will go to efface their own identities to gain social acceptance.

Regarded as the last great immigrant movie of the 1930s, *Uncle Moses* (1932) explores the conflicting impulses of attaining material success and retaining a sense of communal responsibility. This American Yiddish production discloses the inroads that acculturation had made within the Jewish immigrant community, with the dialogue often slipping into English. Moses strives to be a paternal figure for his workers and a patron of the *shtetl* where they and he were born, but he exploits their labor to the point that they unionize and strike. His love for a woman who marries him for financial security ultimately leads to his demise. Moses's character is a transitional figure who futilely tries to bridge the chasm between Jewish collective solidarity and personal enrichment. Happiness eludes him despite his affluence.

The fourth part of the book deals with films about the Jews who pursued revolutionary alternatives to religious passivity in the face of persecution and to the pursuit of individual success within capitalist and liberal societies. The outbreaks of antisemitism such as the pogroms in Russia, the Dreyfus Affair in France, and the violence directed at Jews during the Russian Civil War in 1918–19 shook segments of the Jewish population in these countries out of their complacency. Some copied the national unification movements that had reconfigured the map of Europe in the nineteenth century, prompting disillusioned believers and secularists to forge a new Jewish nation in Palestine. *The Wordmaker* (1991) chronicles Eliezer Ben-Yehuda's lifelong campaign to revive and modernize Hebrew as a spoken language to serve as the unifying language of the future Jewish state. Ben-Yehuda founded a Hebrew newspaper in Palestine and compiled the standard Hebrew dictionary that bears his name. This film is unique in its scope, stretching from the origins of modern Zionism in the 1880s to the Balfour Declaration of 1917 that pledged British support for the establishment of a national home for the Jewish people in Palestine.

They Were Ten (1961) is the first feature-length film made entirely by Israelis. It tells the saga of the early Zionist halutzim (pioneers), who cultivated a parcel of rocky land to grow their own food. In addition to struggling with the inhospitable elements and poor soil, the characters in the film fend off an Ottoman official who tears down the house they build, and Arab peasants who graze their sheep on the Zionists' fields and monopolize the local well. This movie idealized the pioneers "who made the desert bloom," but it also prefigured future Arab-Israeli antagonism.

Though this fact is often forgotten, the Soviet Union initially touted Communist atheism and internationalism as the solutions to antisemitism. Stalin not only sponsored Jewish immigration to the remote district of Birobidzhan as an alternative to settling in Palestine, but he also urged American Jews who had lost jobs in the Great Depression and faith in the American dream of equality as discrimination against African-Americans and Jews rose in the early 1930s, to seek employment and social equality in the Soviet Union. *The Return of Nathan Becke* (1932) recalls this attempt to lure Jews to the USSR during the first Five Year Plan. Far more Jews remained in America or left Europe for Palestine, but a few thousand American Jews went to the USSR in search of the better life it promised.

The fifth and longest part of this volume contains a sampling from the vast corpus of films about the phases of the Holocaust, starting with the disenfranchisement of Jews, expropriation of their wealth, and identification of them in government records and moving through their segregation in ghettos, executions in mass shootings on the German invasion route through the Soviet Union, and ultimately their deportation to concentration and death camps, where they were systematically worked to death or exterminated. The pall that the Shoah casts on the modern Jewish experience is retrospectively apparent in movies like *The Dybbuk* and *The Life of Emile Zola*, which were made before it happened, and deliberately evoked in later films like *Commissar*, *Exodus*, *Hill 24 Doesn't Answer*, and *Prisoner of Honor*. While a debate has raged over whether any cinematic representation of the Holocaust can adequately convey its horrors without softening or trivializing them, filmmakers have felt obligated to try to memorialize the dead, understand the trauma inflicted on the survivors, and remind those who were not directly affected by it about their potential complicity, compassion, and indifference when any minority group is unjustly ostracized and persecuted.

The films I have selected depict aspects of the Holocaust as it unfolded in countries throughout Europe. *The Harmonists* (1997) traces the appeal of Nazism in a Germany embittered by military defeat, impoverished by the Great Depression, and stalemated by polarized political institutions. Though primarily an entertaining tribute to the Jewish and gentile musicians of a popular Weimar sextet, the Nazi threat looms in the background until it assumes ominous proportions, eventually banning the group from performing together and forcing its Jewish members into exile. The Jewish family in *The Garden of the Finzi-Continis* (1970) fails to realize that their high social status does not grant them immunity from the antisemitic laws that Mussolini introduced in 1938 and that became genocidal when Germany occupied Italy in 1943 to prop up his regime. Petty collaboration with local fascists in Slovakia for financial reasons reduces the otherwise benign protagonist in *The Shop on Main Street* (1965) into an inadvertent accomplice in genocide. Both this picture and *The Garden of the Finzi-Continis* won Oscars for best foreign picture. In *Goodbye Children* (1987)— a winner of major British, French, and Italian awards and widely known in the United States by its original French title, *Au revoir les enfants*—the budding friendship between a French Catholic boy and a new boarding-school classmate, whom he eventually discovers is Jewish, is abruptly terminated by a disgruntled informer getting even for being fired from his job at the school.

Although the stories of the aforementioned Holocaust films occur primarily before the deportations of Jews, the next group concerns how Jews endured harsher treatment in the ghettos and death camps in Poland. Honored with seven Oscars, including for best picture, *Schindler's List* (1993) demonstrates that even a pro-Nazi businessman who profited from Jewish slave labor could distinguish between economic exploitation and racist extermination and could intervene to protect Jews. *The Pianist* (2002), another Oscar winner for best picture, shows audiences the viewpoint of a classical musician eking out an existence inside the Warsaw Ghetto and subsequently observing the remainder of the war as a fugitive hiding outside of it. In *Fateless* (2005) a Hungarian Jewish adolescent copes with the harrowing ordeal of concentration and death camps and also comes to appreciate the camaraderie and respites that punctuated the brutal onslaught on his body and mind.

This part on Holocaust films also includes motion pictures about the psychological wounds that scarred the postwar lives of survivors. A multiple winner of the Italian equivalent of the Oscars, *The Truce* (1997) accompanies Primo Levi on his meandering odyssey from Auschwitz to Italy and documents the gradual reawakening of his humanity. *Our Children* (1948) contemplated the difficulties of representing the Holocaust in a creative medium. Yet it also approximates documentary authenticity in casting Jewish orphans in postwar Poland as themselves, eavesdropping on their sharing wartime memories, and recording their responses to a play that reminds them of their suffering. *The Pawnbroker* (1965) simulates the disturbing and progressively intrusive flashbacks triggered by the poverty and crime that a survivor witnesses in Spanish Harlem. His inability to feel anything originates in his suppression of the impotence, pain, and rage he felt as a concentration camp inmate. The lessons he teaches his Puerto Rican assistant summarize how history had consigned Jews to particular economic roles. His explanation accounts for, but does not excuse, his laundering money for the African American gangster who controls the neighborhood. *Enemies, a Love Story* (1989) revolves around the multiple relationships a survivor establishes with a married woman, his gentile wife who rescued him during the Holocaust, and his first wife, whom he had erroneously presumed was dead. With his belief in God shattered by the Shoah, he lacks any moral compass.

The sixth part concerns films that chronicle the most palpable political effect of the Holocaust: the establishment of the state of Israel in 1948. Notwithstanding the economic and institutional foundations laid by the Zionist movement in the fifty preceding years, the United Nations' approval of the partition of Palestine, which was backed by both the Soviet Union and the United States; the plight of Jewish refugees in postwar Europe; and the urgent need to offer them a homeland were inconceivable without the indignation aroused by the revelations of the catastrophe that had befallen European Jewry during the war. That the fledgling state prevailed against considerably larger invading Arab armies became the touchstone of the Israeli national mythology. Directed by a British filmmaker, *Hill 24 Doesn't Answer* (1954) was Israel's first feature film to achieve international success. It flashes back to the formative events in the lives of Israeli soldiers dispatched on a mission to capture a strategic hill. An Irish agent assigned by the English police to ferret out Zionist activists ends up sympathizing with their demand for independence. To him, it resembles the Irish struggle against the British. The son of European Jews who made aliyah avenges the fate of those they left behind by fighting against an ss man who has joined the Arab forces. An American Jewish tourist recovers his ethnic identity and religious faith during the siege of Jerusalem. A sabra—a Jew born in Palestine—displays her deep commitment to her homeland without ever recounting her personal story. *Kedma* (2002) questions the conventional narrative of the War of Independence by showing the mixed responses of Holocaust survivors sent into the fray without adequate military training.

Exodus (1960) was the film most responsible for introducing American audiences to the struggle for Israeli statehood. It opens with the escape of survivors from a British internment camp on Cypress to the ship that ultimately is allowed to ferry them to Palestine. There a Danish Jewish girl joins a kibbutz, while her boyfriend seeks revenge for his suffering at Auschwitz by volunteering for the Irgun. The Zionist organizer of the survivors' escape, Ari Ben-Canaan, played by Paul Newman, epitomizes Israeli manhood with his bravery, handsomeness, and moral decency. Although *Exodus* employs many of the same tropes as *Hill 24 Doesn't Answer*, it also Americanizes the Zionist cause through the figure of an American gentile nurse who becomes Ari's lover and serves as a nurse on the ship and at his kibbutz. The dialogue also draws analogies between the American and Israeli Wars of Independence.

The other large group of immigrants who made aliyah to Israel during this period was the Mizrahim from Arab and Islamic countries. *Braids* dramatizes the exploits of Herzliya Lokai, who joined the Zionist underground in Iraq as the Jews became the target of Arab demonstrators and demagogues. This resulted in her imprisonment in 1947, but she and her family later immigrated with the majority of Iraqi Jews to Israel. The Jews from the Arab world differed culturally and religiously from the Askenazi Zionists who dominated Yishuv politics. *Sallah* (1964) was the first movie to show the "absorption" process from the perspective of a Mizrahi man who learns quickly how to game the Israeli electoral system, the local kibbutzniks, and the government to get new housing for his family. Although the film's director, Ephraim Kishon, was accused of perpetuating negative stereotypes of the Mizrahim, he clearly satirizes sacrosanct Israeli institutions and revels in Sallah's ability to outwit them. Indeed, Sallah's homespun cleverness presaged an evolving admiration of Mizrahi males in films like the Israeli counterpart to *West Side Story*, *Kazablan* (1974). *Sallah* garnered an Oscar nomination for best foreign film and won the Golden Globe in this category.

Part 7 shifts across the Atlantic Ocean to films about American Jews contending with the residual antisemitism in the United States, moving from the Jewish neighborhoods in the big cities to the suburbs, and redefining their Jewish consciousness within a society where they enjoyed economic success. The shocking extent and nature of Nazi antisemitic atrocities created a backlash of sympathy for the Jews in the United States. Moreover, the return of Jewish soldiers from their deployments in Europe or on the Pacific front, the GI Bill benefits they received, and the prosperity of Cold War America thrust them into the mainstream of American life. The Holocaust looms as a catalyst for American Jewish advocacy of Israel in *The Chosen* (1981). The film is unique in its positing two distinctly Jewish responses to equality and modernity: on the one hand, the Hasidic cloistering of its adherents to shelter them from secular influences and, on the other hand, the synthesizing of American freedom, modern Judaism, and Zionist politics. Although the Holocaust is not mentioned explicitly in either *Crossfire* (1947) or *Gentleman's Agreement* (1947), both expose anti-Jewish attitudes and practices. In the former, the result is the murder of a Jewish veteran; in the latter, it is widespread discrimination against Jews in employment, housing, and exclusive hotels. In retrospect both films have been the target of criticism that their protagonists were gentiles rather than Jews, and that they failed to remind viewers of the Holocaust. Yet both struck a responsive chord, earning multiple Oscar nominations, with *Gentleman's Agreement* receiving the award for best picture. Moreover, public opinion polls indicated a sharp drop in the levels of American antisemitism in the immediate postwar period.

Driving Miss Daisy (1989) is one of a handful of films about the Jewish experience in the South. It circumspectly depicts the initially hierarchical, but eventually respectful, relationship between a Jewish widow and her African American chauffeur. Exposing the shared features of the prejudice endured by Jews and blacks, it also distinguishes the less egregious injustices that American Jews experienced and the more tragic legacy of slavery and segregation. Although the rapport and tensions between the two main characters are conditioned by the racial and religious dynamics of the American South, the movie has been charged—unfairly, it seems from a historical perspective—with perpetuating a condescending and racist stereotype of its black protagonist. Nevertheless, it received the Oscar for best picture.

Popular stereotypes of Jewish culture, family, femininity, and masculinity were both reflected and shaped by *Marjorie Morningstar* (1957), *Goodbye, Columbus* (1969), *Annie Hall* (1977), and *A Serious Man* (2009). Marjorie tries to assert her independence from the domesticity of her mother by changing her name and pursuing a career as a dancer. She falls in love with a cad. After he refuses to marry her, fearing that her desire for a nice home and family would hinder him from pursuing his ambition of becoming a theatrical director, the movie suggests that she will wed a successful and less mercurial man whose love she previously had rebuffed. *Goodbye, Columbus* made Brenda Patimkin the archetypal Jewish American Princess and her parents the embodiment of Jewish paternal indulgence and maternal domination. Retaining a sense of Jewish social responsibility, her boyfriend Neil initially is enticed by the allure of Brenda's affluence and uninhibited sexuality. *Annie Hall*, another winner of the Academy Award for best picture, humorously caricatured the cultural stereotypes of a neurotic Jewish New Yorker and a gentile woman from a small Midwestern town. Even their genuine affection for each other cannot bridge their diametrically opposed outlooks on life. *A Serious Man* skewers the ideal of Jewish domestic tranquility in the suburbs, but the main target of its satire is the question of whether science or Judaism can provide any answers or solace when bad things happen to good people.

Although Jews in Israel and the United States far outnumber their coreligionists elsewhere, part 8 considers the postwar Jewish experience in countries that have vibrant but smaller Jewish communities, like Argentina, Canada, France, Hungary, and Mexico. The common thread running through the films in this part is how Jews situate themselves in societies where their concerns seem secondary to those of larger ethnic, political, religious, and racial groups. *Like a Bride* (1993) and *Sunshine* (1999) trace the shifting generational identities of Jews in, respectively, Mexico, whose history and self-definition historically has excluded them, and Hungary, which morphed from a multinational empire into a parliamentary republic, right-wing dictatorship, Communist dictatorship, and democracy in the course of the twentieth century. This category of film imparts a distinctive national flavor to formulaic Jewish stories of upward mobility, as in *The Apprenticeship of Duddy Kravitz* (1974), in which the ambitious Jewish huckster navigates between Francophone and Anglophone elites in Montreal and feels obligated to purchase rural land to earn some respect. *Little Jerusalem* (2005) documents the tensions between Judaism and rationalism, tradition and modern gender roles, and North African Jews and Muslims in a suburban enclave of Paris. It offers a glimpse into how the demographic composition of France has been transformed by immigrants from former French colonies. *The Lost Embrace* (2004) paints a portrait of what once had been a bustling Jewish commercial district in Buenos Aires, but whose residents are now being displaced by other ethnic merchants who are more recent immigrants. Its protagonist knows he wants to escape the district's confines,

but he isn't sure whether he should go to Poland where his grandmother grew up, or to Israel, where his father now resides.

It is generally agreed that the heroic era of Israeli society ended with the Six Day War, and part 9 focuses on films that depict the fissures in modern Israeli society. The defeat of the neighboring Arab countries that fought Israel for the sake of pan-Arabism or Palestinian irrendentism, and the corresponding Israeli occupation of East Jerusalem, Gaza, and the West Bank spawned a vicious cycle of Palestinian terrorist attacks and Israeli reprisals. The less decisive outcomes of subsequent wars chipped away at the aura of confidence Israelis initially exuded after 1967. Moreover, the reunification of Jerusalem and the recovery of "Judea and Samaria" sparked messianic expectations among religious Zionists and their concerted settlement of areas they consider part of biblical Israel. The demographic composition of the Israeli population changed radically too, as the country rescued Jews from Ethiopia and was inundated by those leaving the Soviet Union and its successor states.

The films in part 9 mirror the malaise that has gripped Israeli society in the past three decades. *Munich* (2005) ponders whether the Mossad assassinations of Palestinians implicated in the murders of Israeli athletes at the 1972 Olympics corroded Israel's own democratic heritage. The highly acclaimed *Waltz with Bashir* (2008) looks at the same problem in light of Israel's war in Lebanon in 1982. *Kadosh* (1999) levels a scathing indictment of the repressive sexism of the ultra-Orthodox Jewish community, whereas *Ushpizin* (2004) presents a more sympathetic view of how religious faith can strengthen the bonds between spouses. *Time of Favor* (2000) imagines a plot among several members of an Orthodox platoon of Israeli soldiers who conspire to bomb the

Dome of the Rock. *Live and Become* (2005) is a saga of the Ethiopian Jews, from their airlift to Israel to the religious and racial discrimination they have encountered ever since their arrival there.

Part 10 concludes the book with discussions of films that explore how Jewish identity remains relevant in the lives of American Jews who have achieved the widespread acceptance that eluded their ancestors through most of the history in the Diaspora. These movies touch on how Jews benefit from broader trends in American society, like greater personal choice for both men and women in careers, sexual orientation, and marriage. The decrease in overt antisemitic discrimination has attenuated the Jewish consciousness of being a nation apart within the United States. Consequently, these films reveal a spectrum of Jewish responses to the multicultural relativism that has supplanted Americanization as the paradigm for how minority groups should relate to the dominant culture.

Crossing Delancey (1988) concocts a romance where the *bubbe* (grandmother) and the *shadchen* (matchmaker) pick an Orthodox Jewish man as the soul mate for a single career woman. She eventually realizes that he may be more compatible with her than the manipulative and pretentious author to whom she is originally attracted. *Torch Song Trilogy* (1988) was in the vanguard of American movies about gay Jewish men who seek acceptance from disapproving parents and discern analogies between their marginalization as homosexuals and the historical persecution of Jews in the past. In *Homicide* (1991) the Jewish police officer wonders if he must always prove his bravery to overcome antisemitic stereotypes of Jewish men as cowardly and weak. When assigned to investigate the murder of a Jewish shopkeeper in a black neighborhood, he finds clues that apparently corroborate her family's suspicions that she was killed because she was Jewish. Thus he joins a militant Jewish group that dispatches him to bomb the shop of a neo-Nazi organizer, thereby violating his oath to uphold the law and abandoning his partner in a raid to arrest a drug dealer. The brutal antisemitic skinhead who masks his religious background in *The Believer* (2002) is an extremist who is certainly not typical of American Jews, but the political and theological questions he poses about Judaism and modern Jewish life have crossed the minds of many thoughtful modern Jews. In the last two decades, rates of Jewish intermarriage have risen and rates of synagogue affiliation have dropped. *Keeping the Faith* (2000) playfully draws on the Jewish renewal movement that has rearticulated the moral mission and liturgy of Jewish congregations to make Judaism more relevant to its practitioners. Amid criticism of the film for diluting Jewish tradition, the resolution of the story has been lost: the beautiful gentile woman plans to convert to Judaism because she admires the spiritual fulfillment her rabbi boyfriend derives from his faith.

In the films set in the early decades of the twentieth century, Jewish characters either carve out an economic or political niche for themselves in societies where their equality has been attained or fend off external persecution and internal divisions in countries where antisemitism still curtails their opportunities and endangers their lives. The United States, Palestine, and—briefly—the Soviet Union beckon as havens from antisemitism and as utopias for forging new secular identities. For many Jews, the rise of Nazi Germany and the bloodbath it unleashed on European Jewry dashed the illusory promise of acceptance through acculturation. Its devastating impact has been refracted through the cameras of filmmakers in nations directly implicated in it or that observed it as enemies of the Third Reich or as bystanders. The films dealing with the postwar period to the present portray the repercussions of the Holocaust, the achievement and challenges of Jewish sovereignty in Israel, or the personal quest of protagonists figuring out the relevance of being Jewish when the options of assimilation or communal identification are both viable in contemporary multicultural democracies. The intertwining of these collective themes with the individual narratives they engender on screen provide a view of how the Jewish experience has been depicted in world cinema over the last ninety years.

Bibliography

Altman, Rick. *Film/Genre.* London: British Film Institute, 1999.

Anklewicz, Larry. *Guide to Jewish Films and Video.* Hoboken, NJ: KTAV, 2000.

Avisar, Ilan. *Screening the Holocaust: Cinema's Images of the Unimaginable.* Bloomington: Indiana University Press, 1988.

Aviv, Caryn, and David Shneer. *New Jews: The End of the Jewish Diaspora.* New York: NewYork University Press, 2005.

Baron, Lawrence. *Projecting the Holocaust into the Present: The Changing Focus of Contemporary Holocaust Cinema.* Lanham, MD: Rowman and Littlefield, 2005.

Bartov, Omer. *The "Jew" in Cinema: From "The Golem" to "Don't Touch My Holocaust."* Bloomington: Indiana University Press, 2005.

Bernheimer, Kathryn. *The 50 Greatest Jewish Movies: A Critic's Ranking of the Very Best.* Secaucus, NJ: Birch Lane, 1998.

Biale, David. *Cultures of the Jews.* 3 vols. Boston: Schocken, 2002.

Burgoyne, Robert. *The Hollywood Historical Film.* Malden, MA: Blackwell, 2008.

Carr, Steven. *Hollywood and Anti-Semitism: A Cultural History up to World War II.* New York: Cambridge University Press, 2001.

Colombat, André Pierre. *The Holocaust in French Film.* Metuchen, NJ: Scarecrow, 1993.

DellaPergola, Sergio. *World Jewish Population, 2010.* Storrs, CT: Berman Institute—North American Jewish Data Bank, 2010. http://www.jewishdatabank.org/Reports/World_Jewish_Population_2010.pdf.

Desser, David, and Lester D. Friedman. *American Jewish Filmmakers.* 2nd ed. Urbana: University of Illinois Press, 2004.

Dixon, Wheeler Winston, and Gwendolyn Audry Foster. *A Short History of Film.* New Brunswick, NJ: Rutgers University Press, 2008.

Doneson, Judith E. *The Holocaust in American Film.* 2nd ed. Syracuse, NY: Syracuse University Press, 2002.

Erens, Patricia. *The Jew in American Cinema.* Bloomington: Indiana University Press, 1984.

Ferro, Marc. *Cinema and History.* Translated by Naomi Greene. Detroit: Wayne State University Press, 1988.

Friedman, Lester D. *The Jewish Image in American Film: 70 Years of Hollywood's Vision of Jewish Characters and Themes.* Secaucus, NJ: Citadel, 1987.

Frodon, Jean-Michel, ed. *Cinema and the Shoah: An Art Confronts the Tragedy of the Twentieth Century.* Translated by Anna Harrison and Tom Mes. Albany: State University Press of New York, 2010.

Gabler, Neil. *An Empire of Their Own: How the Jews Invented Hollywood.* New York: Crown, 1988.

Gertel, Elliot. *Over the Top Judaism: Precedents and Trends in the Depiction of Jewish Beliefs and Observances in Film and Television.* Lanham, MD: University Press of America, 2003.

Goldberg, Judith N. *Laughter through Tears: The Yiddish Cinema.* East Brunswick, NJ: Farleigh Dickinson University Press, 1983.

Goldman, Eric A. *Visions, Images, and Dreams: Yiddish Film, Past and Present.* Rev. ed. Teaneck, NJ: Holmes and Meier, 2010.

Haggith, Toby, and Joanna Newman, eds. *Holocaust and the Moving Image: Representations in Film and Television since 1933.* London: Wallflower, 2005.

Hill, John, and Pamela Church Gibson, eds. *Film Studies: Critical Approaches.* New York: Oxford University Press, 2000.

Hirsch, Joshua. *Afterimage: Film, Trauma, and the Holocaust.* Philadelphia: Temple University Press, 2004.

Hoberman, J. *Bridge of Light: Yiddish Film between Two Worlds.* Updated and expanded ed. Hanover, NH: University Press of New England, 2010.

—— and Jeffrey Shandler, *Entertaining America: Jews,*

Movies, and Broadcasting. Princeton, NJ: Princeton University Press, 2003.

Hughes-Warrington, Marnie. *History Goes to the Movies: Studying History on Film.* New York: Routledge, 2006.

Insdorf, Annette. *Indelible Shadows: Film and the Holocaust.* 3rd ed. New York: Cambridge University Press, 2003.

Kellerman, Harry. *Greedy, Coward, and Weak: Hollywood's Jewish Stereotypes.* Fort Lee, NJ: Barricade, 2009.

Landsberg, Alison. *Prosthetic Memory: The Transformation of American Remembrance in the Age of Mass Culture.* New York: Columbia University Press, 2004.

Lichtner, Giacomo. *Film and the Shoah in France and Italy.* London: Valentine Mitchell, 2008.

Loshitzsky, Yosefa. *Identity Politics on the Israeli Screen.* Austin: University of Texas Press, 2001.

——, ed. *Spielberg's Holocaust: Critical Perspectives on Schindler's List.* Bloomington: Indiana University Press, 1997.

Lowenstein, Steven M. *The Jewish Cultural Tapestry: International Jewish Folk Traditions.* New York: Oxford University Press, 2002.

Marcus, Allen, ed. *Celluloid Blackboard: Teaching History with Film.* Charlotte, NC: Information Age, 2007.

Marcus, Millicent. *Italian Film in the Shadow of Auschwitz.* Toronto: University of Toronto Press, 2007.

Marks, Laura U. *The Skin of the Film: Intercultural Cinema, Embodiment, and the Senses.* Durham, NC: Duke University Press, 2000.

Marshall, Edward. "'The Dark Alien Executive': Jewish Producers, Émigrés, and the British Film Industry in the 1930s." In *New Directions in Anglo-Jewish History*, edited by Geoffrey Alderman, 163–87. Boston: Academic Studies, 2010.

Mendes-Flohr, Paul, and Jehuda Reinharz, eds. *The Jew in the Modern World: A Documentary History.* 3rd ed. New York: Oxford University Press, 2010.

Mintz, Alan. *Popular Culture and the Shaping of Holocaust Memory in America.* Seattle: University of Washington Press, 2001.

Nowell-Smith. Geoffrey, ed. *The Oxford History of World Cinema: The Definitive History of Cinema Worldwide.* New York: Oxford University Press, 1996.

Paskin, Sylvia, ed. *When Joseph Met Molly: A Reader on Yiddish Film.* Nottingham, UK: Five Leaves, 1999.

Peleg, Yaron, and Miri Talmon, eds. *Israeli Cinema: Identities in Motion.* Austin: University of Texas Press, 2011.

Picart, Caroline Joan (Kay) S., and David A. Frank. *Frames of Evil: The Holocaust as Horror in American Film.* Carbondale: Southern Illinois University Press, 2006.

Prawer, S. S. *Between Two Worlds: The Jewish Presence in German and Austrian Film, 1910–1933.* New York: Berghahn, 2005.

Rosenberg, Joel. "Jewish Experience on Film—An American Overview." *American Jewish Yearbook* 96 (1996): 3–50.

Rosenstone, Robert A. *History on Film: Film and History.* Harlow, UK: Longman/Pearson, 2006.

——. *Visions of the Past: The Challenge of Film to Our Idea of History.* Cambridge: Harvard University Press, 1995.

Rubin, Scott, Diane Tobin, and Gary A. Tobin. *In Every Tongue: The Racial and Ethnic Diversity of the Jewish People.* San Francisco: Institute of Jewish and Community Research, 2005.

Samberg, Joel. *Reel Jewish.* Middle Village, NY: Jonathan David, 2000.

Saxton, Libby. *Haunted Images: Film, Ethics, Testimony, and the Holocaust.* London: Wallflower, 2008.

Shandler, Jeffrey. *While America Watches: Televising the Holocaust.* New York: Oxford University Press, 1999.

Shohat, Ella. *Israeli Cinema: East/West and the Politics of Representation.* 2nd ed. New York: I. B. Tauris, 2010.

Sorlin, Pierre. *The Film in History: Restaging the Past.* Totowa, NJ: Barnes and Noble, 1980.

Taub, Michael. *Films about Jewish Life and Culture.* Lewiston, NY: Edwin Mellen, 2005.

Toplin, Robert Brent. *Reel History: In Defense of Hollywood.* Lawrence: University of Kansas Press, 2003.

Wright, Rochelle. *The Visible Wall: Jews and Other Ethnic Outsiders in Scandinavian Film.* Carbondale: Southern Illinois University Press, 1998.

Yosef, Raz. *Beyond Flesh: Queer Masculinities and Nationalism in Israeli Cinema.* New Brunswick, NJ: Rutgers University Press, 2004.

PART ONE

Advancement and Animosity in Western Europe, 1874–1924

1. One of Us?

Contesting Disraeli's Jewishness and Englishness in the Twentieth Century

TONY KUSHNER

Disraeli, directed by Alfred E. Green [A]
United States, 1929

Scholarship in literary and cultural studies increasingly recognizes the pervasiveness of anti-Semitic imagery in the popular culture of eighteenth- and nineteenth-century Britain and America. In fiction, drama, ballads, the press, and the new medium of film, the stock anti-Semitic figure of "the Jew"—money-obsessed, foreign, untrustworthy, and physically unattractive—continued into the twentieth century, reinforced by anti-alien agitation against poor Jews and fear about plutocratic Jewish power. Yet there was also change and modification, as typified by American theater and film representations of the former British prime minister in which the myth of Disraeli became established across the Atlantic.

The British-born actor George Arliss established his reputation through playing the lead role in Louis Parker's *Disraeli: A Play* for five seasons. Louis Harap observes that "this favorable portrait of Disraeli virtually identified Arliss for decades with a glorified likeness of the famous man." The play opened in Montreal in 1911 and

transferred to Chicago. In his memoirs, Arliss recalled, "Apart from the Jewish population, I think very few of the theatergoers of Chicago knew anything about Disraeli." In a similar vein, Parker remembered that in Chicago "the title was at first a little against it. People who saw it on the hoardings asked whether it was a new breakfast food."

It is clear that the play struggled initially in Chicago before becoming a success there, followed by even greater recognition and support in New York and across the country. Louise Mayo in her study of nineteenth-century American press and periodicals comments that Jewish leaders were "the sources of far more comments than American Jews. Benjamin Disraeli was a popular topic for articles. Although he was a practicing Anglican, the press always considered him a Jew. Disraeli was often cited as indicative of how far Jews had come in the present 'enlightened' age."

Harley Erdman argues that 1910 was a turning point in American theatrical representations of the Jew. It was not that the old stage Jew disappeared, but that he became rarer and less grotesque while "the exemplary, upstanding Jewish male protagonist" arrived, typified by Parker's *Disraeli* and Augustus Thomas's *As a Man Thinks*, both of which opened in 1911. It was Thomas, a major American dramatist, who publicly opened the debate, in May 1908, on the presentation of the Jews in the theater. Thomas called for a play on the "philanthropic, far-seeing and above all,

George Arliss (as Benjamin Disraeli), second from the left in the first row, dresses differently from other members of Parliament. From *Disraeli* (1929), directed by Alfred E. Green. VITAPHONE AND WARNER BROS./PHOTOFEST

sweetly domestic" Jew, or what Louis Harap has described as "the ideal, middle-class Victorian Jew." Such calls, which were widely reported and discussed, came alongside attempts by a variety of American Jewish organizations to "clean" the stage of the "derogatory characterization of the Jew."

In his note to the published edition of his play, Louis Parker made it explicit that it was "an attempt to show a picture of the days—not so very long ago—in which Disraeli lived, and some of the racial, social, and political prejudices he fought against and conquered." The play, which focuses on the purchase of the Suez Canal, made little pretense at historical accuracy; it was an opportunity to discuss the hostility Disraeli faced. Sir Michael Probert, "the shortsighted, anti-Semitic

head of the Bank of England," refuses to lend money to Disraeli to purchase the Khedive's shares. Disraeli then turns to Hugh Meyers, a financier, described in the notes for the play as a "charming man, with only the faintest traces of the Jew," to fund the purchase. Meyers proves the greater patriot than Probert. But if Meyers, the Rothschild figure, is in essence an Englishman, this is not true of Arliss's Disraeli, who, first in theater and then in film, appeared as an exotic and stereotypically Jewish figure. "Physically," it has been remarked, Arliss's Disraeli "could easily pass for a traditional version of Charles Dicken's Fagin." Arliss took great trouble to portray Disraeli "authentically." He did so by examining contemporary portraits and busts of the man, thereby perpetuating the "semitic discourse" that was instrumental in shaping artistic representations of the former prime minister in the first place. Parker himself played into such constructions, remembering Disraeli's "oriental case of features, his dark curl on a serene forehead, his firm jaws, and piercing, penetrating eyes." Arliss's exaggerated makeup, Gerald Bordman has suggested, "defined Disraeli's appearance for two generations of Americans."

While Parker's Disraeli was a scheming Jew, he was one who used his power and intelligence selflessly for the benefit of his country. Thus in a decisive moment in the play and subsequent film adapted from it, Probert angrily states that he is "an Englishman; the head of a great national institution. I am not to be ordered by an—an alien Jew." Calmly, Disraeli responds: "Ah, but the alien Jew happens to be the better citizen." Eventually, Probert sees the error of his ways and proclaims Disraeli the "kingmaker," to which Meyers quietly adds: "Better than that, Benjamin Disraeli—the Jew—the Empress-maker." All eventually are reconciled to the greatness of Disraeli, whose patriotism and alien status are reinforced by Parker's play and the movie. As Harley Erdman puts it, "Jewish power was performed as actively patriotic, as the play emphasized above all Disraeli's love of country. Any threat of difference was diffused."

Without the endorsement of the Drama League of America, itself a sign that the play and its subject matter were deemed "worthy" of support, it is possible that Parker's *Disraeli*, one of the most successful American plays of the decade, would have folded in Chicago. Nevertheless, it struck a chord with American audiences, in contrast to its reception when it opened in London in 1916. Harley Erdman has emphasized "the American nature" of *Disraeli*. He adds, "Despite its British setting, the play never succeeded

in that country precisely because its audiences would have recognized its simplification and telescoping in ways that clearly lacked verisimilitude." He also argues that the play had immediate relevance to an American audience during "an age of high minded imperialism (when Panama, not Suez, was transparently the canal at issue)."

In his review of the play, the leading American theater critic Walter Prichard Eaton stressed how Disraeli had become Prime Minister of English "in the face of opposition." Eaton highlighted the triumph of power and will over background—in other words, the story of Disraeli could be universalized to be a metaphor for the American rags-to-riches story. The play "enjoyed five full years of excellent business." However, the theater critic and British Jewish communal figure M. J. Landa was scathing about Parker's work. In particular, Landa was concerned about its portrayal of Disraeli's Jewishness, limited in effect, he argued, to "a Jew-badge, no different from the mark of shame of the medieval ages." Seventy years later, Harley Erdman argued similarly. Parker's *Disraeli* reflected a tendency to make Jewishness invisible: "a Jewish character took the lead in a play that was [not] specifically about Jewishness." To summarize, for an American audience, Parker's portrayal of Disraeli appealed at two levels: first, his success, in spite of his alien outsider status, played into the American myth of the self-made man, and second, his Jewish identity was never explored, enabling Disraeli's universalization.

Disraeli's climb "to the top of the greasy pole," however remarkable, was hardly a "rags-to-riches" story. In 1920, Disraeli biographer George Buckle made play of Disraeli's "progress from a middle-class Jewish literary home to Downing Street and the Congress of Berlin." Buckle noted how "in Disraeli's career there was the realization in fact of the dream which has floated before the eyes of many an ambitious youth; a clear proof that there is no eminence to which genius, aided by courage, resolution, patience, industry, and 'happy chance,' may not attain in this free country of ours." But in the 1920s, as earlier, Disraeli's rise to fame was more likely to elicit snide comments about his parvenu status than empathy. Buckle, in his homage to Disraeli and British toleration, pinpointed the appeal of the Disraeli myth across the Atlantic.

Parker's *Disraeli* opened in London at the Royalty Theatre in April 1916. It ran for 128 performances over several months—not a total failure, given wartime constraints, but hardly the phenomenal success it had been in the United States. To the editor of the *Jewish Chronicle*, the play was undoubtedly "quite timely," given that the very loyalty of Jews in Britain was then being brought into question by the war. Elsewhere in the same issue of the paper, Leopold Greenberg concluded: "Our enemies are forever on the prowl. Nothing is easier when loyalty and disloyalty are being balanced, to weight the scale in the popular mind against the Jew." It is for this reason that Parker's *Disraeli* was seen as a godsend by the *Jewish Chronicle*.

Parker had been ambivalent about staging the play in Britain because he "felt that the dramatic treatment of an historical character should be quite different in his own country from what it may be abroad." When it was performed in London he realized that "the play had not the glamour for an English audience with which the American audience had surrounded it." The theater critic of *The Times* was amused and horrified at the historical liberties taken by Parker, mockingly congratulating him "on his revelation of a Disraeli beyond our wildest dreams."

Yet, although Parker's play was not the landmark in cultural representations it had been in America, it was still indicative of changes that were taking place in the British theater with regard to images of the Jew. Harley Erdman suggests that plays such as Parker's which "reform[ed] the Jew to perfection perched on the transitional point between an earlier era of grotesque visibility and a latter one of greater invisibility." Yet however "perfect," Parker's Disraeli could not escape his alien Jewishness. Whether hostile or sympathetic, the "semitic discourse" was too dominant before 1918 to allow an analysis of Disraeli's own construction of his Jewishness and Englishness.

By the time of the First World War, anti-alienism had led to a policy of almost absolute restrictionism and control of aliens within Britain. After the war, this was consolidated in the Aliens Restriction Act of 1919, which, alongside the growth of conspiratorial anti-Semitism in respectable sections of British society (as well as in more extremist circles) made life for a range of Jews in Britain distinctively uncomfortable. What is remarkable in the years after 1918 is how those who were hostile to what they perceived as the malevolent power of Jews were desperately anxious to exempt Disraeli from their strictures. For example, the *Morning Post*, at the forefront of diehard Toryism, which saw the figure of "the Jew" behind international Bolshevism, labor unrest, and the decline of empire, persistently attacked what it perceived as the Oriental/Jewish policy of the secretary of state for India, Edwin Montagu, while at the same time praising "the great Jew," Disraeli.

For non-Jews, especially Conservatives, after 1918 Disraeli was a touchstone of national as well as political identity. Partially in response, but for other reasons as well, he came to play an even more important role within the Jewish world. With the growth of political anti-Semitism everywhere and the challenge of assimilation in an increasingly secular and nationalistic atmosphere, the figure of Disraeli loomed large in images presented to non-Jews and in debates within Jewish circles.

The use of Disraeli as a Jewish superhero was not without its problems. His apostate status and belief in Christianity as the completion of Judaism made him, to say the least, suspect to many Orthodox Jews. Yet for many Jews, especially in the tense atmosphere generated by the growth of conspiratorial anti-Semitism popularized by Henry Ford in the United States, the cult of Disraeli proved to be irresistible. With so much attention devoted to the alleged revolutionary and subversive tendencies of Jews, it was not surprising that Disraeli, whose star was so clearly in the ascendant, should be highlighted as an example of the conservative, patriotic nature of Jewish politicians. According to this stance, in spite of his childhood conversion to Christianity, Disraeli could be praised for contributing to British politics and culture, while managing to keep pride in his Jewishness.

Even more striking was Disraeli's importance to the group of immigrant Jews across the Atlantic, who, in the words of Neal Gabler, were "inventing Hollywood." Gabler's analogy that "like Disraeli, another Jew who felt alienated from and patronized by a class-conscious society, the Hollywood Jews would cope through 'a sustained attempt to live a fiction, and to cast its spell over the minds of others,'" probably would not have occurred to Isaiah Berlin, the author of the quotation within a quotation. Disraeli, of course, with his Sephardic aristocratic pretensions, would have utterly failed to identify with these nouveaux riches Jews of Eastern European origins, even had such an imaginary meeting across time and place been possible. Nevertheless, it is clear that they, or at least two of their leading lights,

Harry and Jack Warner, identified so much with his story that they used it for one of their first historical blockbuster talking pictures.

Disraeli (1929) followed the North American success that Louis Parker's play had enjoyed before the war. There was a direct connection, for the film was based on Parker's play and also starred the now-veteran actor George Arliss. In fact, there were two earlier silent versions: the first scripted by Parker himself and released in 1917, and the second drawing on the play and starring Arliss, released in 1921. As Lester Friedman suggests, "the most popular historical Jew of the silent period is the nineteenth century's most famous politician, Benjamin Disraeli."

It has been suggested that the 1929 film's conclusion, "that the outsider has more loyalty and love for his country than the native Englishman," gave it "dramatic tension." Its attack on an exclusive Englishness probably accounted for its greater success in the United States than in Britain, where it was rejected as historically inaccurate. But the triumph of the outsider over racial prejudice, at a time of rampant American xenophobia and anti-Semitism, was certainly a theme that appealed to the Warner brothers, especially the more thoughtful and sensitive Harry. In this respect, *Disraeli* was the first of a series of Warner Brothers' films about "the contributions and victimization of Jews," including *The Life of Emile Zola* (1937).

Disraeli went further, however, than simply representing the brothers' "vague underdog liberalism" and, as the only one of their interwar films that was explicit in revealing the Jewishness of the victim, reflected their own crisis of identity. As Gabler puts it: "The Warners, split as they were between Harry and Jack, between obligation and aspirations, between the old and the new, between Judaism and America, were actually a kind of paradigm of the tensions of assimilation generally." Making a film about Disraeli appealed to them because of who he was and what he had achieved. But it was also important to them through the respectability it brought by buying into the "theatrical quality" of a serious and well-received Broadway play at a time when Hollywood was being accused of low morality. In many respects, however, the Warner Brothers' film marked the end of the post-1918 infatuation with Disraeli's alien patriotism. Thereafter, until well after 1945, the liberal democratic world attempted to put the genie of his Jewishness back in the bottle.

It is no accident that the Warner brothers' other major treatment of anti-Semitism, *The Life of Emile Zola*, a study of the Dreyfus affair, makes only the most passing reference to the Jewishness of the accused. It has been suggested that what is most revealing about the film is the Warner brothers' total evasion of the anti-Semitic sentiments that motivated the Dreyfus case. Nowhere is this mentioned. Dreyfus is simply presented as an innocent victim, a wronged man. The avoidance is indeed blatant, but it needs to be contextualized rather than condemned. In the late 1930s and during the Second World War, Warner Brothers, like other Jewish film companies, responded to the growth of anti-Semitism at home and abroad largely through the tactic of universalisation. Jewish particularity, even in the form of victimhood, was to be avoided lest it give ammunition to the enemies of the Jews.

From the late nineteenth century, extreme anti-Semites had distorted Disraeli's writings to "prove" the existence of a world Jewish conspiracy. During the Nazi era, however, Disraeli increasingly appeared in their paranoid world as a key player in implementing Jewish control. The 1940 Nazi film *Die Rothschilds* (The Rothschilds) concluded with the statement: "As this

film was being completed, the last descendants of the Rothschilds fled Europe as refugees. The fight against their accomplices, the British plutocracy, continues." The film was an answer to Twentieth Century's *The House of Rothschild* (1934), which, like *Disraeli,* starred George Arliss and other cast members of the earlier film and similarly attacked anti-Semitism, ultimately showing the Jews to be the better citizens—Jewish influence is shown to be a force for the good. In contrast, in *Die Rothschilds* Jewish power is subversive and self-serving.

Formal and informal censorship in Britain during the 1930s reduced cinematic references to prejudice and limited them to the past. By the latter part of the decade, films made on either side of the Atlantic that dealt with modern persecution downplayed or totally ignored the Jewishness of the victims. It is thus not surprising that *The Prime Minister*, released in March 1941, which outlined the whole of Disraeli's career, should fail to mention once his Jewishness. While the tendency to universalize in liberal British culture has been particularly profound, it was far from the case with references to Disraeli before the 1930s: the refusal to acknowledge his Jewishness relates specifically to the context of the war against the Nazis. Even then, the Jewish particularity exemplified in the Warner Brothers' *Disraeli* had been largely abandoned across the Atlantic: such universalizing was hardly specific to Britain.

Disraeli will continue to be a source of fascination, and there will be many who still identity with him. In the process, they will highlight the unstable dynamic categories of "Jew" and "non-Jew." Confrontations with his identity will no doubt continue to be relevant to contemporary and political concerns—Englishness, in particular, has been frequently imagined and constructed in relation to the "alien patriot" with regard to who "belongs" and on what terms. In turn, Jews from a wide spectrum have confronted their own identity through the prism of Disraeli and have been prominent in creating representations of him in a wide range of media.

Abridged and amended from: Tony Kushner, "One of Us? Contesting Disraeli's Jewishness and Englishness in the Twentieth Century," in *Disraeli's Jewishness*, ed. Todd M. Endelman and Tony Kushner, 201–61 (London: Vallentine Mitchell, 2002).

Source: Louis Napoleon Parker, *Disraeli: A Play* (New York: John Lane, 1911).

Background: http://www.jewishvirtuallibrary.org/ jsource/biography/Disraeli.html; http://en.wikipedia .org/wiki/Emancipation_of_the_Jews_in_England.

Bibliography

Custen, George F. *Bio/Pics: How Hollywood Constructed Public History*. New Brunswick, NJ: Rutgers University Press, 1992.

Endelman, Todd. "Disraeli's Jewishness Reconsidered." *Modern Judaism* 5, no. 2 (1985): 109–23.

——. *The Jews of Britain: 1656–2000*. Berkeley: University of California Press, 2002.

Erdman, Harley. *The Performance of an American Ethnicity, 1860–1920*. New Brunswick, NJ: Rutgers University Press, 1997.

Kirsch, Adam. *Benjamin Disraeli*. New York: Schocken, 2008.

Spector, Sheila R. *The Jews and British Romanticism: Politics, Religion, Culture*. New York: Palgrave Macmillan, 2005.

2. Representing the Past and Present in *The Life of Emile Zola*

NICO CARPENTIER

The Life of Emile Zola, directed by
William Dieterle [A]
United States, 1937

On December 22, 1895, Alfred Dreyfus was convicted by a court-martial of the Paris military government for high treason and deported to solitary confinement on Devil's Island in French Guiana. Although he received a pardon on September 19, 1899 (after a retrial in Rennes where his sentence was reduced to ten years' imprisonment), it was not until July 12, 1906, that the French Court of Cassation declared him innocent and ended Dreyfus's tragic Calvary.

His original conviction for espionage was based on extremely weak evidence (mainly a handwritten note, the so-called *Bordereau*, which was obtained from the German embassy), and fed by feelings of anti-Semitism within the leadership of the French army. Moreover, being convinced of his guilt and coming under pressure from the right-wing press, the French minister of war, General Auguste Mercier, unbeknown to Dreyfus's defense team, provided the judges with a secret dossier (containing more circumstantial evidence) to ensure he would be found guilty.

Although initially the majority of French society was convinced that the army staff captain was indeed a spy working for the German embassy, Dreyfus's family (and especially his brother Mathieu and wife Lucie) succeeded in mobilizing a small but influential group of supporters, who became known as the Dreyfusards. At almost the same time, the new head of the French

Paul Muni (as Emile Zola), standing at the center, defends Alfred Dreyfus and himself. From *The Life of Emile Zola* (1937) directed by William Dieterle. WARNER BROS./PHOTOFEST

Intelligence Office, Major Georges Picquart, discovered new evidence (the so-called *Petit Bleu*) that pointed him to the real spy, Major Ferdinand Walsin-Esterhazy. The French general staff decided to protect Esterhazy and had Picquart removed from his position. A new forged piece of evidence (the *faux Henry*) was produced, and Esterhazy's name was removed from the *Petit Bleu* by Picquart's successor, Major Hubert Joseph Henry. A new inquiry was opened and as a result of the trial that followed, Esterhazy was proclaimed innocent.

J'accuse, Emile Zola's famous letter to the French president, Félix Faure, published on January 13, 1898, was the direct result of Esterhazy's acquittal and was aimed at provoking a libel trial against Zola and *L'Aurore*, the newspaper that published Zola's letter. During the new trial, which eventually led to their conviction and to Zola's flight to England, the French chief of staff, General Raoul de Boisdeffre, addressed the jury in a threatening way: "You are the nation. If the nation does not have confidence in the leaders of its army, in those who are responsible for the national defense, they are ready to leave to others that heavy task" (quoted in Johnson, 97).

After the fall of the French government on June 15, 1898, the new minister of war, Jacques Cavaignac, reopened the case, which uncovered the forged *faux Henry* and prompted Major Henry's suicide. On June 3, 1899, the Court of Cassation annulled the verdict of the 1895 court-martial. At a new court-martial held in Rennes that September, Dreyfus's sentence was reduced to ten years' imprisonment. A week later he pleaded for clemency and was pardoned under the condition that no one involved in the proceedings against him could be prosecuted in the future. It took several more years and another inquiry for the Court of Cassation to annul this sentence, this time without calling for a new court-martial of Dreyfus. This decision ended the long legal procedure and rehabilitated Dreyfus.

Out of the courtroom, the Dreyfus Affair had a major destabilizing impact on French political and cultural life, but it was only the tip of the iceberg. The Third Republic (1870–1940), which came into being after the defeat of Napoleon III in the Franco-Prussian war and the bloody suppression of the Paris Commune, was characterized by political instability evidenced by the sixty different government coalitions that ruled France between 1870 and 1914. These events created a backlash of strong nationalist and revanchist tendencies in late-nineteenth-century French politics.

Anti-Semitism was also increasing. Edouard Drumont's 1886 work *La France Juive* (Jewish France) waged a traditional scapegoat strategy against French Jews. Drumont's newspaper *La Libre Parole* (The free word) continued to rail against them until he lost control of it in 1910. His newspaper published lists of "remittance men" involved in the Panama Canal loan scandal between 1888 and 1892, transforming *La Libre Parole* from an insignificant sheet into a newspaper with a circulation of 100,000. The "Jewish threat" became intertwined with the "German threat." Before Russian and Polish immigrants began making their way to France in the 1890s, a migration of French Jews originated from Alsace, which Germany had annexed in 1871. The new outpourings of anti-Semitism marked an important shift in the articulation of this prejudice: it was no longer embedded only in Christian attitudes toward Jews and Judaism, but now was

also fed by economic resentment, nationalism, and racism.

It thus came as no real surprise that when Colonel Jean-Conrad Sandherr and his Intelligence Office began to look for yet another spy in the ranks of the French army, they rapidly decided that the "evidence" pointed to the Alsatian Jewish officer, Alfred Dreyfus. He was "their" traitor. After all, his handwriting resembled that of the *Bordereau*; he spoke German; and his brothers still resided in Alsace and had become German citizens. Finding convincing evidence became of secondary importance.

At its height in 1898–99, the Dreyfus Affair polarized French society and its elites. A famous cartoon by Caran d'Ache from the period showed how a quiet family dinner could be reduced to a brawl between its members over whether Dreyfus was innocent or guilty (see Boussel, 173). The embryonic group of Dreyfusards managed to spread its views through all layers of French society, while resistance to a retrial (or even the release of Dreyfus) led to the establishment of anti-Dreyfusard groups. The Dreyfus Affair transcended the tragic fate of Alfred Dreyfus. Dreyfusard ideology championed the Third Republic's constitutional principles of justice and civic equality. The anti-Dreyfusards championed patriotism, the army, trust in its judicial process, and respect for authority.

A series of conspiracy theories fed into the Affair on both sides. The Dreyfusards suspected a "Jesuit plot" and "military plot" against Dreyfus and the Third Republic. The anti-Dreyfusards charged that there was a "Jewish plot" and a "syndicate of treason" behind the campaign to reverse the verdict against Dreyfus. Both conspiracy theories aspired to give meaning to an otherwise ostensibly incomprehensible set of events, documents, and political strategies, but at the same time provided the rhetorical armory for fighting the enemy.

The Affair tapped into a variety of ideological positions that superseded it in the strictest sense and constituted reactions to the modernization of French society. Integral versus republican nationalism, religious equality versus anti-Semitism, clericalism versus anticlericalism, and civilian versus military control played crucial roles in the Affair. Although some of these positions can be attributed to the Dreyfusard and anti-Dreyfusard split, individual identifications often transcended these binary oppositions. For instance, not all anti-Dreyfusards were anti-Semites. These positions changed over time as illustrated by the socialist Jean Jaurès's belated support of Dreyfus, which broke a tradition of left-wing French anti-Semitism.

While the polemics in the French and international press raged, film was taking its first hesitant steps as a new medium. In the 1890s several short silent films reenacting events from the Affair were produced in France. When one of them provoked riots, the French government banned the making or screening of any films on the subject, a ban that was not lifted until 1950. A second wave of fictional films made in Germany, Great Britain, and the United States surfaced in the 1930s. The 1937 Hollywood version *The Life of Emile Zola*, directed by William Dieterle and starring Joseph Schildkraut as Dreyfus and Paul Muni as Zola, was the most successful and won three Oscars. Dreyfus's Jewish origins were barely mentioned in this second wave of films. However, this important element received more attention in the 1958 British film *I Accuse!*—directed by José Ferrer, who also played Dreyfus in the film. The first postwar French film on the Affair appeared in 1979. In 1991 Ken Russell's *Prisoner of Honor*, an HBO production analyzed in the fol-lowing essay, told the story from Colonel Picquart's perspective.

This essay focuses on *The Life of Emile Zola*, produced by Warner Brothers. This film is especially relevant because of its temporal closeness to the Second World War. It was produced at a time when the National-Socialist regime in Germany was already firmly in power. It is strictly a biographical film whose story was particularly difficult to narrate because of the complexity of the Affair, the immobility and remoteness of Alfred Dreyfus (being locked away on Devil's Island), and the ideological conflicts that fueled the Affair. According to a review published in the *Harrison's Reports* on August 28, 1937, the film was targeted at "better-class audiences" since it purportedly "stuck to the lofty ideal of presenting a drama in the interest of truth and justice."

The film drew upon the biographical film tradition that was flourishing at this time. Warner Brothers and Dieterle collaborated on a series of "prestige" biopics, the Hollywood term for such films, which typically presented famous individuals courageously standing against the cultural, political, or scientific consensus of their times to accomplish things or articulate values that would be relevant to contemporary audiences.

Since the movie portrays Zola's entire life, it includes a much earlier factor that influenced the Affair. The 1870–71 Franco-Prussian War is explicitly mentioned, and French troops are shown triumphantly going to war, followed by shots of newspaper headlines about the defeat of France and the capture of Louis Napoleon, marking the end of the Second Empire and the beginning of the Third Republic. There is a scene in which Zola expresses his dissatisfaction with the "unprepared" generals who led the war.

When the *Bordereau* is brought to the French Intelligence Office, it moves up the hierarchical chain of command to the head of the office, Colonel Sandherr, and beyond. All the officers who read it decry it as "outrageous" and "inconceivable." Finally, the list of potential suspects on the general staff is discussed. Esterhazy's name is mentioned, but he is considered trustworthy. Finally, the name of Dreyfus is settled on. A finger points to the name Captain Alfred Dreyfus and the word "Jew" appears as the designation of his religion.

The remainder of the film contains no other reference to Dreyfus's Jewish origins or to anti-Semitism. Warner Brothers adhered to the film industry's Production Code, strictly enforced by Joseph Breen since 1934, that recommended that no religious or national group be defamed for fear of offending it or inciting further bigotry. Some film reviews, like the one in the August 27, 1937, *Harrison Reports*, applauded this choice as illustrated in the following evaluation: "In presenting the case of Capt. Dreyfus, the producer wisely avoided the 'racial question.'" Other reviewers deplored the omission. Kate Cameron of the *Daily News* called it a "serious flaw," stressing the importance of anti-Semitism in Dreyfus' arrest: "In 1894 an unreasoning wave of anti-Semitism swept through France. It was particularly virulent among army officers and was directly responsible for Dreyfus, a Jew, being falsely accused." The absence of more overt references to the panic over German espionage or the anti-Semitism that cast aspersions on the loyalty of Jewish soldiers decontextualizes the historical factors that prompted the indictment and conviction of Dreyfus.

The circulating secondary texts, like reviews and publicity materials, do provide a context within which the entire film could be read in relationship to past and present anti-Semitism and intolerance. Warner Brothers partially supported this articulation in its press book for the film, which contained a reprint of a letter from Louis Rittenberg, the editor of *American Hebrew*, written to Jewish leaders in New York. This included the following paragraph:

> Today, when prejudices are more rampant than ever, I feel grateful to those who have had the idealism and vision to produce a picture of such tremendous force on behalf of that greater understanding which humanity must have before people of different faith and opinion can live together in peace.

The actual conflict highlighted by the Affair is narrated through a traditional enemy-hero dichotomy, which is reinforced by the presence of the victim. David Denby (1990) summarized its plot in these terms: "When he [Zola] publishes the Truth, he threatens the vested interests of people in power, who become his Enemies." The main enemy is the army and its generals, partially in combination with the police, the judicial system, and the political system, which are seen as accessories of the army.

The army is defined as a class in itself, as evidenced when Lucie charges that they are about to "sacrifice one of their class" upon hearing of Picquart's arrest. The officers frequently proclaim that the army "does not make mistakes." They collude in protecting Esterhazy and treating Dreyfus and his family inhumanely. The latter is illustrated by Dreyfus being denied any physical contact with his wife when she visits him in his Paris cell and by his being shackled to his bed on Devil's Island. The island has so many guards it almost becomes comical. The army's majors, colonels, and generals become interchangeable; they flood the screen, creating a vague, nonindividuated enemy (which discourages audience identification with them).

Books play a highly symbolic role in constructing the antagonism between hero and army. Zola's books are on display throughout the film, symbolizing his wisdom and intellectual capacity, which contrasts with the ignorance of the army generals. When asked if he had read Zola's exposé of the incompetence of the French military command in the Franco-Prussian War, one of the generals comments that "I don't read books, and certainly don't buy them." Finally the army finds itself in a complex relationship with the French people, who initially support the army with anti-Dreyfusard protest marches and mobs shouting abuse. At the same time, the authenticity of this support for the army and the anti-Dreyfusard cause is undermined in scenes showing provocateurs dressed in black (clearly linked to the army and its secret service) stirring up the masses. The French people are portrayed as a passive and manipulated mass.

The depiction of the enemy is juxtaposed to the individual hero, who is, as Denby (1990) describes him, "a great man who stands alone." Zola is self-assured, rational, eloquent, and an intellectual. The movie even compares Zola to Jesus. After Zola is convicted of libel, his lawyer points to a painting of Jesus's crucifixion and says "that too was a closed case." In the *New York Times* of August 12, 1937, one critic glorified Zola by observing that "when he thundered the 'I accuse' message that eventually exposed the army conspiracy against Dreyfus, he was no longer an individual and truly had become, as Anatole France later said of him, 'a moment in the conscience of Man.'"

A threat to Zola's heroic image arises when he is seen fleeing the country to avoid imprisonment. Initially Zola refuses to flee, in contrast to Esterhazy's cowardice and treacherous behavior, but then he reluctantly gives in to his friends who convince him to escape to England. They persuade him that it is "more courageous to be cowardly." However, Zola remains a presence in France through the poster displayed on the front door of the offices of *L'Aurore*, which declares, "Truth is still on the march; read Zola's articles."

The binary opposition between the evilness of the army and the heroism of Zola is reinforced by the presence (or absence when in prison) of the victim Alfred Dreyfus. If his presence were greater, it might diminish Zola's heroism; too strong an absence might render Zola's heroism unnecessary and incomprehensible. Scenes of Dreyfus in captivity remind the audience of his presence, as does the mention of his name in the dialogue. The link with Zola is again forged by books, as we see Dreyfus receiving a copy of a novel by Zola, which subsequently is shown being eaten by ants. By the time Dreyfus gets the letter informing him that his sentence has been annulled and that he must return to France for the retrial, his hair has turned almost completely white.

The only other quasi-hero in the film is Picquart. Rather surprisingly, he is introduced early in the film, critiquing the army's attitudes. Wearing an impeccable and light uniform (contrasting with most other uniforms, which are dark), he is the only military witness to speak out on Zola's behalf during the trial. He too becomes a victim of the Affair, adding to the demonization of the army.

The Dreyfusard leadership barely figures in this film, which adds to Zola's heroism and distances the audiences from political activism. Apart from in the courtroom, the only other group scene involves Lucie and Mathieu Dreyfus and the editors of *L'Aurore* contemplating what Zola will bring to them. This turns out to be the article *J'accuse*, which Zola reads to them. The press is also seen as a crucial and impartial informational source that provides the spectators with all the information necessary to understand the storyline. This overlooks how Drumont's *La Libre Parole* inflamed public opinion against Dreyfus.

The movie's representations of the Dreyfus Affair are intertwined with the present. Despite the absence of explicit references to anti-Semitism, the film contains a strong plea against "fanatical intolerance" and against the vicissitudes, passivity, and gullibility of the masses. It emphasizes the importance of democracy and tolerance. Indeed, the film was, as Denby (1990) puts it, "an early example of Warner's anti-fascist drama." This is exemplified by the book burnings, a clear reference to the burning of "un-German books" by German university students in May of 1933. In his book *Jew Süss and Nazi Propaganda*, Claude Singer (2003, 17) remarks: "We see a stake aimed at burning Zola's books during the Dreyfus Affair in France. This is a purely fictitious event, but it made a clear reference to Nazi Germany."

A pacifist theme also emerges at the end of the film. On the evening of Zola's death, he is working on his new book, *Justice*. It is the day before Dreyfus's reinstatement ceremony. Zola actually died in 1902, four years before Dreyfus was rehabilitated. Zola cannot desist from writing, "What matters the individual if the idea survives," and hopes his book will help prevent a future world war. Whether the film is referring to the First or Second World War is left open.

The Life of Emile Zola promotes individualism, liberty, freedom of speech, human rights, democracy, tolerance, "true" patriotism, and heroism and transposes the Affair into an American context. On the one hand, the anti-Dreyfusard movement is decontextualized and depoliticized, rendering its political motives incomprehensible by reducing them to the self-interest of the army or the irrational behavior of the mob. Thus, the economic, political, religious, and social motivations of the anti-Dreyfusards are forgotten. On the other hand, the heroic individual reunites the French nation, generating closure on the violent times of the Affair. The organized and activist nature of the Dreyfusards is ignored as the film shows Zola leading France back to justice, liberty, and truth. Through these mechanisms, the film optimistically demonstrates how rationalist and enlightened ideologies can overcome militarism, propaganda, and mob passions. By showing how the nation comes to its senses after the crisis, the movie projects the deep-rooted but illusionary hope that totalitarian regimes will eventually vanish and world conflict will be avoided.

Abridged from: Nico Carpentier, "From Individual Tragedy to Societal Dislocation: The Film Representation of Tragedy, Dislocation, and Cultural Trauma in the Dreyfus Affair," in *Culture, Trauma, and Conflict: Cultural Studies Perspectives on War*, ed. Nico Carpentier, 245–70 (New Castle, UK: Cambridge Scholars, 2007).

Source: Mathew Josephson, *Zola and His Time: The History of His Martial Career in Letters* (New York: Macaulay, 1928). [For information on the Zola Trial, see chapter 3, bibliography and background.]

3. The Dreyfus Affair According to HBO

LAWRENCE BARON

Prisoner of Honor, directed by Ken Russell [A]
United Kingdom, 1991

Although the biopic has remained a popular genre, the kind of historical figure whose life is depicted changes to reflect the cinematic styles, political issues, and social values that characterize the time and place in which the film is produced. During the 1930s, *The Life of Emile Zola* simultaneously reenacted the Dreyfus Affair and lionized Zola's intervention in it as a model to inspire Americans to oppose the rise of fascism and racism, both at home and abroad. Evoking the fresh memories of the Holocaust and McCarthyism, José Ferrer's *I Accuse!* (1958) centered on how antisemitism and paranoid patriotism framed an innocent man, whose vindication depended on the mobilization of public opinion spearheaded by the Dreyfus family, Georges Clemenceau, Auguste Scheuer-Kestner, and Emile Zola against the calumnies of the French generals and hatemongers like Edouard Drumont.

These earlier films portrayed Picquart as the exception to the rule of the military cabal against Dreyfus. From the viewer's first glimpse of the general staff in *The Life of Emile Zola*, Picquart emerges as the only officer who agrees with Zola's criticism of the general staff's conduct of the Franco-Prussian War. He bluntly tells his superiors, "We shouldn't be afraid to admit our mistakes." He begins his report on the incriminating evidence he has uncovered about Esterhazy by remarking to the generals, "I've never been fully convinced of Dreyfus's guilt." The Picquart of *I Accuse!* exhibits even more solicitude for Dreyfus. Before any charges have been leveled against Dreyfus, Picquart asks how he is getting along with his fellow officers and assures his former student from the War College that "all armies dislike change in principle and this is something of an innovation, a Jew on the general staff. But I'm glad I recommended you." In fact, Dreyfus was neither the first Jew to have reached the upper echelons of the army, nor the only Jew there when he was accused of treason (Lindemann 1991, 60, 99). Picquart repeatedly expresses disbelief that Dreyfus could be an enemy agent, noting that he was affluent and didn't need the money that the Germans paid their informer. Picquart believed

that incarcerating the real culprit and clearing Dreyfus would enhance France's security and the army's reputation.

To be sure, Picquart deserves credit for advocating the apprehension of Esterhazy and securing a new trial for Dreyfus once the lack of credible evidence against him and the continued flow of French military secrets to the German military attaché became apparent to him in 1896. Yet he hardly qualifies for the sainthood conferred on him in the earlier films about the Affair. Indeed, he harbored an elitist disdain for Jews in general and Alfred Dreyfus in particular. Picquart had been the only one of Dreyfus's instructors at the War College who had given him less than stellar marks. He found Dreyfus arrogant, pedestrian, and pushy. He expressed reservations about appointing Dreyfus to the general staff, fearing it would provide grist for the propaganda mill of the antisemitic press. As an official observer at the first courtmartial, he showed little sympathy for his former student and accepted the verdict as valid. He attended the degradation ceremony, in which all emblems of Dreyfus's rank were cut off his uniform and his sword was broken. Picquart resented the fact that Dreyfus didn't take his punishment like a soldier and instead screamed that he was innocent: "Just like a Jew. Even now he is calculating how much money he lost when he went to the tailor" (Lindemann 1991, 111).

HBO's Prisoner of Honor reenacts the public humiliation of Dreyfus but follows it with a conversation between Picquart and Major Henry over a game of billiards at the officers' club. Picquart does not mince any words about his contempt for the way Dreyfus comported himself at the degradation: "What did he look like? Jailed for life, and, he acted like some Jewish tailor counting the cost of the buttons as they were ripped from his uniform." Henry, who subsequently forged documents to place in Dreyfus's criminal file, believes that any Jew would have acted this way. Most of the other officers share this sentiment, bursting into a song about fighting the "Yids" who don't talk or walk like real Frenchmen. Assigned to review the case by General de Boisdeffre to determine what motivated Dreyfus, Picquart wonders why another inquiry is necessary: "After all, he is a Jew. You know what they're like." After forsaking his mistress and jeopardizing his military career to crusade on behalf of Dreyfus, Picquart muses: "The irony is that I've never been able to think of him as anything but a Jew. I never liked him."

Picquart's prejudice and initial deference to his superiors make him an intriguing protagonist for the HBO biopic. In an interview in the "The Making of Prisoner of Honor," a short documentary that appears on the DVD version of the film, Richard Dreyfuss explains why he was drawn to play Picquart: "What appeals to me about Picquart is not that he is a hero, but that he is flawed. He has at the core of him, an enormous flaw in his character, and from that basis, he does heroic things." The movie typifies the approach that HBO has taken in producing less romanticized biographical and historical films than those traditionally made by Hollywood. HBO often picks as the subjects of its biopics infamous or morally ambiguous personages like the unscrupulous McCarthyist prosecutor Roy Cohen (Citizen Cohen [1992]) and the ruthless Soviet dictator Joseph Stalin (Stalin [1992]).

Some American theatrical releases from this period like Bugsy (1991) and Schindler's List (1993) displayed the same predilection for historical figures with problematic personalities and priorities. It is difficult to pinpoint the reasons for this tack, but the tarnishing of Ronald Reagan's second term by the Iran-Contra Affair, which inciden-

tally is cited as a contemporary, albeit less divisive, parallel to the Dreyfus Affair in the "The Making of Prisoner of Honor"; the recession of the late 1980s; and the reneging of President George H. Bush on his campaign promise not to raise taxes probably contributed to the disillusionment of Americans about the integrity of public figures.

The depictions of de Boisdeffre and the minister of war do not corroborate the common perception that every anti-Dreyfusard was an antisemite. Neither resorts to anti-Jewish slurs when discussing the case with Picquart. Their opposition to a retrial for Dreyfus emanates from their fear that revealing the army convicted an innocent man would diminish its popular support and prestige at a vulnerable moment, when Germany was pulling ahead of France in the armaments race. Oliver Reed, who portrays de Boisdeffre, says in "The Making of Prisoner of Honor" that he considers his character "a man who cares about his regiment, cares about the army, cares about the people he serves with." For much of the film, he serves as Picquart's patron and initially shares his belief that Esterhazy has engaged in espionage. In not stigmatizing all of the generals as bigots, the director Ken Russell echoes the more nuanced interpretations of the Dreyfus Affair advanced by scholars like David Lewis (1973), the title of whose book was borrowed for the film, and Jean-Denis Bredin (1986).

But Russell does not minimize the role of antisemitism in the Affair either. The movie opens with a black screen. In the background the grumblings of a crowd can be heard as an unidentified voice-over proclaims, "Judas sold Christ; Dreyfus sold France." General Gonse and Major Henry trace Dreyfus's treachery to his Jewish origins. When Picquart asks Henry how counterintelligence managed to ferret Dreyfus out as the spy, Henry replies: "It wasn't hard. Not when everyone else was a loyal Frenchmen. What country does a Jew have? Where's his loyalty?" Although Henry also exploited the proceedings against Dreyfus to promote his own career aspirations, he manifests an antisemitic paranoia in the suicide letter he leaves to his wife: "I am a victim of the Jews and their allies. I entreat you to tell our son that I deny to my dying breath having forged anything."

Gonse's antisemitism is even cruder than Henry's. He cannot fathom Picquart's concern over whether Dreyfus received a fair trial: "What does it matter to you and what does it matter to anyone if one Jew rots on Devil's Island?" On hearing that Picquart is a devotee of the music of Gustav Mahler, a Viennese Jew who converted to Catholicism, the general doubts that "a leopard can change its spots." Gonse resembles a voracious predator, gorging himself on pastries and twice staining the front of his white shirt with red wine, symbolizing the blood of the man whom he and his cohort have sacrificed on the altar of the army's credibility.

Prisoner of Honor vividly conveys a sense of the hysteria that swept France during the Dreyfus Affair. The authentic looking and sounding recreations of the furor it caused owe much to an exhibition of documents and posters mounted by the Jewish Museum of New York in 1987 (Kleeblatt 1987). The cabaret skits replicate performances from the period. The "Anti-Jewish Marseillaise" rallies the French "to destroy these filthy Yids." A caped Dreyfus descends as a vampire to drink the blood of Marianne, the symbol of France (see http://www.france.com/docs/472 .html). Members of the audience cheer or jeer when they realize Picquart is in the nightclub. Girls skip rope to the tune of "Frère Jacques," singing the following lyrics: "Captain Dreyfus, Captain Dreyfus / Dirty Jew, Dirty Jew / Stays

on Devil's Island / Stays on Devil's Island / Dirty Jew, Dirty Jew." Irate mobs burn Dreyfus in effigy and pummel a traditionally dressed Orthodox Jew. Wherever the Affair is debated, it triggers heated arguments and leads to fisticuffs. The eyewitness whose interview for a newspaper in 1923 bookends the film exclaims: "You didn't know who you were! You weren't alive unless you knew where you stood on the Affair!"

Yet *Prisoner of Honor* fails to pay attention to underlying elements of the animosity directed toward Jews during the affair. For example, it never depicts the economic resentments of French peasants, skilled workers, and small-business owners who perceived the banks, department stores, factories, and stock market as Jewish enterprises designed to exploit and impoverish French Christians. A more glaring omission is the absence of any portrayal of the Catholic Church's role in fomenting hatred against the Jews. Although much of this rancor tapped into deep-seated theological prejudices against Jews and Judaism, part of it constituted a reaction to recent events like the collapse of a Catholic Union Général Bank in 1882, and the passage of legislation in the same decade to assert state control over primary schools and thereby limit the role of Catholic schools in the educational system. Except for the opening comparison between Judas and Dreyfus, which is reiterated by a man in a mob scene later, the Catholic dimension of French antisemitism remains unexplored in the film.

Like *The Life of Emile Zola, Prisoner of Honor* revolves so much around Picquart's campaign to exculpate Dreyfus that it underplays the crucial role that the Dreyfus family and other Dreyfusards played in keeping the case in the public eye. In the movie, the minister of war responds to Picquart's accusation against Esterhazy in 1896 by briefly noting that Lucie had tried to enlist the support of the press. As early as 1895, Lucie and Mathieu Dreyfus commissioned Bernard Lazare to prove Alfred's innocence. That year Lazare authored an essay exposing the judicial malfeasance, but he delayed its release on the advice of Mathieu and Dreyfus's attorney, who sought to persuade the president of the republic or some other notable to reopen the case. Disillusioned when nothing materialized from these channels, Mathieu authorized the publication of Lazare's piece in September 1896 and subsidized its republication as a pamphlet two months later. He distributed copies to French legislators, journalists, and other prominent figures. Picquart recorded his findings in a confidential letter he entrusted to his lawyer, Louis Leblois. In the film, Leblois arranges for Picquart to meet with Lucie, but Picqart refuses to reveal anything to her. What is overlooked is that Leblois leaked the contents of the letter to the Dreyfus family, who disclosed it to Auguste Scheuer-Kestner, the vice-president of the Senate. Zola entered the fray belatedly, at the beginning of 1898. His trial served as the catalyst for the formation of anti- and pro-Dreyfusard political organizations. The movie reduces this activism to the revelations of Picquart and Zola, with Lucie usually playing a secondary role as a spectator in the courtroom.

The initially unnamed gentleman whose interview introduces and concludes *Prisoner of Honor* turns out to be the unrepentant Esterhazy. To him, the furor over the affair resembles more of a farce than a tragedy. He cynically recounts how the generals protected a mercenary spy like himself and prosecuted a principled patriot like Picquart. Yet he recognizes that Picquart was the "best" among the general staff, "a man of too much honor." Esterhazy's sardonic commentary is placed in perspective at the end, when the reporter conducting the interview asks for his autograph and he signs his name. His bemusement over the folly of the Affair may be counterbalanced by another image in this scene. Esterhazy stands in front of a hearth that is overflowing with ashes. For viewers familiar with the documentary footage of the charred remains of Jewish corpses burned in German crematoriums, this image foreshadows where the antisemitism unleashed by the Dreyfus Affair eventually would lead.

Sources: David L. Lewis, *Prisoners of Honor: The Dreyfus Affair* (New York: Morrow, 1973).

George R. Whyte, *The Dreyfus Affair: A Chronological History* (New York: Palgrave Macmillan, 2008). The film credits Whyte for doing the research on Picquart.

Background: Adam Gopnik, "Trial of the Century," *New Yorker*, September 28, 2009 (http://www.newyorker.com/arts/critics/books/2009/09/18/090928crbo_books_gopnik).

Bibliography

Birdwell, Michael E. *Celluloid Soldiers: The Warner Bros. Campaign against Nazism.* New York: New York University Press, 1999.

Boussel, Patrice. *L'Affaire Dreyfus et la Presse.* Paris: Armand Colin, 1960.

Bredin, Jean-Denis. *The Affair: The Case of Alfred Dreyfus.* Translated by Jeffrey Mehlman. New York: George Braziller, 1986.

Custen, George F. *Bio/Pics: How Hollywood Constructed Public History.* New Brunswick, NJ: Rutgers University Press, 1992.

Denby, David. "Emile and Louis and Mikhail and Václav." *Première* 3, no. 13 (August 1990): 34–35.

Heller, Dana. "Films." In *The Essential HBO Reader*, edited by Gary R. Edgerton and Jeffrey P. Jones, 42–51. Lexington: University Press of Kentucky, 2008.

Hoffman, Robert L. *More Than a Trial: The Struggle over Captain Dreyfus.* New York: Free Press, 1980.

Kleeblatt, Norman. *The Dreyfus Affair: Art, Truth, and*

Justice. Berkeley: University of California Press, 1987. [This is the catalog for the Jewish Museum of New York's 1987 exhibition.]

Johnson, Martin P. *The Dreyfus Affair.* London: Macmillan, 1999.

Lindemann, Albert S. *The Jew Accused: Three Anti-Semitic Affairs: Dreyfus, Beilis, Frank, 1894–1915.* New York: Cambridge University Press, 1991.

Morgan, Owen. "J'accuse!: Zola and the Dreyfus Affair." In *The Cambridge Companion to Zola*, edited by Brian Nelson, 188–205. New York: Cambridge University Press, 2007.

Singer, Claude. *Le juif Süss et la propagande nazie: l'histoire confisquée.* Paris: Belles lettres, 2003).

Wilson, Nelly. *Bernard Lazare: Anti-Semitism and the Problem of Jewish Identity in Late Nineteenth Century France.* Cambridge: Cambridge University Press, 1978.

Wilson, Stephen. *Ideology and Experience: Anti-Semitism in France at the Time of the Dreyfus Affair.* Rutherford, NJ: Fairleigh Dickinson University Press, 1982.

4. Renoir's *The Grand Illusion* and the "Jewish Question"

MAURICE SAMUELS

The Grand Illusion (*La Grande Illusion*), directed by Jean Renoir [A]
France, 1937

In his autobiography, Jean Renoir describes how his cinematic masterpiece *The Grand Illusion* was inspired by the antifascist struggle of the period: "It seemed to me that any honest man had to fight Nazism. As a filmmaker, my only opportunity to take part in this battle was to make a film. I deluded myself about the power of cinema. Despite its success, *The Grand Illusion* did not

stop the outbreak of the Second World War." Renoir's exalted hopes for *The Grand Illusion* derive from the film's espousal of universal brotherhood. Set in a series of German prison camps for army officers during the First World War, the film demonstrates the common bond linking humans across the artificial boundaries of nations. Moreover, in its depiction of the friendship that develops between two French officers, one of whom is Jewish, the film also points to race as another artificial barrier separating men.

Just as the film's pacifist and antinationalist message may not strike all viewers as self-evident today, so too do *The Grand Illusion*'s representations of the Jew prove highly ambiguous. While the film tries to transcend the anti-Semitic ideology that was widespread in France during the 1930s by including the Jewish character within the symbolic national community formed by the French prisoners, it also endows the Jew with a range of negative characteristics reminiscent of anti-Semitic stereotypes. Although André Bazin and other critics have dismissed this anti-Semitic stereotyping as irrelevant to the film's larger message of unity and brotherhood, I argue in what follows that the "Jewish question" provides a key to evaluating and interpreting the film.

An analysis of the representation of the Jew in *The Grand Illusion* also raises larger questions about the reading of race in cinematic culture. By what standard should we evaluate the nature of racial representation? Should works be judged against the norms of the period in which they were produced? Or are critics justified in viewing films through the lens of subsequent historical events and according to more recent standards? *The Grand Illusion* provides a particularly telling case for exploring these vexed questions both because it has given rise to such vehement polemics over the years and because its images of the Jew are so complex.

Critics of *The Grand Illusion* have diverged on the "Jewish question." When the film was released to glowing reviews in 1937, most critics on the Right did not raise the issue. Certain critics on the Left mentioned the presence of a Jewish character, but they did not describe the film as either pro- or anti-Semitic. A controversy over the "Jewish question" erupted, however, when the film was rereleased shortly after the Second World War, in 1946. Writing in a left-leaning newspaper, Georges Altman felt a sense of "malaise" watching the film a second time "that despite Renoir, despite the beauty of the images, or because of it, changed into amazement and distrust." Altman's discomfiture stems in part from the sympathetic treatment of the Germans in the film, a representation that the Nazi genocide caused him to see in a new light. This postgenocide perspective prompts the critic to charge that the very act of depicting a Jewish character, and calling attention to his Jewishness, is anti-Semitic.

Altman's reaction to the film's alleged anti-Semitism is all the more striking in that many of the references to Rosenthal's Jewishness had been edited out of the 1946 version of the film to avoid offending postwar sensibilities. Perhaps because of these cuts, other critics at the time did not share Altman's perception. Amid a general critical and popular appreciation of the film, one left-leaning critic defended *The Grand Illusion* against Altman's attacks, pointing out that the film's producer was Jewish, as was the censor who approved the 1946 version of the film.

More striking is the opinion of those arch anti-Semites and collaborators, Maurice Bardèche and Robert Brasillach, which runs directly counter to

Altman's. In their disturbing *History of Cinema* of 1948, Renoir occupies an ambiguous place as both a despised mouthpiece for the Popular Front and an accomplished cinematic artist. When they come to *The Grand Illusion,* which they call the best French film of recent years, their enthusiasm for an accomplished masterpiece is tempered by what they perceive as the director's philo-Semitism. They praise certain aspects of Renoir's depiction of the "Jew Rosenthal," approving especially of his admission of greed. They are, however, disturbed by Rosenthal's sympathetic qualities.

Despite the criticism from the extreme Right, Renoir's film could not completely escape the charge of anti-Semitism when it was next released in 1958. Henry Magnan singles out the representation of Rosenthal, played by Marcel Dalio. While regretting the depiction of Rosenthal as rich, ostentatious, and given to complaining (especially during the escape sequence, when the proletarian Frenchman played by Jean Gabin remains stoic), Magnan sees the danger not so much in these stereotypes, but in the way the film substitutes cliché for characterization.

The "Jewish question" was foremost on André Bazin's mind when he wrote an important analysis of *The Grand Illusion* in 1958. The legendary film critic begins his review by describing how the new version restored the scenes relating to Rosenthal's Jewishness that had been cut in 1946. Bazin invokes Altman's charge of anti-Semitism right from the start of his article, only to dismiss it as a misguided aftereffect of World War II. According to Bazin, the theme most dear to Renoir was that "men are separated less by the vertical barriers of nationalism than by the horizontal divisions of cultures, races, classes, and professions." Bazin observes that Renoir's theory implies that race remains a fundamental division between men and thus seems to contradict the anti-anti-Semitic "spirit" that Bazin attributes to the film. Bazin thus sees a critical focus on race as a distraction from the film's message of brotherhood.

Another feature of Bazin's analysis that has become a staple of Renoir criticism is his praise of Renoir's realism. Bazin locates this realism in the plurality of languages spoken in the film, in the authenticity of the interactions among the characters, as well as in such technical features as the film's use of real exteriors and of depth-of-field photography. According to Bazin's logic, the film presents reality, which, by its very nature, cannot be prejudiced.

Bazin's view of the film has triumphed. Subsequent cinema scholars have discussed the film's treatment of the Jewish character in passing, but there has been no sustained analysis of the question of anti-Semitism in Renoir's work. In what follows I will present both sides of the question through a close and contextualized analysis of the film's depiction of the Jew. I will show how *The Grand Illusion* raises and tries to answer a series of questions about Jewishness and the nation, questions that circulated through various discourses in France in the late 1930s. While the mere asking of questions like "Does the Jew belong in France?" may implicate the film in an anti-Semitic logic, the film escapes from this logic by subtly undermining the exclusionary categories on which such logic depends.

A first step in evaluating the film's representation of the Jew involves comparing it to other cinematic depictions of Jews from the time. Rémy Pithon's work on the image of the Jews in French cinema of the 1930s allows us to perceive the truly exceptional nature of Renoir's representation. Pithon describes how the first half of the 1930s saw numerous depictions, mainly comical, of Jews on the screen. Explicit references to Jews in French cinema nearly disappeared, however, during the second half of the decade. The same period saw a vast increase in the vehemence of anti-Semitic rhetoric in the popular press. The Stavisky Scandal of 1934, in which a Jewish businessman committed suicide after the revelation of his links with corrupt politicians, as well as the rise to power of the Popular Front government of Léon Blum, who became France's first Jewish prime minister in 1936, provoked a torrent of anti-Semitic writing as well as actual physical violence. To explain the sudden disappearance of the Jew from the French screen in the late 1930s, Pithon suggests that filmmakers may have feared fanning the flames of this violent anti-Semitism. He further hypothesizes that the concentration of Jews in the Parisian cinema world—a concentration that increased as Jewish refugee producers and directors from Germany flocked to France—led to greater reticence and caution.

Pithon goes on to show, however, that despite the explicit disappearance of the Jew, several films of the period included characters who were "vaguely Jewish." Characters had Jewish connotations even if they were not explicitly named as Jews, especially if the actors playing them had played Jews in the past. For example, Marcel Dalio was known for playing shady foreigners in films and on stage. Even if these characters were vaguely foreign rather than explicitly Jewish, Pithon argues that they had Jewish associations for the average viewer of the time.

Viewing it in this context, *The Grand Illusion* stands out all the more strongly as one of the few films from the late 1930s to depict Jews explicitly and to confront head-on the question of their place within French society. According to Pithon, Renoir's clear intention was to combat anti-Semitism with the representation of Rosenthal as a sympathetic Jew. Whether or not he succeeded, however, Pithon leaves in doubt. By casting Dalio as Rosenthal, for example, Renoir may have compromised his intentions, since audiences at the time would have perceived the actor as sinister because of his prior roles. And by depicting Rosenthal as rich, Renoir played into popular prejudices against Jews. For Pithon, the lesson of *The Grand Illusion* is that even with the best intentions it is impossible to avoid falling into stereotype.

The debate over the film's anti-Semitism turns on the issue of stereotypes, the most obvious of which is Rosenthal's extreme wealth. The recipient of packages from home loaded with expensive foodstuffs while a prisoner of war, Rosenthal is introduced as a figure of ostentatious privilege. Presiding over a table set up in the prisoner dormitory, he doles out delicacies from fancy Parisian restaurants to his fellow officers, including the aristocratic de Boieldieu and the proletarian Maréchal. The men accept the "kindness of Rosenthal" with an appreciation mixed with resentment. Rosenthal's display of culinary largesse quickly becomes a pretext for the portrayal of class differences among the officers. Maréchal, a mechanic who has risen through the ranks, emerges as spokesman for the traditional French values of simplicity and thrift, values clearly opposed to Rosenthal's expensive tastes.

In the scene following the lunch sequence, Maréchal inquires about Rosenthal's wealth. "He must be well off," Maréchal states. Another prisoner explains that Rosenthal's family are "great bankers," while Rosenthal himself runs a high-fashion house. He is thus linked to two professions stereotyped as Jewish in 1930s France. As the son of a "great banker," he apparently belongs to that financial aristocracy associated with Jews in France since the early nineteenth century,

when families like the Rothschilds, Foulds, and Péreires presided over France's industrialization. Yet we discover later that Rosenthal's father is an immigrant from Poland, and thus not the type of Jew who would have possessed the capital or connections of those Jewish banking families.

As the son of a Polish immigrant, himself born in Vienna, Rosenthal would have been far more likely to engage in the clothing business, which carried different class associations. As Paula Hyman notes, this business was dominated by poor, Yiddish-speaking, less acculturated immigrants from Eastern Europe. There is thus an element of realism in this occupation designation. I would argue, however, that the film associates Rosenthal with two stereotyped and relatively incongruous professions as a means of reinforcing the Jewishness of the character.

It should be noted that Rosenthal is not explicitly named as a Jew in the early scenes of the film. Instead, his heavily coded name serves as a substitute for any overt reference to his ethnic identity. The film lays stress on the name Rosenthal right from the start, in the first scene when the Germans distribute packages to the French officers. The accentuating of the Jewish name, with its German tonalities, implicitly links the Jew with the enemy and contrasts with the film's treatment of the names of the other French officers, which—with the exception of Maréchal and de Boieldieu—are passed over quickly or not mentioned at all. The name Rosenthal, constantly repeated by the various characters who discuss his wealth, ostentation, and banking connections, substitutes for the word "Jew," which remains absent in the first half of the film. By circling around the "Jewish question" without naming it specifically, the film creates a kind of complicity with the viewer over the tacit recognition of Rosenthal's difference. This implicates the viewer in the logic of anti-Semitic exclusion that the film later seeks to overcome by explicitly including the Jew within the nation and undermining the category of race itself.

The absence of the word "Jew" is felt in the oddness of the dialogue, characterized by non sequiturs. An example of this occurs when the officers take a break from digging a tunnel to discuss their reasons for wanting to escape the German camp. Maréchal wants to rejoin the war effort. For de Boieldieu, a camp is to be escaped just as a tennis court is to be played on. He then asks Rosenthal if he's a sportsman. This unmotivated reference to Rosenthal's athletic prowess gives way to an anti-Semitic slur when another prisoner chimes in: "He was born in Jerusalem." He thus calls into doubt Rosenthal's patriotism and courage by implying that since he was "born in Jerusalem," Rosenthal is not really French and cannot want to return to a country that is not his own.

Rosenthal's deadpan answer about where he was born at once acknowledges the hidden subtext of the dialogue and perpetuates the game of circumlocution. "I was born in Vienna," he emphasizes, referring to his cosmopolitan, partly Eastern European, and hence highly coded, parentage. "Old Breton nobility," adds Maréchal, showing that he too can joke about Rosenthal's Jewishness. But Rosenthal has the last laugh: "That's always possible!" he declares. Speaking as the parvenu immigrant that he is, he reminds the other officers—of "ancient French stock"—that they do not possess a hundred square meters of their country, while the Rosenthals in thirty-five years of residence in France have acquired three castles, along with their hunting grounds and picture galleries of "authentic" ancestors. That, he concludes, is worth fighting for.

Rosenthal's speech provides the cornerstone of the case that would impute anti-Semitism to the film. Not only is he ostentatiously wealthy and involved in stereotypically Jewish professions, but, freshly arrived in France, his family has used its wealth to lay hold of the French patrimony. This reference to Rosenthal's rapaciousness calls to mind the viciously anti-Semitic diatribes of Édouard Drumont—who, in his bestselling *Jewish France* (1886), denounced what he saw as a Jewish takeover of the nation. Rosenthal's very brazenness and unapologetic boast seem calculated to arouse the worst fears of French audiences in the late 1930s, who were all the more alert to the threat of Jews taking over France following the rise to power of Léon Blum.

If Rosenthal's boasts about his acquisitiveness provide rather obvious fodder for critics intent on seeing *The Grand Illusion* as anti-Semitic, closer inspection reveals more subtle—and perhaps for that reason more troubling—ethnic stereotyping. In *The Jew's Body* Sander Gilman describes a tradition of nineteenth-century French and German anti-Semitic discourse that reads racial difference as a series of pathological physical signs. Gilman devotes a chapter to the Jew's supposedly deformed foot, which represented a major sign of inferiority for both German and French anti-Semites because it disqualified the Jew from military service. The limp Rosenthal develops while fleeing with Maréchal taps into these stereotypes. The product of an injury—the film shows the moment when Rosenthal hurts himself—the Jew's lame foot nevertheless acts as an impediment to his escape and, hence, to the accomplishment of his military duties.

The contrast with Maréchal is instructive, for while the proletarian Frenchman grew up in the inner city, he is nevertheless able to establish an immediate bond with the cow of Elsa (played by Dita Parlo), the German woman who shelters the two escaping Frenchmen while they wait for Rosenthal's foot to heal. While hiding out on the farm, Maréchal is continually shown stretching in the outdoors, looking out at the rolling hills; whereas Rosenthal remains confined by domestic space on account of his injury. Whereas Maréchal is filmed against deep-focus landscapes suggesting an affinity with nature, Rosenthal is continually framed or bounded by windows and doors, a sign of his association with culture. While Maréchal engages in rustic farm occupations, Rosenthal occupies himself by teaching the German woman's daughter to count in German. Stereotypical ethnic divisions of labor thus find their echo in these scenes as both men revert to their ancestral occupations: Maréchal returns to his peasant roots, while Rosenthal exercises his innate talent for the calculation associated with banking.

Reduced to the role of interpreter between Maréchal and Elsa (the German woman who hides the fugitives on her farm), Rosenthal watches passively as their mutual attraction turns into a love affair. The feminization of Rosenthal's character, already hinted at through his association with female fashion, is even more accentuated during the scenes on the German farm, when his virility is further compromised.

Of all the elements of the Jewish body marked by anti-Semitic discourse, however, the nose stands out as the most visible and identifiable. *The Grand Illusion* makes much of Rosenthal's nose, or rather of Marcel Dalio's. Renoir films Maréchal and Rosenthal differently, the former often facing the camera, and the latter in profile, his aquiline appendage given full prominence. Rosenthal's silhouette becomes more marked in the scenes when Rosenthal's "race" is at issue, such as when he describes the Jewish tendency toward pride from behind and slightly to the right of Maréchal, who faces the camera head-on.

Defending the film against charges of anti-Semitism would involve recognizing that the characterization of Rosenthal, while invoking a set of anti-Semitic stereotypes, is but one element in a much larger picture. For one thing, the film portrays all nationalities in clichéd terms, and each of the individual French officers embodies a series of stereotypes of his class or profession. While most of these are less threatening than the characteristics associated with the Jew, some might be seen as worse. De Boieldieu's monocle, English cigarettes, and inability to say *tu* (the informal mode of saying "you" in French) even to his wife and mother represent the typical trappings of the effete and painfully remote aristocrat.

Eventually de Boieldieu redeems himself by transcending his stereotype, confirming through his heroic gesture of self-sacrifice that the values associated with his class are doomed to extinction. Acting as a decoy to be shot so that Maréchal and Rosenthal can escape, de Boieldieu forges a link with his fellow officers that makes criticism of his haughty manners seem trivial. Likewise, Rosenthal rises above the stereotype of Jewish acquisitiveness through his generosity. Although he brags of his family's vast fortune, he shares his wealth by feeding his fellow officers. Indeed, the film endows Rosenthal with positive qualities that earn him the esteem of his comrades and the sympathies of the viewer. When Maréchal returns from solitary confinement, the camera cuts to a close-up of Rosenthal's face, showing him wipe a tear away at the sight of his friend's haggard appearance. Moreover, Rosenthal is deeply patriotic and eagerly takes on the project of escape, displaying great personal courage. When von Rauffenstein, the aristocratic German commander of the second camp, makes a disparaging remark about Maréchal and Rosenthal, de Boieldieu declares, "They are very good soldiers."

The affirmation of the Jew as soldier, in the mouth of an aristocratic career officer, had a particularly strong resonance in French culture in 1937. Since the time of Napoleon, when mandatory Jewish conscription was instituted with the aim of "regenerating" a population seen as unfit for soldiering, and, by extension, for citizenship, French Jews had prided themselves on their military accomplishments. By the mid-nineteenth century, Jews had become top-ranking officers, but the Dreyfus Affair opened a rift between the Jews and the army that did not close easily. Perhaps as a result of a nagging insecurity, native-born Jews as well as immigrants supported the First World War enthusiastically, enlisting in large numbers. De Boieldieu's recognition of Rosenthal as a good soldier, and the lack of distinction made between him and Maréchal in soldiering skills, signals the film's acceptance of Jewish military virtue, a deeply felt issue for Jews at the time the film was set and when it was made.

Returning to the comparison between Rosenthal and de Boieldieu, although the Jewish character embodies a series of negative stereotypes, these deficiencies are perceived as less negative than those of the aristocrat. Whereas Rosenthal is genial and generous, de Boieldieu is distant, rude, and snobbish and earns the mistrust—even the dislike—of his fellow soldiers. Once again Maréchal provides the terms for gauging the relative merits of the two men. In a crucial scene Maréchal tells Rosenthal that he would prefer escaping with him rather than de Boieldieu because the latter's "education" erects a barrier between them.

Interestingly, Maréchal does not experience Rosenthal's wealth as a similar barrier. While we know little about Rosenthal's education, he and Maréchal speak in a similar manner. This similarity is displayed most clearly when Maréchal, threatening to abandon Rosenthal because of his

twisted ankle, mimics the Jew's exact words. As Rosenthal intones, "I slipped. It's not my fault," Maréchal echoes, "You slipped. I know that you slipped." The mirroring words underscore the fundamental bond between the two men. Their familiar modes of address and colloquial constructions contrast with the proper and formal French of de Boieldieu.

Maréchal returns to the issue of Rosenthal's generosity in his explanation of why he feels closer to him than de Boieldieu. Rosenthal, however, dismisses his generosity as a function of pride. "I am very proud of my family's wealth," he explains modestly. Rosenthal then engages in a remarkable reflection on the nature of anti-Semitic stereotyping: "The crowd thinks our greatest flaw is avarice. That's a big mistake. We are often generous. Alas, in the face of that quality, Jehovah has given us a more glorious sin." On one level, Rosenthal's statement may be understood as an internalization of the anti-Semitic gesture of viewing the Jews as a group tinged by a collective defect. On the other, the Jew explicitly contradicts the stereotype of Jewish avarice, or replaces it with pride, an arguably less offensive sin. The ambiguity in the scene resolves itself when Maréchal brushes aside Rosenthal's disquisition: "It's all just stories."

Viewers inclined to see Maréchal's gesture of friendship toward Rosenthal as a sign of the film's positive attitude toward Jews receive confirmation during the climactic scenes following the escape. Setting out through the German countryside in the middle of winter with only a few lumps of sugar, Maréchal and Rosenthal experience extreme privation. When Rosenthal hurts his foot and cannot keep up, Maréchal threatens to abandon him after first venting his rage. Calling Rosenthal a "package," thus symbolically returning the packages the Jew has shared, Maréchal states baldly that he cannot stand Jews. The first time the word "Jew" is mentioned in the film, it hits Rosenthal, and the viewer, like a slap in the face. Maréchal leaves him behind to die in the snow. Then follows a justly celebrated scene in which Maréchal returns to help his injured friend. The bond between the two men, temporarily broken, is reforged of much stronger stuff.

Maréchal's generosity, his unwillingness to abandon his injured friend even at the risk of his own life, stands as the film's moral centerpiece. The fact that it comes immediately after the one overt expression of anti-Semitism in the film signals Renoir's elevation of human sympathy over hate and prejudice. Maréchal illustrates the film's message of unity, a message made all the stronger by the venting of repressed animosity. This typical Frenchman's gesture of inclusion indicates French openness to minority and marginality, an inclusion of difference in the nation.

Maréchal's gesture has all the more significance in that the original script for the film showed Maréchal escaping with a non-Jewish officer named Dolette. (Indeed, it did not include a Jewish character named Rosenthal at all.) As Dalio recounts, the tensions between his character and Maréchal were a last-minute addition to the script. The addition of the Jewish theme in the highly charged political atmosphere of the late 1930s no doubt signals the filmmakers' courageous action to take a stand against anti-Semitism.

The case for defending *The Grand Illusion* against charges of anti-Semitism receives further confirmation from the recognition that Rosenthal, more than any other character in the film, serves as a stand-in for the filmmaker. The film points to the resemblance between character and director in the Christmas scene on the farm where Rosenthal and Maréchal are hiding out. The scene begins with a close-up on a miniature

manger with a male voice describing the various members of the Holy Family. The camera pulls back to reveal the Jew arranging the crèche like a director setting up props. He insists on shutting off the lights while cranking up the music and telling Maréchal and Elsa where to stand. Making Rosenthal into a director points to the way his outsider status (as Jew and interpreter for the lovers) is shown to be a source of creativity and productivity. The Christmas scene also helps us see how the film views race itself as a kind of role-playing. The genuine care and interest Rosenthal takes in the *crèche* is that of an artist able to see universal beauties beneath obvious differences: "And the little Jesus? My racial brother," he says playfully. Dalio's delivery, and its accompaniment by a smile directed at Maréchal, contains a definite ironic tinge. In the intimacy of the domestic setting, where he controls not only the two languages spoken but also directs the other's actions, Rosenthal's invocation of the Jewish "race" reveals it playfulness, its theatricality. Just like during the earlier theatrical performance, in which men dressed as women succeed in arousing the silent respect of the assembled prisoners, certain forms of identity—gender or, in this case, race—are seen as a kind of illusion, inessential in the face of a deeper humanity. The film thus undermines the very categorization that underpins the exclusionary logic of anti-Semitism.

The final exchange between Maréchal and Rosenthal as they prepare to cross the Swiss border into freedom reinforces the dismissal of race as an essential category. As they say goodbye, German guards shoot at them while they run for the frontier. Maréchal calls Rosenthal a "filthy Jew" and Rosenthal hurls the less loaded epithet of "old nut." Given the significance that the word "Jew" has taken on during the film, its return at the end as an endearment shows how far the men and the viewer have come. Rendered innocuous through the film's exploration of anti-Semitic stereotypes, the taboo word now has the power not to divide but to unite.

Unlike those critics who suggest that Renoir results to anti-Semitic clichés unconsciously, I would argue that *The Grand Illusion* invokes the discourse of anti-Semitism strategically, the better to lay it to rest. Anti-Semitic stereotypes and clichés can only be neutralized or overcome if they are acknowledged and brought out into the open. By portraying the Jew as a wealthy banker, Renoir makes his character realistic, confirming the audiences' expectations of what a Jew is like. And by showing the character in a positive light, the film negates the negativity of the cliché. Had Renoir chosen to avoid all traces of the stereotype in his depiction of Rosenthal, audiences would not have believed the representation as an accurate depiction of a Jew, and Renoir's attack on anti-Semitism would have failed to hit its mark.

Up to this point, my argument has centered on how the film constructs its message rather than on how viewers understand this signification. Recent film theory, however, has insisted that it is viewers who ultimately determine a film's meaning. As I have shown, certain viewers saw the film as anti-Semitic. For some critics, *The Grand Illusion* proves that filmmakers may end up resorting to anti-Semitic stereotypes despite their best intentions. I think the film teaches a different lesson: that filmmakers cannot ultimately control or fix the meaning of their representations. Perhaps Renoir deserves to be blamed for creating a representation too complex, too liable to be read in the wrong way. Cinematic depictions, particularly realist ones, have a way of escaping the limits prescribed for them, just as audiences have a way of retaining not the subtle

messages of a film but its more overt images, particularly if these confirm their prejudices. The picture of Rosenthal as a large-nosed capitalist may have made a greater impression than the subtleties of his discussions of race. To illustrate this concluding point, I'd like to turn once more to an anecdote from the autobiography of Marcel Dalio, the actor who played Rosenthal.

In the spring of 1940 Dalio was waiting in Portugal, like so many French Jews, for a visa to the United States or any other country that would take him. One night, he ran into an old friend who told him that he had done well to flee Paris. According to his friend, Dalio's face was plastered on posters that purported to show the French how to identify Jewish physical characteristics. The Nazis chose Dalio as the image of the criminalized deviant Jew not merely because of his profile, but because his cinematic roles playing Jewish characters, especially in Renoir's *The Grand Illusion*, had helped fix an image of the Jew in the minds of the French public.

Should Renoir therefore be considered an anti-Semitic filmmaker? A historically informed reading would answer no. But did his films lend themselves to anti-Semitic uses under particular circumstances? Unfortunately, history seems to answer yes. Despite what may have been Renoir's wish to overturn stereotypes to offer up a positive vision of the Jew, the image of the Jew returned in grotesque form, appropriated by the fascist menace it was meant to counter. Perhaps, ultimately, it is not so much Renoir as the medium of film that must be blamed for Dalio's plight, because of the ease with which its images can be isolated, divorced from the subtleties of narrative, captured as a still, and splashed on a poster. Dalio did, however, at least manage to find some humor in his predicament: the actor notes feeling a certain pride that, for once, a poster gave him top billing.

Abridged and amended from: Maurice Samuels, "Renoir's *La Grande Illusion* and the 'Jewish Question,'" *Historical Reflections/ Reflexions Historiques* 32, no.1 (2006): 165–92.

Background: http://www.jewishvirtuallibrary.org/ jsource/vjw/France.html.

Bibliography

Birnbaum, Pierre. *Jewish Destinies: Citizenship, State, and Community in Modern France.* Translated by Arthur Goldhammer. New York: Hill and Wang, 2000.

Crisp, Colin G. *Genre, Myth, and Convention in French Cinema, 1929–1939.* Bloomington: Indiana University Press, 2002.

Dudley, Andrew. *Mists of Regret: Culture and Sensibility in Classic French Film.* Princeton, NJ: Princeton University Press, 1995.

Faulkner, Christopher. *The Social Cinema of Jean Renoir.* Princeton, NJ: Princeton University Press, 1986.

Hyman, Paula E. *The Jews of Modern France.* Berkeley: University of California Press, 1998.

Malinovich, Nadia. *French and Jewish: Culture and the Politics of Identity in Early Twentieth-Century France.* Oxford: Littman Library of Jewish Civilization, 2008.

O'Shaughnessy, Michael. *Jean Renoir.* Manchester, UK: Manchester University Press, 2000.

Pithon, Rémy. "Le Juif à l'écran en France vers la fin des années trente." *Vingtième siècle* 18 (1988): 89–99.

Renoir, Jean. *My Life and My Films.* Translated by Norman Denny. New York: Atheneum, 1974.

Sesonske, Alexander. *Jean Renoir: The French Films, 1924–1939.* Cambridge: Harvard University Press, 1980.

Williams, Allan. *Republic of Images: A History of French Filmmaking.* Cambridge: Harvard University Press, 1992.

5. Chariots of Fire

Bigotry, Manhood, and Moral Certitude in an Age of Individualism

ELLIS CASHMORE

Chariots of Fire, directed by Hugh Hudson [A] United Kingdom, 1981

The values and status hierarchy of Victorian England were fast disappearing at the beginning of the 1920s. Confidence in the power of the free market to deliver personal freedom and material plentitude had receded amid the revulsion at women's work underground, the exploitation of labor in mills, and the squalor of industrial cities. Education reflected a class-divided society, the potential for social mobility being extremely limited. Before the World War of 1914–18, discontents arising from class divisions and industrial labor were held in check by limited expectations and restrained perhaps by religion. By the end of the war, the working class was not so easily placated. Industrial disputes became commonplace, and radical politics centered on the Labor Party, which formed its first administration in 1923.

An incipient consumer culture was taking root. The economic theorist Thorstein Veblen used the term "conspicuous consumption" in 1899 to describe the nascent pattern of displaying social status through consumable items. While the focus of Veblen's analysis was the United States, similar trends were in evidence in Britain. By the 1920s, this growing consumer culture had been complemented by widespread availability of new forms of entertainment like radio and motion pictures. A culture "strongly infused by individualism of a self-interested kind," as Alan Fox puts it, began to coalesce.

Ben Cross (as Harold Abrahams) proves that Jews can win races, too. From *Chariots of Fire* (1981) directed by Hugh Hudson. WARNER BROS./PHOTOFEST

Support for national purposes or any kind of pursuit that transcended individual or group interests was far from assured. Even patriotism was conditional. There was a resistance to combining Englishness with abstract concepts such as state or empire. What good were a strong nation and global empire if there was no individual well-being? Paradoxically this was a time when the English "felt the need to put out the flag, to cultivate national sentiment and to look at national monuments and rituals," as Krishan Kumar reflects. The English superiority that had been undeniable for 300 years was under threat. Charged, as they saw it, with a responsibility for civilizing the world, carrying their language, their culture, their institutions, and their industry to all corners of the Empire, the English rarely showed

the arrogance and all-round superciliousness with which they later became associated. As Kumar points out, "Ruling the roost, they felt it impolitic to crow." But there were portents that the Empire was approaching the end.

The unity of purpose catalyzed by the war had largely dissipated by the 1920s, replaced by the ethic of individualism. The type of Britishness experienced in this period was, as Bernard Crick suggests, "highly and sensibly utilitarian, not emotionally nationalistic." In other words, it was measured in terms of its practical value to the individual. There are, of course, no individuals, in the sense of human beings as separate, independent entities distinct from all others. Every member of society derives his or her identity from membership in a "people" of some kind, whether a group, an organization, or several different kinds of collectivity. Indifferent to the nation and Empire as the English might have been in the 1920s, they still identified or attached themselves to other associations. As traditional ties of geography and occupation weakened, people explored other affiliations: affiliations they felt were central to their being.

Neither Eric Liddell nor Harold Abrahams was overtly patriotic. Even in their triumphant moments, they were not seen draping themselves in the Union flag or heard proclaiming their allegiance to Great Britain. Their behavior suggests they were prepared to defy formal arrangements in pursuit of their own ambitions. Both men's commitments were narrow, specific, and consistent with the individualism of the time.

Liddell was born in 1902 in Tientsin in northeast China. His parents were members of the London Missionary Society. At five, Liddell was enrolled in Eltham College, a private boarding school for the children of missionaries in London. His parents remained in China, and the family met only during furloughs in Scotland. At school Liddell distinguished himself in rugby and cricket, both appropriate for the son of a gentleman, though he excelled in sprinting. He added to his sporting achievements at the University of Edinburgh in 1920 on the track and rugby teams. He became an active member of the Glasgow Students' Evangelical Union, speaking at meetings across Scotland. After the 1924 Olympic Games, he retired from competitive sports and moved back to China, where he was ordained as a minister. He married a Canadian missionary with whom he had two children. After the Japanese invaded China, he was interned by them and died in captivity in 1945 from a brain tumor.

Abrahams, like Liddell, was an all-around athlete, adept at both sprinting and the long jump.

Born in Bedford, fifty miles north of London, in 1899, his family was of Lithuanian ancestry. They were among nearly 250,000 Jews, mostly from Eastern Europe, who migrated to England in the late nineteenth and early twentieth centuries.

Abrahams was privately educated at the Repton School before going to study at Cambridge in 1919. While at Cambridge, he earned a place on the 1920 British Olympic team but failed to place in any of his four events. Four years later, he accompanied Liddell to the Paris Olympiad, which was a more modest tournament than today's Olympics. In 1925 he retired from athletics, having sustained a foot injury, and went into law and journalism. He died in 1978, two years before the film that enshrined him and Liddell in the popular imagination.

Chariots of Fire was director Hugh Hudson's first feature and it was acclaimed globally, winning Academy Awards for best picture, screenplay, costume design, and score. Its plot centers on the efforts of Liddell and Abrahams to win Olympic gold medals. Both did: Abrahams upset the odds by beating two favored US sprinters in the 100 meters, while Liddell, having switched to 400 meters to avoid compromising his convictions about competing on the Sabbath (a 100-meter heat was scheduled for a Sunday), also emerged victorious. Liddell's preparation in the Scottish Highlands parallels Abrahams' endeavors at Cambridge. Both men are depicted as resolute and unwavering in their determination to win gold medals.

There are no villains as such in the film's narrative, just abstract forces that task both men. In Liddell's world, God rather than man is central: he has a pure and immutable faith. When he runs, it is with the same kind of passion he brings to his evangelical orations. In Liddell's mind, there is no doubt that God gave him an intellect with which to comprehend the Almighty. But why was he blessed with being fleet of foot? His sister objects to his athletics, insisting that the time he spends on running should be spent evangelizing. His father assures him that when he races he does so in the service of God: "Run in God's name," he implores him, "and let the world stand back in wonder."

Abrahams' funeral frames the stories: among the mourners is Aubrey Montague, a journalist who recounts his impressions of first meeting Abrahams when he arrived at Cambridge after the war. He recalls Abrahams' ambivalence at the deference of two war veterans who help him with his luggage. While God is a constant presence in Liddell's life, Abrahams has no such comfort. But he has a challenge: as a Jew, he sees himself as "a weapon" representing a group that has an epic history of driven itinerancy and persecution. While his background has afforded him protection from maltreatment, he remains mindful of the anti-Semitism that surrounds him. He confides that he feels "semi-deprived . . . they [gentiles] lead me to water but won't let me drink."

The two men interact when Abrahams, having heard of Liddell, seeks to check out the competition at an athletics meet in Edinburgh. He watches in awe as Liddell grittily picks himself after being knocked over during a race and still prevails. The prospect of running against such an adversary makes Abrahams take the drastic step of securing the services of a coach for his Olympics preparations. Already somewhat marginalized as a Jew, Abrahams distances himself further from his peers by paying Sam Mussabini for his services. The film indicates that it was a dishonor at that time to be trained by a professional. Abrahams is forced to separate from his coach before the competition, and Mussabini waits in a hotel for news of his charge's race. Hiring a professional coach contravened the "Corinthian spirit," so

lauded by true amateurs, who saw the joy of sport in the competing rather than the winning. The move places Abrahams outside the parameters of true sportsmanship. Competition was conceived in a way that permitted honor amid defeat: there was no disgrace in losing, but shame in not trying. A central purpose in sport was to bring all participants to their mettle.

Abrahams is motivated by other priorities. "I run to win," he reminds the actress Sybil Gordon. "If I can't win, I won't run." His remark captures the individualistic, self-interested approach to competition. It is totally at odds with the ethos of sport in the early years of the twentieth century, yet entirely congruent with the "win at all costs" mentality that became prevalent in sport in the decades that followed.

Liddell too is driven by selfish concerns, in his case to satisfy his conviction that he is competing in the service of God. His version of Protestant Christian fundamentalism was underpinned by a sense of certainty and intolerance of other faiths or other versions of Christianity. "I believe God made me for a purpose, but he also made me fast," says Liddell, who is unsettled by the news that a heat for his chosen 100 meters final is scheduled to take place on a Sunday. He will not countenance running on the Sabbath and is offered the alternative of competing in the 400 meters. In fact, the program was known several months in advance, and Liddell made his decision in time to adjust his training accordingly.

Abrahams makes friends and enemies in roughly equal measure. He reminds Montague that, as a Jew, he has "felt the cold reluctance in a handshake," but, as an athlete, he has never felt defeat. Portrayed by Ben Cross, Abrahams has the poker-faced glare of a professional boxer and the gait of a basketball player. He dispenses challenges in a way that advertises arrogance. Within days of his arrival at Cambridge, he succeeds in the Trinity Dash, a sprint around the perimeter of a university courtyard that must be completed in less than forty-six seconds, this being the time it takes for the church bell to chime twelve times. Only two people have accomplished this, Sebastian Coe and Lord Burghley, who is renamed Lord Andrew Lindsay in the film.

The nonchalant aristocrat's training methods are theatrically evocative of the gentleman amateur: he balances full champagne glasses on the edge of hurdles, then negotiates them speedily without spilling a drop. Meanwhile, Abrahams grinds out miles under the ruthless supervision of Mussabini. In one memorable scene, several athletes train on the beach with Vangelis's celestial music matching the slow-motion pace of the runners, prompting the audience to think that the story may be only about two athletes. But the story is also about the moral rearmament of the postwar period.

The Games unite the two stories, if not the two men. Abrahams' race mirrors another theme: America's emerging supremacy as a superpower is represented by Charles Paddock and Jackson Scholz, reputed to be the fastest men alive. Their ambitions are not hampered by Corinthian ideals. They want to win, as, of course, do Abrahams and Liddell, though for different reasons. The Americans' modern approach presages the coming age in sport.

Abrahams and Liddell win their respective events, suggesting a kind of watershed. Abrahams' methodical approach will be duplicated many times over, though few athletes will compete because it is their binding duty to do so. As if to underline his obligation, Liddell pronounced it fulfilled when he left active competition to pursue his calling after the Games.

Chariots of Fire is, of course, drama, not documentary or even docudrama. As such, it mixes fact with fabrication. The timing of Liddell's switch to the 400 meters in a minor historical fudge, as is the omission of any mention of Abrahams' previous defeats in the 1920 Olympics. There is no evidence that Liddell's sister counseled him against running. The sham Trinity Dash is inconsequential. All these add to the film's ethereal quality: its plot may have been rooted in this world, but the main characters embody otherworldly characteristics, including the fortitude, fervor, and redemptive powers typically associated with gods. Abrahams and Liddell were actual people, but their stories are told as fables. The film's title alerts us to this. Taken from William Blake's poem of decline and redemption, *Jerusalem*, it evokes heroism, fearlessness, and valor.

The movie displayed motifs perfectly suited to the time of its release, and, for this reason, can be approached as much as a metaphor for the 1980s as a chronicle of the 1920s. British culture of the early 1980s yoked the breakdown of older loyalties, especially those of class, with a new, unbridled form of ambitious individualism that would by mid-decade effloresce in the yuppies (young, upwardly mobile people driven by acquisitive impulses). The governments of Margaret Thatcher in Britain and Ronald Reagan in the United States conferred respectability on avarice and the inequalities it engendered. Drive, enterprise, and the unswerving will to succeed were hallmarks of a culture in which success was, in many senses, the ultimate value. For this reason, the film was popular at fund-raising events for the Conservative Party.

In the run-up to her election as prime minister in 1979, Mrs. Thatcher memorably warned that British culture was in danger of being "swamped." By 1982, when the Falklands War animated a gung-ho jingoism, a new patriotism lifted Mrs.

Thatcher in the opinion polls. *Chariots of Fire* used a different kind of vocabulary to convey its nationalism, though the repeated signifiers of British perseverance, resolve, and indomitability fit in with the mood of the early 1980s as did the contempt for other nationals shown, especially at Cambridge in the 1920s (Arabs, Italians, and French are disparaged in the film; "Semites" are merely regarded with suspicion).

Interestingly, both athletes' sense of patriotism is brought into doubt. Abrahams "resents" his Cambridge master's accusation that he does not run for his country, but for "individual glory." Elsewhere in the film, he sings with gusto Gilbert and Sullivan's: "He is an Englishman!" while playing in a production of *HMS Pinafore*: "But in spite of all temptations / To belong to other nations / He remains an Englishman." Lidddell's patriotism is questioned by the British Olympic Committee when he refuses to compete on the Sabbath, and he affirms his loyalty—though in another scene, he quotes from the Bible, Isaiah 40:17: "All nations before Him are as nothing; and they are counted to Him less than nothing and vanity." The culture of the 1980s applauded the kind of grit and mercilessness shown by Abrahams and the singularity of purpose Liddell brought to his efforts.

The enchantment of *Chariots of Fire* lies partly in its plausible depiction of Britishness, replete with class distinctions, prejudice, and downright snobbery. Looking backward from the early 1980s, these practices seemed both elegantly civilized and cruelly archaic. But their depiction contributed to a surge of interest in recent British history. When the film won the Oscar for Best Picture and other Oscars, its scriptwriter famously tipped off the Academy audience with the warning, "The British are coming." The film was widely acknowledged as a British achievement.

Chariots of Fire is about men, their dreams, relationships, enemies, strengths, and, very occasionally, their Achilles' heels. Females appear in the drama as fleeting presences, cameos, or staves that make men sturdier in their moments of weakness, reassure them in times of doubt. Olympic founder Pierre de Coubertin announced in 1894 that the event was "an exultation of male athleticism . . . with female applause as a reward." In 1921, there was a separate Women's Olympic Games; by 1928 a limited program of women's events was integrated into the Amsterdam Olympiad. Women did not receive voting rights in England until 1918. The extension of the franchise reflected changing, though not altogether enlightened, attitudes toward women. Manliness was synonymous with moral goodness and physical health, and vestiges of this are apparent in the movie; women are always peripheral to its main narrative.

The English public schools in which Abrahams and Liddell were educated and from which the ethos of "Muscular Christianity" had emerged promoted sport, not simply as recreation, but as a proving ground where boys' resolve would be tested and their resilience taxed. This was wholly consistent with the view that competition would develop the character of the future captains of industry and leaders of the British Empire. "The fear lay deep in English culture that city life was effeminate and that the advancement of material comforts was making men soft," writes Jock Phillips. Disturbed by what they saw as a feminization of Victorian culture, writers such as Charles Kingsley and Thomas Arnold openly praised overt displays of power and aggression to promote the harmonious development of mind, body, and spirit.

The doctrine of "Christian manliness" may have lost strength by the twentieth century, but it finds expression in the efforts of Liddell to discover the theological justification for his pursuit of athletic perfection. He is hailed by his family in the film as a "Muscular Christian." Scholars of this movement observe that "Liddell's decision not to race on Sunday, due to his Christian faith, and his decision to give up his distinguished athletics career to become a missionary . . . demonstrates the virtues of the Muscular Christian ethic."

In Abrahams there is a vision of manhood that resonates with the times. Driven by primal forces, he draws rebukes from Cambridge colleagues who remind him of the importance of esprit de corps, comradeship, and "mutual responsibility." "In your enthusiasm for success, you have lost sight of these ideals," his college master tells him. His quest for "individual glory" is "too plebian." Yet Abrahams' self-centered conduct portrays an individual freely and defiantly pursuing his own course of action. It is congruent with both the laissez-faire doctrine of individual action unrestricted by government interference and a conception of masculinity in which the vigorous pursuit of goals is an ideal antidote to vice, sloth, and indolence.

Abrahams regarded sport as an instrument with which he could fight anti-Semitism. This is part of the film's design, though there are doubters who question whether anti-Semitism occupied such precedence in Abrahams' motivational hierarchy. A report, though contested, that Abrahams converted from Judaism to Catholicism several years after the Games introduced doubts about his purported motives for running. Abrahams talks about his feelings of rejection and alludes to a society seething with antipathy for Jews. He was one of about 250,000 Jews in England in the 1920s, and there is evidence to support the view that anti-Semitism

would have affected the life chances of many of them. Anti-Semitism in its modern form began to emerge in the 1870s, suggesting Abrahams would have lived amid the unfriendly mythology surrounding Jews. Yet there is other evidence that institutional anti-Semitism had been abating for several decades.

Jews were banned from Britain from 1290 until Oliver Cromwell allowed their return in 1655. Benjamin Disraeli, baptized as a child but descended from Sephardic Jews, became prime minster in 1868. By the beginning of the nineteenth century, the Rothschilds were prominent members of society. Elected to the House of Commons in 1847, Lionel Rothschild was barred for his refusal to take the Christian oath of allegiance. It took another decade before he took office. By 1890 all restrictions to politics and commerce based on religion had been removed.

Abrahams' family was part of the great wave of Eastern European Jews migrating to Britain between 1881 and 1914. In 1897 the World Zionist Congress called for the establishment of a permanent state for Jews in what they considered their spiritual homeland, Palestine. With Prime Minister Arthur Balfour's Declaration of 1917, the British government expressed sympathy with this aspiration, though with a certain ambivalence about whether Jews could ever gain full acceptance in gentile societies.

The film records Abrahams' perception of being snubbed and suggests he drew motivation from this. But it is perhaps best regarded as a dramatic device rather an insight into Abrahams' will to win. The available evidence indicates Abrahams' motives were less altruistic. Whatever they were, Abrahams' heroic triumph is a satisfying denouement. The viewer is invited to interpret the victory as a triumph for not just the race's underdog (which Abrahams was), but for society's underdog (which he was not). He wins a race, but as what? An athlete or a Jew? The answer is strongly implied: both. Wounded by the genteel condescending attitudes he encounters at Cambridge, Abrahams takes up the cudgels and fights back in the name of his people. His personal triumph is also a victory over anti-Semites. This lends the film a parable-like conclusion.

The moral in this appears to be that anti-Semitism, like the bigotry that spawns it, can be diminished by symbolic deeds. When African Americans like boxer Joe Louis and track and field athlete Jesse Owens won contests, their achievements were often elevated above the level of sport. *Chariots of Fire* fashions Abrahams' win similarly. There are no radical gestures on victory rostrums or dedications, but the struggle converts Abrahams' victory into an emblem. It is the climatic triumph-of-the-will sententiousness that is simultaneously uplifting yet trivializing. The bigotry so central to the narrative is seemingly broken as easily as the finishing tape. Abrahams' win did little to ameliorate the problems faced by Britain's Jewish population: if anything, the situation deteriorated, as the rise of Oswald Mosley's anti-Semitic British Union of Fascists illustrated in the 1930s.

Abrahams' approach to sport is noticeably incongruous in the 1920s. Yet it prefigures a thoroughly modern attitude toward sport. Lord Burghley, who trains alongside Abrahams, is a more typical athlete of the 1920s. His abiding priority is the protocols of amateurism. He is skillful in the execution of his athleticism and not averse to practicing, though never in a way that confuses his pursuit with labor. He competes out of love. Win or lose, he is fulfilled by the satisfaction of his endeavor. He happily sacrifices his place in the 6400 meters to accommodate Liddell's intransigence.

Abrahams is cut from different cloth. He prompts sneers from his Cambridge colleagues for his insular orientation. For Abrahams, defeat, as athletes were later wont to say, is not an option. The Americans, whom Abrahams beat, were not bound by the gentlemanly code of behavior that prohibited too much preparation or an unseemly desire to win. Abrahams' declaration "I run to win" elicits admiration from his listener. This is a misleading response. More likely, it would have provoked surprise, perhaps even astonishment, and—in some quarters—disapproval, especially in the run-up to the Olympic Games, where the essential thing was "not to have won, but to have fought well."

Abrahams' reversal of this might have been unusual in athletics, though professional sports already depended on the patronage of spectators who were less interested in the experiential aspects of competition. By the 1920s, the sporting world was divided into two halves: those who recognized the positive, morally uplifting, and character-forming benefits of sport, and those who made money from it. As consumer culture began to develop, the two populations were coming together as exploitable markets. Fans of professional sports were not interested in the joys of participating or the rewards of giving one's best: they wanted to be entertained at the end of what might have been a monotonous week of industrial labor.

Even sports that did not depend on spectators' benefaction could not escape the changing attitude of competitors. Abrahams epitomized the change. The wisdom of hiring a professional coach in a sport that barely forty years before had not admitted mechanics [the British term for factory workers in the nineteenth century] must have been doubtful. It was probably a sign of the times. Mussabini was not allowed into the stadium, but Abrahams started a trend. Abrahams introduced a method of preparing and competing that might have upset traditionalists, but was perfectly in harmony with the changes in the role of sport in popular culture. By the mid-1930s, sporting competition had become the instrumental, results-oriented activity we recognize today. Abrahams personified a new type of competitiveness.

"*Chariots of Fire* is a quintessential sports film," tenders David Rowe. "It deals squarely with the mythological possibilities of transcendence of class, ethnic prejudice, and human selfishness through sport." To watch fellow Oscar winner *Rocky* (1976) or any of its sequels is like descending from Mount Olympus to downtown Philadelphia. Rocky Balboa's world boxing title challenge represents a victory for grit and perseverance in the face of adversity and carries the burden of the underclass. But few other films have distilled the "quintessence" of sport quite as perfectly as *Chariots of Fire*. Sport cannot vanquish social inequity, but it transcends it. *Chariots of Fire* treats its characters with reverence, plays up their merits, and alchemizes what might in another era or film seem like vices into virtues.

By centering on what was, in the 1920s, a relatively modest Olympic sideshow and amplifying it into a plausible drama about human lives that intersect momentarily in a context of hope that would soon sink into depression, *Chariots of Fire* manufactured a piece of reality. Its reenactment of that reality is insufficient to explain the why of anti-Semitism. The answer is that the Olympics made no material impact on anti-Semitism, which escalated during the gloom of the 1930s. *Chariots of Fire* finishes with an almost operatically overwrought conclusion, shifting from the prosaic to the sublime. Bigotry is vaporized, uncertainties about God vanish, and affirmations of the ethic of

individualism abound. The film is more an invigorating sermon for the 1980s rather than a literal or an authentic record of the 1920s. Perhaps this is not a legitimate charge to set against a work of art that drew from, but did not purport to be a history.

Abridged and amended from: Ellis Cashmore, "*Chariots of Fire:* Bigotry, Manhood and Moral Certitude in an Age of Individualism," *Sport in Society* 11, nos. 2–3 (March–May 2008): 159–73.

Background: http://www.geschichteinchronologie.ch/eu/GB/EncJud_juden-in-England05-1914-1933-ENGL.html; http://en.wikipedia.org/wiki/Harold_Abrahams.

Bibliography

Alderman, Geoffrey. *Modern British Jewry*. Oxford: Oxford University Press, 1992.

Brenner, Michael, and Gideon Reuveni, eds. *Emancipation through Muscles: Jews and Sports in Europe*. Lincoln: University of Nebraska Press, 2006.

Briley, Ron, Deborah A. Carmichael, and Michael K Schoenecke, eds. *All Stars and Movie Stars: Sports in Film and History*. Lexington: University of Kentucky Press, 2008.

Chapman, James. *Past and Present: National Identity and the British Historical Film*. London: I. B. Tauris, 2005.

Endelman, Todd M. *The Jews of Britain: 1656 to 2000*. Berkeley: University of California Press, 2002.

Hill, John. *British Cinema in the 1980s*. Oxford: Clarendon Press of Oxford University Press, 1999.

Holmes, Colin. *Anti-Semitism and British Society, 1876–1939*. New York: Holmes and Meier, 1979.

Leach, Jim. *British Film*. New York: Cambridge University Press, 2004.

Mayer, Paul Yogi. *Jews and the Olympic Games: Sport; A Springboard for Minorities*. London: Vallentine Mitchell, 2004.

Taylor, Paul. *Jews and the Olympic Games: The Clash between Sport and Politics*. Sussex, UK: Sussex Academic Press, 2004.

PART TWO

The *Shtetl* on the Precipice
Eastern Europe, 1881–1921

6. Fiddling with Sholem Aleichem

A History of *Fiddler on the Roof*

STEPHEN J. WHITFIELD

Tevye, directed by Maurice Schwartz [NCJF]
United States, 1939
Fiddler on the Roof, Directed by Norman
Jewison [A]
United States, 1971

"We are the only great people of the civilized world that is a pure democracy," Henry James asserted in 1878, "and we are the only great people that is exclusively commercial." These are the pressures against which any key text of American Jewish culture struggles for life. Such a context was defined by the forces of vulgarization; and they were surely more formidable than what challenged artists in the Old World, which is where "Tevye the Dairyman" made his first appearance. Sholem Aleichem first published this fifteen-page story in Warsaw in 1895 and added seven related tales, the last in 1914. Exactly half a century later, *Fiddler on the Roof* opened on Broadway and constitutes an intriguing instance of the adaptation of serious literature into a form—really two forms, thanks to the 1971 film—that was expected to satisfy the two characteristics that Henry James ascribed to American civilization.

Those who have championed the standards of the most elevated fiction and who have insisted that Sholem Aleichem satisfied such criteria have managed to restrain their enthusiasm for *Fiddler on the Roof*. It misrepresented his writings as "naive [and] pre-modern," Cynthia Ozick charged, "the occasion of nostalgia for a sweeter time, pogroms notwithstanding." Similar "distortions" included "slickness" (which is what Broadway itself would have called professionalism). Hillel Halkin faulted the show, however "charming," for keeping "within the range of the safely sentimental." The critics in 1964 were even harsher. This adaptation, Robert Brustein asserted, "bears about the same relation to its source as unleavened cocktail wafers do to Passover *matzoth*." *Fiddler on the Roof* is so "slick, colorful, and energetic" that it can offend no one—except "the serious Yiddishist." One exemplar, Irving Howe, found the musical "disheartening," "a tasteless jumble," full of "sentimentalism and exploitativeness," proof of "the spiritual anemia of Broadway and of the middle-class Jewish world which by now seems firmly linked to Broadway." The choreography, which entailed a dance of the village rabbi with a young woman, "shows that if there was a Jewish hand in this production, there was also a *goyisher kop* (Gentile head)," or at least no historical or religious consultant. In the tales themselves, Howe added, "God is a presence to whom Jews can turn in moments of need and

Haim Topol (as Tevye) talks to God. From *Fiddler on the Roof* (1971), directed by Norman Jewison. UNITED ARTISTS/PHOTOFEST

urgency; in *Fiddler on the Roof*, He ends up as Zero Mostel's straight man."

Howe at least was willing to attend the Broadway production (and to praise the bravura, Tony-winning performance of Zero Mostel as Tevye). By contrast Marc Chagall refused to see *Fiddler on the Roof*, even though his paintings of 1912–13 and 1920–21 had suggested to librettist Joseph Stein and director-choreographer Jerome Robbins the title for the show. The artist's canvases of Vitebsk had also helped inspire Boris Aronson to design the expressionistic sets. Because the Metropolitan Opera House had commissioned Chagall to paint the Lincoln Center murals, he and his wife Vava came to New York, where the Broadway hit was playing only a few blocks away. But still the painter stayed away. He seems to have feared that any evocation of his own childhood world of Vitebsk would inevitably misrepresent it, and make it "a dreadful sham."

Chagall exemplified an Old World division between high culture and mass entertainment that is less pronounced in the United States (where the violinist heard on the soundtrack of the movie of *Fiddler on the Roof* is none other than Isaac Stern). In America popular and commercial success are perennial temptations even for the most refined and serious of artists. The aim of the producers of *Fiddler on the Roof* was mass appeal, to pack the house; and very few musicals in history have been more successful in meeting that goal. Winning nine Tony Awards, *Fiddler* ran for 3,242 performances; and when it closed in 1972, anyone in the Northeast who might have wanted to see the show had enjoyed ample opportunity to do so. Until then no other musical had ever run longer on Broadway. Anyone wishing to stage *Fiddler on the Roof* must be licensed by Music Theatre International. This musical consistently ranks in the licensing company's top five.

Even more astonishing is that *Fiddler on the Roof* also became an international smash hit. In virtually every country where the show was scheduled to open, backers expressed the fear of a flop. Audiences were presumed to be indifferent to the Jewish encounter with modernity and to be ignorant of the peculiarities of the *shtetl*—remote from the concerns that this musical addressed. Yet "miracle of miracles"—success occurred everywhere. The Japanese producer was introduced to Joseph Stein, the librettist who had brought Sholem Aleichem to Broadway, and asked him: "Tell me, do they understand this show in America?" Stein answered this question in a Jewish way with another question: "What do you mean?" The producer replied: "It's so Japanese!"

How to account for such popularity is not only the domain of aesthetics, but also the task of the historian, who should treat this phenomenon as an index of the lives and the concerns of the American Jews who put on the show, and whose response at the box office helped to account for the longevity of *Fiddler on the Roof*. Credit for its initial success on Broadway must be given primarily to Jerome Robbins, who won Tonys for Best Director and Best Choreographer. Robbins never forgot a childhood visit to Poland, and in mounting the musical expressed the hope that he would evoke for another generation the devastated culture of East European Jewry.

Zero Mostel's performance as Tevye was pivotal to the initial success of *Fiddler on the Roof*, too. Of the fourteen songs in *Fiddler on the Roof*, all but four Tevye has to sing (in part or whole, solo or with others). He prances, dances, does

pantomime, engages in repartee with the deity. Tevye easily became the most famous role Mostel ever inhabited. The son of an Orthodox rabbi, Mostel was the only member of the original cast to know Yiddish. That "jargon" makes only a very brief appearance in the lyrics. Indeed Mostel insisted upon the universal appeal of Tevye, who "has no nationality really, because he symbolizes the underprivileged in every country." To be sure the matchmaker is named Yente, and some liberal sprinkling of *mazel tov* (plus the Hebrew *l'chaim*—to life) can be detected. But Stein "was very careful not to have any Yiddish words or phrases in the script." Stein had a special ideological purpose, however, since Yiddish would detract from the wider claims that *Fiddler on the Roof* was to advance. Such anxieties were unwarranted. Without provoking irate customers to demand refunds, Yiddish had been spoken on Broadway as early as 1903, when all actors used English in a production of *The Merchant of Venice*, except for Jacob Adler's Shylock.

But the success of *Fiddler on the Roof* cannot be explained merely in terms of sociology any more than by the attribution of luck in the casting of Mostel, whose talent was irrelevant to the planetary popularity of the musical and whose retirement did not seriously hurt box office sales in New York. *Fiddler* is unique; no other musical devoted to an overtly Jewish subject has ever triumphed on Broadway. Those responsible for putting Sholem Aleichem's stories on stage defied the odds, it might be argued, because Robbins and his collaborators knew how to elicit emotions, how to pack a wallop. By 1964 the grandchildren and great-grandchildren of the ghetto were more inclined to romanticize the *shtetl*. Yet that word is unmentioned in the show, which is equivocal about the thing itself: "Underfed, overworked Anatevka. Where else could Sabbath be so sweet?... Intimate, obstinate Anatevka, where I know everyone I meet." Interest in such communities would continue to compete with the old urban neighborhoods of the New World, most prominently the Lower East Side, as places of memory to be summoned from the Jewish past. Since Anatevka was not indigenous to the United States, the allure of *Fiddler on the Roof* suggested the odd vicariousness of a culture that has looked elsewhere, not only to the *shtetl* but also to the Holocaust and Israel, for inspiration and for occasions to confront, however indirectly, issues of validity that might be finessed rather than addressed. The impulse to lift Tevye and his family off of the printed page began with the author himself; and the persistence of that impulse indicates more than the dumbing down of a densely literate "world of Sholem Aleichem," but also of the irrepressible yearning to reconnect with it, and, yes, to tamper with it.

Those responsible for *Fiddler* weren't the first to fiddle with the writings of Sholem Aleichem. Unable to adapt his tales smoothly to the requirements of Second Avenue dramaturgy, the author even worked on a couple of silent film scripts (in Russian), but died in the Bronx in 1916 without having quite finished the stage version of *Tevye the Dairyman*. Three years later Tevye could be seen, but of course not heard, in a movie titled *Broken Barriers* (also known as *Khavah*). Y. D. Berkovitsh, the son-in-law and literary executor of Sholem Aleichem, polished up the play, which, also in 1919, inaugurated the fall season of the Yiddish Art Theater. Directed by Maurice Schwartz, who also cast himself as the protagonist, *Tevye der Milkhiker* (Teyve the dairyman) proved to be a major hit. The play highlighted the heartbreaking decision of Chava to marry outside of the faith and the expulsion of the Jews of Anatevka from tsarist Russia. Schwartz also intro-

duced religious elements (such as the mourning customs when Chava marries a gentile, and the celebration of the *havdalah* at the end of the Sabbath) to draw attention to the rituals that marked the continuity of the Jewish experience under attack.

In transforming *Tevye der Milkhiker* into a Yiddish-language film, shot on Long Island in the summer of 1939, Schwartz made few changes. In both of Schwartz's versions, the final scene depicts Tevye's anguish when Chava, who has left her husband, begs for readmission into the family and community, as they are about to flee from their homes. In the 1919 play, Tevye agrees to a reconciliation and asks himself (or perhaps God): "Must I feel guilty when, after all, she is my child? Deep in my heart, my soul? Come to me, Chavale, you are my child!" Even if the rigor of Judaism is renounced, mercy has been shown; and the generations are reunited. Such gestures of reconciliation may be the grand theme of the Yiddish theater.

To devise the tales as a musical necessarily meant to revise them, since they lacked a carefully constructed plot that could be transposed into a unifying structure. But Sholem Aleichem had highlighted the problem of romantic love as the burden that the family must shoulder, the disruptive force that will finally shatter what this milk-wagon driver cherishes. In the original tales, enlightened ideals of liberalism and individualism have already penetrated the cultural ambience that Tevye inhabits. His sense of order and fitness will be tested when marriages can no longer be taken for granted as arranged, when each daughter wants to choose a husband herself. Tevye must constantly confront the question: is it possible to loosen or even transcend "tradition"? What Stein and Robbins did was to organize their musical around "Tradition," the opening song, and around the sting of modernization that Tevye so painfully feels. *Fiddler on the Roof*, born in the era when fathers knew best, had located a problem at the heart of Sholem Aleichem's stories; and a musical that was itself an adaptation prescribed the need for adaptation, to ineluctable forces such as the personal pursuit of happiness and the decline of austere patriarchy.

Two of the seven daughters Sholem Aleichem gave Tevye are eliminated entirely from *Fiddler on the Roof*; and the two youngest have very minor roles. That leaves three other daughters, whose choices most directly reflect the poignancy of modernity. Tsaytl marries Motel, a likable tailor, rather than the crude but wealthier butcher whom Tevye first favors. An arranged marriage is no longer automatic. Hodel marries the secular revolutionary Perchik; and most shocking of all, Chava marries an educated young villager, Fyedka. Although the first act of *Fiddler* ends with the pogrom that is unmentioned in the original stories, the musical ends with the eviction from Anatevka with which Sholem Aleichem concluded his account of what Tevye told him in 1914.

The cruelest choice is made by the headstrong daughter who is the subject of the story "Chava" (1906). "No Yiddish text has evoked more intense emotions," the Yiddishist Ken Frieden has declared, for she elopes with Fyedka Galagan. (The surname means "roughneck," akin to the Russian "hooligan.") She has not only broken the bonds tying her to her family and her people; she has, in the either/or dichotomy of tsarist oppression and obscurantism, united with the persecutors of the Jews. This is worse than one daughter's choice of a poor man, even worse than another daughter's choice of an assimilated, radical Jew. "In Tevye's universe the loss of a daughter to Christianity, which for him has never shown any-

thing but a murderous face, is the nadir of tragedy," Ozick has observed. "He sobs for her as for a kidnapped child," and of course disowns her and treats her as deceased, as religious law dictates. But not even the devastated father is without ambivalence toward the tradition that now seems so sundered: "Peculiar thoughts came into my mind. What is the meaning of Jew and non-Jew? I regretted that I wasn't as learned as some men so that I could arrive at an answer to this riddle." Nor does his creator solve it, and leaves open the question of whether father and daughter will be reconciled, as Tevye prepares to flee.

Sholem Aleichem's Chava returns to her people, repentant, and hopes to rejoin "her father and her God." She is also without her husband. But in 1964 audiences were already quite familiar with marriages between Jews and gentiles. Such unions were rising, if still statistically insignificant; and "the meaning of Jew and non-Jew" was blurring. So *Fiddler* had to tinker with the original. Now the imminence of a pogrom draws Chava back toward her family and her people—but with the high-minded Fyedka, who abandons Christendom because "we cannot stay among people who can do such things to others." In the musical Chava and her husband decide to find refuge in Kraków. In 1939 Maurice Schwartz's Tevye repudiates Chava after she weds Fyedka, but accepts her when she returns, contrite, and cites the Bible. United Artists' grim Tevye (Topol) maintains his tie to tradition and rejects his daughter, the (proto)-feminist, who refuses to be deflected from her path of independence.

The literary Tevye is far from unshakable, at least subjectively. After recounting the return of Chava, who has asked his forgiveness, her Papa wonders: "Tell me yourself, Mr. Sholem Aleichem, you are a wise man who writes books and gives advice to the whole world. What should

Tevye have done?" No answer is given. On Broadway, after Chava pleads to him ("Papa, I beg you to accept us"), Tevye says to himself: "Accept them? How can I accept them? Can I deny everything I believe in? On the other hand, can I deny my own child?" To betray his religion and people is to realize that "if I try and bend that far, I'll break. On the other hand . . ." But then he concludes: "There is no other hand. No, Chava! No! No! No! No!" Though *Fiddler on the Roof* is told mostly from the father's point of view, the desires and the hopes of his daughters also have their claims. And since one child has chosen to marry a Christian who seems free of prejudice against Jews, the musical does not, cannot, vindicate the need of a tiny minority to honor endogamy. Broadway therefore transformed "a Jewish classic into a liberal classic," the Yiddish scholar Ruth Wisse has argued. While conceding that "*Fiddler* is in many respects an adaptation of genius," she wondered "if a Jewish work can only enter American culture by forfeiting . . . its commitment to group survival," what sort of "bargain" is it that "destroys the Jews with its applause"?

His faith challenged, his family fragmented, the security of his world under assault, Tevye and those who are left are ordered to leave their homes as well. But where can refuge be found? Where can they find relief from persecution? In the original tales, he wants to go to Palestine but tries to find a temporary haven elsewhere in Russia. In the 1939 Yiddish film, the destination is uncertain. When Menachem Golan produced an Israeli version of the tales in 1968, Tevye and Chava depart for Eretz Yisrael. A production conceived by American Jews could not be expected to negate the Diaspora. So Joseph Stein gave Tevye a brother-in-law whom Sholem Aleichem did not realize his protagonist had, named Abram. The land that Abram shows his desperate relatives is

the United States, which was by no means an implausible or an atypical choice, since Palestine was a far less favored option than the "mother of exiles." (Sholem Aleichem is, after all, buried in Brooklyn, not on the Mount of Olives.) America will presumably be the launching site for the upward mobility that so many Jews in the audience had experienced. One of Tevye's daughters is exiled to Siberia; another has converted to Russian Orthodoxy. But Tevye and his wife (who dies in the original stories) will presumably find some success in America, where dreams of being a rich man might someday be fulfilled. The inscrutable forces of modernization and the irrational hatred of anti-Semitism will eventually drive him and his family and his community away. But there is at least a glimpse of a happy ending; eviction may prove to be a blessing in disguise.

Sholem Aleichem had to be Americanized, because Jewish audiences in particular needed to believe in the compatibility of their citizenship with their ethnicity. They would be drawn only to a work that assured them that loyalty to their past generated no friction with the texture of their lives as Americans. In the original Tevye is a widower, alone, forlorn, and beaten down, a wandering Jew at the mercy of fate. Half a century later, Tevye had become a somewhat hopeful immigrant, besieged but still sustained by his family, a non-Zionist ready to face a different promised land. He is, like the text from which he had sprung, adaptable; and the new version, that key text of American Jewish culture, presents such flexibility and resilience as crucial to his survival. He bends tradition in order not to break. The protagonist's "composite nature, a mingling of the spiritual and the practical, the strict and the yielding, the ancient and the modern," made him attractive only if audiences could detect an ambivalence toward tradition.

Fiddler on the Roof was itself suspended between particularism and universalism. Even as the show perpetuated a bit of the cozy faith in the redemptive promise of romantic love that had long been the lullaby of Broadway, even as Tevye was converted from a dedicated reader of the Hebrew Bible into an engaging rustic, anxieties about the viability of the Jewish condition were addressed; and some of the warmth and power of Judaic ritual were presented on stage. *Fiddler* portrayed a distinctive people constituted by both nationality and faith, even as the Broadway production argued for accommodation to historical change as a guarantee of continuity. Admittedly something got lost in translation to the marketplace. The Jewish religious literacy assumed in the Yiddish text is omitted. The culture of Eastern European Jewry became less peculiar, and also became less hermetic. The past became more like the present, and less of a foreign country, as Robbins and his collaborators reached out to a mass audience, indeed a global audience, in which the proportion of their coreligionists was negligible. That so many playgoers found it possible to like *Fiddler* hardly validates its artistic excellence, which cannot be equated with popularity. There is no relation between the integrity and beauty of an imaginative work and its impact in the marketplace. The contrary view is merely an American prejudice, which a democratic and commercial culture encourages.

Fiddler on the Roof is part of the saga of supersession, as the Old World gave way to the New, as the prestige of high culture would yield to the raucous immediacy of popular entertainment, as a sensibility that was tragic and ironic lost traction, defeated by a faith in betterment. That process was epitomized during a US Army benefit show in 1918, when Al Jolson, who was mischievously slated to appear right after Enrico Caruso had sung a couple of arias, bolted out to the stage to announce: "Folks, you ain't heard *nothin'* yet!"

Abridged from: Stephen J. Whitfield, "Fiddling with Sholem Aleichem: A History of *Fiddler on the Roof*," in *Key Texts in American Jewish Culture*, ed. Jack Kugelmass, 105–25 (New Brunswick, NJ: Rutgers University Press, 2003).

Source: Sholem Aleichem, *Tevye the Dairyman and The Railroad Stories*, trans. Hillel Halkin (New York: Schocken, 1996).

Background: http://www.friends-partners.org/ partners/beyond-the-pale/english/28.html; http://www .jewishvirtuallibrary.org/jsource/judaica/ejud_0002_ 0018_0_18416.html.

Bibliography

Baron, Salo Wittmayer. *The Russian Jew under Tsars and Soviets.* 2nd ed. New York: Macmillan, 1976.

Bartal, Israel. *The Jews of Eastern Europe, 1772–1881.* Translated by Chaya Naor. Philadelphia: University of Pennsylvania Press, 2006.

Frieden, Ken. *A Century in the Life of Sholem Aleichem's Tevye.* Syracuse, NY: Syracuse University Press, 1997.

Gittelman, Sol. *From Shtetl to Suburbia: The Family in Jewish Literary Imagination.* Boston: Beacon, 1978.

Hoberman, J. *Bridge of Light: Yiddish Film between Two Worlds.* Updated and expanded ed. Hanover, NH: University Press of New England, 2010.

Klier, John Doyle, and Shlomo Lombroza, eds. *Pogroms: Anti-Jewish Violence in Modern Russian History.* New York: Cambridge University Press, 2008.

Miron, Dan. *The Image of the Shtetl and Other Studies of Modern Jewish Literary Imagination.* Syracuse, NY: Syracuse University Press, 2000.

Wolitz, Seth L. "The Americanization of Tevye or Boarding the Jewish *Mayflower*." *American Quarterly* 40, no. 4 (1988): 514–36.

Zborowski, Mark, and Elisabeth Herzog. *Life Is with People: The Culture of the Shtetl.* New York: Schocken, 1962.

Zipperstein, Steven J. *Imagining Russian Jewry: Memory, History, Identity.* Seattle: University of Washington Press, 1999.

7. *Yentl*

From Yeshiva Boy to Syndrome

PAMELA S. NADELL

Yentl, directed by Barbra Streisand [A]
United States and United Kingdom, 1983

In 1991, in the *New England Journal of Medicine*, Bernadine Healy coined the term the "Yentl syndrome." Two articles in that publication had discovered "sex bias in the management of coronary heart disease." Healy explained: the "Yentl syndrome" referred to the phenomenon that "once a woman showed that she was just like a man," in this case, "by having severe coronary artery disease or a myocardial infarction, then she was treated as a man would be." The "Yentl syndrome" caught on in medical literature.

Meanwhile elsewhere, Yentl kept making unexpected appearances. The *New York Times* headlined "You've Come a Long Way, Yentl" to report on the first women to complete Drisha Institute's Talmudic program. The *Forward* crowed that a female cantor is "no longer the curious Yentl in a man's domain." Third-wave Jewish feminists titled a collection of essays *Yentl's Revenge*.

How did the name Yentl become so iconic of the feminist struggle against gender bias? Yentl, a fictional character created by the Nobel laureate Isaac Bashevis Singer (1904–91), made her first appearance in English as "Yentl, the Yeshiva Boy" in 1964. However, Yentl owes her fame as the exemplary victim of patriarchal bias to the 1983 film *Yentl*, the directorial debut of Barbra Streisand. How did this film emerge as the symbol of the feminist struggle of modern times?

Singer was the only Nobel laureate ever to write in Yiddish. In "Yentl, the Yeshiva Boy," he

imagines Yentl as a young woman of marriageable age born with "the soul of a man and the body of a woman . . . thirst[ing] for Torah." "Yentl knew she wasn't cut out for a woman's life. She couldn't sew, she couldn't knit. She let the food burn." Instead, her bedridden father had taught her, in secret, the sacred texts of Jewish law. After his death, Yentl, who was "tall, thin, bony, with small breasts and narrow hips," succeeds in escaping a life of female drudgery. She cuts her braids, fashions sidelocks, puts on her father's clothes, and feigns she is a man, bent on studying at a yeshiva.

At an inn, Yentl "found herself alone in the company of young men." Taking the name Anshel, she meets Avigdor, follows him to his yeshiva in Bechev, becomes his study partner, and falls in love with him. For his part "Avigdor grew more and more attached to this boy, five years younger than himself, whose beard hadn't even begun to sprout." In time, he confesses that "my life is bound up in your life."

Before Avigdor met Anshel, he was to have wed. When the father of his fiancée, Hadass, discovered that Avigdor's brother hanged himself, he called off the engagement. Out of despair Avigdor marries Peshe, "a cow with a pair of eyes" whose first husband died the year they married, but pleads with Anshel to wed Hadass. When Anshel asks, "What good would that do *you*?" Avigdor replies: "Better you than a total stranger."

Although convinced "that what she was about to do was sinful," Anshel marries Hadass, entangling them both in a "chain of deception." After the wedding, Anshel "found a way to deflower" Hadass, who, "in her innocence, was unaware that things weren't quite as they should have been." Meanwhile, Avigdor, loathing Peshe, began dining with Anshel and Hadass.

For Anshel, "lying with Hadass and deceiv-

Barbra Streisand (as Yentl) is disguised as Anshel. From *Yentl* (1983), directed by Barbra Streisand. UNITED ARTISTS / PHOTOFEST

ing her had become more and more painful. Hadass's love and tenderness" shamed Anshel/ Yentl. Moreover, the town began to gossip: Why didn't Anshel go to the baths before the Sabbath? Why hadn't his beard yet sprouted? Passover approached. It was local custom for young men boarding at their in-laws to travel to nearby cities during its intermediary days. Promising "to reveal an astonishing secret," Anshel persuades Avigdor to journey to Lublin. There, confessing "I'm not a man but a woman," Yentl disrobes to convince the disbelieving Avigdor. He asks, "What will you do now?" She answers: "I'll go away to a different yeshiva."

Yentl tells Avigdor to divorce Peshe and marry Hadass. As they resume their debates over Jewish law, Avigdor "saw clearly that this was what he had always wanted: a wife whose mind was not taken up with material things. . . . His desire for Hadass was gone." Although Avigdor proposes marriage to Yentl, "it was too late for that. Anshel could not go back to being a girl, could never again do without books and a study house." Anshel divorces Hadass. Avigdor follows suit with Peshe and marries Hadass. Within a year she gives birth to a son whom Avigdor names Anshel.

In writing of the "human condition" of the masquerade, Singer employs a time-honored literary device. Shakespeare repeatedly played with the disguise of cross-dressing: Portia as a lawyer in *The Merchant of Venice*; Viola as Cesario in *Twelfth Night*; Rosalind/Ganymede in *As You Like It*. Cultural critic Marjorie Garber finds echoes of these characters rippling through Singer's tale.

Others assert that Singer's inspiration for "Yentl, the Yeshiva Boy" was the life and legend of Hannah Rochel Werbermacher (1806–88?), the Maid of Ludomir. Renowned in Hasidic circles as the only woman ever celebrated like a rebbe, she won acclaim for her deep piety, learning, and healing and mystical gifts. Until she was pressured into a short-lived marriage, she acted like a man—wearing *talit* and tefillin, building her own *shtibl* (a small prayer and study room), holding gatherings, teaching Torah, and leading prayer. Eventually, she settled in the Land of Israel, where she continued to attract a following, and where her grave remains a site of pilgrimage.

But beyond literary and historical sources, Singer had his own real-life inspirations for "Yentl, the Yeshiva Boy." His biographer, Janet Hadda, argues that "everyone in the [Singer] family experienced considerable confusion over gender roles" and that this problem "subsequently absorbed Singer in many of his works."

Whatever inspired the story, critical reception was mixed. When the story appeared in 1964, *New York Times* reviewer Orville Prescott felt that "Yentl, the Yeshiva Boy" "comes perilously close to being silly." Yet, it ultimately captivated a far more influential reader, the "actress who sings," Barbra Streisand. By the time *Yentl* opened in theaters in the United States in 1983, Streisand had been involved with the project for fourteen years. She first read Singer's story in 1968 and acquired the film rights. In the late 1970s, having already rejected Singer's screenplay as well as oth-

ers, she wrote her own film treatment. The movie was reconceived to feature Streisand, the best-selling female recording artist of all time, singing a series of songs that serve as Yentl's interior monologues. Streisand coauthored the film, coproduced it, staged its musical numbers, starred in the title role, and made her directorial debut with *Yentl*.

The film opened to mixed reviews. *Chicago Sun-Times*'s Roger Ebert went into the movie "expecting some kind of schmaltzy formula romance," and found himself "quietly astonished" by its "special magic." He was also convinced that the Hollywood scuttlebutt that *Yentl* would prove "too Jewish" for middle-America was dead wrong. "Like all great fables," he wrote, "it grows out of a particular time and place, but it takes its strength from universal sorts of feelings. At one time or another, almost everyone has wanted to do something and been told they couldn't, and almost everyone has loved the wrong person for the right reason."

The film had broad appeal. It earned five Academy Award nominations—for Amy Irving as best supporting actress as Hadass, for art direction, and for two of its songs—and won the Oscar for best original score. Streisand was snubbed in the Academy's major categories of director, leading actress, and best film but won Golden Globes for her direction and for the best film in the musical or comedy category. Moreover, *Yentl*, which cost $20 million to make, grossed $40 million in the United States and earned more money abroad.

The best remembered criticism came from I. B. Singer. Interviewing himself in the *New York Times*, he decried the film's lack of "artistic merit," its direction, Streisand's monopolization of the camera, the singing, and especially the ending.

In Singer's version, we never learn what happens to Yentl. But in the film, she sets off for

America, dressed as a woman, striding across the steerage deck and belting out a song like Streisand did as Fanny Brice on the prow of a tugboat in *Funny Girl*. Singer felt Streisand's adaptation lacked "any kinship to Yentl's character and her great passion for spiritual achievement." Of Streisand's decision to end the film by sending Yentl to America, Singer wrote: "Weren't there enough yeshivas in Poland or in Lithuania where she could continue to study? Was going to America Miss Streisand's idea of a happy ending for Yentl? What would Yentl have done in America? Worked in a sweatshop 12 hours a day where there is no time for learning? Would she try to marry a salesman in New York, move to the Bronx or Brooklyn and rent an apartment with an ice box and a dumbwaiter?"

Stephen Whitfield has shown us that the transformation of this work from fiction into film gives us an entrée into the creation of American Jewish culture. Streisand's Yentl sings: "Where is it written what it is I'm meant to be?" The film answers that *Yentl* could be other than I. B. Singer imagined her to be. For Whitfield, the clash between Singer and Streisand replays the "clash between the Old World and the New, between the sensibilities of a Warsaw-born man and a Brooklyn-born woman a generation younger." *Yentl*'s "refusal to be confined—either by the religious norms—or by the genre in which her fate was first imagined— is one way of summarizing the individualism and experimentalism, personal freedom and assertion" that have become hallmarks of the Jewish experience in America.

If Singer and critics alike disdained the ending, Whitfield found it "cogent." He perceives "a logic" in the geographic arc of the film. It traces "Yentl's trajectory"—propelling her from one *shtetl* to the next, then to the city of Lublin, "and finally across the Atlantic to another continent, where at its other end Hollywood" and its cinematic imagination lay. Filming *Yentl* allowed for "new artistic choices." A film, Whitfield argues, "should not be judged only by its fidelity to a text." Successful film adaptations enlarge and enrich cultural life, and *Yentl* stands among them.

Others too have used *Yentl* as a prism for reading late-twentieth-century American culture, and their arguments also hinge on the movie's choice to send Yentl to America. American studies scholar Matthew Frye Jacobson explores how, in the 1960s, the once-dominant gospel of American life, the melting pot, gave way to ethnic particularism, making room for white ethnics' proud identification with their immigrant pasts. Mass culture played a key role in conveying that Americans are "'a nation of immigrants'—a national 'we' whose point of origin is the steerage deck of the European steamer." Jacobson reads films like *Yentl* and *Fiddler on the Roof* (1971) as "ratifying the conception of the United States as a nation of immigrants." Thus Yentl's parade among the steerage passengers on the *S.S. Moskva* "melds Yentl's historical moment with Streisand's 'assimilated' present a century later to project an affiliation with steerage as the very soul of 'Americanism.'"

Theater professor Henry Bial locates *Yentl* among a series of films, including Woody Allen's *Play It Again Sam* (1969) and Streisand's *The Way We Were* (1973). He argues that as the strength of the melting pot model waned, performances by publicly identified Jewish American artists were geared "toward the Jewish-specific end of the spectrum." As antisemitism became a negligible factor in American life and ethnic pride surged, Jews felt increasingly comfortable to identify themselves publicly as Jewish. Accordingly, *Yentl*'s warm depiction of Jewish learning communicates "a specific message of Jewish continuity to a Jewish audience." The ending is crucial to the message of the film: "When Yentl is forced to abandon her masquerade," Bial writes, "she does not stand and fight for a reconsideration of gender roles in Russian Jewish culture but instead emigrates to America." *Yentl* affirmed and celebrated that in the United States, American Jews could be both Jewish and American, and in diverse ways.

How did Yentl emerge in the American imagination as shorthand for gender discrimination—and not only in Jewish contexts? The film gave Singer his greatest public exposure, but far more people met Yentl through the film, its album, or its songs than in the written version. In the popular imagination Yentl became synonymous with the film, not with Singer's story. *Yentl* is an undervalued text. It broke new ground for the film industry of its day and deepened public awareness of second-wave feminism.

American feminism burst forth out of a series of events in the 1960s. President John F. Kennedy's 1961 Commission on the Status of Women "implicitly recognized the existence of gender-based discrimination in American society." Betty Friedan's 1963 bestseller, *The Feminine Mystique*, galvanized hundreds of thousands to do something about "the problem that has no name." And the Civil Rights Act of 1964 banned discrimination in employment on the basis of both race and sex. With the founding of the National Organization of Women, in 1966, the "world split open." Soon thereafter the first meetings between second-wave feminism and American Judaism occurred. By 1972 Jewish women demanded equal access to Jewish ritual, Jewish leadership, and Jewish communal life, and the first woman rabbi in America was ordained.

A decade later *Yentl* hit the screen, and its story of the subterfuges required of a girl who wished to learn resonated deeply in a world increasingly sensitized to gender discrimination. *Yentl* was, as noted by scholars Allison Fernley and Paula Maloof, "the first major American film directed, co-produced, and co-written by a woman—who is also its star." Those championing second-wave feminism have repeatedly chronicled triumphant "firsts"—the first woman to sit on the Supreme Court (Sandra Day O'Connor, 1981), to become secretary of state (Madeline Albright, 1997), to win a Golden Globe for directing (Barbra Streisand, 1984), to win an Oscar for directing (nominees, 1927–2010, three; winners, zero). American Jews keep their own lists—the first women to become rabbis (Reform, 1972; Reconstructionist, 1974; Conservative, 1985), and the various glass ceilings they have cracked: the first to have a solo pulpit, to lead a large congregation, to teach in a seminary, to head a rabbinical association.

Streisand was well aware of the challenges she faced cracking the directorial ceiling with *Yentl*. For a documentary produced by the American Film Institute, she recalled that when she tried to make the movie in 1980 there was "a feeling of women, actresses, singers, they should stay in their place. Don't try to be too ambitious; don't reach out beyond your limitations. There is also an inclination to believe actresses could be flighty, not fiscally responsible, responsible for money, finances."

Streisand saw her challenge linked to Yentl's. Yentl wasn't permitted to study. The "only way to study was to be part of a man's world, because women weren't permitted to study, and I was feeling the same feelings . . . I wasn't permitted to direct."

Moreover, not only was the making of *Yentl* a feminist first from behind the camera, but, as Fernley and Maloof argue, what ended up on screen made "accessible to a large audience ideas" of second-wave feminism about gender and identity previously "broached only in the works of 'serious' female fiction writers and academic feminist theorists." Singer saw Yentl's confused sexual identity as "evil" and perverse; Streisand treated Yentl's gender "confusion with an extraordinary empathy."

For Streisand, one of the central questions of the film was "What it feels like to be male, female?" She wants the audience to question its "easy assumptions and presuppositions about life." Anshel thrives intellectually and emotionally with Avigdor as her study partner. At the same time Yentl/Anshel also learns from Hadass. Yentl admires Hadass for her beauty, womanliness, grace, and her domestic gifts. She comes to love both; Anshel and Hadass eventually kiss. None of this homoerotic behavior is ever portrayed as perverse. Instead Yentl's masquerade allows her to discover herself. Streisand deliberately had Yentl cross bodies of water—a small puddle in the opening of the film, later a canal, a river, eventually an ocean—to signify each stage of Yentl's growth. By the end of the film, Yentl refuses to live any longer in the shadows. She must listen to the voice deep inside, "to see myself, to free myself, to be myself at last . . . No matter what happens, it can't be the same anymore." She emerges as "a confident and independent self," who has transcended the rigid sex role limitations of the world she must abandon, because it offers her no alternative but to marry Avigdor and darn his socks. Given this interpretation, the ending flows naturally. Yentl, dressed once more in a woman's clothes, is ineluctably drawn to a "new place . . . the traditional symbol of discovery, change, and promise, America."

The film's entire premise spoke openly of the feminist struggle for equal access. At its core, Singer's story subverted the traditional notion that women lacked the intellectual capacity for serious study. Streisand gravitated toward making a film about why gender should "impact the nature of learning anything." She described her father, who had died when she was fifteen months old and whose spirit she felt hovering over her as she made *Yentl*, as a religious and learned man. She believed that had he lived, he would have taught her. In watching the movie nearly a quarter of a century after it first appeared, two scenes, in particular, stand out for how they resonate with second-wave feminism and its demand for equal access.

The film opens with a still frame on which appear the words: "In a time when the world of study belonged only to men, there lived a girl called Yentl." Riding into the world of the *shtetl* atop a bookseller's wagon, we, the audience, encounter the rigidly gendered world of Jewish tradition. We enter the synagogue and hear men praying. Then the viewer heads out into the bustling square. There the film cuts back and forth between shots of men and women. The men huddle together excitedly discussing what they have learned in the books they have read. The women stand in the marketplace hawking fish, chickens, and flowers. They wash clothes in the river as children splash about. They gossip about engagements, while the men speculate about creation.

Meanwhile, Yentl and the bookseller have a heated exchange:

Yentl: I'd like to buy this one please.
Bookseller: Sacred books are for men.
Yentl: Why?
Bookseller: It's a law, that's why.
Yentl: Where is it written?
Bookseller: Never mind where, it's a law.
Yentl: Well, if it's a law, it must be written somewhere, maybe in here, I'll take it.

Bookseller: Miss, do me a favor, do yourself a favor . . . uh, here . . . buy a nice picture book; girls like picture books.

Yentl: What if I tell you it's for my father?

Bookseller: Why didn't you say? Fifteen kopeks and if you want to know where that's written, it's inside the cover.

By 1983, the critique implicit in this depiction of a society so determinedly gendered and so explicitly inimical to women's learning was familiar to *Yentl*'s American audience. It sympathized with Yentl as she lies to the bookseller. The changes wrought by feminism's demand for women's full access to higher education and what that entailed were well underway. Only a little more than a decade before, the elite Ivy League had opened its admission gates to women. Already, unprecedented numbers of women were entering professional schools that, in the past, had never had more than token female representation. These women insisted on equal treatment when they became students. In 1970 the Women's Equity Action League demanded that institutions of higher education holding federal contracts comply with antidiscrimination regulations. Within a year, over 160 of these schools faced lawsuits for gender bias.

Such blatant denial of women's access to equal education hit especially close to home in the Jewish world. Only weeks before the film opened the Conservative movement's Jewish Theological Seminary had voted, after a decade-long debate, to ordain women as rabbis. That debate had begun with Seminary Chancellor Gerson Cohen conceding: "Qualifying her to teach . . . is one thing. Ordaining her as a rabbi is quite another." It concluded with his applauding his movement's decision "to take a major step in the equalization of women in Jewish religious life." Yentl's desire to learn could be appreciated by Jews and gentiles who had personally or through their daughters, wives, and mothers experienced the repercussions of women's educational opportunities.

The second scene that invites a feminist reading takes place just after Anshel passes the rabbi's admission exam for the yeshiva. Anshel quietly proclaims: "I'm a student." Streisand then launches into one of her private musical commentaries. As she sings, "This is one of those moments that you remember all your life . . . ," a montage of student life in the yeshiva appears on screen. The images and dialogue of the world of the yeshiva contrast pointedly with the world of women of the film's opening scene. Men and boys argue with one another, while the song celebrates Anshel's joining herself to that chain of tradition: "I can travel the past and take what I need to see me through the years. What my father learned and his father before him will be there for my eyes and ears." From atop a ladder Avigdor pulls books off the shelves and throws them to Anshel, while the song celebrates: "There are certain things that once you have no man can take away . . . and now they are about to be mine." As he and Avigdor head out into the rain, even the drizzle cannot dampen their spirited discussion.

As the scene climaxes, Anshel enters the yeshiva courtyard where the rabbi teaches. Descending a long staircase, Anshel moves from the periphery of the students to their center. The rabbi asks: "Where in the Talmud does it say possession is nine-tenths of the law?" The students give wrong answers; Avigdor cites the right tractate, but only Anshel knows the exact page. Yentl/Anshel's learning has earned her this place.

That passage from periphery to center crystallizes the film's feminist message. The first wave of American feminism of the 1910s and 1920s had failed to move women into the center of American life. Women won the right to vote but made only token gains in the political, economic, educational, and social spheres. The second wave would come far closer to transforming society. Its gains, like the disappearance of separate "help wanted" ads for men and for women and the policy of affirmative action for women, thrust women into the center of American life.

The second wave also paved the way for an emerging Jewish feminism, one that has transformed American Judaism, by propelling women onto the bimah as rabbis and cantors; by embracing new rituals like the women's seder and adult bat mitzvah; and by inventing novel and traditional settings where women are fully welcome to encounter the texts of Jewish tradition. Today a woman whose soul thirsts for Torah has an array of choices of where to study and need not disguise herself as Yentl did.

Yentl came to stand in the popular imagination for women's battle against gender discrimination. As a result of the film, Yentl entered our lexicon. Physicians discovered the "Yentl syndrome." Journalists coded stories about Jewish women's growing access to learning and leadership with her name. The editor of *Yentl's Revenge* exclaims, "Now it's Yentl's turn to run the damn yeshiva."

Yentl has become a feminist icon. As she sang, "The time had come . . . to try my wings. . . . What's wrong with wanting more? If you can fly, then soar." Yentl vocalized feminism's aspirations, ambitions, and complexities. The Yentl syndrome is still being reported in newspapers throughout the world. An Irish journalist despairing of violence against women remarks on the "great distance" women have traveled "since Yentl" and ruefully muses how far they have yet to go. In Florida, a journalist probing the "khaki ceiling" and roadblocks to women in the military, remarks, "Today, women don't have to go all Yentl

to join the military." These references to Yentl as the archetypical victim of patriarchal bias suggest that, thanks to the film, she promises to remain so for the foreseeable future.

Excerpted from: Pamela S. Nadell, "Yentl: From Yeshiva Boy to Syndrome," in *New Essays in American Jewish History: Commemorating the Sixtieth Anniversary of the Founding of the American Jewish Archives*, ed. Pamela S. Nadell, Jonathan D. Sarna, and Lance J. Sussman, 467–83 (Cincinnati, OH: American Jewish Archives, 2010).

Source: Isaac Bashevis Singer, *Yentl the Yeshiva Boy*, trans. Marion Magid and Elizbeth Pollet (New York: Farrar, Straus and Giroux, 1983).

Background: http://www.jewishvirtuallibrary.org/jsource/judaica/ejud_0002_0018_0_18416.html; http://jwa.org/encyclopedia/article/jewish-feminism-in-united-states.

Bibliography

Aaron, Michele. "The Queer Jew and Cinema: From Yidl to Yentl and Back and Beyond." *Jewish Culture and History* 3, no. 1 (2000): 23–44.

Bial, Henry. *Acting Jewish: Negotiating Ethnicity on the American Stage and Screen*. Ann Arbor: University of Michigan Press, 2005.

Fernley, Allison, and Paula Maloof. "*Yentl.*" *Film Quarterly* 38, no. 3 (1985): 38–46.

Garber, Marjorie. *Vested Interests: Cross-Dressing and Cultural Anxiety*. New York: Routledge, 1992.

Herman, Felicia. "The Way She *Really* Is: Images of Jews and Women in the Films of Barbra Streisand." In *Talking Back: Images of Jewish Women in American Popular Culture*, edited by Joyce Antler, 171–90. Hanover, NH: Brandeis University Press, 1998.

Jacobson, Mathew Frye. *Roots Too: White Ethnic Revival in Post–Civil Rights America*. Cambridge: Harvard University Press, 2006.

Mock, Roberta. *Jewish Women on Stage, Film, and Television*. New York: Palgrave Macmillan, 2007.

Stuart, Garret. "Singer Sung: Voice as Avowal in Streisand's *Yentl.*" *Mosaic* 88, no. 4 (1985): 135–58.

Whitfield, Stephen J. "*Yentl.*" *Jewish Social Studies* 5, nos.1–2 (1998–99): 154–76.

8. Redressing the Commissar

Thaw Cinema Revises Soviet Structuring Myths

ELENA MONASTIREVA-ANSDELL

The Commissar (*Komissar*), directed by
Aleksandr Askoldov [A]
Soviet Union, 1967

Aleksandr Askoldov's 1967 film *The Commissar* opens with a soft female voice singing a lullaby as the camera lingers on a pale morning sky, before descending to a misty country landscape with a statue of the Madonna by the road. Cinematographer Valerii Ginzburg's camera continues its fluid pan across the steppe until it meets a long procession of Red Army troops, whereupon it accompanies them as it draws back to the holy figure. While clanking metal weaponry temporarily drowns out the lullaby, and the dust raised by the soldiers' feet obscures the peaceful view as the regiment mindlessly bypasses the Madonna, the song soon resumes its affectionate flow over the tired procession.

In this unconventional introduction to a Russian Civil War film intended to commemorate the fiftieth anniversary of the Bolshevik revolution, Askoldov, Ginzburg, and the composer Alfred Shnitke captured "the moral and philosophical tension" defining their subversive reassessment of Soviet legitimating narratives. Rather than celebrating the power of Soviet ideology to shape a better world, the officials who banned the film in 1967 censured it "for distorting the humanist essence of the proletarian revolution." Not surprisingly, they ignored the affirmative stance the movie takes toward the Thaw-inspired, heterodox understanding of the Revolution as a "kind International" in which free individuals could express their philosophical, ethnic, and gender differences, thereby shattering the homogenizing ideological dogma that had prevailed under Stalin. At the time of the film's making, the authorities had begun to reimpose this dogma, leaving no illusions about the possibility of resolving the conflict between the individual and the authoritarian state within the USSR.

Absent from Soviet screens since 1957, the Revolution and the Civil War remerged almost a decade later as the setting for a series of films authorized for the impending half-century anniversary. Younger filmmakers chosen to participate in the series, however, were motivated not by a desire to pay homage to the Soviet regime but rather to question and test its ideological soundness. In the mid 1960s, the Thaw generation's ideal of humane socialism was disappointed by a gradual return to the old authoritarian system. Thus, these filmmakers felt a need to revisit the official myth of creation. In their films, "the artist's personal contemplation of the myth reverberates with the protagonists' probing assessment of the very essence of the faith over which they debate with the antagonist." With the exception of a few films, these introspective inquiries into the country's founding years proved too subversive to the existing system to be allowed to reach wider audiences. Some received limited distribution, while others, including Askoldov's *The Commissar*, were shelved.

As Katerina Clark has shown, the Civil War furnished a metaphor for the Stalinist sense of reality as an unceasing struggle between the revolutionary "us" and the counterrevolutionary "them" (the Whites, the imperialists, the kulaks, the saboteurs, and later the Nazis), all of them commonly represented as hostile elements requir-

Raisa Nedashkovskaia (as Maria) and Rolan Bykov (as Efim, Maria's husband) try to feminize Nonna Mordiukova (as Klavdia, the commissar, right). From *The Commissar* (1967), directed by Aleksandr Askoldov. INTERNATIONAL FILM EXCHANGE (IFEX)/PHOTOFEST

ing subordination or defeat. The hierarchical structure of a military regiment in which ideological allegiances outweigh personal ties provided a blueprint for the organization of Soviet society as a harmonious big family consisting of model sons and wise fathers, with Stalin as the patriarch. In this essentially patriarchal order women generally represented "the ordinary people, who, under the influence of the party (in the form, of course, of a man), embraced the new ways and accepted the wisdom of the revolution."

Following Nikita Khrushchev's proclaimed return to "Leninist ideals" in 1956, Soviet filmmakers in the early years of the Thaw utilized the dramatic possibilities of the Civil War setting to cleanse the Revolution's utopian ideals of Stalinist distortions. Despite their earnest desire to re-

cover the egalitarian and liberating aspects of the Revolution, early Thaw films revealed a hitherto unthinkable tension between the protagonists' ideological loyalty to their big family and their private commitments.

The cultural Thaw was, from its inception, an uneven process, the last years of Khrushchev's rule marked the beginning of the end. Many party functionaries resisted Khrushchev's policy of de-Stalinization, because it undermined party authority and threatened to expose the corruption within the power apparatus. Even before the Central Committee called upon artists in the late summer of 1964 to "plan appropriately triumphant movies for the fiftieth anniversary of the Revolution and hundredth anniversary of Lenin's birth," and prior to Khrushchev's ouster in October 1964, filmmakers felt the tightening of ideological controls.

The Commissar revisits the basic Soviet structuring myths as it tackles the philosophical, societal, and ethnic tensions that tore at the social fabric in the mid-1960s. Askoldov diagnoses the fatal split in Soviet identity as an enduring fissure between the model of society as a semimilitarized "big family" that follows the commands of the state, and the Thaw-era community modeled on a small family, an egalitarian institution that abolishes social, political, and ethnic hierarchies. The film amplifies the existential polarities of the Thaw-era value system before colliding them in a final debate.

Askoldov uses less doctrinaire treatments of the revolutionary theme in early Soviet literature. Two works republished during that period, Vassili Grossman's 1934 short story "In the Town of Berdichev" and Isaak Babel's 1920's short prose cycle *Red Calvary*, both set in the Red Army's 1920s Polish campaign, inspired Askoldov's cinematic revision of the revolutionary myth. The plot of Grossman's short story provided the core narrative for *The Commissar*, while the inquiries of Babel into the nature of revolutionary justice and his potent visual imagery helped flesh out Grossman's somewhat schematic psychological and spatial landscapes.

The Commissar shifts its focus away from the military campaign to a highly personal moment: Red Army Commissar Klavdia Vavilova faces a pregnancy, which she sees as a grave obstacle to her revolutionary struggle and therefore makes every effort to terminate. When various attempts prove unsuccessful, the pregnant commissar moves into the lively Jewish household of Maria and Efim Magazanik for her imminent delivery. After she gives birth to a son, Klavdia must choose between staying with her adopted small family or rejoining the big family of the revolutionary army. Even though she has grown attached to her newborn and her loving hosts, she eventually follows her urge to fight for the better future, leaving the infant with the Jewish family.

Klavidia's flash-forward to the Holocaust notwithstanding, the story seemingly concludes where it began. In the final scene, the commissar again leads Red soldiers in battle, but the film places its major focus upon the profound change that takes place within the protagonist in the course of her home stay. The commissar enters the narrative as an authoritarian leader in command of a powerful and ruthless military force. When she suddenly finds herself outside the military setting, she simply does not know how to function. The stages of Klavdia's emotional and spiritual maturation in the film reverse the symbolic "progress toward consciousness" and ritual initiation into the "big family" that shaped Stalin-era discourse and reappeared in the quasi-Stalinist narratives of the late Thaw. Askolvov's inverted enactment of a conventional Stalinist rite of passage shows Klavdia undergo three main phases: separation from her previous environment, transition to a new system of values, and incorporation into the new community.

The Commissar recasts the image of a manly woman used to denote the unnaturally exaggerated masculinity of Stalinist authoritarian culture, juxtaposing it with the Thaw culture's feminine system of values. At the beginning of the film, Klavdia comes forth as agent and product of a militarized world. Dressed in a heavy military uniform and speaking rough military jargon, the heroine strikes the viewer as more masculine than the men in her all-male army. When the commissar tells the regiment commander about her pregnancy following her cold-blooded order to shoot a deserter, the news comes as a joke both to him and to the audience. The commissar's pregnancy becomes a test for the Revolution's ability to bring forth new life.

Within the movie's visual and nonverbal auditory imagery, Klavdia's changing body becomes a symbolic battleground for the encounter between two opposing sets of ideals. In the war-consumed world of the big family, Klavdia's pregnancy is interpreted as a desertion from the communal cause. When she discloses her state to her commander, she needs to justify her "ideological treason" by describing her attempts at aborting the fetus. To stay loyal to the Revolution, Klavdia has to purge her body and her mind of individualistic impulses. Prior to learning of her pregnancy, the viewer sees Klavdia wash in the town's deserted "Family Baths." Building up the steam to enhance the bath's cleansing effect (and most likely to induce a miscarriage), the heroine violently beats her naked body with birch switches. The camera reinforces the punitive intent of her self-flagellation when it cuts to the flogging that takes place outside, where a mounted orderly whips a helpless deserter, Emelin. Events that follow uncover a deeper correspondence between the expectant commissar and the deserter. Emelin absconded from the regiment to care for his sick wife and children, and a jug of milk that he clutches to his chest confirms his infidelity to the army. Klavida orders his execution in the name of the "bright future." Before the bullets pierce Emelin's chest, they puncture the jug, spilling the milk. This symbolic attack on the small family (the shooting's off-screen victims) undermines the Revolution's promise of the "bright future," whose traditional beneficiaries are children.

Klavdia's relationships within the regiment lack a close familial nature. Equating Klavdia's pregnancy with desertion, the commander threatens her with court-martial, expressing his regret over the loss of a valuable "combatant unit" instead of rejoicing over the emergence of a new life. During this conversation, the camera slowly moves down from the commander's face to the table where he is lining up a row of bullets. It follows the row across the table and slowly rises to connect the commander and the commissar through potentially deadly ammunition. Equally disturbing weaponry resurfaces in the flashback that depicts Klavdia's romantic interlude with her lover next to a cannon stuck in a barren desert. In Civil War films, military weaponry served as a prop that empowered characters or brought romantic lovers together; here it turns into an ominous phallic symbol of official patriarchy.

Klavdia's regiment makes no effort to protect her or her newborn and surely has no inclination to bond with the child. When the commander and his orderly pay a visit to inform her about their retreat from the town, they far too willingly accept Klavdia's decision to stay, especially given that a White occupation would surely be fatal for a Red Army commissar, not to mention those harboring her. Although the sequence has humor, the camera portrays the two men as menacing intruders in the peaceful family abode. They track in dirt with their boots, the commander's cigarette smoke is harmful for the child, and the orderly's gold watch not only clashes with the poor simplicity of the household, but also suggests plundering. Ginzburg's camerawork emphasizes the lack of any deeper connection between the regiment's leadership: avoiding group shots, the camera films most of the conversation in a shot-reverse-shot sequence, isolating the commander and the orderly from Klavdia and her child.

The film presents Klavdia's big family as her and her hosts' chief victimizer; its brutality—epitomized in a massive cannon that threatens to crush Maria and her vulnerably naked children upon the army's arrival in town—becomes associated with the Revolution and the war. Klavdia finds herself in Emelin's shoes when, on a walk around town, her former soldiers start shooting at her, with complete disregard for the child she is holding. The internecine nature of the conflict is vividly conveyed through the Magazanik children's war games, in which siblings attack and torture each other.

Klavdia's inner renewal starts on the day she leaves the military regiment and moves in with the Jewish family. The Magazaniks' inner courtyard presents a stark contrast to the deserted stone-paved streets: it is filled with freshly washed linen, the sounds of cooking dinner, children's voices, and noises from Efim's workshop. Here strong family bonds and respect for elders attempt to keep at bay the martial law of the outside military world. If Klavdia employed a firing squad to protect her regiment's ideological unity, Efim summons his mother, wife, and six children, his "weapon" with which he intends to defend the household from an intrusion when the uniformed strangers appear at their door.

Askoldov's choice of actors for the roles of Klavdia, Maria, and Efim is in line with the film's strategy to amplify the existential polarities of the Thaw-era value scale before colliding them. If Nonna Mordiukova's tall, thickset, resolute, sexually repressed, and uniformed Klavdia epitomizes the big family's paternity, Rolan Bykov's small, poorly dressed, slightly comical, sentimental, and ironic Efim, whose name appropriately means fruitful, incarnates the Thaw-era ideal of parenthood. Raisa Nedashkovskaia's delicately built, compassionate, and family-oriented Maria embodies the ideal of holy motherhood. Maria's and Efim's roles within their small family can be compared to those of the commander and the commissar of the military regiment: Maria takes care of the household's everyday logistics, while Efim is in charge of the children's discipline and intellectual and ethical guidance.

The family soon warms up to Klavdia, starting her initiation into the small family and biological parenthood. The process begins on a purely surface level, when Efim sews a loose light dress to replace her uniform and heavy overcoat. In place of Klavdia's boots, Maria offers Efim's house slippers. The old cradle that Klavdia inherits from the Magazanik children subverts the meaning of the passing of the baton, a symbolic object, gesture, or speech, the passing of which traditionally acted as an ideological blessing that assured the continuity of revolutionary teaching. The familial nature of Maria and Efim's baton reaffirms the continuity of the humane values disregarded in revolutionary lore.

The prolonged sequence of Klavdia's labor constitutes the most physical stage of her transformation, in the course of which her feverish visions of the futile campaign in a barren desert eventually subside, giving way to a heavy rain that welcomes the appearance of new life. When Klavdia sets out on a walk around the town with her newborn, she finally looks comfortable with her new identity. The heroine's visual resemblance to the Madonna with child signals her inner changes and symbolizes the Thaw's hopeful vision of the Revolution as a cradle of humane teaching, launching a new era of internationalism and social equality.

Klavdia's walk around Berdichev—a town situated at the Russian Empire's ethnically, socially, and culturally mixed periphery—allows her to experience life's infinite variety. Askoldov subverts Soviet political and ethnic hierarchies. His ideal and largely utopian community takes shape in opposition to the big family both of the state and of the Soviet peoples. Along with exposing the authoritarianism of the Soviet system, the film reveals the hypocrisy of the official concept of internationalism in a nationalistic and anti-Semitic Soviet Empire. In contrast to internationalism as a homogenizing notion, Askoldov proposes the ideal of ethnic and cultural diversity. The emotional uplift and spiritual enlightenment Klavdia experiences in this multiethnic community is conveyed in the "mother's walk" sequence, in which she ascends to the top of the hill in her search for a unifying moral vision.

The sequence starts with a rapid upward movement of the camera and a dynamic low-angle shot of the Orthodox church cupolas accompanied by tolling bells. As the ringing gets louder, it is joined by the off-screen polyphony of human voices in the market square. The previously desolate market now bustles with music and dance, and its stands abound with farmers' produce and artisans' wares. People interact peacefully in a community comprised of Gypsies, Jews, Poles, Ukrainians, Russians, peasants, intellectuals, craftsmen, and artists. Klavdia continues her walk up to the Catholic church, proceeding to the very top of the hill, the location of the town's destroyed but not abandoned synagogue. An old rabbi looks out one of the synagogue's east-facing windows. When he turns around to greet Klavdia their eyes meet in symbolic communion. Shnitke's nondiegetic music during the walk introduces leitmotifs for each of the religions, and they all intertwine harmoniously with the central musical theme of motherhood. Amid the fragmentation of the film's warring universe, the unity facilitated by the lyrical motherhood theme highlights the ecumenical nature of the scene at the top of the hill.

As she descends, Klavdia leaves the peaceful domain of tolerance and spirituality, to reenter the realm of warring ideologies: at the bottom of the hill her former soldiers accuse her of desertion and shoot at her and her child. Running away from the attack, Klavdia crosses a bridge. She slips on stones and slides all the way to the ground. Her return home is filmed in a long shot, with the small and vulnerable figures of the mother and child viewed against a background of overpowering cliffs. The road is a flat path at the very bottom of the screen. Here Askoldov cinematically visualizes the Thaw's attempt to achieve a nonauthoritarian community and its failure as Klavdia reenters a warring world.

Klavdia's metaphorical baptism during her visit to the town's three temples precedes her complete integration into her adopted small family. When the regiment retreats from the town, Maria and Efim come to Klavdia's room to offer her the protection of their humble home. All three protagonists are grouped around the cradle, conveying a sense of mutual support and close-knit community. The compositional center holds an object that draws the three participants together and emerges as a symbol of hopes for a better future and reconciliation. The newborn child brings out the commonality in people with different ethnic and ideological backgrounds.

As Klavdia sings to her son, a fluid panning shot of the house celebrates the personal ties between her and her new family. Without a single visible cut, the camera moves through the dark house to the accompaniment of a song, hovering over the family's three generations and incorporating their ancestors' portraits hanging on the walls. Klavdia's song is not a lullaby, but short rhymed couplets of urban folklore, known as *chastushki*. It tells the personal story that she could not share with the commander: the loss of the loved one, a mother's sacrifice of her favorite dress for swaddling clothes for her children, and a couple's night walks under blooming locust trees. The secular words of her song merge with the grandmother's Yiddish prayer, an appeal for God to spare the innocent children from murder. Fascinated by the emotion in the commissar's song, Maria joins in with a Jewish tune, and the two melodies complement each other. Despite the difference in language, form, and content, the three genres (prayer, *chastushka*, and lullaby) merge to express the same feeling of compassion for the three women's loved ones.

Klavdia's incorporation into her adopted family does not erase their respective identities and beliefs; instead it helps reappraise their philosophies. Ginzburg's lighting choices for the lullaby scene suggest that Klavdia's emerging identity as a mother exists next to her identity as a commissar: as the singing protagonist paces about the candlelit room, her silhouette doubles as her body casts a shadow on the back wall and reflects the new complexity that has replaced her previous orthodox worldview. Her ideological convictions, suspended during her home stay, eventually become tested in light of her recent experiences and a direct debate with Efim.

As opposed to Klavdia's unwavering endorsement of the party line at the beginning of the film, Efim questions even the most sacred texts and authorities if they fail to take individual people into account. He doubts the wisdom of God's creation when he semi-jokingly complains about his family's meager rations consisting of nothing but potatoes: If God spent the first five days creating potatoes, then why on the sixth day did He create man? Efim uses the newspaper *Speech*, a mouthpiece of official propaganda, to make cutouts for Klavdia's maternity dress. When Efim sadly states that there will be no trams in his town because there will be no people to ride them, he questions the sacrosanct promise of the bright future and denies legitimacy to a state power that asserts itself at the expense of enormous human sacrifice. Efim defies the restrictions that any ideology imposes upon human diversity and individuality by commenting that "a woman who puts on a military uniform does not become a man." His yearning for peace and freedom from authoritarian powers comes true only during brief periods between military occupations, "when one power has left the town and another has not yet arrived."

The film's key philosophical debate takes place when the family, including Klavdia and her infant, hide in the basement during an enemy artillery bombardment. The doom hanging over this underground sequence contrasts with the hopeful spirituality of the scene on the top of the hill. Efim challenges Klavdia to consider the ethical dimension of her doctrinaire assumptions. He echoes Babel's wise shopkeeper Gedali, who supports a "kind International" that ascribes equally high value to each individual, regardless of ethnicity or philosophy. Efim's evocation of the Jewish nation as a symbol of suffering humanity oppressed by ideological systems, and the film's subsequent flash-forward to the Holocaust, make a powerful argument in favor of his viewpoint. The film draws parallels between three autocratic empires—tsarist, Nazi, and Soviet—that used anti-Semitism and nationalism as a means of impressing ideological conformity and unifying the communal "us" against the deviant "them."

Sympathizing with Efim's "kind International," Klavdia nevertheless insists on the use of active and violent means in the struggle for a better future. Her pronouncement about "a free brotherhood of workers," strikes the post-Thaw Soviet viewer as ironically naïve and clichéd. Klavdia begins to question her views on revolutionary ends and means and experiences a clairvoyant flash-forward to humanity's real future. Her verbal defense of an abstract ideology and its utopian promises collapses before the vividly concrete depiction of the Holocaust. Deeply moved by the tragic revelation about the destinies of her small family, Klavdia feels compelled to prevent that future from happening. Doomed to failure, the transformed commissar emerges from the basement to confront the forces of aggression that consume the outside world.

At the end of the film, Klavdia opposes the forces of war to shield her small family, a cradle of interethnic and social communality. Preparing for combat, she puts on her overcoat and heavy boots, but the military garb is no more than an outer shell for her maternal core, as she runs off to battle in her simple dark dress and headscarf. Her overcoat, blown back in the wind in the manner of the Mother of God's mantle, symbolizes the motherly protection she aspires to extend over her loved ones. She now leads a small group of young, idealistic graduates of the Petrograd Academy for Red Commanders who oppose heavy bombardment with nothing but side arms and rifles. Klavdia and a few survivors of the barrage start their final advance to the plaintive, off-key tune of a lonely trumpet playing the "Internationale." The screen freezes in a static view of the snow-covered town, precluding the meeting between the two epochs.

The finale mourns the demise of the Revolution's internationalist and humanist mythology in its ultimate confrontation with the overpowering image of war as an enduring reality in the authoritarian state. In Ginzburg's bird's-eye view of the Magazaniks' empty yard, snow is falling upon the cold stones, obliterating any trace of the life that had flourished there. The actual fate of Klavdia's son is unknown. The snow, the solemn tolling of church bells, and the wailing wind become symbolic of the political freeze of the late 1960s, with its regression to authoritarianism visualized in the final freeze frame.

When *The Commissar* was finally released in the Soviet Union under Gorbachev's policy of glasnost in the 1980s, some Soviet critics and perestroika officials interpreted it as part of the leadership's efforts at reconnecting the crumbling Soviet system with the Revolution's original ideals of compassion and justice. The transformed Klavdia Vavilova embodied for them—as for Askoldov himself—the high moral integrity of the commissars who fought in the Revolution and the Civil War for human dignity. The film's nomination for the Lenin Prize in 1990 seemed particularly appropriate. In the post-Soviet era the film continues to appeal to audiences thanks to its humanistic message, which transcends national, ethnic, ideological, and social boundaries.

Abridged from: Elena Monastireva-Ansdell, "Redressing the Commissar: Thaw Cinema Revises Soviet Structuring Myths," *Russian Review* 65, no. 2 (2006): 230–49.

Source: Vassili Grossman, "The Commissar" [originally titled "In the Town of Berdichev], trans. James Escombe, in "Jews and Strangers," special issue, *Glas* 6 (1999): 6–20.

Background: http://www.yivoencyclopedia.org/article.aspx/Russian_Civil_War; http://www.filmreference.com/encyclopedia/Romantic-Comedy-Yugoslavia/Russia-and-Soviet-Union-THAW-AND-NEW-WAVE-1954–1968.html.

Bibliography

Andrew, Joe. "Birth Equals Rebirth? Space, Narrative, and Gender in *The Commissar*." *Studies in Russian and Soviet Cinema* 1, no. 1 (2006): 27–44.

Babel, Isaac. *Red Calvary and Other Stories*. Edited by Efraim Sicher. Translated by David McDuff. New York: Penguin, 2006.

Clark, Katerina. *The Soviet Novel: History as Ritual*. Chicago: University of Chicago Press, 1981.

Ellis, Frank. *Vasily Grossman: The Genesis and Evolution of a Russian Heretic*. Providence, RI: Berg, 1994.

Gitelman, Zvi. *A Century of Ambivalence: The Jews of Russia and the Soviet Union, 1881 to the Present*. 2nd ed. Bloomington: Indiana University Press, 2001.

Nakhimovsky, Alice Stone. *Russian Jewish Literature and Identity: Jabotinsky, Babel, Grossman, Galich, Roziner, Markish*. Baltimore, MD: Johns Hopkins University Press, 1992.

Roberts, Graham. "The Sound of Silence: From Grossman's Berdichev to Askol'dov's *Commissar*." In *Russian and Soviet Film Adaptations of Literature, 1900–2001: Screening the Word*, edited by Stephen Hutchings and Anat Vernitski, 89–99. London: Routledge Curzon, 2005.

Stishova, Elina. The Mythologization of Soviet Woman: *The Commissar* and Other Cases." In *Red Women on the Silver Screen: Soviet Women and Cinema from the Beginning to the End of the Communist Era*, edited by Lynne Attwood and Maya Turovskaya, 175–85. New York: Harper Collins, 1993.

Turovskaya, Maya. "*Commissar.*" In *Russian Critics on the Cinema of Glasnost*, edited by Michael Brashinsky and Andrew Horton, 97–101. Cambridge: Cambridge University Press, 1994.

Youngblood, Denise J. *Russian War Films: On the Cinema Front, 1914–2005*. Lawrence: University Press of Kansas, 2007.

9. Cinema as Site of Memory

The Dybbuk and the Burden of Holocaust Commemoration

ZEHAVIT STERN

The Dybbuk (*Der Dibuk*), directed by Michał Waszyński [A, NCJF]
Poland, 1937

It is perhaps inevitable that the Holocaust affects the watching experience of the film *The Dybbuk*, shot in Poland in 1937, or, for some viewers, even dominates it. "It's a beautiful film," one friend told me, "but a few minutes into it, I could no longer concentrate on the plot. Instead, I kept thinking about the real people playing in it, about to be murdered." While for this speaker the notion of an imminent calamity disturbed the viewing of the film, for others it may merge with and enhance the film's morbid quality. Cinema scholar Ira Konigsberg regards the doom perspective as a meaningful addition to the film, furnishing it with an elegiac aura and ethical urgency: "*The Dybbuk* is a Kaddish, a prayer for the dead, that asks us to remember its dead. But along with our nostalgia, we bring to the film a sense of the tragic that may not have fully been there to begin with but that makes the film more beautiful and painful to watch." Daria Mazur and Elżbieta Ostrowska, two Polish scholars who have recently written on *The Dybbuk*, echo Konigsberg's interpretation of *The Dybbuk* as a kaddish, which suits their efforts to reclaim this Yiddish film as Polish heritage and commemorate the mass murder of Polish Jews and the destruction of Polish Jewish culture.

Many contemporary spectators view the film as a relic, perhaps even a genuine documentation of Eastern European Jewish life, which was destroyed so shortly after the film's release. The ethnographic display of Hasidic culture, so central to the play on which the film is based, its cinematic stylization characterized by gothic-expressionist tones, the blunt commodification of folklore made to attract mass audiences—these factors might be less significant or apparent for those who wish to watch the ostensibly authentic figures of Yiddish-speaking Hasidim in Jewish Eastern Europe. Such viewers may overlook the various ideological, aesthetic, and commercial motivations behind the film, including those of S. An-Ski, the Russified Jewish ethnographer who transformed life in a nineteenth-century Hasidic community into a mystical tale of social and national significance, or the aspirations of Michał Waszyński, an assimilated Jew and the "king" of Polish popular cinema of the thirties who, twenty years after the play's publication, adapted it for the screen. *The Dybbuk*'s many historical dimensions may easily collapse into one flat image of a world on the brink of annihilation.

In Pierre Nora's terms, the film functions in contemporary culture as a "site of memory" (*lieu de mémoire*), a realm of symbolic representation, a material or spiritual entity that becomes part of the collective memory. In modern times these sites replace the "real" memory of the archaic communities, embodied, unconscious, and often sacred: "There are sites of memory because there are no longer environments of memory." While Nora's ideal image of premodern memory is debatable, he accurately describes modern societies' need for sites of memory and the mechanisms of their construction. The mass destruction of European Jewry presents a special challenge to modern memory, not only due to the immensity of the catastrophe, but also because the survivors and their offspring typically do not live in their pre-

war communities, and because only little is left in the original locations of these cultures, even for the most motivated pilgrim. *The Dybbuk* seems suitable to commemorate the prewar Jewish world in a postwar world—mobile (packaged as a DVD), and yet rooted in prewar Poland where it was filmed (though mostly in a Warsaw studio); foreign by its Yiddish language, understood by very few of its current viewers, and yet international by means of its soundtrack and subtitles. While these qualities characterize every Yiddish film shot in Poland, and thus predispose all of Yiddish-Polish cinema to pedagogical use, *The Dybbuk* is especially susceptible to function as a site of memory. The film's folkloristic nature, its taking place in a distant, vaguely defined Eastern European Jewish past, its tragic romanticism, and the eternal presence of death render *The Dybbuk* an ideal commemorative symbol.

Sites of memory, according to Nora, express a consciousness of the past related to the disappearance of certain living traditions. They essentially involve notions of life and death: "moments of history torn away from the movement of history, then returned. No longer life, not quite death, like shells on the shore when the sea of living memory has receded." Indeed, if *The Dybbuk* resurrects a vanished culture, it creates a world of ghosts. Viewers may ascribe to the film both too much life, regarding it a realistic representation of life in a Jewish *shtetl*, and too little, overtly focusing on the story's macabre elements, read as omens, or on the imminent death of the actors, the language, or the culture as a whole. Turning *The Dybbuk* into a site of memory implies a distance between the displayed "objects," Eastern European Jews before the Nazi genocide, and the audience that watches them today. It may make contemporary spectators overlook the struggles between diverse social agents involved in its creation, from its conception as a play during the First World War to its filming on the eve of the Second.

In what follows I would like counter tendencies of reification and flattening of *The Dybbuk*, related in part to its functioning as a symbol of collective memory. I strive to expose the many "geological" layers in the film, which in itself deals with questions of memory and continuity. Focusing on one prominent symbol in the film—the sacred grave, located at the heart of the market square—I examine the ways in which customs and beliefs become "tradition," folklore, a national drama, a product of mass consumption, and ultimately a site of memory.

Any exploration of the film *The Dybbuk* and its prominent status in contemporary culture should start with the play on which it is based, published in 1918 and staged in numerous productions throughout the twenties and the thirties in various European and American cities and in many languages (including Yiddish, Hebrew, Russian, Polish, English, and German). The legacy of the play, one of the most renowned dramas of both Hebrew and Yiddish theater, has largely contributed to the symbolic capital of Waszyński's *The Dybbuk* from the time of its making to the present. Furthermore, the film's original audiences were likely to have viewed An-Ski's drama in one of its many productions, and the theatrical *The Dybbuk* shaped their watching experience. Thus, for example, a large part of the film review published in the New York Yiddish daily *Forverts* (Forward) in January 1938, on the occasion of *The Dybbuk*'s local cinematic premiere, was devoted to the play.

"It's strange that a play like *The Dybbuk*, which was so remote from life and the relation to things in the years after the World War, that such a play

caught everyone as it did. The play has so much depth, beauty and poetry, that even people who have no idea about the bygone dark *shtetl* life of Polish and Russian *Hasidim*, introduced in this drama, were taken by it."

How could a drama of possession and exorcism in a small nineteenth-century Jewish town be greeted with such an enthusiastic reception after the First World War and the Bolshevik Revolution? Yiddish journalist Y. Kissin ascribes the play's surprising success to its universal "depth and beauty." Himself an Eastern European Jewish immigrant to the United States, he finds fault with the rich folkloristic display in the play, the most renowned work of Shloyme Zanvil Rappaport, better known as S. An-Ski, a pioneer ethnographer of Jewish life in imperial Russia. He also criticizes the exotic nature of the film, which popularizes the drama's ethnographic bent, adding many dances, songs, and religious rituals to it.

Kissin's review reminds us of the gap between the play and the film and the lives of their directors, producers, or original urban audiences. It also sheds light on the various layers of historical memory shaping the film's production and the experience of its viewers at the time of its release: life in the Hasidic *shtetl*; its documentation by An-ski, who in the years 1910–14 headed an ethnographic expedition to Jewish towns, collecting folk customs, stories, melodies, and objects; the literary stylization of these materials in An-ski's only renowned literary work; and finally, the memory of the play's productions in Warsaw, New York, Moscow, Berlin, and Tel Aviv. Kissin, however, attributes "depth and beauty" not to these strata of remembrance and appropriation, but rather to the play's love story, which relies on the familiar formula of *Eros* and *Thanatos*, with a few unique additions, such as the homosocial romance between two Yeshiva students, and possession as a love story, which seem to be An-ski's innovation.

The Dybbuk narrates the story of two young lovers, the rich merchant's daughter Leye (Hebrew: Leah) and the poor Yeshiva student Khonen, who can hardly be considered a suitable match. When Sender, Leye's rich father, decides to marry her to a better qualified groom, the desperate Khonen turns to cabbalistic magic, which ultimately results in his death. Refusing to forget Khonen, Leye becomes possessed by him, in the midst of her wedding ceremony. The exorcism ritual that follows reveals the backdrop love story of Sender and Nisn, Khonen's father, who, as young Yeshiva students, had promised to marry their then unborn children to each other. Leye and Khonen's love is thus a fulfillment of an ancient oath between their fathers, whereas Sender's refusal to marry his daughter to Khonen constitutes a betrayal of his departed friend. Only after a trial against Sender, featuring the conjured up Nisn, does the rabbi succeed in exorcising Khonen from Leye's body. This ostensible triumph over the persistent spirit, however, is followed by Leye's death, perceived as a reunion with her dead lover.

In essence, *The Dybbuk* is a story about the problematic relations between past and present. The narrative, as Naomi Seidman explains, is first and foremost that of the dead who return to the living: Khonen, who takes over Leye's body (or soul), and Nisn, who returns to demand his debt from Sender. The sin that motivates this tragic melodrama is that of forgetting, or rather repressing, since, as Seidman notes, "Sender's love to his friend was actually never forgotten, neither by the children who fulfilled it nor by Sender himself." Nisn's special relationship with Sender, revealed in the play only in the trial scene of the fourth act, is reenacted in the film's first twenty-five minutes. From a secret oath made in the faraway past it thus becomes an integral part of the film's plot, illustrating and fortifying the bonding between the fathers and rendering the love between Leye and Khonen even more fateful.

Whereas in the play the broken oath, also the primal sin causing all the misery, is repressed by the various figures and by the text itself, in the film it is constantly present. The viewers are aware of the homosocial love affair from the very beginning, and Sender discovers Khonen's true identity shortly before the wedding, too late, he believes, to change his decision. Hardly a paragon of the premodern, organic memory revered by Nora, the community in *The Dybbyk* engages with the challenges of remembrance. Is this because An-ski, the modern scholar, created traditional society in the image of his own fractured culture? Perhaps the unmediated collective memory that Nora describes is nothing but a modern fantasy? The sacred grave, a pivotal site of memory in the film, may help us address these questions.

With its odd central location and notable dimensions, the ancient gravestone commemorating a couple murdered on their wedding night serves as one of the *The Dybbuk*'s major visual symbols, amplifying the atmosphere of mystery, ancientness, and death. Whereas the play's staging instruction situates the grave "in front of the synagogue, a little to the side," the film locates it at the heart of the little town's marketplace. It thus conveys a surreal, expressionist effect, with the slanted gravestone intersecting the diagonal lines of the crumbling houses. A hardly subtle foreshadowing device, the grave of the bride and groom slaughtered by Cossacks in 1648 clearly indicates Leye and Khonen's future union in death. The analogy between the two couples is evident in Leye's own retelling of the story, as she testifies to feelings of affinity with the murdered couple. Ignoring the ethnic or political identity of the killers, Leye refers to them as "bad people," and interprets the burial of the lovers in one grave as an expression of their eternal love. The past, for Leye, is clearly not a matter of historical accuracy or national mythmaking, but rather of emotional empathy and projection.

In An-ski's play the grave functions not only as a romantic trope, or an emblem of pogroms and Jewish martyrdom, but also, and even more so, as a symbol of the social strength and continuity of the community, which still remembers and retells this event more than two hundred years after its occurrence. It expresses Jewish solidarity and continuity, and portrays the premodern ways of remembrance. The film, on the other hand, activates the grave first and foremost as an amorous site, the only place of physical contact between the lovers, in the form of an unintentional but meaningful touch of their hands. The local custom of dancing around the grave at wedding ceremonies mentioned in the play is expanded in the film to walking around it every Saturday night. This practice, performed while Khonen and Leye engage in their amorous conversation, endows the scene with stylized and hyperdramatic tones, as the long line of slowly pacing couples operates as a series of mirrors, symbolizing the two couples. The filming of the grave from three different angles further intensifies its romantic meaning: Khonen and Leye next to the grave; then the fateful triangle of the two lovers and the grave between them; and lastly, with the menacing omen of the messenger (which is unintentionally rather humorous). Striving for commercial success rather than for a national drama, Waszyński

emphasizes the grave as a symbol of a romantic unification through death.

Interestingly, in the play the grave evokes not only traditional ways of commemoration but also modern ones. Indeed, this remembrance site is traditionally rooted in the community, which narrates the story throughout the generations and develops symbolic rituals around it. Yet the grave also signifies modern artificial memory, since it involves an external perspective and a conscious effort of reconstruction, marked by the need to decipher the inscription on the gravestone and the story behind it. While in the film Khonen asks Leye about the grave's meaning—thus initiating their intimate discussion of it—in the play it is rather "a guest," appearing out of nowhere and vanishing shortly thereafter, who inquires about the local customs. The figure of the guest, who admires the beautiful synagogue and wonders about the native customs, reminds one of a modern tourist or an anthropologist. Conceivably, he even commemorates An-ski himself and the ethnographic research that originally inspired the play. In An-ski's play the grave evokes the modern effort to retain and reconstruct collective memories, by scientific research as well as by aesthetic transformation. It thus asserts the modern and mediated nature of commemoration in *The Dybbuk* at one of its most "authentic" sites.

After the destruction of European Jewry, a new meaning was ascribed to the sacred grave, the only mention of pogroms and of non-Jews in general in the film. The prologue to the film's restored version by the National Center for Jewish Film, released in 1989, makes the following statement: "The present version, filmed on location in Poland in 1937, brought together the best talents of Polish Jewry—scriptwriters, composers, choreographers, set designers, actors and historical advisors—before they, too, were dispersed or destroyed. The gravestone of a bride and groom who, according to the folk legend, were killed under their wedding canopy, stands as a memorial to them all."

Contrary to the play, which constructs the grave as a symbol of eternal love and social solidarity, and to the film itself, which further exploits the grave's erotic potential, the prologue presents the gravestone as a site of the brutal killing of Jews during the Second World War, thus reducing it to its primitive meaning, cast aside by both An-ski and Waszyński. Furthermore, the opening titles enforce a "backshadowing" perspective on the film, to use Michael Bernstein's term, which views Eastern European Jewish civilization first and foremost as a doomed world. As in other cases in which such a stance is cultivated, here too significant differences may be overlooked, such as the gap between the degeneration of the *shtetl* world through urbanization, secularization, and immigration, which motivated An-ski's ethnographic and aesthetic endeavors around the First World War, and the annihilation of Eastern European Jewish culture in the Nazi genocide. Another distinction erased by the prologue is the one between the participants in the film who were murdered in the Holocaust and those who managed to escape to the United States or to the Soviet Union, continuing to create after the Holocaust. Survivors and those who died are commemorated in one gravestone, which becomes a memorial to Polish Jewry as a whole, and the film itself becomes construed as a gravestone.

How can a gothic love story on possession and exorcism become a site of memory for real human lives—and deaths? How can a film largely shot in a film studio in Warsaw be regarded as a historical document of the *shtetl*? How can a stylized recreation of traditional elements be considered an authentic expression of Eastern European Jewish life

shortly before its destruction? To a certain extant, these paradoxical transformations and cultural projections occurred already at the time of *The Dybbuk*'s cinematic production, and were partly intended by its makers. To create a notion of authenticity, the film was partly filmed in the picturesque *shtetl* of Kazimierz Dolny and used the town's inhabitants as extras. Moreover, since the film was also aimed at non-Jewish audiences, it was conceived from its onset as a Jewish icon. Even modern elements in the film, such as the soundtrack or dances in the style of "Expression Dance," were created with this intention in mind. In an interview for the Yiddish weekly *Literarishe Bleter* (Literary pages) the film's composer Henekh Kohn said he sought to compose in a pure Jewish style, "without any foreign resonance, in order to show to the world what a Jewish musician could create, when given the opportunity."

The indexical nature of photography and growing distance from the traditions portrayed in *The Dybbuk* made even its original audiences susceptible to perceiving it as an expression of an authentic Jewish essence. For certain viewers in the thirties, *The Dybbuk* served as an anthropological finding and evoked alienation and repulsion. Kissin of the Yiddish *Forverts* saw the film as representing "the dark *shtetl* lives" he vehemently rejected. Frank Nugent, the *New York Times* film critic, saw the film as proof of "the religious superstitious mind of the 19th century Polish Jew," and Goebbels wondered how it was that Jews were not aware of the anti-Semitic nature of the film. After the Holocaust, the tendency to view *The Dybbuk* as an ethnographic document has strengthened, along with the urge to construct it as a site of memory. What happens if the film is watched primarily as a kaddish, mourning the decimation of European Jewry? The Nazi genocide may overshadow the culture it destroyed, and the rift it created may hide the traumatic crises of modernity, which lie at the heart of works such as *The Dybbuk*. As a kaddish, the film memorializes the Jewish dead rather than illuminating their lives, including their disappearing folklore and the modern stage and screen reimaginations of their traditions in interwar Eastern Europe.

Excerpted from: Zehavit Stern, "Ghosts on the Silver Screen: The Challenge of Memory in the Film *Der Dybbuk*," in *Do Not Chase Me Away: New Studies on The Dybbuk*, ed. Shimon Levy and Dorit Yerushalmi, 98–119 (Tel Aviv: Assaph Theater Studies and Safra, 2009).

Source: S. Ansky, "The Dybbuk, or Between Two Worlds," in S. Ansky, *The Dybbuk and Other Writings*, ed. David G. Roskies, trans. Golda Werman, 1–50 (New York: Schocken, 1992).

Background: http://www.yivoencyclopedia.org/article.aspx/Rapoport_Shloyme_Zaynvl; http://www.yivoencyclopedia.org/article.aspx/Cinema.

Bibliography

Bernstein, Michael André. *Foregone Conclusions: Against Apocalyptic History*. Berkeley: University of California Press, 1994.

Hoberman, J. *Bridge of Light: Yiddish Film between the Two Worlds*. Updated and expanded ed. Hanover, NH: University Press of New England, 2010.

Konigsberg, Ira. "The Only 'I' in the World: Religion, Psychoanalysis, and *The Dybbuk*." *Cinema Journal* 36, no. 4 (1997): 22–42.

Mazur, Daria. *Waszyński's The Dybbuk*. Translated by Maciej Smoczyński. Poznań, Poland: Adam Mickiewicz University Press, 2009.

Nora, Pierre. *Realms of Memory: Rethinking the French Past*. Translated by Arthur Goldhammer. New York: Columbia University Press, 1996.

Ostrowska, Elżbieta. "Der Dibuk/The Dybbuk." In *The Cinema of Central Europe*, edited by Peter Hames, 25–35. London: Wallflower, 2004.

Saffran, Gabriella. "Dancing with Death: Salvaging Jewish Culture in *Austeria* and *The Dybbuk*." *Slavic Review* 59, no. 4 (2000): 761–81.

——and Steven J. Zipperstein, eds. *The Worlds of S. Ansky*. Stanford, CA: Stanford University Press, 2006.

Seidman, Naomi. "The Ghost of Queer Love's Past: Ansky's 'Dybbuk' and the Sexual Transformation of Ashkenaz." In *Queer Theory and the Jewish Question*, edited by Daniel Boyarin, Daniel Itzkovitz, and Ann Pellegrini, 228–45. New York: Columbia University Press, 2003.

PART THREE

The Americanization of the Jewish Immigrant, 1880–1932

10. From Hollywood to Hester Street

Ghetto Film, Melodrama, and the Image of the Assimilated Jew in *Hungry Hearts*

DELIA CAPAROSO KONZETT

Hungry Hearts, directed by E. Mason Hopper
[NCJF]
United States, 1922

In her autobiography *Red Ribbon on a White Horse* (1950), Jewish immigrant writer Anzia Yezierska recounts how she became a national celebrity in the 1920s. She had been renting a room in the Lower East Side (from which she was soon to be evicted) when a telegram arrived, informing her that the Hollywood studio Goldwyn was interested in purchasing the film rights to her collection of short stories *Hungry Hearts* (1920). Unable to afford the nickel to telephone her agent and the fifteen cents for carfare, she sells her dead mother's antique shawl from Poland to a miserly Jewish pawnbroker. She depicts the pawnbroker in stereotypic terms, "a baldheaded dwarf, grown gray with the years in the dark basement—tight-skinned and crooked from squeezing pennies out of despairing people." Using equally hackneyed terms, she describes the ghetto as cramped and dirty, reeking with "the smell of fish and overripe fruit," her landlady as the "angel of death," waiting for the moment to evict her; and herself as an overworked, underfed writer, living in dire circumstances. The generous contract that she signs with Goldwyn lifts her out of this miserable ghetto existence, and the studio's publicity turns her into an overnight star. The poor immigrant who had once been a cleaning lady and sweatshop worker has thus been magically transformed into a successful writer.

The sensational climax of Yezierska's autobiography reads like the prototypical American success story. Newspaper headlines around the country proclaim the fabulous rags-to-riches rise of the "Sweatshop Cinderella" who has made it "from Hester Street to Hollywood," describing how a poor immigrant Jew who was once a cleaning lady and sweatshop worker has been magically transformed into a successful American writer.

Yezierska's account of this event deliberately exploits the rags-to-riches narrative with its requisite happy ending, only to dismantle it. The myth of assimilation attests to the pervasiveness, persistence, and potential of mass-produced cultural stereotypes. Yezierska not only reiterates the fabricated construction of her immigrant identity but also unravels it at its core. Thus Yezierska's autobiography (like her fiction) uses the myths and icons of assimilation to also explore the in-assimilable and "foreign" elements that help create American culture. Her autobiography shows that she did not live happily ever after, describing her disappointment with the film adaptation of *Hungry Hearts*; her inability to work in Hollywood with its ideology of the "cash register"; the hyping of her immigrant success story, and her disgust at how she had contributed to it; how she attempted to recapture her immigrant lifestyle through writing, but eventually lost her zest to write and found herself during the Depression without money, a livelihood, and a reading audience. Yezierska exposes the fairy tale of the assimilated Jew as an illusion manufactured by Hollywood for profit, revealing how the immigrant experience was informed by and in turn informed the American dream.

These anti-assimilationist messages are also couched within the mass culture idiom of ethnic stereotypes represented in the film *Hungry Hearts* (1922). Like Yezierska's work, the film adaptation exploits popular conceptions of immigrant culture not so much for entertainment purposes, but to point to contemporary social concerns; moreover, the film calls attention to Hollywood's use of these stereotypes and conventions, particularly the image of the assimilated Jew, to legitimate its own agenda of growth and profit. Produced when the Americanization of newcomers was viewed by the public as a failure and was being replaced by severe immigration restrictions, *Hungry Hearts* asks its audience to rethink its assumptions about immigration, reform, and the acculturation of immigrants. *Hungry Hearts* reveals the intimate link between ethnicity and the American dream. Like Yezierska's work, the film reverses the path of assimilation and parallels Yezierska's own return from Hollywood to Hester Street, indicating the failure of

Helen Ferguson (as Sara) still dressed in her immigrant clothes. From *Hungry Hearts* (1922), directed by E. Mason Hooper. NATIONAL CENTER FOR JEWISH FILM

Americanization, which placed immigrants in an inferior status.

In the 1920s, the American film industry, which established itself as a respectable business and the nation's most popular form of entertainment, was largely under the control of successful East European Jews. These immigrant businessmen controlled the production and distribution of motion pictures, making Hollywood a central source of mass culture. Jews were also popular subjects on screen since the earliest moments of film history. In early American cinema, these portrayals were often anti-Semitic and stereotypical, in which Jews were recognizable by their Orthodox dress and appearance, prominent physical attributes, and exaggerated mannerisms. As Jewish immigrants entered the industry at various levels and comprised a significant part of its target audience, the repertoire of Jewish screen images likewise expanded. During this time, as Patricia Erens explains, a variety of Jewish character types were developed and refined as were two major Jewish genres, comedy and melodrama. There was a move away from blatant anti-Semitism to more positive, albeit sentimental, portrayals, often centering on the theme of assimilation. This softening of anti-Semitic content occurred particularly in melodrama since comedy, dependent upon caricature and exaggeration, continued to exploit Jewish stereotypes.

This pattern of assimilation and reward is especially seen in the ghetto film, a popular subgenre that attempted to realistically represent immigrant life in America by emphasizing the cultural and generational conflicts and the hard and unhealthy living conditions of the ghetto. Ghetto films evolved into a more formulaic genre, idealizing the immigrant's assimilation into American society. These films promoted an assimilationist ideology to retain their traditional target audience and to increase their appeal to a larger middle-class and multiethnic audience. Because they were concerned with assimilation, intermarriage, national identity, reform, and upward social mobility, ghetto films proved to be a well-suited vehicle for inculcating immigrants into American consumer and popular culture.

The screen image of the assimilated Jew likewise transformed to meet the demands of this larger and more cosmopolitan public sphere, becoming by the end of World War I what Thomas Cripps has called "a living allegory for the American dream of success" as well as the "nostalgic, benign icon of the ritual of Americanization."

This image of the assimilated Jew, however, can neither be reduced to a sentimentalized reproduction of the "assimilationist experience of the Jewish studio bosses" in which they appear as "the most dramatic example of the ethnic success story," as Cripps claims, nor, as Lester Friedman believes, an attempt on the part of Hollywood "to make Americans less nervous about Jews and Jews more conscious of themselves as Americans." Equated with democratic consumerism, the image of the assimilated Jew created a powerful myth of a nation united not only culturally and politically but economically as well, representing an America bound together by democratic values and the affluent lifestyle of its consuming masses. In this way the rags-to-riches sagas of immigrants submerged the divisions of class, culture, and ethnicity into a homogeneous mass of American consumers. These myths of universalism and democracy provided Hollywood with a marketing strategy that legitimated its ideology and exploitative economic practices as essentially American and democratic.

A late example of the ghetto film, *Hungry Hearts* (1922) depicts the potential of the younger generation to move itself out of the ghetto and into mainstream American life. At one level it employs a formulaic treatment of assimilation, conflating concerns of love, marriage, social mobility, and economic consumption with the American dream. The immigrant quickly assimilates and rises in status, overcoming ethnic, cultural, social, and class differences. However, unlike other romanticized ghetto films, the subtext of *Hungry Hearts* acknowledges a profound disenchantment with the promises of America's melting-pot democracy, providing a criticism of Americanization. This ambivalence is first seen in its ironic manipulation of the conventions of ghetto film, parodying the Americanization ritual and its expectations. This light parody gives the film its humorous and entertaining aspects, reflecting skepticism toward the rhetoric of assimilation and immigrant culture. It also exhibits an enlightened consumerism that exposes the deceptions of ruthless capitalism as an essentially democratic enterprise. Toward the film's end, this ironic ambivalence reaches a feverish pitch and calls attention to the assumptions underlying the film's construction. Here, the viewer unexpectedly confronts disturbing images of ethnic self-hatred, trauma, and resentment that disrupt the transition from immigrant to American. The contrived happy ending does not repair this rupture but highlights the improbability of assimilated immigrants living happily ever in America, thus radically calling into question the entire project of assimilation and Americanization.

The film presents the rags-to-riches story of the Levin family's immigration and assimilation in the short space of a year in three parts: the first section takes place in a *shtetl* in Russia and depicts the reasons for leaving; the second section depicts the Lower East Side ghetto as the transitional and economically deprived space that must be traversed on the way to American affluence; the third section, the happy ending, portrays the family successfully ensconced in middle-class American society. In its adherence to the conventions of the ghetto film, *Hungry Hearts* parodies its own genre and the underlying ideology of the classic American success story. Since immigration had come virtually to a halt in 1914 due to World War I and was drastically reduced by the restrictive immigration laws of 1921 and 1924, the film's subject matter was part of a past that was being romanticized and sentimentalized in ghetto films.

The film opens with an idyllic view of Russian *shtetl* life in 1910. In a setting of abundant natural beauty, we see the daily affairs of the community, including people working and children playing. Moving into the hut of the Levin family, we meet the protagonists: Abraham Levin, the father, described as a "gentle, pious, unpractical and, who in 1910, solved all problems according to a book written in 1200"; Hanneh, his hard-working wife and head of the household; the eldest daughter, Sara; and the other Levin children. In their home, Abraham conducts Hebrew classes while Hanneh and Sara perform household chores. This peaceful routine of *shtetl* life is rudely interrupted by a Cossack, who enters the Levin home to enforce the rule prohibiting teaching Hebrew. The Cossack threatens Abraham, steps on the family's bread, attempts to whip the children, and briefly struggles with Hanneh as she protects them. After the Cossack's departure, a letter arrives from America. As one of the *shtetl*'s few literate people, Abraham reads it to the community. It describes in humorously inflated rhetoric the luck of the former water carrier, now a businessman (fruit vendor) in America. The writer proudly tells of his $2 daily profit, his private room, and American democracy where he "has as much to say as Rockefeller, the greatest millionaire." He also mentions the American social practice of "ladies first," which forces men to wait upon their wives and even wash dishes.

The mistreatment by the Cossacks and the optimistic letter foster a longing to move to America to obtain its guarantees of equality in spite of religious differences. These events foreshadow the future dominance of the mother and daughter, who in America will be responsible for the family's social mobility as the main consumers of the household. By contrast Abraham is represented as the "Pathetic Patriarch," an inept figure incapable of handling practical affairs. His point-of-view shots are relegated to written texts (religious texts and letter), establishing his position as patriarch, but indicating the narrowness of his theological and learned outlook. That these texts are in Hebrew further estranges Abraham from the viewer. This portrayal of the father anticipates the later use of two immigrant clichés: that it takes hard work (manual labor) rather than learning to become successful; and that America is the land of "ladies first." America is associated with marriage opportunity, a place where a poor immigrant woman without a substantial dowry can overcome poverty by marrying for "love." Since Abraham is unconcerned with practical matters, he occupies a sentimental role, serving as the head of family in name only. Conversely, Hanneh proves herself to be the courageous and independent "Long-Suffering Mother." We first see her carrying water into the house and later shoveling coal into the stove. She argues with the Cossack and realizes what $2 daily profit would mean to her family. Assisted by Sara, she decides the family will immigrate and raises the travel funds.

In his study of Jewish immigrants and mass consumption, Andrew Heinze explains how Jewish women "served as a catalyst for the adaptation of newcomers to the American standard of living." Since Jewish men in Eastern Europe achieved status by studying the Torah and Talmud, they left the running of the household in the hands of women who bought kosher food and prepared and served it in accordance with Jewish dietary codes. With these skills, Jewish women quickly adapted to the domestic realm of the American economy, namely budgeting, managing the home, and shopping. In turn they significantly contributed to the rapid social and economic mobility of the new Jewish immigrant population from working to middle class in the span of one to two generations. *Hungry Hearts* illustrates the role Jewish women played in this social mobility and how they conformed to the American assimilationist model.

The authority of Hanneh and Sara in America is immediately established in the film's next section, which depicts the family's adjustment to New York as part of the urban poor and their attempts to escape the ghetto and their despised condition as "greenhorns." Hanneh disembarks from the boat at Ellis Island, wearing typical immigrant clothes, and stares admiringly at Gedalyeh Mindel, the former village water carrier and now a respected American citizen, who has come to meet them. The comical Mindel is dressed to the nines and fastidiously adjusting his accessories. As he leads the family through the Lower East Side, the poverty and unhealthy living conditions of the ghetto are seen through the women's eyes. However, in spite of their privileged point-of-view shots, Hanneh and Sara remain nonassimilated immigrants. When Sara asks, "Ain't even a greenhorn also a somebody in America?" Mindel replies, "Nobody's a somebody before he can earn money in America!" In a shot viewed from Mindel's perspective, Sara appears peasant-like in un-American clothes, wearing old-fashioned stockings and clumsy shoes. "But can't I work and earn money—and make myself a somebody?" she wonders. "Sure," he assures her, "but not in those greenhorn clothes." Sara quickly realizes what she needs to be somebody in America. Sara begs her father to "make money quickly for American clothes. I'm burning to work and make myself a somebody!"

This importance of dress in the New World had become a convention in immigrant literature. The ritual of taking a picture in American clothes upon landing at Ellis Island to show relatives in the Old World one's remarkable transformation already had been firmly established. This association of American dress and social mobility is comically presented in the film, cynically exploiting the twisted logic in which one needs money for clothes before one can find work. Consumption is promoted at the expense of production, exploiting the labor of the immigrant worker while promising liberation through consumption. Thus, consumption is flatly equated with assimilation, especially the purchasing of American clothes. Consumption, however, involves the exploitation of the labor of working-class women. In this vicious circle, freedom is accompanied by further enslavement and enslavement is endured by accepting consumption as an illusionary freedom. Sara's dual ability to work and to clothe herself in American fashion demonstrates her worthiness to become an American citizen.

Since Abraham's endeavors to earn money fail, the women must earn the family keep. Hanneh takes in laundry, and Sara first works as a janitor of the tenement building to earn money and free rent, and later as a garment worker. The assimilative process of working for clothes leads to the reward of love American style through which Sara is able to leave the ghetto. The first meeting between Sara and David, the landlord's American-born nephew who has just received his law degree, does not end in romance because she has not yet been able to purchase American clothes. In their second encounter, however, her stylish American clothes combined with her good looks succeed in catching his eye. In a point-of-view shot recalling that of Mindel, he looks at her American dress and fashionable shoes and falls in love. The film not only represents acculturation as the only viable alternative, it shows that those who acculturate are richly rewarded.

Whereas Sara's assimilation centers on love and clothes, Hanneh desires a beautiful white kitchen like that of her American employer, Mrs. Preston. Like Sara, she works to earn the money

that will turn her kitchen into a suitable space "so that even the President from America will be proud to step into such beautifulness." In the Progressive Era, the reform of the immigrant focused on personal and household cleanliness, with special attention given to the kitchen as the center of the domestic sphere. To instill American domestic culture and its values of order, function, and cleanliness in the immigrant home, reformers designed model tenement kitchens with white walls and bare wood floors to fit into an overall "scheme of simplicity." In reality, the kitchen of the average immigrant of the Lower East Side fell short of this ideal and was used for eating, doing homework, conversing, and manufacturing various commercial products. According to Jenna Joselit, most immigrants disliked the austere look of whitewashed walls, preferring instead, to the dismay of reformers, "colored wallpaper, brightly patterned linoleum, and yards of lace and fabric trimmings" that were "anything but visually comprehensive and ordered." Like Sara's American clothes, Hanneh's white kitchen reveals the great extent to which she has become Americanized. It is fitting that the kitchen is presented as a tribute to Sara's engagement, the reward for assimilation that will raise the Levin family to middle-class status.

Likewise, the complication in the film—David's uncle threatens to withhold his financial support if his nephew proceeds with the marriage—brings together the concerns of marriage and the kitchen. He not only attempts to break the engagement but doubles the rent of the Levin family, claiming Hanneh's new kitchen has made the property more valuable. Unable to pay, the family faces certain eviction and Hanneh the loss of her kitchen and prospective son-in-law. In a traditional ghetto film, this complication would restore the balance of power to the younger generation or, more precisely, to David, the native-born

American and hero of the film. The strengthened position of the women would be held in check and not allowed to threaten the hero's position as the head of the household and representative of American culture. At this crucial point, however, the film disrupts its own assimilationist logic.

In the most remarkable scene of the film, Hanneh's sorrow over losing her kitchen erupts into violent rage, revealing her ambivalence toward Americanization. Told by a policeman that the landlord has the right to raise the rent, Hanneh returns downtrodden to her kitchen. In a sudden revelation, however, Hanneh cries out, "No! The landlord ain't going to get the best from me" and grabs a large meat cleaver hanging on the wall. We see the cleaver in her hand gashing the white wall and causing the plaster to scatter. This shot alternates with close-ups of Hanneh's grimacing face. She turns to the cupboards and hacks the shelves, sending dishes and cups crashing to the floor. The duration of her rage is visualized not only in lengthy close-ups, but in crosscutting sequences showing Sara and Abraham buying meat and heading home as the janitor who, upon hearing the noise, enters the apartment. Spotting the janitor, Hanneh swings her cleaver at him, forcing him out. Subsequent crosscutting shots show him rushing across town to fetch the landlord. When Sara and Abraham return, Hanneh is still hacking away and Abraham attempts to restrain her. Meanwhile, water is boiling over on the stove, and a small stove fire starts. A group of neighbors enter and attempt to restrain Hanneh, but she swings at them with the cleaver. Finally, the landlord arrives with two policemen, who restrain Hanneh. In a last fit of rage she yells "The Cossack! The Cossack!" and faints from exhaustion.

Exceptional in its intensity, violence, and duration, this scene of destruction not only drama-tizes the irrational and uncivilized nature lurking within the female that must be contained by the male hero, but more importantly interrupts the otherwise chronological, if condensed, timeline of the film and its assimilationist model. In contrast to the seamless conventional plot, this scene underscores the violence that underlies the model of acculturation and foregrounds the resulting reactions of ethnic self-hatred, resentment, and frustration. A film meant to provide entertainment begins to destroy its own cinematic appeal, reflecting Yezierska's stance. The light ironic humor that poked fun at assimilation has been transformed into a subversive force, questioning the models of assimilation and consumerism and the filmic conventions employed to affirm these ideologies. At this point, the cynicism and pretense of the film come undone and radically express disenchantment not only with the ideology of Americanization but with cinema's manipulative projection of social illusions. The white kitchen wall that Hanneh destroys symbolizes the white screen upon which Hollywood projected its idealized America.

This scene further discloses how the ghetto is constructed as a transitional place in the Americanization narrative, where it is neither a site of legitimate residence nor culture. Yezierska's notion of a hybrid Anglo-immigrant culture emerging from the ghetto is contradicted by a socioeconomic reality that does not tolerate domestication and affluence within it. Hanneh cannot remain once she has remodeled her kitchen, since that marks an attempt to make herself at home in the Lower East Side. The rent is raised to demarcate the socioeconomic difference between the immigrant and the upwardly mobile Americanized immigrant. Social dignity, white kitchens, and clean rooms are reserved for Americans who can afford higher rents, not for "greenhorns."

Capitalism emerges as the only criterion of Americanization, setting a limit to any other form of acculturation that falls short of economic affluence. By film's end, David replaces Hanneh as the hero, since his success as a lawyer propels the family into middle-class status.

Hanneh's trial appears to restore the broken plot structure through the reestablishment of patriarchal dominance. However, the viewer finds it hard to accept that a woman who had struggled with a Cossack, brought her family across the Atlantic, and wreaked havoc on her kitchen, now sits before the court, crushed and afraid to speak. David, who is defending her, must coax her story out of her. Upon telling it, she faints. The judge dismisses her case and scolds the landlord for exploiting his fellow immigrants. The judge functions not only as a legal and moral adjudicator but also as an agent of social reform and assimilation. Hanneh's submissive behavior is rewarded, while the disrespectful demeanor of the landlord is punished. As anticipated, the film delivers the traditional happy ending, displaying the rich rewards of assimilation. The family, after only "their second summer in a new land," is now shown living happily in a large white house with a large yard. This idyllic scene, with the father and mother on the front porch and the children playing the American games of skipping rope and catch and wearing American clothes, recalls the film's opening shot of *shtetl* life in Russia that has been enhanced by the affluence of America. Meanwhile, David has become a successful defense lawyer who, as Mindel notes, is now earning "fat fees" by freeing murderers.

According to Yezierska, who disliked this happy ending, Samuel Goldwyn hired Montague Glass to give the film "laughs and a happy ending." A popular Jewish writer, Glass was described by Yezierska as a man who "turned out his caricatures of Jews like sausage meat for the popular weekly and monthly magazines." Yezierska claimed that upon meeting her, Glass commented: "I hear your book is a great tear-jerker. With a few laughs to set off the sob stuff, a story like yours could put you on Easy Street for the rest of your life." Because Glass relied heavily upon Eastern European Jewish stereotypes in his caricatures and humor, Yezierska believed his ending, like his stories, had anti-Semitic overtones. She complained that his readers "thought those clowning cloak and suiters were the Jewish people." For Yezierska, Glass's happy ending ruined *Hungry Hearts*, turning it into sentimental pulp that exploited immigrant culture for profit. In one of her subsequent stories, the narrator begins, "This is a story with an unhappy ending, and I too have become Americanized enough to be terrified of unhappy endings." Unhappy endings, albeit painful, she implies, are more truthful when writing about Americanization.

In Yezierska's story "The Lost Beautifulness," upon which the closing scenes are based, the outcome is decidedly different. Hanneh is punished for her belief in America's democratic system, which is revealed as a sham. She loses her court case to the landlord, and the family is evicted. Her unsupportive husband blames the unhappy outcome solely on her: "and all because you, a *meshugeneh yideneh* [a crazy Jew] a starved *beggerin* [beggar], talked it into your head that you got to have for yourself a white-painted kitchen alike to Mrs. Preston. Now you'll remember to listen to your husband." The kitchen ultimately serves to mock the immigrant who naively buys into Americanization, revealing the extent to which the immigrant *cannot* assimilate. The proud son, for whom the kitchen was painted, returns home from the war with a Distinguished Service Medal pinned to his uniform only to find his mother and the family's entire belongings in the street.

While apparently stressing an ideology opposed to Yezierska's work, the screen adaptation ultimately articulates her anti-Americanization message. Hanneh's outburst calls into doubt the film's entire mode of address, pointing to its own complicity in promoting assimilation. The happy ending appears mechanical and staged purposely to affirm Americanization as part of an institutional and national formula. If the happy ending is the natural heritage of a democratic country, an ending that highlights an immigrant family living off of "fat fees" earned by freeing murderers provocatively subverts this message. The film's ending exposes a nation ruled by a savage capitalism that lurks beneath the social concerns of Americanization, immigration, philanthropy, and reform. Whether or not he intended it, Glass's ending also exposes Hollywood's image of the assimilated Jew as an empty one motivated by commercial profit. The joke concerning David's financial success indirectly makes it clear that Americanization has its limits, reminding the audience of the inassimilable ethnic difference between Jews and the dominant Anglo-Saxon culture.

According to Magdalena J. Zaborowska, Yezierska purposely used happy endings to deflate the illusions of acculturation. Yezierska, she maintains, "did not fall prey to her clichéd romantic endings, as most critics suggest, but, rather, used them for an ironic self-conscious contrast highlighting the unglamorous side of female Americanization." Indeed, many of Yezierska's stories and novels employ the same stilted happy ending, prompting the reader to question the assumptions about the American dream. Yezierska's complaints about the ending of the film and Hollywood centered largely on its cash register ideology and its relegation of her power as an author to a secondary position; however, it could not have been, as she claims, due to the violation of her work. In her critique of Hollywood, Yezierska may ironically have fallen prey to her own stereotypes pertaining to popular cinema, thereby overlooking its equally disruptive potential to convey disturbing images and deliver a strong social criticism through a provocative rendering of melodramatic and hackneyed plots.

Abridged from: Delia Caparoso Konzett, "From Hollywood to Hester Street: Ghetto Film, Melodrama, and the Image of the Assimilated Jew in *Hungry Hearts*," *Journal of Film and Video* 50, no. 4 (1998–99): 18–34.

Source: Anzia Yezierska, *Hungry Hearts and Other Stories* (New York: Persea, 1985). An earlier edition (Cambridge, MA: Riverside, 1920) is available online (digital.library.upenn.edu/women/yezierska/hearts/hearts.html).

Background: http://www.history.umd.edu/Faculty/BCooperman/NewCity/Jewishwomen.html; http://jwa.org/encyclopedia/article/yezierska-anzia.

Bibliography

Brownlow, Kevin. "*Hungry Hearts*: A Hollywood Social Problem Film of the 1920s." *Film History* 1, no. 2 (1987): 113–25.

Cripps, Thomas. "The Movie Jew as an Image of Assimilation, 1903–1927." *Journal of Popular Film* 4, no. 3 (1975): 190–207.

Erens, Patricia. *The Jew in American Cinema*. Bloomington: Indiana University Press, 1984.

Friedman, Lester D. *Hollywood's Image of the Jew*. New York: Frederick Ungar, 1982.

Gabler, Neal. *An Empire of Their Own: How the Jews Invented Hollywood*. New York: Crown, 1988.

Heinze, Andrew R. *Adapting to Abundance: Jewish Immigrants, Mass Consumption, and the Search for American Identity*. New York: Columbia University Press, 1990.

Joselit, Jenna Weissman. *The Wonders of America: Rein-

venting Jewish Culture, 1880–1950. New York: Hill and Wang, 1994.

Weinberg, Sydney Stahl. *The World of Our Mothers: The Lives of Immigrant Jewish Women.* Chapel Hill: University of North Carolina Press, 1988.

Yezierska, Anzia. *Red Ribbon on a White Horse: My Story.* New York: Persea, 1985.

Zaborowska, Magdalena J. *How We Found America: Reading Gender through East European Immigrant Narratives.* Chapel Hill: University of North Carolina Press, 1995.

11. The Right Film at the Right Time

Hester Street as a Reflection of Its Era

HASIA DINER

Hester Street, directed by Joan Micklin Silver
[A]
United States, 1975

Scholars of film, like those who study other forms of popular culture, have rightly insisted that creative documents like movies, music, "middlebrow" literature, cartoons, and the like tell us much about the concerns and sensibilities of the times and places of their creation. Feature films reflect and absorb the values that predominated in the shared world of the producers who made them and the audiences who consumed them. Not concerned with offering aesthetic evaluations of these works, historians have analyzed films as vehicles by which to understand the cultural contexts of their production and reception. They ask why a filmmaker made a particular film at that specific time. What accounts for the fact that audiences flocked to it? How can we under-

stand why this film moved its viewers, and what contemporary issues propelled audiences to embrace it?

Some films stand out as perfect exemplars of the social and cultural trends that prevailed when they were being made and when audiences had a chance to accept or reject them. Joan Micklin Silver's 1975 film *Hester Street*, an adaptation of Abraham Cahan's 1896 short story, "Yekl: A Tale of the New York Ghetto" offers an excellent case in point. In the period that commenced in the late 1960s and continued into the 1970s, America became the setting for a revival of interest in the "roots" of the many minority groups who constituted its people. It also became a kind of battleground in a struggle between men and women, with women demanding equality in multiple spheres. (Jacobson: 2006; Evans: 2003)

The quest for their origins and for answers to questions about gender rights took the filmmaker and her producer-husband, Rafael Silver—both American Jews—to New York's Lower East Side, a neighborhood that became in that period a symbol of the authenticity of the immigrant era. Contemporaneously a newly energized wave of feminist activism and consciousness-raising sent women to history, searching for a usable past that would provide them with models to emulate in the present. Jewish women sought to reclaim their past even as they tried to radically improve their present conditions. *Hester Street* resonated with people involved in both of these trends in the late 1960s and 1970s. (Diner: 2000)

The plot of the film, which hewed quite closely to Cahan's short story, told a gripping tale of love, marriage, betrayal, and starting over in New York's Jewish ghetto in the late nineteenth century. Jake, called "Yekl" when he lived in his small town in Eastern Europe, has changed his name and style of clothes to reflect his new iden-

Zvee Scooler (as the rabbi), in the center, explains the *get*, the writ of divorce, to Steven Keats (as Jake), on the left, and Carol Kane (as Gitl), on the right. From *Hester Street* (1975), directed by Joan Micklin Silver. MIDWEST FILMS/PHOTOFEST

tity as an American. The arrival of his wife, Gitl, from the "old country" upsets his newly acquired lifestyle.

Many married immigrant Jewish men, like Jake, came to America first, to earn enough money to bring over, as soon as they could, their wives and children. Like so many others, Jake worked in a sweatshop, having arrived with the intention of reuniting with his wife and son, Yossele. But something happened to Yekl. He not only became "Jake," but he plunged so enthusiastically into the process of becoming someone new that he lost touch with his past and his family back home. The audience gets an insight into Jake, and how he has become disconnected from his Jewish origins, when he receives word that his father has died. Jake thinks that he should recite

the obligatory prayer, the kaddish, for his deceased father, but he cannot. He just does not remember how.

More central to the plot is the fact that Jake did not stick to the script in terms of doing what an immigrant Jewish man ought to have done in his years alone in America. He used some of the money intended for the support and reunification of his family for upgrading his clothing, going to dance classes, and courting a woman, the fancy and Americanized Mamie. Over the years, he managed to avoid telling Mamie that he happened to have a wife and child back home.

Gitl's arrival jeopardizes his new American persona as a happy-go-lucky, bachelor sweatshop worker. The key conflict in the film—as in the short story penned by the long time editor of the

Forverts (*Forward*), the Yiddish newspaper with the largest circulation in America—flares between Jake, the dapper Yankee with the secret romance on the side, and the traditional Gitl, the normative Jewish wife wearing a dowdy dress and a wig perched atop her head, conforming to the Jewish law that a married woman must not appear in public with her own hair exposed. Jake expresses revulsion at Gitl's appearance and withholds his affection from her. Clearly, trouble looms for this marriage.

Gitl initially does what she can to win Jake's affection back. When a peddler knocks on her door, she inquires if he sells a love potion. Desperately wanting her marriage to work, she reluctantly doffs the wig and replaces it with a kerchief. When that fails to attract Jake, she takes it off and appears showing her own hair. But to no avail. Jake persists in his revulsion against her and never breaks off his relationship with Mamie.

Mamie's presence, however, complicates what could be a straightforward story of acculturation and its discontents. Mamie persuades Jake to divorce Gitl and marry her. That means Jake must obtain a ritual *get*, a Jewish divorce. In order to do this, he has to spend Mamie's money, squirreled away from her years of toil in a sweatshop, to pay a settlement to Gitl. Stripped of his and her savings, he and Mamie marry in a simple civil ceremony at City Hall and leave for their new and impecunious married lives on foot, wanting to save the nickel needed to take the streetcar.

Gitl, on the other hand, makes out just fine. Over the course of the film and during her struggle with the unloving and unfaithful Jake, she has fallen in love with the pious scholar Bernstein, Jake's co-worker and the family's boarder, who has been smitten by her. At the film's end, the two traditionalists go off together. Gitl has decided that with the money from her divorce settlement,

she will open a grocery store and get started on her path to the American dream. Her entrepreneurship will enable Bernstein to pursue his Talmudic studies, which he was unable to do during his years of labor in the sweatshop.

Gitl's agency, her ability to chart her own future, allows her to organically blend her commitment to tradition and her adoption of aspects of American culture. She appears in the last scene sporting a modish pompadour hairdo, a stylish hat, and a form-fitting shirtwaist, a far cry from the baggy immigrant garb and mushroom-shaped wig in which she first came on the screen. Like Jake, she now calls her son Joey, instead of the Yiddish Yossele. But unlike Jake and Mamie, she has not exchanged her birthright as a Jew for a kind of tawdry Americanization. She strives for a synthesis that keeps her connected to the authentic.

Joan Micklin Silver's film stands out in the long history of films made by Jews about Jewish subjects for American audiences, of whom Jews constituted only a small minority. Although this was not the first movie to use the backdrop of the Jewish quarter, it did so in a novel way. During the era of the silent films, movies like *The Ghetto Seamstress* (1910) and *Humoresque* (1920) depicted immigrant life, but that genre—known as "ghetto films," regardless of their theme or emphasis—came to an end with the 1927 "talkie," Al Jolson's *The Jazz Singer*. Even in that film "the New York ghetto," referred to directly in the titles in the first frame, served as just a backdrop to the action that launched Jake, in this case Jake Rabinowitz, into a singing career on Broadway. After that watershed film, the Lower East Side slipped away as a setting for Jewish-themed movies, surfacing only to provide a starting point for a narrative about paths out of the ghetto.

That Joan Micklin Silver turned to the ghetto, and to a tale written by one of the most astute and most published commentators on the Lower East Side's trends, personalities, and places, meant that that long avoidance had come to an end. Starting in the years immediately after World War II, the old Jewish neighborhood of New York had begun to emerge from its obscurity, and an array of artists, writers, and others turned to it for inspiration. It became not just acceptable but culturally *au courant* in the wake of the tumultuous 1960s to think about, perform, and represent that neighborhood and the immigrant era. In 1966 the Jewish Museum staged a blockbuster exhibit, "Portal to America," followed by the publication and robust sales of its catalog by the same name. (Schoener: 1967) In 1966 Schocken Press reissued an immigrant-era text, *The Spirit of the Ghetto*, with a running commentary by the humorist Harry Golden. Three years later Milton Hindus published *The Jewish East Side*, and Ronald Sanders brought out *The Downtown Jews*. The early to mid-1970s witnessed a quickening of the pace of production of Lower East Side texts. Not only did Abraham Cahan's *Yekl* become available to late-twentieth-century American readers, including the Nebraska-born Joan Micklin Silver in 1970, but in 1971 Isaac Metzker (1971) also availed himself of the Cahan repertoire in his *A Bintel Brief*, a selection of questions posed to Cahan by the immigrant readers of the *Forverts* and the columns he published in reply. There is good evidence that Cahan penned most of the questions himself. The release of *Hester Street* in 1975 coincided with the Feminist Press's publication of the forgotten work *The Bread Givers*, a 1925 novel by Anzia Yezierska, which was set in the Lower East Side. Finally, and hardly incidentally, the year after *Hester Street* premiered, Irving Howe's magnum opus, *World of Our Fathers*, became a bestseller and popularized terms like "the Lower East Side," the "Jewish quarter," and "the New York ghetto," on television talk shows and reviews in publications of all kinds.

The revival of the Lower East Side in popular memory offers one context for thinking about *Hester Street* and why it worked so well for a 1970s America. Indeed, the fact that Silver changed the title of the film reveals the degree to which the Lower East Side mattered to it. Although the film was originally called *Yekl*, Silver chose *Hester Street* as the final title, reflecting the emergence of the neighborhood as a sacred symbol of American Jewish culture.

The vigor of the image of this neighborhood—its ability to inspire, and the eagerness of audiences to consume works set on its streets—mirrored the general cultural ferment of "the sixties," a shorthand term commonly used to denote the vast upheavals of the decade. Those upheavals can be seen in a number of different but related ways, all of which pointed to a desire to escape to more authentic times and places—if only momentarily, while sitting in a darkened theater.

One reason is that, starting in the middle of the 1960s, America experienced an across-the-board change in the nature of public discourse. As the civil rights movement went out into the streets and into the consciousness of the white public, bringing the nation to a legislative and judicial revolution, Americans began to talk, volubly, about their relationship to the American experience, what had brought them or their ancestors there, and what price tag America had affixed to their integration.

In what is often dubbed the "ethnic revival" of the 1960s—or, as the historian Matthew Frye Jacobson (2006) has called it, the claim of "Roots Too"—the grandchildren of the forty million or so Europeans who had immigrated to the United States launched a two-pronged discussion about these matters. Some wrote fiery diatribes against what they considered the inexorable process of assimilation, which had robbed them and their forebears of their ethnic origins. Michael Novak's *The Rise of the Unmeltable Ethnics* (1972) wagged an accusatory finger at the larger hegemonic cultural forces that had tried to melt down the Poles, Greeks, Italians, Hungarians, and other "ethnics" into bland, ordinary Americans. As the title implied, he pointed out that some of these resilient people had refused to abandon their ethnic heritage. At the grass-roots level, these ethnic groups engaged in new cultural endeavors to revive what they believed to be the authentic cultures of their immigrant forebears. Although much of what they created can rightly be considered innovative rather than traditional, their efforts to return to their origins in the late 1960s and 1970s constituted a shift in American cultural history.

These undertakings may have reflected in part an antiblack backlash, sparked by the triumph of civil rights legislation and the emergence of affirmative action, bussing, and other policies that offended the sensibilities of an essentially white, working-class population. In any case, they also reflected a transition in American culture in which many people of diverse backgrounds sought to explore, think about, and indeed hallow their roots, sharing with the public their personal, and also their group's, narrative about arrival, struggle, tragedy, and ultimate triumph. In 1972 Congress passed the Ethnic Heritage Studies Act, introduced by Congressman Peter Rodino, with the aim of having the federal government partner with ethnic communities in the preservation of languages and cultural customs.

The quest for roots in the late 1960s and 1970s represented a powerful cultural movement of that era. Millions of Americans were riveted to the television when the generational saga of a slave family, *Roots*, aired in 1977, based on Alex Haley's book of the same title—which had topped bestseller lists the previous year. The 1970s saw the beginning of a mass volunteer effort to restore Ellis Island, the gateway to America for so many immigrants in the late nineteenth and early twentieth centuries, whose grandchildren in the last quarter of the twentieth century started to search for the authentic in their own pasts.

If the civil rights moment made this quest salient and extensive, so too did the counterculture that swept America's youth from the middle of the 1960s onward. A broad and spontaneous critique of America's culture, voiced by young people, particularly although not exclusively on college campuses, was associated by the rebels with the blandness of the culture of the 1950s and the superficial materialism of suburbia. The culture of suburbia became a target for ridicule and serious criticism. These critics, in and out of academia, asked what had been lost in the quest for the comfort and privacy of suburbia and the embrace of consumerism. They claimed that little had been gained as Americans moved en masse into cookie-cutter suburban houses dubbed "little boxes" by Malvina Reynolds in her satiric song of 1962.

Jews, especially Jewish youth, play a significant role in these cultural transformations of the late 1960s and 1970s. They participated well out of proportion to their numbers in the population in the great social movements of those years, leading many of them as well. They definitively cast their lot with the insurgents among their peers and protested for civil rights and women's liberation and against the Vietnam War.

Some also helped shape a specifically Jewish counterculture, directing the same kind of criticism at what they called the "Jewish establishment" as they did at the administrators who ran their universities, the officials who governed the country, and the owners of corporations. They chided that "establishment" for compromising too much with American middle-class values and currying favor with the non-Jewish majority. That is, the Jewish counterculture saw the adults who ran Jewish institutions as not having been authentically Jewish enough. In their broadsides, magazines, newspapers, and other texts, they criticized both America and the Jewish leadership for having relinquished too much to attain power and wealth. (Staub: 2004)

Certainly much of the literary and artistic work about the Lower East Side revealed a yearning to engage with a time and place so different than the suburbs to which Jewish families had moved in the years after World War II. The Lower East Side may have been crowded, poor, dirty, riddled with tuberculosis, and odoriferous. Women and men may have toiled in sweatshops and faced dangers to life and limb as they worked in unsafe factories. They did not worry about fitting into a genteel, middle-class American mold but eagerly grabbed items from the pushcarts that lined the streets, haggling with vendors and yelling at each other. They slept on the rooftops, shouted from the stoops, and lived a life that seemed authentically Jewish.

As depicted in these texts, the Lower East Side pitted groups against each other. On its streets Jews argued volubly over matters of class, family, ideology, and religion. Jewish radicals took on the evils of American capitalism, and socialism reigned supreme as the political affiliation of the immigrant Jewish masses, in this romantic version of the past. The romance of the Lower East Side, so manifest in the late 1960s and 1970s, idealized these struggles. Immigrant Jews had fought with each other because these issues mattered. The countercultural radicals appreciated that their ancestors had not papered over their

differences and settled for middle-of-the-road solutions.

Much of the appeal of *Hester Street* grew out of the combined salience of the Lower East Side in this age of "roots too," set against the intense cultural criticism and the triumph of the image of the authentic over that of the fake. Walking away from the conflict with the prize in their hands and an upbeat future, Bernstein and Gitl represented a commitment to tradition, which helped make their tale so attractive to audiences in the 1970s. In *Hester Street* and presumably on Hester Street, not only did good win out over evil, but authenticity triumphed over shallow Americanization.

In *Hester Street* the struggle also pitted a man, Jake, against a woman, his wife, who seemingly possessed no power. After all, he had the American lifestyle and skills. Only he could grant her a *get*. Yet Gitl not only made off with the money Mamie had saved, but strode off from the divorce with a plan to control her own life. The particular gender twist in this tawdry tale of marital infidelity also reflects much about the era in which it appeared, and how and why audiences embraced it.

What has commonly been called second-wave feminism, or the women's liberation movement, stood at center stage of American political and cultural discourse in the 1970s. In 1972 Congress passed the Equal Rights Amendment, sending it off to the states for its ultimately unsuccessful journey toward ratification. The first issue of *Ms.* magazine appeared on the newsstands, and newspapers, other publications, and Americans in general began to get comfortable with the idea of not addressing women in terms of their marital status. The years leading up to *Hester Street* with its triumphant Gitl saw the Supreme Court's landmark *Roe v. Wade* decision in 1973, giving women the right to choose to have an abortion, and the publication by the Boston Women's Health Collective of the wildly popular *Our Bodies, Our Selves,* intended to empower women through knowledge. The years in which Joan Micklin Silver embarked on her project of turning Abraham Cahan's tale of the New York ghetto into a film and projecting the image of a woman at first despised, then triumphing over the man who controlled her destiny, were years in which the issue of men, women, and women's agency over their own lives pervaded American public discourse.

In those same years, Jewish women also agitated to achieve equality in the name of Jewish tradition. A few examples will have to suffice here. In 1972 the Reform movement's Hebrew Union College conferred the degree of "rabbi and teacher in Israel" on a woman, Sally Priesand, making her the first American woman to be ordained a rabbi, and insurgent women within the Conservative movement organized themselves into a group called Ezrat Nashim, to demand that the Jewish Theological Seminary follow suit. In 1976, the same year that Irving Howe published *World of Our Fathers,* two other books came out, to less fanfare and fewer sales. Both reflected the desire of Jewish women to tell their history in the context of the great Eastern European Jewish immigration to America. Both also helped explain why Gitl became the hero that she did. One of the books—the slim *Jewish Grandmothers,* by Sydelle Kramer and Jenny Masur (1976)—tackled the subject of the experiences of ordinary Jewish women who, much like Gitl, had journeyed to America from Europe, settled in poor neighborhoods, struggled with poverty, and diligently contributed to their families and communities. Broader in historical scope, the second book—Paula Hyman, Charlotte Baum, and Sonya Michel's *The Jewish Woman in America* (1976) —

served both to tell Jewish women's past and to nudge the Jewish community into rethinking the roles and rights of women in the present.

These books also drove home a message to the Jewish public. The history of their immigration to the United States and the process of settlement had involved dislocation and disruption as well as success and achievement. The desire of the "establishment" to project the image of Jews as good, law-abiding, hardworking women and men, whose families seemed so strong and intact, needed to be set against the reality of the strains that resulted from migration. Jews in their days as poor people had endured the kinds of family breakdowns that seemed pervasive among African Americans in the 1970s, a subject of much public discussion then. These books and *Hester Street* were reminders of the fact that Jews had had their share of these "pathologies"—a phrase associated with the 1965 report on the black family issued by Daniel Patrick Moynihan—when they had lived in slums. These texts by Jewish authors, committed as they were to liberal politics and racial equality wanted to show that American Jewish history also ought to be seen as a history of family difficulties amidst social change and just as in the case of African American history, women had made the crucial difference in steering their families through troubled times.

Jewish women in the late 1960s and 1970s experienced a women's movement of their own. They turned for inspiration to the women of the immigrant era, who seemed so passive on the surface, yet who found multiple ways to exert their agency. Rather than being victims of the forces around them, these Jewish immigrant women became heroes who organized unions, managed their families' meager resources, operated grocery stores, and weathered the process of Americanization. Like Gitl, they played no incidental role in the Jews' negotiation of the differences between tradition and America.

Hester Street stands on its own after the passage of time, still enthralling students in classes and audiences in synagogues and Jewish community centers who are interested in Jewish films. While it continues to reverberate some three decades after its release, it seems impossible to imagine it being made the way it was in any period other than those years of turmoil, the late 1960s and 1970s. For a society engaged in public debates about ethnicity and gender, *Hester Street* served both Jewish and general audiences in a distinctive manner, both echoing and informing those debates.

Source: Abraham Cahan, Yekl *and* The Imported Bridegroom *and Other Stories of the New York Ghetto* (New York: Dover, 1970).

Background: http://www.history.umd.edu/Faculty/BCooperman/NewCity/Jewishwomen.html; http://www.myjewishlearning.com/culture/2/Literature/Jewish_American_Literature/Immigrant_Literature/Abraham_Cahan.shtml.

Bibliography

Antler, Joyce. "*Hester Street.*" In *Past Imperfect: History According to the Movies*, edited by Mark C. Carnes. New York: Henry Holt, 1995. 178–81.

Baum, Charlotte, Sonya Michel, and Paula Hyman, *The Jewish Woman in America*. New York: Dial, 1976.

Chametzky, Jules. *From the Ghetto: The Fiction of Abraham Cahan*. Amherst: University of Massachusetts Press, 1977.

Diner, Hasia. *Lower East Side Memories: The Jewish Place in America*. Princeton, NJ: Princeton University Press, 2000.

Evans, Sarah. *Tidal Wave: How Women Changed America at Century's End*. New York: Free Press, 2003.

Glenn, Susan A. *Daughters of the Shtetl: Life and Labor in the Immigrant Generation* Ithaca, NY: Cornell University Press, 1990.

Hapgood, Hutchins, *The Spirit of the Ghetto: Studies of the Jewish Quarter of New York*. New York: Schocken, 1966.

Hindus, Milton, *The Old East Side: An Anthology*. Philadelphia: Jewish Publication Society of America, 1969.

Howe, Irving, with the assistance of Kenneth Libo. *World of Our Fathers*. New York: Harcourt Brace Jovanovich, 1976.

Jacobson, Mathew Frye. *Roots Too: White Ethnic Revival in Post–Civil Rights America*. Cambridge: Harvard University Press, 2006.

Kramer, Sydelle and Jenny Masur, *Jewish Grandmothers*. Boston: Beacon, 1976.

Michel, Sonya. "*Yekl* and *Hester Street:* Was Assimilation Really Good for the Jews?" *Literature Film Quarterly* 5, no. 2 (1977): 142–47.

Novak, Michael, *The Rise of the Unmeltable Ethnic: Politics and Culture in the Seventies*. New York: Macmillan, 1972.

Schoener, Allon, ed., *Portal to America; The Lower East Side, 1870–1925*. New York: Holt, Rinehart and Winston, 1967.

Staub, Michael. *The Jewish 1960s: A Sourcebook*. Waltham, MA: Brandeis University Press, 2004.

Weinberg, Sydney Stahl. *The World of Our Mothers: The Lives of Jewish Immigrant Women*. New York: Shocken, 1990.

12. Cultural Erosion and the (Br)other at the Gateway of Sound Cinema

JOEL ROSENBERG

The Jazz Singer, directed by Alan Crosland [A] United States, 1927

Today, more than eighty years after *The Jazz Singer*'s release, it is customary to see the film in all its loss of innocence, its morally compromised iconography, its enmeshment with racial and cul

Eugenie Besserer (as Sara Rabinowitz) backs her son, Al Jolson (as Jakie), against the denunciation of Warner Oland (as Cantor Rabinowitz). From *The Jazz Singer* (1927), directed by Alan Crosland. WARNER BROS./PHOTOFEST

tural guilt, its Oedipal obsessions, and hysterical bathos. It has become a cardinal point on the map of cultural studies, an archetypal historical crime: Jewish entertainer, a cantor's son, borrows face of antebellum black slave to escape Jewish particularity, gaining acceptance among gentiles, winning the love of a shiksa (a gentile woman), romancing his own mother, and achieving success in white America at the expense of African Americans. We are chiefly indebted to the late Michael Rogin for this by no means unwarranted argument, and his work on this subject is a genuinely

disturbing reflection, even if marred by overstatement, careless film scholarship, and poor readings of film language. We shall return to the subject of blackface, but it serves to note that in one respect classical cinema histories and postclassical political critiques of the film have something in common: a view of *The Jazz Singer* as a drama of Jewish assimilation and social mobility, a matter whose contours deserve closer attention.

Common, as well, to both approaches is a view of Al Jolson's function in the film as Janus-like gatekeeper of the sound-film era. Jolson's trademark line: "You ain't heard nothin' yet!" seemed tailor-made even in its own time as a kind of auditory logo, not just for Jolson but for the new technology, and it has served similarly in popular histories of cinema since then, even though the more complex events surrounding the advent of sound have long been known. In truth, in these transitional years there were many dozens of films worldwide that variously heralded, emblematized, manipulated, and, in some cases, resisted and subverted the new technology. But Jolson's presence as a symbol of the sound-film era is significant, nonetheless, and closely bound up with the fact that the film itself, based on a short story and play by Samson Raphaelson, was first inspired by a live Jolson performance Raphaelson had heard in his college years.

The politically charged interest in Jolson and blackface has focused attention on another important phenomenon: the symbolic uses of the Jew in a period that coincided with Hitler's eventually successful rise to power in Germany. Can one indeed ask about a connection between the advent of sound film and the advent of Hitler? Sound cinema was indeed not a negligible factor in the malevolent turn of world politics in these years. What had been a truly international cinema soon became an archipelago of self-enclosed national cinemas, and voice was a principal catalyst. It exaggerated difference and singled out the foreigner. It displayed a rich variegation of regional identities, but also intensified pressure for conformity and censorship. The nearly simultaneous blossoming of the recording industry, radio, and sound cinema helped solidify national identities, with both benign and baneful consequences. The sound media served as creative arenas of national self-discovery even as they soon became, in a worldwide atmosphere of economic despair, weapons of war. If Jewish performers

such as Molly Goldberg, Jack Benny, and George Burns thrived on American radio, so did the anti-Semitic demagogue Father Coughlin. It seems no surprise that in this period, film censorship in America acquired a new stringency. It was in fact not Jolson who first spoke to American audiences through Vitaphone but the great silencer, Will Hays of the Production Code Administration, the agency in charge of film censorship.

The Jazz Singer would be among the last for a long time of what was by then a sizable tradition of American films on immigrant life. Giving formal completeness to the purported absorption of the Jew into the American melting pot, this film would linger briefly as an emblem of America's heterogeneous unity. It would soon be supplanted by other paradigms of Americanness, more rooted in idealizations of small-town America and the Western frontier, more preoccupied with the New England Yankee and the Midwestern heartland. The main vestiges of *The Jazz Singer*'s ambience would be found in the streamlined film musical of the 'thirties, the big-city pressroom comic drama, the gangster flick, the biopic, and the antics of the Marx Brothers. But if the absorption of the Jew was seen as a *fait accompli* in America, it should be understood in the context of an era when, in Europe, Jewish assimilation would come to be redefined as a crime. If the alternating image of Jake Rabinowitz / Jack Robin, in cantorial garb and with open arms in blackface, helped to introduce the world to the era of sound film, its corollary was Leni Riefenstahl's filmed images in 1934 of Adolf Hitler, in Wagnerian procession, his back turned to the world. To shed light on the American component of this dichotomy, I will focus on the dimension made especially conspicuous by the coming of sound film: language and human utterance.

In addition to being the first sound film in

English, *The Jazz Singer* was also the first to display utterances in Yiddish and in Aramaic. The film's multilingual fabric has generally been ignored, though it has long been recognized that the film's structure is established by the six vocal performances, totaling ten songs that punctuate the story. But a proper assessment of the meanings opened up by the Jewish music in the film has yet to be made. The film's decision to leave the Jewish languages untranslated has created a literal embodiment of the mutual incomprehensibility of Orthodox Jewish and American popular culture. The film's polyphony, its interlacing of voices, is thus riddled with undelivered or misconstrued meaning. This allowed the strangeness of Jewish religious life to remain undiluted, while the film's Jewish texts play admirably well against the action of the story, opening new dimensions of meaning.

The languages of *The Jazz Singer* consist of Yiddish, Aramaic, English, and, arguably, Hebrew, whose absence from this film is a kind of spectral presence. Hebrew was accorded considerable prominence in the stage play, opening act 1, where Cantor Rabinowitz attempts to instruct an unenthusiastic ghetto pupil in the singing of the Hebrew hymn *Mah Tovu* ("How beautiful [are your tents,] O Jacob."). This hymn is a preface to the daily morning service, and, as such, a major point of embarkation into all Jewish prayer. Its omission from the film falls just short of the threshold of narrative significance. Hebrew's disappearance from the film, its replacement by the languages of the Diaspora and secularism, is almost totally unnoticeable to the spectator but coincides remarkably well with the story's narrative meanings and this accretion of meaning, precisely amid a *subtraction* of meaning, is now irreversibly part of the story.

A comparable process is at play in the film's use of Aramaic, the Hebrew language's viceroy in the liturgical life of the Jews. Perhaps most familiar to Jews as the language of the mourner's kaddish (only the opening word of which is actually spoken in the film), Aramaic is also the language of Kol Nidre, the formal renunciation of unfulfilled vows opening the evening service at the start of Yom Kippur, the Jewish Day of Atonement. Kol Nidre receives prominent attention twice in the film, though it is significant for what is subtracted and how it is changed.

Strictly speaking, Kol Nidre is not itself a prayer but a preface to prayer: a legal declaration limiting the force of one's vows and oaths, premised on a belief that one who has sworn an oath to do or not do something incurs divine punishment if eventually unable to carry out the promise. The formula thus aims to protect against divine retribution one might unwittingly incur for a vow uttered and then forgotten. It acquired deeper significance when, during the Spanish Inquisition, many Jews who had been forcibly converted to Catholicism continued to practice Judaism in secret and used Kol Nidre as a means of renouncing vows imposed by Inquisition authorities. The text thus bore a special relation to the situation of apostasy, and to the state of the Marrano, the crypto-Jew. Here is a translation of the Kol Nidre text commonly found in High Holiday prayer books:

> All vows [*kol nidre*], and formulas of prohibition, and declarations of taboo, and promises of abstinence, and names of God, and pledges one assumes on penalty, and oaths—whatever we might vow [and then forget], whatever we might swear [but not uphold], whatever we declare taboo [but violate], whatever prohibitions we assume upon ourselves [to no avail], from this Day of Atonement to the next Day of Atonement—may the day come upon us for

the good!—from all of them, we now request release. Let their burden be dissolved, and lifted off, and canceled, and made null and void, bearing no force and no reality. Our vows shall not be vows, our oaths shall not be oaths, our prohibitions shall not be prohibitions.

Although the full text is not used in the film, we can readily see that where it first occurs carries considerable dramatic force. The Rabinowitz household has just been shattered. The cantor father (Warner Oland) has thrashed his son for singing in a saloon, and the son (thirteen-year-old Bobby Gordon) has resolved to run away, while his mother (Eugenie Besserer) looks on in dismay. All three enter the Day of Atonement's fasting with empty stomachs. As the Cantor soon afterward prepares to sing before his congregation, a congregant asks him if something is wrong. He replies that his son was supposed to stand by his side and sing Kol Nidre with him that night— "but now," he says, "I have no son." Raising his spectacles, he blots tears from his eyes with a corner of his prayer shawl. As the Cantor's chant fills the house of worship, we view the son as he stealthily reenters his parents' apartment, stares tearfully at a photo of his mother (intercut briefly with a live image of his mother in the synagogue looking longingly in a far-off direction), turns sharply as if he has heard a noise, and then, with his head hung in dejection, exits, carrying with him no belongings except the photo. The camera returns to the synagogue, where we again see the Cantor singing, flanked by Torah scrolls and congregants, intercut with views of the anguished face of Sara Rabinowitz in the women's section as she recites the penitential prayers. What vows are renounced in these moments? What oaths are dissolved, what promises and pledges are left unfulfilled for the three Rabinowitzes?

At such a juncture, we can appreciate the importance of the Kol Nidre text to the film's theme of assimilation. Unlike in Samson Raphaelson's original tale, there seems to be no middle ground between assimilation and apostasy. The drama of the apostate stands for the process of second-generation assimilation that has led to the family rift. This common squabble is a spiritual rupture, equivalent to the excommunication traditionally prescribed (though rarely enacted) against the Jew who denies God or adopts an alien faith. The situation of the Marrano is an apt metaphor for Jewish modernity, which has increased the number of minimally observant Jews. In our own time, the typical overcrowding of synagogues, during the Kol Nidre service, with "once a year Jews" remains poignant testimony to the pull of Kol Nidre and the absolution it offers.

The Kol Nidre formula, however, presupposes a reverse situation to that portrayed at this point in the film: the *return* of the apostate to the fold; the *release* from vows of servitude to "other gods," or to no god. Here it occurs paradoxically at the moment of the protagonist's apostasy. That the Cantor should say "but now, I have no son" expresses the full gravity of Jake's departure, for in rabbinic law, the apostate is mourned by his or her parents as if deceased. Since Jake moves in a reverse direction from the "returned" penitents, the question of his return will loom large over the story.

As noted, only part of the Kol Nidre formula is heard in the film:

All vows, and formulas of prohibition, and oaths, and declarations of taboo, and promises of abstinence, and pledges one assumes on penalty, and names of God, whatever we might vow, whatever we might swear, whatever we declare taboo, whatever prohibitions we assume upon ourselves, upon ourselves.

The final words "upon ourselves," literally "upon our souls," are repeated, as is common in cantorial art, but here phrased as a conclusion, ending both the scene and Jake's childhood. It leaves concealed from the spectator the Kol Nidre's decisive formula of *release* from vows. It is as if the recitation, with its cascade of oaths and vows and prohibitions, has been heaped higher and higher upon the already burdened soul of each Rabinowitz. Part 1 ends with each soul enclosed within its social itinerary, gender, generation, and linguistic horizon. Each soul's burdens are unrelieved.

Kol Nidre is sung by Cantor Rabinowitz (dubbed by the renowned Cantor Yossele Rosenblatt). When the chant is reprised by Al Jolson near the film's end, the Cantor's son Jake, now Jack Robin, a rising star in the show-biz world, temporarily returns to the fold to take his dying father's place in the synagogue on the Day of Atonement. The chant itself, its melody still intact, is now transformed into something resembling jazz:

> All vows, and formulas of prohibition and oaths and declarations of taboo, and promises of abstinence, and pledges one assumes on penalty, and names of God, and pledges one assumes on penalty, and names of God, and oaths, and declarations of taboo, and promises of abstinence, and pledges one assumes on penalty, and names of God, and pledges one assumes on penalty, and names . . .

As a Kol Nidre this is little short of a meltdown—its riffs circling endlessly around the same first clause in a kind of atonement reverie. Jack is still caught in the bramble of I-shall-nots that had enmeshed young Jakie and his parents on that night when he first left home, but his Kol Nidre text, both mangled and creatively transformed, is a token of American Jewry's cultural erosion, a hidden slaying of the past, visualized in the image of the Cantor's ghostly apparition bidding his son farewell.

A similar process is at work earlier in the story. While on tour with a show in Chicago, Jack attends a performance of Yiddish songs, sung in a cameo appearance by the actual Yossele Rosenblatt. The song Jack hears is called *Yartsayt* ("Year Tide"), a popular contemporary ballad, sung in the untranslated original, in praise of the candle lit annually in commemoration of the death of a loved one. The following is the song's text in English—but note the twice-uttered Aramaic word intruding on the Yiddish song, here echoing the first word of the traditional mourner's kaddish prayer, *yisgadal, yisgadal* ("May [God's name] be magnified, be magnified"):

> We kindle you now with a passionate sigh,
> let your flame shed its light upon days now
>   gone by,
> and pour out its shine upon darkened
>   roadways,
> to find there a heart and hand's touch
> of one who had lived but for us,
> *yisgadal, yisgadal.*
>
> Ah, *yartsayt* light, there in a corner alone!
> May you make us mindful how lowly we are,
> reminding the heart, with a flame's glowing
>   fire,
> to call to our thoughts our holy peo[ple's
>   line] . . .

This sentimental song summons potent metaphors of spiritual journey—the darkened road, the journey of a wandering soul, perhaps a prodigal son, the rituals of memory among the living, the solemnity of communing with a "holy people," and, depending on the Jew who recites the kaddish it refers to, varying degrees of "bygone-ness" of the past to which it harkens. But for whom is the kaddish it betokens? It is inevitable that we try to read it into the film's story. Is it for a parent, who presumably has died while the son is away on prodigal wanderings? Or for the son himself, who has long ago been declared dead in his apostasy? As the song suggests, the Jew of that era might sooner or later be reciting kaddish, not just for a departed parent, but also for a people of ancient lineage, for its culture of study and prayer, and the delicate architecture of the sacred it had long striven to make a place for in this world. As Cantor Rosenblatt sings, his image is superimposed by that of Jack's father, Cantor Rabinowitz. This visualization of a double cantorate—that of prayer and that of public entertainment—carries the film's central dilemma: its preoccupation with cultural succession. The issue here is more than a career, more than an art form, more even than questions of whether Jack is a believer or a faithful son. We confront here the realm of articulation between tradition and modernity, where the internally coherent life of a traditional culture disperses itself into the multiple and incompatible coherences of modern mass culture.

Acts of erosion, forgetting, and revision; riffs of jazz improvisation imposed on texts of the past; rituals of memory and commemoration that are also rites of separation and estrangement—by means of these, *The Jazz Singer* traces a widening gulf between the Jewish past and the modern present. Jolson's Jack Robin is a figure of energy and exuberance whose every gesture is unintentionally filled with the forgetfulness of cultural adaptation. Consider Jack's enthusiastic romancing of his mother upon their reunion (the famously ad-libbed scene that sold American audiences on sound film): "Mama, darlin,' if I'm a success in this show, we're gonna move from here. Oh, yes, we're gonna move up in the Bronx. A lot

of nice green grass up there, and a whole lot of people you know. There's the Ginsbergs, the Guttenbergs, and the Goldbergs. Oh, a whole lotta Bergs. I don't know 'em all."

From the vantage point of the twenty-first century, Jolson's precipitous words seem to pinpoint the historical moment when Jews of America's urban tenements and ghettos were just beginning to move to the suburbs (as the Bronx then was). Jolson's song and patter in this scene are so energetic that he borders on Dionysian abandon. But there is also restraint, carried in the obvious fact that whatever love he lavishes on his mother, Jack is working her the way he works a crowd. Jolson's forgetfulness, the torrential demolition wrought by his unknowing, reigns here. It reduces American Jewry to a string of surnames: "the Ginsbergs, the Guttenbergs, and the Goldbergs. Oh, a whole lotta Bergs, I don't know 'em all." Does he know *any*? We cannot be sure. At most, he has ransacked a few conjoined pages of the Bronx telephone directory. But at least he knows they're all "Bergs"—which is to say, in this context at least, Jews.

What, then, *is* the Oedipal territory trodden here? If the ancient myth of Oedipus was grounded in a suspicion that the crowning achievements of its hero's kingship were perched precariously on some hidden flaw at the heart of the genealogical gerrymandering—that relentless marrying *out*—on which the health and continuity of royal alliances depended and out of which cosmopolitan culture was sustained, then we have a useful paradigm for understanding the situation of that budding king of entertainment, Jack Robin. Jack's scene with his mother, despite the homage it pays to a parent, is a kind of celebration of self-creation, of emergence fully formed, like Cadmus's warriors sprung from dragon's teeth—and a basking in those freely willed alliances with the wider world that Werner Sollors has dubbed "the culture of consent."

In such a light we return to the film's use of blackface. Jolson's donning of a cartoonish image of the antebellum slave soon became obsolete as an entertainment convention, as actual African American performers—themselves often in self-caricature—entered into white America's cinema and popular entertainment. Jolson's own career would fall into obsolescence from this pivot. The blackface numbers of *The Jazz Singer* are actually the least memorable and surely an insufficient homage to jazz. They seem present in the film for only one reason: to be introduced by a scene of Jack donning black greasepaint. That ritual was the symbolic underpinning of blackface entertainment since its use by Irish immigrant minstrel performers in the nineteenth century: marking the *artifice* of a blackness *appropriated* by marginalized whites seeking to make themselves more "white" in the eyes of white America. If "black" is only how I show myself for finite moments on a stage, then I can call myself, and be, whatever I want for all the rest. The ritual, in the form of exaggerated "blackness" in speech and gesture, was popular as much among black performers as the greasepaint was among whites, and had a counterpart in the "Jewface" adopted by many a Jewish performer in vaudeville and radio, conveyed through Yiddish humor, Jewish dialect, and Borscht Belt ironies.

After Jake puts on the makeup, he is visited by his Mama and ghetto notable Moisha Yudelson. "Jakie, this ain't you?" cries Mama. "He talks like Jakie," says Yudelson, "but he looks like his shadow." The original line, excised by film censors, was more blatantly racist (" . . . but he looks like a n****r . . ."), but either way the words tap into the biblical Isaac's utterance in Gen. 27:23: "The voice is the voice of Jacob, but the hands are the hands

of Esau," Jacob's disguise thus betokening an archetypically intimate convolution of self and other that haunts the ancestor of the people Israel. Esau is at once Jacob's twin, the closest of kin, and remotest of foreigners, the disowned alter ego we can call "the (br)other." In rabbinic exegesis, Esau paradoxically became a symbol of the Roman Empire and triumphant Roman church—late antiquity's cosmopolitan society—thus signifying the broader social order, which, in the landscape of modernity and mass culture, translates into the inescapable mutual otherness of all. Jacob's relation to Esau was one of theft, displacement, guilt, and historical rift, but also of kindred feeling and shared identity. American Jews in the modern era had a similarly convoluted relationship with African Americans, but in America of 1927, their plights still overlapped, their ghettos adjoined, and the divisor of race was not limited, then or thereafter, to skin color alone. If the fate of American Jews soon diverged sharply, in socioeconomic terms, from a majority of African Americans, it contrasted still more sharply with the wholly racialized fate of the Jews of Europe who would descend to a state below slavery. Meanwhile, the "black" Jew of America—the Jew of caftan and skull cap; of Hebrew, Aramaic, and Yiddish; of Talmud, Halakha [Jewish law] and prayer, this Jew whose subjectivity and inner universe are, but for the texts we have examined, mostly concealed in the film—is quietly and respectfully laid to rest. Still a murder, in its way, of which the film keeps careful account. And, in the film's final scene, the blackface performer serenades his "Mammy" from the stage with haunted words:

Mammy, I'm comin,' I hope I didn't make
    you wait,
Mammy, I'm comin'! Oh, God, I hope I'm
    not late.

Late, indeed. The tone of desperation in these lines, the wistful sense of belatedness and disconnection from Mama, from *Mameloshn* (the mother tongue, Yiddish) and from an ancestral past, is highly palpable in this symbolic figuration of Jack's now-dubious spiritual return. Jack seems trapped in a posture of pleading, snared in the sentimental claptrap of his own stage persona, and giving voice to a deeper anxiety of the Jew amid this land of reputedly gold-paved streets. He seems to be progressively sinking into the depths of a blackness assigned not by skin color or by greasepaint but by the capricious torrents of modern history and the scandal of a flawed and uncompleted social realm, the destiny of which was then far from certain. While *The Jazz Singer* displays an America making peace with its multiple heritages, the film's hidden unease and cultural ambivalence are palpable. They remind us of what Walter Benjamin would call, in 1933, the impoverishment of experience—encompassing, in part, the eclipse of richly verbal cultures handed on orally from one generation to the next. Paradoxically, Benjamin welcomed the "barbarism" of modern mass culture (including film, broadcasting, newspapers, advertisement, shopping arcades, avant-garde art, etc.) that was supplanting traditional cultures, but he would grow progressively uneasy at its rapidly growing power to wreak destruction.

Excerpted and revised from: Joel Rosenberg, "What You Ain't Heard Yet: The Languages of *The Jazz Singer*," *Prooftexts* 22, nos. 1–2 (2002): 11–54.

Sources: Samson Raphaelson, "The Day of Atonement," in *The Jazz Singer*, ed. Robert L. Carringer, 147–67 (Madison: University of Wisconsin Press, 1979). This volume also contains Albert A. Cohn's screenplay for the film, as well as Carringer's insightful introduction.

Samson Raphaelson, *The Jazz Singer* [play] (New York: Samuel French, 1925).

Background: http://www.jewishjournal.com/arts/article/think_you_know_the_jazz_singer_you_aint_heard_nothin_yet_20070921/.

Bibliography

Alexander, Michael, *Jazz Age Jews*. Princeton, NJ: Princeton University Press, 2001.

Benjamin, Walter. "Experience and Poverty." In Walter Benjamin, *Selected Writings*, edited by Marcus Bullock and Michael W. Jennings, and translated by Rodney Livingston, 2:731–36. Cambridge: Belknap Press of Harvard University Press, 1999.

Gubar, Susan. "Blackface Lynchings." In Susan Gubar, *Racechanges: White Skin, Black Face in American Culture*, 53–94. New York: Oxford University Press, 1997.

Lott, Eric. *Love and Theft: Blackface Minstrelsy and the American Working Class*. New York: Oxford University Press, 1995.

Melnick, Jeffrey Paul. *A Right to Sing the Blues: African Americans, Jews, and American Popular Song*. Cambridge: Harvard University Press, 1999.

Rogin, Michael. *Blackface, White Noise: Jewish Immigrants in the Hollywood Melting Pot*. Berkeley: University of California Press, 1996.

Rosenberg, Joel. "Rogin's Noise: The Alleged Historical Crimes of *The Jazz Singer*." *Prooftexts* 22, nos. 1–2 (2002): 221–39.

Sollors, Werner. *Beyond Ethnicity: Consent and Descent in American Culture*. New York: Oxford University Press, 1986.

Walker, Alexander. *The Shattered Silents: How the Talkies Came to Stay*. London: Elm Tree, 1978.

Weber, Donald. *Haunted in the New World: Jewish American Culture from Cahan to "The Goldbergs."* Bloomington: Indiana University Press, 2005.

Whitfield, Stephen J. "Black Like Us." *Jewish History* 22 (2008): 353–71.

13. Ethnic and Discursive Drag in Woody Allen's *Zelig*

RUTH D. JOHNSTON

Zelig, directed by Woody Allen [A]
United States, 1983

Woody Allen's *Zelig* is a film about a Jewish man's chameleonism, which enables him to assume the accent, appearance, profession, and ethnicity/race of those he comes into contact with. Chameleonism functions in the film as a metaphor for ethnic assimilation in general. More particularly the film explores a tradition of secular Jewish identity that has been linked with a Jewish politics of vicarious identity, described by Michael Rogin (1996) as a kind of blackface. At the same time, chameleonism operates not only on the diegetic level (storyline), but also on a discursive level (narration) insofar as the film parodies *The Jazz Singer*. Thus *Zelig* anticipates contemporary theories of performativity, such as Judith Butler's definition of identity as "the repetition or citation of a prior authoritative set of practices" (1993, 227), implying the overlapping of identity and intertextuality, since such practices can include textual practices and conventions.

On the diegetic level, chameleonism in *Zelig* is a metaphor for different models of ethnic/racial assimilation. This historical perspective is enabled by the fact that the film was made in 1983, when the multicultural model prevailed, but is set in the interwar period of the 1920s and 1930s, when the concept of the melting pot and 100 percent Americanism or Anglo-conformism was at its peak. The ideology of multiculturalism, which emphasizes the public display of cultural diversity and insistence on cultural identification

with sites outside the United States, arose from the disillusionment with prior models of ethnic assimilation because of the failure of such models to accommodate racial difference in the United States.

The film offers a broad spectrum of representations of ethnicity as Leonard Zelig (played by Allen) transforms himself into an American Indian, a Chinese, a Mexican, and a black. As a Jew, Zelig is a particularly appropriate figure to explore the possibilities of ethnic and racial assimilation. As David Desser argues, "Jews may be understood as a kind of 'free floating ethnic signifier,' a signifier of otherness across a wide spectrum of discourses" (1991, 391). More specifically, Jews have been equated with blacks, women, gays, and Orientals. Thus Sander Gilman observes, "Jews were black, according to nineteenth-century racial science, because they were not a pure race" (1991, 99). Their status as a mixed race or mulattos was opposed to the status of the Germans (Aryans) as a pure race. Moreover, Gilman demonstrates that dating back to the Middle Ages, Jewish men were considered feminine in European culture largely because of the ritual practice of circumcision (1993, 38). This equation is based on the analogy of the circumcised penis and the clitoris: each was seen as a truncated penis. In short, circumcision functioned as a racial and sexual sign, the latter serving also to link the Jewish male and the homosexual because the homosexual was associated with effeminacy and sexual deviance. Eastern European Jews were also frequently called Orientals, and a vestige of that connection continues to exist in the use of the word "mogul" to designate Jewish heads of motion picture studios (Desser 1991, 392). Thus Robert Stam and Ella Shohat claim, "Zelig sums up in his metamorphoses the plurality of the Jewish experience and even the reality of Jews as a trans-racial people who literally range in appearance from blonde Hollywood actresses to the black Falashes of Ethiopia" (1987, 188).

Ella Shohat insists elsewhere that, "a critical analysis of ethnicity in films also involves historicizing the question of the specific and evolving articulations of cultural and political power" (1991, 246). Thus it is important to take into account the American context, where Zelig's transformations are not confined to transformations into obviously oppressed minorities. Zelig also chameleonizes vertically, gaining access to both European and US centers of power: the Vatican, the Third Reich, American café society, and Hollywood. Significantly, the horizontal transformations are registered by visible physical changes in appearance as well as the assumption of stereotypical ethnic and racial cultural traits (Desser and Friedman 1993, 63) and include other, not necessarily ethnic or racial, transformations of the body, as when Zelig chameleonizes into a fat man. The vertical metamorphoses emphasize class differences and entail insertion and blending into a social context. Though Stam and Shohat argue that Zelig's vertical "mimicry is incomplete, always producing what Homi Bhabha calls its slippage, 'its excess, its difference' " (1987, 188), resulting, for instance, in Zelig's ejection from the papal balcony and from the Third Reich rostrum, Zelig's vertical mimicry actually seems quite successful in the US context. For at the end, his marriage to Eudora Fletcher (played by Mia Farrow), who comes from a prominent Philadelphia family, indicates Zelig's full cultural and ideological assimilation. Eudora teaches Zelig civility, provides him with an entrée into Anglo-American society, and "cures" his chameleonism. Yet as Stam and Shohat observe, "Zelig is never more conformist than when he starts to 'be himself' " (1987, 189–90).

In other words, Zelig is never cured of chameleonism; rather he merely exchanges one form of chameleonism for another. On the one hand, therefore, the film deconstructs the distinction between coming out and assimilating, as Zelig demonstrates that both are forms of (ethnic) drag. Here I am extending Judith Butler's definition of drag as gender parody (1990, 137) to apply to race and ethnicity: drag implicitly reveals the imitative and contingent structure of all racial and ethnic identity. On the other hand, despite the structural similarity of both forms of chameleonism, their effects are radically different, depending upon context and reception.

In the historical and geographical context depicted in the film, Zelig's bifurcated chameleonism exposes its disparate effects as it retraces the history of Jewish assimilation in the United States from ethnic immigrant status to conformity to both Anglo-American culture and the ideology of individualism via racial masquerade. The Jews' history of enforced cultural mimicry in Europe was transformed into a strategy to achieve assimilation by the enactment of racial difference in the US context. Blackface, the flip side of Jews' capacity for cultural syncretism, was deployed to achieve assimilation and whiteness because it emphasized the distinction between the black mask and the real race underneath. Therefore, the two forms of chameleonism are linked insofar as horizontal chameleonism is the means for achieving vertical chameleonism.

"During the period of mass European immigration, roughly the 1840s to the 1920s, the racial status of Irish, Italians, Jews, and Slavs was in dispute" (Rogin 1996, 12). From the 1920s on, whiteness was extended not only to Jews, but also to other immigrant groups from Eastern and Southern Europe, and the landscape of American culture came to be inhabited simply by blacks and whites. In this connection, Jon Stratton distinguishes between acceptance into American society and assimilation to whiteness (2001, 145–46). Becoming American involves subscribing to the Enlightenment ideology of liberalism, individualism, and freedom. Assimilation to whiteness involves acceptance of Anglo-American culture: "the groups which were whitened were not thought to be white. Rather, they had to learn to be white, in the process transforming some of their most basic cultural attributes, such as the extended family" (145).

Furthermore, Zelig's cultural and ideological assimilation is facilitated by a form of blackface, or horizontal chameleonism. For according to Rogin, minstrel shows "served a melting pot function by insisting on the distinction between race and ethnicity" (1996, 56). Reading horizontal chameleonism as a form of blackface calls to mind *The Jazz Singer*. Shohat insists on the added significance of Jewish entertainers' employing blackface (1991, 229). Jews had almost entirely taken over blackface entertainment by the early twentieth century (Rogin 1996, 97).

If *Zelig* parodies the use of blackface in general, it may be read more particularly as a parodic repetition of *The Jazz Singer*, made in 1927, the time when *Zelig* is set. Certainly there are striking parallels between the two films. *Zelig*'s revision of the earlier film functions as a discursive form of chameleonism. This implies an overlapping between identity and the citation of antecedent texts and practices (Butler 1993, 227).

But before exploring these parallels, it is important to clarify the relation between the two texts. In this connection Elizabeth Langland develops a definition of intertextuality, which she differentiates from influence (1994, 247). Langland argues that the distinction between influence and intertextuality is that they involve different notions of repetition. Influence establishes a hierarchical relation between an original text and the imitation, while the theory of intertextuality calls into question the very notions of agency, property, and especially origin that support the dualism of influence. If I focus especially on *Zelig*'s relation to *The Jazz Singer*, it is not to view the earlier film as a precursor, but to throw into question *The Jazz Singer*'s status as the original talking picture by exposing its imitativeness and contingency.

The Jazz Singer alternates between sound and silence, musical and melodrama. As a generic hybrid, *The Jazz Singer* gives rise on the one hand to the race-ethnic social problem film manifest in intergenerational conflict and on the other to the blackface musical (Rogin 1996, 169).

Zelig also juxtaposes the old and the new technologies; in addition, it is a generic hybrid that incorporates the forms of both documentary and fiction. Accordingly, its mimicry of documentary forms includes the formal marking of past and present by the use of color to designate present tense and black-and-white film stock to mark the past. Both past and present accounts blur history and fiction. The present tense sections consist of interviews with actors in the roles of people who knew Zelig well in the past. The present tense sections also include comments by recognizable authorities (for instance, Susan Sontag, Irving Howe, Saul Bellow, and Bruno Bettelheim) who interpret Zelig's cultural and aesthetic significance as if he were an actual historical figure. The past tense sections use a disembodied male narrator, clips from Movietone, Pathé, and Nazi German newsreels, eyewitness testimony, headlines, and newspaper reports about Zelig.

Actual film clips from the 1920s and 1930s show figures such as F. Scott Fitzgerald, Fanny Brice, and Josephine Baker, as well as clips doctored to place Zelig in historical shots. Therefore, the historical data can by themselves be considered hybrid insofar as they are composed of both archival and pseudo-archival footage in approximately equal parts. Cinematographer Gordon Wills imitated the grainy texture, the unsteady lighting, the jerky movement, and the low-fidelity recording of the archaic footage, making it impossible to distinguish the new from the old (Stam and Shohat 1987, 177–80). *Zelig* also includes scenes from *The Changing Man*, a film about Zelig supposedly made in 1935, which draws on 1930s' melodramatic conventions and glamorous stars, overly dramatic acting, romantic music, and a formulaic happy ending (181).

Rogin argues that in *The Jazz Singer*, the death of silent film and the death of the Jewish patriarch are closely related since each scene featuring sound is linked to generational conflict. On the discursive level, the cantor's silencing of Jack's voice involves a rejection of the musical genre and a return to silent melodrama. The generational conflict deflects attention away from racial prejudice and anti-Semitism by reducing the conflict to a matter of family, which places it in the domain of melodrama.

Zelig, unlike *The Jazz Singer*, situates familial conflict and romance in a larger social context of racial prejudice. The Ku Klux Klan regards Zelig as a triple threat because of his multiple Otherness as black, Jew, and Native American. People in France propose sending Zelig to Devil's Island—where Alfred Dreyfus was imprisoned— after he transforms himself into a rabbi. In fact, familial conflict is itself linked to anti-Semitism. When as a child Zelig is bullied by anti-Semites, his parents side with his attackers. Finally, a miniature anatomy of Jewish self-hatred is symbolized by Zelig's attendance at a Nazi rally (Desser and Friedman 1993, 64).

Zelig also changes the family dynamics of *The Jazz Singer* and their connection to technological innovation. Here, family conflict divides sister and brother, not father and son, and is subordinated to romance. Zelig's half-sister Ruth forces him to perform at freak shows. Eudora wants to rescue and cure Zelig, but her methods reveal striking parallels to his exploitation by his sister. Both women have a personal, economic stake in Zelig's chameleonism. Ruth wants to get rich by forcing Zelig to perform, while Eudora wants to make her reputation as a psychiatrist. The freak shows, which display Zelig's ability to transform himself, resemble the therapy he receives from Eudora, which is just another form of performance, for the famous white room sessions conducted at Eudora's country home are recorded on film by her cousin Paul Deghuee.

Though initially Ruth Zelig is associated with melodrama and Eudora with documentary, these generic alignments are undermined. The elderly Eudora challenges the accuracy of *The Changing Man*, especially the ending. She states in an interview that her reunion with Zelig at the Nazi rally was not at all accurately represented in *The Changing Man*, which ends in a close-up of a kiss between the reunited Eudora and Zelig, accompanied by romantic music. The real story, however, presented in pseudo-archival clips from a Nazi newsreel, is even more wildly implausible than the fictional melodramatic ending: the couple escapes in a private plane; Eudora, who is a pilot, loses consciousness, and Zelig mobilizes his chameleonism to transform himself into a pilot. He reverses Lindbergh's achievement and flies the plane across the Atlantic in the opposite direction and upside down. Thus the incredibility of the details of the supposedly historical account exists in tension with the apparent authenticity of its documentary form. In other words, just as the story line collapses the distinction between the cure and the disease (chameleonism), the discursive level undermines the difference between fiction and history.

The use of blackface in *The Jazz Singer* does not appear in either the short story "The Day of Atonement" by Sampson Raphaelson or the stage play *The Jazz Singer*. "Blackface reinstated the exaggerated pantomime that had supposedly been made unnecessary by the use of the close-up, montage, and crude shot/reverse shot editing that accompanied the introduction of sound" (Rogin 1996, 91). Yet paradoxically, this regression to "blackface's imaginary realm of music, image, and a specular, histrionic self" serves to free the past and promote Jakie/Jack's assimilation (Rogin 1996, 102). Like the protagonist of *The Jazz Singer*, Jews seeking to assimilate adopted the more restrained body language of Anglo-American culture, which associated melodramatic gestures with less civilized societies. Blackface functioned at the expense of blacks as a ventriloquist strategy that projected emotionality onto a group regarded as inferior. Blackface thus promoted assimilation, not merely by freeing the performer from the Old World Jew, but by relegating blacks to a subordinate status. Jack's mobility depends on differences of race (the black/white binary) rather than ethnicity.

Zelig parodies *The Jazz Singer*'s use of blackface in a number of ways. *Zelig* extends the partial play of identity in the earlier film by diversifying the transformations to include multiple ethnicities and races, thereby reversing the function of traditional blackface to differentiate ethnic from racial difference. At the same time, horizontal chameleonism performs a similar function as blackface in *The Jazz Singer* insofar as it promotes Zelig's assimilation through upward mo-

bility and especially his access to women. However, Eudora is not Zelig's only wife, just his last one. His monogamous stable relation with her is achieved after a number of other marriages. Thus in contrast to *The Jazz Singer*, which uses blackface both to mimic a forbidden interracial romance and remove the threat of miscegenation, *Zelig* comically literalizes and multiplies that threat. For when Zelig's fame as a chameleon man spreads, many women of disparate ethnic and racial backgrounds claim that he married them during one of his transformations. Of course he does not recall any of these past relations, and when he is hunted down for his former activities, he disappears. Despite the fact that the ending of the film endorses the marriage to Eudora as the authentic union, the fact that it occurs in a series of marriages undercuts such pretensions, for their marriage is part of a successive process.

Zelig's depiction of chameleonism may be described as technologically produced ethnic and discursive drag. Ethnic and discursive forms of drag are primarily explored through the juxtaposition of archival and pseudo-archival footage. Zelig's diverse racial and ethnic transformations are surely a testament to the achievements of the make-up artist. But they also reveal how small are the physical changes required to signal ethnic and racial difference and also how conventional they are, depending as much on context as on physical transformation. In addition, the proliferation of these transformations insists on ethnicity as a serial process, displacing the original/copy binary with a relation of one copy to another. At the same time, Zelig's appearances at the Vatican and the Nazi rally expose the flipside of chameleonism as a drive to conform that motivates participation in totalitarian/authoritarian regimes. Moreover, since chameleonism is so tied up with technological innovation, the effects of the latter are similarly rendered ambiguous, though their threatening aspects are presented as comic.

On the discursive level, the juxtaposition of melodrama and documentary suggests that the difference is purely formal and conventional and not a matter of adherence to the facts. This is demonstrated in the two endings, both equally implausible, but implausible in accordance with different sets of conventions. If the melodrama presents the reunion of Eudora and Zelig at the Nazi rally through the use of close-ups, romantic background music, and exaggerated gestures while eliding the escape by ending with a Hollywood kiss, the documentary is no less hyperbolic, though drawing on another representational tradition. It uses long shots and voice-over narration as it emphasizes the escape, in other words action, rather than gesture. At the same time, the fact that archival footage is virtually indistinguishable from pseudo-archival footage suggests that fiction can pass for history via formal imitation, or masquerading as documentary. And just as ethnic drag recasts the relation of original to copy into that of a relation of copy to copy, so on the discursive level, history loses its authenticity and is exposed as an alternative fictional form.

Abridged from: Ruth D. Johnston, "Ethnic and Discursive Drag in Woody Allen's *Zelig*," *Quarterly Review of Film and Video* 24, no. 3 (2007): 397–406.

Background: http://nationalhumanitiescenter.org/tserve/twenty/tkeyinfo/jewishexp.htm.

Bibliography

Butler, Judith. *Bodies That Matter: On the Discursive Limits of Sex*. New York: Routledge, 1993.

——. *Gender Trouble: Feminism and the Subversion of Identity*. New York: Routledge, 1990.

Desser, David. "The Cinematic Melting Pot: Ethnicity, Jews, and Psychoanalysis." In *Unspeakable Images: Ethnicity in American Cinema*, edited by Lester D. Friedman, 379–403. Urbana: University of Illinois Press, 1991.

——and Lester D. Friedman. *American-Jewish Filmmakers: Traditions and Trends*. Urbana: University of Illinois Press, 1993.

Gilman, Sander L. *Freud, Race, and Gender*. New York: Routledge, 1993.

——. *The Jew's Body*. New York: Routledge, 1991.

Langland, Elizabeth. "Dialogue, Discourse, Theft, and Mimicry: Charlotte Brontë Rereads William Makepeace Thackeray." In *Understanding Narrative*, edited by James Phelan and Peter J. Rabinowitz, 246–71. Columbus: Ohio State University Press, 1994.

Rogin, Michael. *Blackface, White Noise: Jewish Immigrants in the Hollywood Melting Pot*. Berkeley: University of California Press, 1996.

Shohat, Ella. "Ethnicities-in-Relation: Toward a Multicultural Reading of American Cinema." In *Unspeakable Images: Ethnicity in American Cinema*, edited by Lester D. Friedman, 215–50. Urbana: University of Illinois Press, 1991.

Stam, Robert, and Ella Shohat. "*Zelig* and Contemporary Theory: Meditation on the Chameleon Text." *Enclitic* 9 (Summer 1987): 176–94.

Stratton, Jon. "Not Really White—Again: Performing Jewish Difference in Hollywood Films since the 1980s." *Screen* 42, no. 2 (2001): 142–66.

14. *Uncle Moses*

The First Artistic Yiddish Sound Film

HANNAH BERLINER FISCHTHAL

Uncle Moses, directed by Aubrey Scotto and
Sidney Goldin [EM, NCJF]
United States, 1932

Uncle Moses was the first Yiddish sound film
that aspired to—and reached—artistic excellence.
Based on Sholem Asch's novel, it is a wonderful
movie that deals with many important issues: the
Jewish-American immigrant experience, the socioeconomic realities of the American dream, the
rise of the labor union, including its corrupt political ramifications, as well as conflicts between
socialism and capitalism, between the traditionalism of the old country and newer American life-
styles. The movie additionally explores human relationships in families, in the sweatshop, in love,
and in marriage. The central concern of *Uncle
Moses*, however, focuses on the relationship between wealth and happiness. Gifted actor Maurice Schwartz uses humor, drama, and even pathos
to portray the nouveau riche Moses as a benevolent despot of the sweatshop whose money ultimately does not decrease his essential loneliness.

Sholem Asch was the most popular, prolific,
and critically acclaimed Yiddish writer in the period between the two World Wars, and the first
Yiddish writer to have an international reputation. Maurice Schwartz, director of the renowned
Yiddish Art Theater on Second Avenue, had put
several of Sholem Asch's works on the stage.
Schwartz wrote his own adaptation of *Onkl Mozes*, in which he starred from 1930 to 1931. In fact,
he was one of the biggest stars on Second Avenue.

The idea of a movie version of Sholem Asch's

Uncle Moses, starring Schwartz, was very promising. "No previous Yiddish talkie had so much
prestige: if Schwartz was America's foremost Yiddish artiste, Asch was the nation's most popular
'serious' Yiddish writer," states J. Hoberman. Yiddish Talking Pictures, set up by Louis Weiss and
Rubin Goldberg, commissioned Sidney Goldin
and Aubrey Scotto to codirect Schwartz as Uncle
Moses in the only film the company would produce. Goldin had already directed every other
Yiddish sound picture to date. Scotto was hired to
upgrade the technical aspects. Except for the jerky
opening track down Orchard Street, the entire
film was shot in the two rooms belonging to Metropolitan Studios in Fort Lee, New Jersey. Dovid
Matis explains that shooting *Uncle Moses* in New
Jersey was a significant statement about the importance of the project, since all previous Yiddish
silent and sound films made in the United States
had been produced in a rather "primitive film studio on East 38th Street, New York."

The cast was chosen with extreme care. Nobody could portray emotions as well as Schwartz.
The other actors in leading and supporting roles
were also effective. The fine acting, improved cinematic technique, and absorbing thematic material distinguish *Uncle Moses* from all previous
Yiddish sound films. As Matis points out, *Uncle
Moses* was the first artistically serious Yiddish
sound movie to be made in an era when "tasteless-
ness and lack of refinement ruled most Yiddish
films."

The story begins in Uncle Moses's clothing
sweatshop, located on the Lower East Side of
New York. The factory is on the second story of
the building; downstairs is the retail store. Moses
Melnick had immigrated, penniless, from Kuzmin years ago, but had since become extremely
wealthy in America. In his shop, Moses oversees

his fellow Kuzminers, toiling fourteen hours a day, six days a week, sewing clothing. For this they receive very low wages and a filthy, ugly, work area complete with broken windows, a gas leak, and a stove that doesn't work. As boss he has absolute power, and can dismiss anyone at whim. These conditions, however, were normal for the times. As a matter of fact, Moses was a kinder boss than most. In his shop the workers were kept on throughout the dreaded "slack season," when other employers would dismiss their people for months at a stretch. In addition, Moses closed his shop on the Sabbath and Jewish holidays. He supported the Kuzminer synagogues and cemeteries on both continents; provided ship tickets for others coming to America; gave generous dowries and wedding gifts; and brought in doctors when needed.

Both Asch and Schwartz portray Moses as a complex figure. He regards his workers as family, and is genuinely fond of them; he is respectful and tolerant toward his old father, who insults him to his face in front of his workers. And they, in turn, have sincere family feelings toward him as well. At the same time, however, Moses shamelessly exploits these workers, who are completely dependent on his beneficence. Moses has led the Israelites to the promised land, but they are still servile.

All the older immigrants, including Uncle Moses, waver between homesickness for their idealized Kuzmin, and their desire to assimilate and profit from America's bounty. The images of Kuzmin are associated with the beauties of nature. America, in contrast, is physically ugly. In their repulsive sweatshop, the workers cannot even see the sky. They are, as Shmuel Niger notes, trapped between their "enslavement in the present" and "memories of free life in the past."

Perhaps nothing symbolizes the dichotomy between the old country and the new as much as the music in the film. In the beginning of the movie, the rebbe from Kuzmin comes to Moses for money. He enthralls everyone by singing *Avinu malkeynu*, traditionally chanted in the synagogue on fast days and during the ten days of repentance, between and including Rosh Hashanah and Yom Kippur. The prayer asks, "Our Father, our King, remember us . . . for a good life." The tune brings a wealth of memories and images to mind: the sacredness of the holidays back in the old country, the old cantor, the old synagogue, the old (romanticized) way of life, all so different from crass America, where the dollar takes priority over everything else. Even Moses is touched, and he donates generously. After the rebbe leaves, a different *nign* [tune] is taken up by Moses's father, who sings "Hayom" [today], also in a way that reminds the Kuzminers not of today, but, indeed, of yesterday. Rapoport asserts that the Jews of the transposed *shtetl* "long for the harmonious melody which used to rule over and spread sunshine over their lives from the cradle to the grave." The traditional tunes were the poetry, art, and harmony of the shtetl. The younger generation, that of Masha and Charlie, is not affected by, or even interested in, the songs emblematic of Europe. On the contrary, they are looking forward to attending the symphony in Jackson Park. Later on, Charlie invites his sweetheart to Carnegie Hall to hear another symphony.

Moses first meets Masha (played by Judith Abarbanel) when she comes into the shop to plead for her father, who had been fired for foolishly insulting his boss's belly when he thought Moses could not hear him. When Moses refuses to reinstate Aaron, beautiful Masha calls him a "brute, beast, dog." Enchanted by her filial devotion and courage, Moses gives Aaron his job back with a raise, while he starts planning to court the much younger girl, mainly by dazzling her with his wealth. Masha is not impressed with either Uncle Moses or his money, for she and Charlie, a student and a Marxist (played by Zvee Scooler), are in love. Nevertheless, at the age of eighteen, she tearfully agrees to the unwanted match, because Moses has showered her impoverished family with gifts, and, more importantly, he has brought her parents financial security and peace at home.

The wedding itself indicates the conflicts between values of the old country and those of the new. Moses has declared that he wanted an old-fashioned, Jewish-European wedding. Yet anyone back in Kuzmin would have been astonished indeed to witness this mishmash of tradition and modernity. Moses has hired klezmorim [musicians who play a distinctive Eastern European Jewish type of music], but they are wearing tuxedos. A throng of stylishly dressed (in the 1930s mode) men and women are wildly dancing in a scene that reminds J. Hoberman of *Freaks*. (How did they all fit in the tenement anyway?) There is a *badkhn* [wedding entertainer, jester], but very little else that would signify a wedding back home. Moses's father is dancing in a separate room with other elderly immigrant men, in the midst of which he announces he will return to Poland. The scene closes with a shot of Charlie sitting alone in his darkened apartment, sadly looking at the wedding celebration through his window.

The marriage, however, collapses after the birth of a son. Moses is a devoted and loving husband and father, and amazingly respectful to his especially silly mother-in-law. But Masha, suffering from postpartum depression (in luxury), cannot keep up the pretense any longer. In the meantime, Charlie has incited the workers in the shop to strike and hold out for unionization and

the eight-hour workday, along with an increase in salary and improvements in the workshop. Moses is eager to settle and not have any trouble, but Sam, the jealous and greedy nephew (played by Sam Gertler), has taken over and hired *shtarkers* [tough guys] to suppress the protesters with violence. Charlie is arrested. The thugs go so far as to inform the strikers they are available for future work of this nature, no matter which side, as long as they are paid well.

All this is too much for Moses, who, unlike Sam, has real affection for his workers. He insists that Sam get Charlie out of prison. He grants Masha the divorce she wishes, as he does not want her to be unhappy. After he has a heart attack, his lawyer draws up his will: 25 percent of his money will go to his fellow Kuzminers in the shop; 15 percent will go to the hospital to which he has been a steady contributor; 10 percent will go back to Kuzmin. Sam, although Moses does not like him, will still inherit $15,000 and the house, only because he is a relative; the rest of the estate will go to Masha and their son.

Gravely ill, Moses returns to his people in the sweatshop. He talks about a sermon he heard about the nature of man. Somberly, he concludes that "in the end, there's an open grave waiting for him." No longer omnipotent, Moses asks Yosl, one of his tailors, to sing his father's old *nign*, but he is drowned out by the sound of the new electric sewing machines. This is the last scene of the film, and it sets a grim tone and message. Although Moses has attained the American dream of wealth, he is not happy in his personal life.

Moses Melnick is a multidimensional figure, who both exploits and succors his *landslayt*, immigrants from Kuzmin. Maurice Schwartz makes an imposing, self-centered, and vain Uncle Moses. He also brings humor into his courtship of Masha. When, for example, Sam tells the overweight, aging widower, who is exercising in preparation for his visit to Masha's home, that he looks as good "as the president," the smug, pleased look on Moses's face is quite hilarious.

His relationships with women were problematic. His first wife died from lack of love. He had at least two affairs: one with the married woman in the luncheonette he frequents, who claims that he fathered her son; the other with a *poylishe shikse* [Polish gentile woman]. Moses is cold and indifferent to both of these women. When he meets young Masha, however, he truly falls in love. His love is not reciprocated.

In the workplace, too, Moses is not a simplistic character, not just a slave driver. Certainly, he takes full advantage of his position as boss in his nonunion sweatshop to become very wealthy while keeping his *landslayt* poor and laboring about eighty hours a week in his dark and dingy shop. Certainly, he reminds them of all the favors he has bestowed on them. On the other hand, Moses cares about them and generously sets up and maintains the Kuzminer society. He provides medical and emergency care, ship tickets, gives gifts, and so on. The difference between Moses's real concern for his workers, and Sam's indifferent show of force after he takes over the shop, is quite clear.

In contrast to Schwartz's Moses, Arbarbanel's Masha is disappointing and shallow. Sholem Asch, in his novel, develops her character and makes her heroic as she sacrifices herself to save her family. In the film, however, Masha is a pretty young woman whose father is a wimp and mother is a shrew. She has only one sister at home, as opposed to the many siblings she has in the novel. In the movie, when Moses comes to visit, bestowing gifts on everyone, Masha is looking at herself in her mirror. This family, unlike the one depicted by Asch, is not in terrible financial distress.

When Masha agrees to wed Moses in the movie, it is more to please her fawning, obsequious parents than because she is making a necessary moral choice. After the baby is born, Masha languishes on the couch, attended by her mother, nurse, and maid. In the novel, by contrast, Masha rushes out to the aid of the striking workers. Abarbanel's performance has no real depth, nor do any of her lines. She is a sad, passive victim of her patriarchal society, in which she marries without love. Asch made her more of a forceful feminist.

Moses's father is an even more wretched creature who cannot or will not assimilate. He does not need to work, but he appears in the shop often. He is always a little drunk, singing his tune, or insulting America and his son, whom he calls "Pharoah, King of Egypt" and "Tsar Nicholas." The older Melnick decides to repatriate to Kuzmin during his son's wedding, declaring "to hell with my son and America." He is played by coproducer Rubin Goldberg, in a role originated onstage by Joseph Buloff, who was no doubt very comical. Old Melnick is an unsympathetic drunken victim of nostalgia.

Charlie is a good-looking young student who keeps a picture of his hero Karl Marx on the wall. His goal is to unionize Uncle Moses's sweatshop. Even though this would mean higher wages and shorter workdays, it would also involve keeping the factory open on Saturdays and Jewish holidays, a great hardship for many of the immigrants. Charlie and Masha are in love, and they make a fine-looking, happy couple (as opposed to the mismatched appearance of Uncle Moses and Masha). When Masha gets engaged to Moses, Charlie, who is used to making persuasive political speeches, is strangely silent. The socialist dream is more important than the personal one.

As J. Hoberman indicates, *Uncle Moses* readily lent itself to the mood of the early 1930s and its

focus on the Great Depression, when labor problems and the rise of trade unions were extremely
important issues. There is no attempt to set the
film in the earlier decades of the century, the era
Asch wrote about in his novel.

Uncle Moses was unquestionably an American-
Yiddish film in theme, style, and even language.
The use of a sizable English vocabulary is deliberate. As David Roskies puts it in a *Commentary*
article (April 1992), Uncle Moses moves from
"the comforting familiarities of Yiddish, which he
uses to mask his exploitation of the workers, to an
Americanese designed to show who's boss." Business transactions, too, are conducted in English.
Moses and the younger generation have a command of English, unlike the older immigrants.
The switching from Yiddish in the upstairs shop
to English downstairs is indicative of Maurice
Schwartz's brilliance.

Uncle Moses played steadily until 1939, with
great acclaim. The tragedy of Moses Melnick's life
was that he could never quite escape his slaugh-
terhouse roots. In Kuzmin he had butchered
calves. In his New York sweatshop, in spite of his
grandeur, he cuts his nails with the big tailor's
shears. He is too ostentatious about his wealth,
derived basically from the labors of his *landslayt*.
He can mask his background, but not completely.
Uncle Moses buys cemeteries, synagogues, supports charitable organizations, and he even buys
Masha; nevertheless, his inability to make his father, wife, and himself happy, in spite of his riches,
is a sad commentary on ambition and achievement. Yet, Moses's life was not meaningless; he
accomplished more than just filling an empty
grave. His son will inherit his wealth, but none of
the nostalgia for Kuzmin. The children of the
immigrants in the sweatshop will all have better
lives in America.

Abridged from: Hannah Berliner Fischthal, "Uncle
Moses," in *When Joseph Met Molly: A Reader on Yiddish
Film*, ed. Sylvia Paskin, 217–30 (Nottingham, UK: Five
Leaves, 1999). The translations from the Yiddish are by
Hannah Berliner Fischthal.

Source: Sholem Asch, *Onkl Mozes* (New York: Forverts, 1918). The English translation of the novel differs
considerably from the original Yiddish version.

Background: Howard Sachar, "Into the Sweatshops,"
http://www.myjewishlearning.com/history/Modern_
History/1700–1914/America_at_the_Turn_of_the_
Century/Factory_Workers.shtml.

Bibliography

Bliss, Steven J. "Inventing Yiddish: Observations on the
Rise of a Debased Language." *Judaism* 46 (Summer
1997): 333–45.

Fischthal Berliner, Hannah. "*Onkl Mozes*: Novel and
Video." *Yiddish* 10, no. 1 (1995): 79–82.

Goldberg, Judith N. *Laughter through Tears: The Yiddish
Cinema.* Rutherford, NJ: Fairleigh Dickinson University Press, 1983.

Goldman, Eric A. *Visions, Images, and Dreams: Yiddish
Film, Past and Present.* Rev. ed. Teaneck, NJ: Holmes
and Meier, 2011.

Hoberman, J. *Bridge of Light: Yiddish Film between Two
Worlds.* Updated and expanded ed. Hanover, NH:
University Press of New England, 2010.

——. "Der ershter Talkies [sic]: *Uncle Moses* and the
Coming of Yiddish Sound Film." *Film Comment*
(November–December 1991):32–39.

Howe, Irving, with the assistance of Kenneth Libo. *World
of Our Fathers.* New York: Harcourt Brace Jovanovich,
1976.

Lifson, David S. *The Yiddish Theater in America.* New
York: Yoseloff, 1965.

Matis, Dovid. "Tsu der geshikhte fun yidische films." In
YKUF Almanakh, 439:65. New York: YKUF, 1961.

Roskies, David G. "Sholem Asch and I. B. Singer." In
Sholem Asch Reconsidered, edited by Nanette Stahl.
New Haven, CT: Beinecke Rare Book and Manu-
script Library, 2004.

——. "Yiddish on Screen." *Commentary* 93 (April 1992):
47–50.

PART FOUR

Revolutionary Alternatives
Zionism and Communism, 1880–1932

15. The Birth of a Language,

or the Man Who Loved Hebrew

YVONNE KOZLOVSKY GOLAN

The Wordmaker [Ish She'Ahav B'Ivrit],
directed by Eli Cohen [NCJF]
Israel, 1991

In Israel during the 1990s, very few producers were willing to risk making a high-budget film for a limited audience without government subsidization. The director Eli Cohen was an exception. He and his crew succeeded in filming an excellent movie that compressed the biography of the so-called father of modern Hebrew, Eliezer Ben-Yehuda, into one and a half hours. Produced for the Israel Broadcasting Authority at a total cost of $200,000, the director used cinematic shorthand and extremely original artistic manipulations of backdrops for his film.

The Wordmaker was shot entirely in Israel, in an old hangar that was formerly the British Customs House. The café scenes were filmed in Jaffa, while the meeting in Vienna was filmed in the Railroad Museum, in Haifa. Scenes set in Jerusalem were filmed in the ancient alleys of Ramleh and Lod, which resemble the streets of Ottoman Jerusalem. Adhering closely to the reality of Ben-Yehuda's era, the actors speak English, French, Russian, and Hebrew, emphasizing their origins and cultural contradictions.

The man who was born Eliezer Perlman Eliyanov renamed himself Eliezer Ben-Yehuda, meaning the son of Judah. He revived the Hebrew language from a "dead" language, preserved only in the Jewish Bible and prayers, and transformed it into the spoken language of daily life of the Jews who lived in Palestine. The film depicts him as a man of fiery temperament motivated by a burning passion. Despite his long struggle with tuberculosis, he persistently devoted not only his life to this cause, but the lives of his family as well. He attempted to restore to the Jewish people its language, the third element of its nationhood along with the Land of Israel and a shared history of nearly four millennia. Ben-Yehuda will forever be remembered for authoring the first Hebrew dictionary after approximately two thousand years of Jewish exile. To do so, he coined new words to expand the language's vocabulary. He is known as "the first Hebrew teacher" (although of course others taught Hebrew) for reviving the Hebrew language.

Eli Cohen begins his film during World War I, when Ben-Yehuda was living in New York City for economic and security reasons. The story moves back and forth in time to depict the past and show its impact on his later decisions. The supporting actors play the people on whom

Sinai Peter (as Eliezer Ben-Yehuda) plays the father of modern Hebrew. From *The Wordmaker* (1991), directed by Eli Cohen. BELFILMS AND M. SLONIM PRODUCTIONS/NATIONAL CENTER FOR JEWISH FILM

Ben-Yehuda depended financially and morally throughout his life. Because they believed in his mission, they stood by him in times of distress, despite pressures that almost cost some of his relatives their lives.

When Ben-Yehuda arrived in Eretz Israel in 1881, it was ruled by the Ottoman Turks, whose corrupt empire was sometimes called the "Sick Man of the Bosphorus." The Turkish authorities set up obstacles to Jewish settlement, in the hope of discouraging it. Above all, the regime placed numerous restrictions against any expression of nationalism by minorities throughout the Ottoman Empire, and particularly in the *sanjak*, or district, of Jerusalem. The Jews in Eretz Israel were mostly concentrated in very old commu-

nities in the four holy cities of Jerusalem, Hebron, Safed, and Tiberias, called the Old Yishuv. This name, meaning the old settlement, was coined by Ben-Yehuda for his newspaper articles, to contrast it with the New Yishuv.

The Old Yishuv was divided into two major groups: Ashkenazi Jews and Sephardic Jews, from the old Hebrew words for Germany and Spain, respectively. The Ashkenazim originated in countries that were part of the old Germanic empire, while the Sephardim were from countries under Spanish-Portuguese domination and in the Balkans. The Ashkenazim spoke mostly Yiddish as well as local languages, primarily Russian and Romanian, while the Sephardim spoke Ladino (a hybrid of Hebrew and Spanish) and Arabic. The

Ashkenazi Jews did not work for their livelihood. They did not engage in small businesses or agriculture, but mostly studied in yeshivas, institutes of Jewish learning, supported by the *halukah*, literally "distribution," of charitable funds raised from Jews abroad to support the Jewish residents of Eretz Israel. The Sephardic Jews were wealthier and believed in working for a living as well as engaging in Torah learning. Each group had its own chief rabbis representing it, based on the members' various geographical origins.

A new wave of Jewish immigrants arrived in Ottoman Eretz Israel between 1885 and 1904 in what was to be called the First Aliyah, or ascent to the Holy Land, following the outbreaks of pogroms and increased anti-Semitic discrimination in Russia's Jewish Pale of Settlement. These were the Biluim, activist Jewish pioneers who were sick of life in the Diaspora and wished to begin new lives in their ancestral homeland. Their ambition was to work the soil and settle in Eretz Israel, but most if not all were supported financially by Baron Edmond de Rothschild and later by Baron Maurice de Hirsch, too. The relations between the new immigrants—pioneers for whom agricultural work was a priority—and the members of the Old Yishuv were sometimes tense. Although they observed Jewish rituals, the newcomers' commitment to tilling the soil rather than studying Torah and Talmud seemed like a rejection of Judaism to the old-timers.

Ben-Yehuda arrived in the midst of this political and social unrest with the goal of creating revolutionary change in the community's cultural and social fabric. Aided by a handful of supporters from the Old Yishuv, he was backed up by people from the New Yishuv who eagerly embraced their identity as "New Jews" with a language of their own. Between 1905 and 1914, a second wave of Jewish settlers immigrated to Ottoman Eretz Israel. Unlike their predecessors, they were "barefoot peasants," secularist thinkers, and ideologues intent on redeeming the land through their own labor. They avoided settling in the four holy cities or in colonies supported by Baron Rothschild. Espousing a synthesis of Marxism and Zionism, they founded the first agricultural collectives. They spoke Hebrew and developed their own defense force.

Ben-Yehuda's great-grandson provided most of the details for the screenplay, which was based on Ben-Yehuda's biography. This chapter examines the filmmaker's selection from Ben-Yehuda's overall legacy, and discusses whether the film succeeded in challenging and expanding Israel's collective image of him.

The first scene opens in Ben-Yehuda's apartment in New York City, where he and his family had been living for about three years, financially supported by wealthy Jewish patrons under the auspices of the World Zionist Organization. Hemda Ben-Yehuda, Eliezer's second wife and the younger sister of his first wife, Devorah, had convinced her husband to move there from Jerusalem when World War I began.

It is November 1, 1917, the eve of the Balfour Declaration. Ben-Yehuda's visitors are Nissim Bachar, a wealthy donor named Weintraub (a fictitious character), and a Catholic priest (played by Kevin Patterson). The purpose of the evening is to raise donations so that Ben-Yehuda could complete the fifth volume of his *Dictionary of the Hebrew Language, Ancient and Modern*. He is late for the meeting, and the group awaits him in the living room.

In the film as in Ben-Yehuda's life, Nissim Bachar played a very significant role, and the director has placed him at most of the important milestones of Ben-Yehuda's life, despite presenting him one-dimensionally and focusing entirely on Ben-Yehuda's work as a linguist. Bachar was a French Sephardic Jew who was born in Jerusalem and appointed by the Alliance Israelite to build a school in Jerusalem to teach French culture, thereby raising the educational level of Jewish Jerusalemites. The school, called Torah Umelacha, taught both Jewish and vocational studies. Bachar met Ben-Yehuda and became enchanted with his ideas. However, Ben-Yehuda's financial situation in Eretz Israel was extremely poor. He could not support his family on his salary as an assistant editor of a Hebrew newspaper. Thus, Bachar offered him a job teaching at his new school, albeit at a very low salary. Ben-Yehuda actually taught there for only a year, but he earned the reputation as the first Hebrew teacher because he allowed only Hebrew to be spoken in his class and forbade his students to speak the languages they used at home. Ben-Yehuda transformed Hebrew from a sacred "Sabbath language" used only for prayer and study into an everyday language. During his tenure at the school, Ben-Yehuda and David Yellin developed a curriculum for teaching Hebrew.

The film depicts Ben-Yehuda's work as a teacher in a very short scene that condenses two important pieces of information: first, his work as a teacher, and second, the ridicule his eldest son Ben-Zion (who later changed his name to Itamar Ben-Avi) suffered from the other students for being "the first Hebrew child." This did not really happen since Ben-Zion/Itamar was not of school age during the year that Ben-Yehuda taught at his school. However, it is a cinematic shortcut intended to cover two overlapping dimensions of the school. The conflict between father and son appears later in the film, when Itamar accuses his father of subjecting him to a traumatic pedagogical experiment by forbidding him to speak to other children in any language

but Hebrew. Until he was five, Itamar had no friends of his own age.

In 1882 Ben-Yehuda and Bachar formulated an agreement for a semi-clandestine association, *Sefer Habrit* (Book of the Covenant), which had to be kept secret because the Turks forbade any nationalist manifestos. The association's major goals were to "be Israelites in the Land of their Forefathers" and to urge people to earn their daily bread through commerce and industry. Ben-Yehuda intended to establish colonies in Eretz Israel that would be self-sufficient and even learn how to use arms. These ideas were not associated with the revival of the Hebrew language, but since Ben-Yehuda's primary contribution to Zionism was his revival of Hebrew, these other aspects of his activities are not shown in the film.

In a sharp transition from the family home with children and guests aplenty, the scene cuts to Ben-Yehuda, sitting alone in the New York City Public Library, as was his custom. It is closing time, but Ben-Yehuda refuses to leave the reading room, since he is searching for a word he "lost." The noun "word" runs through the film as a theme. Indeed, Ben-Yehuda coined a new word to mean "dictionary"–*milon*–from the Hebrew word for "word"–*milah*. This neologism encapsulates his lifetime, which was almost entirely focused on words. He even recruited his family to coin new words and "ordered" them to spread the new words everywhere they went. Ben-Yehuda forbade his wife to speak with his young son in any other language but Hebrew, so that Ben-Zion would grow up with Hebrew as his mother tongue. She finds it difficult to find Hebrew words to calm the child down during the night. In the film, numerous fights break out in the family due to the pressure of being forbidden to speak with neighbors and tradesmen who do not know Hebrew.

The next scene shows Ben-Yehuda going out into the street and meeting Yevgeny Chirikov, known by his underground name of Nikolai Nikolaevitch Tschashnikov, at the newsstand. Tschashnikov was a distributor of Communist newspapers, and the film allows viewers to infer his political leanings. Like Bachar, Tschashnikov was a major figure in Ben-Yehuda's early life. They met for the first time in 1877 in Paris (although in the film, they know each other when they meet on the train to Paris, where Ben-Yehuda was headed to study medicine). During the course of their conversation in the film, it is evident that Tschashnikov is a trusted comrade who introduced Ben-Yehuda to the pleasures of Paris and later accompanied him to the Land of Israel. Tschashnikov was not Jewish, and his motives are unclear. Tschashnikov finances Ben-Yehuda's stay in Eretz Israel. When he leaves, he introduces him to the Russian consul, Kozivnikov. The interpreter of the consulate (a former Jew who converted after being conscripted into the czarist army) now becomes Ben-Yehuda's patron and helps him financially.

Most of Ben-Yehuda's biographers are convinced that Tschashnikov was an agent of the Russian secret police, operating in Europe and the Middle East. It may be that he employed Ben-Yehuda to obtain information, but this has not been proved. Since his relationship to Ben-Yehuda is unclear, he appears sparingly in the film.

Meanwhile, in a flashback to the family apartment in New York, the hostess engages her guests in conversation. When one of the guests asks how Eliezer embarked on his quest, Hemda attributes it to a vision he had in his sleep after the Balkan Wars. This happened when he was a gymnasium student, before he contracted tuberculosis. The viewer is now aware that Ben-Yehuda knew about his illness before his first marriage. This triggers a flashback to Vienna, when Eliezer learned that his illness is a death sentence and that he should not marry. He informs Devorah that their wedding is off, but she decides to meet him there, marry him, and remain at his side as his wife. In Vienna they still speak Russian and French, but they make a covenant to speak only Hebrew with each other. In reality, the two were married in Alexandria and then traveled to Constantinople, where they met Tschashnikov and journeyed on to the Land of Israel. This point disappears from the film because the director preferred to focus on the newlyweds as they arrive in the country, and on their passionate devotion to the Hebrew language.

Ben-Yehuda's concern for Hebrew language and culture was not free of the nationalist aims that became the cornerstones of the entire Zionist movement, but these have no place in the screenplay. One example is a political article that Ben-Yehuda published in Paris, under the headline "A Burning Question." This extremely important article was the first of many for Ben-Yehuda. He used unambiguous language to resolve questions discussed by Jews throughout history. His opinion was that a political solution was the only alternative to the historical and current diasporic situation of the Jewish people. He wrote: "The nationalist feeling is deep-seated in the human spirit, and all modern history is an unceasing struggle between each nation's desire to preserve its separate nationalist identity and the transcendence of nationalism in the universalist and classless utopia envisioned in Socialist and Communist theories. In reality, there is no difference between the aspirations of the nations and the aspirations of the Jewish people" (quoted in Even-Zohar, 1980).

To promote the cause, Ben-Yehuda stated that the Hebrew language would be the foundation for a Jewish national revival and constitute a counterweight to Yiddish. The Sephardic pronunciation would prevail instead of the Ashkenazi pronunciation, which symbolized the Diaspora. Ben-Yehuda refuted the "Father of the Enlightenment," Moses Mendelssohn, who stated that the Jews do not need national sovereignty because they are only a religious community. He enumerated the values that Jews have in common, and that give them the right to be defined as a nation: a common historical past and a shared faith in an ancestral homeland. For the first time, he signed his name as Eliezer Ben-Yehuda instead of Eliezer Perlman.

In a scene set back in New York, Ben-Yehuda finally comes back to his apartment to be with his friends. The director portrays him as a capricious person, a stubborn man with mood swings, distracted from everyday matters by his obsession with writing the dictionary. He begins by speaking of his dream to return to the Land of Israel and his discomfort about living in the United States: "I feel that I am betraying everything that I preached about. Until the end of the film, the viewer never realizes why he temporarily left Eretz Israel for the United States.

The film reveals how the New Yishuv subsisted on donations from abroad. Under the Ottoman Empire, then under the British Mandate, and even through the establishment of the state of Israel in 1948, the New Yishuv benefited from monetary contributions from the Jews of the Diaspora to the settlers in the barren country. Funds collected by the Jewish Agency, the Jewish National Fund, the Joint Distribution Committee, and other relevant organizations financed the settlers' purchase of land and investment in industry. American Jews played a major role in funding the pioneers, and Eli Cohen portrays this very precisely in the next scene. Ben-Yehuda arrives

home to find that an American donor has been waiting for him. Their conversation concretizes the tension—familiar now as well as then—between donor and recipient, between the man who holds the purse strings and the recipient of the funds. Ben-Yehuda hates having to grovel before his guest, but finally Bachar pressures him to give in.

During the film, Ben-Yehuda experiences flashbacks of his imprisonment by Turkish authorities in Jerusalem after ultra-Orthodox Jews informed on him as someone calling for revolt against their rule. The film does not explain precisely why he was sent to prison, but it does convey the fact that the experience was extremely traumatic for him and his family. In one of the most moving scenes of the film, the entire Ben-Yehuda family is excommunicated by the ultra-Orthodox community, which accuses them of desecrating the holy tongue by using Hebrew for daily use and in his articles in *Hatzevi*, the Hebrew newspaper he founded. Ben-Yehuda called on people to stop accepting *halukah* money for religious study and to begin building the Land of Israel by the sweat of their brow. Things reached such a point that when his first wife, Devorah, died in 1891, the Ashkenazi Burial Society refused to bury her. Mourning her deeply, Ben-Yehuda appealed to the Sephardic society, which buried her.

In an interview, the director Eli Cohen told how during the filming on the Mount of Olives, ultra-Orthodox men gathered around the grave to find out what was going on, and to see if, in their view, the shoot would desecrate the holiness of the place. The trouble his film crew experienced illustrates the tensions that reigned in Jerusalem in the past and the present. The Zionists build the land with their labor, while the ultra-Orthodox Askenazim feel justified living off donations, considering "their Torah scholarship to be their craft," as a common adage puts it. The latter regarded Ben-Yehuda as a heretic.

The film concludes with the arrival of a telegram from the Jewish Agency, communicating the good news about the Balfour Declaration issued in November 1917. It stated that England would "favor the establishment in Palestine of a national home for the Jewish people" and would "facilitate the achievement of this object, it being clearly understood that nothing shall be done which may prejudice the civil and religious rights of existing non-Jewish communities in Palestine, or the rights and political status enjoyed by Jews in any other country."

Ben-Yehuda is revered in Israeli memory as the father of modern Hebrew. He transformed the biblical language into a spoken one. His influence was also obvious on Theodor Herzl and his ideas. Soon after Herzl's utopian book, "*Altneuland*" (The old new land), appeared, he emphasized that the Jewish state should be established in Eretz Israel and that the language of the state should be Hebrew. The perspective of many years allows us to see that what the two visionaries had in common was more than could have been imagined during their lifetimes, not only in terms of their philosophies, but also in the details of their lives. As one historian has observed, the initiatives by BenYehuda and his colleagues were the philosophical infrastructure that Herzl used to develop his ideas.

Despite the unique status accorded to Ben-Yehuda in Israeli historiography, there are those who object to him being dubbed the father of Hebrew, since other teachers of modern Hebrew had preceded him. Ben-Yehuda's other ideas—such as establishing a state for the Jewish people, or at least trying to concentrate as many Jews as

possible in their own territory—have disappeared from the collective memory because they were ahead of their time. It was in the context of Balkan nationalism that Ben-Yehuda developed his ideas for reviving the Hebrew language as a rallying point for cultural autonomy, but Eli Cohen's film does not refer to that context. The film mentions only briefly the critical tension between Ben-Yehuda and the ultra-Orthodox Jews, and does not discuss the "language wars" of 1913, the debates about whether German or Hebrew would be the language of instruction at the Technion, the Institute of Technology in Haifa.

The film depicts BenYehuda as a paragon of nationalist identity. But viewers should remember that no film can tell everything about a person. Especially in a low-budget film like this—which may have been censored—the director must make choices about what information to include. Some critics charged that during the years the film aired on television, government representatives at the Israel Broadcasting Authority, which had a nationalist and religious orientation, wanted a film that would be acceptable to a broad spectrum of viewers without being controversial. However, this is not how things seemed to the film's director. In an interview I had with him, Eli Cohen emphasized that this was the material he was given to work with. "The canvas was too small, the budget ran out, and we had to make a film that would be short and to the point. . . . All the rest, of course," he hinted to his critics, "arose from simple ignorance and lack of back-up support." Viewers can only regret not knowing more about one of the founding fathers of Israeli culture. Still, the film constitutes a media jewel from the television productions of that period.

World War I ended in 1918. In the spring of 1919, the Ben-Yehuda family returned to Eretz

Israel. In 1922, British High Commissioner Sir Herbert Samuel declared that the Hebrew language was one of the three official languages of Eretz Israel. In December of that year, Eliezer Ben-Yehuda passed away from tuberculosis, while working on his dictionary's entry for the Hebrew word for "soul."

Source: Ben-Yehuda, Eliezer, *A Dream Come True*, trans. T. Muraoka, ed. George Mandel (Boulder, CO: Westview, 1993).

Background: http://www.jewishvirtuallibrary.org/jsource/biography/ben_yehuda.html.

Bibliography

Brenner, Michael. *Zionism: A Brief History*. Translated by Shelley Frisch. Princeton, NJ: Marcus Wiener, 2003.

Even-Zohar, Itamar. "The Birth and Formation of Local and Indigenous Hebrew Culture in Eretz Israel, 1882–1948 [in Hebrew]." *Cathedra*, no.16 (July 1980): 165–93.

Fellman, Jack. *The Revival of a Classical Tongue: Eliezer Ben Yehuda and the Modern Hebrew Language*. The Hague, Netherlands: Mouton, 1973.

Saposnik, Arieh Bruce. *Becoming Hebrew: The Creation of a Jewish National Culture in Ottoman Palestine*. New York: Oxford University Press, 2008.

St. John, Robert. *Tongue of the Prophets*. Garden City, NY: Doubleday, 1952.

Stavans, Ilan. *Resurrecting Hebrew*. New York: Schocken, 2008.

16. *They Were Ten* Revisited

Zionism, Trauma, and New Identity

ELDAD KEDEM AND BENJAMIN BEN-DAVID

They Were Ten (*Hem Hayu Asarah*), directed by Baruch Dinar [EM]
Israel, 1961

They Were Ten tells anew the story of the pioneering act of Eastern European Jews who immigrated to the Land of Israel at the end of the nineteenth century. The film is considered a remake of Aleksander Ford's *Sabra*, also known as *Chalutzim* (1933), which was one of the first action feature films to be shot in Palestine. In 1987 the director Uri Barbash created an updated version, *Ha-Holmim* (*The Unsettled Land*, also known as *Once We Were Dreamers*) in which he critically examined, from a post-Zionist perspective, the ideological values of the two earlier versions. This phenomenon of repetition and the desire to retell reflect the obsession of Israeli culture to engage with the components of the national Israeli identity: the Jewish past and the Jewish Israeli present, issues of territory and establishing roots on the land, personal and collective identity, the Israeli-Arab conflict, and universal themes of morality and justice.

Israeli cinema experts have labeled both the period when *They Were Ten* was made, and its genre, "national heroic." Between 1955 and 1968, a handful of films were made in Israel that related to the struggle against the British Mandate, the War of Independence (1948), and the Six Day War (1967), including *Hill 24 Doesn't Answer* (1955), *Pillar of Fire* (1959), and *He Walked Through the*

Fields (1967). These films, some of which were influenced by Hollywood Westerns and war films, reflected the transition from Zionist settlement to Israeli statehood; they presented narratives of heroism and sacrifice by Israelis—in situations of war, military operations, and under siege—and of the integration of new immigrants, refugees and survivors of the Holocaust, into the national struggle and nascent society.

The plot of *They Were Ten* involves the attempt to establish an agricultural commune by a group of nine men and one woman, including a married couple, Joseph and Manya. The group arrives at a desolate and arid area in the Galilee, and the plot shows the many hardships they deal with in order to turn the Zionist dream into a reality. These hardships can be grouped into three categories. First are environmental hardships: the group must confront the harsh climatic conditions, the lack of access to sources of water, drought, their lack of agricultural knowledge, the shortage of food, and their cramped living conditions, inside one small hut. The second category is external hardships: the hostility of some of their Arab neighbors, who prevent their access to the land, do not let them draw water from the well, steal their only horse, and try to drive them away; and the hostility of the Turkish policeman who oversees the new settlers. The third category is internal hardships: personal tensions within the group; illness, hunger, and exhaustion; and feelings of disappointment, helplessness, frustration, and despair, in spite of their hope for a better future. Some members of the group wish to react violently to their Arab neighbors, while others are more moderate, and some wish to abandon everything and return to the Diaspora. The people in the last group eventually leave the commune. The film also touches on sexual tensions, when one of the men lusts after Manya, and on the difficulty of creating privacy and time for the married couple to be together.

When violence threatens to break out following the theft of the horse by the Arabs, the Arab *mukhtar* (village head) succeeds in stopping the village extremists, and in making peace with Joseph and the other Jews. Manya gives birth to a daughter but then contracts malaria and dies. Her death and burial are accompanied by symbols of redemption and birth: her baby, rain that breaks the drought, and a blossoming tree.

This essay offers a reading of the film as divided into two different stages: the first stage is the opening sequence, and the second stage is the events that follow. The film presents a transformation of the settlers from an amorphous group with separate pasts, devoid of a unified narrative, into a collective, secular entity with common concrete aims, seeking to realize these aims in light of the Zionist enterprise.

The opening sequence depicts the return of a group of Jews to their ancestral homeland as an abstract event, devoid of any historical context. It is therefore packed with connotations, from both the actual past and the imagined past of the Jewish nation, as well as from other films, which provide a structured and familiar framework relating to the Zionist enterprise. The condensed blocks of images characterizing the opening sequence also create a condensed space and time, characterized by hybridism, liminality (the blurring of boundaries) and heterotopias (the realized versions of a utopian ideal). This first stage constitutes both an entrance into the film itself and also a brief introduction to the history of the Jewish people up to the return to the homeland, at the end of the nineteenth century.

The opening of the film reveals the pioneers

arriving at a desolate and rocky area. They are pushing a cart and seem to be gathered together to protect it and themselves from the forbidding, alien space, or from some unseen enemy. They pass in front of the camera and are presented individually, thereby receiving a face and a history. Together they represent a collective portrait of all the Jewish pioneers. They unload their belongings by the abandoned house atop the mountain, and this English text appears on the screen in the subtitled version:

> At the end of the nineteenth century, driven by the outbreak of the pogroms in Europe, groups of Jewish youth abandon their studies and businesses and go to Palestine to redeem the land of their forefathers. The land is barren, infested with malarial swamps, and the Turkish rulers create further obstacles to plague the new settlers. These unsung heroes were the forerunners of the multitudes that followed. Without them the Israel of today would still be a dream.

This exposition defines the stage of return to the homeland, incorporating several contradictory aspects. First, although the narrative of immigration to the Land of Israel and its Jewish settlement are circumscribed in time, those events are also mythical and allegorical, and thus not bound by a concrete place or period. The result is a plot located in a particular era—the end of the nineteenth century—that nevertheless has an ahistorical quality. Second, the pioneers return to the familiar space of their ancestral land, but this is also a return to an alien, threatening territory that initially seems more like a place of exile. The opening sequence consequently depicts a liminal and hybrid space: the pioneers enter into the very heart of the Land of Israel, but they remain outside it. Third, although the pioneers

are steeped in Zionist ideology, they are also following the tradition of the wandering Jew who was rejected and persecuted. These effects demonstrate the essence of the notion of immigration and renewed Jewish settlement of the Land of Israel, while exposing the contradictions of the Zionist enterprise.

The text on the screen provides the film's viewers with a concrete historical framework for the group of young Jews, pioneers, who have immigrated to settle the Land of Israel following pogroms and overt anti-Semitism in Europe. This framework changes the status of the collective from one that appeared from out of nowhere into one that appears from everywhere. This transition from nowhere to everywhere establishes the mythic dimension of *They Were Ten*. The film seeks to blur the original and specific place from which this collective had come. Thus, not only do the wheels of the cart symbolize the Zionist movement and change, but the ten pioneers themselves also symbolize the national awakening that resulted in the waves of immigration to the Land of Israel during the first half of the twentieth century. The collective is perceived as one that arrives from nowhere or from everywhere, and also one that settles everywhere. The specifics of the historical event are deliberately blurred into a generic Jewish migration. The emphasis is on the transition from one world to another: from the Diaspora to the lost homeland, from slavery to freedom.

In this respect, the opening sequence presents a version of the cycle of movement from the outside inward, from exile to the homeland, that is both old and new. And the return always involves building and restoring the devastated and neglected land. This is why the group is shown moving across desolate spaces, in what looks like a chaotic journey, without direction or clear aim.

The journey echoes two central biblical myths: the story of the Creation and the story of the Exodus from Egypt. The story of the Creation enables the film to advance the notion of renewal, of transforming the wilderness and desert. The creation or restoration of the space is expressed by renovating the abandoned, ruined house, by working the land, and by the woman's pregnancy. The story of the Exodus from Egypt emphasizes the temporal dimension, the infinite movement in the desert, when the promise of a land flowing with milk and honey seems an unattainable fantasy. The disoriented movement of the members of the collective in the opening sequence echoes the forty-year journey of the people of Israel in the desert. Thus, the pioneers' movement represents their actual journey in exile, even though it is now taking place in the Land of Israel.

The fact that the film opens with the group's journey in an unfamiliar wilderness turns the space represented in the opening sequence into a liminal and hybrid space: it replicates the journey of the people of Israel in the Sinai, the journey from Europe to the Land of Israel, and the journey within the Land of Israel itself. For the pioneers, the land constitutes a nostalgic territory, an imagined space, mediated by the mythic historical narrative of the Jewish people. In this connection, Gideon Eran and Zali Gurevitch (1991) note that the modern-day return to the desolate Land of Israel is but a return to the working of the land. The Bible constitutes a sort of meta-narrative, whose entire continuation is both a return to the Land and the agricultural development of the land.

Consequently, the gap between imagined knowledge—their expectations in exile—and their actual encounter with the land creates among the pioneers a hybrid concept of space: they understand cognitively that they have ar-rived in the Land of Israel, but through their senses they experience that same alien land as an exilic space. This is not yet a protected space but an open one, lacking borders or defenses. The transition from one world to the other assumes the existence of the two worlds, simultaneously separated and joined by means of a border or threshold. The connection and separation between two territories joins them structurally. The threshold always indicates two directions—one can cross a border precisely because it indicates a spatial closeness. This structural connection between separation (between exile and the Land of Israel) and joining (the Land of Israel is still exilic) is expressed in the way the group experiences the migration from the old world to the new one.

The lack of specific characterizations of any of the members of the group reflects their collective identity. They have immigrated to the Land of Israel, but at this stage of the narrative their faces are those of the desert and wilderness. This is a blurred group portrait, erased, stricken by trauma. This shock is expressed in the plethora of symbols of death: the coffin, the bare branches of the carob tree, the slow movement of the characters, the cloudy sky, and the darkness that descends on the land. The signs of Europe and the Diaspora are still present at this stage of the film, depicting the entrance into the Land of Israel as strangeness, alienation, disconnection, passivity, and connotations of death. The signs of exile, the yearnings, and the acute sense of disconnection persist: the pioneers sing Russian folk songs in Hebrew and refer to the homes and families they have left behind.

Realizing the Europeans' exilic space in the space of the Land of Israel establishes a space that Michel Foucault (1999) called a heterotopia, a place outside any place, but whose location can in fact be determined. This is a heterotopic space in several senses: it is simultaneously physically and mythically present, both landscape and idea; it is the Land of Israel and the Diaspora; it is the land of milk and honey and the valley of the shadow of death. In the minds of the pioneers, this territory incorporates two spaces that coexist incompatibly and incoherently. Although the opening shots present the Land of Israel as representing hope, renewal, and optimism, this is expressed in terms of a march in a graveyard, with the pioneers walking as if at a funeral.

Thus, the opening of the film disconnects the specific arrival from the historical and confers on the return a mythic hue characterized by a compression of Jewish suffering through the generations, beginning with the destruction of the Second Temple and extending up to the methodical annihilation of Jews during World War II. Throughout the film, images of siege appear to express the settlers' latent anxiety, a consequence of the traumatic memories whose source lies in the ghetto experience. This is the reason why the journey of the collective is located in the Land of Israel itself, in a geographic and mental space that blurs the spatial borders (from there to here) and the temporal ones (from then to now).

Benedict Anderson (1991) notes that the narrative of a nation requires stories of war and struggle. These stories engage with the origin of the nation, with the myths of the founding fathers, and with tales of heroes with high moral values who are willing to endanger and even sacrifice their lives for the collective or the country. The frontiers constitute a space in which conflicting forces are reconciled or at least find a common denominator. This is a space of disconnection and coalition, of separation and articulation, containing stories of past heroism and sacrifice, which constitute the broad common denominator of the

concept "nation." *They Were Ten* should be understood as a film that tells anew the story of the origin of the state of Israel, the genealogy of the founding fathers and their heroic deeds.

The main theme of the film involves the transformation that the members of the group have to undergo to cast off their old, exilic Jewish identity and acquire a new one. This is expressed by the contrasts between dream and reality, with the plot comprising a series of obstacles and difficulties that the group must confront. The first part of the film stresses the difficulties and unsuitability of the pioneers to the new reality: their attire is unsuitable for the climate; they don't know how to plough the land; they don't possess suitable tools; they are unable to start a fire; and the Arabs not only prevent their access to water but also drive them from the pasture.

The pioneers' overcoming of these obstacles— depicted in the film with great pathos, flowery language, low focus angles, agonized faces, and dramatic music—intensifies the difficulties on the one hand, and the successful fulfillment of the personal and collective mission on the other hand. The success enables the pioneers to become natives who merge with the environment and its geography. The Jewish settlers learn from the Arabs how to ride the horse and work the land. One of the few functions of the Arabs in the film is to teach the Jews the language of the land and its secrets. This Zionist theme manifests itself in the transformation that the Old Jew must undergo to give birth to the New Jew, the antithesis of the weak and submissive Diaspora Jew. This Zionist transformation is expressed in a movement of binary contrasts as shown in the two columns below. The column on the left presents the negative connotations from the past, and the column on the right, the positive connotations of the present:

Europe and the Diaspora	> Land of Israel/ Palestine
Old identity	> New identity
Insubstantial work	> Productive work
Passivity	> Activity, initiative
Inferiority, submission	> Heroism, victory, revenge
Weak, diseased body	> Mental and physical strength
Death	> Revival and rebirth
Schism and dispersal	> Coalescence and unification
The past	> The future

An additional important theme is revealed in the relationship between the individual and the collective and the glorification of socialist or communist values such as collaboration, egalitarianism, and solidarity. During the course of the plot, the arguments and disputes within the group become prominent, with individual settlers at various points compromising their personal needs for the sake of the national or group mission. Hardships such as hunger, crowding, a lack of water, and the death of Manya are represented as the personal price that must be paid for the success of the collective mission. An additional compromise results from the need to create a private space for the young married couple, with the fear that such a step will undermine the solidarity and interests of the group. In this context, the fact that there are nine men and one woman in the group is linked to the concepts of gender equality— namely, that women too will participate in the hard, "masculine" mission. Moreover, the film minimizes individual close-ups while providing many mid- and long-distance shots and compositions of the entire group or of several members together. The formal cinematic composition, greatly recalling the aesthetics of the Western

genre, also transmits the importance of the group and individual sacrifice for the sake of the majority. In other words, the film suggests the possibility of harmony between the individual and the collective, and the importance of individual sacrifice for the sake of the group and the collective's or nation's aims.

This viewpoint reflects the literature and cinema of the 1930s and 1940s in Israel, and it articulates the utopian vision of the socialist Zionists and the first waves of immigration. Ideologically, representations of the pioneer benefited the dominant Zionist labor movement of the period. The pioneer communal settlement emblematizes a revolutionary dimension in the life of the individual and the Jewish nation, by shaking off the characteristics of ghetto life and constructing a new identity in the Land of Israel. The importance ascribed to labor in the film idealizes the notion of productivity subscribed to by the socialist streams in Zionism: in order to let the Jewish people "recover," to become a nation like any other, and to assert control over their personal and collective fate, the Jews had to return to physical labor in general, and to agricultural and productive work in particular. The commune embodies the socialist ideas of independent Hebrew labor, equality, and social justice: the New Jew would live by his labor, to rehabilitate himself and to establish a more just society for his people. The cinematic representation of the prototypical pioneer epitomizes the Zionist revolution, with its aims of a return to the homeland, redeeming it by making it flourish, productive labor, strengthening solidarity among disparate groups of immigrants, stressing values and norms such as cooperation, volunteering for national missions, readiness to make do with little, and so on.

The film contains additional echoes from the socialist Zionist rhetoric. The pioneers return to the land and work it to develop enduring roots in the land. The scenes of working on the land indicate ownership and belonging based on primordial claims. In an early scene, ownership of the land is signified by the furrow left in the field by the plow. Working the land is also connected to a cosmic or primordial rhythm, in the sense of the cyclical nature of plowing, sowing, blooming, and harvesting. The depiction of the pioneers hard at work in the fields strengthens the idea of an organic connection to the land, and even of an erotic link with the land and nature. The body of the pioneer becomes a work tool in the socialist Zionist ideology that glorifies work and symbolizes modernity and efficiency. These images were part of the national rhetoric that linked the new identity with authenticity and the locale of the Land of Israel.

Nonetheless, the film introduces two motifs that depart from the socialist Zionist ethos of the 1930s, and that mirror the nationalistic and militaristic ethos of the 1960s in Israel. The personal conflicts and interests within the group are clearly expressed, hinting that the stage of collectivism and cooperation is merely a transitional one. The film emphasizes individual initiatives, mainly through the character of the group's leader, Joseph. It stresses his strong leadership qualities: he is someone who displays courage, determination, and pride in himself, but he is also willing to compromise and live in peace with the Arab neighbors. The arguments that arise within the group imply that their cooperation is a temporary state to allow them to survive, and it will not last forever. The need to clear a space for private purposes, the family unit, and the birth of offspring reveals that the commune is only a transitional step toward a stratified society and not necessarily a truly egalitarian cooperative. The dispute between the Arabs and Jews in the film, and the

understanding at which the two leaders arrive, is based on the norms of law and order connected to the state and not on a utopian, universal brotherhood between two nations.

The second motif differentiating the 1930s and 1960s relates to the significant difference in the approach to the Israeli-Arab conflict, which correlates with the historical changes that followed the establishment of the state of Israel. For example, in the film *Sabra* the contrasts between the Jewish and Arab societies are presented and stressed, with the Arabs depicted as a tribal society, backward, and violent, whose members are consumed by hatred and manipulated by their leaders. In contrast, in *They Were Ten*, the two societies are portrayed as possessing similar aspirations; their differences lie mainly in their customs and cultures. Violence between the Jews and Arabs is attributed to youthful anger or misunderstandings that can be settled by wise and moderate leaders. These social and cultural differences between the two groups constitute a basis for the friendship woven between Joseph and the Arab leader. This optimism is extraordinary in the national cinema of the 1960s (in comparison, for example, with the Egyptian officer who is revealed as a Nazi soldier in *Hill 24 Doesn't Answer* or the representation of the defeated Arab enemy and the subtextual message that the Arabs understand only force, in films made following the Six-Day War). According to Nitzan Ben-Shaul (1997), these differences emerged in the period following the establishment of the state of Israel, during which the Israeli Arabs were gradually freed from military rule, and attempts were made to integrate them into Israeli democracy and halt their nationalist ambitions.

Why does the film return to stories of the pioneers sixty years later, and why docs it return to the plot of the film *Sabra* twenty-five years later?

The reason lies in the historical context and zeitgeist in which *They Were Ten* was made. The 1950s and first half of the 1960s are considered a relatively calm period in the history of the young state of Israel. Following the physical damage and psychological trauma of the War of Independence (1948); absorption of the waves of mass immigration from Europe, Asia, and Africa (1949–51); a severe economic depression (1953–54); and the 1956 war (the Sinai campaign), Israeli society underwent a transition from the upheaval of creation to the stage of consolidation, a process that included a transition from the pioneering ethos to one of statehood and sovereignty.

Dramatic changes took place, the most prominent of which were the weakening of the collective norms and the legitimization of more capitalist and individualist aspirations, such as attaining a livelihood, career, family, education, housing, and material possessions. Those years saw the emergence of a bourgeois middle class of civil servants, professionals, and white-collar workers. With them arose a culture of consumption and leisure. National policy shifted from the pre-statehood emphasis on village and agricultural settlements to a focus on urban development. After the major waves of immigration, every other person in Israel was a new immigrant, most of whom had not immigrated for socialist Zionist motives.

Within this historical context, we should understand *They Were Ten* in Fredric Jameson's (1981) terms, as a symbolic and strategic social act of containment. The film attempts to revive the old collective ethos while domesticating the contradictions and conflicts stemming from changes in the means of production and social attitudes noted above. Against the historical horizon of the 1960s, it offers an imagined return to the pioneering values and merges this with the new reality of social classes and private interests through the collective remembrance of the past.

A symbolic synthesis is thus created between the two spaces and ways of existence, which have become disconnected in reality. For example, in order to create a festival of Jewish unity, the film attempts to synthesize the secular pioneering practices and religious practices such as the harvest festival and threshing, on the one hand, and Hasidic dances and the kiddush, on the other hand. To a great extent, this is one of the central functions of the national cinema: to create the story of the national awakening of the Jewish people as a collective narrative, as part of the melting-pot policy—a doctrine that incorporated a deep anxiety about the idea of a multicultural society, which would be conducted according to what is commonly known today as identity politics. What lies behind the desire to retell the history of the origins of Zionist settlement in the Land of Israel is the aim of presenting a myth. The rebirth of the past by cinematic means fosters a collective Israeli memory, a basic component in constructing a new nation, most of whose citizens are immigrants who have only just arrived from different places around the world. The specific historical past becomes a mythic, collective past, based on an imagined memory that replaces actual memory.

Background: http://www.jafi.org.il/JewishAgency/English/Jewish+Education/Compelling+Content/Worldwide+Community/Connecting+to+Community/Zionist+Dreams.htm.

Bibliography

Anderson, Benedict. *Imagined Communities: Reflections on the Origin and Spread of Nationalism.* London: Verso, 1991.

Ben-Shaul, Nitzan. *Mythical Expressions of Siege in Israeli Films.* Lewiston, NY: Edwin Mellen, 1997.

Bennington, Geoffrey. "Postal Politics and the Institution of the Nation." In *Nation and Narration*, edited by Homi K. Bhabha, 121–37. New York: Routledge, 1990.

Foucault, Michel. "Different Spaces." Translated by Robert Harley. In Michel Foucault, *Aesthetics, Method, and Epistemology*, vol. 2 of *Essential Works of Foucault 1954–1984*, edited by James D. Faubion, 175–86. New York: New Press, 1999.

Gavron, David. *Kibbutz: Awakening from Utopia*. Lanham, MD: Rowman and Littlefield, 2000.

Gluzman, Michael. *The Zionist Body: Nationalism, Gender and Sexuality in Modern Hebrew Literature* [Hebrew]. Tel Aviv: Hakibbutz Hameuchad, 2007.

Gurevitch, Zali, and Gideon Eran. "About the Place [Hebrew]." *Alpayim* 4 (1991): 9–44.

Jameson, Fredric. *The Political Unconscious: Narrative as a Socially Symbolic Act*. Ithaca, NY: Cornell University Press, 1981.

Rogoff, Irit. *Terra Infirma: Geography's Visual Culture*. London: Routledge, 2000.

Shohat, Ella. *Israeli Cinema: East/West and the Politics of Representation*. 2nd ed. New York: I. B. Tauris, 2010.

Troen, S. Ilan. *Imagining Zion: Dreams, Designs, and Realities in a Century of Jewish Settlement*. New Haven, CT: Yale University Press, 2003.

17. Jews of Steel

J. HOBERMAN

The Return of Nathan Becker (*Nosn Beker Fort Aheym*), directed by Boris Shpis and Rokhl Milman [NCJF]
Soviet Union, 1932

That the first Soviet sound film, Abram Room's compilation documentary *Plan for Great Works* (1930), would celebrate the Five Year Plan was hardly coincidental. Talking pictures arrived just as the Communist Party began implementing a crash program for industrialization, collectivized agriculture, and the consolidation of state power.

If the party's new emphasis on building socialism in one country mitigated the significance of foreign revolutionary movements—and hence the propaganda value of Soviet policy toward certain of its own internal nationalities—the Soviet Union's first and only feature-length Yiddish talking picture, *The Return of Nathan Becker*, suggests the importance of addressing American Jews. If nothing else, the Belgoskino Studio film gave the idea of Jewish national aspiration a unique twist: After twenty-eight years in America spent "laying bricks for Rockefeller," Nathan leaves the land of bread lines and the Depression for his Belorussian hometown and thence, having been reunited with his aged father, on to the new industrial center of Magnitogorsk.

Nathan Becker spoke to the failure of American assimilation while offering a non-Zionist *aliyah* (return to Zion). Moreover, in dramatizing the liquidation of so-called "declassed" and "nonproductive" Jews and their migration out of their primitive *shtetlekh* (villages) and into the industrial cauldron of Great Russia, *Nathan Becker* was the first Soviet film to address the 150-year old "productivity" debate over whether agriculture was productive and trade was not. Jews and gentiles, Communists and Zionists, had long engaged in both theoretical and practical attempts to transform Jewish middlemen into a "productive" social element.

Aesthetically as well as ideologically, *Nathan Becker* is a complex artifact. The film was directed by Boris Shpis and Rokhl Milman from an original scenario by Peretz Markish, then the most widely published and translated of Soviet Yiddish writers. It weds a self-conscious Yiddish folk culture to the optimistic methods of the first Five

Year Plan, melding the theatrical stylization of famed Yiddish actor Solomon Mikhoels's Jewish Academic People's Theatre of Moscow to that of Leningrad's avant-garde Factory of the Eccentric Actor.

The "eccentric" elements of *Nathan Becker* are indistinguishable from the propagandist ones. America the decadent is briefly (and pragmatically) represented by stock footage of the Manhattan skyline. A startling *hommage* to the most radical aspects of silent Soviet technique depicts a boat sailing out of New York harbor intercut with a stroboscopic montage of cars, cosmetics, and can-can dances—the images culled mainly from German magazines. A mock lyrical shot of garbage floating in the harbor provides a segue to Nathan [Nosn] on the ship. Nosn is returning to his native village to serve the Revolution. "Well, Mayke, we are going home," he tells his dubious wife (Elena Kashnitskaya). The couple is traveling with Nosn's black colleague, Jim (Kador Ben-Salim). "You, too, are going home," Nosn adds.

An actor whose mere presence signified American injustice, Ben-Salim had recently appeared in *Black Skin*, a 1931 Ukrainian film production that favorably compared Soviet racial attitudes to those of the United States. Although Ben-Salim is used more as a prop than a performer in *Nathan Becker*, his appearance in the Belorussian *shtetl* is a subject for mild vaudeville humor. "Is he a Jew too?" asks Nosn's father, Tsale (Mikhoels). "He is a bricklayer," Nosn replies with consummate political correctness. The town cantor rushes over to Tsale's hovel, shakes Jim's hand, and is suitably impressed: "This is Nosn? Your Nosn from America? How did he get so blackened . . . like the earth?"

Unlike Jim, however, the figure of Nosn was not completely exotic. The early thirties saw a small immigration from the United States back to the Soviet Union. In his memoirs, Eugene Lyons reports that "the news that Russia had liquidated unemployment and was in dire need of labor power brought hundreds of foreign job hunters to Moscow." Most, however, were disappointed. "Even when they had specific mechanical trades, only one in a hundred managed to cut through the jungles of red-tape around Soviet jobs." According to Lyons, by the year of *Nathan Becker*'s release, "these hordes of stranded Americans became a real problem."

As though consigning the misery of the Diaspora to the dustbin of history, *Nathan Becker* gives less authority to tradition—even as an adversary—than any previous Soviet Jewish film. The movie opens in a miserable tumbledown *shtetl* populated mainly by old men, stray dogs, and ragged children. This dilapidated Belorussian village is eerily underpopulated, halfway toward becoming a ghost town. Although the *shtetl*'s haunting sense of emptiness and abandonment carries inadvertent associations with the catastrophic, manmade famine that even then was decimating the Ukraine, the film is probably an accurate representation of *shtetl* conditions. In his *Where the Ghetto Ends*, a survey of Jewish life in the new Russia published in 1934, Leon Dennen interviews a lonely old woman in a *shtetl* outside Kiev: "The revolution has robbed them (the inhabitants of the *shtetl*) of their children. The youth has deserted them. It has gone off to the cities, where new industries are rising, where there is activity and life."

Nosn's arrival draws a crowd of urchins, vagrants, and beggars. The rumor has spread that he represents "a commission from America bringing dollars." A pathetic *klezmer* (a Jewish folk musician) plays his clarinet and sings a toneless ballad about poverty and starvation: "With such a song you would become a rich man in America," Nosn

tells him. Intentionally or not, the opening parodies the 16mm home movies made by successful
immigrants of their Old World villages. But, even
as the returning son is greeted by old Tsale, the
town is honored with another distinguished visi-
tor. A pretty *Komsomulka* (female member of the
Communist Youth League) appears in an official
car to recruit workers to help build Magnitogorsk. An enthusiastic mob abruptly materializes, chanting the mysterious name "Magnitogorsk" as though it were a sacred spell, falling over
themselves in their desire to leave the *shtetl* for the
steel city beyond the Urals.

Constructed in the first frenzy of the Five Year
Plan on an empty steppe in the Urals, Magnitogorsk symbolized Soviet industrial growth: "A
quarter of a million souls—Communists, kulaks,
foreigners, Tartars, convicted saboteurs and a
mass of blue-eyed Russian peasants—making the
biggest steel production *combinat* in Europe in
the middle of the barren Ural steppe," the American welder John Scott wrote in his firsthand account of the city's rise.

The new arrivals included 40,000 Jews. Indeed, one of the outstanding figures of Five Year
Plan literature, David Margulies, the "positive
hero" of Valentin Kataev's 1932 celebratory novel
of Magnitogorsk, is nominally Jewish. However, as an engineer, Margulies was distinguished
mainly by his profession; most of the workers
who flocked to Magnitogorsk were unskilled,
with bricklayers in particular demand at the beginning of 1933.

Nosn is assigned to the Central Institute of
Labor as an instructor, along with a German spe-
cialist who has been imported to teach the workers movements that combine efficiency, artistry,
and pleasure. As Magnitogorsk produces steel,
it also transforms the unproductive. "Are they
studying to become actors?" the incredulous

American asks. "The worker plays his work as
though it were a piano," the instructor explains,
and the optimistic construction leader Mikulitch
adds that "the backs of the workers are as important to use as the building of the wall." Uncon-
vinced, Comrade Becker petulantly overturns the
table on which the bricks have been arranged:
"Piano they play? Why not hire musicians then?
Meshugoim [crazy people]!" Unpacking his trowel,
he proposes an "American-style" competition. "I
will show them who works better, Soviet klezmer
or an American bricklayer."

The *Daily Worker*, America's leading communist newspaper, observed that "twenty-eight years
of intense economic struggle to live have left their
mark on Nathan Becker. He has become a machine, an automatic robot. . . . The new type of
Soviet worker whom he now meets, a new man
with a new outlook on life, is incomprehensible
to him." The *Worker*, however, missed the nu-
ance. Nosn is not robotic enough. The industrial
utopia envisioned during the Five Year Plan embraced such automation.

Tsale Becker watches the contest intently,
along with the Jewish elders who have also left the
shtetl for Magnitogorsk. By the seventh hour,
their American champion is exhausted. As the
unflustered Russian forges ahead, Nosn vainly remembers the movement class he scorned. Humiliated, he decides to return to America: "Any boy
here knows how to work better than I do." His
wife reminds him of the American unemployed
fighting for soup, and his father explains that
"these are different times," but Nosn is determined to leave until Mikulitch confronts him:
"You're not in America. We're not going to fire
you. We're going to learn from you. But you must
learn from us, too." The chief of operations
praises Nosn's work—he was working more effi-
ciently, but tired sooner than his rival—and sug-

gests combining the systems. The synthesis of American and Soviet techniques will increase production.

Clearly, *Nathan Becker* was made with at least one eye on the American audience—Yiddish-speaking elders as well as ardent young Communists. Virtually every ad in New York's Yiddish press stresses the spectacle of "old Jews in the new Russia." In the end, the know-it-all American must acknowledge his father's wisdom. "You keep on quarreling with us, Nosn. You keep on fighting," is Tsale's fond, recurring reprimand. Structurally, at least, the movie has a conservative bias. In the Yiddish literature of the Five Year Plan, the generational schism is wider and the emphasis more upon the new Soviet youth.

Despite its tendentious narrative, *Nathan Becker* is a surprisingly playful movie. One advertisement in a New York Yiddish paper proclaimed, "Jewish workers, this is your *yontev* [holiday]!" Subsequent ads advised readers to "Share May Day with the First Yiddish Talkie from Soviet Russia." In fact, *Nathan Becker* did celebrate a relative improvement for many Soviet Jews: the popular anti-Semitism of the NEP (the New Economic Policy instituted by Lenin in 1921 and ended by Stalin in 1928) receded as the Five Year Plan created tens of thousands of new jobs. (Not only were previously "unproductive" Jews now able to find acceptable "proletarian" occupations but, in the tensions that arose when disparate peoples were brought together in work projects, Asians more often bore the brunt of prejudice and violence.)

Nathan Becker is at least as full of comic routines—one of them devoted to the old men of the *shtetl* signing up for the "shock brigade"—as it is steeped in Stalinist propaganda. "There's a definite strain of the native Jewish sense of humor," *Variety* would observe. In the role of Tsale, Solomon Mikhoels, who uses a mysterious mixture of Russian and Yiddish, is delightful. Indeed, the fractured language he speaks is virtually his own—interspersed with chuckling, clucking, and the continual humming of a *nign* [a religious melody with no words].

Mikhoels constructs his persona out of stylized bits of business. It's an overwhelming tactile performance, as precise as ballet. In one comic throwaway, Mikhoels picks up a handy bust of Karl Marx, stares at it, and reflectively strokes his own beard. David Gutman, who plays Nosn, is a solid proletarian type who looks more like Mikhoel's brother than his son. As Nosn's wife, Elena Kashnitskaya is also something of a comedienne whose constant confusion about the date (she is always asking when it will be Sabbath) is a joke on the Five Year's Plan's "continuous-production week" of four workdays followed by one day of rest.

Given the light mood, it seems appropriate that a circus provides the site for the competition between Nosn and the Soviet bricklayer. (According to John Scott, the circus was Magnitogorsk's most popular form of entertainment. Although "the performance was of third-rate Barnum and Bailey quality" and "occasional attempts to tie up the program with the construction of socialism in one country or with plan fulfillment in the plant tended to be ludicrous," seats had to be booked well in advance.) Despite the absence of a harsh moral or positive hero, *The Return of Nathan Becker* fulfills the Soviet formula for socialist realism, "a combination of the most matter-of-fact, everyday reality with the most heroic prospects."

True to its genre, the movie ends with a hymn to labor. "We must win. We will win," the chorus sings. "Long live the day of victory!" Meanwhile, the camera peers up at happy Nosn perched on the scaffolding beside old Tsale and the ever beaming Jim. "Here the workers work not only with their hands but also with their hearts," the American rhapsodizes. "And also with their heads," his father adds. In a final gag that recalls the exercises of the Institute, Tsale instructs Jim in the fine points of his ubiquitous *nign*, complete with appropriate hand gestures.

Excerpted from: J. Hoberman, *Bridge of Light: Yiddish Film between Two Worlds*, 170–77. Updated and expanded ed. Hanover, NH: University Press of New England, 2010.

    Background: http://www.friends-partners.org/partners/beyond-the-pale/english/44.html; http://www.friends-partners.org/partners/beyond-the-pale/english/45.html.

Bibliography

Dennen, Leon. *Where the Ghetto Ends: Jews in Soviet Russia*. New York: Alfred H. King, 1934.

Estraikh, Gennady. *In Harness: Yiddish Writers' Romance with Communism*. Syracuse, NY: Syracuse University Press, 2005.

Levin, Nora. *The Jews in the Soviet Union since 1917: The Paradox of Survival*. New York: New York University Press, 1988.

Lyons, Eugene. *Moscow Carousel*. New York: Knopf, 1935.

Scott, John. *Behind the Urals: An American Worker in Russia's City of Steel*. Boston: Houghton Mifflin, 1942.

Shneer, David. *Yiddish and the Creation of Soviet Jewish Culture, 1918–1930*. New York: Cambridge University Press, 2004.

Shternshis, Anna. *Soviet and Kosher: Jewish Popular Culture in the Soviet Union, 1923–1939*. Bloomington: Indiana University Press, 2006.

PART FIVE

The Holocaust and Its Repercussions

18. Muffled Music

LAWRENCE BARON

The Harmonists (*Comedian Harmonists*),
directed by Joseph Vilsmaier [A]
Austria and Germany, 1997

Since the reunification of Germany in 1990, German directors often have dramatized love stories between Jewish and German characters set in the Weimar Republic or Third Reich as a way to reconstitute the public memory of the Jewish contribution to German culture and history. Recent films that focus on positive German-Jewish interactions in these bygone eras are called heritage films. Some German film scholars accuse heritage films of divorcing ordinary Germans from Nazism's assault on the past bonds of artistic collaboration, friendship, and love between Germans and Jews. According to Lutz Koepnick, conventional melodramas about how the Third Reich's racism stigmatized personal relations between gentiles and Jews "produce nostalgia for successful moments of German Jewish symbiosis" and idealize pluralism without confronting the Holocaust. I contend that because the directors of these films assume the audience already knows that antisemitic discrimination led to genocide, they tragically highlight how these cordial and intimate ties were destined to be torn asunder by the expulsion or the execution of the Jewish part-

ner. When genocide is part of a nation's historical legacy, nostalgia, as the joke goes, is not what it used to be. Instead, it serves as a painful reminder of a shameful past.

Most of these love stories blend different genres. Genre mixing increases marketability by fitting a movie's plot into several narrative formulas that appeal to different segments of the viewing public. *The Harmonists* amalgamates many genres. It has been categorized as a comedy, a show biz biopic, a musical, a buddy movie, and a love triangle.

Publicity for *The Harmonists* varied from country to country according to what its distributors thought would have the greatest audience appeal. In Germany, the poster for the movie catered to the nostalgia of older Germans and the historical curiosity of younger Germans by advertising the film with the tag line, "A legend returns." The publicity logo in the United States evoked comparisons with *Cabaret* (1972) by revealing the face of a woman tipping a fedora over her eyes and looking very much like Liza Minnelli in her role as Sally Bowles. The tag line sold it as a buddy movie about friendship. The connection with *Cabaret* was not publicity hype, since production designer Rolf Zehetbauer created the sets for both films to capture the ambience of Berlin during the Weimar Republic. The French poster superimposed swastikas cascading down onto bars of music. At the bottom of the poster, the lead actress walks between her two lovers as they rush with the other members of the group to stay one step ahead of the Nazi avalanche. In visual terms, Nazism buries both love and music.

The striking parallels between *The Harmonists* and *Cabaret* invite a broader consideration of the usage of music as an element in Holocaust feature films. *The Producers* (1968, 2005) relied on the incongruity of a Broadway musical about Hitler as a humorous paradox intended to guarantee the box-office failure of the show. *Cabaret*'s nightclub songs parallel the disintegration of Germany's embattled democracy during the late 1920s and early 1930s. For example, Nazi thugs beat a political opponent as women mud-wrestle to the cheers of an audience. The angelic looking and sounding Hitler Youth who sings "Tomorrow Belongs to Us" at a rustic beer garden epitomizes Aryan purity and solidarity in sharp contrast to Berlin's squalor and the sexual kinkiness of the Kit-Kat Club patrons. Assuring one's fame by catering to the musical tastes of the leaders of the Third Reich provides the motivation for collaboration in *Lili Marlene* (1981). Music emerges as a key to survival in *Playing for Time* (1980) and a sublimated form of resistance in *Swing Kids* (1993).

Like the *Swing Kids*, the German crooners in *The Harmonists* simply like the instrumentation and rhythms of American jazz. They do not create their fusion of vocal harmonization and syncopation as a political statement. Nazi ideologues, however, perceived jazz as a seductive Black and Jewish import that contaminated traditional Aryan culture. Donning tuxedos to entertain an elegantly dressed audience, the five singers and pianist who comprise the Comedian Harmonists sing the ditty *Veronica, Spring Has Sprung*, which abounds in witty double-entendres. The movie flashes back to 1927, when Harry Frommermann was unemployed. Harry is infatuated with Erna, who works at a music shop. Together they listen to the latest American recording by The Revellers, whose catchy arrangements of "Negro music" inspire Harry to form a German version of the group. Harry puts on a yarmulke to visit his parent's graves and confess to them that he loves a "shiksa" [a gentile woman].

As Harry conducts rehearsals for the group, he recruits a bass opera singer, Robert Biberti, who introduces him to the pianist Erwin Bootz; two tenors, Erich Colin and the Bulgarian Ari Leschnikoff; and the Polish Jewish baritone Roman Cycowski. Sticking to the clichés of the rags-to-riches show business saga, Vilsmaier endows each character with a distinctive trait, like Ari's womanizing or Bootz's oversleeping, and follows the success story of the group. The rhythm of the tune they perform at their first audition is so slow that Harry's agent dismisses it as "funeral parlor music." Their artistic breakthrough comes when the bickering members of the group are on the verge of splitting up. In a stroke of genius, Bootz quickens the tempo of a Duke Ellington composition, and the singers improvise the sounds of the instruments in a big band orchestra. The next audition assures them a booking, which catapults them to fame. The impresario who hires them articulates the movie's theme: "The darker the times, the brighter the theater lights."

As the group revels in its success, the first omen of Nazi antisemitism disrupts their celebration. Hans, a former boyfriend of Erna's, taunts her for hanging out with a Jew. Roman retorts, "I'm a Jew and proud of it." Erna defiantly kisses Harry. Two years pass. It is now May 1930. On the radio, Hitler denounces the chaos caused by the Weimar Republic's political factionalism. The Comedian Harmonists' latest hit advises the young to enjoy themselves because "the happy days will soon be gone." The Nazis vandalize the music shop. Its Jewish owners shake their heads in disbelief and erase the swastikas and slogans painted on their windows. They believe Germany is a land of "law and order and will stay that way." Harry quips, "The teacher asks Moshe, 'What race do the Jews belong to?' 'The Semites,' Moshe answers. 'And what race do the Germans belong to? 'The antisemites,' Moshe replies."

Personal rifts in the group mirror the political polarization of the Weimar Republic. Robert courts Erna and invites her to one of the group's concerts. Afterward, Robert accuses Harry of being an egomaniac who hams it up too much on stage. Taking umbrage at this insult, Harry disputes it until Robert reveals that Erna had confided to him that Harry only talked about his musical career and never inquired about her university studies. The overall tone of the film, however, remains light. When Roman proposes to his gentile girlfriend, she agrees to convert to Judaism. The ensuing Jewish wedding scene with festive klezmer music diverts attention away from the looming threat of Nazism. Indeed, when German focus groups previewed the movie, this scene proved to be the film's most popular one, particularly among viewers who were under twenty. The revival of klezmer music in reunified Germany has been viewed as cultural atonement for the annihilation of European Jewry and as an expression of the receptivity progressive Germans want to exhibit toward minority groups in the Berlin Republic.

The movie abruptly shifts to October of 1933. Hitler now holds the reins of power. Nazi strongarm tactics are symbolized by a boxing match that Robert attends with Erna. He professes his love to her and suggests she move into his apartment where she will be safer. The Reich Music Association summons Harry and Robert to order the group to dismiss its three Jewish members and to stop singing songs composed by Jews. The two

are amazed to learn that according to Nazi racial criteria, even Erich is Jewish despite his conversion to Christianity. Yet the Nazi official also asks them to autograph an album for his nephew, who is a big fan of their music. For the first time, the trappings of the Nazi dictatorship are omnipresent. Swastika flags are hung in the halls where civil servants greet each other with the Hitler salute. Storm Troopers ransack the music store, and the police advise its Jewish owners to "disappear." Robert fights back while Harry stands helplessly by because a Storm Trooper holds a knife under his neck. Erna exits with the bloodied but undaunted Robert.

Esther Fuchs claims this scene reinforces traditional male stereotypes of gentiles as virile and Jews as cerebral. Lutz Koepnick charges that Vilsmaier "encodes the male Jew's sexuality as muted, mediated, and decidedly non-aggressive." While this contrast between Robert and Harry exists, a more plausible reason for Harry's passivity is that the Nazis consider his Jewish ancestry a mortal threat to Aryan supremacy and point the knife at him rather than at their fellow racial comrade, Robert, who is merely defending his girlfriend.

Still the members of the group believe that their status as international stars will shield them from further harassment. This assessment of their situation seems validated when Julius Streicher, the notorious antisemitic propagandist, summons them for a command performance. The sextet sings the ideologically innocuous, "I have an uncle in Kalumba where politics have been forgotten." Streicher invites the group to his home and requests they sing a German folk song popular among Nazi supporters. They comply, but Harry becomes nauseous and refuses to resume singing the politically tainted tune.

Just as the group's future appears bleak, they

receive an offer to perform in New York. Vilsmaier depicts the United States as a utopia of racial tolerance. The antics of the group there replicate scenes of the Beatles frolicking on their American tour in a *Hard Day's Night*. With American flags rippling in the wind and the Statue of Liberty in the background, the group performs on a US Navy battleship. Despite the segregation of black sailors in this period, the camera captures the faces of African Americans listening intently among the crew. On the ferry ride back to the city, the group debates whether they should remain in America. Harry argues they should stay: "It is not about me; it is about us! Us Jews!" Robert thinks Harry has a "persecution complex" and envies the relationship between Erna and him. Nevertheless, Robert confesses that he is actually worried if his elderly mother could adjust to the move. When five of the six decide to return, Harry overcomes his qualms and joins them.

Streicher grants the group permission to perform one concert before disbanding. Swastika banners dwarf the stage, and a few members of the audience walk out when informed that three of the Comedian Harmonists are Jews. Harry insists that the concert is for their fans. Their last song expresses their realization that fame provides them no refuge from fanaticism. "Our fairy tale is over. Give me one last kiss goodbye." Erna sobs throughout the number, distraught about the prospect of never seeing Harry again. The group receives a standing ovation. The camera alternates between views of the gargantuan swastika banners and the enthralled audience. Harry dutifully visits the graves of his parents to the accompaniment of a clarinet playing a mournful klezmer melody. He carries his parrot's cage and resembles Alan Bates seeking asylum from the carnage of World War I in the final scene of *King of Hearts* (1966).

As the group's Jewish members ready themselves to leave, Erna runs to the train station platform and melodramatically declares, "I belong with Harry." The closing shot of a train carrying the exiles to Switzerland evokes associations with transports that soon will shuttle Jews to death camps. The camera assumes the perspective of the Germans who stay behind. In my opinion, this vantage point heightens the sense that Germany was impoverished by the banishment of talented Jewish artists. Koepnick contends that the ending implies that Jews and Germans suffered equally under Nazism: "What makes audiences weep is not that Hitler's Germany exterminated the Jews of Europe in the name of the German nation, but rather that the Nazis betrayed the nation by prohibiting Germans to love their Jewish compatriots."

The postscript informs the audience of what became of the members of the group. The Aryan and Jewish members formed separate singing groups, both of which broke up in 1941. Bootz divorced his Jewish wife and married the daughter of a Nazi sculpture. Robert became one of the designers of the V-2 rocket. Ari returned to Bulgaria. Erich became an eyeglass frame manufacturer. Harry and Erna got married, but divorced in 1952. Harry obtained American citizenship and entertained Allied troops during World War II. Roman became a cantor and settled in San Francisco with his wife. The audience learns that the group's music has remained popular.

Vilsmaier avoided being too controversial in his portrayal of the rise and fall of the Comedian Harmonists. A renewed interest in their music began two decades earlier, with the broadcast of Eberhard Fechner's television documentary about the group. In 1988 Fechner authored a book on the subject. *Autumn Milk* (1988) and *Stalingrad* (1996), Vilsmaier's previous movies about the Nazi period, respectively depicted Nazism as a movement with little support among German peasants and the plight of German soldiers as cannon fodder for Hitler's grandiose military ambitions. Films like *Stalingrad*, *Sleeper's Brother* (1995), and *The Harmonists* earned Vilsmaier the record as the most commercially successful German director of the nineties. Since then, he has directed two more historical films about the Holocaust: *Leo and Claire* (2001), about the trial and execution of a Jewish man for having an affair with a younger female German employee, and *The Last Train* (2006), about the last transport of Jews deported from Berlin to Auschwitz.

The Harmonists won many of the major Bavarian and German film awards for 1998. In interviews about the picture, Vilsmaier admitted that he subordinated the Nazi theme to focus on the musical legacy of the sextet. He marveled that the members of the group were so "totally apolitical" that they themselves were unaware of who among them was Jewish. Ultimately, the movie is about how Hitler's policies hurt German culture. As Jürgen Büscher, who scripted *The Harmonists* and *Stalingrad*, commented, "The film wants to express the sorrow of what it meant—and what it still means—for Germany that the country's best creative talents were persecuted, suppressed, driven away, and finally murdered."

Excerpted from: Lawrence Baron, *Projecting the Holocaust into the Present: The Changing Focus of Contemporary Holocaust Cinema* (Lanham, MD: Rowman and Littlefield, 2005).

Background: http://www.comedian-harmonists.com/?lang=en&open=history; http://www2.facinghistory.org/campus/weimar.nsf/howtousethissite?OpenFrameSet.

Bibliography

Friedlander, Saul. *Nazi Germany and the Jews: The Years of Persecution 1933–1939*. New York: Harper Perennial, 1998.

Gay, Peter. *Weimar Culture: The Outsider as Insider*. New York: Harper and Row, 1968.

Gruber, Ruth Ellen. *Virtually Jewish: Reinventing Jewish Culture in Europe*. Berkeley: University of California Press, 2002.

Kater, Michael H. *Different Drummers: Jazz in the Culture of Nazi Germany*. New York: Oxford University Press, 1992.

Koepnick, Lutz. "'Honor Your German Masters': History, Memory, and National Identity in Vilsmaier's *Comedian Harmonists*." In *Light Motives: German Popular Film in Perspective*, edited by Randall Halle and Margaret McCarthy, 340–75. Detroit: Wayne State University Press, 2003.

———. "Reframing the Past: Heritage Cinema and Holocaust in the 1990s." *New German Critique* 87 (Fall 2002): 47–70.

Laqueur, Walter. *Weimar: A Cultural History, 1918–1933*. New York: Putnam, 1974.

Niewyk. Donald. *The Jews of Weimar Germany*. Baton Rouge: Louisiana State University Press, 1980.

Steinweis, Alan. E. *Art, Ideology, and Economics in Nazi Germany: The Reich Chambers of Music, Theatre, and the Visual Arts*. Chapel Hill: University of North Carolina Press, 1993.

19. "In Italy There Has Never Been Anti-Semitism"

The Garden of the Finzi-Continis

GIACOMO LICHTNER

The Garden of the Finzi-Continis
(*Il giardino dei Finzi-Contini*),
directed by Vittorio De Sica [A]
Italy and West Germany, 1970

Elie Wiesel has said of De Sica's *The Garden of the Finzi-Continis* that "it succeeds in moving us without falling into sentimentality." Adapted from Giorgio Bassani's novel, the film relies greatly upon symbolism and metaphor to portray the decadence of a class and investigate collective behavior. Set in Ferrara between 1938 and 1944, it is the story of a young middle-class Jewish university student, Giorgio, who is in love with Micòl Finzi-Contini. She belongs to an exclusive and exclusivist Jewish family that lives in what De Sica described as "a bourgeois and aristocratic climate of egoism and comfort." The love story is not destined for a happy ending, both because Micòl prefers the gentile worker Malnate, and because she will be deported and murdered. Hints of incest between Micòl and her brother, Alberto; questions over his sexual orientation; and the Giorgio-Micòl-Malnate triangle come across as pretentiously provocative. They are in keeping with the cultural concerns and artistic productions of that time; yet they also explain Bassani's rejection of De Sica's adaptation of his book.

Despite its romanticism and aestheticism, which sometimes spill into oversimplification and rhetoric, the film succeeds in addressing the historical events that constitute the unique context of this story of adolescence and love. The personal relationships are played out against the background of fascist Italy: the 1938 anti-Semitic laws, the start of the war, and Italy's first defeats, ending with the deportation of the Jews of Ferrara. The recreation of the historical setting, though by no means free of contemporary interpretations, is what separates *The Garden* from other films of the period. As Annette Insdorf notes, De Sica's neorealist roots are as evident in his treatment of Jewish patricians as they were in his portrayal of impoverished Italians in postwar movies like *The Bicycle Thief* and *Shoeshine*.

De Sica directly attacks gentile and Jewish complacency over the rise of fascism, and the Nazi persecution of the Jews. The gentile bourgeoisie is epitomized by the director of the public library, who regretfully expels Giorgio by explaining that he has "a family [to feed]." Giorgio remonstrates that "the whole of Italy has a family [to feed]." The Jewish middle class is represented by Giorgio's father, a card-carrying member of the Fascist Party who, even after the racial laws, excuses Mussolini's actions with the confidence that "Mussolini is not Hitler." Giorgio accuses his father of "not having raised a finger," when fascism persecuted other people. De Sica was fascinated by these characters, though he understood their situation as bourgeoisie better than their predicament as Jews: "This is what drew me to the book. Italian Jews were completely unaware. They could not bring themselves to believe what was threatening them." Perhaps he unfairly criticizes them for lack of foresight, but he levels his critique of them as members of the bourgeoisie who had welcomed Mussolini's law and order.

The Garden is as much about the decadence of a social class as it is about the persecution of Italian Jews. De Sica centers his film around the Finzi-Continis' magnificent garden—quiet, green, and luxurious. The walled private grounds; extensive library where Giorgio is symbolically imprisoned; the tennis courts, where a fictitious harmony reigns, are all at once a defense, a hiding place, and a prison. The Finzi-Continis deliberately chose their isolation, but it is one motivated by class, not religion or political discrimination.

Their Judaism is therefore passive. It seems to be little more than the reason why they are persecuted. They are Italians before being Jews; they feel closer to members of their class or profession than to those of their religious community; they respect their religion out of convention rather than devotion. With occasional scenes of domestic and public religiosity, however, De Sica manages to capture these people's way of being Jews. In this respect too, his film has scant company in the history of prior Italian Holocaust films.

De Sica's characterization of the Finzi-Continis is faithful both to history and Bassani's memoirs. Most Northern Italian middle-class Jews of the 1930s were indeed completely integrated into Italian society. Bassani wrote: "That we were Jews still counted fairly little in our case. For what on earth did the word Jew mean? It derived from the fact that our families, not through choice, but thanks to tradition belonged to the same religious rite." Other Northern Italian Jewish authors such as Primo Levi and Natalia Ginzburg have also expressed their memory of being well-assimilated Italian Jews along similar lines.

The relations between characters are played according to the rules of the class system. Giorgio's father tells him to forget Micòl because she is "a class apart" or "of a different social class." At the same time, he suggests that this was the very reason his son was attracted to her: she was different and unattainable. In a similar way, Micòl despises and at the same time is attracted by Malnate, the gentile factory worker. Her interest is strongly determined by his being a member of the working class: "too industrial, too Communist, and too hairy." Insdorf suggests that his class is even reflected in his name: "Malnate: badly or lowly born."

The film's Jewish characters can achieve a collective Jewish identity only when the class distinction is removed by their arrest. Still, this unity is tainted by their inability to identify themselves as a people beyond geographical boundaries: in the classroom where they are being held, Giorgio's father comforts Micòl by stating that "at least we are together, us Jews of Ferrara." His idea of unity is contradicted by the painful implication that Giorgio's family can survive only through its separation: his brother had left for France before the war, and Giorgio himself, warned by a friend, manages to escape with his mother and younger sister.

While the emphasis on class and personal relations unequivocally places *The Garden* in the 1970s, the film's apparent willingness to describe the persecution of Italy's Jews as an Italian phenomenon, rather than a purely German one or a universal crime against humanity, puts it well ahead of its time. In acknowledging this persecution as an outgrowth of generally accepted anti-Semitism, De Sica's film constitutes an important breakthrough within Italian cinema dealing with the Holocaust. Whether or not there was a deliberate decision to "Italianize" the Holocaust, this remains a fundamental virtue of the film. Nevertheless, a very significant question mark remains over De Sica's approach as his comments from 1971 testify: "In Italy there has never been anti-Semitism. In this domain the fascists have been merely the imitators of the Nazis. And these arrests of Jews took place without the least violence, indeed with great courtesy, which is the height of cruelty."

This statement confirms the ambiguity of Italy's relationship to the Shoah in the 1970s. On the one hand, the film uncompromisingly portrays the rise of anti-Jewish feeling in Italy and the Italian role in the genocide, specifically depicting Italian militiamen—and not German troops or SS—carrying out the arrest of the city's Jews. On the other hand, the film's director facilely dismissed Italian anti-Semitism as copying Germany's, thus reiterating one of the most popular explanations for the Italian racial laws.

At the end of the film, the policeman arresting Micòl calls her Mícol in accordance with fascist rules for pronunciation. This significant and understated detail reinforces the message that the anti-Jewish persecution depended not on the actions of a single person, but on a climate of xenophobia and anti-Semitism, inextricably linked to fascist nationalism. Along with several other anti-Semitic incidents in the film, it implies either that Italy was predisposed to anti-Semitic sentiment or that anti-Semitism was opportunistic—revealing that if Italians were not genuinely racist, they were at least not *brava gente* [decent people]. Yet De Sica denied the existence of Italian anti-Semitism. It is hard to make sense of the film in light of his words.

Analyzing the reception of *The Garden* in both Italy and France illuminates how contemporaries reconciled these contradictory elements. It is almost impossible to establish what contemporary moviegoers thought of De Sica's representation of wartime Italy, but this particular aspect was almost entirely ignored by Italian critics. The film, however, was commercially and critically successful. It garnered many awards, including the Golden Bear at the Berlin Film Festival in 1971 and an Academy Award for Best Foreign Language Film in 1972.

At the same time, *The Garden* was widely dismissed as a mediocre film. As a psychological portrayal of ambiguous relations, it seemed both conceptually and artistically inferior to Luchino Visconti's works; as an interpretation of the country's history, it fell short of the merciless criticism of Bertolucci's *The Spider's Strategem* and *The Conformist*, both released in the same year. Only as an adaptation of a respected literary work did it attract much attention, though Bassani's disavowal hurt the film's reception. De Sica's fame assured the film a high profile, and yet proved a disadvantage: following a decade of many uninspired directorial and casting choices, he had come to be seen by many as not politically engaged enough for the 1970s, or in any case, past his prime.

Despite the fact that fourteen years had passed since his last neorealist film, *The Roof* (1956), De Sica's reputation affected the reception of *The Garden*. An Italian newspaper hailed De Sica's "rehabilitation" in 1959 for his starring performance in Rossellini's *General della Rovere* but drew a comparison with his previous works. At the premier of *The Garden* in Rome, the Communist daily, *L'Unità*, called his effort "a return to the dignity, if not the coherent inspiration of his best years." On the same day, *Il Popolo*, the Christian Democratic Party paper, deemed the final sequences of *The Garden* a return to the "the best De Sica, his neo-realist tone."

In fact, the film's finale is also its least realistic section, as the scene of the arrests is followed by slow-motion flashbacks to the Finzi-Contini siblings playing tennis, dressed in white and bathed in a striking bright light, accompanied by a lyrical voice singing the names of the extermination sites: Auschwitz, Majdanek, Treblinka. What reviewers did was pay tribute to the parts they liked by calling them "neorealist," even though they clearly were not. While neorealism had long been dead and filmmakers experimented with different styles, critics in 1970 continued to use the word "neorealist" as a term of general praise in reference to the immediate postwar film school. This manifested the privileged place neorealism held in postwar Italian culture, carrying the connotations of aesthetically beautiful, thematically important, and ideologically sound.

The controversy between De Sica and Bassani diverted attention from the film's content and tone. The author took the film's producers to court and dissociated his name from it, though the judge allowed the film to be distributed under its original title. On the day the film premiered in Milan, newspapers reported the judge's decision to add a disclaimer to the film indicating it was only loosely based on the book. On the same day, an article reported that Israeli Prime Minister Golda Meir had praised the film for its artistic and moral virtues after watching it at the Jerusalem Film Festival. The same article mentioned that an Israeli paper simultaneously had published an essay by Bassani entitled, "The Betrayal of My Garden."

De Sica's film does differ from Bassani's novel in both detail and overall tone. In the novel, the memory of the time, people, and places of Bassani's youth plays as central a role as the events he recounts. The lingering sadness of the memory of the loss makes it superfluous to delve deeper into the circumstances surrounding it. De Sica sacrificed the subtlety of the relationship between narrator, witness, and character by changing the book's narrative structure, mixing Giorgio's reminiscences with those of an omniscient narrator. He struggled to adapt the text into the conventional narrative structure of a film. In the novel, Micòl neither returns Giorgio's love nor betrays him, denying the filmmaker the traditional outcomes of romantic entanglements. Consequently, De Sica added, cut, and changed the plot freely.

He invented the secret affair between Micòl and Malnate, who are caught in the act by Giorgio; he transformed the closeness of the two siblings into a relationship with more than a hint of incest; he added anti-Semitic episodes and roundups to give a sense of time passing and to allow the tension to mount to its climax with the arrest of the Finzi-Continis and Giorgio's father, whereas the latter had escaped capture in the novel.

Nevertheless, De Sica's film should not be assessed merely as an adaptation of a literary text, but rather to address the question of what the film says and how. This is precisely what contemporaries were unable or unwilling to do. Only one Roman daily paid any attention to De Sica's representation of wartime Italy and the anti-Jewish legislation. It noted that Italians took the Finzi-Contini family away. Instead of commenting any further on this significant detail, the critic simply confirmed its historical accuracy. Bassani's novel says nothing about the circumstances in which these arrests took place, and, thus the filmmaker's representation is at best the result of speculation.

Other reviewers ignored the theme of Italian history altogether and focused on aesthetics and acting, narrative structure, and the judicial controversy. Discussion of the ambiguity of Micòl's relationship with her brother and between the latter and Malnate outweighed analysis of class relations and political struggle. A renowned critic contended that the "suspicion of incest and abnormal friendships" contributed to the film's "languid atmosphere, foretelling the approaching catastrophe." Much was made of the film's commercial success, which allegedly was achieved at the expense of fidelity to the novel and good taste. Both French and Italian reviewers referred to the gratuitous nude shot of Micòl and criticized the acting.

Why then was the theme of Italian history so

blatantly ignored? An initial explanation may be found in Italian cinema's preference for using historical settings for its stories. From its beginnings to the resurgence of films about the Second World War in the early 1960s, historical recreations had been a successful genre. In general, these films did not require prior historical knowledge or curiosity on the part of the audience to be entertaining, nor did they aspire to comment on the historical period in which their stories were set. For example, the immensely popular Roman mythology films comprised about 10 percent of all Italian films between 1957 and 1964. In these films, which did not hesitate to feature Hercules alongside Zorro and Genghis Khan, history was either distorted or remote. At other times, history was merely an excuse for topical criticism. If Italian historical films traditionally had an escapist or presentist flavor, perhaps there was no reason for *The Garden* to be any different.

It can be argued that in the politically charged post-1968 environment, reviewers and the public immediately recognized that the film was more about class than about fascism. They may have believed that De Sica had made a romantic melodrama set against a background of individual and collective tragedy, without any intent to reevaluate the fascist period in Italian history. The director's failure to present his film as anything but an exploration of youth, love, and class relations reinforced such assumptions.

Finally, the standard interpretation of that history, in which the persecution of Italy's Jews was viewed as entirely the work of the Germans, had become too deeply rooted to be shaken by a subtle, and perhaps unwitting, voice to the contrary. While all three of these explanations have some validity, the last one is the most convincing. The 1972 Italian response to the television broadcast

of Ophüls's *The Sorrow and the Pity*, a documentary about the extent of French collaboration in the implementation of Nazi policies, indicated the common wisdom that stressed German guilt and minimized local complicity continued to affect the analysis of even those few works that dared to challenge it.

Several other elements confirm this explanation. The reviewers failed to draw any basic conclusions about Italian responsibility for the persecution of the Jews from the film's content. Even the one paper that mentioned the arrests by Italian personnel did not explore the question about what this signified, or attempt to place the incident within the wider corpus of Italian films about the Second World War. Many reviewers considered the film an indictment of Jewish passivity, while neglecting the passivity of the Italian population at large. One described Giorgio's father as "a man who naively has deluded himself that he can collaborate with the regime" but overlooked the repeated acts of Italian cowardliness and anti-Semitism. This reviewer's criticism of conformism did not target a social class, as De Sica did, but only the Jews.

Conversely, French newspapers did remark on *The Garden*'s representation of Italian fascism and anti-Semitism. One states that the subject of the film was "the slow and inexorable rise, between 1938 and 1943, of the persecution of Jews in the conditions specific to Italy," and considered it "a testimony on this phenomenon and period in question." Another praised De Sica's "documentarian rigor" in the representation of "fascism and its corollary, anti-Semitism." In stark contrast with Italian reviewers, the French critics uniformly touched on this subject.

Yet the French reviewers also persisted in viewing anti-Semitism as alien to Italy and Italian history. One critic maintained anti-Semitism had been "imposed by fascism onto a country which did not know the very meaning of the word." This contradiction provides proof of the durability of this version of the events. The image of the decent Italian people had spread in France and elsewhere: decades of self-deprecating Italian war films—simultaneously mocking the Italians' lack of discipline, organization, and military courage, and glorifying their compassion, charity, and human warmth—had played their part in this process.

Finally, the persistence of this particular vision of the country's history is supported by De Sica's own statement about Italian anti-Semitism. The apparent contradiction between his film and his subsequent comment can ultimately be explained by the fact that the Italian narrative of innocence had been so pervasive and persuasive in his mind and in those of his audience that the two visions had ceased to be incompatible.

Abridged from: Giacomo Lichtner, *Film and the Shoah in France and Italy* (London: Valentine Mitchell, 2008).

Background: http://www.ushmm.org/wlc/en/article.php?ModuleId=10005455.

Source: Giorgio Bassani, *The Garden of the Finzi-Continis*, translated by Isabel Quigly (New York: Atheneum, 1965).

Bibliography

Curle, Howard, and Stephen Snyder, eds. *Vittorio De Sica: Contemporary Perspectives*. Toronto: University of Toronto Press, 2000.

De Felice, Renzo. *The Jews in Fascist Italy: A History*. Translated by Robert L. Miller. New York: Enigma, 2001.

Hughes, H. Stuart. *Prisoners of Hope: The Silver Age of Italian Jews, 1924–1974*. Cambridge: Harvard University Press, 1983.

Insdorf, Annette. *Indelible Shadows: Film and the Holo-caust*. 3rd ed. New York: Cambridge University Press, 2003.

Marcus, Millicent. *Filmmaking by the Book: Italian Cinema and Literary Adaptation*. Baltimore, MD: Johns Hopkins University Press, 1993.

———. *Italian Film in the Shadow of Auschwitz*. Toronto: University of Toronto Press, 2007.

Michaelis, Meir. *Mussolini and the Jews: German-Italian Relations and the Jewish Question in Italy, 1922–1945*. Oxford: Clarendon Press of Oxford University Press, 1978.

Sarfatti, Michele. *The Jews in Mussolini's Italy: From Equality to Persecution*. Translated by John Tedeschi and Anne C. Tedeschi. Madison: University of Wisconsin Press, 2006.

Schneider, Marilyn. *Vengeance of the Victim: History and Symbol in Giorgio Bassani's Fiction*. Minneapolis: University of Minnesota Press, 1986.

Zuccotti, Susan. *The Italians and the Holocaust: Persecution, Rescue, and Survival*. New York: Basic, 1987.

20. "All Men Are Jews"

Tragic Transcendence in Kadár's *The Shop on Main Street*

JEFFREY SAPERSTEIN

The Shop on Main Street (*Obchod na Korze*), directed by Ján Kadár and Elmar Klos [A] Czechoslovakia, 1965

Like many films of the Czech New Wave, *The Shop on Main Street* blends comic and tragic elements in a disarming fashion. The film begins as a leisurely paced, gently ironic observation of a henpecked carpenter, Tono Britko, who is appointed "Aryan Controller" of a small button shop owned by an elderly Jewish widow, Mrs. Lautmann. As the narrative proceeds, however, it becomes an increasingly urgent study of an ordinary man caught up by forces he does not understand.

Much of the film's disturbing power is a result of dramatic irony. In 1965, when Ján Kadár, in collaboration with Elmar Klos, made *The Shop on Main Street*, the shock of the Holocaust was beginning to register on the world's consciousness. Taking for granted the viewers' awareness of what lies just outside the film's frame, Kadár can afford to be suggestive and understated. We know, as the characters within the world of the film do not, that the Aryanization program in this quaint village will lead to Auschwitz and Treblinka.

But if it is the force of history that will doom Tono Britko, it is also the choices necessitated by history that will grant him a measure of freedom. Although its focus is a particular moment in time, *The Shop on Main Street* clarifies a timeless human crisis: within the prison of our immediate circumstances, we have the potential to choose our actions freely and thus define who we are. This paradox is central to tragedy. In its sense of fatality, its portrayal of suffering and guilt, and especially its emphasis on moral responsibility, *The Shop on Main Street* evokes a tragic sense of life. Though Tono Britko is no King Lear, he too achieves a painful self-knowledge, which is his salvation. As Tono's false identity as "Aryan Controller" is stripped away, his true identity as a "Jew" is made plain. The narrative forces this awareness upon him.

Tono Britko is an appealing character from the very start. His long-nosed, melancholy face gives him a saintly, yet somehow comical, expression. And his ungainly mutt, Brandy, is equally sad-faced. On the soundtrack, Tono's rambles through town are accompanied by a slightly off-key melody for strings. Henpecked, not particularly bright, a bit of a drinker, Tono is like some

Ida Kaminska (as Mrs. Lautmann) doesn't understand the warning Jozef Kroner (as Tono) is giving her. From *The Shop on Main Street* (1965), directed by Ján Kadár and Elmar Klos. CRITERION COLLECTION/ PHOTOFEST

Slovakian Rip Van Winkle: harmless, likeable, out of touch.

As the narrative unfolds, however, Kadár will not allow such a complacent reading of the protagonist. There are no innocents in the world of the film: naïveté itself has its price. The creation of a Nazi puppet state in Slovakia has forced ordinary citizens to declare themselves as either "patriots" (that is, collaborators) or to be labeled "white Jews" (gentiles who protect, assist, or befriend Jews). At the outset of the film, Tono has refused to participate in the Guard's project of building a great tower in the city square, their monument to Fascist rule. His motives are not political: he holds a grudge against his brother-in-law, Marcus, the head of the local militia, who cheated Tono out of his wife's inheritance. In his unwillingness to salute the Fascist regime, Tono is already something of an outcast. In effect, he is a "Jew" though he doesn't realize it. In the remainder of the film, he will be forced to embrace rather than evade this hidden identity.

Despite his reluctance to join the Fascists, Tono is vulnerable to his wife's desires for status and respectability. In a crucial scene early in the film, Marcus and his wife make an unexpected visit to Tono's home. Ready to make amends, Marcus comes laden with gifts: a string of fat sausages, a pearl necklace for Tono's wife, a gold cigarette case for Tono, and, most importantly, the official notice of Tono's new position as "Aryan Controller" of Mrs. Lautmann's shop, a position that his wife assumes will bring wealth. After all, Mrs. Lautmann, as a Jew, must have a treasure hidden away somewhere. Soothing his conscience with alcohol, Tono accepts the gifts, telling Marcus, "You're calling the tune now." During this scene, Tono holds a tumbler up to his eye and, in a memorable point-of-view shot, we see the image of the others fractured by the multifaceted glass. In the same sequence, Tono's own image is comically distorted when he gazes into the shiny mirror of the gold cigarette case. Thus, Tono's passive complicity in the Aryanization program not only distorts his perception of reality; it also warps his self-image. *The Shop on Main Street* is structured to make Tono realize to the fullest extent who he is and to conjoin the splintered pieces of his vision.

Nominally the "Aryan Controller," Tono soon discovers that he is actually in the employ of the Jews of the community. The great fortune his wife has conjured up proves to be an illusion.

Mrs. Lautmann's button shop is a relic of the past, occasionally doing a brisk business but largely empty of profit. In fact, unbeknown to her, Mrs. Lautmann is being supported by a Jewish Aid Society. Now that Tono has become "Aryan Controller," the Society has no choice but to pay him off. As Mr. Blau, the treasurer of the fund, says, while handing Tono his first cut, "The Lord has chosen you to protect Mrs. Lautmann." These words are spoken with an irony born of desperation at the new turn of events and in the hope that Tono will indeed prove himself one of the "chosen people." Thus, on a financial level, Tono finds himself directly affected by the plight of the Jews. As his relationship with the Jewess develops, we will see that Tono has an emotional, as well as a financial, stake in Mrs. Lautmann's well-being.

At first, the shop offers Tono an escape from his overbearing wife, a haven where he can practice his carpentry in peace. And as he spends more time at the shop and less at home, he comes to appreciate the natural, uncomplicated human exchanges that take place there. Mrs. Lautmann's living-room window is always open to her courtyard neighbors. There is Mrs. Andoric, the young gentile woman, or *Shabbos Goy*, who helps the elderly Jewess with her chores; and Elias Danko, a fatherless Jewish boy who is intrigued by Tono's craft and becomes something of a surrogate son to the childless carpenter. The casual and supportive intermingling of Jew and gentile creates a familial atmosphere that is much more spontaneous and genuine than the one Tono is used to at home.

The importance of the family theme is suggested as soon as Tono enters the shop for the first time. Trying to explain the Aryanization policy to the nearly deaf and totally uncomprehending Mrs. Lautmann, Tono is forced to express himself in the simplest of terms. He says to her, "I'm your Aryan, you're my Jew." Without realizing the full significance of his words, he thereby articulates the theme of mutuality that is at the heart of *The Shop on Main Street*.

When Mrs. Lautmann's friend Kuchar explains to her that Tono will be her new assistant, she smiles sweetly and says, "You'll be like a son." Later, when Tono discovers that Mr. Lautmann's old suit fits him perfectly, he becomes a symbolic spouse. As he spends more time in the shop and less at home, Tono's emotional allegiance begins to shift. During the earlier banquet scene, Marcus had said to Tono, "We're one family. We must get rich. It's our duty to God and the Führer." Now, in the shop, Tono rejects this narrowly self-serving concept of family and joins the larger human community.

Unfortunately, Tono is too short-sighted to comprehend that the financial and emotional security that the shop offers also calls for a political and moral commitment. His guise as "Aryan Controller" gives him a kind of protective coloring; he can appease everyone without risk to himself. Hoping to get along as best he can, Tono is all things to all people. To Marcus, he is a good Fascist; to his wife, he is a wealthy entrepreneur; to the Jews of the community, he is an ambiguous special protector; to Mrs. Lautmann, he is a son and husband, as well as clumsy assistant. The increasing urgency of the moment, however, will not allow Tono to maintain this convenient multiplicity of roles. Twice, Tono is explicitly told that he must choose sides. Just before the lighting of the "tower of Babel," Marcus's lieutenant eyes Tono and says, "Those who aren't with us are against us." And the barber Katz, in response to Tono's question of why the Jews don't resist the roundup, asks him rhetorically, "Will you join us, Mr. Britko?" As events close in on him, Tono will

be disarmed of his political innocence. With that he will recognize his true identity.

Tono's dilemma is conveyed most forcefully in the film's final reel. As the roundup of Jews begins, Tono remains holed up in the shop, unable to decide on a course of action. This sequence is the most subjective in the entire film, Kadár's camera remaining, for the most part, locked in the shop. The confinement creates an almost unbearable tension; it also identifies Tono with this space in a visually explicit manner. As Tono paces around the counter, his complacent sense of possession is undermined. The shop on Main Street has become his in a way he hadn't anticipated when he accepted Marcus's gift. Now the shop becomes a symbolic prison—the prison of self—and Tono must bear the full responsibility of "ownership."

The final sequence occurs on a Saturday, the Jewish Sabbath. It begins with the blaring of a loudspeaker in the town square—"Attention all Jews"—sharply penetrating the storefront. Throughout this sequence, Kadár masterfully uses the soundtrack to bridge space. Although Tono inhabits his own separate world, visually shut off from the events in the square, the obnoxious drone of the roll call serves as a constant reminder of the outside reality. Kadár selectively controls the level of amplification here to great effect; the names of those Jews whom Tono knows personally come through more clearly and loudly than others. When Katz, the barber, is called, the name registers almost too sharply, as if Tono himself were being hunted down.

In an impulsive gesture of rebellion against the transport, Tono rushes to the door and begins to shout out a protest. Kadár cuts to a reverse angle, the camera peering in on Tono, whose voice cannot be heard from outside. The sudden cutting off of sound suggests Tono's ineffectual resistance. Torn between his roles as chosen protector and Aryan Controller, Tono is paralyzed with indecision. The ambiguity of his position is also underscored in one of the most remarkable shots in the film. On the words "Silence for the Commandant," Kadár uses one of the few zoom shots in the film to rivet Tono's attention on his brother-in-law, who is on the podium outside assuring the assembled Jews that they have nothing to fear. The shot has a paradoxical effect: while maintaining Tono's point of view from within the shop, it simultaneously creates the impression that Tono is among the crowd of gathered Jews, for we seem to be placed right behind the shoulder of one of them. Thus the use of the zoom lens captures Tono's duplicitous identity in a purely cinematic way. He is both insider and outsider, both a member of the protected class of citizens and, exposed and objectified by the camera's gaze, one of the persecuted.

This shot concludes the first part of the final sequence. Now Tono stops pacing and sits down in Mrs. Lautmann's chair, Kadár's high angle emphasizing his stillness and confusion. A new act begins when Mrs. Lautmann enters the shop from the back room. Although she has never heard of "Aryanization," she does recognize all the signs of a "pogrom" outside the window. Such overt anti-Semitism brings home her own identity as an outsider; she speaks Yiddish, not Slovak, for one of the few times in the film. Finding Tono nearly hidden in the back of the store, she perceives him now as a potential enemy. As he has done before, Tono acquiesces in the role others have assigned him, chasing the frightened woman around the shop and packing her suitcase so that she can join the transport, which has just started moving.

That Mrs. Lautmann never receives a deportation summons highlights Tono's personal rela-tionship with her. With or without official notice, it is up to Tono to decide her fate. One moment pathetically justifying his actions, the next moment humbly asking for Mrs. Lautmann's forgiveness, Tono is seen here in all his contradictions. The climax of the film occurs shortly after the transport has left, when Tono sees Marcus approaching the shop. Still torn between protecting Mrs. Lautmann and saving his own skin, Tono panics and shoves her into a closet. A moment later he discovers what he has done when he reopens the closet door and finds Mrs. Lautmann crumpled on the same wicker suitcase he had started to pack, her dead eyes staring ahead. This frozen image compresses the full meaning of Tono's passive complicity in the anti-Jewish campaign. All rationalizations and evasions must be abandoned in the face of this horror. Tono's acceptance of Marcus's gift has led, as if in a straight line, to Mrs. Lautmann's death. And in killing the old woman—his Jew—Tono has in essence murdered himself. Tono comes to this double realization in the film's final scene.

Attempting to evade accountability for his actions, Tono becomes his own doppelgänger. Pursued by a hand-held camera, Tono slips out of the frame three times, trying to elude its gaze. His movements take him from the shop to the kitchen to the bedroom, in the direction of greater intimacy with Mrs. Lautmann. Here the camera discovers Tono on Mrs. Lautmann's sofa, from which she said her final prayer, then pans to the twin photographs of the young Mr. and Mrs. Lautmann. At this crucial point, the pursuit ends. The image of wife and husband, occupying separate but symmetrical oval frames, speaks to Tono of his own spiritual kinship with Mrs. Lautmann. Tono now acknowledges the camera's presence with an accepting nod. He then retrieves a rope and footstool from the cupboard.

Tono's suicide is not presented as an act of despair. It is an acknowledgment of his failure to commit himself fully to his proper role as protector of Mrs. Lautmann and, more deeply, an acknowledgment of their common humanity. It would be soon after the period of the film's setting that the Czechs themselves would be persecuted by a repressive Communist regime. In Bernard Malamud's famous formulation, "All men are Jews, except they don't know it." That is, all people suffer, and so each of us is obligated to offer sympathy and support to "the other." Or as Malamud's character Morris Bober, the owner of a small grocery store, tells his gentile assistant, Frank Alpine, in the 1957 novel *The Assistant*, "I suffer for you . . . I mean you suffer for me." Tono's nod, then, is an affirmation of that fundamental Judeo-Christian code of mutuality. As the film's idyllic epilogue makes clear, it is also a kind of spiritual union with Mrs. Lautmann.

This fantasy/dream vision blends in seamlessly with Tono's death. Here, Tono, wearing Mr. Lautmann's suit, and a younger Mrs. Lautmann, holding the same parasol that appeared in the photograph, skip through the sun-drenched town in slow motion. We note some important changes: gone is the "tower of Babel," with its flag signifying Fascist domination; instead, the bandstand has been restored and the band plays the light-hearted waltz from the film's opening. Now husband and wife, Tono and Mrs. Lautmann move screen right and, holding hands, recede deep into the frame, down the same street from which the transport had departed. Thus, Tono, who was unable to fully declare himself in life, joins the Jews in death. In its purifying brilliance, the film's final vision evokes a transcendent realm of being, a world in which pragmatism and accommodation have been replaced by kindness and responsibility, a world that might have been.

Excerpted from: Jeffrey Saperstein, "All Men Are Jews: Tragic Transcendence in Kadár's *The Shop on Main Street,*" *Literature/Film Quarterly* 19, no. 4 (1991): 247–51.

Source: Ladislav Grosman, *The Shop on Main Street,* trans. Iris Urwin (Garden City, NY: Doubleday, 1970).

Background: http://www.ushmm.org/wlc/en/article.php?ModuleId=10007324.

Bibliography

Avisar, Ilan. *Screening the Holocaust.* Bloomington: Indiana University Press, 1988.

Baron, Lawrence. *Projecting the Holocaust into the Present: The Changing Focus of Contemporary Holocaust Cinema.* Lanham, MD: Rowman and Littlefield, 2005.

Hames, Peter. *The Czechoslovak New Wave.* 2nd ed. London: Wallflower, 2005.

Kirschbaum, Stanislav J. *A History of Slovakia: The Struggle for Survival.* New York: Palgrave Macmillan, 2005.

Liehm, Anthony J. *Closely Watched Films: The Czechoslovakian Experience.* White Plains, NY: International Arts and Science, 1974.

Mendelsohn, Ezra. *The Jews of East Central Europe between the Wars.* Bloomington: Indiana University Press, 1987.

Mistriková, Lubica. *"Obchod na Korze: A Shop on the High Street."* Translated by Janet Livingstone. In *The Cinema of Central Europe,* edited by Peter Hames, 97–106. London: Wallflower, 2005.

Vago, Bel, and George L. Mosse, eds. *Jews and Non-Jews in Eastern Europe.* New York: Wiley, 1974.

21. History, Memory, and Art in Louis Malle's *Au revoir les enfants*

CHRISTOPHER SHORLEY

Goodbye Children (*Au revoir les enfants*), directed by Louis Malle [A]
France and West Germany, 1987

"More than forty years have gone by, but until the day I die I shall remember every second of that January morning." The final words the audience hears were, in fact, Malle's starting point. Until the mid-fifties, as he several times pointed out, he was unwilling or unable to deal with his memories of occupied France in 1944, even though they had an immense influence on the rest of his life, and perhaps even made him into a filmmaker. But when, in the summer of 1986, he felt the moment was right, he said, "these lines were the first thing I wrote, before I even started the screenplay." He eventually abandoned his initial idea of beginning the opening sequence with a voice-over, "but the line at the end and the fact that I would inject my own voice—suddenly jumping forty years—that was always my intention. . . . I thought it was important for people watching the film to understand at the end that this . . . was a true story and . . . came from my memory. And I knew it would come on the close-up of Julien." Capturing as it does the overlapping and interweaving of experience, recollection, and narrative—recorded history, personal memory, and artistic technique—the statement offers a telling paradigm for *Au revoir les enfants* as a whole. What is more, the use of an external narrator for the only time in the film is a unique feature in a closing sequence that is, throughout, exceptional in its impact.

"All Malle's best work," it was long ago claimed, "grows out genuine personal feeling," such as suicidal despair, anarchistic revolt, or an intense mother-son relationship. A cluster of characteristic features is apparent as early as his first feature film, among them a certain contempt for the bourgeoisie, an instinct for moments of social change, and a sense that his characters are trapped in some web of fate. And Malle himself has, in retrospect, underlined what he sees as two of his major themes: "people who suddenly find something . . . that diverts them from their expected path," and "a child, an adolescent, who is exposed to the hypocrisy and corruption of the world of adults." *Au revoir les enfants* not only draws in most, if not all, of these concerns, but locates them firmly in the events of Malle's own past.

He wanted the film to cover his life at his privileged Carmelite boarding school near Fontainebleau, and claimed it was "truest in its sociological observation of upper-middle-class pupils." With that setting, he aimed to show the realities of the war breaking in. At a general, quotidian level this means the appalling food, the vitamin biscuits, the electricity cuts, the air-raid warnings, and the rumble of bombing heard in the cellars. Various details recall more specifically the ambience of the Occupation: a young man wearing a yellow star emerges from the public baths beside a notice proclaiming that Jews are banned; Julien and a friend chant a mocking slogan about the pro-German Radio Paris. More topically, in January 1944, a group of *miliciens* [members of a French fascist paramilitary group], newly active in northern France, come to school in search of *réfractaires* avoiding compulsory labor in Germany, then check the customers in the local restaurant. Likewise, contrasting views are expressed about Pétain [the head of the collaborationist

Raphael Fejtö (as Jean Bonnet/Kippelstein), on the left, and Philippe Morier-Genoud (as Father Jean), on the right, are marched away with two other Jewish boys by German guards. From *Goodbye, Children* (1987), directed by Louis Malle. ORION CLASSICS/PHOTOFEST

French government in Vichy] now that his authority and credibility may be slipping away from him. Julien himself draws attention to the historical moment one day when he explains to his indifferent classmates that there will never, ever, be another 17 January 1944 [the date of the Allied attack on Monte Cassino, which began the battle to liberate Rome].

As Malle was quick to point out, the film has "many more dimensions." It is also a "portrait of a child," and Julien's "very emotional relationship with Mme. Quentin, the first character Malle had ever based on his own prejudiced but lovable mother. Accordingly when she sees her son off at the Lyon train station and her visit three weeks later are key sequences. Julien's personal life is explored in other ways, too, through the influ-

ence of his likeable if patronizing elder brother, the references to his perpetually absent father running his factory in Lille, and the various embarrassments and puzzlements of adolescence.

Just as crucially, Malle insisted that the film was never intended as a straightforward reconstruction of the past. History has to give place to memory and memory to art: "Inevitably, when a film is based on a true story that took place forty years earlier, the process of representation is tortured and complicated. I had no interest in making a film that was merely a personal account. I think that what has happened is that I have injected my thinking about these events over the past forty years into the history. In the end I kept what I thought I remembered, even though I knew it was somehow fictionalized."

The initial situation is a simple one. After the Christmas holidays Julien Quentin returns to his school with its familiar rhythms and well-worn rituals: a seamless succession of dormitory pranks, washroom routines, Mass, recreation (typified by a particularly brutal playground game whose players try to knock each other off their wooden stilts), rudimentary gymnastics, piano lessons. The vital change in Julien's existence, and the central element in the plot, occurs with the unexplained arrival of a pupil called Jean Bonnet, one of three newcomers. The pair move rapidly from mutual suspicion and rivalry to respect, trust, and affection, helped by their common passion for reading and their shared experiences, notably getting lost together during a "character-building" treasure hunt in the forest. And their friendship is a major part of the fictionalization, as Malle and the real-life Bonnet were apparently far less close. Parallel with the narrative of deepening intimacy runs Julien's desire to penetrate the mystery surrounding Bonnet. Not for nothing does their very first encounter in the dormitory revolve around one of the books Bonnet is unpacking: *The Adventures of Sherlock Holmes.* As Malle put it, "Julien does not know what to make of Bonnet. He is intrigued by him.... The dramatic energy of the film is driven by Julien's curiosity." Through a series of clues that Julien alone picks up—Bonnet's incomprehensible prayers late one night, his aversion to pâté, a book prize awarded to "Jean Kippelstein"—the spectator comes to realize that Bonnet is a Jew; and Julien stumbles toward an understanding of what Jewishness might be, as in the confused questioning of his mother—"Aren't we Jewish? . . . Aunt Reinach? Isn't that a Jewish name?"—which are all drawn straight from Malle's own reminiscences.

What will be the final routine event, a Sunday film show, the subject of a resonant sequence, is also a piece of poetic license. Chaplin's *The Immigrant* is a significant choice, given that all "Anglo-Saxon" films were banned, and that Chaplin was unpopular with the Germans on account of *The Great Dictator* and, according to Malle, his perceived Jewishness. The showing offers a simulation of the whole cinematic experience; and within it the Jewish boys, whose reactions to the shot of the Statue of Liberty are carefully observed, find a replica of their own sense of persecution and yearning for freedom. The film is crucial to the plot, as this is the last occasion when the school functions as an integrated and self-sufficient community. The camera pans over row after row of intent faces—pupils, teachers, priests—enjoying a common pleasure, and dwells not only on Julien and Bonnet but also the austere principal, Father Jean, and Joseph, the wretched kitchen boy, seated together and laughing more than anyone at the slapstick.

This convivial, relaxed mood is soon dispelled forever. As Malle explained, "It mattered to me that the first part of the film should seem like a chronicle about what it was like to grow up and attend boarding school at that time. Then there is a shift and things get more dramatic." The vital factor, he went on, was "getting this shift right, from period chronicle to tragedy." The shift occurs the day after the film show, when Joseph is summarily dismissed by Father Jean for black-market dealings that have involved pupils including Julien and his brother, whose only punishment is to be gated [confined to the school grounds] until Easter. The outcome is rapid and disastrous. In the next classroom scene, after the math teacher has shown the progress of the Allied armies on a map of Europe, a flatulent pupil asks to be excused. Immediately after Sagard steps outside, a German voice shouts "Halt," and the boy totters backward through the door and the whole established order of things is just as abruptly thrown into reverse.

Before this scene there were a number of potential threats that for the time being came to nothing: an inoffensive off-duty German soldier, seen from the same classroom, was simply asking for confession; the *miliciens* who entered the school and the restaurant left empty-handed; the young soldiers at the baths were too caught up in their own horseplay to pay any serious attention to Bonnet; nothing, seemingly, has come of a disturbing telephone call to Father Jean. Moreover, the portents of disaster have been discreet and underplayed: no one paid much attention to Julien's claiming that he was the only one capable of foreseeing death; a static camera showed the figure of Father Jean blotted out by a largely unsympathetic congregation after his virulent anti-Establishment sermon, but did not linger.

Now these subtle hints take on a more sinister connotation. When writing the screenplay, Malle began with the scenes of the final tragedy: "I knew that sequence was not going to change. That was the whole point of the film." All the earlier motifs, images, and patterns, then, have been devised and minutely organized in view of a known, predetermined denouement. Sagard is followed back into the room by a large, fully armed, and genuinely menacing German MP, the first incursion of its kind into the classroom, which is immediately repeated with the entrance of a Gestapo officer, Doctor Muller. Having asked which of the pupils is Jean Kippelstein, Muller angrily removes the pins from the classroom map, and Julien cannot help turning to look at his friend. Muller glimpses this and has Bonnet taken away. By deliberately and explicitly implicating Julien in Bonnet's capture (this incident, too, is not a memory but an invention), Malle generates the most intense moment of the film so far. While

emphasizing that "it didn't actually happen that way," he maintained that Julien's look crystallizes two forms of guilt: one "at having belonged to a world where such things could happen," the other "a kind of guilt that is rooted in my sense of curiosity, of knowledge." Going further in the same direction, Lynn Higgins interprets the look as a primal scene: an act of traumatic and inadvertent looking akin to that of Freud's Wolf-Man.

Higgins' reading still leaves room for a different focus. For the look that Julien directs at Bonnet on the fateful morning cannot be considered in total isolation, as it is part of an extensive pattern stretching from their first meeting to the very end of the film, and, taken in the context of the film as a whole, conveys concern and complicity, not ultimately betrayal. Malle even went as far as to suggest that "the screenplay is entirely about looks." Moreover, in Malle's terms, the final classroom scene, in which the look occurs, is inseparable from the rest of the compulsively written and delicately constructed closing sequence. For the tragedy is played out through an intricate pattern of echoes, contrasts, and negations.

Muller announces that the school is to be closed, in a reversal of the New Year reopening at the beginning of the film. At this point, too, the preceding mystery is unraveled: it is explained that the school's three newcomers have been exposed as Jews, and that Father Jean, a Resistance activist, has been arrested. In the following scene Julien finds himself briefly alone in the dormitory with Bonnet, now packing his case instead of emptying it as when they first met. This time, however, they exchange books (Julien handing over *The Thousand and One Nights* they read together the previous evening), and Bonnet tells Julien not to blame himself as his capture was inevitable. A scene in the infirmary, witnessed by Julien, has an overt act of betrayal, contrasting with Julien's involuntary glance, when the nurse gives away another of the Jewish pupils, and screams a profanity entirely at odds with her nun's habit. Back outside Julien comes face to face with Joseph, no longer the scruffy urchin of the "chronicle," but wearing an expensive new coat: his reward for denouncing the school to the Germans. The encounter is particularly shocking to Julien given the total change in his erstwhile friend, and his absolute indifference to his victims. It ends with Joseph blaming Julien and the others in the black-market ring for his sacking and what has followed. His terse "Don't worry about it. It's only Jews!" both echoes and contrasts with Bonnet's "Don't worry about it. They'd have got me anyway."

In just a few minutes—and four brief scenes—the "little world has fallen apart." The closing sequence in the yard, with the whole school gathered for a roll call organized to find more Jews, brings home—to Julien and the viewer—the endless repercussions. Cinematically everything confirms that a line has been definitely crossed: that a new "world," with its own sights, sounds, and effects, has suddenly replaced the old. There may have been little relief, in the rest of the film, from the prevailing bleakness—Julien's mother's lipstick, candles in the chapel, a torch in the dormitory—but here there is absolutely none. What dominates is the drabness of the uniforms and the setting, and the paleness of the sky: Malle had specifically told his cameraman that he did not want to see the sun. The soundtrack during the "chronicle" phase was strikingly rich, especially in music, culminating in Bonnet and Julien the previous day playing joyous boogie-woogie in a deserted music room; and it was also full of noise and bustle, in keeping with the rowdiness of normal school life. Now it is reduced to a stunned silence punctuated by wintry birdsong, the tolling of a bell, and departing footsteps.

Through most of the film the camera has followed the swift movements of its subjects, and the editing has emphasized continuity and connection, making brisk transitions from one episode to the next, sometimes with the soundtrack running ahead of the images on the screen, linking gym and piano lesson, private study and confession. The pace here, on the contrary, is slow and measured: this is no longer a case of fleeting impressions, but of weighty implications gradually sinking in. Moreover, there is a changed sense of scale. A long shot at the beginning of the scene takes in the whole yard and, for the first time in the film, the snow-covered hills beyond. A collection of diminished and vulnerable figures now inhabits a much larger, grimmer, and more inhospitable sphere than before. And if it does return to individuals, at the end the camera—which previously brought Julien and Bonnet together in any number of frames—now, as their eyes meet for the last time, holds them apart.

The changed environment not only looks and sounds different: the new conditions of existence make for radical change within it. The imposing presence of the wall surrounding the school has earlier been stressed, as by the corporal bringing Julien and Bonnet back from the forest ("Is it the big wall, beside the church?"). Malle was clear about its symbolic significance: "We were surrounded by walls, somewhat pretending the war was not taking place, feeling protected." In the last few minutes the walls have been irrevocably breached, and, with them inner sanctuaries such as the classroom and the infirmary. Whereas at the beginning the pupils found security after entering by the school gate, the end sees Father Jean, Bonnet, Négus, and Dupré disappearing through it into the ultimate danger.

Previously Germans have acted specifically as

rescuers, like when the patrol finds Julien and Bonnet in the forest, or the Luftwaffe officer throws the *miliciens* out of the restaurant. As Malle recalled, "The French collaborators were more aggressive and active than the German soldiers." Now the military police and the Gestapo are the agents of catastrophe. More fundamentally, authority has been usurped, and the old order replaced. Discipline, as in the lining up of the pupils and the reading of the roll call, has passed to the invader, while the teachers are reduced to voiceless spectators and literally sidelined, and the school's principal and presiding father figure is removed.

The physical setting is a grim metaphor. What was previously a place of relaxation and play now has the look and feel of a freezing prison camp. All the games and make-believe from earlier on have been superseded by the harshest of realities. The stilt contest as a "parody" of the conflict between Crusader and Saracen, one pupil's putting on a German accent and "confiscating" Julien's jam, and another's clicking his heels and giving a Nazi salute—all belong in a milder past. On this latter occasion a teacher wearily comments that Ciron should not always feel the need to "act the clown," an image that is recalled when one of the priests scolds Julien for "playing the fool." The time for these antics, like those of Chaplin, "the little clown," has gone. Escapism of any kind— *The Three Musketeers* early on, *The Thousand and One Nights* only hours before—is out of question: capture and confinement are inevitable. Most important of all is the passage from initial arrival to present dispersal, from the community of the Mass to the fragmentation of individuals lined up against the wall: the friendship of Julien and Bonnet turns to absence, and Bonnet's life is being lost. The film began with the *au revoir* between Mme. Quentin and her sons at the train

station in Lyon: painful enough, but still a standard event to be followed by foreseeable reunions. The cries of *au revoir* at the end are, of course, the complete opposite. And through them comes a further separation: for it is at this point that Julien—bewildered as he still is—realizes that he is definitely taking leave of childhood, ignorance, and innocence, and that the territory he now glimpses is called adulthood.

France still exhibits symtoms of what the historian Henry Rousso calls "the Vichy Syndrome" in the seminal study that appeared in the same year as Malle's film. Rousso himself identified four phases in France's collective memory of the Occupation years: first, between 1944 and 1954, a "mourning phase" during which the country had to "deal directly with the aftermath of civil war, purge, and amnesty"; second, from 1954 to 1971, a period dominated by the myth of the Resistance, which minimized the role of the Vichy regime while promoting the importance of the Resistance and identifying it with the nation as a whole; a third phase, a "return of the repressed," from 1971 to 1974, saw this "carefully constructed myth" shattered; and a fourth phase, one of obsession, continuing to the late eighties, was marked by a reawakening of Jewish memory and renewed concern with the Occupation in French political debate. Rousso focuses on cultural forms he calls "vectors of memory" and pays close attention to cinema, particularly after Marcel Ophüls's *The Sorrow and the Pity* (1969), a documentary that exposed the extent of French collaboration with the German occupation during World War II. This was when a number of those filmmakers and writers who were only children during the war began to come to grips with it. Malle obviously fits into this group given his film *Lacombe Lucien*, which appeared in 1974. On its release, this fictional story of an uncomprehending young collaborator stirred up controversy by refusing to endorse the simplistic certainties of the myth of the Resistance. In the longer term, Rousso would argue it did as much as *The Sorrow and the Pity* to develop a more complex image of the war years.

Malle admitted that he would not have dared to make *Lacombe Lucien* a decade earlier, and it would be another thirteen years before he would make *Au revoir les enfants*. In the meantime he had been working in America, so when he returned he was at a different stage of his own evolution, and France had entered the fourth phase of the Vichy syndrome. He later claimed that he discerned no great interest in his project when he was trying to raise money for it; but during the editing Klaus Barbie, the Gestapo chief in Lyon, was put on trial, and two weeks before the film opened, Jean-Marie Le Pen created a controversy by minimizing the enormity of the Holocaust. For France and Malle, Vichy has become "an ever present past." Nowhere is this better conveyed than in the final seconds of the film. The close-up of Julien, enhanced as the surrounding faces go out of focus, recalls the shot of him looking out of the railway carriage window as he started out: but these final frames also suggest everything that has happened in between, and how the memory will not go away. Julien's eyes slowly fill with tears; his image is not frozen, and he looks toward the open gate. Before the soundtrack ends with the Schubert *Moment musical* Bonnet had played, Malle's adult voice-over recounts the fate of Bonnet and the others, which he learned only later. Thus, Higgins observes, "accuser, child, and narrator are three distinct but related characters, facets, perhaps of a single historical consciousness able to recognize the graduations of complicity." Then come the closing words that carry memory forward into the narrator's present, and project it into the future. "Ultimately," writes Higgins, "it

matters less what Julien knows in 1944 than what Malle knows in 1987, and what we know with him. "Memory," said Malle, "is not frozen; it's very much alive, it moves, it changes." It is the achievement of the mature filmmaker that the complex shifting perceptions of his own past history come to haunt his audience too.

Abridged from: Christopher Shorley, "History, Memory, and Art in Louis Malle's *Au revoir les enfants*," in *The Seeing Century: Film, Vision and Identity*, ed. Wendy Everett, 49–59 (Amsterdam: Rodopi, 2000).

Background: http://www.ushmm.org/wlc/en/article .php?ModuleId=10005429.

Bibliography

Audé, Françoise, and Jean-Pierre Jeancolas. "Louis Malle on *Au revoir les enfants*." In *Projections 9: French Film-makers on Film-making*, edited by John Boorman and Walter Donahue, 33–50. London: Faber and Faber, 1999.

Frey, Hugo. *Louis Malle*. Manchester, UK: Manchester University Press, 2004.

Higgins, Lynn. *New Novel, New Wave, New Politics: Fiction and the Representation of History in Postwar France*. Lincoln: University of Nebraska Press, 1996.

Malle, Louis. *Malle on Malle*. Edited by Philip French. London: Faber and Faber, 1993.

Marrus, Michael R., and Robert O. Paxton. *Vichy France and the Jews*. New York: Basic, 1981.

New, Elisa. "Goodbye, Children; Good-bye, Mary, Mother of Sorrows: The Church and the Holocaust in the Art of Louis Malle." *Prooftexts* 22, nos. 1–2 (2002): 118–40.

Rousso, Henry. *The Vichy Syndrome: History and Memory in France since 1944*. Translated by Arthur Goldhammer. Cambridge: Harvard University Press, 1991.

Southern, Nathan, and Jacques Weissgerber. *The Films of Louis Malle: A Critical Analysis*. Jefferson, NC: McFarland, 2006.

22. A Reel Witness

Steven Spielberg's Representation of the Holocaust in *Schindler's List*

FRANK MANCHEL

Schindler's List, directed by
Steven Spielberg [A]
United States, 1993

Although released in December 1993, *Schindler's List* has become for the present generation the most important source of historical information affecting popular perceptions of the Holocaust. Such reactions make it clear that *Schindler's List* is not just a movie. It has become part of an ongoing worldwide cultural war that for decades has been debating both the nature and causes of the Holocaust and the advisability of having artists interpret the events surrounding the Nazi genocide. The distinguished film remains continuously embroiled in controversy.

Rather than confining itself to a straightforward review of the movie, this essay examines Spielberg's treatment of the Holocaust in light of his prior cinematic career. The plan is to position the film in its historical and cultural context and then to speculate on why it took so long for the book to be adapted to the screen. I will focus on three major areas: the subject matter and its visual presentation; the challenges that filming the Holocaust presents; and Spielberg's interpretation of this uniquely monstrous event.

At the end of World War II, Holocaust survivor Leopold Pfefferberg became obsessed with persuading some gifted individual to tell the inexplicable story of Oskar Schindler, an apparently amoral German-Austrian businessman who nonetheless saved the lives of 1,100 Jews. Finally, in 1980, a chance meeting with Australian writer Thomas Keneally resulted in the publication two years later of the novelist's critically acclaimed book, *Schindler's List*.

Based on interviews with the Jews saved by Schindler, the narrative recounts the story of the lustful Catholic industrialist and Nazi spy who came to occupied Poland in 1939 to exploit the persecution of the Jewish population. Schindler took over a confiscated enamelware factory and manufactured pots and pans for the Nazi war effort. Rather than pay higher wages to Polish workers, Schindler used Jewish slave labor. Eventually, he convinced the authorities to house his workers at the factory. Scheming, bribing, and black marketeering, he amassed a fortune and endeared himself to the Nazi bureaucracy. Then, for reasons never explained, this unlikely hero underwent a transformation and risked his life and squandered his wealth to protect his Jewish laborers. As the Nazi war effort faltered in 1944 and orders came to deport all surviving Jews to Auschwitz, Schindler persuaded the authorities to relocate his factory and its "essential workers" to his hometown in Czechoslovakia and convert the plant into a munitions factory. A list of 1,100 Jewish names, "Schindler's List," was prepared. To get on the list was to escape extermination in the gas chambers. Shortly after Germany's defeat in May of 1945, Schindler, now a presumed war criminal, fled. His marriage and subsequent business ventures failed, but his courageous actions during World War II earned him the gratitude of Jewish survivors. In 1962, a carob tree was planted in his honor on the Avenue of the Righteous of the Yad Vashem Holocaust Museum in Israel. When he died in 1974, his body was transported to Israel and buried in the Catholic cemetery of Jerusalem.

Ben Kingsley (as Itzhak Stern), seated, and Liam Neeson (as Oskar Schindler) decide how to save the Jews who work for Schindler. From *Schindler's List* (1993), directed by Steven Spielberg. UNIVERSAL STUDIOS/PHOTOFEST

Recognizing the dramatic possibilities of the story and inspired by its heroic tale, Music Corporation of America president Sidney Sheinberg immediately purchased the screen rights to Keneally's book. Sheinberg saw it as a perfect vehicle for his protégé Steven Spielberg. More than ten years elapsed before Spielberg began shooting the film. Why? It was not a matter of financing. Spielberg did not have to worry about financing or distribution. The problems involved the director's cinematic stature and confidence about making a Holocaust film. Ironically, film is a medium where the more successful you are commercially, the less acceptable you are to the critical community.

Sheinberg was one of the few people who thought Spielberg capable of adapting Keneally's book to the screen. The artist differed from other prominent Hollywood directors like George Lucas, Francis Ford Coppola, and Martin Scorsese, who had studied film in college. His more educated peers frequented art house theaters, appreciated subtitled masterpieces, and aspired to be cinematic masters, but he preferred the world of B movies: the serials, science-fiction films, action thrillers, and war movies.

After working a few years in television, the twenty-six-year-old Spielberg made his feature film debut, *The Sugarland Express*, in 1974. In reviewing the movie, critic Pauline Kael identified the strengths and weaknesses that would define Spielberg's work up to *Schindler's List*. She characterized him as "commercial and shallow and impersonal," but praised his ability to make the mundane entertaining. Within six years, Kael blamed Spielberg, along with Lucas, for representing everything that was wrong with modern American cinema, especially the industry's emphasis on marketing rather than creativity. By 1982, most critics echoed Kael's judgment, but few doubted that Spielberg's films were distinctive. The director's cinematic technique had made him film history's most popular and successful director. Thanks to works like *Jaws, Close Encounters of the Third Kind, Raiders of the Lost Ark*, and *E.T.: The Extra-Terrestrial*, Spielberg became a modern Walt Disney whose movies entertained the child in all of us.

In *Schindler's List* one can easily recognize the master film technician in love with the classical Hollywood tradition. Audiences recognize not only what they know about the Holocaust from past films but also a format with which they are comfortable. A central figure, Oskar Schindler (played superbly by Liam Neeson), overcomes a series of obstacles by the film's conclusion. Through a spectacular reconstruction of historical events—the rounding up of the Polish Jews in 1939, the establishment of the Podgórze Ghetto in 1941, the construction of the Płaszów Forced Labor Camp in 1942, the destruction of the ghetto in 1943, the dehumanization of helpless people, the exhuming and burning of ten thousand Jewish bodies in 1944, and the horrors of arriving at Auschwitz—Spielberg and his ingenious collaborators "document" historian Raul Hilberg's description of the evolution of anti-Semitism: "The missionaries of Christianity had said in effect: You have no right to live among us as Jews. The secular rulers that followed had proclaimed: You have no right to live among us. The German Nazis at last decreed: You have no right to live."

In classical Hollywood style, the story of millions is symbolized by the fortunes of the few.

Individuals plead hopelessly for help from the Jewish Council, which supervised and administered the conqueror's law. A rich Jewish family is displaced from its home and joins other refugees on a forced march to the Kraków ghetto. The sound of Polish onlookers yelling "Goodbye Jews" is chillingly presented. Equally memorable are the images of atrocities committed in the ghetto, the labor camp, and finally Auschwitz.

The narrative dictates the action, the pace, and the imagery. This is a story of a culture that disappeared in six horrifying years, and how the efforts of one man made a difference to the few survivors. Our emotions are evoked as the opening shots, in color, focus on a Jewish family observing the Sabbath and then proceed to quick dissolves eliminating the parents, then the one remaining child, to the single flickering candle and finally to a wisp of smoke that transports us back to the black-and-white era of 1939, with the smoke rising from a locomotive carrying Jews to the Kraków railway station. A single clerk sets up his typewriter, ink pad, pens, and table to register Jews forced into the urban trap created by the Nazis. In rapid order, clerks register the bewildered victims. Spielberg synthesizes Hitler's process, by which his minions meticulously constructed their death lists. Later in the film, Schindler and Itzhak Stern (magnificently portrayed by Ben Kingsley), his Jewish accountant, repeat the process by compiling another list, but this time one of "essential workers," a list of life.

Interpreting history through the main characters, Spielberg contrasts the fate of Poland's 3.3 million Jews with the fortunes of Schindler. The camera introduces us to the avaricious opportunist by showing his decadent lifestyle. First, we see his preparations for dining out. Keeping Schindler's identity hidden, the film shifts to a nightclub scene where he curries favor with the top

Nazi brass. Slowly, Spielberg acquaints us with the protagonist: physically suave, stylishly dressed, and presumptuous. After several people wonder about his identity, we are told, "That is Oskar Schindler!"

In hindsight we appreciate how the camera records Schindler's hypnotic style. Spielberg repeatedly shows the successful results of Schindler's charming behavior. Each encounter with the Nazis brings rewards with greater significance. It is visually foreshadowed that Schindler's unique talents will enable him to save over a thousand Jews from annihilation. Yet the reasons for his heroic metamorphosis remain an enigma.

Besides its scenes of nudity, terrifying violence, outstanding performances, brilliant production values, and spectacular cinematography, the film also contains a macabre sense of humor. One is grateful for the momentary relief of tension. Consider the first exchange between Schindler and Stern. The former tries to enlist the accountant as his bookkeeper. Stern points out that most people have more urgent problems. Schindler replies incredulously, "Like what?" He then explains his scheme to acquire the enamelware factory. Stern listens and then says, "Let me get this straight. The Jews put up the money, and I do the work. What do you do?"

As the fate of the Jews becomes more perilous, this humor is given greater scope and visual power. When Stern is threatened with deportation, Schindler goes to the train station and demands that Stern be removed from the transport. The clerk refuses, and Schindler tries a bluff. He demands to know the clerk's name. The stakes escalate when a German officer says that nothing can be done. Schindler threatens both adversaries that they will be in the front lines within a week. Cut to the three men walking along the train and yelling, "Stern! Stern!"

In addition Spielberg creates one of the cinema's most unforgettable villains, Amon Goeth (memorably played by Ralph Fiennes), who epitomizes Nazi barbarism. While the brass takes bribes and soldiers obey orders, Goeth murders indiscriminately. He kills an educated Jewish woman overseeing the construction of the labor camp, not because she is incompetent, but because she criticizes Nazi incompetence. Elsewhere, he stands on his bedroom balcony watching the morning camp roll call and randomly shoots Jews for target practice. In the end, the Poles execute him for crimes against humanity.

Schindler's List transformed both Spielberg's and the Holocaust's image in the public's mind. *New York Times* critic Janet Maslin echoed the sentiments of most of her peers when she declared, "Mr. Spielberg has made sure that neither he nor the Holocaust will ever be thought of the same way again." Emilie Schindler, Oskar's ex-wife, announced, "It shows some ugly things, but when you realize it's the truth, it's more powerful. The truth was even worse than the film."

Schindler's List also stimulated other interpretations. Various Muslim governments dismissed the film as Israeli propaganda. Art Spiegelman, the author of *Maus: A Survivor's Tale*, insisted the movie was not about the Holocaust, but about Clinton and capitalism: "Capitalism can give us a health care program, and it can give us a Schindler." President Clinton, seeking public support for military action in Bosnia to stop two years of "ethnic cleansing," urged everyone to view Spielberg's film.

Whatever interpretation one gives to *Schindler's List*, it is undeniable that the public reacted strongly to Spielberg's supposed docudrama, applauding its seeming authenticity, visual virtuosity, storytelling genius, and towering humanity. Serious film students already knew about his artistry in creating imaginary worlds and making them visually unforgettable. His emphasis had always been on the emotional rather than on the intellectual. He enjoyed making the epic event personal. Why should anyone be upset with such a virtuous production?

To understand the backlash to *Schindler's List*, we need to return to the years between 1982 and 1993. Clues about his reluctance to make the film surfaced in statements to the press. After receiving the 1994 Directors Guild Award, he commented that "when I first read the book, I said, there are a lot of directors in this world who are much better than me to make this picture." On another occasion, he said, "I've never given up the ghost of my childhood. . . . I really feel I stopped developing emotionally when I was 19." Spielberg attributed the film's length and black-and-white monochrome photography to "remaining true to the spirit of documentaries and stills from the period." Interviews also dwelled on his bornagain Jewishness, how "I was so ashamed of being a Jew and now I'm filled with pride." In talking about his Arizona childhood, he frequently admits that "I was always attempting to assimilate into popular culture."

Who knows definitively the uncertainties Spielberg overcame to promote the picture, change his image, and win awards? He knew that to make his Holocaust film attractive to mass audiences it had to be a box-office hit, and that required a marketing approach guaranteed to produce major awards and public approval.

These problems are part of the critical tools that scholars use to discipline our imaginations. The issue of whether European genocide is an appropriate subject for the arts started when Auschwitz was liberated. Many Holocaust scholars and survivors argued that silence was preferable to fictional reconstructions. For them, it is incomprehensible that art can reconstruct atrocities, beautifying unimaginable horrors, and profiting from depicting human misery. Those who raise these issues draw an aesthetic line for anyone who makes a movie about the Holocaust, but especially for American productions marketed primarily as entertainment. Yet it is important to appreciate that artists create illusionary worlds to provide experiences that enable us to better understand the human situation. They force us to examine the unexamined, to imagine the unimaginable. Even mawkish melodramatic works like the TV miniseries *Holocaust* (1978) force the public to rethink its attitudes toward the role of the media, the meaning of the event, and the responsibility of individuals in our society.

Imagine the questions that Spielberg probably considered. His entire career had been devoted to making sentimental movies with optimistic endings, reassuring his audiences that they can triumph over their fears. Is that approach appropriate for interpreting the death of six million Jews? His box-office appeal rested largely on his ability to manipulate people's emotions through the recycling and revitalization of film clichés and stereotypes. Moreover, if cinema demands stars more than statistics, fun more than fact, is film a suitable vehicle for examining the essence of evil? Does it make sense to mix entertainment and education? Does one's drive for popularity require misrepresentation? And are factual distortions about the Holocaust, or history in general, insignificant? If a film becomes a visual witness for future generations, is it reasonable to assume that audiences will distinguish between perception and reality?

I suggest that Spielberg's approach to these types of questions in *Schindler's List* is related to his shame about being Jewish, his orientation to filmmaking, and his exposure to films he had seen about the Holocaust. I further contend that the film's reception is related to legacies associated with class, age, race, education, and status. Moreover, the cultural and historical context in which a film is received assures us that one cannot control the public's reactions or the use it will find for the movie. For example, only in the last fifteen years have educational institutions elevated the Holocaust from a footnote in twentieth-century history to a serious place in the curriculum. Thus it is not surprising that different groups not only saw *Schindler's List* differently but also battled each other over its historical and social relevance.

For Spielberg's generation, the mass media were the primary classrooms on racism and the Holocaust. During the first half of the twentieth century American films struggled to make Jews acceptable to the gentile world. The representations changed from decade to decade, to keep pace with the Jews' ability to achieve economic, social, and political freedoms. During Spielberg's formative years, the screen image of Jews underwent radical changes. Freedom from studio domination and the conservative Motion Picture Production Code allowed filmmakers to reexamine attitudes toward ethnicity and to stress diversity rather than conformity. This revolution produced a range of new Jewish characterizations. Spielberg was influenced by the intellectual debates over whether stereotyping contributed to or undermined racial bigotry.

Another legacy of American film history that influenced Spielberg's Jewish identity was the Holocaust productions themselves. Informed viewers realized that most popular productions stressed how catastrophic World War II was for groups other than the Jews and that performances are prized more than are honest scripts. It is difficult to identify an American film or television miniseries on this monstrous subject that was not accused by at least one noted commentator of being too melodramatic, simplistic, and trivial.

Conventional wisdom castigates American Holocaust films on four specific grounds: (1) too much emphasis on emotional rather than informational issues; (2) the emphasis on the sensational rather than the factual; (3) underestimating the intelligence of audiences by oversimplifying complex material; and, worst of all, (4) diminishing the specificity of Jewish victimization by universalizing the Holocaust experience. Moreover, only European filmmakers seem acceptable to scholarly audiences, mainly because foreign films take greater intellectual risks, stress original interpretations, explore complex moral positions, and deal sensitively with the painful memories of the past.

Sensitive to these issues, Spielberg began a new cinematic journey after 1982. He broke out of his "Peter Pan" mode by making serious films like *The Color Purple* (1985) and *Empire of the Sun* (1987), although to very mixed reviews. In 1983, he commented that *The Color Purple* was his first movie about people and that he felt badly when critics accused him "of not having the sensibility to do character studies." His forays into World War II started with *1941* (1979) and *Raiders of the Lost Ark* (1981), and continued with the other Indiana Jones films (1984, 1989) and *Empire of the Sun* (1987). Clearly, his sensitivity to Jewish pride had evolved from *An American Tail* (1986) and *An American Tail: Fievel Goes West* (1991), two animated cartoons starring Jewish immigrant mice.

By now, Spielberg's approach to Keneally's novel was paramount. To help determine his treatment, Spielberg and his team studied previous movies about the Holocaust: for example, *The Shop on Main Street* (1965), *Wallenberg: A Hero's Story* (1985), and *Shoah* (1985), all of which featured Christians who risked their lives to help Jews. Clearly, he benefitted from the 1955 documentary *Night and Fog*, where Alain Resnais contrasted the past, using black-and-white photography, with the present, using color film, to present a point of view of how the Nazis made use of everything the Jews owned or wore. Spielberg must have studied *The Sorrow and the Pity* (1970) and *Shoah* to grasp the importance of displaying anti-Semitism rather than merely describing it. And certainly he was aware that impolitic casting (Vanessa Redgrave in *Playing for Time*) and inappropriate analogies (comparing the Vietnam War to the Holocaust in *The Memory of Justice*) had created storms of controversy in the past.

And how could Spielberg have ignored the fact that the Europeans were the only ones to win Oscars for films about the Holocaust? For example, only four American Holocaust movies prior to 1990 had even been nominated, and none of them won. In contrast, ever since the foreign film category was introduced in the late 1950s, seven European features about the Holocaust had been nominated, and only three failed to receive an Oscar. For a man who by 1983 had been nominated three times for best director and yet had failed to receive the honor, the European successes must have meant something to Spielberg. What was just as evident was that American films did well at the box office, while their European counterparts were rarely seen outside intellectual circles.

My contention is that this ingenious filmmaker designed a self-study program to discover what distinguished filmmakers like Alain Resnais, Marcel Ophüls, Claude Lanzmann, George Stevens, Stanley Kramer, Sidney Lumet, and Alan Pakula had done successfully. He attempted to merge the documentary approach of Europe with the box-office appeal of Hollywood. Moreover, he embraced the positive attitudes of Holocaust survivors toward the subject matter.

In essence then, Spielberg the businessman and Spielberg the artist knew that getting his movie across to the public and having the film's message have a significant impact depended on approaching the project in a specific way. The film had to account for the attitudes of Holocaust survivors toward the subject matter. The screenplay must incorporate Hollywood's tradition of making an epic story personal. Spielberg also needed to convince the public that his film grew out of a commitment beyond personal gain. Moreover, the sheer number of Holocaust films on television and the big screen required his approaching the by-now-familiar material with a "new look." Depicted properly, the screen narrative offered him the opportunity to improve his stature in film history. Finally, he had to find the right time to release the movie—not just the season of the year but also the moment when society could appreciate its relevance to the present.

Nowhere is there a greater danger of misunderstanding or misusing *Schindler's List* than in the area of recreated historical incidents. With all due respect to the film's imaginative depictions of the destruction of the ghetto, the selection scenes in the labor camp, and the shower incident at Auschwitz, they are dramatizations, even though a large portion of the public assumes that what they see are the actual events. Audiences must recognize that fact. Scholars need to curb their enthusiasm for an extraordinary piece of filmmaking while disciplining their students' imaginations to the difference between fact and fiction. After all, they, not filmmakers, are responsible for teaching the distinctions between perception and reality.

Turning to the issue of the black-and-white photography, one clearly sees the lessons Spielberg learned from European film culture. The quasi-documentary style, making masterly use of German Expressionist lighting, offers striking allusions to the perils of living in Nazi-occupied Poland from 1939 to 1945. Working with Janusz Kaminski, the great Polish cinematographer, the director uses hand-held cameras to show how human beings were degraded, humiliated, and dehumanized. Unforgettable images of Nazi soldiers who enjoyed killing, horrifying reminders of the lengths the Germans went to to get gold from their victims, and the painful choices the hunted made in their struggle to survive are brilliantly portrayed.

But black-and-white cinematography and abandoning Hollywood cranes and dolly shots do not translate into documentary footage. No pictures, "documentary" or otherwise, can capture the misery, fear, illness, and suffering that occurred. It is foolish to assert that *Schindler's List* replaces the eyewitness accounts of the Holocaust. More to the point, Spielberg ignores how European directors employed humility in the presence of complexity. His fast-paced shooting and Hollywood voyeurism placed more emphasis on emotion than on the intellect, on the art rather than on the event. One style is not better than the other. Stirring emotions is one powerful way to get millions of uninvolved and uninterested audiences to examine a complex issue.

Much thornier than these aesthetic concerns are the intellectual issues raised by *Schindler's List*. Consider the question of how the film presents the question of survival. Spielberg demonstrates the conventional wisdom that survival depended on chance. One sees scenes of hiding places being discovered, accidental encounters with murdering soldiers, and random shootings of prisoners when one of their peers escapes from a work detail. But the film also shows that there

were things people could do to improve their chances of survival. The daughter who dresses up to gain entrance to Schindler's office does save her parents from death. The quick-thinking child who identifies the dead man as the thief who stole the chicken is rewarded by Schindler and transferred to the factory. Goeth does not kill prisoners randomly from his balcony. He shoots only those who are resting. Once the other prisoners begin running, the shooting stops. J. Hoberman argues: "In the Holocaust, Jews were not saved, were not snatched from the jaws of Auschwitz." But some people did survive. With hundreds of movies about the absence of choices, what is wrong with skillfully created films examining another perspective?

That daring stance is overshadowed by the film's brilliant approach to Oskar Schindler and Amon Goeth. How one becomes virtuous is developed in the film through the use of editing and irony. Consider the parallels between Schindler and Goeth. Neither acts virtuously at first. Schindler goes to the Jewish Council to get Stern's help. Goeth arrives at the construction site of the forced labor camp to assert his authority. Both use Jewish slave labor to operate their "businesses." Just as Schindler interviews Jewish women for a secretary's job, Goeth "interviews" Jewish women for a maid's position. When Schindler first meets Goeth, their initial conversations are about clothes, money, and business pressures. Both are consumed with material pleasures, and both eventually are perceived to be "mad" by those closest to them.

The differences are not as obvious as one might suspect. There is a crucial scene where Schindler defends Goeth to Stern, arguing that you have to understand the commandant's position: "He has a lot to worry about." It's the war that's making Goeth behave as he does. (Earlier

Schindler told his wife that the war was the reason for his success.) Schindler argues that Goeth is not a bad fellow, and the two of them have a lot in common: womanizing, drinking, and a love of the "good life." Stern reminds Schindler that the chief difference between the two men is that Goeth is a killer. Spielberg then intercuts Goeth's random shooting of twenty-five laborers in a returning work group. The point is again brought home in a drunken balcony scene, where Schindler lectures Goeth about the importance of temperance, power, and justice. He tells him the parable about the emperor who had the ability to execute, but preferred to pardon. Goeth tries but fails to apply this principle. After seeing countless examples of Schindler bribing officials, Goeth imitates his friend to get him out of jail and fails. Schindler subsequently bribes the commandant of Auschwitz to free three hundred imprisoned Jewish women. Of particular importance is that the film omits the novel's references to how much Schindler hated the Nazis. That omission intensifies the parallels between the industrialist and the commandant.

The difference between the virtuous man and the tyrant becomes clearer when comparing the compassion Schindler feels for his Jews and the indifference Goeth feels toward them. In a telling scene, the two men bargain over the fate of Schindler's Jews while a window post divides the pair. Schindler gives away everything he owns to save his workers. Goeth takes all he can get but admits he does not understand the scam Schindler is playing on him. At the ring-giving scene, Stern explains that its inscription is from the *Talmud*: "Whoever saves one life saves the world entire." Schindler's triumph lies not only in seeing the error of his ways but also in doing something about it.

Crediting Spielberg with a quantum leap in

intellectual content is a double-edged sword. On the one hand, it acknowledges the brilliant filmmaking and rejects the idea that either Spielberg or Hollywood remains subservient to European artists in matters of the Holocaust. On the other hand, it illustrates how the uniqueness of the Holocaust can be misinterpreted and/or misused. True, it is useful as a means of combating racial intolerance. At the same time, it obscures the fact that the Holocaust is a specific event in history, not a generalized horror.

My last concern is with the final scenes of the film. Schindler gathers his factory workers, persuades Nazi soldiers to disperse, explains why he has to flee, and breaks down over the realization that he could have saved more Jews. Most reviewers comment negatively about the scene's melodramatic nature. Others attack its "dishonesty," noting that Schindler was too scared to say anything, that the car was lined with money, and that he fled not only with his wife, but also his mistress. Screenwriter Steven Zallian admitted that including the ring-giving ceremony was done precisely to remind the audience "that although Schindler saved some 1,200 people, 6 million more died during the Holocaust."

During the final scene where the actors and their true counterparts file past Schindler's grave on Mount Zion, a printed statement informs us that only four thousand Jews still live in Poland, but that there are six thousand survivors and descendants of Schindler's Jews. The statement is necessary because audiences presumably are mourning Schindler, not the Jewish victims. Yet some viewers see the statistics only as further testimony to Schindler's heroism.

Schindler's List illustrates the issues associated with Holocaust films. First, its images remind us of movies on the subject. A careful study of this film reveals Spielberg's debt to other works, as well as his new contributions to the subject. Second, the questions raised about the movie's authenticity and historical relevance arise from the ongoing debate surrounding aesthetic representations of the Holocaust. The discussion distinguishes between what Professor Garth Jowett calls "history *on* film and history *in* film." The former refers to historical dramas like *Schindler's List* that try to recreate the past. As historical records, they fail to measure up to the criteria used in judging historical evidence. History in film, however, refers to how it reflects and affects people in a particular place and period in history. Spielberg's work provides a portal to the attitudes and values of society in 1994. Third, the movie's worldwide popularity reveals traces of the director's earlier cinematic techniques. Fourth, the accolades bestowed on Spielberg and his film, while richly deserved, also remind us how belatedly the critics recognized the talented filmmaker. Fifth, the film's critical reception illustrates that artists cannot control how an audience interprets and uses their motion pictures.

Schindler's List demonstrates that art is not about factual truth, but about experience; and that experiences are provided by artists who use the legacies of the past to interpret the present. Recognizing that each experience is different, we should realize that one film need not compete with or replace other works on the Holocaust. In this case, *Schindler's List* takes its place as one of the great achievements in film history, for it teaches us that momentous experiences must always be critically examined both as history and art.

Abridged from: Frank Manchel, "A Reel Witness: Steven Spielberg's Representation of the Holocaust in *Schindler's List*," *Journal of Modern History* 67, no. 1 (1995): 83–100.

Source: Thomas Keneally, *Schindler's List* (New York: Simon and Schuster, 1982).

Background: http://www.ushmm.org/wlc/en/article .php?ModuleId=10005169; http://www.ushmm.org/ wlc/es/article.php?ModuleId=10005787.

Bibliography

Crowe, David M. *Oskar Schindler: The Untold Account of His Life, Wartime Activities, and the True Story behind the List.* Boulder, CO: Westview, 2004.

Doneson, Judith E. *The Holocaust in American Film.* 2nd ed. Syracuse, NY: Syracuse University Press, 2002.

Fensch, Thomas. *Oskar Schindler and His List: The Man, the Book, the Film, the Holocaust and Its Survivors.* Forest Dale, VT: Paul S. Erickson, 1995.

Friedman, Lester D. *Citizen Spielberg.* Urbana: University of Illinois Press, 2006.

Loshitzky, Yosefa. *Spielberg's Holocaust: Critical Perspectives on Schindler's List.* Bloomington: Indiana University Press, 1997.

Mintz, Alan. *Popular Culture and the Shaping of Holocaust Memory in America.* Seattle: University of Washington Press, 2001.

Picart, Caroline Joan (Kay) S., and David A. Frank. *Frames of Evil: The Holocaust as Horror in American Film.* Carbondale: Southern Illinois University Press, 2006.

Schindler, Emilie, with Erika Rosenberg. *Where Light and Shadow Meet: A Memoir.* Translated by Dolores M. Koch. New York: W. W. Norton, 1997.

Weissman, Gary. *Fantasies of Witnessing: Postwar Efforts to Experience the Holocaust.* Ithaca, NY: Cornell University Press, 2004.

23. *The Pianist* and Its Contexts

Polanski's Narration of Holocaust Evasion and Survival

MICHAEL STEVENSON

The Pianist, directed by Roman Polanski [A] France, Germany, Poland, the United Kingdom, and the United States, 2002

I want to place Polanski's *The Pianist* within the context of Holocaust and specifically deal with questions of representation. I have decided to produce three lines of discussion on *The Pianist*: first, to reprise some of the general arguments about Holocaust representation; second, to place the entwined narratives of Wladyslaw Szpilman and Polanski in relation to a particular mode of Holocaust narration that includes Primo Levi and Tadeusz Borowski; third, to link these with other issues more directly contextual, the construction of the Warsaw ghetto and those who survived and hid in the city.

In the latter I am indebted to Gunnar S. Paulson's *Secret City: The Hidden Jews of Warsaw, 1940–1945*. It is situated somewhere between an ethnography of events in the ghetto and a detailed analysis of the vagaries of evasion and survival. Paulson's study provides a useful contextual parallel with Szpilman's memoir and Polanski's film. This is to be found in its concentration on small, everyday processes and the changing and often improvised nature of Nazi oppression that constantly shifted the parameters in the possibilities of evasion and survival.

This is not to claim the film is attempting an unusual strategy for Polanski, a kind of everyday "realism," as may be claimed for Spielberg's *Schin-*

dler's List. The film does have a clear sense of documentary drama, but with a striking sense of controlled artifice. There are elements not present in Szpilman's memoir that broaden its historical perspective and provide a sharpened representation of the family. Polanski adds explicit scenes of the Ghetto Uprising of 1943 and the start of the Warsaw Uprising of 1944 that go beyond the book.

Paulson reminds us of the exceptional nature of the Warsaw ghetto experience and the extraordinary nature of life in Warsaw during the Second World War. To summarize the complex city experience as a key context for the film is important in understanding the reasons for *The Pianist*'s firm sobriety. Paulson states the reality succinctly: "Ninety-eight percent of the Jewish population perished together with one quarter of the Polish population . . . some 720,000; a number that dwarfs the destruction of Hiroshima and Nagasaki combined . . . the greatest slaughter in a single city in human history. Warsaw thus had far more Holocaust victims than any whole country save the USSR and Poland itself."

He then notes: "The flight of twenty-odd thousand Jews . . . seems by comparison a negligible phenomenon . . . almost unnoticed by historians . . . yet it was the greatest mass escape in history . . . and the life of these fugitives in hiding for up to four years is a story with few parallels."

Given the continuing presumptions of an overwhelmingly hostile environment outside the ghetto, it is surprising that Warsaw accounted for the largest number of Jews hiding in one city. Therefore, Warsaw also provided the largest number of helpers, institutions of aid, charitable organizations, as well as those who preyed on the vulnerability of evaders and survivors.

Yet the book and the film are not about direct

the dangers of the corrupting fascination that may be elicited by their stories if there were any recourse to an excessive mise-en-scène. Instead, they want to establish a small, even ironic distance between the events and themselves. This kind of witnessing marks the dissonance between the extraordinary and the everyday, avoiding an overwhelming clamor of terror in an attempt to find a way to provide space for a thought, a distance, a breathing moment.

Immediately following the bombing of the radio station, Szpilman arrives home. Polanski shows how members of his family learn about the engulfing events. In eighteen shots and two minutes, they express a range of contrasting attitudes from passivity to bustling action to evade and survive, to go to the country. Two well-known British actors head the family as Mother (Maureen Lipman) and Father (Frank Finlay). For British audiences, this brings a strong sense of artifice as they see familiar and comfortable faces represent a bourgeois family in an atrocious situation. The interplay between these elements provides a useful distance for the viewer as he or she oscillates rapidly between familiarity and strangeness. In this way the film uses a range of artifice to shed new light on what has become too conventional in Holocaust films. It asks the audience to look again at a family on the edge, to see their uncertainty afresh.

Mother is full of a premonitory trepidation. Henryk (Ed Stoppard), Wladyslaw's brother, is developed more than in the book into a knowing and cynical figure. Polanski contrasts him with Wladyslaw as knowing more than Wladyslaw, though he does not act upon that knowledge. He would rather die in his own home. The family members and the camera quickly slide in and out of exits. Father talks about new lines of defense across the Vistula. Regina (Julia Rayner)

mocks this. Wladyslaw enters and the Steadicam holds him central, sliding past and around him as he stares bewildered at the activity. His self-absorption is evident. Our identification with him is made more complex and troubled by the processes of distancing these strategies enable.

Finally, an authentic voice of reassurance emerges as Henryk tunes in to BBC news. "There are other stations than Warsaw you know," he rather condescendingly avers. Britain has declared war and France will soon. Given our perspective on the betrayals of Poland this is not reassuring, but Father is delighted. The Polish national anthem plays on the BBC but is interrupted by Hitler's speech on defending the German nation. The radio is firmly knocked and BBC returns. The whole family gathers together and embrace in confidence for the future. They think they are together again in security. The terrible inklings of doubt are gone. This is a quite spurious coherence, one of underlying desperation and only a momentary safety.

A special dinner introduces the theme of food in relation to survival. There will be several more of them before the final meal at the Umschlagplatz. Polanski with spectacular precision develops his key task, his need to examine, within the specific possibilities of narrative fiction, the ways in which small steps of understanding the genocidal process were gained.

It is useful to group Polanski's attitude with a number of other first-person accounts, specifically in relation to the question of why the Holocaust occurred. The reference here is to a moment in Primo Levi's *Survival in Auschwitz*: "Driven by thirst, I eyed a fine icicle outside the window, within hand's reach. I opened the window and broke off the icicle but at once a large heavy guard prowling outside brutally snatched it away from me. '*Warum* [why]?' I asked in my poor German.

Adrien Brody (as Wladyslaw Szpilman) is in a crowd of Jews in the Warsaw Ghetto. From *The Pianist* (2002), directed by Roman Polanski. FOCUS FEATURES/PHOTOFEST

resistance. Rather, Szpilman and Polanski present a specific type of response to the Holocaust. Historian Raul Hilberg proposed five categories of Jewish response to genocidal oppression: resistance, alleviation, evasion, paralysis, and compliance. Hilberg and early Holocaust scholars emphasized paralysis and compliance as most typical. Then there was a counter wave of material emphasizing resistance. The stress on paralysis and compliance is seen in this response as a slur, a too excessive highlighting of the failure to resist and counterbalancing it with an emphasis on resistance. What was left out in both accounts of the Jewish experience was the fifth category, that of evasion. It is this recent area of debate that chimes so powerfully with Polanski's concern in the film, driven by his reading of Szpilman and his own experience in hiding during the war. Recent

writing on the Holocaust has stressed different ways of thinking about resistance in order to see evasion on a continuum with resistance. In this sense *The Pianist* is quite unlike other Holocaust films and is more related to the experience of Anne Frank.

These revelations of the apparently small experiences of the Holocaust represent material that tries to bridge the abyss between despair at never being able to understand and the possible extending of the knowledge to understand. The two million or so Jews who fled or went into hiding were in Paulson's opinion driven by "surely the most reasonable and human of all responses to an overwhelming hostile force." These evaders evince characteristics of the continuity between the ordinary and the extreme and the moralities that then are questioned.

I have selected three scenes from the early part of *The Pianist* to represent the processes of the film as a whole. These have been selected to represent a characteristic narrative strategy adopted by Polanski. Polanski's mise-en-scène [the composition of a scene] and camerawork to indicate how he is attempting to grapple with issues of how representation may be able to produce knowledge of this extreme experience. He uses many strategies from his earlier work, especially his mastery of precise, specific placement of the camera in relation to the deeply troubling issue of a scene. He also produces new elements, most particularly a stillness and quietness of means, in narrative and mise-en-scène that enable a gap to be opened up between horror and contemplation. The often calm and steady narrative pace thus enables a most profound sense, quieter and yet more troubled, of the frantic experience of attempts at survival.

The film begins with a prologue of the quiet and calm of a C-sharp Minor Nocturne; no title sequence; twelve fleeting black-and-white shots, newsreel with scratches, not reconstructed, suggesting urgency, each lasting only two to three seconds. This contrasts with the calm content of the shots: a sunny day, possibly Sunday, with many walking in the park with prams, flower baskets visible, a great city at rest, peace, and leisure. Only the twelfth shot breaks the security of the content. Here a newsboy hurries toward the camera and there is a close-up of his pale, serious face. Immediately the cut takes us to Polish Radio, to the final broadcast on September 23, 1939. Thus the newsreel shots suggest a time before, because by the time of the broadcast Warsaw had been under bombardment and siege from the beginning of the month. The film moves across a sharp break into an absolute insecurity. The nocturne plays over all this, and even the explosions outside

the studio hardly stop Szpilman from playing. Indeed, at first he refuses, shaking his head. Only the violent incursion of a bomb can finally do that.

Adrien Brody's quiet performance gives no answers to our many questions. We have to invest ourselves in a far more painful way into these experiences. This mode of acting only breaks up at moments of extreme stress, at the Umschlagplatz [the transfer point for deportations of Jews] after being dragged unwillingly from his family, and, because he is an artist, at the final moments of realization, signified by his wan smile as he returns to playing the nocturne. If we could identify with Szpilman as an active agent in the narrative, much would be lost. Our identification with him is rather more distant. Cooler, it is thus more icily terrifying in developing our sense of Szpilman's helplessness, reminding us of the worst nightmares of being lost and with little chance to find a way out. He meanders through the confined space of the ghetto and Warsaw. As he looks obliquely through windows, small gaps, and around corners at the catastrophe, he never sees the totality of the action, the complete picture, and neither do we.

Thus, Polanski provides a means of helping us to experience the improvisations of terror, played out day by day as oppressors seek to entrap and make the victim passive. In this Polanski follows the events of Szpilman's memoir closely, but often uses an icy and clinically calm mise-en-scène that renders the events nearly unbearable. In *The Pianist* everything must be at one remove, with no clear linear psychology. Szpilman must wander, hope, evade, make a small move, think that all is impossible and coincidental, and yet continue, , making the most of the faint and ephemeral chances that come his way. This is a description of a survival strategy. In 1945, Szpilman will return

to the same Polish Radio studio, apparently picking up exactly where he left off in 1939. This could be seen as a satisfying rounding out, as escape from darkness. But the gaze by Szpilman's returning musician friend Lednicki through the studio window suggests rather a kind of rebirth amid great sorrow and knowledge.

The Pianist represents an explicit culmination of discourses that have been a troubling undercurrent in Polanski's work, especially of the nameless, faceless, ever-present threat that exists just beyond an illusionary zone of security. The lack of reference to his wartime experience has been a significant structuring *absence* for critics of his work. *The Pianist* represents an opportunity grasped to finally open up that experience and provide a thoroughly revisionist way of representing it. For many, an initial line of enquiry would lead to the influence of Polanski's childhood in the Cracow Ghetto on his films. In his earlier works, this is characterized by a recurrent mise-en-scène of entrapment, of steadily increasing pressure, of uncertainty as to its cause, and an avoidance of generically familiar closure.

In his autobiography, Polanski devotes some twenty-five pages to his ghetto experience. The general tone of his survivor recounting is sometimes light: "I played with Polish, not just Jewish kids" and "It would be wrong to think that fear dominated our lives during this preliminary period. I had some good times too." Yet this is after another iconic moment that he uses in *The Pianist*: " 'What are they doing?' I asked. 'They're building a wall.' Suddenly it dawned on me: they were walling us in. My heart sank." The tone oscillates between the ordinary life of a child and isolated moments of realization that a gradual process of elaborate deception is enveloping the ghetto. Yet even the ghetto is better than the out-

side. After one of his many small escapes from the Podgórze Ghetto, Polanski comments, "It wasn't until I was back inside, after slipping through the wire again, that I felt entirely safe."

Other incidents from Polanski's recollections of the Cracow Ghetto appear in *The Pianist*. The most notable are the following: "Near us, guarding the assembled ghetto inmates, stood a young Polish militiaman. . . . I went up and tried out our story on him. He must have seen through it but pretended not to. His nod of assent was barely perceptible. We started running. 'Walk slowly,' he growled, 'don't run.' We walked."

He recalls when his father was being deported, "I headed back to the ghetto. . . . I saw a column of male prisoners being marched away . . . among them was my father. He didn't see me at first. I had to trot to keep up. . . . At last he spotted me. . . . He dropped back with the tacit assistance of others . . . to be farther from the nearest guard and closer to me. Then out of corner of his mouth, he hissed, 'Shove off!' "

Polanski works these autobiographical experiences into *The Pianist* as well as other incidents generically present in Holocaust representation—for example, the street executions in *Schindler's List*—but retains a narrative tone that is faithful to Szpilman's memoir. Laconic, cool, and underplayed, Polanski's account works against the tendency in other memoirs to represent the unspeakable in more graphic detail. Polanski provides a detailed if brief account, but avoids any attempt at judging what had happened to him. Again, in this approach to narrative he resembles Szpilman and others.

The ambiguities of Polanski's and Szpilman's accounts resemble those found in the narratives of survivors like Borowski and Levi. Their recounting of survival stems from an awareness of

'*Hier ist kein warum* [here there is no why],' he replied, pushing me inside with a shove. The explanation is repugnant but simple: in this place everything is forbidden, not for hidden reasons, but because the camp has been created for that purpose. If one wants to live one must learn this quickly and well." The tone of this passage, suggesting a very limited compass of view to the implications of the iconic "here, there is no why," is shared in the key survivor texts of Levi, Borowski, Szpilman, and Polanski too. Polanski's film surely attempts to find possible ways of understanding a little more of these events even though, as George Steiner has noted, "the very business of rational analysis grows unsteady before the enormity of the facts."

Szpilman apparently has had a very different experience from a camp survivor—he moves from ghetto constraint to fugitive isolation. However, the stages of the experience are in every case similar. The movement is from a search for reassurance coupled with a growing dread to the point of discovery of the very worst. This is followed by the shock of immediate survival on the ramp or at the Umschlagplatz and then the processes of survival. The need to depend upon others was a paramount principle. Anyone who hoped to make it on their own, by whatever means, was likely to fail in the attempt. No matter how small or infrequent, the processes of solidarity and help were crucial, whether from fellow Poles in Warsaw or fellow scavengers in the Auschwitz work details. No matter how cynical, self-serving, and demanding of reciprocity such sharing might entail, complete aloneness meant no chance at all. Szpilman, Polanski, Levi, and Borowski do not admit to being passive victims. All seem to be, in a sense, contemplative of an extraordinary and largely inexplicable event about which it is necessary to bear witness.

In relation to witnessing and the need to continue it as long as possible, it should not be forgotten that there is an animus against the attempt to counter the "here, there is no why" syndrome, most spectacularly by Claude Lanzmann in his documentary *Shoah* (1985). In attacking *Schindler's List*, Lanzmann proposed that, "after *Shoah* certain things can no longer be done." Indeed, he felt that feature films dramatizing ghetto and death camp experiences should be forbidden. Given Lanzmann's position, a case has to be made that Polanski and others, in making complex narratives of evasion and survival based on firsthand accounts, are essential in developing an understanding of the minutiae of the events, of the microprocesses, to preserve memory otherwise to be eventually lost and to continue analyses of the irrational monstrosity that nearly overwhelmed Szpilman, Borowski, Levi, and Polanski. Doing this with a calm and rational curiosity is an aesthetic tact that does not mask a controlled rage.

The scene at the Umschlagplatz occurs at the center of Spzilman's memoir but earlier in the film, as Polanski wants to give weight to later scenes of isolation in peeling and dilapidated apartments, echoing voices, and threatening neighbors, with only partial, sidelong looks at the history unfolding outside. Polanski adheres very closely to the book but makes some telling additions. In particular he maintains the relatively calm tone that Szpilman exhibits until the end, when he finally understands what is transpiring: "In a flash I realized what awaited the people." The family enters the Umschlagplatz searching with their eyes about what may be happening. Despite the immediate killing of the young woman in the previous scene as she asks, "Where are you taking us?," they have not yet lost hope. The scene is poised around this issue, as characters variously demonstrate a range of attitudes to this uncertainty. In ten minutes and forty-six shots, Polanski presents us Szpilman's precise description with a quiet and ferocious clarity. The option might have been to develop the scene like the selection on the camp square in *Schindler's List*, with racing camera, hysteria, and explicit terror. Instead, Polanski uses calm camera movement and analytical cutting, shot–reverse shot (set-ups) of the most conventional kind as conversations occur. The audience sees the how of the process in a series of small vignettes, of family, of children. Only near the end does the camera enable a release from this. There is an intense and sharp tilt down as a soldier throws the bolt on the door of the train carriage. Such camera usage allows for a more developed thinking about the emotional processes of courage, love, despair, of family, of knowledge that we must know but can hardly bear to know.

Polanski concentrates more on Szpilman than the book. He is the uncertain center of the scene, stumbling clumsily against people. He stares in astonishment as Halina (Jessica Kate Meyer) and Henryk return, desperate to be reunited with the family. "Stupid, stupid," he mutters to himself about their bravery and his incomprehension of the events he and the camera pick out.

There are fifteen of these short vignettes: the everyday civility of the man's doffed cap to Szpilman contradicts the audience's knowledge of the terrible inexorability of the events; the story, narrated three times, of the smothered child, contrasts strongly with the heroic silence of children in *Schindler's List*; the strangeness of the child with the bird cage looking for a lost pet; the fierce argument about resistance between the dentist (who does resist on behalf of a pregnant woman at the train and is instantly killed), the businessman, and Mr. Szpilman. The book mentions Henryk reading Shakespeare, and Polanski includes this but adds lines from *The Merchant of Venice*. This may seem contrived but is appropriate, given Henryk's ironic distancing of himself from the events contrasted with Szpilman's mystified uncertainty.

The scene draws to its terrible climax. Father divides a caramel into six pieces for each member of the family, returning to the theme of food in relation to love and survival. A train whistle sounds, with a few dark chords from the understated score. Guards gather; the emphasis is on the young Jewish Police, with a few Germans and Ukrainians in the background. These well-fed young men know what is happening. "Off to the melting pot," is the last line of the scene, delivered by one of them to a German guard. One of the most mysterious moments of the film now occurs, one not in the book. Szpilman says to Halina, "It's a funny time to say this but I wish I knew you better." Halina thanks him. I assume Polanski added this strange yet deeply touching moment to emphasize that kinds of knowing/not knowing are at stake in Holocaust representation, even knowledge of ourselves and those close to us. Szpilman's last chance to know his sister has gone, echoing in reverse the loving "shove off" of Polanski's father.

Many reviewers noted the understated tone of Szpilman's account of his experiences. For example, Lisa Appignanesi wrote: "The immediacy of Szpilman's account goes hand in hand with a rare tone of innocence. We are drawn in to share his surprise and then disbelief at the horrifying progress of events. His shock and ensuing numbness become ours, so that acts of ordinary kindness or humanity take on an aura of miracle." Szpilman's book has something also of the quiet desperation and submerged anxiety in Chopin's music as well. The key piece of the film is the C-sharp Minor Nocturne that Szpilman reports playing on the last broadcast of Polish Radio in 1939. It is also the piece he played for Captain Wilm Hosenfeld (Thomas Kretschmann) when they met late in 1944 (not the Ballade in G Minor that is used in the film). This nocturne was valued by some critics for its modesty and balance, with "an inexplicable yet compelling unity . . . as if passing through a dreamlike landscape . . . with a quiet and solemn expectancy and having a melody that is one of the most vocal in Chopin."

The coolness and balance of Szpilman's writing can be quite disconcerting even when he recalls extreme events, like when he is starving and visited by the treacherous Szalas (Andrew Tiernan), the only Polish helper who fails him. He achieves this through slight deprecation, wit, and even here not wanting to apportion blame: "Beaming, evidently with his mind on something else, he would always enquire, 'Still alive then, are you?' I was still alive, even though the combination of malnutrition and grief had given me jaundice. Szalas did not take that too seriously, and told me the cheering tale of his grandfather, whose girlfriend had jilted him when he suddenly went down with jaundice."

The film remains largely true to this tone throughout, constantly drawing back when there might be a temptation to impose something more, a point of view explaining human behavior and attributing unambiguous blame. At the end Polanski allows himself to break the rule he has imposed upon himself to wind his experience into that of Szpilman in order to create a world of evasion that had paralleled his own. Only then, over the end credits, does he allow an explosion into the exuberance of a concert performance of the Grande Polonaise Brillante.

Polanski has delineated another way of handling a narration of the Holocaust through film. Those familiar with parallel texts such as *Schindler's List* will notice many elements in common, down to particular scenes deemed necessary to include. But Polanski redirects these details away from sentiment and melodrama, consoling as these are, and toward difficulty. When asked about his method of writing about being in Auschwitz, Primo Levi responded: "I prefer the role of witness to that of judge. I can bear witness only to the things that I myself endured and saw. My books are not history books. Remembering is a duty. These experiences were not meaningless. The camps were not an accident, unforeseen historical accident." This quiet and even mode of reporting atrocious events is also the task of Szpilman and Polanski.

Abridged from: Michael Stevenson, "*The Pianist* and Its Contexts: Polanski's Narration of Holocaust Evasion and Survival," in *The Cinema of Roman Polanski: Dark Spaces of the World*, ed. John Orr and Elżbieta Ostrowska, 146–57 (London: Wallflower, 2006).

Source: Wladyslaw Szpilman, *The Pianist: The Extraordinary True Story of One Man's Survival in Warsaw, 1939–1945* (New York: Picador USA, 1999).

Background: http://www.ushmm.org/wlc/sp/article.php?ModuleId=10005069.

Bibliography

Appignanesi, Lisa. "Notes from the Warsaw Ghetto." Review of *The Pianist: The Extraordinary True Story of One Man's Survival in Warsaw, 1939–1945*, by Wladyslaw Szpilman. *Observer*, March 28, 1999.

Bauer, Yehuda. *Rethinking the Holocaust.* New Haven, CT: Yale University Press, 2001.

Borowski, Tadeusz. *This Way for the Gas, Ladies and Gentlemen and Other Stories.* Translated by Barbara Vedder. New York: Viking, 1967.

Hilberg, Raul. *The Destruction of the European Jews.* London: Holmes and Meier, 1985.

Levi, Primo. *Survival in Auschwitz.* Translated by Stuart Woolf. New York: Touchstone, 1996.

Liebman, Stuart, ed. *Claude Lanzmann's Shoah: Key Essays.* New York: Oxford University Press, 2007.

Mazierska, Ewa. *Roman Polanski: The Cinema of a Cultural Traveler.* New York: I. B. Tauris, 2007.

Paulson, Gunnar S. *Secret City: The Hidden Jews of Warsaw, 1940–1945.* New Haven, CT: Yale University Press, 2002.

Polanski, Roman. *Roman / by Polanski.* New York: Morrow, 1984.

24. A Hungarian Holocaust Saga

Fateless

CATHERINE PORTUGES

Fateless (*Sorstalánság*), directed by Lajos Koltai [A] Germany, Hungary, and the United Kingdom, 2005

In the spring of 2004, on the eve of Hungary's admission to the European Union, the nation commemorated the sixtieth anniversary of the Holocaust, engaging in sustained reflection on the intensive massacre of Hungarian Jews in 1944. After decades of relative silence, writers, artists, scholars, and filmmakers were in the vanguard of this process, opening new spaces for discussion and research. By the 1970s, the Shoah had begun to reappear in literary texts produced by a generation of writers such as Imre Kertész, who bore witness to their experience as an adolescent survivor of the camps. In his essay "Long Dark Shadow," Kertész writes:

> Nothing would be simpler than to collect, name and evaluate those Hungarian literary works that were born under direct or indirect influence of the Holocaust. . . . However, in my view that is not the problem. The problem,

dear listeners, is the imagination. To be more precise: to what extent is the imagination capable of coping with the fact of the Holocaust? How can the imagination take in, receive the Holocaust, and, because of this receptive imagination, to what extent has the Holocaust become part of our ethical life and ethical culture? . . . This is what we must talk about.

Born in Budapest in 1929, Kertész was awarded the Nobel Prize in Literature in 2002 "for writing that upholds the fragile experience of the individual against the barbaric arbitrariness of history" (The Nobel Prize in Literature 2002). His semi-autobiographical novel, *Fateless* (or *Fatelessness*, in the later translation discussed below), completed in the mid-1960s and published in 1975, draws on the author's own tragic experience as a fifteen-year old Hungarian Jew in Auschwitz and Buchenwald. Following his liberation from Buchenwald in May 1945, he returned to Budapest to work as a journalist, but he was fired in 1951, after the Communist takeover, for refusing to submit to the party's cultural policies. The Nobel Prize catapulted Kertész onto the international stage, eliciting accolades as well as ambivalence and hostility in his native Hungary. Still relatively unknown and unappreciated in Hungary in the 1980s, at the time of the Nobel award he was already a fellow at the Institute for Advanced Study in Berlin, and in 2005 he was awarded an honorary doctorate by the Free University of Berlin. According to the Swedish Academy, "In his writing Imre Kertész explores the possibility of continuing to live and think as an individual in an era in which the subjection of human beings to social forces has become increasingly complete. . . . [*Fateless*] upholds the fragile experience of the individual against the barbaric arbitrariness of history" (Nobel Prize in Literature).

Marcell Nagy (as Gyuri Köves) prostrate on a cart for corpses in a concentration camp. From *Fateless* (2005), directed by Lajos Koltai. THINKFILM/PHOTOFEST

The Nobel committee acknowledged the novel's more disturbing aspects, in particular its "lack of moral indignation,"(Nobel Prize in Literature) an assessment that may be attributable in part to the writer's spare, unsentimental prose and mordant Central European wit. Its first English translation was disavowed by Kertész, who, however, approved the second, by Tim Wilkinson, published in 2004 and titled *Fatelessness* rather than *Fateless*. Narrated in the first person from the point of view of György "Gyuri" Köves, the novel did not enjoy international recognition until 1990. Kertész may have anticipated criticism of the novel's "lack of moral indignation" in 1991, when he asserted: "My country has yet to face up to the skeleton in the closet, namely, awareness of the issue of the Holocaust, which has not yet taken root in Hungarian culture, and those writing about it [still] stand on the sidelines. . . . I

think it is a success if my book has made even a slight contribution to this process" (quoted in Riding, 2002).

A significant gesture toward reinscribing the Holocaust in Hungarian memory was made by Hungarian Motion Picture Foundation in 2003, when it decided to fund a film adaptation of *Fateless*. That a large-scale, multinational project based on this highly controversial novel was approved for production in difficult economic times demonstrates the extent to which both the author and the Hungarian Ministry of Culture embraced the opportunity afforded by the Nobel laureate's new status. With a budget of $13 million (one of the largest in the history of Hungarian cinema), over 500 extras, and a screenplay also written by Kertész, *Fateless* was Hungary's entry for best foreign language film at the 2006 Academy Awards (the South African entry, *Tsotsi*, won that year).

Paradoxically, perhaps, the frenzy of media attention brought to the surface deep and persistent layers of Hungarian antisemitism.

Fateless inaugurates the directorial debut of Lajos Koltai, the distinguished Oscar-winning cinematographer who had worked on more than seventy features, including such renowned films as István Szabó's *Mephisto* (1982), *Sunshine* (1999), and *Taking Sides* (2001). Kertész approved of the selection of Koltai as director; in turn, Koltai proposed that Kertész adapt his own novel for the screen, after the author's rejection of an earlier synopsis that had transformed the project into the story of a wealthy New York violinist who, one day in Budapest, remembers, in flashback, what had happened to him fifty years earlier. The collaborators agreed on the fundamental question posed by *Fateless*: to whom does time belong? (Kertész has written a long article on this issue, titled "To Whom Does Auschwitz Belong?") Having taken fifteen years to complete, Kertész and Koltai seem to conclude that it is the perpetrators rather than the protagonist who determine temporality. Accordingly, the novel's force derives from a unique style of language that creates a certain distance vis-à-vis the events it recounts. Adapting it to the screen required the coordination of each shot and color choice with image and music, a process that, according to the filmmakers, risked altering the novel's intention. "We did not want sentimentality; we wanted to keep a distance," Koltai has said. "After Imre had finished the screenplay, he said, 'I give you this as a present, and then you give me the present back as a film.'"

Crafting the screenplay some thirty years after he had written the novel, Kertész found that the reality of his lived experience had become integrated with the novel itself, thereby combining his memory of the real camp experience with that of his alter ego, Gyuri. "The film is more autobiographical than the book," he said in an interview (http://isurvived.org) at his Berlin home: "I'm not even sure if I wrote the screenplay from memories or from memories of the book." The paradoxical nature of this statement evokes the perplexing nature of memory and its transformation by writers into what Serge Doubrovsky has called *autofiction*, ("L'autofiction") a combination of the genres of autobiography and fiction—the liminal zone inhabited by the writer.

The production was quickly targeted for criticism by some Hungarians, who objected to plans to film scenes in their villages where the camp of Buchenwald was to be recreated—an unwelcome reminder, they contended, of a chapter of history better relegated to the past. Kertész has stated, perhaps in reference to his refusal to endorse the reading of his protagonist as a victim, as well as his literary use of irony and humor within the novel's tragic framework: "It is a proud work—people will never forgive the book or me. . . . The Holocaust is a state that has not yet come to an end. I feel it everywhere. There is no catharsis. You cannot come to terms with the Holocaust. . . . Hungary has not yet taken its turn in coming to terms with the past. It is true that Hungary has indeed known great suffering as a country under threat, which makes its people understandably more sensitive to distress. But its time for reflection will come, even if the nation has not yet acquired the power or solidarity or generosity to complete the process. Membership in the European Union now gives the country *carte blanche* to do so" ("The Holocaust").

The film's historical context warrants a brief overview. Of the 825,000 Jews living in Hungary in 1941, approximately 63,000 died or were killed before the German occupation of March 1944. During the occupation, more than 500,000 died from maltreatment or were killed or deported. Some 255,000 Jews, or fewer than a third of those living in Greater Hungary in March 1944, survived the Shoah. In mid-May 1944, the Hungarian authorities, in concert with the SS, began systematically deporting Hungarian Jews; Adolf Eichmann, the Nazis' chief deportation expert, worked with the Hungarian authorities. The Hungarian police proceeded to conduct raids, brutally forcing Jews into deportation trains. In less than two months, nearly 440,000 Jews were deported from Hungary. The great majority went to Auschwitz, although several thousand were also sent to the Austrian border as slave laborers. By the beginning of July 1944, the only Jewish community remaining in Hungary was that of Budapest, the capital.

Fateless chronicles the experiences of Gyuri, a fifteen-year-old Jewish boy from Budapest. His youthful innocence is revealed in the opening scene—photographed in muted, autumnal hues—when, as he walks down a bustling thoroughfare in the metropolis, he adjusts his jacket lapel to boldly display his yellow Jewish star. During a farewell dinner for his father in the family's well-appointed home, there is fearful talk of war among the family and guests, all of whom are wearing the yellow star. Separated from Gyuri's mother, the father—a prosperous merchant who has lost his business due to the imposition of a quota discriminating against Jews—has been ordered to join a forced labor battalion the following day. His departure initiates Gyuri's traumatic odyssey and his ongoing quest for surrogate father figures.

Gyuri leaves school after his father's deportation to work in a factory with other Jewish boys. When the bus taking him there is stopped at a random checkpoint, a Hungarian policeman orders all passengers wearing the yellow star to dis-embark. Along with other boys, Gyuri is arrested and detained. Members of the Arrow Cross, the Hungarian equivalent of the SS, register the boys and deport them to Auschwitz-Birkenau. The color palette drains out during this section of the film, shifting to a pale blue-gray, monochromatic tint as Gyuri is transferred from one camp to another. Starvation, illness, boredom, forced labor, dehumanization, and death become part of his daily life, as dissociation and dissolution threaten to overwhelm his still-developing adolescent personality. Speaking neither Hebrew nor Yiddish, and rationalizing incomprehensible events as "probably natural" or "probably a mistake," he wonders whether he is the pawn of an absurd, arbitrary destiny, asking: "Who can judge what is possible or believable in a concentration camp?"

The lack of control over his own fate is foregrounded when the internees are forced to stand for countless hours in formation on the Appellplatz. As they grow faint, staggering from exhaustion, the camera remains at ground level, tracking through their ranks. In visually striking overhead shots, the hypnotic pattern of the lineup is captured as if to suggest, in an abstract and boldly daring fashion, the prisoners' solidarity in the face of the annihilation of their identities. In the subsequent scene, weak, terrified, and suffering from starvation, Gyuri leaves his bed in search of the latrine, barely able to slog through the mud. The next day his friend, Bándi Czitrom (Áron Demé), a fellow Jew from Budapest a few years older than Gyuri, takes him under his wing, offering the younger boy, now extremely debilitated, his own jacket and lecturing him on survival strategies. When I interviewed Koltai in Budapest during the film's production, he addressed this aspect of his interpretation of the novel and screenplay: "What I learned from the books of

Kertész is that . . . boredom in the camps was a serious difficulty that few have written about or discussed. There will be intervals in the film where nothing happens, when all you can do is watch a sunset. There were sunsets in the camp; there was still beauty. . . . The composer, Ennio Morricone, wants the music to be completed first, and the editing to harmonize with the music. . . . I have read that the only language of the Holocaust should be silence."

Although Koltai minimizes the cinematic use of dramatic climaxes and violent moments, the sumptuous beauty and mastery of his visual compositions (he is credited as both director and cinematographer) and the quality of the film's production values imbue *Fateless* with a degree of emotional symbolism and affective power that are at odds with the ironic, understated dialogue and brutal settings. Similarly, the minimalist score (with vocal chants by Lisa Gerrard) by honorary Oscar-winning composer Ennio Morricone tends to match the screenplay's starkly unsentimental language, evoking unease and horror while at the same time suggesting the struggle for sanity and survival, through the dreamlike, even surreal, internal world of the youthful protagonist. The film thus paradoxically exploits its musical sound design through vocal chants and a composed score, despite the director's stated position that the Shoah is better represented by silence. Further challenging this view are Roman Polanski's *The Pianist* (2002), based on Wladyslaw Szpilman's autobiography, in which music plays a key role in the Polish protagonist's wartime survival, and Steven Spielberg's *Schindler's List* (1993), in which a German soldier sits at a piano in an abandoned apartment, playing Mozart, as his comrades seek out and slaughter Jews attempting to avoid being moved out of the ghetto. Less plot-driven than either *The Pianist* or *Schindler's List*, *Fateless* is

surely among the most existential of Holocaust reconstructions, evoking (as its title suggests) a state of being.

Although Gyuri's individual odyssey is closely documented in every scene, Koltai and Kertész remind the viewer of the machinery behind the torment of ghettoization, deportation, and extermination. How, wonders Gyuri, can happiness be justified in such a context: "I would like to live a little longer in this beautiful concentration camp." Kertész writes: "In Auschwitz, you hope that nothing happens" (*Fateless* film script). The author's nuanced and deeply philosophical exploration does not exclude the possibility of moments of friendship and even fleeting happiness (he has said that whenever the system, founded on the destruction of the individual, marked a pause, he experienced a form of happiness) (*Koltai Napló 2001–2003*) as part of the boy's experience of incarceration. We are invited to imagine that such moments are experienced through the small thoughts that comfort the deportees: memories of the sun's warmth, of loved ones from the past, or of the taste of a family meal arise unprompted, in contrast to the experience of hunger and deprivation.

Kertész has criticized *Schindler's List* for portraying those who did not die in captivity as in some sense victorious; for him, there was no victory possible in the concentration camp system. Yet perhaps unconsciously, *Fateless* disconcertingly shares certain of its predecessor's perspectives and cinematic techniques. A scene in the showers, for instance, may be seen as echoing and paralleling a similar sequence in Spielberg's film, in which a train carrying Jewish women is accidentally redirected to Auschwitz. The women are taken to what they believe to be the gas chambers, and the camera lingers on Helen Hirsch as she removes her blouse. The women then weep with joy when water falls from the shower heads. Critics and viewers have found this scene to be exploitative, a manipulation of suspense in the interest of intensifying the viewer's anticipation of the sequence's dramatic denouement.

Koltai's directorial decisions, however, may be seen to a certain extent as entering into dialogue with the ethical positions of Claude Lanzmann, director of the documentary masterpiece *Shoah* (1985), an oral history shot without archive footage or historical reconstruction, utilizing only first-person testimony from Jewish, Polish, and German survivors, camp guards, and local villagers whose indifference made them passive collaborators. For Kertész, a member of the last generation of survivors, the major question since *Shoah* remains whether or not to depict scenes of the concentration camps. (Kertész has been a vocal critic of *Schindler's List*, yet he expresses esteem for Roberto Begnini's *Life Is Beautiful* (1997). In Lanzmann's view, new technologies of representation capable of deconstructing images of the camps and thereby of creating new connections may "undermine the status of the image as visual evidence, as a reliable witness." Interrogating Hungary's role in the Holocaust and offering an engaging young protagonist with whom audiences can identify, the film exposes the difficulty and contradictions of these overriding questions of representation without providing definitive answers.

Temporality—the chronological passage of time as well as the protagonists' subjective experience of it—is a fundamental aspect of Gyuri's journey in *Fateless*. Throughout the course of his harrowing ordeal, the narrative itself seems to unravel and become depersonalized, as if reflecting the protagonist's own emotional and physical disintegration, and the psychic effects of separation and dissociation. When the boys sit in the shadow of the Birkenau crematoria discussing another boy who has been selected to be gassed, the looming smokestacks and heavy gray skies above seem a harbinger of their destiny. And when Gyuri looks on as a guard savors his meal, he mimes the guard's gestures as if to internalize and vicariously consume the food of which he has been deprived. At another point a man throws the boy over his shoulder, and we see the world from Gyuri's delirious perspective—upside down—as he passes mound after mound of corpses. Deploying these visual and rhythmic strategies, Koltai eschews conventional narrative structure and transforms the moment into a nearly indecipherable perception.

Despite his mastery of the narrative's epic scope, the filmmaker suggests that it is rather the intimate gestures, connections, and observations that enable the protagonist to survive his devastating internment, against all odds. The unique power of *Fateless*, then, derives in part from a commitment to recast and interrogate accepted notions of dehumanization in the death camps, while remaining faithful to the bildungsroman's mission to document a young protagonist's coming of age and ultimate survival. Marcell Nagy performs the role of Gyuri with an extraordinary depth of maturity and understated intelligence, aloofness, and wonderment, projecting an uncommon authenticity in his evolution from innocent Budapest boy to adolescent Holocaust survivor.

Koltai's precise, gray-toned lighting opens up in the final section of *Fateless*, flooding the screen with a vivid color scheme when, after a series of random experiences and devastating twists of fate, and still clad in striped concentration camp garb, Gyuri returns to Budapest, now under Soviet control. (Likewise, *Schindler's List* begins in color, which disappears as the lot of the Jews deteriorates, reappearing only in the concluding scenes as Jews survive their ordeal.) Bereft and dazed, Gyuri makes his way back to the family's apartment, only to be turned away by its current inhabitants. Although some of his Yiddish-speaking fellow inmates had rejected him as "Gentile Gyuri," he misses the solace and camaraderie he had received from others; their gestures of kindness and humanity contrast sharply with the incomprehension that greets him in the irrevocably transformed city, leaving him profoundly alienated from the postwar community and his own relatives, well-meaning though they may be. Like many survivors confronted by indifference or rejection from those unable or unwilling to serve as empathic listeners to the narrative of the returning deportee, Gyuri misses the empathic response of a resonating "other," an interlocutor or community indispensable for enabling the traumatized survivor to rebuild his inner and external worlds and counter his fear that his fate may have been deserved.

In a scene that is not part of the original novel, an American army officer (Daniel Craig), himself Jewish, encourages Gyuri to emigrate to the United States, but the boy insists on returning to his family in Budapest. "The officer is a composite of various Americans who said the same thing," Kertész has explained. "For everyone, it was an important decision whether to return home or go somewhere else. Those who had an idea there would be socialism in Hungary did not go back. I couldn't imagine going anywhere except home. I was like a stray dog" (http://isurvived.org).

But home was not as Kertész—or Gyuri—imagined it: his father had perished in Mauthausen; his stepmother had remarried; and he found his old apartment occupied by another family. The magnitude of the loss of more than half a million Hungarian Jews in the Shoah remains beyond his grasp; asked about atrocities in the camps, he remembers his happiness. "Yes," the novel concludes in Gyuri's voice, "the next time I am asked, I ought to speak about that, the happiness of the concentration camps. If indeed I am asked. And provided I myself don't forget."

The psychoanalyst Dori Laub has called the Holocaust "an event without a witness"("An Event without a Witness"), in reference to the inability of some survivors to acknowledge and express the trauma they experienced. Realizing that he misses the sense of community he experienced in the camps, Gyuri feels alienated from both his Christian neighbors, who turned a blind eye to his fate, and the Jewish family friends who avoided deportation and who now want to put the war behind them. His indifference, detachment, and hostility toward the Hungarians he encounters mirror the profound dislocation and shattering alienation reported by many survivors and returning deportees. It is as if his very physical existence is experienced as a threat by friends, relatives, and neighbors, who—while making an effort to ask about his experience—betray deep discomfort when he attempts to respond. They reject the opportunity to engage him in authentic exchange, instead urging him to forget the traumatic experience that has so comprehensively transformed him. This dynamic of severed connection to others bears out recent research on the role of witness, suggesting that what had long been assumed to be the survivors' censorship of their own experiences—their own affective responsiveness—may well have been as much a result of others' inability to hear them than a self-imposed silence. The indirect language of fiction may serve to shield the subject from raw affect, as when Gyuri encounters a Holocaust denier during his odyssey, while it simultaneously expresses trauma. Gyuri's testimony implicates everyone; in order to transcend his isolation and return to life, he must abandon the generalized hatred he feels and weave together his life before and after liberation.

Kertész has suggested that he did not know even as a child what to make of the Jewish identity that had been thrust on him: "What kind of a Jew is one who did not have a religious upbringing, speaks no Hebrew, is not very familiar with the basic texts of Jewish culture, and lives not in Israel but in Europe? . . . But as a Jew, I was taken to Auschwitz, as a Jew I was in the death camps, and as a Jew I live in a society that does not like Jews, one with great anti-Semitism. . . . I am Jewish, I accept it, but to a large extent . . . it was imposed on me."

Like the author, the protagonist must assume the Jewish identity imposed on him, seeking to claim within it his own agency, in part by rupturing the master narratives that are overwhelmingly applied to the Holocaust. By upholding "the fragile experience of the individual against the barbaric arbitrariness of history," *Fateless* problematizes and foregrounds questions that confront filmmakers who focus on Holocaust memory: how to transmit the Shoah—the profound destruction of life, the absolute pain—to contemporary audiences, especially younger viewers, who, as Koltai told me in 2005 during an interview," "fall in love with the boy and realize that his fate could be theirs . . . it could happen to anyone anywhere in the world today." Sustaining a respectful historical, generational, and aesthetic distance from the protagonist's quest for meaning in his tragic life, the film suggests that if indeed the notion of "happiness" in such circumstances is shocking, it was nonetheless the author's intention. "I took the word out of its everyday context and made it seem scandalous," says Kertész. "It

was an act of rebellion against the role of victim which society had assigned me. It was a way of assuming responsibility, of defining my own fate" (http://isurvived.org). As Kertész confessed in his Nobel acceptance speech, he has gazed into the eye of the Gorgon and has been able to continue living in the aftermath of catastrophe.

Source: Imre Kertész, *Fatelessness*, translated by Tim Wilkinson (New York: Vintage International, 2004).
    Background: http://www.ushmm.org/wlc/es/article.php?ModuleId=10005457; http://www.ushmm.org/wlc/es/article.php?ModuleId=10005458.

Bibliography

Bori, Erzsébet. "The Second Wave: Speaking out on the Holocaust." *Hungarian Quarterly* 177 (spring 2005). http://www.hungarianquarterly.com/no177/11.html.

Braham, Randolph. *The Politics of Genocide: The Holocaust in Hungary*. New York: Columbia University Press, 1981.

Deák, István. "The Holocaust in Hungary." *Hungarian Quarterly* 176 (winter 2005). http://www.hungarianquarterly.com/no176/6.html.

Doubrovsky, Serge, "L'autofiction: Definition de Serge Doubrovsky." http://serieslitteraires.org/site/article.php3?id_article=191; http://isurvived.org/InThe News/Kertesz_Imre-movie.html.

Hirsch, Joshua. *Afterimage: Film, Trauma, and the Holocaust*. Philadelphia: Temple University Press, 2004.

Kértesz, Imre. *Fateless* film script, Magvetö, Budapest: 2001 (English subtitle).

Kértesz, Imre. Nobel Laureate for Literature 2002, Guest of the Artists-in-Berlin Programme 1993, "The Holocaust is a state that has not yet come to an end." http://www.daad.de/alumni/en/4.2.6_07.html.

Kertész, Imre. "Long Dark Shadow," trans. Imre Goldstein. In *Contemporary Jewish Writing in Hungary: An Anthology*, ed. Susan Rubin Suleiman & Eva Forgacs. Lincoln: U. of Nebraska Press, 2003. 171–177.

Kertész, Imre. "The Nobel Prize in Literature 2002." Nobelprize.org, 23 May 2011. http://nobelprize.org/nobel_prizes/literature/laureates/2002.

Kertesz, Imre, speaking in *Koltai Napló 2001–2003*, documentary of the filming of "Fateless," directed by András Muhi and Klára Muhi, Budapest: Muhi Productions, 2004.

Lanzmann, Claude. *Shoah: An Oral History of the Holocaust; The Complete Text of the Film*. New York: Pantheon, 1985.

Laub, Dori M.D. "An Event without a Witness: Truth, Testimony and Survival" in Shoshana Felman & Dori Laub M.D. *Testimony: Crises of Witnessing in Literature, Psychoanalysis and History* in (New York: Routledge, 1991.

Nádas, Péter. "Imre Kertész's Work and His Subject." *Hungarian Quarterly* 168 (winter 2002). http://www .hungarianquarterly.com/no168/3.html. Nobel Prize in Literature: The Laureates (2002). http://www .nobel.se/literature/laureates/index.html.

Portuges, Catherine. "Jewish Identity in Post-Communist Hungarian Cinema." *Assaph-Kolnoa Studies in the Cinema and Visual Arts* 1, no. 1 (1998): 83–101.

Riding, Alan. "The Holocaust, from a Teenage View." *New York Times*, January 3, 2006 http://www.nytimes .com/2006/01/03/movies/MoviesFeatures/03fate .html.

Riding, Alan. "Nobel for Hungarian Writer Who Survived the Death Camps" *New York Times* (11 October 2002): A7–A8.

Spiró, György. "In Art Only the Radical Exists." *Hungarian Quarterly* 168 (winter 2002). http://www.hun garianquarterly.com/no168/2.shtml.

Zoklos, Magdalena. "Apocalyptic Writing: Trauma and Community in Imre Kertész's *Fateless*." *Angelaki* 15, no. 3 (2010): 87–98.

25. Filming the Text of Witness

Francesco Rosi's *The Truce*

MILLICENT MARCUS

The Truce (*La tregua*), directed by Francesco Rosi [A]
France, Germany, Italy, and Switzerland, 1997

In his decision to film Primo Levi's *The Reawakening* [entitled *The Truce* in its Italian edition], Francesco Rosi faced a doubly formidable challenge. Not only was he adapting a text of indisputable literary merit and thus risking the invidious comparisons that such projects routinely invite, but he was adapting a work that testifies to what Primo Levi called "the central fact, the stain" on twentieth-century European history. Because Levi's book is a text of witness, it is expected that the filmmaker not deviate from the original, to avoid charges of violating the sacrosanct relationship between the language of witness and its referent. This expectation is intensified by the moral and historical truth claims inherent in first-person accounts of the Shoah.

Such intolerance to the interpretive freedom of the filmmaker works against the driving force of Holocaust testimony, which is to keep the story alive through constant elaboration, adaptation, and retelling of it to engage new generations of listeners. The text of witness is an ongoing, open-ended narrative that resists definitive formulations and rejects closure. "What the testimony does not offer," writes Shoshana Felman, "is a completed statement, a definitive account of those events. In the testimony, language is in process and in trial, it does not possess itself as a conclusion, as the contestation of a verdict or the self-transparency of knowledge."

Levi's own literary production offers eloquent proof of the need constantly to rewrite the text of witness. After his most straightforward rendering of his experiences in *Survival in Auschwitz* (1947), Levi saw fit to reprocess the story by chemical means in *The Periodic Table* (1975) and then to revisit it at a still higher level of abstraction in the thematically organized essays of *The Drowned and the Saved* (1986). Not only does Levi feel compelled to rewrite and rethink his story at various times, he denies that there could ever be a definitive Holocaust writing, a truly referential account of what happened at Auschwitz. In his refusal to claim a privileged relationship between his writings and the Holocaust referent, along with his own compulsion constantly to reinvent the text of witness, Levi invites others to take up the challenge—to interpret, elaborate, adapt, and in so doing to keep the testimony alive.

There is another way in which Rosi's adaptation fulfills the testimonial imperative of Levi's writing. Integral to the retelling, according to psychoanalyst Dori Laub, is the presence of a listener, an "addressable other" who enables the victim to contain the enormity of trauma, which has "no beginning, no ending, no before, no during and no after." Testimony cannot occur in the absence of an addressable other, an "authentic listener" willing to take on the cognitive and moral responsibility of receiving the narrative. This is what I call "the covenant of witness," an agreement on the part of the listener to accept the full burden of knowledge, and, to quote Levi's poem from *Survival in Auschwitz*, "meditate that this has happened." The recurrent nightmare that frequently haunted Levi's sleep involved the terror of not finding listeners willing to enter the covenant of witness, of returning home and telling the story to a group of family and friends who remain indifferent, distracted, and who finally withdraw from his presence.

By retelling the story with the creative latitude justified by Levi's own refusal of absolute authority and by adapting the story to a mass medium that will exponentially increase the audience of "addressable others," Rosi becomes an "enabler" of witness as his film takes its place in the ongoing process of testimony. In what I consider the directorial center of the film, Rosi conflates two episodes from the book to make explicit the moral impulse behind his adaptation of Levi's text. Rosi brings together the scene in the market of Cracow, where Primo learns to sell shirts under the flamboyant mentorship of the Greek, with that in the train station of Trzebinia, where a group of onlookers marvel at the protagonist's Auschwitz attire. In the memoir, the presence of a kind and cultured lawyer in the crowd who could speak French and German convinced Levi that he had finally found the interlocutor he had sought so long—"the messenger, the spokesman of the civilian world" who would enable him to put into ordered narrative terms the inchoate experience of Auschwitz—in other words, the listener who would allow him to bear witness. As the lawyer translates his outpouring of testimony into Polish for the benefit of the crowd, Primo soon realizes that his account has been censored, that "Italian political prisoner" has been substituted for "Italian Jew" as the explanation for his internment at Auschwitz. When Primo questions the lawyer about the mistranslation, the response—"It is better for you. The war is not over"—offers chilling proof of the difficulty he will face in finding and engaging the sympathies of an "addressable other."

That Levi's translator is a lawyer is laden with irony. Not only has Levi's advocate failed to win his client a fair public hearing, he has subverted the metaphoric system on which all Holocaust testimony is based—that of a court of law whose judges "are you," according to the author's charge to his readers in a subsequent edition of *Survival in Auschwitz*. The passage ends with the dispersal of the crowd, which has somehow understood the substance of Primo's quarrel with the lawyer and refuses to receive the testimony.

Because the corresponding scene in the film is accompanied by an extremely obtrusive cinematic device—one that calls attention to the presence of the filmmaker and his perspective—we may see this as the moment in which Rosi explicitly accepts the imperative to witness. When Primo asks the lawyer, "Why didn't you tell them I am a Jew?" the patronizing French answer in the text is not forthcoming. Instead, the camera cranes up high enough to afford an aerial view of the crowd withdrawing from Primo. In foregrounding the technology of the medium, Rosi announces his own role as a translator of Levi's memoir, a mediator between the written word and the language of audiovisual spectacle. The lawyer is the foil for Rosi, who corrects the character's deliberate misrepresentation of the chronicle. Accordingly, John Turturro's Primo Levi is far more aggressive than his textual counterpart, confronting the Polish crowd with the evidence of Holocaust history. "At Auschwitz, not far from here, there was a camp full of innocent people—men, women, mothers, children, burned in crematoria, in ovens."

Rosi demonstrates his awareness of the filmmaker's role as translator of the written text, but also of the unconsumability of his message. By conflating the episode in the marketplace with the scene of the need for translation, Rosi acknowledges his film's status as consumer object in search of a mass audience. When Primo holds up the Greek's white shirt for sale but is unable to peddle it because of his own striped jacket with its ominous number and yellow star, Rosi announces the "discomfort" of his message and challenges his audience not to withdraw like the crowd at the marketplace. Rosi consciously invokes the audience not to deny Levi's witnessing, but to be morally accountable and not turn away from the truth of Auschwitz.

In convening us as the audience of witness, Rosi inscribes his own awareness of the challenge facing the director to invent a film language adequate to the task. One of Rosi's most effective strategies is to make explicit through a series of performed moments the power of spectacle to bring about social transformation. A moving example occurs in the scene in the Russian variety show staged in celebration of the Allied victory in Europe. Halfway into the entertainment, a Soviet officer performs an imitation of Fred Astaire, using a Cossack sword in place of a cane and making a number of Bolshoi adjustments to the American dancer's choreography. With the introduction of a Hollywood musical into this scene comes the invitation to a collective wishfulfillment fantasy that exceeds national borders and ideological divides. The Fred Astaire–Ginger Rogers collaboration signifies glamour and romance, enabling the Holocaust survivors to identify so powerfully with Hollywood exemplars that they can imaginatively overcome their wretchedness and be swept up in the magic of myth. Exchanging shy looks of desire, the men and women in the audience do as the lyrics suggest, slowly beginning to dance "cheek to cheek," oblivious to the distance separating their threadbare, emaciated selves from the luxury and elegance of the Hollywood icons. What more poignant proof of triumph over the bestiality of the camps than to be able to feel the first stirrings of sexual desire through the elegant filter of Hollywood romance?

If the appeal of the text of witness to the addressable other is verbal in nature, then the film of witness must find a medium-specific equivalent to that address. Rosi achieves this by establishing a regime of gazes mediated by the character of Primo within the film that he turns back on us at the conclusion. The director attributed his decision to cast John Turturro as Levi to the actor's "way of interiorizing experiences and re-externalizing them through delicacy, humor, but also the great firmness with which Primo Levi expresses his ideas." The act of looking translates the first-person narrative of Levi's memoir into cinematic terms, making Primo's gaze the conduit through which the Holocaust and its aftermath are registered and conveyed to us.

Rosi's decision to have Turturro wear glasses privileges Primo's function as a visual mediator between the events of the Liberation and our perception of them. Like the written text, the film is bracketed by acts of seeing, of raising the eyes up from the bondage of the ground-level existence to begin the "return to life," as co-scriptwriter Stefano Rulli described the story. When the Russian soldiers arrive to liberate the camp, Primo lifts his eyes in a gesture that signals the start of the journey from Auschwitz to Turin—an itinerary at once geographic, ideological, personal, and cinematic. From the exchange of intense gazes between Daniele, who chooses to burn his Auschwitz jacket, and Primo, who decides to retain his and "remember," Rosi establishes his protagonist as an observer whose act of seeing is also a writing of history. As the film progresses, that gaze will register a variety of responses to the journey, ranging from the bewildered disbelief when the Italian officer at Cracow denies him and the Greek entrance to the barracks, to the astonishment of his eyes within the dream of Auschwitz, to desire for Galina, to shock at the spectacle of German prisoners in their turn reduced to hard labor and starvation.

Though usually the "owner" of the gaze and a participant in gazing at others, Primo becomes the object of visual spectacle in two important scenes. The task of communicating with a family of Russian peasants to obtain a roasting chicken for the Italian refugees falls to Primo, who knows more languages than his fellow survivors. Having exhausted his stock of Indo-European poultry synonyms, however, Primo is reduced to performing a most undignified pantomime, making him the source of the peasant family's delight and prompting the daughter to furnish him with a savory chicken. Primo's gesturing is doubly successful, disarming the audience by playing the fool and predisposing them to reward him for their comic pleasure.

By the end of the film, Primo becomes the object of a far more serious gaze—that of a German officer in the train station at Munich. Primo informs us in voice-over, "We felt as if we had enormous things to say to every single German, and every German should have something to say to us." As the train stands in the station, the camera cuts from window to window, each one filled with survivors, all mutely observing the German prisoners who refuse to return the gaze as they work repairing the tracks. Against a backdrop of Allied banners, lit sporadically by the sparks of soldering irons, this is indeed a spectacle—one that ironically reverses the heroic propaganda documentaries of German industrial and military strength. When Primo succeeds in making eye contact with one of the prisoners, this man kneels down at the sight of the Auschwitz jacket with its embroidered Star of David and bows his head in contrition. This ending signals both a departure from Levi's text and an acknowledgment of his reflections on the subject: "I surprised myself in seeking among them, among that anonymous crowd of sealed faces, other faces, well defined, many linked by a name, of those who could not *not* have known, not have remembered, not have answered; of those who had commanded and obeyed, killed, degraded, corrupted. A vain and foolish attempt because not they, but others, the few just ones, would have answered in their place."

In the one German prisoner who does not withhold his gaze but bows down before a survivor of the Shoah, Rosi dramatized a minority stance, that of "the few just ones." The penitent kneeling of the German prisoner alludes to West German Chancellor Willy Brandt's famous act of reverence before the Warsaw ghetto monument in 1970. By making Primo the object of the gaze of remorse in Munich, Rosi reverses the terms of the earlier episode in the Cracow marketplace, where the spectacle of the Star of David had prompted a mass withdrawal from him. Though the contrite soldier is only one in a group of otherwise unrepentant Nazis, his willingness to take moral responsibility for the Holocaust indicates Rosi's guarded hope that his film will find its audience of "just ones" who will awaken the slumbering consciences of the rest.

It is appropriate that *The Truce* ends with the visual sealing of the covenant of witness between Rosi and the spectators of his film. To do so, the director has Primo recite in voice-over two excerpts from the prefatory poem to *Survival in Auschwitz*:

> You who live secure in your warm houses,
> You who find warm food,
> And friendly faces,
> Returning home each evening:
> Consider if this is a man
> Who works in the mud,
> Who knows no peace,
> Who struggles for half a piece of bread,
> Who dies for a yes and a no.
> Meditate that this has happened.

In the second-person plural imperative of the poem, Levi convenes his readers as the community of witness. He wrenches them out of their complacency by attacking the material foundations of civilized life—a secure domestic space, regular meals, familial solidarity—and compels them to confront what is left of the human condition when all its vital supports are removed. In the commands "consider" and "meditate," Levi exhorts his readers to travel the distance separating the world of warm houses and convivial dinners from the mud-infested quarters and starvation rations of Auschwitz, and to accept the moral demands that such an imagined journey imposes.

This direct address to the reader finds its cinematic equivalent in the protagonist's gaze into the camera at the end of Rosi's *The Truce*—a technique that shatters the fourth wall of theatrical illusion and makes us the object of the filmmaker's gaze, as Levi's direct address shatters the walls of his readers' "warm houses" and forces them into the cold and muddy spaces of history. By looking us straight in the eye, Rosi's protagonist dispels the comfortable fiction that we are invisible spectators, forcing us to accept that this reconstruction is being staged *for our sake*. In Rosi's words, such a restaging is "an operation indispensable to renewing the necessity of not forgetting, in times like these in which the risk of a general denial of the Holocaust and of the traumas imposed on Europe by Fascism and Nazism seems ever more threatening."

By concluding his film with excerpts from the poem that marks the threshold of Levi's first concentration camp chronicle, Rosi makes his work a retroactive commentary on all of Levi's Holocaust writings. He indicates that the end of Levi's journey from Auschwitz is no end at all, but a circle that revolves ceaselessly around the all-encompassing horror of the camps. With this ending, which takes us to the beginning of Levi's ordeal of bearing witness through writing, Rosi demonstrates his profound sensitivity to the meaning of Levi's title. Whether construed literally as "cease-fire" or figuratively as "respite" or "truce," the film proclaims its transience as the pause between hostilities. One meaning Levi attributed to his title is the military one: "It was the great truce: because the other hard season that was to follow had not yet started, nor had the ominous name of the Cold War yet been pronounced." In a more immediate sense, the truce was a time spent betwixt and between stable orders, a time of fluidity, experimentation, and freedom from personal constraints.

Implicit in this title is an invitation to historicize, to interpret the truce as a period that is over. For Levi, writing in 1961–62, knowing how difficult reentry would be and how painful the task of bearing witness, the period of "wandering at the margins of civilization" was a privileged time, as was the Russians' enjoyment of "that happy moment of their history" before the onset of the Cold War. For Rosi, the idea of a utopian season that has drawn to an end dilates and expands to include Italy's entire journey from World War II to the present.

It is in this context that Rosi redefines an Italian national identity in the wake of Fascism and war. This begins with Primo's cry to Daniele, "See you in Italy," when they are separated. Such an exhortation makes Italy the goal of the journey in more than a geographic sense. Italy is the place of reunion, the promised land where the Holocaust will end, and Levi's ordeal of exile will be over, where the loss of everything that defined him as a man—family, community, national identity, and cultural heritage—will be reversed. Throughout the journey, Primo seeks out compatriots not only to communicate, but to reconstruct his Ital-

ian identity. "Does anyone speak Italian?" is the first thing he says after being hauled onto a truck. "I'm Italian," he announces as he arrives at a new encampment. "You're not Italian!" exclaims the good German woman who opposed Hitler and was exiled to Katowice for her temerity. "Italians have black hair and passionate eyes. Your eyes have no passion. You must be Croatian!" "We are very much Italian," Primo responds, "but we come from a place where people forget passion, family, country, culture." To be Italian, to have passionate eyes, means to rededicate one's life to the ideals of family, community, political struggle, which Auschwitz had sought to destroy.

Primo finally does manage to find a semblance of Italy in the motley crew of compatriots who become his fellow travelers through the countryside of Europe after his liberation from Auschwitz. From the pages of Levi's memoir, there is Daniele, the sole survivor of his family, which had been deported after the raid on the ghetto of Venice; Ferrari, a pickpocket from Milan; Cesare, the mattress maker from Rome; and D'Agata, the Sicilian crazed by food and sex. Each member of the band tells his story. In recounting these individual stories, and representing the band's collective adventures en route, the film lapses into a picaresque mode whose fragmentary structure is appropriate to the discontinuities and contradictions of postwar Italian identity.

From his contemporary perspective, Rosi focuses with special nostalgia on the relationship of the intellectual Left with the myth of the Soviet Union—a relationship that was central to the Italian dream of postwar cultural renewal. Levi, too, elevated Russia to mythic status, but in terms that were more anthropological than political. Although often invidiously compared with the Nazis, the Russians are depicted as benignly anarchic and truly heroic. As the memoir proceeds and the odyssey is beset with bureaucratic obstacles, Levi grows more disenchanted with the Russian regime and its arbitrariness and administrative ineptitude. In the film, however, the disappointment that Levi overtly shows toward the Soviets is banished to the margins. It is projected onto an awareness of a future beyond the events represented on screen, but one that provides the perspective on "that happy moment of their history" and what it signified for the Italian Left. The most powerful vehicle of that myth is the recurrent image of the Soviet locomotive, often shot in low angle as it races across the screen to drive the narrative to its destination. What gives the image its iconic power is the imprint of the bright red star at the center of the huge engine, whose contours are blurred by the billowing smoke accompanying its forward progress.

But it is in the scene of the Russian victory performance that Rosi expresses the yearning of the Italian Left for the myth of Soviet redemption. The scene represents the Russian collectivity as irresistibly attractive, with the jolly Marja Fjodorovna and the benign Dr. Dancenko in the front row of the soldiers who sing their song of victory—a song that emphasizes the Soviet responsibility for defeating the Nazi scourge. When Galina, the object of Primo's unrequited desire, comes on the stage, dressed as a traditional Russian maiden, she personifies an idealized Soviet national identity. Primo's infatuation with her partakes of a long-standing literary and cinematic tradition whereby the desires aroused by the individual erotic body can be applied metaphorically to matters of state.

The object of Rose's nostalgia, then, is Italy's love affair with the myth of the Soviet Union—an affair doomed to disaster when the reality of the regime revealed itself in the decades-long vicissitudes that led to its final collapse in 1991. Yet Rosi mourns the grandeur of the vision sustained by the myth—a vision of epic dimensions that dared to dream of a better world. In *The Truce*, the possibility of a new postwar order is built into the choral dimension of the film, whose vast numbers of extras give visual expression to a Europe in the throes of communal rebirth. In its insistence on the mass scale of the experience, the film is as much about Europe's quest for identity as it is about one man's personal ordeal. The interplay between collective and individual experience finds musical expression in the counterpoint between Primo's motif, entrusted largely to a solo flute, and the choral theme, which is large and orchestral in range.

If the grandeur of the political vision sustained by the Soviet myth is the object of Rosi's nostalgia, so too, is the film's cinematic style. In terms of cinema history, the truce—the privileged season that has come to an end—is certainly that of directors like Rosi's master, Visconti, but also of Rossellini, De Santis, and De Sica; of Bertolucci before he abandoned Italy; of the Tavianis. The truce is the season of socially committed cinema, when the industry was epic in purpose, if not always in scale; when filmmaking was seen as an intervention in the life of the country; when motion pictures mattered. In turning to the Holocaust as its privileged subject and in memorializing Italy's foremost survivor of this "central fact, the stain" on twentieth-century European history, Rosi is bringing together the best tradition of his country's committed art with the most solemn act that a historical reconstruction can perform—that of bearing witness. It is up to us, then, to become the "addressable others."

Abridged from: Millicent Marcus, *After Fellini: National Cinema in the Postmodern Age* (Baltimore, MD: Johns Hopkins University Press, 2002).

Source: Primo Levi, *The Reawakening*, translated by Stuart Woolf (Boston: Little Brown, 1965).

Background: http://www.ushmm.org/museum/exhibit/focus/auschwitz/.

Bibliography

Felman, Shoshana, and Dori Laub. *Testimony: Crises of Witnessing in Literature, Psychoanalysis, and History.* New York: Routledge, 1992.

Hughes, H. Stuart. *Prisoners of Hope: The Silver Age of Italian Jews, 1924–1974.* Cambridge: Harvard University Press, 1983.

Levi, Primo. *Survival in Auschwitz.* Translated by Stuart Woolf. New York: Touchstone, 1996.

Marcus, Millicent. *Italian Film in the Shadow of Auschwitz.* Toronto: University of Toronto Press: 2007.

Patruno, Nicholas. *Understanding Primo Levi.* Columbia: University of South Carolina Press, 1995.

Sarfatti, Michele. *The Jews in Mussolini's Italy: From Equality to Persecution.* Translated by John Tedeschi and Anne C. Tedeschi. Madison: University of Wisconsin Press, 2006.

Wyman, Mark. *DPs: Europe's Displaced Persons, 1945–1951.* Ithaca, NY: Cornell University Press, 1998.

26. *Our Children*

Responding to the Holocaust

IRA KONIGSBERG

Our Children (*Unzere Kinder*), directed by Natan Gross [NCJF]
Poland, 1948

For twenty years after the end of the Second World War, the West responded to the Holocaust with relative silence. During more recent decades, the West has sought to make the Holocaust part of history, an event described and inter-preted through the eyes and sensibility of each culture that tells its story. As the historical episode has become more manageable, our responses to it have become ritualized. This ritualized diminishment of the horrors and suffering of the victims has motivated historians to argue that the trauma of the Holocaust has not been worked through on either the individual or the collective level. What appears to be going on now is a process of mourning, but, as psychotherapist Sheldon Roth warns us, "Mourning is designed for loss, not catastrophe!"

It is certainly true that the enormity of the event seems to defy comprehension, but what also anguishes us, especially in the representation of the Holocaust in art, concerns the internal psyches of the vast number of people involved in this event: the terror and despair felt by the victims and survivors, the will to destruction shown by the perpetrators, and the complicity demonstrated by those who watched and knew. Lawrence Langer cites the proposition of several writers on the subject of atrocity "that before 1939 imagination was always in advance of reality, but that after 1945 reality had outdistanced the imagination so that nothing the artist conjured up could equal in intensity or scope the improbabilities of *l'univers concentrationnaire* (the universe of the concentration camps)."

Our Children was one of several postwar feature films made by European Jews trying to acknowledge the decimation that had just happened to them and to find a way into the future. The filmmakers attempted to link themselves with and continue the prewar Jewish past after the Final Solution by working in Yiddish. The motion picture painfully demonstrates the struggle and inability to comprehend and mourn that characterized cinematic responses to the Holocaust for decades. Made by artists forced to confront the countless deaths of friends, relatives, and strangers, it is a remarkable document revealing the limitations of art and the problems of coming up against those limitations.

While most Jewish survivors immigrated to Israel after the war, some tried to convince themselves that they had a home in Europe. There were some 60,000 to 70,000 Jews in Poland at the end of the war, and they were joined by another 175,000, who returned, mostly from the Soviet Union. Only 245,000 people survived out of 3 million Polish Jews. Despite Poland's continuing anti-Semitism and the large number of Jews fleeing the country, a significant group still remained, trying to forge a new life under the banner of communism. Since a popular film industry had existed as part of the Yiddish culture in Poland before the war, it was natural that Jews should turn to the cinema as a means of expressing their hopes about the future while attempting to cope with the horrors of the past. Film producer Shaul Goskind, who had spent the war years with his brother in the Soviet Union, returned to Poland, where he formed a film cooperative called Kinor (the Hebrew word for harp) to make Yiddish films. Kinor hired Natan Gross, who had survived the war years in Poland hiding with a gentile family, as a director.

While completing *We Are Still Alive*, a documentary, about the resumption of Jewish life in postwar Poland and the cooperation of Jews and Poles to build a communist society there, Kinor planned a narrative film about reconciliation and the bright future of the Jewish people in Poland. When Shimon Dzigan and Yisroel Schumacher, two well-known Polish-Yiddish entertainers, returned to Poland from the Soviet Union, Goskind approached them about making a film. The idea for *Our Children* seems to have been a collaborative effort—a film about Dzigan and Schu-

macher's discovery of the Nazi atrocities with a positive emphasis on the future of the Jews, especially children. Young survivors who resided in the Helenowek Colony near Lodz would play the children. *Our Children* also seems to draw inspiration from the 1938 documentary *Here We Are*, about the Medem Sanitarium for Jewish children with tuberculosis. These children died in the gas chambers of Treblinka in 1942. *Our Children* is about the rebirth of Jewish children and attempts to bridge the abyss from 1942 until the present.

Although the film was made with the approval of the communist government in 1947 and 1948, it was banned from any public screening because it did not show enough Poles in a positive light; however, the film was screened privately at a number of Jewish homes. It was the last Yiddish film made in Poland. In spite of the hopes for a new alliance of Jews and Poles under the banner of communism, Poland was still not a home for Jewish people, who continued to be subject to violence, pogroms, and political purges. Many of the remaining Jews in Poland fled, reducing the number to some 70,000–80,000 by 1949. Dzigan, Schumacher, Gross, and Goskind immigrated to Israel. Goskind smuggled prints of the film to Israel and France in 1950. *Our Children*, as it had been shot in Poland, finally premiered in Tel Aviv in 1951. It then dropped out of sight until a copy was found and screened in 1980 at a reunion of the children in the film with Dzigan, Goskind, and Gross in Tel Aviv. It was restored and released by the National Center for Jewish Film at Brandeis University in 1991.

Our Children is not only one of the first narrative films to draw its subject matter from the Holocaust, but it is the first film to confront the issue of whether the Holocaust is a suitable subject for art. The film asks whether remembering is beneficial and whether it is even possible to deal with this subject in art. The questions, then, are, "How should we?" and "Should we at all?" with the second clearly following from the inability to resolve the first. In raising these questions so soon after the Holocaust, the film provides important insights into the thinking and spiritual state of the Jews in Poland immediately after the war. Its inability ultimately to confront the reality of the past also prefigures the decades of silence that were to follow.

The opening documentary footage indicates that the events of the film must be taken seriously. It is dealing with enactments of situations that happened and are happening. The focus is on the children, not only the children seen in the movie, who are themselves survivors, but all the young victims and survivors whom they represent. The piles of shoes and dolls in the documentary clip create powerful images because we know these objects actually existed; they symbolize the more than one million Jewish children who did not survive the Final Solution. The shoes and dolls themselves are signifiers, traces of the children to whom they once belonged. Because Dzigan and Schumacher had themselves been behind Soviet lines during the war years, the film portrays their journey of discovery when they returned to Poland and learned of the Holocaust. The locations of the film, from the streets of Lodz, to the Polish countryside, and to the Helenowek Colony, are carefully documented as real places that testify to the authenticity of the experiences the film portrays.

But such reality plays off an unreality that the film explores: the unreality of art. The film questions whether art itself can ever encompass the reality of an event such as the Holocaust. This dichotomy is evident at the start of the film, when the children visit the theater in Lodz and are less than enthusiastic about a musical skit by Dzigan and Schumacher about two beggars in a ghetto. After the children have heckled the ghetto sketch, they come to the actors' dressing room to apologize for their behavior and perform some reenactments of their ghetto experiences. Their performance makes the actors' skit seem naive and uninformed. Schumacher suggests that he and his partner received creative inspiration from the children's performance, but Dzigan says, "And you want to perform this? For me this is a theme to lament and not to play." The film then explores whether to lament the past or move toward the future.

After he and Dzigan finish a dramatization of Sholem Aleichem's story "Kasrilevke Brent" (Kasrilevke Burning) at the colony, Schumacher asks the children to describe or dramatize what they saw or experienced during the German Occupation, but the directress forestalls such confessions by sending the young people off to their rooms for bedtime. Yet she acknowledges that, "if they don't deal with these memories by day they will suffer them at night as terrible nightmares," and that "the only way for adults as well as children is to express their experiences creatively." These words justify the kind of psychodrama that the children enact when, later that night, they tell one another of their experiences during the Holocaust. It also explains the children's astonishing caricature of Hitler and his followers in their performance in the actors' dressing room.

Our Children explores the limitations of art in dealing with reality and the possibilities of art as therapy for social trauma. Even though Dzigan initially voices skepticism and upon overhearing the children's experiences cries, "This is not a house of children. It is a house of nightmares," he too is converted the morning after when he sees the children playing and comically mimicking "Kasrilevke Brent." "Look, they're imitating us. . . . This morning proved that the children are healthier than we are." The artists' challenge to the children to express their past experiences succeeds in encouraging them to testify for the first time. The film suggests that such testimony serves as a kind of purgation and helps the children move from their nightmares and into the sunny morning by allowing them to leap from repression to artistic play.

But what of the artists who create without having experienced that which they create? Dzigan and Schumacher had escaped the Holocaust. They seek to discover what actually happened, so that they may absorb such events into their art. From one perspective, the film is about the pilgrimage of the two men, not only the physical one from Lodz through the bucolic world of the Yiddish farmer to the home of the children, but also an intellectual, spiritual, and artistic journey. Their trip is also an act of contrition because these children have suffered and they themselves have not. In this sense, both Dzigan and Schumacher are the surrogates within the film for many who sit in the audience.

Our Children moves inevitably to the stories the children tell and the dramatizations of their experiences. Each child tells a story of abandonment, of being separated from his or her parents. As a little girl tells her story, the screen shows her pulled off a truckload of children and sold to an old peasant by a sadistic guard. The audience is touched by the concern of the Polish peasants and moved by the old man holding her in his arms, but the viewer must also remember that the truck is driving away and carrying the other children to their destruction. What the audience does not see and is forced to imagine is more heinous than what it does see. It is not so much what the audience sees happening to the children in these stories that disturbs—the dramatizations themselves are generalized and weakly staged—as the fear of what will happen to them. The old peasant's act of caring is especially moving because it is an action not often associated with the Polish response to Jewish victims during the Holocaust. Once again, the picture achieves its impact from what is missing. Missing, on one level, is what the audience knows from all they have learned since the film was made, a knowledge that motivates them to overlay images from their own imagination upon the actual images on the screen. The movie ignites their imagination to bring to the film what is not there, but what is present in absences.

A small boy recalls how he was hidden by a doctor after being separated from his parents. A second abandonment occurs when he hears the Nazis arrest the doctor and his family. Once more the power of the story arises from the horrors the audience is forced to imagine, from overhearing what is happening to the doctor and his family, but through how the boy imagines the capture to have been while he remained alone in the dark room. He rolls himself in a carpet in order to survive. In the third story, a young boy is forced to run from his mother to save his life, but returns to find her dead. His mother died not knowing that he was still alive. "Until this day her voice rings in my ears," he says to the other children. Time after time, we are struck by the same themes of abandonment, helplessness, and victimization.

In spite of their ability to evoke powerful responses, fictional films about the Holocaust must remain a ritual act, an homage to the past, since the very act of fictionalizing makes something real into the unreal. *Our Children* recognizes this problem by presenting the fictionalizing of the past through the performers' ghetto skit at the start of the film and later in their dramatization of "Kasrilevke Brent." We realize that the children are acting and their scenes are staged, but at the same time this staged quality undermines the unreality, boldly announcing that we are to distinguish between the children as performers and the children as survivors. Their authenticity is painfully clear when we eavesdrop on their private conversations and hear them recall their Holocaust memories. These scenes become psychodrama since we know that the young actors had to undergo similar experiences in order to be alive at the orphanage and in the film. These are moments of discovery and truth for the children and for the audience, and yet the irony is that the children's testimonies take place in their sleeping quarters, away from the adult world. The children never speak directly to the performers of their experiences; there is no public expression of their traumas. Dzigan and Schumacher hear them only by accident, because they have lost their way in the building and stumbled upon the children's bedrooms. And they hear them surreptitiously, secretly intruding into their privacy. What is the significance of this?

For one thing, the children do not have to perform to turn their experiences into material for the professional performers. Instead, their confessions seem spontaneous and natural. The very telling of their experiences is the hidden heart of the film, the core that undermines its unreality and fictions. One feels that this must be the first time that the children had revealed their stories. Dzigan and Schumacher appear to have had a positive effect in allowing them to work through their trauma. This is supposed to be evident when we see the children at play the following morning, playing imaginatively with the actors' dramatization of "Kasrilevke Brent."

And yet the dynamics between the performers and the children are even more complex, espe-cially when we consider Dzigan and Schumacher's performance of "Kasrilevke Brent." The inclusion of this long skit in the middle of a relatively brief (sixty-eight-minute) film might seem confusing, especially since it is so skillfully done and stands apart from the more serious tone of the rest of the film. On the one hand, the skit is a reminder of the *shtetl* reality and culture that once existed in Eastern Europe but was destroyed during the war years. Schumacher describes the skit as "a bit of the old way of life." But this dramatization of the past prepares us for the movement toward the future with which the film concludes. The skit portrays the past culture in a comic and exaggerated manner: scenery and stage props are suddenly available for this impromptu performance, the stage lighting against the black background puts us into a theatrical context, and the two performers, playing many roles and changing costumes in an impossibly short time, challenge credibility. The dramatization emphasizes itself as art and as separate from reality, and, along with the earlier ghetto skit, contrasts with the authenticity of the children's Holocaust memories, which they acted out in the dressing room and described in their bedrooms. Certainly the children laugh, momentarily relieved of the burden of reality. But immediately after the performance, Schumacher asks the children if any have ever seen a fire, and a number respond that they saw the burning of the Warsaw ghetto. Once more art is overwhelmed and seems almost superfluous to reality.

The skit is a remarkably overdetermined object in the context of the entire film. How can it not be when the film itself must be seen in the larger context of the Holocaust? "Kasrilevke Brent" is both an object of pleasure and humor, but also an object of pain. The world it depicts has been wiped out by the Nazi onslaught. It is also impossible not to respond to the subject of burning itself with discomfort. How can we not be struck by the way in which the children are encouraged to recall the burning of the homes in the *shtetl* to the burning of the ghetto? How can we not feel discomfort when we hear such lines as "Flames reaching high- / higher, higher! / Screams! Alarm! Fire! Fire!" in the context of the actual burning that the children witnessed and now are forced to remember.

One of the most famous songs associated with the Holocaust was "Es Brent" (It Burns), written by Mordecai Gebertig, a Krakow carpenter and poet who wrote it in 1938 in response to the Polish pogrom in Przytk in 1936. He also wrote a series of poems about his experiences in the Krakow ghetto until he, his wife, and two daughters were killed by the Nazis on June 4, 1942. "Es Brent" became a song that Jews in the ghettos and forests of occupied Poland sang, as did Holocaust survivors after the war. The refrain demonstrates why the song served as a clarion call both to Jewish resistance and to an indifferent world: "And you stand there looking on, / With folded arms, / And you stand there looking on / While our *shtetl* burns." More striking, however, is the song's relevance to the dramatization of Aleichem's piece in *Our Children*: "It burns, brother, it burns! / Oh, the moment can, alas, come, / When our city with us in it / Can go up in flames / Leaving it, like after a battle, / With empty, charred walls!" Dzigan and Schumacher's drama makes a potentially tragic situation comic and alleviates the children's pain, only to be followed by the strange questioning that forces the children back into the real and painful world of the ghetto. The problem is that the associations cannot possibly stop there. The flames and burning remind the children of the ovens and the burning of the Jewish victims in the camps—just as the song "Es Brent" has always done.

Whether or not the filmmakers were aware of such associations, it is important to recognize that the film downplays the suffering and anguish of the children and demonstrates an inability to deal with the subject openly and directly. This limitation is reflected in the performers' lack of awareness and their general clumsiness when they probe deeper into the experiences of the children, asking them to relive trauma as they themselves increasingly feel their own helplessness and guilt. Although Schumacher and Dzigan claim that they are asking the children to remember to collect material for their art and although their journey is one of contrition, the result of their visit indicates some confusion about their roles and their feelings toward the children. Despite their eulogies and encomiums about the children's resilience, the actors seem ready to expose them once again to past traumas. Certainly the manner in which they wander about the house after the children have been put to bed and act as interlopers as they eavesdrop on the children telling their stories diminishes their stature. Dzigan and Schumacher meant to be sincere and well intentioned, but, like the filmmakers themselves, they seek the truth while simultaneously defending themselves against discovering it. At the same time the atrocities and suffering of the past threaten to overwhelm them. Dzigan and Schumacher's idealization of the children and denial of their pain create a gap between themselves and the young people, leaving the two artists uninformed and helpless.

The adults' feelings of helplessness are poignantly demonstrated in the directress's response to Schumacher's singing of the Yiddish song "Doves" after the children have gone to bed. The song itself, with lyrics by Zishe Weinper and music by Joseph P. Katz, was originally published in New York City in 1924, but apparently was known in Europe and sung in the ghettos during the Holocaust as an expression of mourning and loss. In the film the lyrics are: "Above at my window / two white doves are perched / I will open the window for them" and "In night's sorrowful stillness I hear them / Hear them cooing at my window / two white doves." Schumacher's sorrowful singing sends the directress to her room in tears where, still hearing his song, she also hears the voice of her little girl, her own little dove, pleading with her mother for help as she is carried away by the Nazis. The scene emotionally confronts the utter helplessness of parents to protect and save their young and depicts their agony at the loss of their children. When two female kitchen workers discuss the murder of children during the Holocaust and one exclaims how she would have saved her children at any cost had she been in such a situation, her words seem hopelessly naive. *Our Children* celebrates the resilience of the young Jewish survivors while it mourns the loss of those who did not survive. But its narrative is very much concerned with the responses of adults, especially those who were not survivors of the camps, to these young people—not their guilt but, in the case of Schumacher and Dzigan, their unconscious exploitation of the children they seek to probe, understand, and use as a subject for art.

Because of the movie's self-reflexivity, its exploration of representing the Holocaust in art, and of the outsider's ambivalent position in learning about and responding to this catastrophe, the film speaks powerfully to us today. We share the responses of Schumacher and Dzigan as we sit in the theater and seem to exploit these children ourselves. Such viewing is fraught with terror because of the privileged status it allows us, a privileged status we do not wish to have. But like Schumacher and Dzigan, we continue to watch, feeling compelled to make a similar contact, no matter how complicated and painful our responses. Just like the Holocaust survivors, who to this very day continue to tell us their experiences on film and videotape, the children are our only links to this past. It is only in their presence made present through the image that we can feel some trace of the horror, through their imprint upon reality made visible by the film.

Abridged from: Ira Konigsberg, "*Our Children* and the Limits of Cinema: Early Jewish Responses to the Holocaust," *Film Quarterly* 52, no. 1 (1998): 7–19.

Background: Joanna B. Michlic, "Who Am I? Jewish Children's Search for Identity in Postwar Poland 1945–1949," *Polin* 20 (2007): 98–121 (http://www.lehigh.edu/inber/whoamI.pdf).

Bibliography

Brenner, Ira, and Judith S. Kestenberg. *The Last Witness: The Child Survivor of the Holocaust*. Washington: American Psychiatric Press, 1996.

Cooper, Leo. *In the Shadow of the Polish Eagle: The Poles, the Holocaust, and Beyond*. New York: Palgrave Macmillan, 2000.

Dwork, Debórah. *Children with a Star: Jewish Youth in Nazi Europe*. New Haven: Yale University Press, 1991.

Goldman, Eric A. *Visions, Images, and Dreams: Yiddish Film, Past and Present*. Rev. ed. Teaneck, NJ: Holmes and Meier, 2011.

Hoberman J. *Bridge of Light: Yiddish Film between Two Worlds*. Updated and expanded ed. Hanover, NH: University Press of New England, 2010.

Portuges, Catherine. "Intergenerational Transmission: The Holocaust in Central European Cinema." In *Projected Shadows: Psychoanalytic Reflections on the Representation of European Cinema*, edited by Andrea Sabbadini, 73–91. New York: Routledge, 2007.

Schatz, Jaff. *The Generation: The Rise and Fall of the Jewish Communists of Poland*. Berkeley: University of California Press, 1991.

Steinlauf, Micheal C. *Bondage to the Dead: Poland and the Memory of the Holocaust*. Syracuse, NY: Syracuse University Press, 1997.

27. "Teach Me Gold"

Pedagogy and Memory in *The Pawnbroker*

ALAN ROSEN

The Pawnbroker, directed by Sidney Lumet [A]
United States, 1965

The story of a Holocaust survivor unable to mourn, *The Pawnbroker* is clearly of the postwar era. But the strategies of the novel (1961) and, particularly, the film (1965) draw on earlier efforts to represent the ambiguous cultural position of the Jew. Most notably, both book and film recall Shakespeare's Shylock, associating the transactions of the pawnshop to Shylock's early modern money lending. The pawnshop has played this cinematic role since the emergence of moviemaking at the end of the late nineteenth century, fashioning the pawnbroker either to emphasize allegations of Jewish greed or to contest them.

But the film challenges the conventional depiction of the cinematic pawnshop. It represents the shop's primary relationship between Sol Nazerman, professor turned pawnbroker, and Jesus Ortiz, his assistant, as one of teacher and student, with lessons constituting an alternative kind of transaction. These lessons provide the assistant with skills that will help him "get legit"—to give up a life of crime in order to acquire economic, social, and cultural legitimacy—and also school him in a broader circle of cultural awareness. The film transforms the pawnshop into a classroom and relates Sol's story to urgent issues of the 1960s: urban blight, integration, and the plight of blacks and Puerto Ricans in New York City.

These issues recoil back on the film: as a Hollywood artifact, *The Pawnbroker* has often had its own legitimacy questioned. Held in suspicion generally when it comes to Jewish themes, Hollywood has fared even more poorly with regard to the Holocaust. Distant from the events, Hollywood has been viewed as indifferent to the subject, or, at best, as able to represent the Holocaust only within inappropriately melodramatic conventions. This dubious record was and is contrasted with European cinema. Proximate to the death camps, less beholden to popular taste, European cinema had early, if infrequently, found innovative means to deal seriously with the Holocaust. Yet the specter of the Holocaust has cut two ways. Europe's proximity to the events and its responsibility for them has tainted its credentials for comprehending or explaining them.

Itself a kind of hybrid, *The Pawnbroker* tries to "broker" this divide between Hollywood and Europe, between popular and art film, between commercial and moral enterprise. The idiom of teaching has also shadowed (and preceded) the film's quest for legitimacy: Edward Lewis Wallant's novel satirizes the notion that postwar Europe teaches America; the film, in a modified form, takes up this critique. Scholars debate whether the film's use of the flashback derives from European cinema or has native origins. Director Sidney Lumet's own assessment challenges European dominance, positing an American pedigree for representing the Holocaust.

Hence, the film's quest for legitimacy also hinges on its representation of memory. Annette Insdorf, for instance, sees the manner in which memory figures centrally in the film—"a cinema of flashbacks"—as its defining as well as legitimizing feature. Yet in the framework of pedagogy, the striking aspect of the film's conception of the memory of trauma is that it cannot be taught, an impasse that the film shows by making the scenes of memory inarticulate.

Rod Steiger (as Sol Nazerman) is a prisoner of his past and his present. From *The Pawnbroker* (1965), directed by Sidney Lumet. AMERICAN INTERNATIONAL PICTURES/PHOTOFEST

What would it mean for a Jew to write *The Merchant of Venice*? In his novel Edward Lewis Wallant toyed with this question: his protagonist confesses to a "sense of kinship, of community with all the centuries of hand-rubbing Shylocks." The plural here intimates that Wallant was aiming not only at Shakespeare's Jew but at the greater number of "Shylocks" in the history of representations of Jews. When Wallant made his hero a pawnbroker, he knew it would play into anti-Jewish stereotypes. But the "sense of kinship" implies that Wallant's Jew knows what images he evokes and yet chooses to live with them nonetheless. The pawnbroker recalls Shakespeare, "You [the Jew] are a

merchant," says Nazerman in a lecture to his assistant Jesus Ortiz. "You are known as a usurer, a man with secret resources, a witch, a pawnbroker, a sheenie, a mockie, and a kike!" The lecture joins Nazerman to Shylock: merchants, usurers, and pawnbrokers share occupations and defamations. Nazerman's list progresses from reputable to disreputable (merchant to usurer) and from reality to image ("You are. . . . You are known as"). Whatever corruption has infiltrated the Jew's business relations and perceptions of it, it was not there at the beginning. The Jew's supposed penchant for disreputable occupations has devolved from socially integrated to stigmatized professions or images.

Pawnbroking and pawnshops are found in some of the earliest cinematic productions, including those by influential early filmmakers. Charlie Chaplin produced the best-known silent film dealing with pawnbroking, *The Pawnshop* (1914). Chaplin evokes the exotic Jew as a pawnshop owner, but shows him capable of generosity and forgiveness. Its climax, with an assistant thwarting a robbery by a gun-wielding assailant, foreshadows the denouement of *The Pawnbroker* in which Jesus, who had initially collaborated in planning the robbery of the store, nevertheless intervenes on the Jewish owner's behalf. Whereas Chaplin's assistant succeeds in subduing the assailant; Lumet's assistant can prevent the robbery and murder of Sol only by sacrificing himself. In the years separating Chaplin's and Lumet's films, nearly a hundred films represented pawnbrokers or shops. Some of the proprietors were shown to be charitable, but many were not. Pawnbroking served as one of the chief cinematic vehicles for negotiating the perplexing status of the Jew, a role that both invoked the malevolent stereotype of Jewish greed and contested it by showing the charity of which such figures were capable.

In truth, Nazerman serves as a front man for an organized crime operation and merely plays the role of a pawnbroker. This role-playing may be why the film sets its opening sequences outside of the city and the pawnshop, thereby placing a buffer between Nazerman and his occupation. Once in the pawnshop, the film reveals this masquerade by having Nazerman repeatedly offer a minimal amount for almost every item. Not compelled to depend for a livelihood on the money he receives in the shop (he is paid well by the crime syndicate), he can simply go through the motions. The fact that Nazerman previously was a university professor deepens the sense of masquerade; pawnbroking seems the garb he wears

over the professor who resides within. Though Nazerman seemingly renounces his previous vocation—"the word 'professor,'" he says, "I don't like it"—his concern with a radical kind of pedagogy nonetheless governs the action in the film.

Renunciation of the word "professor" complements the film's rejection of Europe as mediator of culture. Nazerman's relatives—his sister-in-law, Bertha; her husband, Selig; and their children—wish to travel to Europe at Sol's expense and argue such a trip is warranted because of Europe older cultural heritage:

> *Sol*: Why do you want to go to Europe, Bertha?
> *Bertha*: Mostly, it's him. He says it'd be very good for his standing with the School Board if he went there. And he's always wanted to visit there anyhow. The shrines and the old cities. There's an atmosphere we don't have here.
> *Selig*: Something mellow . . . age lends its own charm . . . why, you can almost smell the difference.
> *Sol*: Rather like a stink, if I remember.

To Nazerman's family, Europe is culturally superior to America, but Nazerman reminds them of the "stink"—presumably the odor from the crematoria—and implies it is more representative of Europe's legacy than its culture. The scene is important in that Nazerman's caustic assessment of Europe is the last thing spoken before the film moves from the suburbs into the city itself.

Once there, the hope for learning comes in an unlikely setting: a Harlem pawnshop in the 1960s. Having once served as an enclave for Jews who had left the Lower East Side, Harlem had long before the 1960s become a neighborhood dominated by people of color. As in most major American cities, Jews had moved their residences to the suburbs while continuing to operate businesses in the inner city. The Jewish presence became synonymous with the shops, stores, and tenements they owned or managed. Represented as they were largely by businesses, whites generally, and Jews particularly, were targets of resentment among local residents.

Special anger was often directed toward the pawnshops and their predominantly Jewish owners. Jews had entered pawnbroking as an outgrowth of dealing in textiles and second-hand goods. Making high-interest loans to those desperate for cash, pawnshops were often viewed as the symbol of white colonization of the black inner city: when in the context of the civil rights movement, the formidable urban insurrections of the early 1960s first erupted in Harlem in 1964 and reached their climax in Los Angeles the following year, pawnshops were particularly hard hit, both because of their notoriety as a symbol of exploitation and also because they contained weapons. *The Pawnbroker* was released into this unaccommodating environment in 1965.

Combating discrimination of all kinds, the civil rights movement also had education at the top of its agenda. *Brown v. Board of Education of Topeka*, the 1954 Supreme Court decision, pronounced school segregation unlawful. However, the pace of integration thereafter was uneven, and some ten years later de facto segregation continued to be the norm in New York. This prompted public school boycotts by black and Puerto Rican students in 1964.

By staging scenes of pedagogy in a pawnshop, *The Pawnbroker* implies that integrated education is the norm. Nazerman lectures to two students of color: the assistant, Jesus Ortiz, and the "boss," Rodriguez, the crime syndicate figure who uses the pawnbroker as a front for financial transactions. Positioned at the two social extremes—the younger man, Ortiz, impressionable yet yearning for respectability; the older man, Rodriguez, powerful and established in a life of crime—both characters emerge from the inner city. A light-skinned black in the novel, Ortiz, the assistant, becomes in the film a Puerto Rican. The syndicate boss is the only character who is radically altered in the film adaptation of the novel: his name is changed from Murillio, a Sicilian immigrant, to Rodriguez, an African American with a Spanish name.

Ortiz, however, is Nazerman's foremost student. The film devotes three scenes to teaching sessions with him. Although the lessons turn on various subjects relevant to the trade of pawnbroking, each one also deals with forms of knowledge—literacy, history, values—that can secure for Ortiz cultural and social legitimacy. In the initial session, Nazerman teaches Ortiz how to test precious metals: how to plumb beneath the surface, how to distinguish one kind from another, and how to establish its authenticity: "You see you take an object like this. . . . Watch. . . . Right. It's a touchstone. . . . Now you rub it on the touchstone like that. . . . Now if that turns a bright green, then that means it's brass. And if it turns a milky white, that means it's silver." It is a lesson in learning to read properly. The nature of the text—brass, silver, and gold—evokes alchemical associations, suggesting occult knowledge that Jesus is learning. The sense of the lesson as an initiation dovetails with Jesus's desire to join a "secret society." Noticing the tattoo on Sol's arm, Ortiz seeks an explanation for what it means:

> *Ortiz*: Mr. Nazerman? You wanna tell me, Mr. Nazerman, what is that? Is that a secret society or something?
> *Nazerman*: Yeah.
> *Ortiz*: What do I do to join?

The "secret society" consists of those who were tattooed upon entering Auschwitz. Brushing off Jesus's wish to join such a society, Nazerman nonetheless then proceeds to teach him secrets of a different, alchemical-cultural order, the latter set of secrets compensating for the untold secrets that neither teacher nor student is ready to divulge or assimilate.

Yet the lesson comes up short in several ways: although Ortiz sets it in motion by his request, "teach me gold," Nazerman never gets the chance, for the lesson is interrupted by the arrival of Savarese, the agent of the crime syndicate boss who runs the pawnshop. Precluded from reaching the goal, Ortiz's first lesson nevertheless takes hold, prompting him to fantasize a path on the road to legitimacy: "That man Nazerman, he knows things," Ortiz muses to his girlfriend, Mabel Wheatley, continuing: "I wonder how much it takes to open a pawnshop?" Linked again to secrets, the pawnshop symbolizes one who knows how to gain such knowledge.

With the second lesson, Ortiz calls class to order by intoning, "Teachin' time, Mr. Nazerman. Time to teach." This lesson schools Ortiz in the history of the Jews. Lumet situates this scene in the middle of the film, giving it a dramatic position parallel to Shylock's "Hath not a Jew eyes" speech in Shakespeare's play. Yet the argument about the nature of the Jew moves the film in the opposite direction from the play. Ortiz asks, "How come you people come to business so natural?" Nazerman's lecture places the notion of "natural" in its proper context:

First of all, you [the Jews] start off with a period of several thousand years during which you have nothing to sustain you but a great bearded legend. No, my friend, you have no land to call your own to grow food on or to hunt. . . . All you have is a little brain . . . a little brain and a great bearded legend to sustain you and convince you that you are special, even in poverty. But this . . . this little brain, that's the real key. You see, with this little brain, you go out and buy a little piece of cloth and you cut that cloth in two and you go out and sell it for a penny more than you paid for the one, then you run out and buy another piece of cloth. Cut into three pieces, and sell it for three pennies profit. But my friend, during that time you must never succumb to buying an extra piece of bread for the table nor a toy for a child. No, you must immediately run out and get yourself a still larger piece of cloth, and so you repeat this process, over and over and suddenly you discover something. You no longer have any desire, any temptation to dig in the earth or grow food, or to gaze at a limitless land and call it your own, no, no. You just go on and on and on repeating this process over the centuries, over and over and suddenly, you make a grand discovery: you have a mercantile heritage. You are a merchant. You are known as a usurer, a man with secret resources, a witch, a pawnbroker, a sheenie, a mockie, and a kike!

In Shakespeare's play, Shylock emphasizes reflex as a basis for behavior and the common denominator between Jew and non-Jew alike. His set of claims, "If you prick us, do we not bleed?" is based on an assumption that any physical body, Jewish or Christian, will react identically to the same provocation or violation. In contrast, Nazerman argues that what is assumed to be reflex, a form of "natural" behavior, is actually learned. Hence, natural talent is learned behavior, habits of survival taught, as it were, through inflicted privation ("no land," "never in one place long enough"). While the specific lesson accounts for (and parodies) the acquisition of Jewish business acumen, the broader lesson historicizes the notion of instinct, making it, too, a product of learning. At bottom, then, the lesson is about learning, about how to take what seems natural and, by examining its lineage, to see how history taught it to be what it is.

The lesson resides not only in its content but in the lesson of teaching itself. In the scene that follows, Jesus appropriates the belief in teaching as a mode of affecting behavior and brings it home. The film cuts from the lecture in the pawnshop to the Ortiz apartment. Taking a bath, Jesus converses with his mother in Spanish. The dialogue evolves into a language lesson, whereby Jesus teaches his mother how to say in English "good boy." The drift to English is no surprise since Jesus's first appearance in the film showed him outlawing Spanish in favor of English: "No Spanish, mama, no Spanish; English." Jesus justifies this decree by associating it with legitimacy. Just as he gives up illicit ways of making money and aims to pursue a respectable career, so English will assist him on that path, a path that seemingly demands aggressive acculturation.

The lesson from Nazerman makes Jesus rethink how to transform habitual behavior, particularly language. In contrast to the opening scene, Jesus no longer decrees language policy to his mother. Jesus works for change from within, speaking Spanish while teaching his mother English words. By not providing subtitles, the film legitimates the Spanish they speak and holds at bay the English Jesus plans to master. The English phrase Jesus uses to conduct the language lesson—"I am a good boy"—refers to the boy he hopes to become rather than the boy he is. His mother initially confuses the phrase "good boy" with "good bye." Despite Jesus's correction of her

mistake ("it's another thing"), we hear the play between the phrases as foreshadowing the tragedy that will ensue when Jesus attempts to live up to his ideal and protect Nazerman from the gunman; the final "good bye" will come when Jesus endeavors to be the "good boy."

Nazerman's lesson about transforming habit cannot, however, shape public behavior. When Jesus later orchestrates the robbery of the pawnshop, he once again tries to decree that "There'll be no shootin,'" to modify, in other words, the greed and ruthlessness of his cohorts. But his attempt to *impose* a certain standard of action predictably fails. His own death then testifies tragically to the distance between a proclamation to which behavior is expected to conform and a process by which the student learns how to appropriate the behavior as his own.

The final lesson begins with an event that introduces memory as a crucial component in the act of teaching. Savarese appears on the scene once again and tears pages off the wall calendar, violating the pawnbroker's attempt to freeze time and memory rather than be forced to endure the anniversary of his family's murder. Several times previously the assistant has tried to flip the page, a gesture that the pawnbroker enigmatically refuses to condone and about which he refuses to speak. The refusal to speak, to refrain from saying why the calendar should not be changed, not only puzzles the one who tries to change it (Ortiz) and the one who eventually does (Savarese), but also has left its mark on the film's interpreters. Some see the anniversary as marking a wedding, others as commemorating a death. Although the novel clearly states the date is the anniversary of his family's death, the film never says so directly. A number of critics mistakenly claim that the first date shown on the calendar in the film (September 29) marks the anniversary. The audience is left in the dark, trying to understand not only how memory is being violated but even what memory it is.

Imbued with struggle and silence, the third lesson then begins on the eve of the anniversary of the family's death with the violation of memory that Saverese's act connotes. Both anniversary and violation set the context for the lesson "'bout money," a lesson that insists that money is the "whole thing," that it is the only value:

> Sol: Now come here. Firstly, money can in-crease or decrease in value. Secondly, money is risky, but at a given moment one has some idea of its worth. Thirdly, money can buy you many things: comfort, luxury, relief from pain, sometimes even life itself. And now you listen to me, and you listen very carefully. Next to the speed of light, which Einstein says is the only absolute in the uni-verse, second only to that, I rank money. Yes, you believe me, that's all you need to know.
> Jesus: That's what life's all about?
> Sol: That's what life's all about.
> Jesus: You mean money is the whole thing?
> Sol: Money is the whole thing.
> Jesus: I'll see you later, Mr. Nazerman.

The context of the soon-to-be anniversary, however, suggests that money is the only value because what had value, Nazerman's family, was annihilated. So the emphasis on money must be read against the loss of his family. Ortiz fails to read this lesson dialectically and gets involved in planning the robbery that, by carrying out the implications of Nazerman's teaching, will get the money—an act that will ostensibly show (with paradoxical effect) what a good student Ortiz is. Having transformed the pawnshop into an edu-cational domain, the camera now follows Ortiz

off to plan the robbery with his collaborators, conceding that the final lesson has rendered the classroom obsolete.

Yet Nazerman gives one more lecture. Once he discovers that prostitution finances his pawn-shop operation, he visits Rodriguez to refuse the tainted money:

> Nazerman: I said, I don't want your money if it comes from that place.
> Rodriguez: Why?
> Nazerman: Because it's money that comes from filth and from horror.
> Rodriguez: That's what it is, Professor.

Rodriguez frames the visit as an ethics lecture given by a "professor," the unwanted title that Rodriguez uses repeatedly. In contrast to Ortiz, Rodriguez labels Nazerman a professor to disre-gard the lesson at hand. Rodriguez draws up the curriculum: "Professor, you don't know it but the lecture is over; now you're gonna listen to me." If Ortiz absorbs each lesson, thereby radicalizing his behavior, Rodriguez challenges the lesson and substitutes it with one of his own.

Like Ortiz, Rodriguez is also homegrown. In Wallant's novel, the figure who pulls the strings is a Sicilian immigrant, Murillio. Like Nazerman, he, too, is an outsider, a European who has little connection to the people of color whose lives he manipulates. Like the pawnbroker, Murillio sur-rounds himself with relics of European culture. Thus, for Wallant, the chain of exploitation, from the syndicate chief to the pawnbroker to the pop-ulation of Harlem replicates that of European colonialism. For Lumet, however, the agent of oppression comes from within, not from a white European but from a black American who him-self comes out of Harlem. This shift revises the victim's relation to his own victimization. In the film version, blacks are complicit in their own exploitation and persecution. Moreover, Rodriguez is the most brutal figure in the film, overshadowing Nazerman, in the fear he inspires and the power he wields. Finally, Rodriguez not only heads the operation but supplies the ideology that carries it forward.

The film was produced from 1961 to 1965, years marked by the publication of Hannah Arendt's controversial *Eichman in Jerusalem*, which argued that European Jewry during the Holocaust played a crucial role in its own destruction. The film's representation of the victim seemingly echoes Arendt's claim that the victim was an important cog in his own persecution. But the shift of villain from foreigner to local universalizes Arendt's thesis by making the victim/victimizer dynamic apply not only to Jews but to blacks. Lumet implies that groups of victims generally have members who are willing to collaborate with the persecutor, whereas Arendt and historian Raul Hilberg accounted for the alleged complicity of European Jewry by positing a historic and specifically Jewish propensity for such behavior. The film suggests that whatever the Jews did, they did as any victim would have done—and does.

Wallant's novel already links the issue of teaching to the modes of cinematic production, using film and the film industry to set forth and context neat categories of culture. The initial references occur in one of the brutal family discussions that punctuate the novel. Here, film promotes the excellence of Europe at the expense of America:

"The thing is," Selig said, "Hollywood is just interested in making money." Now, he sighed in wan regret. "No, to Hollywood, culture is just a dirty word. Callow, that's the word for American culture. They have so much to learn from the Europeans." Selig and [his daughter] Joan went back to talking about

movies, and Selig observed that another trouble with Hollywood was that they were unwilling to face life. "Does that make sense to you, Solly [Nazerman], that the Europeans are more willing to face life?" "Oh yes, they are willing to face life," Sol answered, without intonation.

The discussion sets in opposition European versus American movies and the motivation (culture versus money) and ethos (facing life versus being unwilling to do so) of the industries that purportedly fashion them. Ostensibly, Europe will teach America the meaning of culture. But Selig's juxtaposition quickly comes undone. "Making money" describes not only Hollywood but also Sol Nazerman, who came from Europe. In contrast, the American Selig, as a grade-school teacher, works not for money but for his version of culture. Wallant uses the survivor to satirize a notion of culture—a "facing life" that is not informed by life, but by history—that would not take account of the Holocaust but would see America as derivative of a more accomplished Europe.

The notion that Europe teaches America underlies accounts of *The Pawnbroker*'s cinematic innovations. These innovations refer mainly to the film's strategies for representing memory. As Ralph Rosenblum, film editor for *The Pawnbroker*, puts it:

The time was right for an overhaul of the flashback. In the thirties and forties the flashback had been very popular and always happened in the same way. Joan Crawford or Bette Davis said, "I remember . . ." or began reminiscing in a dreamy way about her first marriage, the camera moved in on her entranced face, an eerie "time" music saturated the sound track, a shimmering optical effect crept over the screen as if oil were dripping across it, and everyone in the audience knew, "Uh-oh, we're going into memory." And sure enough, during a long, slow "ripple" dissolve, the star's face gradually disappeared, to be replaced by a scene from the past or perhaps the same face looking twenty years younger.

Rosenblum's condensed history of America cinema implies that the standard technique of signaling smooth transitions between present and past could not properly represent traumatic memory of a historically unprecedented sort. "The time was right" refers to experiments in French cinema that had recently developed a new idiom for representing filmic memory.

Rosenblum elsewhere refers to French director Alain Resnais's use of memory in *Hiroshima, mon amour*, released in 1959, as the crucial influence on *The Pawnbroker*, on which work began in 1961. Rosenblum's emphasis on Resnais's influence casts a European art film (high culture) as providing the model from which *The Pawnbroker* drew. Rosenblum's view matches that outlined (but critiqued) in the novel: Europe leads, America follows; in Selig's formulation, Europe "teaches," America learns; Europe remains the source of culture. America can at best provide a crude, more popular version. To be sure, Rosenblum praises *The Pawnbroker*'s innovations. Yet the flow of transmission parallels that expressed by the novel's satirized Europhiles.

One can see this more sharply when contrasting Rosenblum's view with Lumet's. In 1964, a year prior to *The Pawnbroker*'s American release, Lumet tried to distance the film's innovations from European high culture and instead sketched an American pedigree: "We did a lot of this kind of insane cutting in the early days in TV, when often television technique was far in advance of

movies. I'm always amused by avant garde critics who'll probably sit down and say about this film, 'Well, the two frame cuts came from [another film by Renais] *Last Year in Marienbad*, and this came from,' which is nonsense."

By anchoring the technique in television, Lumet grounds the innovations of the film in popular culture. Whatever innovations the French may have devised, Lumet suggests, the Americans did it earlier. *The Pawnbroker* specifically, and American films generally, are not required to turn to Europe to "learn" essential strategies. As in Wallant's novel, Lumet contests a model of cultural transmission from Europe to America, and from high culture to low. By its skepticism toward Europe as a cultured teacher, the film version of *The Pawnbroker* mirrors the stance of the survivor who is its hero: although appearing to be a European intellectual, Nazerman has rejected the legacy that shaped as well as destroyed him. Lumet's claim of an American pedigree for *The Pawnbroker* has a polemical edge: it implies the film's innovative (if not unprecedented) technique for representing memory is not derivative of Europe. The memories shown may be European, but the means of recovering memory, at least in Lumet's eyes, is American.

The relation between teaching and memory in the film is especially provocative because it seems, at first glance, that memory is represented precisely as that which cannot be taught. In contrast to the scenes of teaching, the scenes of memory—the flash cuts that may or may not be borrowed from the French avant-garde—are radically inarticulate. The opening scene establishes this pattern: filmed in slow motion, the scene shows a family picnic—children, wife and husband, grandparents—taking place in a pastoral setting. Graceful at play, content with rest, busy with menial tasks, those in the scene are strangely bereft of dialogue. When the woman calls and waves to the man, we paradoxically *see* the call but hear nothing. This voicelessness, moreover, becomes symbolic of the scene's relation to the rest of the film.

The next scene—a second family gathering in the backyard of a suburban home—introduces the flash cuts of memory, the technique most reminiscent of European art cinema. Prompted by a remark about an upcoming anniversary, Nazerman briefly recalls the woman, his wife, from the first picnic scene. The recollected fragment is that of the soundless call of the woman. Indeed, the soundless call becomes emblematic of the flash cut technique: appearing on the screen barely long enough for the eye to register, it is too brief to produce articulate sound.

Once the film brings the spectator into the city itself, inarticulate memory goes in two directions: toward the animal and the foreign. Leaving the pawnshop, Nazerman hears the barking of a dog, which triggers the memory of a barking German shepherd that, along with a guard, chases after a concentration camp prisoner. The barking continues, accompanied by German commands—without subtitles—and eventually the dog pins the prisoner on a fence. The "trigger" recalls something *analogous* from the past on the basis of an aggressively nonverbal sound in the present. The strategy suggests that the present and past are connected by that which is inarticulate. Left without subtitles, the German commands imply a malevolence intensified by being incomprehensible. The German commands infuse the barking with a kind of predatory intelligence, and the barking makes the German sound animalistic. In this scene memory begins to speak, but it does so without being conventionally articulate or comprehensible.

The next scene returns to the soundlessness of the opening. The pawning of a fake diamond ring acts as the trigger. The flash cut shows a German guard taking rings from outstretched hands and creates a tableau of plunder, emptied of sound and word. Memory exists as a ritualized violation of European Jewry that says nothing about the one who remembers. This is the only extended memory sequence in which Nazerman does not appear. The sequence suggests a memory so general, so undistinguished by personal violation, that it can be detached from Nazerman. Anonymous and detached, it likewise remains soundless and inarticulate.

In contrast, the memory sequence that follows, showing Nazerman's wife serving as a prostitute in a Nazi concentration camp brothel, focuses on extreme personal violation. This memory is jarred when Mabel Wheatley, the black prostitute girlfriend of Ortiz, pays an after-hours visit to the pawnbroker, hoping to make extra money by offering him a "private session." To spark his interest, the prostitute undresses, and the sight of her naked body eventually triggers the memory of Nazerman's wife's forced prostitution. The violation is made more terrible by the fact that Nazerman himself, by requesting information about his wife, has induced the Nazi guard to take him to witness her humiliation by an SS man. Yet the scene never gives voice to Nazerman's inquiry. This memory too is left inarticulate, the soundless gestures of most of the actors alternating with the Nazi guard's single insistent question in German (without subtitles): *"Willst du was sehen?"* (Do you want to look at something?)

Without subtitles, the German remains incomprehensible and thus barbaric; the tongue of the persecutors reflects the tortures they inflict. The film further nuances the effects of the incomprehension. Once naked, Mabel repeatedly commands Nazerman to "Look. . . . Look. . . . That's it. . . . Look," believing that "looking" will increase the likelihood he will accede to a deal. On one level, the command to look only serves to drive Nazerman deeper into the past. But on another level, Mabel's command to "look" nearly approximates the German, almost permitting memory to speak in the English of the present. It is nevertheless the nearness of translation that reminds the audience that memory continues to operate in a foreign language, further underscoring the opacity of German as a figure of memory. Indeed, in the final flash cut, memory will claim English and emerge as articulate.

The Pawnbroker explores and ultimately rejects a different mode of representing memory during Nazerman's visit to Marilyn Birchfield, the social worker who has tried vainly to strike up a friendship or romance with the pawnbroker. The scene is original to the film, and it is here that Nazerman for the first, and only, time openly alludes to memories of prewar Europe—"We had . . . we had . . . a river in Germany"—and attempts, if tentatively, to recount what happened during the war. But what started as a narration of memory quickly becomes inhibited: "It's just that there have been memories that I had, well, I thought that I had pushed them far away from me and they keep rushing in, and then they're words, words that I thought I had kept myself from hearing . . . and now they flood my mind."

The sequence moves from memory to words to flood. The metaphor of water for memory takes over, disabling articulation through speed ("rushing in") and excess ("flood my mind"). Paradoxically, English here can begin to speak about memory even while memory itself is kept at bay. The scene plays off a previous meeting between Nazerman and Birchfield. She had confided to him her memory of a suitor who had died to make her situation analogous to his own. On the balcony of her apartment, Sol tells her about his loss to make a gesture that mirrors hers. But he informs her not what happened but what didn't: "What happened? I *did not* die."

In refusing to allow memory to be narrated, the film veers away from the course taken by *Hiroshima mon amour*. In Resnais's film, a man and a woman discover in their brief but poignant romantic encounter the occasion to tell, for the first time, of their mutual if distinct loss. Romance enables the couple to express haunting memories associated with the Second World War. In bringing Nazerman and Birchfield together, Lumet nods toward *Hiroshima* and flirts with this mode of representing memory of loss. And indeed there was pressure in the early stages of production to end the film by having Birchfield and Nazerman touch hands. But the film dismisses this option: when Birchfield extends her hand to Nazerman, he does not take it.

Nazerman's awkward attempt to relate the memories of the war allows English to emerge as a language of memory in the flashback to the deportation by trains that follows his scene with Birchfield. Leaving the apartment, Nazerman boards a subway and looks for a seat, during which time the camera grotesquely pans the accompanying passengers. The crowded subway car soon triggers flash cuts to the crowded boxcar in which Nazerman and his family were deported. And here, memory becomes articulate: Nazerman and his wife call to one another—*in English*—trying to save the life of their son. There are other reasons why English is used here. It would be appropriate to use German since those in the freight car are presumably German Jews like Nazerman, but German already has been associated with animalism and barbarism, rather than with the victims. So the film inverts the terms that it has used up till now: the present, the subway car that "triggers" the memory, is soundless; while the flashback brazenly borrows the English of the present to represent the past. The inversion suggests that with the terrible death of Sol's son in the train, the past has taken over, supplanted, even erased, the present.

The death of the assistant Ortiz follows soon after the flashback of the son's death. The logic of inarticulate memory nevertheless accounts for the silent scream at the film's conclusion, Nazerman's reaction to the assistant's death. Generally viewed as an unprecedented gesture, the silent scream proceeds from the strategies of memory, utterance, and silence pursued throughout the film. For just as English takes over the past in the train, the soundlessness from past memory takes over the present, forming the idiom of grief. Nazerman's silent cry alludes to the soundless call of his wife. The film's idiom of past and present merge: the death of Ortiz bears witness to the peril of teaching, even as his memory of loss speaks through silence.

Teaching fails because memory intensifies. *The Pawnbroker* differs from other great films on the Holocaust. Both *Night and Fog* and *Shoah*, different though they may be, for example, share a concern for place, usually the vacant, and vacated, concentration camps. *The Pawnbroker*, for its part, features time, making an anniversary and hence memorialization, the governing agency of the film. The film preceded widespread Holocaust memorialization. To see memory regulated enough to be read and interpreted came only later. *The Pawnbroker* shows memory when it still refused to be domesticated, or conveyed in public rites and rituals. The film teaches that memory is dangerous, explosive, even deadly.

The tragic account of teaching and memory shaped the film's form and reception as it was released at a time when the classic style of narration in Hollywood film was breaking down. Having provoked the criticism that the film equated the collective suffering of American cities with those of wartime Europe, the film and the subsequent scholarship on it have figured prominently in the legacy that the Holocaust leaves to America, and America to the Holocaust. By doing so, *The Pawnbroker* developed a hybrid style as a response to trauma. Coming into being after *Hiroshima mon amour*, the film that established (or revolutionized) the paradigm for responses to trauma, *The Pawnbroker* articulated a view of its own, a view that, in turn, set forth a radical response to dilemmas particular to America at a crossroads.

Abridged from: Alan Rosen, "Teach Me Gold: Pedagogy and Memory in *The Pawnbroker*," *Prooftexts* 22, nos. 1–2 (2002): 77–117.

Source: Edward Lewis Wallant, *The Pawnbroker* (New York: Harcourt, Brace and World, 1961).

Background: http://peterfelix.tripod.com/home/Dia.pdf; http://www.jewishvirtuallibrary.org/jsource/judaica/ejud_0002_0003_0_03042.html.

Bibliography

Cunningham, Frank R. *Sidney Lumet: Film and Literary Vision.* Lexington: University Press of Kentucky, 1991.

Desser, David, and Lester D. Friedman. *American Jewish Filmmakers.* 2nd ed. Urbana: University of Ilinois Press, 2004.

Hass, Aaron. *The Aftermath: Living with the Holocaust.* New York: Cambridge University Press, 1996.

Hirsch, Joshua. *Afterimage: Film, Trauma, and the Holocaust.* Philadelphia: Temple University Press, 2004.

Langer, Lawrence L. *Holocaust Testimonies: The Ruins of Memory.* New Haven, CT: Yale University Press, 1991.

Leff, Leonard. "Hollywood and the Holocaust: Remembering *The Pawnbroker*." *American Jewish History* 84, no. 4 (1996): 353–76.

Lumet, Sidney. *Sidney Lumet: Interviews.* Edited by

Joanna E. Rapf. Jackson: University Press of Mississippi, 2006.

Rosenblum, Ralph, and Robert Karen. *When the Shooting Stops, the Cutting Begins: A Film Editor's Story*. New York: Da Capo, 1986.

28. "What *Is* the Way?"

Finding Meaning and Purpose after the Holocaust

ASHER Z. MILBAUER

Enemies, A Love Story, directed by Paul Mazursky [A]
United States, 1989

"If I should tell it all, anyone listening would think I was out of my mind."

—Isaac Bashevis Singer,
Enemies, A Love Story

In his "Author's Note" to *Enemies, A Love Story*, Isaac Bashevis Singer establishes his credibility to write about the unspeakable catastrophe that befell the Jewish people during World War II. He points out that, although he "did not have the privilege of going through the Hitler holocaust," he knew its survivors' milieu intimately. Singer lived among them in New York, spoke the same vernacular, frequented the same cafeterias, and shared their love for a culture and a people who had been murdered by a power whose evil was aided by the zeal of collaborators, the silence of bystanders, and the indifference of the Allied powers. Singer's "credentials" as a chronicler of the Holocaust are reinforced by the personal losses he sustained as a result of the Nazi invasion of Poland, his birthplace, on September 1, 1939. Along with nearly three million other Polish Jews, almost all of his family was wiped out in Nazism's fanatical obsession to rid the world of Jewish people. Had Singer not left Poland in 1935 to join his brother Israel Joshua Singer (also a novelist) in America, he probably would have shared the tragic fate of his people.

The lucky few who survived to bear witness and give life to a new generation of Jewish children were forever scarred by the horrors they experienced and witnessed. Their explicit and implicit "otherness" is irrevocable: the memory of the nearly incommunicable anguish and loss forever set them apart from people and societies untouched by the horror of victimization, isolation, and abandonment. Yet Singer implies that what makes the tragedy of the survivors even more pronounced is that none of them was a saint, entitled to be worshiped. By and large, they were just like the rest of humanity, defined by the strengths and weaknesses of their respective characters. Victimized for one reason only—they were born Jewish—the survivors, Singer maintains, were also "victims of their own personalities and fates" (Author's Note, *Enemies, A Love Story*). They defy being typecast. If a writer fails to create survivor characters who seem like flesh and blood and who are inclined to do both good and bad, he will victimize the real survivors further by setting them apart and denying them a sense of shared humanity, a prerequisite for anyone to be the master of his or her own fate.

Published in 1966 in Yiddish in installments in the *Jewish Daily Forward*, a newspaper conceived by its founder and editor, Abraham Cahan as a means of helping Jewish immigrants become full-fledged American citizens, the novel reflects the artistic dictum of its creator. It is populated by characters whose desires, inclinations, passions, and doubts are not unlike those of the novel's readers. But Singer's mastery extends beyond his ability to create characters his readers learn to both love and hate, to fear and pity. With the Holocaust always in the background, he reminds his audience that unless they remain vigilant and mindful of the curse of "otherness," the tragic destiny of the survivor might very easily be their own.

When contemplating how to adapt the novel into a movie, the director Paul Mazursky took great care to understand I. B. Singer's intentions fully and follow them closely. He was aware that he was dealing with a novel whose characters live in the shadows of the Holocaust and cling fiercely to the memories of a civilization, people, culture, and language that were almost completely destroyed. He knew that by focusing on a small group of Jewish survivors transplanted to America in the aftermath of the Shoah, Singer was not just exploring the usual and obvious hardships that immigrants face while trying to build a meaningful life in an alien environment. The noted Yiddish writer had created a *matzevah*, a rhetorical monument to pay tribute to the millions who fell prey to Hitler's Final Solution, as well as issuing a warning that unless the lessons of the Holocaust are heeded, history may repeat itself.

Although a number of Mazursky's films deal with Jewish themes, he waited until he was almost sixty to do a film centered on the Holocaust. He approached the project cautiously, not only because of its subject matter, but also because he was aware of Singer's disappointment with Barbra Streisand's adaptation of his short story "Yentl the Yeshiva Boy." Streisand's movie lacked both "artistic merit" and good directing, according to Singer ("I. B. Singer Talks to I. B. Singer," 2A). Moreover, Mazursky must have felt that he had to address Singer's reservations about translating fiction into film. "It is not easy to make a film from a story," claimed Singer. "In most cases it is impossible" ("I. B. Singer Talks to I. B. Singer," 2A). In his commentary on the DVD of *Enemies, A Love Story* (1989), Mazursky states that he made a point to visit Singer in Miami Beach to reassure the writer, and himself, that he would handle the subject of the Holocaust with the utmost sensitivity. Mazursky took pains to cast actors who would be able to create authentic and believable characters. He thus assembled a highly accomplished cast: the Swedish Lena Olin (Masha), the Polish Margaret Sophie Stein (Yadwiga) and the Americans Anjelica Houston (Tamara), Ron Silver (Herman), and Judith Malina (Shifrah-Puah). These actors could be relied on to deliver masterful performances. However, according to Singer's biographer, Janet Hadda, Mazursky immersed them in Holocaust history, too. He made them watch Holocaust documentary footage and invited them to the restaurants frequented by survivors and often staffed with survivor waiters. He also had his wife, Betsy, who worked with Holocaust survivors, arrange meetings between her clients and the cast (Hadda, 205).

Many writers question the ability of art to communicate the incommunicable suffering of Holocaust victims and survivors (Milbauer, 104). Twenty years after his liberation from Auschwitz in 1945, Elie Wiesel, the prolific writer and author of *Night*, still maintained that "Auschwitz negates any form of literature. . . . A novel about Auschwitz is not a novel, or else it is not about Auschwitz" ("For Some Meaure of Humility," 314). He was even more dubious about the capacity of cinema to "imagine the unimaginable." Wiesel also questioned the power and legitimacy of the filmed image: "Can it be more accessible, more malleable, more expressive than the word? I am as wary of one as the other." Nevertheless, Wiesel concedes that "certain films resonate with us . . . [and] succeed in moving us without falling into cheap sentimentality" ("Forward" to *Indelible Shadows: Film and the Holocaust*, xii). Mazursky's *Enemies, A Love Story*, released the same year that Wiesel voiced these reservations, succeeds in resonating with the audience and avoiding "cheap sentimentality." It does what Annette Insdorf expects a film dealing with the Holocaust to do: it "manifest[s] artistic as well as moral integrity" (*Indelible Shadows*, xv).

The film opened to considerable critical acclaim. Hal Hinson described it as a "deeply, fully human work" (B1), and the critic Annabelle Boyd called it "unusually complex . . . heart-breaking and funny." It brought the "vitality of Singer's novel to the screen," she claimed.(9). And Janet Maslin's perceptive characterization of the film as "Paul Mazursky's deeply felt, fiercely evocative adaptation of Isaac Bashevis Singer's brilliantly enigmatic novel" (C24) identified the source of the film's success: the synergy between a talented film director and a literary masterpiece. The screenplay, written by Mazursky and Roger Simon, closely follows the novel's plot and draws heavily on the text for dialogue. It captures what Mazursky most valued in Singer's story: the writer's ability to "shift constantly from tragedy to comedy," enabling the reader to "believe in the utter despair of [the characters'] lives" (DVD Commentary). Furthermore, the meticulously replicated Jewish neighborhoods of New York in the 1940s and 1950s created a "visually authentic" (DVD Commentary) film inhabited by credible characters who were devoid of sentimentality and kitsch.

Given the plot's twists and romantic entanglements, the film adaptation could have easily turned into a melodramatic production about a neurotic polygamist. Herman Broder continuously crisscrosses three New York City boroughs while visiting the homes of three different women—a second and current wife, Yadwiga; a first wife whom he thought had died, Tamara; and a long-time mistress whom he has just married, Masha. Sexually and emotionally involved with all of them, he avoids their demands to settle down and take responsibility for his actions. None of these women, however, is a playful courtesan; nor is the man profligate. The film discourages viewers from perceiving them in that way. Instead, they are survivors, marked for life by their experience.

The film's opening scene makes it clear that what the audience is about to watch has very little to do with a set of sexually active women and a Jewish libertine's romantic shenanigans. Herman is awakened by a nightmare in which he secretly watches Nazi soldiers invade his Polish hide-out and mercilessly beat Yadwiga, his gentile rescuer, to force her to reveal his whereabouts. Drenched in cold sweat, Herman stands by the window of his Coney Island apartment, gazing at the circular motion of the nearby Wonder Wheel, a recurring image in the film, as if he is trying to decide whether the entertainment value of a Luna Park attraction goes beyond its intention to delight visitors and points, rather, to its traditional symbolic connotation: an ever-turning wheel of fortune. His querying gaze seems to reflect his preoccupation with life's big questions: Is the history of the world, and especially that of the Jews, a history of pain, suffering, and perpetual loss? Can one find meaning in life after the Holocaust? How can one live with memories of horror? Is there any redeeming value in having had the privilege or luck to survive? Why bring children into a world of evil? Could a holocaust happen in America? Where was God when His chosen people were mercilessly exterminated? As Edward Alexander observes, the story "treats the survivors of the Holocaust as if they were now the central bearers of Jewish fate, and as if the definition and the resolution of the ultimate questions of philosophy, politics, and religion can never again be made without reference to their experiences" (99). Neither can these questions be treated without understanding that the Holocaust is not an isolated incident in the history of the Jewish people. Rather, the Jewish people had been in a state of permanent exile, in which they were repeatedly subjected to the whims of majority cultures and ideologies, be they religious, racial, or political.

Despite the promise of the Statue of Liberty to welcome "the huddled masses yearning to breathe free," breathing free in America does not come naturally to the film's characters. "The past followed [them] like a dog," to invoke the words of Henryk Grynberg, a Polish poet-survivor in America (51). The klezmer melodies and the image of the slowly revolving Wonder Wheel that mark the beginning and end of the film make the viewer realize that the present lives of the characters are inseparable from their past. Whether they find themselves in the depths of the New York subway system or in the pastoral setting of the Catskill Mountains, they are repeatedly haunted by nightmarish visions and dreams of Nazi persecution—the ominously reverberating noises of moving cattle cars transporting Jews to the camps, the howling of watchdogs, and the piercing screech of watchtower sirens.

In *Enemies, A Love Story*, Mazursky conveys the conflicted lives of survivors by making the viewer keenly aware of their unstable situation as post-Holocaust immigrants in the United States. He develops multidimensional characters whose complexity precludes them from being regarded simply as victims. By highlighting the intricate relationships among various pairs of characters, Mazursky makes viewers cognizant of the inherent complications and injustices that resulted from the shattering of their pre-Holocaust lives. Traumatic experiences undermine the survivors' ability to form consequential relationships that could endow their lives with a sense of meaning.

This is especially true in Herman Broder's case. Herman found his traditional prewar Jewish-Polish milieu to be restrictive and suffocating. He married Tamara, a leftist activist, whose intellectual restlessness matched his own. Herman's self-absorbed egoism doomed the marriage from its inception. The birth of their children, David and Yocheved, brought even more discord into their lives, leading to estrangement and separation.

The German invasion of Poland that led to the extermination of Polish Jewry seemed to have severed their marital ties forever. During a mass execution, David and Yocheved were shot to death by the Nazis. Miraculously, Tamara, two bullets lodged deep in her hip, managed to crawl out from under the dead bodies. Aided by a kind gentile couple, she recovered from her wounds, survived the hardships of Russian camps, and joined her uncle, Reb Nissin Yaroslaver, and her aunt, Sheva Haddas, in Brooklyn. Herman was also lucky enough to survive: for three years he hid in a hayloft, protected by Yadwiga, his parents' maid. Having had a witness confirm that both Tamara and the children had perished, Herman married the virtuous Yadwiga out of gratitude for saving his life, and the two made their way to America after waiting for American visas in a displaced persons camp in Europe. There Herman formed an intimate relationship with Masha, a Jewish survivor from Poland, whose Holocaust experiences left her emotionally unstable. Masha, too, left Europe and settled in the

Bronx with her mother, Shifrah-Puah, and Leon Tortshiner, a charlatan, whom Masha had married out of convenience after the war.

At the time of the film's opening, Herman and Masha have rediscovered each other in America and resumed their tumultuous and destructive relationship. Although both his wife and his mistress plead for "exclusivity," Herman can neither forsake Yadwiga nor give Masha up. With intermittent stops in the Manhattan office of Rabbi Lampert, who employs him as a ghostwriter, he shuttles between Coney Island, where he lives with Yadwiga, and the Bronx, where Masha shares a flat with her mother, Shifrah-Puah, trying to balance his moral obligation to Yadwiga with his sexually charged passion for Masha. And as if his life were not complicated enough, Herman discovers that his first wife, Tamara, is in New York, trying to reunite with him and share her stories of her survival and their children's murder. Herman has gained yet another destination to run to and from.

Exhausted by his inability to settle on one of the three women, Herman seeks refuge in Jewish teachings. Several attempts to live according to the Torah fail to resolve Herman's doubts about the validity of faith in the aftermath of the Shoah. Rather, these attempts reinforce his belief that God had turned His face away when Jewish children were mercilessly slaughtered. Although he knows that straying from Judaism and, in Singer's words, "yearning to be like a gentile" (*Penitent*, 90–91) might lead to a "spiritual holocaust" (*Meshugah,144*), he often finds himself either standing indecisively in front of the subway signs that point toward the different locations where his lovers await his return, or gazing at the Wonder Wheel and trying to understand why, according to Singer, "Cain continues to kill Abel," why

"Nebuchadnezzar is still slaughtering the sons of Zedekiah and putting out Zedekiah's eyes," and why "the Jews are forever being burned in Auschwitz" (*Enemies, A Love Story*, 30).

"We are running away and Mount Sinai runs after us. This chase has made us sick and mad," (*Shosha*, 255) cries out Aharon Greidinger, the protagonist of *Shosha*, a Singer novel set in prewar Poland, as he sums up the tragedy of the exilic existence of a nation caught between the desire to preserve its identity as the People of the Book and the longing to assimilate and join the people of the world. This exasperating chase assumes even more severe manifestations of sickness and madness after the Holocaust. "Evil spirits are playing with us," Shifrah-Puah, Masha's mother, laments in the novel. "We came out of Gehenna, but Gehenna followed us to America" (*Enemies, A Love Story*, 184).

Each of the film's major characters lives in his or her personal hell, confirming Jean Améry's observation in his survivor memoir: "Whoever was tortured, stays tortured" and will no longer be able to feel comfortable in the world (34). Herman's three-year confinement in a barn and constant fear of exposure left him psychologically scarred, mentally fatigued, and severely guilt ridden for failing his children and the Jewish community in time of need. The German bullets lodged in Tamara's hip have caused more than a limp: they serve as a continuous reminder of the most painful loss she sustained—the loss of her children. Masha's forearm tattoo, acquired in the concentration camp, was more than skin-deep; it penetrated her very being, engendering a sense of vulnerability that she would never be able to overcome. And the persistent smell of burning food, a direct allusion to the crematoria, pursues Shifrah-Puah even in her American kitchen. "Maybe I am no longer part of this world," is Herman's response to Rabbi Lampert's exhortations that he forget his past and start living as a normal human being. "I am not the same. I am dead," Tamara confesses to Herman during a rare moment of intimacy. "I don't want to live any more," Masha screams bitterly when it turns out that she is not pregnant. Watching her daughter suffer breaks Shifrah-Puah's heart. "I wanted so much to have a grandchild, if only somebody to name for the murdered Jews," she laments, just days before she succumbs to her grief. Although Shifrah-Puah's anguish seems to confirm Tamara's belief that "a slit throat cannot be sewn together again," Shifrah-Puah's prayer does not go entirely unanswered, as Yadwiga names the child she conceives with Herman after Masha, who, even if her death comes belatedly, is ultimately one of the murdered Jews. As several critics have observed—among them Alexander, Milbauer, Desser, and Friedman—this yearning to see a new generation of Jewish children born into the world recurs throughout the novel. In Mazursky's film adaptation the issue becomes especially prominent.

In the pastoral setting of the Catskill Mountains, Herman admonishes Masha not to drink, telling her that alcohol "is not the way" to alleviate life's agonies. "What *is* the way?" asks Masha, thus positing a question that permeates the whole of Mazursky's film. How does one transcend the sense of irrevocable loss that the survivors feel so acutely? How is one to deal with the anxieties, depressions, nightmares, insomnias, personality disorders, and suicidal inclinations that the noted psychiatrists William Niederland and Leo Ettinger consider pivotal elements of what they defined as the "survivor syndrome"? (quoted in Hass, 2) What will give the survivors an opportunity to "establish new, adequate, interpersonal contacts"

(quoted in Hass, 3) and regain what Améry considers the biggest losses engendered by the Holocaust: "trust in the world" and the sense of rootedness in one's homeland (28). Contrary to Améry's belief that neither "trust in the world" nor one's feeling of being at home can ever be regained, Mazursky offers at least partial answers to Masha's query: each of the main characters recreates deeply felt human bonds and becomes attuned to his or her own deeply felt longings and desires.

Many of Herman's encounters with his three lovers take place in their respective apartments, with the kitchen table taking center stage most of the time. The traditional Jewish foods served on these tables, the festive radiance of the Shabbat candles, and the serene Jewish rituals appeal to Herman and expose his craving to belong to a community. In their own ways, each of the women would like to provide a permanent address for Herman. However, his tragic understanding of history as a rotating wheel with evil as its axis makes it impossible for him to answer Yadwiga's plea for a child. During a rare outing to Coney Island's Luna Park, with the Wonder Wheel providing a backdrop for fun, Yadwiga implores Herman to settle down and have a family: "I want to become a Jew. I want to have your child." For the righteous Yadwiga, who endangered her life to save a Jew and forsook her family, the act of childbirth and a commitment to Judaism serve as antidotes to a world where the sanctity of human life is disparaged. Herman recognizes the cruelty he is inflicting on a woman he calls an angel by denying her the pleasures of motherhood; he also knows that by turning his back on his roots, he is unwittingly completing Hitler's efforts to eradicate the Jewish people. "If we don't want to become Nazis, we must remain Jews," Herman proclaims during one of his short-lived returns to Judaism. And then he is on the run again into the arms of Masha, who demands that he marry her and give her a child, in spite of her bitter tirades against a God who "doesn't care" about his own creation. "I wanted your child since the day we met," she tells Herman. When, during their Catskills outing, she informs Herman that she is pregnant, he decides to marry her rather than lose his *femme fatale*. However, Masha's pregnancy turns out to be a figment of her imagination. She is denied the experience of motherhood and the bonds of love that accompany it; all she has left in her life to make her feel alive is an animalistic sexuality that she substitutes for love. On learning that Yadwiga is pregnant and before taking her own life, Masha expresses a generosity of spirit that even the Nazis could not completely repress: "At least go back to your peasant," she entreats Herman. "Don't leave your child."

Masha's plea parallels that of Tamara. When Herman rejects Tamara's offer to help him stabilize his life and informs her of his decision to leave New York, she puts aside whatever feelings she still has for him and begs him to stay with Yadwiga: "God blesses you with a child, you spit in His face." Herman, however, sees no way out of his predicament but escape. So great is this survivor's despair that, short of taking his life, Herman sees only one way to alleviate his pain. Singer writes: "Those without courage to make an end to their existence have only one other way out: to deaden their conscience, choke their memory, extinguish the last vestige of hope" (*Enemies, A Love Story, 30*).

However, Herman's defeatist stance is forcefully repudiated by Yadwiga and Tamara, and even by Masha, who finds the act of leaving a child behind to be utterly abhorrent. For these women, living without hope for a better future and without remembering the victims of the Holocaust would only encourage the kind of evil that, in the estimate of Debórah Dwork, took the lives of nine out of ten Jewish children (*Children with a Star,* xi). The anticipated birth of a child changes Tamara's and Yadwiga's lives. To steady her physical and moral standing, Tamara has one of the two bullets lodged in her hip removed through surgery; and Yadwiga, as her pregnancy progresses and her Jewish identity strengthens, regains the self-confidence and moral courage she exhibited when she saved Herman's life. Their decision to create a home for a child, rebuild a community, and run a Judaica store in the aftermath of the Holocaust translates into a refusal to accept a world where people conduct their lives according to the law of the jungle. These women understand that by giving birth to a new generation of Jewish children, they are celebrating life and rejecting evil. In this respect they adopt the position of the noted philosopher Emil Fackenheim: "Jews are forbidden to hand Hitler posthumous victories. They are commanded to survive as Jews" (188).

The film ends with Tamara and Yadwiga caring for baby Masha in Herman's absence. The two women lovingly fuss over the little girl, whose name sustains the memory of their former rival, who has succumbed to the suffering caused by the Holocaust. As Yadwiga watches her daughter with awe and pleasure, Tamara feeds the child apricot purée, holding her close with a tattooed arm. With Yadwiga and Tamara as her guardian angels, Masha has a hopeful future. Born to a Righteous Gentile, one of the "undeniably heroic and principled few," as Cynthia Ozick labels rescuers of Jews in the Holocaust (xvi), little Masha will be able to learn from her mother that "to

be human," in the words of Sister Carol Rittner, "means to care for people who are in danger . . . and that each one of us can make a difference" (xv).

Moreover, Tamara's tattoo will always remind
Masha of her obligations as a second-generation
witness to preserve the memory of her half-
brother and -sister—Herman and Tamara's murdered children, David and Yocheved—and to
commemorate the woman after whom she is
named. And who knows—she might still be able
to share her joys and sorrows with her father, a
ghostwriter in perpetual search of his own voice,
who in Mazursky's cinematic adaptation chooses
to maintain at least a marginal contact with his
daughter by sending her money, rather than vanishing completely, as he does in Singer's novel.
After all, an American-born Jewish cinematographer has more reason to be optimistic about growing up in America than an old-fashioned Yiddish
writer whose life and writings were defined by
exile and loss. But Mazursky and Singer share a
firm belief that the birth of baby Masha provides
at least a partial answer to the painful question
that Masha Broder poses in the pastoral setting of
the Catskill Mountains: "What *is* the way?"

Source: Isaac Bashevis Singer, *Enemies, A Love Story*,
trans. Aliza Shervin and Elizabeth Shub (New York:
Farrar, Straus and Giroux, 1972).

Background: http://www.myjewishlearning.com/
beliefs/Theology/Suffering_and_Evil/Responses/
Modern_Solutions.shtml.

Bibliography

Alexander, Edward. *Isaac Bashevis Singer*. Boston: Twayne
Publishers, 1980.

Améry, Jean. *At the Mind's Limits: Contemplations by a
Survivor of Auschwitz and Its Realities*. Trans. Sydney
Rosenfeld and Stella P. Rosenfeld. Bloomington: Indi-
ana University Press, 1980.

Blacher-Cohen, Sarah. "Hens to Roosters: Isaac Bashevis
Singer's Female Species." *Studies in American Fiction*.
10 no.2 (1982): 173–184.

Boyd, Annabelle. "Enemies, A Love Story." *The Tech*.
109/60 (January 24, 1990) 9.

Desser, David, and Lester D. Friedman. *American Jewish
Filmmakers,* 2nd edition. Urbana: University of Illinois Press, 2004.

Dwork, Debórah. *Children with a Star: Jewish Youth in
Nazi Europe*. New Haven and London: Yale University Press, 1991.

Fackenheim, Emil L. "The Voice of Auschwitz," *Mod-
ern Jewish Thought: A Source Reader*, edited by
Nahum N. Glazer, 188–196. New York: Schocken
Books, 1977.

Grynberg, Henryk. "Writing about Uprootdness," *The
Writer Uprooted: Contemporary Jewish Exile Litera-
ture*. Ed. Alvin H. Rosenfeld, 50–74. Bloomington:
Indiana University Press, 2008.

Guzlowski, John. "Isaac Bashevis Singer and the Threat to
America." *Shofar* 20, no.1 (2001): 21–35.

Hadda, Janet. *Isaac Bashevis Singer: A Life*. New York:
Oxford University Press, 1997.

Hanson, Hal. "Enemies, A Love Story." *Washington Post*.
(January 19, 1990) B1.

Hass, Aaron. *The Aftermath: Living with the Holocaust*.
New York: Cambridge University Press. 1995.

Insdorf, Annette. *Indelible Shadows: Film and the Holocaust*. 2nd edition. New York: Cambridge University
Press, 1989.

Maslin, Janet, "Tale of Hope and Fatalism." *The New York
Times*. (December 13, 1989) C24.

Mazursky, Paul. *Show Me the Magic*. New York: Simon &
Schuster, 1999.

Milbauer, Asher Z. *Transcending Exile: Conrad, Nabokov,
I. B. Singer*. Miami: University Presses of Florida/
Florida International University Press, 1985.

Ozick, Cynthia. "Prologue," *Rescuers: Portraits of
Moral Courage in the Holocaust*. Eds. Block, Gay, and
Malka Drucker. New York: Holmes & Meier,
1992.

Rittner, Carol, and Sandra Moyers, eds. *The Courage to
Care: Rescuers of Jews during the Holocaust*. New York:
NYUP, 1986.

Singer, Isaac Bashevis. *Meshugah*. Trans. Isaac Bashevis Singer and Nili Wachtel. New York: Farrar, Straus & Giroux, 1994.

——. *Penitent*. Trans. Joseph Singer. New York: Farrar, Straus & Giroux, 1983.

——. *Shosha*. Trans. Joseph Singer. New York: Farrar, Straus & Giroux, 1978 .

——. "I. B. Singer Talks to I. B. Singer About the Movie *Yentl*." *New York Times*. (January 29, 1984) 2A.

Wiesel, Elie. "For Some Measure of Humility." *Sh'ma*. 5/100 (October 31, 1975), 314–315.

——. "Foreword," *Indelible Shadows: Film and the Holocaust*, by Annette Insdorf, 2nd edition, New York: Cambridge University Press, 1989, xi–xii.

PART SIX

Israel's Heroic Years, 1947–1967

29. Filming the Israeli War of Independence

ARIEL L. FELDESTEIN

Hill 24 Doesn't Answer (*Giv'a 24 Eina Ona*), directed by Thorold Dickinson [EM]
Israel, 1955
Kedma, directed by Amos Gitai [A]
France, Italy, and Israel, 2002

The Israeli side paid a heavy price for the 1948 war. The deaths of six thousand soldiers raised questions about who was to blame for this war, and whether the sacrifice was necessary. One way to deal with these issues was to present the war and the fallen soldiers as the "silver platter" (referring to a famous line from a 1947 poem by Natan Altherman, conveying the understanding of the sacrifices that would have to be made for the sake of Israel's independence) that saved the nation from annihilation by the Arabs. Official history depicted this conflict as necessary because the Arab states and Palestinian Arabs had refused to accept the existence of the Jewish state. Armies of seven Arab states, well equipped with state-of-the-art weapons, invaded the territory of the young state, which defended itself with a smaller number of poorly armed soldiers. In newspaper articles, poetry, prose, plays, and films, the hero of 1948 was portrayed as a brave and idealistic young man who lived in harmony with nature as an agricultural laborer. He waged war in self-defense, dedicating himself to the Zionist settlement of the country. He spoke fluent Hebrew. In all of these characteristics, he was the antithesis of the Jew of the Diaspora.

However, not only sabras—the native-born Israelis—fought in this conflict. The 1948 war served as a melting pot for Israeli society as sabras, Holocaust survivors, and new immigrants fought side by side. Did the divisions between the latter and the sabras disappear in the course of combat? Were the differences blurred due to the camaraderie of battle? Did the immigrants' participation in the struggle enable them to shed their diasporic skins to be reborn as natives and prove they belong to Israeli society?

This essay discusses these questions as they are addressed in movies about the 1948 war. It is a comparative study of *Hill 24 Doesn't Answer* and *Kedma*. The former was produced in the 1950s and the latter in the early years of the twenty-first century. I will analyze the cinematic, narrative, and ideological codes highlighting the way the diasporic Jew, the Holocaust survivor, and the new immigrant, were represented and the changes in these representations over the years.

Hill 24 Doesn't Answer opens in newsreel style, presenting the partition map of Palestine accepted by the UN General Assembly on November 29, 1947. An announcer explains the progression of the Arab armies from the beginning of the invasion on May 15, 1948, until 5:45 A.M. on July 18, when the UN declared a second ceasefire. This first sequence links the events of the war and the film's plot, guiding the viewer toward the opening scene—a rocky hill, with explosions in the background, smoke rising, and four bodies filmed in close-up and medium shots. Their names (James Finnegan, Allan Goodman, Esther Hadassi, and David Amiram) are announced in a voice-over, and the film shifts back to when they were all still alive. The flashback returns the viewer to the briefing before their fatal mission. The goal was to improve the Israel Defense Forces' (IDF) positions in outposts overlooking the road to Jerusalem by conquering Hill 24. Since the IDF was overextended, only four soldiers could be sent. From here on, the plot splits into three episodes depicting the fighters' personal stories, with the threads eventually woven together into a common tragic conclusion.

Kedma opens with a close-up of a woman's bare back. She takes her nightgown off and gets into the bed where a partially naked man lies. A slow-moving camera reveals additional details, raising questions as to the scene's location. The couple's sex scene contradicts the frame's background. Suddenly, the man gets up and swiftly dresses. The surroundings consist of many metal bunk beds, with people crowded together and suitcases, sacks, and clothes hanging everywhere. The viewers slowly understand that they are watching people in the steerage of a ship. The man climbs up a ladder, and the sky comes into view. People are sitting on the deck wearing winter clothes, with their suitcases, bags, and sacks next to them. There is hardly any room to pass between them. This is a ship carrying refugees or immigrants to their new country. The expanse of the sea, the noise of the waves, and the cries of

seagulls contrast with the overcrowding on the deck and the roar of the ship's engines. From a distance, the ship's name can be seen painted on its bow: Kedma.

One episode in *Hill 24 Doesn't Answer* records the transformation of an American Jew, Allan Goodman, into a "New Jew." Allan arrived in the country as a tourist before the founding of the Israeli state. He intended to visit various sites, first and foremost Jerusalem's old city. During his visit in Jerusalem, his travel agent convinces him not to enter the old city because it is too dangerous. Allan witnesses a sudden attack of stone-throwing Arabs. He experiences Arab aggressiveness at first hand, when his cheek is slightly hurt. Confused, Allan converses with a Jewish resident and asks, "What will you do when the British leave?" He receives this determined reply: "We will fight, of course." "But," Allan continues, "there are millions of Arabs. You would simply get mixed up with another pogrom." The Jerusalemite replies: "If there is a war, we will fight alone, if necessary. . . . We have no choice. That is our secret weapon: lack of choice." Thus, Allan learns about the Jews' resolve and their lack of alternatives when Israel was invaded by Arab states in 1948.

In a sequence at a hotel swimming pool, Allan is no longer the neutral observer when he asserts his views to his Arab and British companions: "I have only been here for three weeks, but of one thing I am sure, Jews have a real interest in this country. . . . [The Jewish refugees] will not return to Germany and Poland . . . they came here to live. . . . This is our homeland; the promised land." The Arab unequivocally retorts that "either you push us into the desert, or we throw you into the sea" (and he pushes Allan into the swimming pool). Allan now knows the Arab side's approach and symbolically experiences the Jews' future if the Arabs win the war. After falling victim twice to Arab aggression, he understands what it means that Jews in Palestine have "no alternative." Thus, he decides to join the defense of the Jewish Quarter in Jerusalem.

Preceding the battle for the old city, the commander speaks about the Jewish return to the Holy Land: "Israel's soldiers, you are standing in front of the Jerusalem walls. For 1,878 years these walls have been waiting for you. Since the days of King David no Jewish force has burst through the walls of the old city. Tonight you will climb on them." While he talks, the camera pans the Jerusalem walls and the formation of soldiers, visually linking the city to those who will redeem it. The liberation of the city by the soldiers will reestablish the connection between the state of Israel and the kingdom of the House of David, reviving the Jewish historical right to Jerusalem in particular and the Land of Israel in general. The commander also spells out the dire circumstances faced by the residents of the Jewish Quarter: "For three weeks our troops have been occupying the place against superior Arab forces, suffering from lack of food, water, weapons, and ammunition." He describes the strategy of drawing the enemy's attention to the Jaffa Gate and then entering through the Zion Gate.

To highlight the importance of the battle and justify it, a scene of women, the elderly, children, and wounded soldiers crammed into a building that serves as a shelter and hospital is presented. The Sh'ma Yisrael prayer can be heard as nurses treat the growing number of wounded soldiers. The commander says off camera: "There are 3,000 Jews in the old city in contrast with 40,000 Arabs. The [Jordanian] legion has brought in heavy artillery, artillery against guns." Despite the poor odds, the importance and implication of the battle outweigh the risks.

Kedma presents several Holocaust survivors. They have left Europe on a ship sailing to the Land of Israel. Until they reach the shore, the viewer does not know their names. The camera scans their faces. Instead of human voices, only the earsplitting noise of the ship's engines can be heard. A young man and a young woman lean on the railing. The man turns around and starts vomiting. Little children try to find refuge on their parents' laps. These people are exhausted by their wartime ordeals and the difficult journey on the ship.

The camera returns to the face of the male character seen at the beginning of the film. Suddenly he begins speaking: "My family lived in Lodz before the war." That is the first sentence heard in the film. It explains that these are Holocaust survivors on their way to Palestine, on an illegal immigration ship. The man continues: "I don't know. It could be [that my family] had expired during the rebellion in the ghetto." The woman sings. The man sitting next to them says: "Rosa was my student. . . . She was sent to Siberia. Rosa speaks Russian. Everything will be all right."

The camera shifts to a landscape near the seashore, a rocky terrain with typical coastal vegetation. A group of uniformed people approaches, speaking Hebrew. Their commander looks toward the sea, scanning the horizon for the ship. These are soldiers in an underground military organization, involved in smuggling new immigrants into Palestine. The open scenery and their faces are juxtaposed with shots of the Holocaust survivors on the ship. Both the surroundings of the two locations and the types of people inhabiting them are contrasted. The soldiers are masters of their own fate, while the Holocaust survivors depend on others.

On land, British soldiers emerge from among the bushes. They start marching: left, right, left.

They are equipped with weapons and are very organized. They clearly differ from the underground soldiers in their attire, weaponry, and regimented behavior.

Back on the ship, the immigrants chaotically board boats, carrying their personal belongings. They hope to evade capture by the British. The next scene pits an illegal immigrant, the Holocaust survivor, against the British occupier who is unwilling to open the gates of the Land of Israel for him. With the ship in the background, the immigrants land on the beach and try to organize. Underground fighters hand out oranges, one of the symbols of Zionist cultivation of the land. Shouts in English and gunshots are heard. The immigrants flee, pursued by the British. The well-armed soldier is positioned opposite the Holocaust survivor who must fight with his bare hands. A chaotic flight erupts, accompanied by shouts in Hebrew, Yiddish, and Polish. The underground fighters sneak the immigrants in, while the British soldiers chase them. A rocky landscape and hedges of prickly pear cactus (*sabra*) appear in the background. The native sabra is contrasted with the Holocaust survivor. This shot recurs in films contrasting the "Old Jew" with the Israeli landscape. In this arid region, only those with the characteristics of the *sabra*—toughness and coarseness, intimidating protective thorns, cleverness, and creativity—survive. The *sabra* wisely uses the scarce water to bear juicy, sweet fruit. This scene concludes with a flock of birds migrating like the Holocaust survivors.

Both films impart only minimal details about the Old Jews' lives prior to immigration. The viewer learns only that some characters are Holocaust survivors, one is an American Jew, and so forth; otherwise, the Old Jew's diasporic life is not explored. His past is dwarfed by his present redemption. In this process of salvation and re-birth, the past functions only as a point of departure. The Old Jew usually does not have a surname, land of birth, family, or roots. The Israeli landscape emphasizes the transition from the past to the present. It is initially filmed from the Old Jew's point of view. The scenes are closed, the scenery confined within a frame. At this stage, the landscape and open space are not depicted. The Old Jew is still incapable of observing the landscape and merging with it; this will occur only through a long process of conquering it and fusing with it.

In *Hill 24 Doesn't Answer*, Allan undergoes salvation. He enlists in the fighting forces planning to break through to the Jewish Quarter: "I may be crazy, but to fight for Jerusalem did something for me." Allan has not been involved in the country's pioneer experience and has lived in the land of freedom, where he enjoys equality. Yet he decides to fight in Israel rather than simply send contributions, like most American Jews. The ultimate change occurs when Allan is wounded by a sniper's bullet during combat. Despite his injury, he demonstrates heroism by warning the other fighters of an impending attack.

Lying wounded in the hospital, Allan opens his eyes but does not understand where he is. There he meets a rabbi who wants to discuss God and faith with him. Allan protests: "I hate God. He has no love or compassion. Where is He anyway? Where was He when millions of Jews were slaughtered in Europe? Where is He now when Jerusalem is dying? He doesn't care." The rabbi replies: "God cares. If we allow evil to exist, we abandon God." This dialogue poses the questions of the Jews' fate and of whether history results from divine or human will. According to Zionism, Jews must redeem themselves rather than wait for a miracle to happen.

A nurse enters Allan's room, announcing that

the forces defending the hospital have decided to surrender. The old city's evacuation is filmed in a long shot, showing Jews (some of them carrying Torah books and other holy items) walking amid flames and smoke and loudly singing "If I forget you, Jerusalem." Nearby, Jordanian soldiers loot property as the muezzin calls them to prayer. The face of an Arab Legion officer exhibits amazement over the spirited chanting of the brave Jewish fighters. The emotion conveyed by the sight of the evacuees' convoy is more intense than in any other scene in the film. The stream of Jewish refugees evokes associations with the deportation of Jews from Jerusalem after the destruction of the Second Temple. This scene culminates with a shot of Allan and the rabbi holding hands, symbolizing the solidarity between religious and secular Jews from different places. The battle over Jerusalem combines the historical and religious claims of the Jews to the Promised Land. It also symbolizes the continuity between the ancient destruction of Jerusalem and the deportation of the Jews from the old city in 1948. The war expedites the process of reintegration, which occurs in front of the viewer's eyes.

In *Kedma*, three Holocaust survivors relate their stories. Rosa remembers how she escaped from the ghetto and looked for a place to hide. Her story is interrupted to indicate how trauma prevents Holocaust survivors from fully recounting their memories. Rosa does not want to continue escaping. She loves Yanosh. She does not want her terrible memories to deprive her of her *joie de vivre*. Rosa has endured many hardships, and now she wishes to live a normal life: "I do not want to say goodbye any more." Yanosh announces, "This is the first time I am happy." He loves Rosa and cannot stop hugging and kissing her. He quickly joins the underground fighters.

The former occupation of a young man called Menachem, who was a cantor in the Diaspora, evokes the underground fighters' laughter. They ask him to sing, and he begins with the Rosh Hashanah prayer "*Yehi Ratzon*" [May it be your will, our God]. They tell him: "This is not a synagogue here. . . . Why don't you sing something happier?" Menachem starts singing "Shoshanat Yaacov was happy and joyful." The underground fighters sit around a bonfire, away from the Holocaust survivors. The physical separation signifies the cultural, ideological, and behavioral differences between the Old Jew and the New Jew. The past has opened an abyss between the two. Menachem talks about his Holocaust ordeal. Weeping, he says: "Now I am fatherless and motherless. . . . If God loves us so, where was He when the Jews were killed in the extermination camps?" The fighters ignore him.

At the end of the journey, everyone meets at a makeshift army camp, where they prepare for battle. The Holocaust survivors are taught how to use weapons. The young, fierce-looking instructor says, "You must learn how to fight." He explains the use of the Sten submachine gun. His words are spoken with force, determination, and authority. Slowly, the camera leaves the tent and pauses on the fighters waiting to depart for battle. From afar it is difficult to distinguish between them, implying that the underground fighters and the Holocaust survivors have started to merge. Menachem sits with a weapon in his hands: "I want to fight for the country. . . . I was hungry not for bread, I was thirsty not for water, but for your bullet-pierced flesh, my soul has craved." The commander announces that they must leave to attack the neighboring Arab village.

The concluding sequence of *Hill 24 Doesn't Answer* delineates the four fighters' nighttime arrival at Hill 24. As they descend from it, shots are heard in the background. The scene now shifts to a pan of the Jerusalem hills and focuses on the arrival of a UN jeep carrying representatives of the Arab Legion and the IDF. Each representative calls for his fighters but gets no reaction, and each claims ownership of the hill. They climb the hill and see the four fighters' bodies. The legion's representative declares: "It is clear that the hill belongs to us. The defenders were killed." But the UN representative opens Esther's hand, which clutches an Israeli flag, and announces, "Gentlemen, Hill 24 belongs to Israel." Although each male fighter displayed military prowess, it was Esther's act that determined the outcome of the battle on Hill 24.

The other three fighters had won a place in the Zionist pantheon, and Esther is admitted into it, too. Her story is little more than her role in this battle. Esther's portrayal reflects the general attitude to women in the films produced in Israel during this period: women usually had marginal roles, in contrast with the comprehensive representation of the male soldiers' world. The films' approach to them derives first and foremost from their gender, regardless of their ethnic origins. We are told detailed stories about the three male fighters, but all we know about Esther's past is that she was born in the Jerusalem area. Esther enters the film during Allan's story about the occupation of the old city, when she assists the wounded soldiers. She volunteers to join the mission to occupy Hill 24 and entertains her comrades on the trip there by singing.

At the end of the film, the camera returns to the dead heroes' faces. Now the viewer's identification with them peaks, and the reaction is quite different from that at the beginning of the film, when the viewer still felt unattached to the characters. Death is linked in the final scene with shots of Jerusalem and the Israeli landscape. The individual stories of each fighter intertwine with the narrative of the nation, whose existence was made possible by their personal sacrifice.

In *Kedma*, the fighters are filmed attempting to attack an Arab village without any battle plan. Yanosh storms forward with a weapon in his hand, but he still wears his tattered diasporic clothes. He observes the killing and the killed around him. In the course of the battle, one of the underground fighters turns to Menachem and asks him for his name. "Menachem Teitelboim," he answers. "Starting now you are Menachem Tamari." The fighter Hebraizes Menachem's surname and thereby severs him from his past and roots. Shortly after Menachem is born again as a New Jew, he is hit by a bullet and dies. When he becomes a fighter, the antithesis of the diasporic Jew, he sacrifices his life for the homeland.

During the battle, the fighters meet Palestinian villagers who have become refugees finding their way through the smoke of the battlefield. When asked where they are heading, they reply: "When the area was conquered, everyone escaped to Jerusalem. . . . This is our land. . . . They heard what the Jews did and were scared." The Arab villagers exhibit courage but also express helplessness. They have been uprooted from their land and separated from their leaders for reasons that are unclear to them. This scene draws an analogy between the Arab villagers and the Holocaust survivors. Both are swept into the whirlpool of war. Both want to live, and neither knows where to turn. Gitai implies that everybody is the victim of the war, though nobody knows when it started, what its goals are, and when and how it will end. Arab and Jewish fighters both feel their cause is just and will die for its sake. Yet deep inside their souls, doubts emerge.

When the battle is over, it is unclear who won. Rosa is near one of the trucks. Rain is falling. The wounded and killed are transported away from the battlefield in stretchers. In vain, the fighters try to identify the wounded and dead, who are now just anonymous soldiers in a war. The shell-shocked Yanosh cries: "We have no history. . . . I would forbid our children to study history. . . . From the moment we were thrown from our country, we became a people without history." He feels he cannot find rest and comfort: "I don't care about bravery. That bravery is evoked by desperation. Anybody can be a hero." Yanosh challenges the ethos of New Jew who is willing to sacrifice himself for the new Jewish state. Yanosh and Rosa are reunited and push their way into a jeep in a convoy. The rain intensifies; the sky is gray, the earth muddy. The convoy disappears in the distance. There is no victory, no end.

In both films, the climactic moment focuses on the rebirth of the "other." The war enables him to redeem himself from his diasporic nature and integrate himself into the collective ethos of the New Jew. The narrative leads to a climactic point, when the transformation takes place. The major part of these films is dedicated to this process, while the story of the "other's" past is reduced to several sentences. The war creates unity among various time levels, groups of people, and even between the Jew and the Arab. But in *Kedma* the Holocaust survivor doubts the necessity of the war and questions the demand for sacrifice. He does not accept destiny with blind faith and does not consider a hero's demise as the high point of his life.

The Zionist storyline positions the New Jew—the sabra—at the core of the Zionist movement, which informs every aspect of life in Palestine. Like his forefathers, the "New Jew" was expected to be brave and proud. He was healthy, worked the land, and waged war against those aiming to harm him. His culture and language were Hebrew. He was the quintessential opposite of the diasporic Jew. Immigrating to Israel and dedicat-ing his life to its settlement, he paved the way for the masses following him. Like him, the Holocaust survivor and the new immigrant were required to discard their diasporic traits.

A comparative discussion of *Hill 24 Doesn't Answer* and *Kedma* sheds light on the Holocaust survivor and the diasporic Jew's transformation as a result of the war. This process is reflected in the plot and staged by the camera. The Old Jew is erased as an independent character. His prior life is relevant only insofar as it plays a role in his redemption. The metamorphosis receives both visual and ideological expression. The protagonist accepts this initiation without any doubts or fears. He proves by fighting that he is as qualified for the mission as the sabra.

The films' examination of the Old Jew does not require a simultaneous presentation of the sabra, whom the viewer encounters for just a few moments. The "other's" path, ideas, and war are modeled after the sabra's. The "other" acquires his Hebrewness and new identity according to the Zionist definition of Hebrew identity as the one and only identity. The "other" follows the sabra, who has shown him the way. The film-makers assume that the audience is familiar with the sabra's traits. As a mythical figure, the sabra serves as an entity that is both present and absent, and that informs the plotline. When the diasporic Jew changes into his opposite, he is reborn. Thus, the sabra disappears because the space is fulfilled by the diasporic Jew.

Hill 24 Doesn't Answer presents a linear historical narrative from the Diaspora, equated with destruction and the Holocaust, to the rejuvenated settlement in the Land of Israel. The "other" has one role, and that is to assimilate and contribute to the Jewish state's construction and development. The camera follows the "other" as he adopts the Zionist ideology and erases the details of his past suffering. The plot reduces the presentation of the past to the minimal details required by a happy ending.

The war is viewed as a necessary sacrifice for the homeland and an existential victory. It forges the unity between "New" and "Old Jews," whether secular or religious, male or female. The war connects the Jewish history of different eras and events. It provides the opportunity for the diasporic Jew's rebirth by returning to the homeland.

In contrast, *Kedma* presents an essentially different historical narrative. The beginning and end of the film signal a change in the Old Jew's redemption process. The film begins with an intimate event and concludes with a sense of failure. The Holocaust survivor is sent straight into battle with little training. Doubts about the righteousness of his cause bother him. Menachem and others follow in Allan's footsteps, but Yanosh and Rosa are unwilling to reconcile themselves to the war.

Sixty years after the establishment of the State of Israel, Israeli society's approach to the 1948 war has changed. These two films reflect the shifts. The "other" is denied his past and must be reborn in the war. Each of the protagonists goes through such a process. Immediately after the founding of Israel, the war was perceived as a heroic struggle forced on a community of only 600,000 Jews, who had to defend themselves against the Arab armies that came to annihilate them. The fighter's courage, heroism, and willingness to die for the homeland were core values. *Hill 24 Doesn't Answer* displays the rebirth, discarding the Diaspora and the heroic sacrifice under fire. This film engages in no criticism of the demand for the diasporic Jew to shed his past skin, deny his origins, and undergo a test of courage. The consensus among Israelis in the 1950s was that the new immigrant must become like the sabra. He submitted to this demand, and, if he had qualms, he repressed them.

Filmed almost fifty years later, *Kedma* articulates a different perspective. It still conveys descriptively and visually the contrasts between the Old Jew and the sabra, but the former is portrayed more humanely and tragically. Rosa and Yanosh express doubts about the righteousness of the war and the sacrifice of many lives. They do not passively accept the process of salvation. Throughout the film, they remain in their diasporic clothes. It is never clear to the viewer what the purpose of the battle is, which target was conquered, why so many fighters were killed, and why Holocaust survivors, who did not even know how to use guns, were not given time to train. They are led straight from the ship into battle. The viewer is left questioning the waste of human life, the sacrifice of everything for statehood, the need to live by the sword, and the policies of leaders who seem detached from the will of the people.

Background: http://
www.mfa.gov.il/MFA/History/Modern+History/Israel
+wars/Israels+War+of+Independence+-+1947+-+1949
.htm.

Bibliography

Almog, Oz. *The Sabra: The Creation of the New Jew.* Translated by Haim Watzman. Berkeley: University of California Press, 2000.

Avisar, Ilan. *Visions of Israel: Israeli Filmmakers and Images of the Jewish State.* New York: Jewish Media Fund, 1997.

Ben-Shaul, Nitzan. *Mythical Expressions of Siege in Israeli Films.* Lewiston, NY: Edwin Mellen Press, 1997.

Gertz, Nurith, and Hermoni Gal. "Deconstructing History: Trauma and Subversion in *Kedma* and *Atash.*" *Israel*, 14 (2008): 13–34.

Kronish, Amy, and Costel Safirman. *Israeli Film: A Reference Guide*. Westport, CT: Praeger, 2003.

Morris, Benny. *1948: The First Arab-Israeli War*. New Haven, CT: Yale University Press, 2008.

Shohat, Ella. *Israeli Cinema: East/West and the Politics of Representation*. 2nd ed. New York: I. B. Tauris, 2010.

30. Screening the Birth of a Nation

Exodus Revisited

YOSEFA LOSHITZKY

Exodus, directed by Otto Preminger [A]
United States, 1960

His masculine naked torso bathed in moonlight and gently wrapped in white soft foam created by the light waves of the Mediterranean Sea, a necklace with a big Star of David adorning his neck—this is how Ari Ben Canaan (Paul Newman), the protagonist of Otto Preminger's *Exodus*, first "penetrates" the spectator's space of desire. This sensual image of male beauty, resembling Botticelli's *Birth of Venus*, has engraved, for world audiences at large and American audiences in particular, the ultimate image of the birth of the "new Jew." Ari Ben Canaan symbolizes the sabra [native-born Israeli], a Rousseau-like "noble savage" born from the sea who epitomizes a powerful eroticized counterimage to the on- and off-screen image of the Jewish neurotic, intellectual, urban persona of Woody Allen. Ari, personified by the handsome Newman, demonstrated that the way the new Jew was represented to himself was not far from how he was perceived by others. Self-representation and "objective" perception, self-presentation and projection of the "other," narcissistic fantasies and fantasies of the "other" have thus become one in the long and traumatic historic affair between the Jew and the non-Jew. Hence it is for the birth of the mythic "new Jew" that the *Exodus* film stands.

Although *Exodus* is not an Israeli film, it has become an inspiring model for the heroic-nationalist genre in Israel cinema. Released shortly after *Exodus*, the Israeli film *They Were Ten* (1961), starring Oded Teomi, provides evidence of the compelling new image that Preminger's film created. A comparison between Newman and Teomi and the characters they play reveals many similarities. Both are handsome European-looking men whose devotion to the Zionist project of establishing a Jewish state is total. Both are admired by women who, despite their courage, occupy a less central place in the narrative. Both films are loaded with symbolism of sacrifice and sanctification of death, and both came to be known as the ultimate shapers of the image of the new Israeli (identified with the Askenazi male). Newman as Ari Ben Canaan (whose name ironically fits into the film's ideological scheme) has become a model of pride for both Israeli and American Jews. Furthermore, *Exodus* has reinforced the view of America and Israel as mirror images of the promised land.

I approach the film as a conscious cinematic attempt to turn history into a contemporary Zionist myth to create a new national tradition for modern Israeli society. Like the biblical story whose name it bears, *Exodus* is a story of origin. My reading of the film centers on the question of how it reenacts the foundational Exodus narrative to support the Zionist project of establishing Israel and eliminating the "Palestinian question." A close reading of the film opens the way for fresh interpretations of the "mythical structure" of

the Palestinian-Israeli conflict and its representation in Hollywood cinema and later in Israeli
cinema. The film reinforces the universalist and
liberationist "classical reading" of the Exodus
myth (thereby universalizing Zionism itself)
while suppressing the potential threat of reading
this mythical archetype as a paradigmatic narrative of conquest, colonization, and domination
(the ethnic cleansing and oppression of the native
Canaanites and, by implication, of the indigenous
Palestinians).

The interpretation of the story of the real ship
Exodus serves as a site of struggle in what has
become known as the post-Zionist debate. Israeli
historians, sociologists, and cultural critics have
questioned the dominant narrative of the Israeli
nation. The Holocaust, the 1948 War (known in
Israel as the War of Independence), the Palestinian refugee problem, the massive immigration of
Jewish survivors and refugees from Europe after
World War II and that of Oriental Jews to Israel
in the early fifties, and the different wars Israel has
fought since its establishment have emerged as
important components in this contemporary debate. How to construct the nation's history in
ways that challenge official memory has become a
major theme in current Israeli life. The *Exodus*
affair occupies a major space in this debate.

The ship *Exodus* was purchased in the United
States by the Mossad, the organization in charge
of illegal immigration of Holocaust survivors and
refugees from Europe to Palestine. The ship symbolized the "Ha'apala" [illegal immigration to the
British mandate of Palestine]. The ship set out
from France with 4,500 Jews from displaced persons' camps in Germany. Upon arriving in Haifa
on July 18, 1947, while still outside Palestinian
territorial waters, it was attacked with live ammunition by British soldiers. Three passengers
were killed, including a small boy, and dozens

Paul Newman (as Ari) takes down the hanged and
defaced body of his Arab friend John Derek (as Taha).
From *Exodus* (1960), directed by Otto Preminger.
UNITED ARTISTS/PHOTOFEST

were injured. The British unintentionally maxi-
mized the Zionist propaganda value of the *Exodus* by sending passengers back to France instead
of to refugee camps in Cyprus. Since the French
did not force the passengers to disembark, only a
few left the ship. The drama lasted three weeks,
drawing enormous media attention. Sympathy
for the *Exodus* passengers reached its peak when
the British government announced that they
would be returned to Germany. In September
1947, the passengers found themselves in Germany in fenced compounds not far from Lübeck.
The journey of the *Exodus* with its heavy symbolism had served its purpose from a Zionist point of

view: it helped persuade the world that the Jewish people needed their own state.

The story of the ship, regardless of its interpretation by Zionist or post-Zionist historians (the latter accuse Zionist leaders of exploiting the suffering of Holocaust survivors for political ends), demonstrates the power of revisiting national symbols and myths. Such myths can be appropriated not only by the nation itself but also by the so-called enemy of the nation. Indeed, the symbolism of national rebirth embedded in the story of the *Exodus* did not escape the Palestinians. In 1987 the Palestine Liberation Organization planned to send a ship named *Safinat al-Awda* [Boat of Return] with Palestinian refugees and Israeli and European peace activists from Cyprus to Israel. Just days before embarkation, the Mossad blew it up. By appropriating Israel's national symbols, the PLO was hoping to draw worldwide attention to the suffering of the Palestinian people and to Israel's denial of their right of return to their homeland, Palestine. This strategy also emphasized the transformation of the Jews from victims into oppressors.

Hollywood's *Exodus* imagines the nascent modern Israeli nation as a handsome American actor, Paul Newman, who plays the character of Ari Ben Canaan, the "new Jew." But the handsome Newman is not the only metaphor of the birth of the modern Israeli nation in *Exodus*. The ship that plays such a crucial role in the Zionist narrative of the birth of Israel is also used as metaphor of birth in the film. It not only evokes Moses's cradle and crossing of the water, which are part of the Exodus myth, but it follows the cinematic tradition of the "boat film" genre (a claustrophobic counter-genre to the more personal and open space–oriented "road film") that mobilizes boats, ships, and submarines as metaphors of national birth and death in films such as

Potemkin (1925), *Das Boot* (1984), and *Titanic* (1997). As closed spaces, enclaves surrounded by water, ships, boats, and submarines are associated with a womb that can also become a tomb, as *Titanic* shows. In fact, the founding myth of America (a birth story that echoes the Exodus myth) is associated with two ships: Columbus's ship *Santa Maria* and the *Mayflower*. Recalling these mythic ships could only evoke sympathy in an American audience through the identification between America and Israel as the two promised lands.

The Zionization of the American Jew and non-Jew alike is embodied through three of the main characters: Ari Ben Canaan, Kitty Fremont (Eva Marie Saint), and Karen Hansen (Jill Haworth). The casting of Paul Newman as the ultimate "new Jew" plays on the tension between difference and sameness. Newman's "classic" looks, invoking the beauty of an ancient Greek sculpture, are a far cry from the stereotype of the old Jew. His salient Americanness redeems him for the American Jewish male from racial and ethnic difference, and makes him a source of narcissistic identification. This mechanism of the identification enables the American Jewish male to overcome the split in his identity caused by the perceived pressure of Zionism to identify with Israel more than with his own country. The Americanization of the new Jew and the construction of the sabra as an American star embody, as Ella Shohat observes, "the virility of both the *Sabra* soldier and the American fighter, merging both into one myth, reinforced and paralleled by the close political and cultural Israeli-American links since the sixties."

Kitty, the Waspish, soft anti-Semite, enables gentiles in the American audience to identify with Zionism. Kitty is from Indiana, a Midwestern state, traditionally perceived as part of the heartland of America. She is blond and admits to "feeling strange among Jews." Yet, she falls in love with Ari Ben Canaan, the model sabra. This recruitment of the American gentile woman can also be read as an allegory of the growing involvement of the United States in the Middle East, beginning in the 1960s, and America's increasing support for Israel. Significantly, Kitty is cast as a nurse. Her ideological function is to nurture, as she heals the traumatized survivors through her work at the camp in Cyprus, and saves the life of Ari Ben Canaan. Her nurturing fits the self-image of America as an omnipotent healer of weak nations. When Kitty is still slightly anti-Semitic, the only person with whom she admits not feeling strange is Karen, her younger blond double, whose Aryan/Waspish look makes her a perfect candidate for American citizenship. Although Karen possesses the qualities that could have turned her into a model American citizen as Kitty's adopted daughter, she ultimately chooses Zionism and sacrifices her young life for her new chosen homeland.

Exodus, as a parable of the "love story" between America and Israel, recruits Kitty, the all-American woman, to mediate between the American audience and the "alien" Jewish people. Symbolically the film's portrayal of sympathetic and unsympathetic British military personnel also signals the new reality in the Middle East after the failure of the 1956 Suez operation. The disappearance of Britain as the former imperialist power broker of the Middle East, followed by the emergence of America and the Soviet Union as the new superpowers in the region, is presented through the love story between Ari and Kitty. This love story is an educational process whereby Kitty "learns to love the Jews" and respect them. Her initial "soft" anti-Semitism is gradually transformed into total love, admiration, and devotion.

Exodus is only one cultural manifestation of the love story between America and Israel that became more pronounced in the 1960s. A wave of novels and films such as *Ben Hur* (1959) that dealt with Jewish liberation stories emerged at that time in the United States and enjoyed immense popularity with American audiences. On the Israeli front, interest in America and American popular culture began to develop. To a certain extent these changes in cultural taste also reflected political changes related to the role of Israel in the new Middle East of the Cold War, with the Soviet Union becoming an ally of the Arab countries and the United States an ally of Israel.

Exodus transforms the Israeli-Palestinian conflict into a utopian reconciliation, following Hollywood's epic tradition of personalizing historical conflicts. The film portrays the conflict through the story of Taha (John Derek), the son of the mukhtar of Abu Yesha, an Arab village neighboring the fictitious kibbutz Gan Dafna. In a speech delivered by Barak Ben Canaan (Lee J. Cobb) to the child survivors who join Gan Dafna, he states that, "we [Arabs and Jews] live as brothers." Barak presents a picture of the Jewish settlement of Palestine even more radical than the official Zionist version. According to him, the mukhtar voluntarily gave the land of his village to the Jews to build a village where Arab and Jewish youth could work and study together. The obvious message of Barak's speech is not that the Zionists took Arab lands, but rather that the Arabs gave them the land because they knew the Jews would bring progress to the region. To further strengthen this version of enlightened colonialism, Ari and Taha are presented as "brothers" who sanctify and validate their voluntary brotherhood through a ritual of blood mixing that imbues their bond with a "biological" and historical status.

The culmination of the "Zionizing" of Taha is

his sanctification as a Zionist martyr along with Karen, the young and pure Holocaust survivor. Their common sacrifice, symbolized by their shared funeral and grave, enables the old/young nation to be reborn. Taha's act of martyrdom (he is ultimately murdered by Arabs for collaborating with the Jews) reconciles the iconography of the three great monotheistic religions. Although Taha is a Muslim, the scene where he is found dead is rich with Judeo-Christian symbols. A Star of David is tattooed in blood on his bare chest (echoing his blood oath to Ari), and his dead naked body is positioned in a crucifix-like way. Karen, who is also killed by the Arabs, is also a "sacrificial lamb" whose martyrdom redeems the nation. This scene suggests that the hybridization of the Palestinian and the Holocaust survivor constitutes the moment of the birth of modern Israel. Paradoxically, the shared grave may lead the viewer to acknowledge the victimization of the Palestinian and that of the Holocaust survivor. This image suggests that in Palestinian collective consciousness the Holocaust occupies a significant role, since the memory of the Holocaust is "forced" upon them by the European "exodus." The burial implies that Israel was literally built on the graves of the Palestinians and Holocaust survivors, a charge not too far from the post-Zionist critique.

Taha's role in the birth of modern Israel affords a multiplicity of readings. The dominant reading legitimates Zionism through the symbolic annihilation of Palestinian identity and selfhood; whereas a subversive reading acknowledges that the Zionist state was established on the graves of Palestinians and Holocaust survivors. This reading suggests that Taha and Karen are too pure to bear the tragic contradictions of history generated by the competing narratives of the Palestinians and Israelis. According to the dominant

reading, however, Taha and Karen must die because they "contaminate" the Zionist project of creating a "new Jew." As an Arab, Taha has no place in a community dominated by Zionist values. Karen too came from the land of the "old Jew," the Holocaust victim. The "new Jew," the American sabra, can be reborn only on the grave of the impure ones: the Palestinian and the Holocaust survivor.

In *Exodus* the moment of the birth of modern Israel is also a moment of death. The oscillation in the burial scene recapitulates the story of the birth of ancient Israel, a story of trauma and recovery. The birth of modern Israel is also based on recovery from the trauma of the Holocaust, which constitutes the ideological core of the film as much as it constitutes the formative myth of modern Israeli identity. In the Zionist narrative the illegal immigration of European survivors and refugees to Palestine during the British mandate (the European "exodus") is described as if it were an inseparable part of the Holocaust.

Three Holocaust survivors personify this story of trauma and recovery: Dov Landau (Sal Mineo), whose fictional character is loosely based on the historical figure of Dov Gruner; Karen; and her mentally traumatized father. Only Dov and Karen are purified by "redemptive Zionism" from Jewish victimhood associated with the Holocaust. Their purification necessitates their transformation into heroes and martyrs of Zionism. Karen's father, however, who represents the "old Diaspora" Jew and a "contaminated" Holocaust survivor, is beyond Zionist redemption. He is doomed to remain in an insane asylum in a catatonic state. The scene of Karen meeting her mute father in the asylum epitomizes the trauma of the Holocaust. Although physically alive, emotionally the father is dead. He cannot communicate with his own daughter. The father's silent presence represents the threat that the survivors posed to the nascent Jewish state, the threat of "Diasporic weakness" and of Jewish vulnerability. In a society where military heroism was the priority, there were fears that the survivors' stories could turn the whole country into one "big insane asylum." The father's silence manifests the self-suppression and alienation experienced by the survivors in pre- and post-state Israel. Only the young survivors can partially escape the "impurity" associated with the Holocaust. Dov is purified in a ceremony in which he joins the Irgun (the Etzel underground) and thus symbolically regains his Jewish phallus. Karen joins the kibbutz and relinquishes her dream to build a new, comfortable life in America. She is killed by an "Arab gang" defending her new homeland.

The two young Holocaust survivors, Dov and Karen, represent through their love the film's reconciliation between the Zionist Right and Left. The film blurs the internal conflicts between the Right and the Left (the Irgun and the Haganah, respectively) to show them as marginal. The leaders of the two military undergrounds, Akiva (David Opatoshu) and Barak Ben Canaan, are biologically brothers, as if to say "it is all in the family." Akiva tells Ari, "In your optimism you are Haganah; in your methodology you are Irgun, but in your heart you are Israel." The representation of the conflict as a family disagreement fits Hollywood's tradition of personalizing history and reducing politics to family romance. Contemporary Israel tries to patch over its internal divisions by calling for the unity of the people of Israel.

Despite their initial resistance to Zionism, both Karen, who dreams about America, and Dov, who rejects his Jewish compatriots, eventually join the two major Zionist political groups.

Karen joins the kibbutz associated with the Zionist Left, and Dov joins the Irgun, associated with the Zionist Right. Their choosing of sides represents the traditional schism between the Zionist Left and Right regarding the interpretation of the Holocaust. The Left's humanism and racial tolerance is represented by Karen, the blond "child of light" who was saved by the Danes and therefore, unlike Dov, trusts the non-Jewish world despite the Holocaust. Dov Landau, on the other hand, the young, dark, and slightly misanthropic survivor, represents the "lessons" that the Right derived from the Holocaust: isolationism, mistrust of the "goyish" world, fetishistic militarism, and ultranationalism.

Dov's initiation into the Jewish Right verges on Holocaust pornography, playing on the voyeurism of the audience. During the course of a brutal interrogation by the Irgun, Dov reveals his "dark secret": his subjection as a sexual slave by the Nazis in Auschwitz. Following his revelation, Akiva forgives Dov, who is redeemed by his initiation into Zionist nationalism. His broken manhood, his phallic pride, and his "normal Jewish heterosexuality" are regained as he swears to sacrifice his life for the nation on a Bible, menorah, and rifle, three fetishes that symbolize phallocentric, homophobic, and militarist Judaism. The ceremony conveys the message that only through armed struggle can lost Jewish pride be regained and the humiliation of the Holocaust revenged. It is not an accident that the Arabs replace the Nazis, and the delayed revenge for the Holocaust is displaced into the struggle against the Arab (the local "goy"). The equation between the Nazis and the Arabs (developed in a number of Israeli films in this nationalist-heroic genre) occurs when a mysterious Nazi officer, wearing a white Panama hat and white gloves, and evoking the glamorized colonialist attire depicted in *Casablanca* (1942), incites Taha to attack Gan Dafna, referencing the historic visit of the Jerusalem mufti Haj Amin Al-Husseini to Berlin, where he reclaimed a promise of Nazi support.

The cinematic rhetoric used by the film reveals a multiplicity of ideological ruptures between "history" and "legend." At times Preminger's *Exodus* shows that the historical and legendary aspects of the national narrative can be seen as essentially complementary. The film combines psychohistory (the view that personal history is not less important than public history) with the epic genre. As an epic film exploring both the psychology of the individual and the nation, *Exodus* invokes the difficulties of representing national struggles in cinema. As psychohistory, it renders the Israeli-Palestinian conflict through its characters' psychology, as well as through a dialectical process of political augmentation whereby each party to the conflict presents his or her version of the political and historical events. Part of the fascination of the film derives from its eclectic mélange of elements and influences borrowed from a variety of cinematic, literary, and theatrical traditions such as the social problem film, the psychodrama, the melodrama (with a leaning toward the woman's melodrama), the war film, and the action film. The historical approach imposes moral closure on reality. In preferring the imaginary to the real, *Exodus* surpasses the boundaries of history and becomes a moral drama on Zionism.

The promotion of Zionism as a liberation movement by *Exodus* was an imperative because in 1960, when the film was released, the propagation of the myth of Palestine as "a land without people" prior to Zionist settlement was no longer tenable, creating a need to rewrite the history of the Palestinian conflict for the international community and the American audience. Following the colonialist tradition, the film presents Zionism as fulfilling a "civilizing mission" with regard to the indigenous Arab population (the "Canaanites" of the biblical narrative). Moreover, the film shows that the native Arabs actually welcomed the Jews and gave them the land of Palestine as an act of gratitude for the progress they brought. The film implies that the new Jews are in fact the real "Canaanites." It is no accident that Newman's surname in the film is Ben Canaan, which literally means son of Canaan. Moreover, the film Zionizes the indigenous Arab Taha, whose enthusiasm for the Jewish settlement in Palestine elevates him into a Zionist martyr. Finally, transforming the old European Jewish victim into the new heroic Jew, the film uses the Holocaust to justify Zionism. To idealize Zionism, *Exodus* naturalizes the differences and tensions between the Irgun and Haganah, and the sabras and newcomers from Europe. These tensions existed within the Jewish community in the years the film depicts, and still permeate Israeli political life. Full of intentional historical mistakes and the mingling of fact and fiction, the film constructs an idealized cinematic representation of the foundation of the state of Israel, naturalizing differences and symbolically annihilating "others."

The kind of history refracted by imagination that *Exodus* so beautifully constructs paved the way for other Hollywood narratives that celebrate Zionism, such as *Cast a Giant Shadow* (1966) and Steven Spielberg's *Schindler's List* (1993), which is perhaps the master of Hollywood's Zionist narratives. These films submit the experience of the Holocaust to the Zionist perspective, which interprets the creation of the State of Israel as a process of Jewish redemption culminating in the creation of a new Israel free of the burden of the Jewish Diaspora.

Abridged from: Yosefa Loshitzky, *Identity Politics on the Israeli Screen* (Austin: University of Texas Press, 2001).

Source: Leon Uris, *Exodus* (Garden City, NY: Doubleday, 1958).

Background: http://en.wikipedia.org/wiki/SS_ Exodus.

Bibliography

Gruber, Ruth. *Exodus 1947: The Ship That Launched a Nation*. New York: Times Books, 1999.

Halamish, Aviva. *The Exodus Affair: Holocaust Survivors and the Struggle for Palestine*. Translated by Ora Cummings. Syracuse, NY: Syracuse University Press, 1998.

Mart, Michele. *Eye on Israel: How America Came to View the Jewish State as an Ally*. Albany: State University Press of New York, 2006.

Moore, Deborah Dash. "*Exodus*: Real to Reel to Real." In *Entertaining America: Jews, Movies, and Broadcasting*, edited by J. Hoberman and Jeffrey Shandler, 207–19. Princeton, NJ: Princeton University Press, 2003.

Segev, Tom. *The Seventh Million: The Israelis and the Holocaust*. Translated by Haim Watzman. New York: Hill and Wang, 1993.

Shohat, Ella. *Israeli Cinema: East/West and the Politics of Representation*. 2nd ed. New York: I. B. Tauris, 2010.

Silberstein, Laurence J. *Post-Zionism: A Reader*. New Brunswick, NJ: Rutgers University Press, 2008.

Weissbrod, Rachel. "*Exodus* as Zionist Melodrama." *Israel Studies* 4, no. 1 (1999): 129–52.

Zertal, Idith. *From Catastrophe to Power: Holocaust Survivors and the Emergence of Israel*. Berkeley: University of California Press, 1998.

31. Feminism, Zionism, and Persecution in Iraq

The Story of Herzliya Lokai and Her Imprisonment in the Baghdad Women's Jail

DAPHNE TSIMHONI

Braids (*Tzamot*), directed by Yitzhak Halutzi
[NCJF]
Israel, 1989

This film is based on the story of Herzliya Lokai (born Regina Sameh), a fourteen-year-old Jewish girl who joined the Zionist underground movement in 1947, in her northern Iraqi hometown of Arbil. Her underground Zionist activity led to her arrest and imprisonment in Arbil for six months and then in the Baghdad women's jail for another year and a half.

The making of this film was the outcome of several trends and processes that took place during the 1970s and 1980s: the growing interest of the Israeli public and academy in the aliyah (immigration) to Israel of Jews from countries all around the world; the expansion of research on the history of the Jews of the Middle East and their mass immigration to Israel; and the search for roots and self-empowerment by Jews from the Middle East, particularly Iraq. The latter trend was strengthened by the shift of government in 1977 from the Labor Party to the right-wing Likud Party, whose victory can be partly attributed to the growing influence of Jews of Middle Eastern origin on Israeli politics. Moreover, political activists from Iraq and other Arab states sought to demonstrate to the general Israeli public that their involvement in Zionist activities was a major incentive for their aliyah, to counter common stereotypes of Jews from these countries as being passive, poor, and lacking any ideology or culture of their own.

Iraqi Jewish activists in particular wanted to portray the narrative of the almost total immigration of Iraqi Jews to Israel in an organized airlift in 1950–51 as the outcome of the community's ancient religious yearning for Zion that had been transformed into modern Zionist ideology. In 1974 former Zionist activists from Iraq—headed by Mordechai Ben Porat, the Israeli emissary to Iraq between 1949 and 51—established the Babylonian Jewry Heritage Center in Or Yehuda, near Tel Aviv. The center declared its aim to be the presentation and preservation of the cultural heritage and history of the Jews of Iraq. Its permanent exhibitions, archives, and library have emphasized the underground Zionist activities of the Jews of Iraq rather than their ancient Babylonian heritage or religious and cultural contribution to the development of Judaism at large.

In 1981 Israeli Educational Television (IET) started screening the film series *Eretz Moledet* (*Homeland*), which surveyed the immigration of Jews to Zion from the early nineteenth century to 1950. It became one of the most acclaimed series broadcast by the IET, which then approached Yitzhak Halutzi, an IET screenwriter and producer at that time, to make a film on Zionism in Iraq that would appeal to Israeli Jewish youth. Born in Mosul, the largest city of northern Iraq and home to the largest Jewish community in that area, Halutzi had immigrated to Israel at the age of four with his family, as part of the mass immigration of 1950–51. Halutzi recalled in an interview with me on April 21, 2010, that he was inspired by the book *'Ad 'Amud Ha-tliyah—'Alilot Hamahteret Be-'iraq* (*Up to the Gallows: The Story of the Underground in Iraq*) by the renowned author Yehuda Atlas, which was published by the De-

fense Ministry Publishers (Ma'arkhot) in 1969. Recording the exploits of the clandestine Zionist movement in Iraq, the book became very popular. Among its stories was that of Herzliya Lokai, the only Jewish female ever jailed in an Iraqi prison for her involvement in the Zionist movement. Fascinated by her story, Halutzi thought it would appeal to Israeli youth. He based the core of his script on Lokai's story but changed parts of it and expanded its scope to represent the experiences of Iraqi Jewry in general. Although it was based on historical evidence, Halutzi said he wrote the script as a feature film rather than a documentary, and the IET accepted it. The movie aired on Israeli television three times in prime time. It won several prizes and has been incorporated into several educational enrichment programs. The National Center for Jewish Film at Brandeis University gave it English subtitles and has screened it at film festivals in the United States.

The Jews of Iraq formed one of the largest and most affluent Jewish communities in the modern Middle East. After experiencing invasions and wars over the course of their long history, Iraqi Jews embarked on an era of unprecedented prosperity and relative freedom in the twentieth century. By the 1920s, about 80 percent of the Jews of Iraq were living in the capital of Baghdad or the port town of Basra. Over half of them made their homes in Baghdad, where they were approximately one-third of the population. Only 20 percent of Iraqi Jews lived in small towns and villages, mostly in the Kurdish-dominated northern part of the country. That region includes the town of Arbil, where the story of *Braids* began.

During the British Mandate (1920–32), the Jews of Iraq flourished economically and socially. Many had been prominent in international British trade between Iraq, India, and the Far East since the late nineteenth century. Pioneers of Western education and modernization in Iraq, Jews worked as bankers, government administrators, and engineers for the Iraqi railways and the port of Basra. A number of young, educated Jews excelled in Arabic and won recognition as journalists, poets, and novelists. However, Jewish leaders were acutely aware of their community's vulnerability as a minority, dependent on British protection and the good will of the Muslim majority of Iraq.

Jews and other non-Muslim minorities in northern Iraq continued their traditional lifestyle as *dhimmis* (protected people), whose status was protected but inferior to that of Muslims in the Ottoman Empire. Although occasionally attacked by Muslims, the Jews in northern Iraq generally had good relations with their Muslim neighbors. From the late 1930s until 1947, they attracted less political criticism from nationalist extremists than the Jews of Baghdad did.

Iraqi Jews had yearned for Zion from the beginning of their exile in Mesopotamia. This found expression in the prayer "next year in Jerusalem." Jews from Iraq participated in the first Zionist congresses in the late nineteenth century. Zionist organizations became active in Iraq shortly after the British occupied the country, in 1917. Several Zionist associations offered Hebrew study groups, maintained libraries, and organized cultural and educational activities. They also raised funds for the Zionist cause. Relative to its size, the Jewish community in Iraq contributed more to Zionist funds than all but a few other Jewish diasporic communities. However, Zionist activities remained on the margins of Jewish communal life in Iraq, and none of the community leaders accepted the invitation of the World Zionist Organization to chair the local Zionist federation, fearing that open support of Zionism would damage the fragile relationship of the Jews with their Muslim neighbors.

With the growing involvement of Iraq in the Jewish-Arab conflict in Palestine from 1929 on, the Iraqi government limited Zionist activities in the country. It gradually expelled Hebrew teachers from Palestine, until Zionist activities stopped completely in Iraq in 1935. The Hebrew libraries were closed, and the books hidden.

The position of the Jews deteriorated after Iraq gained independence in 1932, as a result of government instability, the rise of pan-Arabism, the involvement of Iraq in the 1936–39 Arab revolt in Palestine, the growing fascist and Nazi influences in Iraqi politics, and the Iraqi government's granting of asylum in 1939 to the exiled Palestinian national leader, the Mufti Hajj Amin al-Husayni, and his entourage. World War II and the pro-Nazi coup by Rashid Ali al-Kaylani in May 1941 changed the treatment of the Jewish community in Iraq. Anti-Semitic Nazi propaganda was disseminated, and attacks on Jews occurred. British army forces from Egypt, Palestine, Trans-Jordan, and India reoccupied Iraq. Rashid Ali and his entourage fled from Baghdad as the British forces approached the capital. The pro-British regent of Iraq reentered the city in early June 1941, while British troops waited on the outskirts of the city. During this power vacuum, attacks by Muslim mobs developed into a horrifying and bloody two-day pogrom against the Jews of Baghdad, known as the *Farhud* (an Arabic word meaning serious destruction of order). More than 130 Jews were killed, many were wounded, and much Jewish property was damaged and looted. The pogrom stopped only after the regent realized the danger that the upheaval might cause him and his entourage. He called in a loyal Kurdish regiment from the north of Iraq, which soon stopped the massacres and lootings. A spontaneous movement to flee started among the Jews, but there was nowhere for them to go. The new pro-British Iraqi government established a committee of inquiry into the events of May and June 1941 and paid reparations to some of the victims. On the surface, everything was back to normal, but life could never be the same for the Jews. Memoir writers, other authors, and scholars consider the *Farhud* to be the beginning of the end for the Jewish community in Iraq.

When the news about the pogrom in Baghdad reached Palestine, it shocked the leaders of the Yishuv (the Zionist settlement there) and prompted them to establish a clandestine Zionist movement in Iraq to train activists, as well as supply them with arms, so they could defend themselves if necessary. The movement's ultimate aim was to persuade Iraqi Jews to immigrate to Palestine. Founded in 1942 by emissaries from Palestine, the Babylonian Pioneer Movement (Tenu'at he-Halutz) or in short the Tenu'a, organized Zionist groups in the major Jewish centers of Baghdad and Basra, and in smaller provincial Iraqi towns. The movement smuggled in arms, ammunition, and Hebrew teaching materials via Jewish soldiers and drivers who served in British army camps in Iraq until the end of World War II. Because of the remoteness of northern Iraq and the traditional lifestyle of the Jews there, the Zionist movement started its activities in that region later than in Baghdad and Basra. The Arbil branch was established in 1946 by Zionist emissaries from Baghdad and Palestine.

The Zionist movement in Iraq had two major branches: The Tenu'a organized educational and ideological activities. It propagated socialist Zionism, taught Modern Hebrew, and encouraged its members to immigrate clandestinely to Palestine. The Hagana (self-defense) or Ha-Shura (the line) trained Jewish youth to use firearms

and organize groups for self-defense. These two branches operated separately in Baghdad, where a number of Jewish youth who were not attracted to Zionism nonetheless joined the self-defense organization in case of another pogrom. Smaller branches, like the ones in northern Iraq, combined self-defense and educational activities.

During the 1940s, the Zionist movement in Iraq competed with the rising Communist movement that preached to Jews and other minorities that they could become fully integrated in Iraq under a future egalitarian regime modeled after that of the Soviet Union. After the *Farhud*, some Jewish youth embraced Communism; some wanted to study abroad and eventually emigrated; others tried to assimilate into the new educated Iraqi elite; and still others joined the Zionist movement. However, the majority of Jews carried on their daily lives within the Jewish community and worried about their future in Iraq, disregarding both Zionism and Communism.

The United Nations' 1947 plan to partition Palestine made the position of Iraqi Jews even more precarious, as establishment of the Jewish state in Palestine became imminent. The Arab League decided to discriminate against and persecute Jews in Arab states as revenge for the plight of the Palestinian Arabs. Iraq was among the first states to execute these decisions. On the eve of the 1948 Israeli War of Independence it prohibited Jews from leaving Iraq and criminalized both Communist and Zionist activities. Possessing Hebrew books and letters was punishable by jail and banishment; hundreds of Jews were charged with this offense and banished, fined, or imprisoned. Muslim mobs attacked Jews, particularly in Baghdad, the largest Jewish center.

With the establishment of the state of Israel in 1948 and the ensuing Arab-Israeli War, the persecution of Jews was expanded and their prohibition from leaving Iraq became harsher. Zionist activities in Iraq reached their peak. The Zionist movement now counted 3,000 men and women members, including 600 who belonged to the Hagana. They still constituted a small minority of the 140,000 Jews who lived in Iraq. But as the position of the Jews deteriorated in Iraq, the Zionist movement increased its influence over the Jewish youth and through them over their families.

Persecution of the Jews reached its peak in 1949 under Prime Minister Nuri al-Sa'id. As a result of their persecution and the lack of a legal way to leave Iraq, increasing numbers of Jews fled illegally to Iran with assistance from the Tenu'a. From Iran, the Jewish Agency for Israel organized their air flights to Israel. With the resignation of Nuri al-Sa'id's government in December 1949, persecution of Zionist activists and Jews somewhat eased. The rise to power in early 1950 of Tawfiq al-Suwaydi, a moderate pro-British politician, changed the policy of the Iraqi government toward the Jews. International pressure, the porous Iraqi-Iranian border, and the amicable relations of some prominent Iraqi Jews with the country's new prime minister resulted in the issuance of a regulation in March 1950 that enabled Jews to forfeit their Iraqi citizenship and leave Iraq permanently. Shlomo Hillel, a representative of the Israeli Mossad La-Aliya (Institute for Immigration), disguised himself as a representative of an airline company and met Prime Minister Suwaydi. The two agreed to evacuate the Jews who wanted to leave Iraq. Unexpectedly, the majority of the Jews registered to forfeit their Iraqi citizenship and leave Iraq permanently. It was tacitly understood that the final destination of the airlift was Tel Aviv. The Tenu'a, organized the registration for emigration from Iraq, its members ostensibly working as clerks for the Jew-

ish community. This semi-clandestine operation, known as Operation Ezra and Nehemiah, ended with the mass exodus of 135,000 Jews to Israel, leaving no more than 6,000 Jews in Iraq.

The participation of women in the Communist and Zionist movements improved their position in Iraq. Of the two movements, Zionism was much more revolutionary in this regard. Whereas the Communist movement in Iraq maintained separate sections for women, women in the Zionist movement were in the same groups as men and participated in most of the men's activities. They attained leadership positions in Zionist educational efforts. At one time a woman was elected as deputy chair of the Tenu'a. Another woman led an operation to smuggle a group of Jewish youngsters across the border to Palestine. This radical shift in women's roles was most obvious among the conservative Jewish communities of northern Iraq. In Arbil, recalled Herzliya Lokai in an interview with me on April 2, 2010, most girls did not attend school. Of the six local girls who joined the Zionist movement in Arbil, Lokai was the only one who had a formal education. Hence, quite a number of Jewish girls in northern Iraq learned Hebrew as their first written language in study groups conducted by the Tenu'a. The girls also went on trips and attended seminars outside Arbil. Expected to be married by the age of sixteen, the younger female members of the Tenu'a rebelled against their parents and refused to be wed. Although women were involved in educational activities and the smuggling of Jews across the borders, in northern Iraq only men received arms training in the Hagana, recalls Lokai.

The film *Braids* opens with a line of women prisoners holding metal plates, waiting to receive their meal of a thin soup. They throw their soup away and declare a hunger strike, protesting against the harsh prison conditions, bad food, and long hours of washing the clothing of the nearby male prisoners. The warden, Nuriyya, is portrayed as a tough, somewhat sadistic, woman of lower-class Muslim origins. She enters the cabin of the guard Abduh while he is listening to the popular (Jewish) singer Salima Pasha and rebukes him for listening to such music "while our best guys are fighting in Palestine." She reads him an order from Baghdad to suppress the hunger strike before it sparks a Communist overthrow of the government. Nuriyya goes with Abduh, who is carrying a bowl of curried lentil soup, to the hall where the prisoners are gathered. She tries to break the hunger strike by urging Su'ad to eat, assuming that as the youngest prisoner, she would not be able to withstand the smell of her favorite lentil dish. Su'ad resists the attempts to feed her by force. Despite the objections of other prisoners, Nuriyya orders Abduh to cut Su'ad's braids. In the film, the organizer of the strike is a Jewish Communist, Munira; all the other political prisoners are Communists of Muslim Arab origin. Nuriyya then tries to turn the prisoners against their Jewish leader but fails. Herzliya Lokai remembers that altogether there were fourteen political prisoners in a separate section of the women's jail. Twelve of them were Jewish Communists, one was a Shiite Arab Communist, and only Herzliya (Su'ad in the film) was a Zionist. In reality, as in the film, the prisoners' strike succeeded in getting better conditions, food, and access to reading materials.

In the film, Munira and Su'ad develop a friendship, based on their being the only two Jews and having a strong sense of belonging to the same persecuted community. They argue about the future of the Jews of Iraq: should they stay in their homeland and try to change its regime into a Communist one, in which the Jews would be accepted as equals? Would Communism solve the issue of minorities and religious persecution in Iraq? Or should they immigrate to Palestine and help build a nation-state for Jews? Su'ad reminds Munira about the 1941 pogrom, and Munira warns that once the Jews achieve statehood in Palestine, a war with the Arabs will erupt. "The Jews of Europe have no place to go to except Palestine, but we have," asserts Munira. "Can you call this our place?" replies Su'ad. Herzliya Lokai recalls her discussions with Communist prisoners: "I used to tell Munira and the other Communists, be Communist—but in our own state of Israel."

Munira tries to comfort Su'ad after her braids were cut: "To my mind it is irresponsible to recruit a girl of your age to the underground; they [the Zionists] should have realized the risk that they were taking." Su'ad responds: "It's not them, it's me. I knew where I was heading; the underground used to meet in the cellar of our house." Su'ad recounts her role in the Zionist underground, arrest, trial, and imprisonment.

The second part of the film opens with a flashback to a swearing-in ceremony held in Su'ad's home cellar in 1947 administered by five Zionist Iraqi Jews and the Zionist emissary from Palestine. The Israeli flag and the Bible have been placed on the table; photographs of Theodor Herzl, the founder of modern political Zionism, and David Ben-Gurion, the leader of the Yishuv—and, later, the first Israeli prime minister—hang on a wall. Su'ad secretly watches the swearing-in ceremony. Since the Jews of Arbil formed a close-knit community, the Zionist group already included some of her cousins. Su'ad convinces them and the emissary to accept her into the underground. She explains what motivated her. She had witnessed an old, blind Jewish beggar woman—who used to bless children in return for food—blessing a Muslim boy in Hebrew.

He burst out laughing, and his friend punched the woman's back with all his might. Though stunned, she continued to sing. Su'ad went home sobbing. Her father comforted her that "when we're in the Land of Israel this will never happen again." (In her interview in 2010, Herzliya Lokai explained that the assault on the old woman was actually due to her being old, blind, and strange, not because she was Jewish.) Su'ad is required to read a text in Hebrew to demonstrate her fluency. After identifying the photos of Herzl and Ben-Gurion and expressing her admiration for them, she is initiated into the clandestine Zionist group and receives her Hebrew name Herzliya, after Theodor Herzl.

The next part of *Braids* flashes back to the police search of Su'ad's home, a traditional house of a well-to-do Jewish family. Just minutes before the raid, Su'ad's father and a cousin from the underground manage to remove the Zionist publications from the cellar and hide them on their neighbor's roof. The policemen, who knew Su'ad's father (Abu Habib) explain, "We are looking for traitors, wicked people that are threatening the Arab nation." According to the new regulations, traitors meant Zionist collaborators. When the search fails to turn up anything incriminating, the policemen accept her father's invitation to share a drink, "for the Arab nation." At that time Su'ad heard about the search and hurried to her home to hide some Hebrew newspapers that she had left in her jacket. By rushing in, putting on the jacket, and trying to leave quickly, she arouses the suspicion of the police chief, who then discovers the Hebrew newspapers and letters from Palestine. The policemen drag her to the police station and comment about the respectable Jews who had become collaborators with the enemy. Su'ad's father begs the police officer to let him go to jail instead of his child, but his offer is rudely rejected. Some of the Muslim neighbors ask the police officer to leave the "good girl" alone, but they are roughly pushed aside.

For six months, Su'ad is confined in the local jail in Arbil, which had no facilities for women prisoners. She is then sent to Baghdad for further interrogation and a trial. Her mother is allowed to accompany her on the train, together with a guard who monitors them to prevent Su'ad from escaping. In this scene, the guard and other Iraqi bystanders emerge as poor; some are good-natured, but others extort bribes to keep them from molesting Su'ad during the trip. The incitement against local Jews becomes evident as the news of the Iraqi victims in the Palestine war reaches Iraq. When Su'ad and her mother request to go to the toilet alone, the guard initially refuses, fearing Su'ad might escape and telling them that "the Jews and Arabs have changed since the trouble in Palestine. They (the Jews) have become our enemies." Finally, he agrees. Su'ad's mother (Umm Habib) shows her the gold and money that she has brought for their expenses during the trial. Her father had sold his shop for that purpose. The mother convinces Su'ad not to try to escape because that would provide a pretext for jailing and torturing her father, perhaps to death. The guard also warns Su'ad not to bring disaster on her family. Arriving in Baghdad, Su'ad faces interrogation, but not before she receives a good meal to eat after her long trip and is transferred to a jail.

In a scene set in 1949, during the peak of the persecution of Zionists, Su'ad is grilled by the police to disclose the names of Zionists involved in smuggling Jews across the border. To break her spirit, she is placed in a cell where she is assaulted by a prostitute. The rabbi of her community is summoned to convince Su'ad to reveal the names of her Zionist comrades. In the presence of the guards, he loudly begs her to submit the names but simultaneously whispers to her to resist her interrogators.

The film climaxes after Munira is taken to the hospital and dies. The government suddenly announces that Jews may relinquish their Iraqi nationality and leave Iraq. The warden summons Su'ad, declares that she is free, and gives her back her sheared braids. Abduh parts with her amicably. Outside the prison, her family waits for her to immigrate together in the airlift to Israel. The Muslim neighbors' son from Arbil comes to say goodbye and give Su'ad's family money from his father to help them with travel expenses. He regrets that the Jews are leaving. This happy ending, which has some basis in truth, suits a film for adolescents.

Although *Braids* is a dramatization, its historical background was well researched, and it realistically portrays the story of Herzliya Lokai and Zionism in northern Iraq. To be sure, it overemphasizes how easily the Jews of Arbil in particular, and the Jews of Iraq in general, transformed their religious attachment to Zion into modern Zionism. When depicting the persecution of Zionism and the Jews before their aliyah to Israel, it does not demonize the Iraqi people and tries to show their humanity. It is first and foremost a fascinating story of a brave Zionist girl from Arbil who survived the horrors of Iraqi jail, made aliyah to Israel, and became an Israeli patriot, but did not succumb to hatred for the Iraqi people despite her persecution.

Acknowledgment

This essay was written at the Truman Research Institute, the Hebrew University of Jerusalem. Thanks are due for the assistance given.

Background: http://www.google.com/search?hl=en&source =hp&biw=960&bih=447&q=Maurice+Shohet+%2B+History+of+Iraqi +jews&btnG=Google+Search.

Bibliography

Interviews with the Author

Yitzhak Halutzi, April 21, 2010

Herzliya Lokai, April 2, 2010

Publications

Haim, Sylvia, G. "Aspects of Jewish Life in Baghdad under the Monarchy." *Middle Eastern Studies* 12 no. 2 (May 1976): 188–208.

Hillel, Shlomo. *Operation Babylon*. Garden City, NY: Doubleday, 1987.

Kedourie, Elie. "The Break between Muslims and Jews in Iraq." In *Jews among Arabs: Contacts and Boundaries*, edited by Mark R. Cohen and Abraham L. Udovitch, 21–64. Princeton, NJ: Darwin, 1989.

Meir-Glitzenstein, Esther. *Zionism in an Arab Country: Jews in Iraq in the 1940s*. London: Routledge, 2004.

Rejwan, Nissim. *The Jews of Iraq: 3000 Years of History and Culture*. London: Weidenfeld and Nicolson, 1985.

Tsimhoni, Daphne. "Activity of the Yishuv on Behalf of Iraqi Jewry 1941–1948." In *Organizing Rescue: National Jewish Solidarity in the Modern Period*, edited by Selwyn Ilan Troen and Benjamin Pinkus. London, England: Frank Cass, 1992. 222–68.

——. "The Pogrom (*Farhud*) against the Jews of Baghdad in 1941: Jewish and Arab Approaches." In *Remembering for the Future: The Holocaust in an Age of Genocide*, edited by John K Roth and Elizabeth Maxwell, 1. Houndmills, Basingstoke, Hampshire: Palgrave, 2001. 570–88.

——. "Why the Majority of the Jews of Iraq Emigrated to Israel in Operation Ezra and Nehemya, as Viewed by Jewish Memoirs." In *Encyclopedia of the Jewish Diaspora*, edited by M. Avrom Ehrlich. 1, 378–82. Santa Barbara, CA: ABC-Clio, 2009.

32. From Black to White

Changing Images of Mizrahim in Israeli Cinema

YARON PELEG

Sallah (*Sallah Shabati*), directed by Ephraim Kishon [EM]
Israel, 1964
Kazablan, directed by Menahem Golan [A]
Israel, 1974

The cinematic "birth" of Israel's ethnic divide between Ashkenazi and Sephardi or Mizrahi Jews occurs in the opening scene of the famous 1964 comedy, *Sallah Shabati*. The differentiation between two kinds of Jews is set up from the beginning of the film, which opens with the landing of an airplane in the Tel Aviv airport. As the door to the plane opens a middle-aged American couple briskly steps down the stairs, smartly outfitted in matching suits, coiffed hair, and a multitude of suitcases. Following the Americans is a very different immigrant family: Sallah Shabati (Haim Topol), his seven children, his wife, and an assortment of relatives. The family's non-Western origin is immediately clear from their disheveled, Levantine dress; from their Arabic accents and their traditional religiosity: as they step onto the tarmac, Mr. Shabati kisses the ground and says the *shehecheyanu* blessing [a prayer said on holy days and special occasions]. His entire clan rejoins him with a resounding "Amen."

Thus begin Sallah's adventures in the Holy Land, where he is hoodwinked into accepting a "temporary" shelter in a decrepit *Ma'abara*, a transit camp for immigrants, where he is put to work in various mindless public works, where his vote is disingenuously solicited, and where he is patronized by callous Ashkenazim, social workers, politicians, and others. Sallah rarely loses his sweetness and good cheer. His mischievousness and street smarts enable him to beat the system, get decent housing, and no doubt an honest job as well.

The hit movie made Sallah Shabati a household name in Israel and established him as the stereotypical Mizrahi whose image influenced the Bourekas—ethnic comedies that flourished during the 1970s—serious social commentaries, and crime dramas from that time, and finally the Mizrahi identity films of the 1990s. Those works comment in some way or another on Sallah's iconic image and explore his most identifiable characteristics: the Mizrahi as an artless and good-hearted fool and as a degenerate criminal. Sallah wins at the end of the film because of his good heart, not because he works hard or fights bravely for social justice. But he is also presented as illiterate, dirty, lazy, alcoholic, and abusive of his family. The cinematic images of Mizrahim that followed had to contend with the two sides of his image.

In light of the film's unprecedented success, much has been written about it. Most of the criticism has been negative. Early critiques of the film faulted it as a misrepresentation of Israel's immigration and social policies, and later ones focused on the "colonial" nature of a Mizrahi image written and directed by an Ashkenazi, Ephraim Kishon, and played by an Ashkenazi actor, Haim Topol. I reexamine these contentious images and discuss their more positive aspects based on three related propositions that deal with the perceived inferiority of Mizrahim. The first is that early Israeli films attempted to validate Mizrahim as Jews. The second is that, once their Jewish identity was confirmed, Mizrahim were then made part of the Jewish-Israeli family through marriage. The third proposition is that many films bolster the masculine credentials of Mizrahi men as part of the national family and even as leaders of it. Accordingly, I demonstrate how subsequent Mizrahi images in Israeli cinema decreasingly denigrated or marginalized Mizrahim. Indeed, they frequently came to epitomize the very idea of Israeliness.

Politicians and film critics initially were anxious about the negative and "false" image of Israel the film portrayed. Very few, however, doubted the veracity of the film's portrayal of Mizrahim. Sallah's character as played by Topol was perceived as emblematic of Mizrahim. This was perhaps the film's most damaging aspect with respect to early cinematic portrayal of Mizrahim. Sallah's naiveté serves a satirical function: to expose the ills of the Zionist establishment. Ella Shohat argues that the joke is also on Mr. Shabati, who is ridiculed for being a primitive "oriental." On the negative side, he is a potential criminal: lazy, drunk, illiterate, and violent. On the positive side, this primitive Mizrahi is warmer and more genuine than his cold and disconnected Ashkenazi counterparts. Filmmakers returned to these opposing characteristics of the Mizrahi image time and again in subsequent Israeli films.

The first significant evolution of the image of Mizrahim after *Sallah Shabati* occurred in the Bourekas ethnic comedies that proliferated in Israel during the 1970s and 1980s. The film became the prototype of a chain of "sequels," which capitalized on its success by copying its premise. Eventually termed Bourekas, named after the cheap savory pastries sold on Israeli streets, these films followed the cinematic formula that was first laid out in *Sallah*. Most Bourekas films involved the struggles of a Mizrahi underdog against an Ashkenazi social, cultural, and political

Haim Topol (as Sallah), at top center, disembarks from an airplane with his large family, on their arrival in Israel. From *Sallah* (1964), directed by Ephraim Kishon. PALISADES INTERNATIONAL CORPORATION/PHOTOFEST

establishment; struggles that were often resolved through "intermarriage": the Mizrahi character generally marries into the more established Ashkenazi family. The tension between the two poles of the Mizrahi character first seen in *Sallah* is evident in most Bourekas films, which use comedy and sentimentality to avoid serious involvement with the problematic issues they raise. This was the most ingenious invention of Bourekas films, which largely managed to maintain a delicate balance between these two poles.

If the directors' balancing act may explain the popularity of the genre, which was almost the only kind of film that made money in Israel during those decades, the public's tolerance of a genre that in some ways perpetuated negative Mizrahi stereotypes may be harder to explain. The dismissal of the critical establishment can be explained by a disinterest in the plethora of B films produced under the Bourekas imprimatur. But the films' appeal to Mizrahi audiences, who made up at least half of the movie-going public at the time, is more enigmatic.

One explanation for this paradox is the visibility that these films gave to an ethnic community that was underrepresented in Israeli public culture and politics. Bourekas films may have provided a fictitious sense of triumph and control that was divorced from reality, but satisfied an important psychological need until more tangible gains were made later by Mizrahim. Bourekas films offered an initial measure of recognition for the Mizrahim themselves. The institutions of the state may have all but ignored them, but here were these popular films that not only depicted them and their traditions, but accorded them a measure of respect as well.

The initial introduction of Mizrahim to Israeli culture took the form of such ethnic sentimentalism. It was later when Mizrahim were more integrated into Israeli culture that such expressions were labeled "Mizrahi Disneyland." During the 1970s and 1980s, however, they were not perceived so negatively, as box office receipts attest. Nearly every Bourekas film included depictions of Mizrahi religious rituals. Although it may appear today as a paternalistic public relations effort to endear Mizrahim by familiarizing audiences with their traditions, Bourekas films legitimized them as Jews. Since the Jewish world in Muslim countries was unfamiliar to Ashkenazi Jewry before the Holocaust, Mizrahi Jews appeared almost "un-Jewish" to their Ashkenazi brethren when they arrived en masse in Israel after 1948. The phrase *koolanu yehudim*, we're all Jews, can

be frequently heard in Bourekas films, beginning with *Sallah Shabati*. It is a telling glimpse of the genre's most important agenda, the construction of an Israeli nationality that included the Mizrahim as Jews.

Another recurring component of the Bourekas plot, marriage between Mizrahim and Ashkenazim, completed this inclusion by bestowing conjugal sanctity on it. After being verified religiously as bona fide Jews, Mizrahim were then aligned to the Jewish-Israeli family and made part of it through marriage, whereby a member of the new immigrant community married a member of the veteran or native community. This simplistic plot device, part of the genre's rules to untangle the [melo]drama by providing an easy way out, a happy ending, elided the entrenched inequality between the two communities. But as contrived and fictitious as it was, one cannot ignore the sanguine assumption on which it was based, that the offspring produced by such unions would combine the ethnic traditions of their parents and transcend them.

Although this marriage plot was often criticized as a shameful evasion of the harsher reality it ignored, its cumulative effect legitimized Mizrahim by including them as part of the Jewish-Israeli family. Following their legitimization as Jews, Bourekas films then drew Mizrahim closer by making them wives, husbands, and in-laws of Ashkenazim. This is a matter of seeing the glass half full rather than half empty. The genre peaked during the 1970s, when Israel's ethnic communities were jostling for their place in the emerging Israeli nationality. Bourekas films reflected these tensions although, again, their underlying assumption was always *koolanu yehudim*, we're all Jews. And nothing said that more clearly than a wedding.

The Bourekas genre introduced a new kind of

masculinity that competed with that of the New Hebrew masculinity that was constructed by Ashkenazi Zionists at the beginning of the twentieth century. The reference here is to the "muscle Jew" as formulated by Max Nordau, which emerged in early Zionism as a reaction to common anti-Semitic stereotypes of Jews as weak, passive, and effeminate. The image of the New Hebrew man was burnished during Israel's War of Independence in 1948. The long and bloody war cost the Jewish community in Israel 1 percent of its members. Its outcome was credited to the heroism of these New Hebrew men of the fledgling state and its nascent army.

The image of the New Hebrew continued to reverberate in Israeli culture after independence. It eventually came to be associated with the Israeli soldiers of the IDF [Israel Defense Forces] rather than the smaller group of pioneering fighters of the pre-state, mostly Ashkenazi, Jewish community. Since the IDF drafted everyone to serve in it, Ashkenazim and Mizrahim, the ability to excel and attain the masculine status it conferred was potentially open to all, irrespective of ethnic background. The playing field for achieving "true" Israeli manhood was ostensibly leveled, allowing both Ashkenazi and Mizrahi men to become New Hebrews.

The 1974 musical *Kazablan* is predicated on this premise. The protagonist of the film, Yosef Siman-Tov (Yoram Ga'on)—nicknamed Kaza after the city of his birth, Casablanca, Morocco—had been a decorated soldier in the Six Day War (1967). After the war, however, he cannot parlay his heroic service to the state into anything tangible, like a good job or a business. Unemployed, he roams his poor neighborhood with a bunch of other unemployed Mizrahi young men, whom many of the neighborhood's Ashkenazi residents think of as gangsters. Kaza is in love with his beautiful Ashkenazi neighbor Rachel (Efrat Lavi), an affair that is strongly objected to by her parents on account of Kaza's alleged criminality and his ethnic background. In the course of the film Kaza is wrongfully blamed for stealing money from Rachel's parents, but is eventually acquitted when the real thief is identified. Kaza then gets together with Rachel to begin a brighter future.

Kaza's negative traits are both exaggerated and domesticated through the conventions of the musical. Styled in the image of the contemporaneous African American Black Panthers, Kaza and his gang strike an exaggerated masculine pose, with their Afro hairdos, tight outfits, muscular bodies, and confident swagger. All of these are elaborated not just by the flashy outfits and gold jewelry but especially by the song-and-dance numbers that draw attention to their flamboyant display. It is precisely the alleged hostility and violence that attract the sheltered Rachel, who is flattered by the attention of the neighborhood's "bad boy." The eventual love affair between the two allows the film to offset, harness, or domesticate Kaza's frustration and rage, which threaten to disrupt the socioeconomic order.

Kazablan is clearly a modern Israeli fairy tale about a "fair princess," Rachel, and her brave and dashing "Oriental prince," Kaza. But it also reflects a community's hidden anxieties, desires, and values. Kaza's placement in the role of the prince is telling. Even if we look at the story as a sublimation of Ashkenazi fears of Mizrahi violence and rage, the fact remains that the prince, the desired male and the paragon of manhood, is Mizrahi. The film stresses this fact by exaggerating Kaza's virility and reflecting and refracting it through the machismo of the men who surround him. Kaza is not only a war hero who was decorated for his bravery under fire, but also the leader of a gang of tough guys.

Kaza's marriage to Rachel is again a cheap narrative device; a shortcut to avoid a more serious contention with the obstacles that prevent him from translating his military heroism into a successful postarmy career. *Kazablan*, like many Bourekas and other films that deal with Ashkenazi-Mizrahi tensions, is explicit about the cultural marginality of Mizrahim, which Kaza epitomizes. This is why the construction of a Mizrahi masculine image became such an important issue in those films. The temporary inability to penetrate the real centers of Israeli power is initially overcome by the much easier manipulation of their image as compensation; an image that often takes the shape of exaggerated masculinity.

The emergence or cultivation of an exaggerated Mizrahi masculinity should be seen in the context of two interrelated developments. One is the decline of the image of the heroic New Hebrew as exemplified by the *Palmachnik* after the establishment of the state, and especially the transition into a more normal, national existence. The other is the concurrent emergence of a unique Mizrahi masculinity as a response to the crisis many Mizrahim experienced after immigration to Israel, especially the erosion in their patriarchal traditions. As the old Ashkenazi, Zionist, pioneering masculinity waned between about 1960 and 1980 a new Mizrahi masculinity challenged it. Both, however, exhibit surprisingly similar patterns of development, in which an image that is first formed as an aesthetic response to adversity eventually shapes culture and then history in a much more tangible sense.

But the success of the *Palmachnik*, the paramilitary soldier-farmers of the pre-state period, who helped the Jewish settlement in Palestine to victory and secured its independence, also led to his retreat from the forefront of the Zionist revolution once his job was done. As Israeli society became less mobilized and the zeal that was directed at founding the state was channeled into the more mundane business of running the country, the epic *Palmachnik* gave way to a more professional soldier. The romance of the nation's birth became less romantic. The heroes of the past gradually became the businessmen, citizens, and workers of the new country.

Mizrahi masculinity filled the space that was vacated by the retirement of the New Hebrew man. Here, too, the emergence of an overt, non-Ashkenazi masculinity as depicted in *Kazablan* originated as a reaction to negative stereotypes of Mizrahim, very much like the dynamic that gave rise to the New Hebrew image at the end of the nineteenth century. The hurried immigration to Israel of many Mizrahim during the 1950s led to a breakdown in their traditional ways of life, which were drastically disrupted during and after their move. The move to Israel exacted an especially high toll on Mizrahi families. Unlike many of the Ashkenazim, who came to Israel prior to independence as young, single, and ideological pioneers, men and women who rebelled against their diasporic families, most Mizrahim moved to Israel as intact family units. The opening scene of *Sallah Shabati* illustrates this well.

The position of the Mizrahi father as head of the family was undermined by immigration. Unlike their younger children, who adapted quickly to the new culture, Mizrahi fathers were slower to do so. The loss of property, professional accomplishments, the security that comes with cultural familiarity, as well as middle age, made the transition much more difficult for the generation of Mizrahi parents. It did not help either that the traditional Arab cultures they came from were more patriarchal in comparison to the young and irreverent Israelis. The idea of honor, which was inextricably connected in Arab cultures to the traditional role of men as fathers, brothers, and husbands, was eroded in the dynamic, socialist, and more sexually permissive Israel. All of these forces wreaked havoc on the actual function as well as the self-image of Mizrahi men, especially fathers and husbands.

The hypermasculinity of Mizrahi men in Israeli culture compensated for the emasculation of the immigrant and acculturation experiences. Their loss of control over individual, family, and community life was channeled into the construction of an alternative fantasy of control, that of the macho male. Kaza's gang members offset their socioeconomic marginality with an accomplishment that was shorter lived, but quicker to attain: menacing their neighborhood. Brandishing their muscular bodies and bravado, they gain the respect that otherwise eludes them, not just from neighbors but from the police too. The fact that they are feared rather than respected does not matter. The hunger for respect is so pressing that it suffices in the short run. Indeed, the most famous song from the musical is literally called *Kol hakavod*, honor or respect. The song, performed by Kaza (singer Yehoram Ga'on), has four stanzas, each describing an aspect of Kaza's manly honor. The first one touts the respect he is paid everywhere he goes; the second publicizes his military credentials; the third lauds him as a just but tough peacekeeper; the fourth flaunts his irresistibility to women but also his deep respect for them. The words of the catchy refrain are "Everyone knows very well / who has more honor or respect."

The formation of the Mizrahi macho man developed not just because of the disproportional concentration of Mizrahim in the lower rungs of society, but also in connection with the decline or metamorphosis of Ashkenazi masculinity. *Kazablan* links the machismo of Mizrahi images to

crime. One of the most visible places where this shift occurred was in the realm of sex. In many films from the 1970s and 1980s, Mizrahi men clearly emerge as sexual objects. Sex, writes Raz Yosef, "offers for Mizrahi males a space for emotional and bodily expression, self-encouragement and self-affirmation that contests the oppressive conditions of Israeli social reality." For Yosef, however, this cultural construction derives from "Orientalist beliefs of Zionist racist ideology," which sees Mizrahim as people who "think" with their bodies rather than their minds. If we consider the marriage ceremonies that conclude many Bourekas films and look at the gender division of these "mixed" marriages, a different picture emerges. In many of these films the desired male is Mizrahi while the desired female is Ashkenazi. Kaza is attractive partly because he is a bad boy who defies social conventions. His defiance is expressed through his criminal associations.

Having proved their masculinity during the War of Independence and secured their financial future after 1948, Ashkenazi men no longer had to prove anything and could relax—hence the leftist political leanings and the willingness to compromise with the Arabs, of many of them. At the same time, the Mizrahi man developed the image of being confident, brash, and attractive, someone who expended most of his energies on ensuring that others respect him either aggressively, toward men, or sexually, toward women. The preoccupation with *kavod*, respect, and political nationalism sheds some light on the increasing electoral support the Mizrahim gave the hawkish Likud, which culminated in the formation of a coalition government by Menachem Begin in 1977.

The negative representation of Mizrahim in Israeli cinema has been discussed at length since the early 1990s, especially the tendency to serve up *Mizrahiyut* as a cultural curiosity, a performance of exotic ethnicity that came at the expense of economic and political integration. At the same time, many films also drew Mizrahim closer to the bosom of the expanding Israeli family, as I show in this essay. If we are cautioned against negative images of Mizrahim and their power to shape culture, we must also acknowledge the power of positive images to do the same.

Abridged from: Yaron Peleg, "From Black to White: Changing Images of Mizrahim in Israeli Cinema." *Israel Studies* 12, no. 2 (2008): 122–44.

Background: http://en.wikipedia.org/wiki/Mizrahi _Jews.

Bibliography

Arzooni, O. G. J. *The Israeli Film: Social and Cultural Influences, 1912–1973*. New York: Garland, 1983.

Avisar, Ilan. *Visions of Israel: Israeli Filmmakers and Images of the Jewish State*. New York: Jewish Media Fund, 1997.

Ben-Rafael, Eliezer. *The Emergence of Ethnicity: Cultural Groups and Social Conflict in Israel*. Westport, CT: Greenwood, 1982.

Goldscheider, Calvin. *Israel's Changing Society: Population, Ethnicity, and Development*. Berkeley: University of California Press, 2001.

Kimmerling. Baruch. *The Invention and Decline of Israeliness: State, Society, and the Military*. Boulder, CO: Westview, 2001.

Loshitzky, Yosefa. *Identity Politics on the Israeli Screen*. Austin, TX: University of Texas Press, 2001.

Presner, Todd. *Muscular Judaism: The Jewish Body and the Politics of Regeneration*. New York: Routledge, 2007.

Shohat, Ella. *Israeli Cinema: East/West and the Politics of Representation*.2nd ed. New York: I. B. Tauris, 2010.

Talmon, Miri, and Yaron Peleg, eds. *Israeli Cinema: Identities in Motion*. Austin, TX: University of Texas Press, 2011.

Yosef, Raz. *Beyond Flesh: Queer Masculinities and Nationalism in Israeli Cinema*. New Brunswick, NJ: Rutgers University Press, 2004.

PART SEVEN

Acceptance in Postwar America, 1945–1977

33. *The Chosen*

The Jew as Both American and Alien

MICHAEL W. RUBINOFF

The Chosen, directed by Jeremy Kagan [A]
United States, 1981

When Chaim Potok's novel *The Chosen* appeared in the spring of 1967, American Jewry was complacently enjoying the growth of suburban Jewish life, the spread of Conservative Judaism, the decline in antisemitism, and two decades of Israeli statehood. Within days of *The Chosen*'s arrival in bookstores, the smugness of postwar Jewish American security was challenged by the Six Day War. The threat to Israel's survival reminded older Jews and their baby boomer children about World War II and the need for a Jewish state. By 1967, the major Jewish organizations had become adjusted to the fraternal tension between Israel and the American Diaspora. But this new relationship coexisted uneasily in the suburban Jewish enclaves of the 1950s like Levittown, Skokie, and the San Fernando Valley, where the manifestation of ethnicity was muted. This was epitomized by the radio show *The Goldbergs* which originally was set in the Bronx but was shifted to Long Island when the program became a TV sitcom.

Both the 1958 best-selling novel *Exodus* by Leon Uris and the Otto Preminger film of the same title which was released two years later—were designed to rekindle Zionist fervor after a decade of Israeli independence. Though set in Palestine, the characters of Ari Ben-Canaan (Paul Newman) and Kitty Fremont (Eva Marie Saint) played directly to assimilationist thinking.

Potok's book harkened back to another kind of Jewish past and recalled the forgotten issue of American Jewish anti-Zionism. Often associated with classical Reform Judaism, anti-Zionism had long been a spiritual anathema to many Orthodox Jews too. In this respect, the novel's publication on the eve of the Six Day War was fortunately timed. Israel's stunning military victory transformed Zionism into an expression of American Jewish pride. Potok's book was a curious reminder of American Jewry in the 1940s. Despite American Jewry's passionate support of the 1942 Biltmore Platform, non-Zionism and anti-Zionism had significant support among Reform and ultra-Orthodox communities, respectively. Although older generations were familiar with these internecine battles, younger Jews were learning something new. Through the Six Day War and Potok's novel, the boomer generation received a quick history lesson about the wartime era.

Seventeen years passed before Potok, the Bronx-born rabbi-turned-novelist, saw his work appear on screen. Just as his story's protagonist had a passion for secular studies and literature, Potok found his intellectual excitement in the

The Hasidic Robby Benson (as Danny Saunders) and the Americanized Barry Miller (as Reuven Malter) first meet at a baseball game. From *The Chosen* (1981), directed by Jeremy Kagan. ANALYSIS FILM RELEASING CORPORATION/PHOTOFEST

public library. He admitted: "There are pieces of me in all four of the major characters" (Nichols). *The Chosen* garnered tepid, but respectful early reviews when it first appeared. There was nothing then to suggest that the book would be on the *New York Times* bestseller list for thirty-nine weeks. But Potok had the advantage of making his literary debut at a time when American Jewish writing was gaining a wide readership. The prolific careers of Joseph Heller, Norman Mailer, Philip Roth, Isaac Bashevis Singer, Irwin Shaw, Leon Uris, Irving Wallace, and Herman Wouk signaled the rapid mainstream acceptance of American Jewish authors. Potok, a chaplain dur-

ing the Korean War, readily identified with authors who wrote about World War II. Hence, *The Chosen* tenaciously clings to mid-1940s subjects—which in a specifically Jewish context meant the Holocaust and birth of Israel. Indeed, a montage of radio clips in the film's beginning aggressively proclaims the period: Fiorello La Guardia's New York. The only voice missing from the montage was that of the mayor himself. The opening pan shot of the Brooklyn Bridge in *The Chosen* sets the film's tone. Clearly for certain generations, the weather-beaten structure served as a physical link between the world of commerce (Manhattan) and the old neighborhood (Brooklyn). Whereas the

Bronx-accented Gertrude Berg carefully avoided offending gentile norms in *The Goldbergs*. Potok and his contemporaries Woody Allen, Mel Brooks, and Neil Simon cast such constraints aside. In fact, confronting the greater society might have been one of their goals. Along with a bevy of Yiddish words served up by many Jewish comedians, the Borscht Belt milieu increasingly carved itself into everyday idiom.

Sales for *The Chosen* skyrocketed in June 1967; eventually 3.4 million copies would be published. On the surface, the writing was not cutting-edge fiction, considering the fact that Norman Mailer and Philip Roth had bestsellers on the *New York Times* list along with Potok. His was a Jewish coming-of-age story set a generation earlier and not particularly concerned with breaking new ground. Potok focused on fairly safe plots and subplots: friendship, Old World versus New World, father-son relationships, Jewish-Gentile interaction, career goals, and the proverbial issue of growing up. The single-parent angle, although occasionally maudlin, served to strengthen the characters of both Reuven Malter and his father. In contrast with the sexual revolution of the 1960s, Potok carefully avoided hormonally driven scenes. Retaining an air of simple dignity for his readers, he left dating and marriage primarily to the realm of secondary adult characters. Whenever the possibility arose in the story for Potok to explore sexuality, he quickly rescued the characters from these dilemmas and turned to other key themes. One might explain this restraint as reflective of classic American fiction. Another reason was because the novelist was a conservative rabbi, not a humorist like Woody Allen or a sensationalist like Philip Roth.

Allen and Roth aside, probably the exploration of American Jewish differences was the starkest revelation for novices. After reading the novel in April, Eliot Fremont-Smith wrote, "I wanted to like the book very much" (Fremont-Smith). Instead, he only liked the book "somewhat." Less than sixty days later, and with the once-embattled Israel triumphant in battle, Smith concluded that he now liked the book "a lot." Without mentioning the Middle East, he admitted that "perspective has also placed it in larger and more settled (because time has passed) context—the context of recently published, commercially successful American fiction." Israel's creation as related in *The Chosen* had been re-ratified in the space of six weeks since the book's publication. With the Israeli army sitting on the east bank of the Suez Canal, and holding the Golan Heights against Syrian bombardment, Jews praying again at the Western Wall, and Potok's book topping the bestseller list for weeks, it was hard to dispute current events. For one golden season, Israel's eye-patched General Moshe Dayan, Barbra Streisand's concert in Central Park, and *The Chosen* made it trendy to be Jewish.

The seventeen years between the publication of *The Chosen* and its appearance as a film was highly eventful for the American Jewish community. First, the confidence seen in the aftermath of June 1967 lasted until the Yom Kippur War in 1973. But with the Egyptian invasion that October, Israel suddenly seemed vulnerable again. Second, the Jackson-Vanik Amendment made obtaining the release of Soviet Jews a major US priority. Third, the revelations of President Richard Nixon's taped conversations, released in the aftermath of Watergate, revealed lingering animosities toward Jews—even to the extent that Nixon aide Fred Malek was asked to do a census of Jews working in the US Department of Labor. Fourth, Israel itself underwent a political catharsis, with the resignations of Prime Ministers Golda Meir and Yitzhak Rabin and the ascension to power of the revisionist Herut Party, under Menachem Begin. Fifth, the Carter administration had its own difficulties with Israel over West Bank settlements and the gradual US acceptance of the PLO as spokesman for the Palestinian community. Last, within the American Jewish community itself, the years between 1967 and 1981 saw a major increase in the rate of intermarriage, coupled with the fall of Conservative Judaism from its position as the largest branch. The film version of *Fiddler on the Roof* (1971) seemed to nostalgically mark the contradictions of American Jewish life: Orthodox or Hasidic tradition versus modernity. Most Jews would have opted for modernity, albeit with guilty reservations. Oddly enough, it was in the Lubavitcher world where the ultra-Orthodox started to contend with their secularized coreligionists for the soul of American Jewry.

When Edie and Ely Landau produced *The Pawnbroker* (1965), they adapted to screen Edward Lewis Wallant's novel about a tormented Holocaust survivor. Shot on location in New York in film noir style, the movie had a powerful impact and helped make Holocaust horrors a part of mainstream American cinema. When they produced *The Chosen* (which won the Edward Lewis Wallant Prize for Potok), they inserted into the film graphic footage of the liberation of Nazi concentration camps. Another unsettling feature of both movies was the use of the pejorative "kike." With *The Pawnbroker*, Sol Nazerman (Rod Steiger) deploys the word in an extended rejoinder to an antisemitic reference. When used by several teens tormenting the Jewish protagonists in *The Chosen*, it uncomfortably reminded older audiences about prior twentieth-century realities. In both motion pictures, the Landaus conveyed the experiences and insecurities once all too common in the American melting pot.

Perhaps the baseball game in the opening of *The Chosen* served as a positive memory. The setting of the game—a gritty, enclosed yard—quickly introduces the audience to Potok's story. The gist of his novel's first page is summarized in the voice-over spoken in the first person by Reuven Malter (Barry Miller):

I suppose Danny Saunders and I would never have met had it not been for America's entry into World War II and the desirability of American Jews to show the world they were as physically fit as any other American. We would prove this by playing tough games of neighborhood baseball. But even though Danny and his team lived within five blocks of us, it might have been 5,000 miles. Danny was a member of a very Orthodox group of Jews called Hasidim. They wore their hair and clothes the same way their ancestors did hundreds of years ago in Eastern Europe. You could see them on Saturday—*Shabbes*—they would hurry off to their small synagogues to pray and study the holy books, the Torah and the Talmud.

One of the film's challenges was to simultaneously show the competitive nature of the two distinctly different-looking Jewish teams. The director, Jeremy Kagan, acknowledged his intent to make the Hasidim look "alien" (Kagan). The Hasidic boys, with broad-brimmed hats and flowing sidelocks, show up in the yard dressed in black suits. Their one concession for the game was to take off their hats and jackets and put them in a pile. This revealed that they were wearing long-sleeved, white shirts. They also appeared to be playing in dress shoes. In depicting them this way, Kagan caught the essence of Potok's description of their bizarre appearance. If the Hasidim looked "alien," Reuven's team appeared as all-American types, wearing caps, T-shirts, and jeans—a cross between *Boys Town* (1938) and *The Bad News Bears* (1976). Kagan briefly outlines the history of the Hasdism and their traditions, but he also lingers on their "alien" nature. By the film's end, he has turned the principal Hasidic character, Danny Saunders (Robby Benson), into a well-dressed, clean-cut, American male. But Danny's efforts to understand the greater secular world result in this fairly predictable conclusion. Perhaps unintentionally, Kagan rekindled the older assimilationist film ideology, dating back to *The Jazz Singer* (1927). Potok's novel sought to explain a relationship between two Jewish youths from entirely different backgrounds. In transferring *The Chosen* to the screen, Kagan emphasizes this theme, perhaps beyond Potok's original intent. Thus, the film dramatically transforms the novel from what is primarily an off-beat adolescent tale into a confrontation between the new and the old (normal versus alien). Perhaps in keeping with the persona of his actor, the star Robby Benson, Danny is consistently shown as sensitive, bright, and charming. Reuven is a more tempermental, serious, and not necessarily a very likable kid. In their own ways, both boys are sharp and snooty—which is what seemingly brings them together. Kagan focuses on how friendship can overcome different backgrounds and quarreling fathers. In fact, both boys repeatedly overcome their own peer group's suspicions and prejudices.

Potok established baseball as the common ground between the "Americans" and the Hasidim. Rather than belabor the sport's symbolism and myths, once the two boys reconnect in the hospital, there is no further mention of the game. Both the book and film internalize Reuven's anger toward Danny. The cutaway shots of their batting sequence with wry smiles and smirks reveal many unspoken tensions. On one close pitch, Danny catches the ball in his hand and tosses it back at Reuven. At a time of widespread Jewish vulnerability, the two Jews were battling one another—and an irreverent baseball game was serving to continue the century-old struggle between the Hasidim and the more modern *Mitnagdim* (Potok uses the pejorative word for heretic, *apikoros*), the followers of the Vilna *Gaon*. In the novel, this arises when Danny doubles and has a few words with Reuben at second base. He says, "I told my team we're going to kill you *apikorsim* this afternoon." Reuven later repeats this to his teammate Sydney Goldberg (Evan Handler). It was clear to Reuven and his friends that the Hasidim actually viewed them as "alien." This is played out in the hospital scene, following Danny's line drive shot into Reuven's left eye. First, David Malter (Maximilian Schell) and then Danny appear in the ward. The dialogue carefully replicated from the novel conveys a panoply of emotions—pain, belligerency, and youthful despair:

> *David*: Danny Saunders' father called me twice today and once last night. He just wanted to know how you were, and he tells me his son is very, very sorry.
> *Reuven*: He's sorry that he didn't kill me.
> *David*: Reuven, what kind of talk is this?
> *Reuven*: It wasn't an accident. He wanted to hit me.

Then Danny shows up at the hospital and tries to apologize.

> *Danny*: I'm sorry.
> *Reuven*: *(nods his head up-and-down)* Is that it? Huh? That's it?
> *Danny*: *(shrugs)*.
> *Reuven*: Great! *(turns the radio volume up)*.

Danny: I didn't come here to fight with you. If all you want to do is fight, I'm gonna go home.

Reuven: Yeah—good, go home!

Edwin Gordon's script completely changed this scene from Potok's novel. Whereas the book showed a less contentious hospital encounter, the film made it a continuation of the baseball game. Reuven wonders if Danny can speak English, a question that turns into a double-edged sword. Danny is both indignant and emotionally scarred by the line. He quietly says, "Of course I understand English." Downcast by the rejection and the insulting question, he leaves. Again, Kagan emphasizes the alien aspect of the Hasidic figure: the American Jew, Reuven, speaks English without any accent, which is surprising for a presumed Brooklyn native. The Hasid, Danny, has to defend his very ability to speak English. *The Chosen* is told through Reuven's eyes; the more effective character portrayal is convincingly done by Danny Saudners (Robby Benson) because of the raw emotions he conveys with both dialogue and gestures.

After Reuven returns home from the hospital, Danny drops by for a second attempt at reconciliation. He confides to Reuven that he really wanted to kill Reuven at the baseball game, but he didn't understand why. Then Reuven expounds on how "weird" Danny is.

Reuven: You are. You look like you walked out of another century. You play baseball like Babe Ruth and talk like you are from outer space.

Danny: Thanks for the compliment.

With this exchange, Danny confirms Reuven's belief he harbored an inexplicably murderous in-

tent toward him. The reason for this hostility is never alluded to again. The intensity of their baseball game was a Jewish "War of the Worlds." But the conflict between the two boys is ended. Reuven lets Danny know in 1940s parlance that he is "weird," and Danny simply responds, "I am?"—showing that for the Hasidim, it is the "Americans" who are strange. With the ground rules for their respective definitions of "weird" and "alien" set, they can befriend one another. Gordon altered Potok's original dialogue. In the book, Reuven says, "I was fascinated just listening to the way perfect English came out of a person in the clothes of a Hasid." The film deliberately heightens the alien nature of Danny's character so that the assimilationist conclusion would fit the expectations of both Hollywood and Jewish audience. Next, Danny reveals how different his father's views of faith and child rearing are from Reuven's:

Danny: You see, my father believes that words distort what someone feels in their heart.

Reuven: Your father doesn't speak with words?

Danny: Actually, he doesn't talk much. At least not to me. We talk when we study Talmud, otherwise . . . My father wishes everyone could speak in silence.

This dialogue not only segues to the main storyline, but it also sets up almost every remaining scene. Reuven and Danny will become fast friends from this point on. Their respective backgrounds will pull them together even as external, paternal circumstances try to divide them. In essence, their commonalities as young Jews in a tough time will overcome whatever earlier barriers existed. Kagan advances his story by the Hasid's immersion into the *apikorsim* world and Reuven's gradual, begrudging appreciation for

Hasidic Judaism. This is satisfying for viewers, who bond with the young men.

But the plot twists soon hinted at by Danny's discussion of his father's "silent" treatment will eventually overwhelm the subsequent story. Rather cautiously, Reb Saunders (Rod Steiger) is presented as a *tzaddik* (righteous man), revered by his community. Reuven concedes the rebbe's reverence but is troubled by the elder Saunders's penchant for playing Talmudic games, isolation from the outside world, and intolerance of Zionism. The rebbe uses Reuven as a conduit for speaking to his son. But the very public, ultra-Zionism of David Malter leads to Reuven's being excommunicated from Danny's world. The scenes surrounding this ban are among the most emotionally charged in the film. Not until Reb Saunders accepts the secular establishment of Israel can the two boys resume their friendship. Given that *The Chosen* was published just weeks before the Six Day War, this underscored the serious split that once existed in the Jewish world. With the film recreating this in 1981, the split appears to be a relic form of anti-Zionism which made it synonymous with the alien "other."

Ultimately in *The Chosen*, the *tzaddik* Reb Saunders realizes his son does not want to succeed him as the community leader but has different goals for himself. Lester Friedman sees this as not as a repudiation of Judaism (or of the father), but as "an affirmation of Jewish freedom of choice" (244). The "alien" (Danny) agrees to complete his rabbinical training but decides to pursue graduate studies in psychology at Columbia University. This is not a balanced ending, because there is no hint that Danny retains much of his Hasidic background. Indeed, the final scene is faithful to Potok's novel, with the two boys conversing about their futures. Reuven is deter-

mined to become an "American" rabbi, which in the story's context denotes Conservative Judaism. Danny—shorn of sidelocks, black suit, and hat—is off to start classes as a newly secularized Jew. Accepting the inevitable, his father has canceled Danny's arranged marriage and is grooming Danny's brother to be the next rebbe. The film ends with Danny happily walking away from the audience until he disappears from view. The unabashed symbolism of triumphant modernity as "liberating" is striking. Kagan presents "his" kind of American Jews with Reuven: secularized, smart, proudly Jewish, and willing to help smuggle weapons to Israel. At the film's end, Danny has left the Hasidic fold and is seeking out the secular Jewish world: confident, optimistic, and apparently pro-Israel.

Equally telling, the Landaus showcased their film's Hollywood premiere as a fundraiser for Israel's thirty-third anniversary. Within a year, the widely heralded movie played on 1,000 screens in some twenty countries. Janet Maslin praised it for not showing Hasids as a Woody Allen–style gag. She concluded, "This is a gently evocative movie, with its glimpses of a strict and self-contained culture, and its memories of a time gone by" (Maslin). In other words, the movie was another spin on *The Way We Were* (1973). With the "alien" protagonist becoming "more American," the film formulaically projected a satisfying, if not a particularly original, ending. With a safe assimilationist message conveyed and a subtle form of Zionism thus embedded, *The Chosen* immediately carved its own niche among major American Jewish films.

Source: Chaim Potok, *The Chosen: A Novel*. New York: Simon and Schuster, 1967.

Background: http://www.jewishmag.com/117mag/zionism/zionism.htm.

Bibliography

Abramson, Edward A. *Chaim Potok*. Boston: Twayne, 1986.

Cohen, Naomi Wiener. *The Americanization of Zionism, 1897–1948*. Waltham, MA: Brandeis University Press, 2003.

Fremont-Smith, Eliot, "Books of the Times: Looking Back: Two Good Novels Reconsidered," *New York Times*, June 16, 1967, 41.

Friedman, Lester D. *The Jewish Image in American Film*. Secaucus, NJ: Citadel, 1987, 244.

Glazer, Nathan. *American Judaism*. Chicago: University of Chicago Press, 1988.

Kagan, Jeremy Paul, *The Chosen* (Director's Audio Commentary), The Chosen, Hen's Tooth Video, 2010.

Maslin, Janet, "As Time Gone By," *New York Times*, April 30, 1982, C5.

Miles, Margaret R. *Seeing and Believing: Religion and Values in the Movies*. Boston: Beacon, 1996.

Mintz, Jerome. *Hasidic People: A Place in the New World*. Cambridge: Harvard University Press, 1992.

Nichols, Lewis, "Mr. Potok," *New York Times*, April 30, 1967, 301.

Rubel, Nora L. *Doubting the Devout: The Ultra-Orthodox in the Jewish American Imagination*. New York: Columbia University Press, 2009.

Sternlicht, Sanford. *Chaim Potok: A Critical Companion*. Westport, CT: Greenwood, 2000.

Urofsky, Melvin I. *American Zionism from Herzl to the Holocaust*. Garden City, NY: Anchor, 1975.

Waldman, Daniel, ed. *Conversations with Chaim Potok*. Jackson: University Press of Mississippi, 2001.

34. Jew and Not-Jew

Antisemitism and the Postwar Hollywood Social Problem Film

STEVEN ALAN CARR

Crossfire, directed by Edward Dmytryk [A]
United States, 1947
Gentleman's Agreement, directed by Elia Kazan [A]
United States, 1947

Both *Crossfire* and *Gentleman's Agreement* have come to epitomize Hollywood's immediate postwar response to the Holocaust, which historians conventionally have characterized as not amounting to much of a response, either in terms of tackling Nazism or of addressing the specifically Jewish dimension of the Nazi genocide. Explicit critiques of American antisemitism, both films at best implicitly invoked the European Holocaust by setting anti-Jewish attitudes against postwar domestic backdrops more familiar to American moviegoers: Washington, D.C., in *Crossfire*, and Manhattan and New England in *Gentleman's Agreement*. Both films revealed a brief, bifurcated response to the Holocaust: heightened American consciousness of domestic antisemitism as a serious social problem, on the one hand and, on the other hand, the structuring absence of Nazi atrocities that newsreels had so vividly depicted just a few years earlier. Then, just as quickly as the topic had entered the genre, antisemitism in the Hollywood social problem film disappeared from view.

Or so the story of *Crossfire* and *Gentleman's Agreement* goes. In *Hollywood and Anti-Semitism*, I argued that both films "condemned anti-Semitism, not because of its prevalence, but because of its aberration" (Carr 2001, 281). and that

Gregory Peck (as Phil Green) being told there are no rooms at the Flume Inn by Roy Roberts (as the hotel manager). From *Gentleman's Agreement* (1947), directed by Elia Kazan. TWENTIETH CENTURY FOX FILM CORP./PHOTOFEST

such views were completely at odds with American democratic and assimilationist ideals. I still believe these films function this way, pitting antisemitism as a distinctly un-American presence coexisting but at odds with the core values of American democracy. There were indeed historical reasons why these films functioned like this, and why antisemitism as a subject just as quickly seemed to vanish from the social problem genre. Indeed, after *Gentleman's Agreement*, Hollywood did not make a mainstream film that explicitly tackled both antisemitism and the Holocaust until *The Young Lions* (1958).

There also were political and economic reasons for this absence, though it probably was not a conscious decision. A number of people have argued that anticommunism and American antisemitism

had a chilling effect on Hollywood's treatment of the Holocaust. However, this explanation fails to account for other pressures on the industry, or even for the potential benefits of not making a film that dealt overtly with the Holocaust. Postwar discussions between Hollywood and those involved in the reconstruction of Europe typically stressed the need for films to help aid efforts at German reeducation. "The films . . . listed for use in Germany are entirely insufficient," General Robert A. McClure told a group of Hollywood executives at a meeting in occupied Germany on July 4, 1945. "What can you gentleman do to help us in our main job of winning the peace?" (Harmon 1945). As one representative of the German film industry observed a few years later, so-called message pictures made by Hollywood were particularly unpopular in occupied Germany (Segrave 1997, 171). Eager to cooperate with postwar reconstruction efforts and tap new audiences, the US film industry had powerful incentives to favor making certain kinds of films over others, even if their efforts were not successful in reaching the desired goal, or in commercial terms.

In terms of what *Crossfire* and *Gentleman's Agreement* failed to do or launch, I have revised the view of a bifurcated response to the Holocaust to consider what these films were doing. Each film addressed antisemitism within the constraints of the Hollywood social problem genre, explicitly referencing American antisemitism while only incidentally referencing the Holocaust. The two films did this quite differently, with *Crossfire* depicting antisemitism as a pathological aberration, and *Gentleman's Agreement* depicting it as a nasty personal habit tolerated in polite society, but with corrosive consequences for democratic ideals. Although explicit references to the Holocaust remained noticeably absent from these films, that absence is key to understanding the logic of a broad-based view shared by Hollywood and the federal government: the injustice of antisemitism was that it singled out everyday people who just happened to be Jewish; and American democracy upheld universal ideals that not only minimized religious, ethnic, or racial differences, but stubbornly denied the fact that they existed in the face of a normative comprehensive national identity.

Whether antisemitism is a pathological aberration or a nasty personal habit with corrosive effects on democracy, this consensus on antisemitism fit within the formula of the social problem film. As Peter Roffman and Jim Purdy have argued, the Hollywood social problem film was meant to arouse indignation over some facet of contemporary life, carefully qualifying criticism so that the problem can in the end be reduced to simple causes, to a villain whose removal rectified the situation. Allusions to the genuine concerns of the audience stir up antisocial feelings, only to divert them to safe targets contained in a dramatic rather than a social context. Key to the resolution of the "problem" in *Crossfire* and *Gentleman's Agreement*, then, were two distinct but related narrative strategies: the displacement and projection of antisemitism onto identifiable villains, such as the murderer in the first film, or less viscerally in the latter film, onto narrow-minded and petty individuals incapable of seeing the collective harm they inflict on the democratic polity. Most striking is that even though both films were about antisemitism, neither offered a Jewish protagonist. From a dramatic standpoint, this was a key characteristic: their narratives were not about what it is like to be Jewish and encounter antisemitism, but what it is like to be *not* Jewish and encounter this phenomenon.

Both *Crossfire* and *Gentleman's Agreement* reflected a powerful, negotiated consensus through which the Hollywood social problem genre could neatly align with President Franklin Rooosevelt's Four Freedoms. These freedoms, as articulated in Roosevelt's January 6, 1941, State of the Union address, presented a distinctly American vision of the modern world meant for wartime and postwar cultural export: freedom of speech, freedom of worship, freedom from want, and freedom from fear. As a guiding set of principles in determining how Hollywood could better support the war effort, the Four Freedoms asserted the positive aspects of the American way of life, rather than demonizing the enemy.

The revised view outlined here of what *Crossfire* and *Gentleman's Agreement* did offer, beyond just a criticism of Nazi antisemitism, thus suggests a kind of wish fulfillment for what American democracy, warts and all, could offer the rest of the world as it faced postwar reconstruction. In a draft memo written in August 1944 to outline how government might offer better guidance to the film industry, the Office of War Information outlined the kinds of themes that Hollywood should use in dramatizations of social problems.

Films dealing with the American domestic scene run the risk of presenting America in an unflattering light to foreign audiences unless the treatment maintains a balance on the positive rather than the negative side. Thus, a film should show that men of goodwill are actually in the majority, even though it is only a passive majority until aroused. In other words, good should not only triumph over evil but the result should be brought about through wilful [sic] and purposeful action rather than through fortuitous circumstances. The difficulties arising from these films are largely due to the problem or theme, but this principle should underlie the treatment of all films dealing with the seamy side of American life. Showing our problems frankly and objectively reflects very well upon American freedom of discussion, but we must remember that movies are made for a mass audience not necessarily given to such reflection and analysis. For this reason, the overall impact of a film should be one in which problems are shown with relation to the measure being taken to adjust them. (Draft Motion Picture Guidance 1944)

With such guidance, the lack of explicit reference to the Holocaust did not necessarily prevent actual audiences from connecting these films to Nazi antisemitism. Rather, as the quote above indicates, the emerging consensus between government and Hollywood stressed the impor-

tance of winning the peace through promoting a realistic but positive view of America for mass consumption.

The narratives in both *Crossfire* and *Gentleman's Agreement* fit in this paradigm and reflected the outcome of this consensual vision of America. In *Crossfire*, the negative aspect of isolated, pathological antisemitism is outweighed by the civilian and military status quo, which, once "aroused," undertakes a "purposeful" investigation of the ugly motivation for what slowly emerges as a hate crime. When the police shoot the murderer at the end of the film, diligent good has triumphed over irrational evil. *Gentleman's Agreement* is a more complicated narrative, but it fits the same basic formula. An investigative reporter pretending to be Jewish in order to write an exposé of American antisemitism finds this prejudice completely endemic in polite society, including the workplace, schools, hotels, and even in personal relationships. Although the film suggests that antisemitism is prevalent, it contains enough men and women "of goodwill" to confront what it portrays more as a tolerated evil than a pathological one. The most interesting aspect of *Gentleman's Agreement*, though, is how the reporter methodically roots out instances of antisemitism in polite society, as the homicide detective in *Crossfire* amasses evidence of a hate crime. By the time the reporter in *Gentleman's Agreement* writes his story and has his mother approvingly read a passage from it, the film no longer needs to show a heretofore "passive majority" aroused. His story has marshaled the preponderance of American history against an insidious personal habit. Read by his mother, the passage implicitly invokes Nazism through its contrast between the metaphor of a fruit tree and the mythology of the founding fathers as framed by Roosevelt's Four Freedoms:

Driving away from the inn, I knew all about every man or woman who'd been told the job was filled when it wasn't. Every youngster who had ever been turned down by a college or a summer camp. I knew the rage that pitches through you when you see your own child shaken and dazed. From that moment, I saw an unending attack by adults on kids of seven and eight and ten and twelve. On adolescent boys and girls trying to get a job or an education or into medical school. I knew that they had somehow had known it too. They, those patient stubborn men who argued and wrote and fought and came up with the Constitution and the Bill of Rights. They knew that the tree is known by its fruit, and that injustice corrupts a tree. That its fruit withers and shrivels and falls at last to that dark ground of history, where other great hopes have rotted and died. Where equality and freedom remain still the only choice for wholeness and soundness in a man or in a nation.

When she finishes reading the passage, the mother solidifies this consensual view of American history at a deeply personal level, observing that the reporter's recently deceased father "would have liked to have you say that, Phil."

Neither *Crossfire* nor *Gentleman's Agreement* was simply about antisemitism, but rather both were about encountering antisemitism from the perspective of not being Jewish. Framing antisemitism as a social problem in this way was crucial to the consensual view of antisemitism as unjustly singling out individuals who just happened to be Jewish. A pivotal scene from *Gentleman's Agreement* underscores this ideology. In order to write his exposé on antisemitism, the journalist Schuyler "Phil" Green realizes that he can pose as Jewish, as he gazes into a bedroom mirror. He

effectively erases the difference between himself and his best friend, Dave Goldman, who does happen to be Jewish: "Dark hair, dark eyes, sure, so has Dave. So have a lot of guys who aren't Jewish. No accent, no mannerisms, neither has Dave. Name: Phil Green. Skip the Schuyler. It might be anything: Phil Green! Ma, it's a cinch!" When Phil asks his mother not to reveal his true identity to any new people she meets, she responds, "if you're Jewish, I am too, I guess."

In keeping with the film noir genre, which stressed more tawdry social issues, the formulation for being not-Jewish appears secondary to the solving of a senseless murder in *Crossfire*. In fact, the victim, Joseph Samuels, is apparently the only Jewish character in the film, and he gets killed in the opening scene. Like *Gentleman's Agreement*, *Crossfire* emphasizes the point of being not-Jewish by underscoring the senselessness of the crime. During an interrogation, Finley, a homicide detective played by Robert Young, questions Mitch, a soldier wrongly held on the murder charge:

> *Mitch*: I didn't murder anyone. Why would I murder him? What motive would I have?
> *Finley*: Maybe you didn't like him. Maybe you hated him. Hate's a good motive.
> *Mitch*: Why would I hate him? I hardly knew him. I only talked to him for a couple of hours. He seemed like a nice guy.
> *Finley*: You knew he was a Jew.
> *Mitch*: No . . .
> *Finley*: You mean to say you didn't know he was Jewish?
> *Mitch*: No, I didn't think about it. What would that have to do with it? What's that got to do with me?

The scene ends when another detective brings in Samuels's medical discharge as a result of wounds he received at Okinawa, thus subtly refuting the canard that Jews evaded military service during World War II while other Americans fought what was essentially a "Jewish" war.

The production history behind *Crossfire* underscores the fluidity of Jewish identity and its happenstance status, relative to a larger umbrella of national identity. In the original novel on which the film is based, *The Brick Foxhole* by the future Hollywood director Richard Brooks, the murder victim is not Jewish but gay. Given the film industry's self-regulation apparatus at the time, this narrative would have been rejected outright before RKO shot a frame of film. Although some have noted that in the postwar era, interchangeable gay and Jewish identities suggest an intrinsic commonality between the two, the film's adaptation and domestication of a plotline from a relatively obscure novel also pointed to the idea that confronting antisemitism flowed from a universalized position of being not-Jewish, or not-gay for that matter. In other words, the victim could indeed be anyone: black, Jew, or gay. The depiction of a victim who coincidentally happened to hold a particular identity other than "American," as well as the relatively fluid manner in which anyone could occupy that identity, became a hallmark for how American films depicted and did not depict the Jewish specificity of the Holocaust.

If such representations of antisemitism actually ended there, they arguably would have amounted to not much of a response. However, the revised view of these films proposed here sees them not as an endpoint, but—to use the terminology of the media scholar John Fiske (24)—as way stations pointing both to and through other, more varied and disjointed responses to antisemitism, Nazi or otherwise. In another article I have discussed the possibility that American audiences

may well have come to understand the European art film, such as Wanda Jakubowska's 1948 Polish film *The Last Stage*, as the appropriate way to depict the Holocaust (Carr 2010). A scene from that film was the only depiction of a concentration camp appearing in *The Diary of Anne Frank* (1959), which otherwise took place almost exclusively in the attic where Anne and her family hid in Amsterdam. Meanwhile, in downplaying a specifically Jewish dimension to the Holocaust, and instead emphasizing universal ideals of democracy and assimilated pluralism, Hollywood, following the urging of the Roosevelt administration, believed that it was offering a viable response to Nazism by *not* singling out Jews as victims of fascist ideology.

In continuing to reassess how *Crossfire* and *Gentleman's Agreement* addressed antisemitism and the Holocaust, this investigation needs to go beyond just a close reading of these films. A comprehensive study of these films would encompass a close reading but also include tracing them from their inception to their reception. Researching the relevance of both films to the Holocaust, then, would also include both production and reception histories that use primary historical resources. For production history, this involves archival research, such as studying studio memos and scripts. However, even production history alone is insufficient, as this would tell only what Hollywood personnel might have intended, or how they imagined a particular audience. Ultimately, a history of these films must include consideration of how actual, rather than imagined, audiences made sense of these narratives. This reception history would use film reviews, publicity, and discussions in the popular press to understand the range of meanings that real audiences made of these narratives.

The revised view proposed here thus moves

beyond looking at *Crossfire* and *Gentleman's Agreement* as discrete and ultimately failed confrontations of antisemitism trapped within the social problem genre, instead considering these films as part of a broader process of consent and negotiation between Hollywood, government, and audiences. Analysis of these films should begin by examining the particular circumstances of their production, and how they were initially laden with potential relevance to the Holocaust. This analysis also must consider the ways in which these films underwent a highly regulated studio production process meant to standardize and domesticate the controversy inherent in these topics for a mass audience. Finally, this analysis must consider the ways in which these films emerged from that process overlaid with various publicity strategies meant to restore some of the films' resonance and narrative potential to speak to the Holocaust, even if that resonance and potential remained highly ambiguous. An uncritical and ahistorical embrace of today's identity politics may miss how, by asserting an unspecific, universal identity, these films did offer a postwar response to the Holocaust.

This research was supported by a grant from the United States Holocaust Memorial Museum.

For an extended version of this essay: see "Anti-Semitism and the Postwar Hollywood Social Problem Film," at http://d.pr/Eq1S, where you can also find media clips and primary documents.

Background: http://nationalhumanitiescenter.org/tserve/twenty/tkeyinfo/jewishexp.htm; http://nationalhumanitiescenter.org/tserve/twenty/tkeyinfo/jewishexpb.htm.

Sources: Richard Brooks, *The Brick Foxhole* (New York: Harper and Brothers, 1945).

Laura Z. Hobson, *Gentleman's Agreement: A Novel* (New York: Simon and Schuster, 1947).

Bibliography

Baron, Lawrence. "Picturing Prejudice in Hollywood's First Films About Anti-Semitism." In *Studies in Jewish Civilization*, edited by Leonard J. Greenspoon and Ronald A. Simkins, 17–37. Omaha, NE: Creighton University Press, 2006.

Carr, Steven Alan. *Hollywood and Anti-Semitism: A Cultural History up to World War II.* Cambridge: Cambridge University Press, 2001.

———. "Hollywood, the Holocaust, and World War II." In *Studies in Jewish Civilization*, edited by Leonard J. Greenspoon and Ronald A. Simkin, 39–58. Omaha, NE: Creighton University Press, 2006.

———. "To Encompass the Unseeable: *The Last Stage* and Auschwitz in the Mind of Cold War America." October 2010. http://stevenalancarr.pbworks.com/w/page/24704810/The-Last-Stage.

Dinnerstein, Leonard. *Antisemitism in America.* New York: Oxford University Press, 1994.

"Draft Motion Picture Guidance." Office of War Information, Motion Picture Bureau, Overseas Branch, New York Review Board. Records Relating to the Overseas Branch, Compiled 1945–45. Records of the Historian. Record Group 208: Records of the Office of War Information, 1926–51. MLR Number NC148 6B Box 2. National Archives and Records Administration, College Park, MD.

Harmon, Francis S. *Western Europe in the Wake of World War II, June 17–July 18, as Seen by a Group of Motion Picture Industry Executives Visiting the European and Mediterranean Theatre of Operation as Guests of the Military Authorities.* Washington: Department of War, 1945.

Higham, John. *Send These to Me: Immigrants to Urban America.* New York: Atheneum, 1975.

McWilliams, Cary. *A Mask for Privilege: Anti-Semitism in America.* Boston: Little, Brown, 1948.

Roffman, Peter, and Jim Purdy. *The Hollywood Social Problem Film: Madness, Despair, and Politics from the Depression to the Fifties.* Bloomington: Indiana University Press, 1981.

Segrave, Kerry. *American Films Abroad: Hollywood's Domination of the World's Movie Screens from the 1890s to the Present.* Jefferson, NC: McFarland, 1997.

Short, K. R. M. "Hollywood Fights Anti-Semitism, 1945–

1947." In *Feature Films as History*, edited by K. R. M. Short, 157–89. Knoxville: University of Tennessee Press.

Weber, Donald. *Haunted in the New World: Jewish American Culture from Cahan to "The Goldbergs."* Bloomington: Indiana University Press, 2005.

35. Southern Jewishness on Screen

ELIZA R. L. MCGRAW

Driving Miss Daisy, directed by Bruce Beresford [A]
United States, 1989

The release of the film *Driving Miss Daisy* in 1989 made American moviegoers aware of the presence of southern Jewishness. Alfred Uhry adapted the film's screenplay from his 1987 autobiographically informed Pulitzer Prize–winning play, the story of the relationship between Daisy Werthan, a Jewish Atlanta matron, and Hoke Coleburn, her African American chauffeur. Hoke, played by Morgan Freeman, and Daisy, played by Jessica Tandy, come together inauspiciously. Seventy-two-year-old Daisy crashes her car, and her son, Boolie (Dan Akroyd), deciding she needs someone to drive her, hires Hoke. At first Daisy will not even enter the car, but eventually Hoke wins her over. As they age, the two forge a complicated bond challenging some socially proscribed southern mores, but leaving others intact. The film demonstrates the inseparability of Jewishness within a southern context. Daisy simultaneously exists within and without the dominant culture, as representative because of her status as a white southern matriarch and exceptional because of her Jewishness.

With its inclusion of southern Jewishness and the topic of race relations, however, the film extends cinematic conventions of southernness. *Miss Daisy* offers a visual vocabulary for southern Jewishness with its wide, bright shots of the Temple in Atlanta and southern-accented voices discussing synagogue carpooling and singing hymns in Hebrew. Noting that Daisy imperiously orders Hoke around while lauding Martin Luther King Jr., critics have cast *Miss Daisy* as a portrait of naive and reactionary white liberalism. Daisy's Jewishness, however, makes this depiction itself seem naive. In the film, southernness and southern Jewishness become interdependent, with Daisy's Jewishness the lens through which questions about southern race relations are viewed.

Atlanta, Georgia, *Miss Daisy*'s setting, provides an appropriate forum for such complicated questions. As the site of Leo Frank's arrest, as well as the Temple bombing depicted in *Miss Daisy*, the city has been the setting for tragic episodes for Jewishness in the South. Frank, a northern Jewish superintendent in an Atlanta pencil factory, swore he was alone in his office when Mary Phagan, a young white girl employed by the factory, was murdered on Confederate Memorial Day, April 26, 1913. Although the evidence was not conclusive, Frank was nevertheless charged and sentenced to death. Governor John Slaton later ruined his own political future by commuting that sentence to life imprisonment. Frank survived an attack in prison in which a fellow inmate slit his throat, only to be kidnapped from his cell and lynched. During the turmoil of the Frank case, Jewish Atlantans, who had felt safe in their city, were treated as outsiders and experienced new fear when a white supremacy group, the

Jessica Tandy (as Daisy) in the back seat, being chauffeured by Morgan Freeman (as Hoke). From *Driving Miss Daisy* (1989), directed by Bruce Beresford. WARNER BROS./PHOTOFEST

Knights of Mary Phagan, arose as a reincarnation of the Ku Klux Klan.

The 1958 Temple bombing, like the Frank case, constituted a moment of crisis for Jews in the South, and the two events stand yoked as tandem instances of Atlanta in turmoil. While Frank represented unwelcome northernness, the Temple community embodied southern Jewishness. The Jewishness under attack could no longer be portrayed as "foreign" when the Atlanta Benevolent Hebrew Congregation, known as the Temple, was bombed with a nitroglycerine device roughly equivalent to fifty sticks of dynamite. Five white extremists were indicted for the crime, and their successful defense was built on a foundation of anti-Semitism. The first lawyer for the five was an Imperial Wizard of the National Knights of the Klan. The second assigned his re-search staff to tasks like discovering if it were true that *Kol Nidre*, the Yom Kippur eve prayer, permitted Jews to invalidate all oaths, rendering it impossible for them to swear in a court of law. The jury decided that the state's evidence was too circumstantial to convict the accused, and no one was ever punished for the bombing. The verdict made Atlanta Jews realize that they did not enjoy the same privileges as white Christians, no matter how many Christmas trees they displayed in their homes to fit in.

Atlanta is the setting for another fictional mistress-and-servant pair more famous than Hoke and Daisy: *Gone with the Wind*'s Mammy and Scarlett O'Hara. Mammy's obligation to Scarlett comes from her affiliation with Scarlett's mother's family, while Hoke's desire to work for the Werthans stems from his expressed preference to work for Jews. A kind of reverse noblesse oblige runs through both scenarios. In each case, the African American subordinate knows the white mistress better than she knows herself. Hoke and Mammy are concerned with appearances: Hoke reprimands Daisy for wanting to take public transportation to the Piggly Wiggly, while Mammy constantly reminds Scarlett what makes her seem like "poor white trash," such as revealing her bosom early in the day or consorting with Rhett Butler. Both Mammy and Hoke have strong opinions about employers. Mammy stays on with Scarlett even after the Emancipation Proclamation, deriding those who obstruct them on the streets of Atlanta as "trash." Boolie and Hoke have a similarly class-conscious exchange when Hoke informs Boolie that although he would not want to work for "trash" like Jeanette Harris, he appreciates her offer of a higher salary. Boolie asks if he will take Jeanette's offer, and Hoke tells him, "Get on with you, Mr. Werthan. What you think I am? I ain't studying about going to work for no trashy something like her." Hoke both flatters Boolie and explains how class plays a role in his choice of employer. Boolie gives him a raise. The Mammy/ Scarlett template for Hoke and Daisy epitomizes the stereotypical southern servitude that some critics have chastised *Miss Daisy* for romanticizing.

Daisy wrecks her car and requires Hoke's services in 1948, the same year the Dixiecrats (the States' Rights Democratic Party) achieved political success and Israel achieved statehood. *Driving Miss Daisy* demonstrates that in the wake of these events, southern Jewishness strove to define itself, even as it remained bound by its American traditions of simultaneous assimilation and distinction. The film does not explicitly refer to Israel or the Dixiecrats, but the choice of opening date resounds as Israel, the Dixiecrats, and Daisy fight for independence and validation.

Uhry draws his characters and ambivalent view of southern Jewishness from his own experiences. "That really was my grandmother and her driver," he claims. "There is something about being Jewish, even as un-Jewish as I was brought up to be, that's in the marrow of your bones." The term "un-Jewish" implies that Atlantans like himself fall outside an authentic site of Jewishness, but he insists their identity is still "Jewish."

Hoke works for Daisy, in part, because of her Jewishness. "I'd rather work for Jews," Hoke tells Boolie. "Oh, I know folks be saying they stingy, cheap, one thing and another, but don't be saying that around me." Hoke has worked for a Jew before, mentioning his former Jewish employer and friend of Boolie's father, Judge Stone. Just as Boolie asks Oscar, an African American employee, if Hoke works in his factory, indicating a "they all look alike" kind of prejudice, Hoke believes his experience with Judge Stone qualifies him to work for all Jewish people. His comment gently reminds Boolie that Hoke knows his new employer's different status. Although the Werthan family business is a printing press in the play, in the film it is "Werthan Cotton and Bag Co.," a change that positions the Werthans as purveyors of the *authentic* crop of Dixie.

Daisy and Hoke do not begin their tenure together in Eden, however. The following exchange takes place as Daisy insists she does not require Hoke's services even as he tries to persuade her that she does:

Hoke: A fine rich Jewish lady like yourself ain't got no business dragging herself up the steps of no trolley carrying no grocery store bags. How about I come along and carry them for you?

Daisy: I don't need you. I don't want you. And I don't like you saying I'm rich.

Hoke: Well, I won't say it no more.

Daisy: Is that what you and Idella talk about in the kitchen?

Hoke: No, Miss Daisy.

Daisy: Oh, I hate this. I hate being talked about behind my back in my own house. I was born on Forsyth Street and believe you me, I know the value of a penny.

Hoke's servility gives him the authority to pronounce what Daisy "should" do as a "fine rich Jewish lady." In his view, such individuals do not take public transportation or carry their own groceries. "Fine," "rich," and "Jewish" come together as one epithet for Hoke, defining a type of person "like" Daisy. "Rich" is the adjective Daisy rejects, taking Hoke to task for making presumptions about her background. He rejects her refusal, telling her that he "won't say it no more." He will humor her, but not change his original characterization. To Daisy, being from Forsyth Street is proof of modest financial circumstances that do not fit Hoke's stereotype. Not wishing to be perceived as rich, she commands Hoke not to wait for her directly in front of the synagogue, "like I was the queen of Romania." "Jewish" remains the unspoken modifier for Daisy, but her fear of being viewed as rich demonstrates a fear of being stereotypically Jewish, amassing fortunes nefariously as charged by the anti-Semitic populist Tom Watson during the Frank case. Daisy would have been in her late twenties when that happened and Hoke some ten years younger. As native Atlantans, both would have understood the legacy of Frank's lynching and the implications of the phrase "rich Jews." Hoke's comment is not intended as anti-Semitic, but Daisy's reaction indicates that its tainted past, even when diluted, still rankles.

Hoke and Daisy only edge toward camara-derie. While the two travel to Mobile for Daisy's brother's birthday, they each share something about their pasts. Hoke confides that the trip is his first outside Georgia, and Daisy tells him about a train ride she took as a child. They eat lunch in typically separate style, with Daisy in the back seat and Hoke leaning against the car. As Daisy reminisces, the camera remaining on her face while Hoke laughs, two white Alabama policemen approach them. Calling Hoke "boy," one officer asks where he got the car. Daisy pipes up that the car is hers. The policeman looks at the car's registration and mispronounces her name. She corrects him, and he says, "Never heard of that one before. What kind of name is that?" Daisy announces that Werthan is "of German derivation." His questioning reveals that he sees her as somehow illegitimate. She may appear white, but he suspects she is merely passing. As Daisy and Hoke drive away, the policeman remarks to his partner, "An old nigger and an old Jew woman taking off down the road together. Now that is one sorry sight." He pairs them as a pitiful duo, their togetherness multiplying their degradation. His view is a distortion of Boolie's, who sees the two off from Daisy's garage, yelling, "Good luck!" before adding a benevolent, "Good God," audible only to himself and the audience. The spectacle of Daisy and Hoke reminds audiences of the tenuous position each bears in racial terms in southern society at midcentury. The audience, along with the police officers, watches them continue down the highway, considering whether this is a pitiful image or one with its own power, embodied in the confidence Daisy and Hoke have in each other as well as the tension between them.

Daisy's formal, stiff, sometimes authoritarian attitude toward her servants appears lenient when compared with that of her daughter-in-law.

Florine cannot keep help because of her temper. This is illustrated by her impatiently demanding coffee from Gaynelle and raging at Katie Belle because there is no coconut for her Christmas ambrosia. Florine's behavior reminds the audience that Daisy and Hoke have an exceptional, if troubled, relationship. Florine's impatience with servants and toadying assimilation are a foil to Daisy's relationship with Hoke and affirmation of her faith.

But Daisy and Florine display similar insensitivity to Atlanta's racial complexities before the Temple bombing. When Daisy and Hoke drive to Boolie and Florine's, Hoke notes that he always enjoys Christmas with the Werthans. Daisy remarks that she is not surprised, since he is the only Christian there. Daisy imagines herself far ahead of Florine in matters of interracial relations and Jewish identity, but ultimately behaves similarly to Florine by asking Hoke to work on Christmas Eve.

These complexities emerge when Hoke and Daisy go to the cemetery to visit her late husband's grave. Daisy asks Hoke to place flowers on the grave of Leo Bauer, a friend of the family. He hesitates, ostensibly because he cannot read the Hebrew etched on the tombstones. When Daisy asks why he does not put flowers on the grave, he confesses his illiteracy. Since English names appear on the stones, Daisy teaches him how to sound out Bauer. Hoke eventually finds the grave. Daisy later presents him with a copybook—although "it isn't a Christmas present," she stresses. "Jews have no business giving Christmas presents." She mediates her gift through Jewishness, while Hoke enters Jewishness by proxy though reading Jewish names.

Like the gravestones, mirrors serve visual and thematic functions in *Miss Daisy*. The film navigates questions of identity through the constant presence of reflections. The rearview mirror in which Daisy and Hoke exchange looks distances them from each other. The frame used to advertise the film depicts Hoke looking in the rearview mirror at Daisy. This image shows how the two characters view each other. The mirror—he in front, she in back, commanding—frames their relationship. Daisy decides what to do, but Hoke actually drives. Hoke reminds Daisy that she can no longer drive, but she tries to make him an extension of herself by insisting he drive slowly, or out of his way. Although the mirror bridges the space between Daisy and Hoke, they regard each other in it without ever getting too close.

Mirrors also augment the moment at which Boolie explains to his mother that he cannot go to hear Martin Luther King Jr. with her because his business might suffer if customers heard about his attendance. The audience sees both Boolie and Daisy reflected in a series of small mirrors. Framed photographs of Daisy's late husband stand between the two of them. As the older generation does what the younger does not dare to do, the remove offered by the framing and mirrors conveys distance. Even though Daisy and her son stand near each other, they are in different frames of mind. While Boolie moves around, Daisy remains in the frame, never doubting she will hear King speak. She maintains the high moral ground with her husband, as their son faces conflict over the personal and financial burdens righteousness might force him to bear.

Boolie reminds his mother that if she is as unprejudiced as she claims, perhaps she could take Hoke with her to the King lecture. She tells Hoke that King is "wonderful," but does not invite him to attend his speech. Her belief that Hoke could "hear [King] anytime he wants" demonstrates her continuing bigotry. The empty chair next to her throughout the speech symbolizes that there is space for Hoke, but also reminds the audience that Hoke and Daisy do not sit next to each other as a matter of course.

For Daisy and Hoke, the pairing of southern Jewish and black experiences extends beyond their encounter with King and the civil rights era to the Temple bombing. The audience sees Daisy alone in the car, clearly stuck in traffic while rain drums loudly on the roof. Hoke returns and tells Daisy why they are not moving:

> *Hoke*: Somebody done bombed the Temple.
> *Daisy*: I don't believe it.
> *Hoke*: Well, it's what the policeman just said up yonder . . .
> *Daisy*: Who would do such a thing?
> *Hoke*: You know as good as me, Miss Daisy. It will always be the same ones.

Hoke attempts to establish camaraderie, placing Daisy's experience in a larger context of oppression. As they drive home, Daisy stares straight ahead while Hoke, glancing in the rearview mirror, tells her about a lynching he witnessed as a child. When he finishes, Daisy asks, "Why did you tell me that story?"

> *Hoke*: I don't know, Miss Daisy. Just seem like that there mess back there put me in mind of it.
> *Daisy*: That's ridiculous. The Temple has nothing to do with that.
> *Hoke*: Yes'm. If you say so.
> *Daisy*: We don't even know what happened. How do you know that policeman was telling the truth?
> *Hoke*: Well, why would he go and lie about a thing like that?
> *Daisy*: You never get things right anyway.
> *Hoke*: Now, Miss Daisy, somebody done bomb that Temple back yonder and you know it.

> *Daisy*: Go on. Just go on, now. I don't want to hear any more about it.

This exchange reveals Hoke's belief in a basis of community between himself and Daisy. She rebuffs him, dissociating the Temple crisis from Hoke's lynching story. Daisy doubts everything, from the policeman's report to Hoke's veracity. Instead of recognizing the gravity of the Temple bombing as an event that could be discussed in the same conversation as a lynching, Daisy denies that it has happened. A place in which she felt safe—the Temple, and by extension southern Jewishness—lies in ruins, and she dreads confronting the ramifications of the violence. Hoke's story becomes conflated with the Temple bombing, as Daisy progresses from not wanting to hear it to disbelieving the policeman to silencing Hoke. He believes that the Temple bombing brings them together, and Daisy finds this a daunting revelation, even as she repeats, "I'm not prejudiced." The South may be prey to brutal racism, but now *her* Jewishness becomes paramount through the assault, threatening to dismantle the stability of her identity. Julian Bond called the bombing a "proxy attack," suggesting that the perpetrators were demonstrating prejudice against African Americans by assaulting the Jewish community. By portraying the vulnerability of southern Jewishness, *Miss Daisy* demonstrates the *inseparability* of Jewishness and blackness in the South. Southern Jewishness and African Americanness become linked through violence and prejudice.

Miss Daisy came out in 1989, when the American quest for colorblindness sought in the seventies and eighties became a search for multiculturalism. As Todd Gitlin writes, the decades' symbols turned from 1987's July 4 cover of *Time* bravely announcing "We the People" to 1991's fife and drum corps made up of all ethnic types and asking, "Who Are We?" Daisy and Hoke do not attempt the colorblindness of 1987 or the move in 1991 toward inclusive recognition. When Daisy and Hoke look at each other in the rearview mirror, their reflection gives rise to entanglements such as Hoke's consistent subjugation and Daisy's refusal to identify with him, as well as both characters' mutual reliance. Neither's identity erodes, but the two eventually demonstrate a shaded form of communion—a vexed but challenging partnership.

Miss Daisy was widely reviewed and primarily deemed a testament to the bonds that form over racial lines even in a stratified society. Uhry won an Academy Award for his screenplay adaptation, and the film won three other Oscars, including best picture and best actress for Jessica Tandy. For many reviewers, *Miss Daisy* was an "odd couple" film, a mild-mannered depiction of an unlikely interdependence. The film's marketers desired it to be perceived as a messenger of good will. Richard Schickel wrote in *Time*, "Mostly it is the simple presence of a good man that grants her age's greatest benison, expanding rather than shrinking her humanity." In *Playboy*, Bruce Williamson added, "All the . . . implications regarding racial harmony are more implied than socked across." Though some abhorred its sentimentality, other critics considered it a rewriting of *Uncle Tom's Cabin*, starring Hoke as the idealized slave.

Most reviews of *Miss Daisy* glossed over the complexity of the film's treatment of Jewishness in the South, which Pauline Kael understood in her review for the *New Yorker*: "The movie is about the love between blacks and whites (Jewish division) at a time when a wealthy Southern Jewish matron plays mah-jongg, is addressed by her servants as Miss Daisy, and eats alone in the dining room even after she has become an advocate of civil rights." Kael positioned the film as a portrait of a time and place rather than a morality play. She noted that the "whites" in the film belong to a "Jewish division" and links this to Daisy's presumed Jewish brand of liberalism. In popular culture the figure of Miss Daisy has been cited to denote imperiousness. In her humorous book *Clara, The Early Years: The Story of the Pug Who Ruled My Life* (1998), Margo Kaufman writes: "If I attempted to leave home alone, she skittered under my feet, dashed out the gate, and bounced defiantly into the passenger seat of my car. I felt like Morgan Freeman in *Driving Miss Daisy*." In a more direct critique, the rap group Public Enemy's song "Burn, Hollywood, Burn," ends with an announcer who booms, "Ladies and gentlemen, today's feature presentation, *Driving Miss Daisy*," followed by groans and deriding comments, "No, no, no" and "Bullshit." The song includes the phrases, "As I walk the streets of Hollywood Boulevard / Thinking how hard it was to those that starred / In the movies portraying the roles / Of butlers and maids, slaves and hos." Public Enemy denounces *Miss Daisy* as an example of a painfully long line of racist films depicting black servitude.

Daisy may not succeed in conquering her own racial bias, but her story, framed by her relationship with Hoke, is more than either a depiction of an unlikely friendship or white southern condescension toward African Americans. Instead, Daisy tackles the closed world of southern Jewishness, within which she feels secure, and the more open concept of an ethnically intertwined society. *Driving Miss Daisy* depicts southern Jewishness independently and in conjunction with race relations. The film acknowledges the complexity of southerners as individuals and the complexity of their relationships with each other; southern Jewishness smudges the color line laid down by southern custom. The film demonstrates that the snug world of southern Jewishness outgrew its close fit within the larger, changing panorama of the South. From 1948 to 1973, *Miss Daisy* tells us, the southern cultural landscape, preoccupied with racial issues, challenged southern Jewish identity as well.

Abridged from: Eliza R. L. McGraw, "*Driving Miss Daisy:* Southern Jewishness on the Big Screen," *Southern Cultures* 7, no. 2 (2001): 41–59.

Source: Alfred Uhry, *Driving Miss Daisy* (New York: Dramatists Play Service, 1987).

Background: http://www.georgiaencyclopedia.org/nge/Article.jsp?id=h-2731.

Bibliography

Bauman, Mark K., and Berkley Kalin, eds. *Quiet Voices: Southern Rabbis and Black Civil Rights, 1880s to 1990s*. Birmingham: Alabama University Press, 1998.

Evans, Eli. *The Provincials: A Personal History of Jews in the South*. Chapel Hill: University of North Carolina Press, 2005.

Ferris, Marcy, and Mark I. Greenberg, eds. *Jewish Roots in Southern Soil*. Hanover, NH: Brandeis University Press, 2006.

Greene, Melissa Fay. *The Temple Bombing*. Reading, MA: Addison-Wesley, 1996.

Gitlin, Todd. *The Twilight of Common Dreams: Why America Is Wracked by Culture Wars*. New York: Metropolitan, 1995.

Oney, Steve. *And the Dead Shall Rise: The Murder of Mary Phagan and the Lynching of Leo Frank*. New York: Pantheon, 2003.

Kael, Pauline. "The Current Cinema." *New Yorker*, December 25, 1989, 76

Public Enemy. "Burn, Hollywood, Burn." *Fear of a Black Planet*. New York: Def Jam. Columbia CD: CK-45413, 1990.

Schickel, Richard. "Of Time and the River." *Time*, December 18, 1989, 91.

Williamson, Bruce. "Movies." *Playboy*, February 1990, 18.

36. Jewish Women and the Dilemmas of America's Postwar Middle Class

RIV-ELLEN PRELL

Marjorie Morningstar, directed by Irving Rapper [A]
United States, 1958

Following World War II, most Americans inhabited a nation that was changing dramatically in the aftermath of the Great Depression and the war years. This emerging culture was both more urban and more suburban than in previous decades. New media, television in particular, shaped Americans' understanding of the world around them. At the center of this culture were the parents of baby boomer children, who turned increasingly to "experts" in magazines and on television to learn how to live happier lives and how to raise "better-adjusted" boys and girls. They pursued religion and spirituality more avidly than their peers had in the previous decades. Jews and Jewish life changed dramatically in this era as well. The majority of them were now native born and members of the middle class; their primary language was English rather than Yiddish; and many felt that to be a good Jew was equivalent to being a good American and a member of the middle class.

The Cold War shaped Americans' private lives as much as it did global policies because of a persistent fear of invisible enemies at home and abroad, and the anxieties created by the possibility of nuclear destruction. A new generation of young literary writers and social scientists addressed a wider audience about the problems that beset an increasingly affluent and anxious society.

The United States was changing not only because of the economic success that followed its wartime victory, but because the nation was increasingly diverse. Both racial discrimination and civil rights activism persisted and grew. In addition, the descendants of Eastern European immigrants—once thought to be unfit for citizenship because they were not Protestants—Jews among them, were moving to the center of American life as cultural producers, commentators, and critics.

Jews were as intensely engaged in the making of American mass culture after World War II as they had been at the beginning of the twentieth century. One of the hallmarks of the films, television shows, and other media in which they worked after the war was how rarely these cultural products engaged the Jewish experience. There were a few important exceptions, of course. *The Goldbergs*—a radio program from 1929 to 1946, and then a television show from 1949 to 1956—focused on a Jewish family. Its television incarnation was very similar to other programs that featured urban, ethnic, and working-class families, all of which disappeared from television by the end of the 1950s. The media of the late 1950s and 1960s, in contrast, favored a narrow vision of American life that was white, suburban, and timeless. Paradoxically, much of the postwar era's culture was driven by mass media that reflected (almost exclusively) white, Protestant views of American life, even while the diversity of the US citizenry was touted under the banner of American freedom.

In the midst of this era, Herman Wouk's novel *Marjorie Morningstar* was the best-selling book of 1955. It was condensed for *Reader's Digest* subscribers and was featured as a Book-of-the-Month Club selection. The 565-page coming-of-age novel about a Jewish college-age woman from New York and her newly affluent family during the period from the Great Depression through the war to the postwar era in suburbia captured the nation's imagination. Wouk portrayed a version of some of the much-debated tensions of the era. What was the proper balance between individual freedom and the attachment to family and religious and social traditions? Did Americans' growing affluence end any limits on personal desires, including sexual ones? What would become of increasingly independent young, educated women? Was the conformism of the period really such a bad thing?

In Wouk's novel, the struggles involved in these questions took shape around the conflicting aspirations of Marjorie Morgenstern, a beautiful young woman who is nineteen at the outset of the novel. Her parents both represent and advocate for the importance of marriage, chastity, and loyalty to Judaism and family. The beautiful daughter who is to fulfill these dreams is one of their rewards for the sacrifice and hard work that facilitated their climb into the upper middle class. Meanwhile Marjorie aspires to be an actress— hence her stage name of Morningstar—and to pursue love and freedom. Wouk depicted these tensions in the novel through Marjorie's relationship with Noel Airman, a much older man she meets in the 1930s at South Wind, an adult summer camp where he, as the music and dramatics director, hires her to work on productions. Noel is the charismatic star of the camp. The young adults who summer there adore his musicals and songs. His bohemian life style and passion for theater draw Marjorie into a struggle between virtue and her desire to be an actress and pursue their affair.

The novel follows Marjorie's life for seven years and devotes 500 pages to the questions of whether or not she will become an actress and remain a virgin. In this epic battle, Marjorie is initially a naive young woman pursuing not only a first love but also her ambition to act. Noel Airman is a fraudulent, pseudo-intellectual who is afraid of commitment. She believes that he possesses talents he actually lacks. He labels her a "Shirley," a woman who simply wants conventional love, marriage, and a life in the suburbs. However, their attachment is passionate, and they profess their love for each other.

The novel was by no means considered a work of significant literary merit, although it was widely reviewed and became the source of some cultural debates. Wouk was an accomplished and well-known author by the time of the novel's publication, and it was compared unfavorably to his Pulitzer Prize–winning *Caine Mutiny* (1951). *Marjorie Morningstar*'s literary reputation has not grown with time. Nevertheless, its popularity makes it a source of some interest, all the more so because it focused on the American Jewish experience. Given its wide readership, one can conclude that the majority of its readers had never before encountered Jews on the page, and perhaps not in real life either. The novel simultaneously registered changes in American Jewish life and Jews' increasing acceptance by other Americans, some continuing antisemitism notwithstanding. For the first half of the twentieth century, many Americans viewed Jews as outsiders, enemies, or aliens. The fact that the Morgensterns experienced the personal and cultural conflicts facing many middle-class Americans seemed quite remarkable. Gordon Hutner (47) refers to the novel as the first "cross over book," a work about the Jewish experience that was embraced by the broader society.

Wouk's story of American Jewish life most likely appealed to this postwar generation of readers because it resonated with the experiences of the children of many immigrant American ethnic groups, as well as the children of native born Americans living in suburbia. The themes of morality and traditional authority under attack, changing ideas about sex and family, and a beautiful young woman seeking new freedoms clearly fascinated American readers. Wouk's tale was ultimately conservative; virginity was to be preserved; traditions were to be honored; young women's aspirations were probably foolish, if not dangerous: and mother was right. Readers might be titillated by the novel's focus on sex, but by the book's conclusion, order has been restored, with a clear condemnation of intercourse outside of marriage. The issues of sex, affluence, love, and social mobility—Jewish dramas in the novel—concerned most Americans in the 1950s.

Four years later Philip Roth, the great American writer, launched his literary career with the publication of his novella *Goodbye Columbus*, which positioned the struggles of the middle class through another beautiful daughter, Brenda Patimkin, and her experiments with sex and freedom. Roth's first major work attracted only a fraction of the readership of Wouk's novel, but both writers focused many of the cultural conflicts of the period on the sexuality and beauty of a young Jewish woman and her newly affluent parents. It may not be possible to identify the roots of the stereotypical Jewish American Princess, but Brenda and Marjorie certainly may be her literary sources.

Marjorie Morningstar was released as a film by Warner Brothers in 1958. The studio was rumored to have paid a million dollars to acquire the script. The translation of the book to the screen raised two problems. It was almost six hundred pages long, and it was a book about Jews. Despite the novel's broad appeal, the Hollywood studio system still viewed films about "minorities" as a threat to box office success. Wouk had written a novel about Jews, their history, rituals, and harrowing experiences during the genocidal World War II. Marjorie confronts the Holocaust and is transformed by it; her brother is killed in the war. These challenges apparently lengthened the process of creating a script as well as finding the female lead. The director, Irving Rapper, and the screenwriter, Everett Freeman, took up the challenge. Rapper directed films for over thirty-five years, beginning his career in 1941. Freeman was a well-known writer for radio, films, and television, especially renowned for adapting books to the screen. The film featured a number of Hollywood stars. Natalie Wood portrayed Marjorie. The role marked her transition from a child star to a prominent actress. Gene Kelly, the famous dancer and actor, portrayed Noel, who was nearly twenty years Marjorie's senior. They were supported by a cast of prominent actors and actresses.

The film radically condensed the novel, gave it a different ending, and shifted the time frame to the 1950s. It retained the novel's focus on the family, the love affair, and Marjorie's inability to succeed as an actress. The film never matched the novel's popularity. Despite much publicity and numerous reviews, not to mention an entire line of clothing based on the costumes designed for Marjorie, it earned far less than other films of that year. Many of them—like *Auntie Mame*, *Gigi*, *South Pacific*, and *Cat on a Hot Tin Roof*—also explored issues of sexual freedom and repressive culture, but they found a larger audience.

The Jewishness of *Marjorie Morningstar* is paradoxical. The film broke new ground for portraying the Jewish experience, even as it emptied the story of much of its Jewish content. Thus the film captures some of the interesting ways in which Jews interacted with American society in the mid-1950s, as members of the mainstream yet not fully integrated. That integration was much

sought after by Jews, but often decried by Jewish intellectuals, rabbis, and other leaders because of the assimilation it promised.

Jews were absent from the silver screen for most of the three decades that preceded *Marjorie Morningstar*. In 1947 a film about antisemitism, *Gentleman's Agreement*, won the Oscar for best picture. However, it really depicted very little Jewish life, focusing instead on prejudice in order to celebrate the triumph of democracy and America over fascism.

Ultimately, *Marjorie Morningstar* did not portray the Morgensterns as incidentally Jewish, but neither did their Jewishness define them. They participated in Jewish rituals, both a Passover seder and a synagogue service that included the bar mitzvah of the Morgensterns' younger son. These scenes included Jewish music, ritual objects, and food. One of the film's characters, Uncle Samson, portrayed by the famous comic actor Ed Wynn, was beloved by audiences. Though often amusing and clearly a relative of almost no means, his dignity was established in his role as a leader of the seder; he embodied Jewish tradition. Cinematic portrayals of synagogues and family rituals ended in the 1920s. Their reappearance in the 1950s, first in a 1952 remake of *The Jazz Singer* and then in *Marjorie Morningstar*, suggests that cultural and ethnic differences became acceptable in American popular culture in this period.

Many reviews took the film to task for excluding too much of the novel's Jewish content and focus. However, the film also introduced Jewishness in a way that the novel did not. For example, Noel extolled the virtues of family and tradition as he left the Morgensterns' Passover ritual, an innovation that is completely inconsistent with Wouk's contemptuous portrayal of Noel in the novel.

When Marjorie's parents appealed to her to

guard her virtue and to seek marriage, it was in the context of their commitment to traditions. Jewishness, then, stood for respect for the past, for family, and for sex only within marriage. Jack Moffitt's review for the *Hollywood Reporter* wished that the film had been released during Brotherhood Week because "I have yet to meet a gentile who read it and was not made more friendly and considerate in his attitudes toward his Jewish fellow citizens." For the *Hollywood Reporter*, Jews were objects of a week devoted to getting along with "others." Wouk's book and Rapper's film are, in themselves, an act of brotherhood.

Nevertheless, the presence of a distinctive Jewish culture on screen signaled not only a shift in Hollywood's portrayal of Jews, but also the nation's new boundaries of inclusion of (some) social differences. Jews were incorporated into popular culture portrayals of American life through families. Both the novel and the film version of *Marjorie Morningstar* appeared at a cultural moment when ethnic family stories crossed over from radio to television. *I Remember Mama* and *The Goldbergs* were examples of what historians Judith Smith and George Lipsitz described as the most popular use of the family to explore issues of memory, Americanization, and values (Lipsitz; Smith.) Virtually all conflicts in family dramas were resolved in ways that were strikingly parallel to those in the film version of *Marjorie Morningstar*. The older generation adapted to American ways by promoting their children's success, and children accepted, sometimes with considerable angst, the wisdom of their parents.

These family dramas reinforced the emerging values of the postwar nuclear families, and a strongly gendered division of labor that put middle-class men in the workplace and women at home, often in isolating suburbs. Marjorie Morningstar's cross-over power was at least in part related to Jews' embrace and eventual personification of this middle-class life. The film's first scene links three generations of the Morgenstern family. The immigrant generation, embodied in Uncle Samson, is Old World, poor, and unrefined. The Morgenstern parents are new to affluence. Mr. Morgenstern chides his wife for spending too much money and being too indulgent, but he is proud of his achievements, which made their affluence possible.

Mrs. Morgenstern closely watches and manages her daughter, Marjorie, the member of the most American generation. In the first scene, she rouses Marjorie after a late date and pumps her for details of her evening. The mother offers advice about marriage and aspirations as she hurries Marjorie to dress for synagogue. The younger generation restlessly seeks experience and resists expectations.

The intimate portrayal of this family avoided the protest and tensions that characterized earlier and later American Jewish fiction and film. Mrs. Morgenstern lacks the vituperative domineering qualities of the stereotypical Jewish mother. The family is less tormenting and tormented than families in other popular films about Jews that would appear in the following decades. The Morgensterns' blandness emphasizes the similarity between middle-class white Americans and their newly affluent ethnic neighbors. The viewer is to believe that, for all of their religious distinctiveness, the Morgensterns are, like most middle-class Americans, engaged in containing a generational rebellion and maintaining traditional family authority.

Through the medium of these popular culture family dramas, Jews were written into an American story of the nation in a way that African Americans and other Americans of color were not in this period. The film version of *Marjorie Morningstar* did not include racially integrated neighborhoods, or integrated theater productions at Hunter College, where Marjorie is a student. If the Morgensterns are American, it is in part because they are white.

At the heart of the story were both tensions between generations and questions about sex. A young beautiful woman whose beauty and sexuality were a preoccupation of the story seemed capable of transforming the drama into a tragedy and threatening the happy ending of the tale of Jewish inclusion. The film portrays Marjorie's transformation from a naïve young college student to a woman who, in the words of one of the minor characters, "has finally grown up." Her transformation unfolds both in her long-term love affair with the older Noel Airman and in her aspirations to act in the theater. For a young woman portrayed on the screen as dazzlingly beautiful and remarkably persistent, it is somewhat surprising that both of her pursuits are heart-breaking failures. Not only does she fail to win what she most wants, but, in both the film and the book, what she yearns for proves to be illusions. She lacks the talent to be an actress and cannot succeed in the theater. Noel Airman, whom she sees as brilliant and gifted, lacks talent and integrity. Marjorie's attempts to deviate from middle-class Jewish propriety give her little more than the hard-won lessons of life experience.

Herman Wouk's obsession not only with his character's lack of talent but with that of most aspiring young actresses is striking. In an article he wrote about the casting of Natalie Wood as Marjorie, a choice he initially resisted, he focused on that theme. He wrote: "It evidently never occurred to the hundreds, I may say the thousands, of girls who besieged Warner Brothers for a chance to play the part that they were really describing themselves as infatuated youngsters who could not act." Wouk continued: "In my novel I believe I told the truth. The unknown youngster never gets the chance, does not deserve it, most likely cannot handle it if she does get it, and is better off putting such dreams out of her head" ("My Search for Marjorie").

However politically, religiously, or culturally conservative Herman Wouk was in the 1950s, his refusal to imagine that a talented young woman, other than Natalie Wood at least, could exist is at best overwrought, and at worst advocacy for limiting women's lives. For all of her beauty and aspirations, her attractiveness to legions of men, and her capacity for love, the film and novel both make Marjorie little more than a cipher, a figure of hardly any significance. Only as daughter or wife could she live a suitable life. The rest is illusion. Her efforts to resist the fate of becoming a "Shirley" were, according to Wouk, nearly disastrous, threatening her chance for marriage by having sex.

The film portrays freedom's illusions even more harshly in the character of Noel Airman. Marjorie took the romantic stage name Morningstar. Noel similarly changed his German Jewish name Ehrman, which means an honorable man, for the more American Airman. Airman is the English equivalent of the Yiddish word *luftmensch*, an impractical person without a livelihood. The film savages Noel less than the novel does, but it ultimately portrays him as weak, lacking real talent, and irresponsible. His bohemianism is treated as the source of his irresponsibility, a cover for his shallowness of character and lack of true talent.

Noel and Marjorie both chase dreams and freedoms that the film suggests have no place in the lives of mature men and women. The film resolves the characters' dilemmas differently. Noel initially takes jobs in advertising in an attempt to work in an adult world, but he leaves them in anger. Finally given the opportunity to finish his play and stage it on Broadway, he meets with failure. Noel literally runs away, and Marjorie pursues him through Europe and finally back to the summer camp where they met. When she finds him once again surrounded by adoring young men and women, she accepts that this was where he will remain, trapped in perpetual youth.

In turn, Marjorie is reduced to playing a predictable role in the family while Noel is consigned to eternal immaturity, demonstrated by his refusal to accept the responsibility of marrying a beautiful wife. He rejects not only Marjorie, but the hard-won status of his parents, who have now made it into American affluence. Marjorie Morningstar and Philip Roth's Brenda Patemkin were the glittering prizes of Jewish affluence. These novels and films were as much about sons who reject their fathers' mobility and success as they were about men who flee "Shirleys."

The film's conclusion is less harsh than that of the novel. Marjorie has many suitors, proof of her beauty and apparent uniqueness. Her most persistent one is Wally, Noel's assistant at the adult summer camp. Wally, in contrast to Noel, becomes a very successful playwright. In the film's final scene, he is waiting for her after her realization that Noel is not the person she had hoped he would be. At last she will turn to Wally.

The novel's ending is strikingly different. Wally appears in the book's conclusion as a commentator, explaining that Marjorie now lives a dull, predictable, and religious life in the suburbs with her husband and children. Faced with the mature Marjorie, he cannot understand why he ever found her special, daring, or interesting.

Marjorie does fall in love with and marry the sort of man her parents had hoped she would find, a successful lawyer. But their love is forever changed by Marjorie's revelation to him that she is not a virgin. Though devastated, he marries her, but the reader is assured that he never loved her in the same way again. In the end, Marjorie is redeemed only by the forgiveness of her parents and husband; she is chastened.

This bleak work of cultural conservatism ironically appealed to more than a single generation of postwar readers. The film is available on DVD, and the novel continues to attract new readers, selling about 5,000 copies a year. The amazon.com page devoted to the book boasts over fifty comments that debate its greatness as a literary work, its aptness as a moral tale, and how to understand an ending that reduced the heroine's coming-of-age experiences to something only to be forgotten by a suburban matron.

Variety announced in 1998 that Al Pacino had acquired rights to the remake of the film for Castle Rock Pictures. In July 2004 the renowned film actress Scarlett Johansson agreed to play the new Marjorie. In several interviews she declared, "I read it and thought, 'Oh my God, this is me,' and I called my mom and told her 'I'm Marjorie Morningstar,' and she said, 'I know you are'" (Newhouse). However, the *Jewish Daily Forward*, a national Jewish weekly, broke the news in 2007 that Johansson had abandoned the film. She explained: "It was one of those heartbreak projects that you had to let go. Sometimes when you have a book like that, there are a lot of rights to it, and everyone's been involved for such a long time. It was a 'Too many cooks spoil the broth type of thing'"(Heifitz).

Alana Newhouse, a perceptive journalist, reflected on the novel on its fiftieth anniversary for the online cultural magazine *Slate*. She concluded her essay by commenting on the novel's persistent popularity: "Almost everyone loves the Marjorie of the first 556 pages. This Marjorie evokes the period when girls are still free to dream about their future, before they actually have to start making choices about it. Wouk might wince at the thought, but what women enjoy about his book is the promise of adolescence. As she enters middle age, Marjorie continues to defy her paternal creator, like the rebellious teenager she was meant to be" (Newhouse). The story's power on film and in the novel is its ability to capture, despite the author's intentions, the experiences of a young woman coming of age and her wish to chart her own destiny.

If *Marjorie Morningstar* was indeed the first cross-over novel and an early attempt to link Jewish family dramas to the white middle class, it was no accident that it did so through the medium of a young Jewish woman. Rather than her hopes and aspirations leading to "near disaster," as Wouk put it ("My Search for Marjorie"), in barely more than a decade following the film's release, young women—with Jews central among them—fought the battle for feminism and women's liberation, both within Judaism and in American society. By invoking American Jewish culture, what Wouk unintentionally accomplished was to show how ready women were to change their lives and the world. The dreams of Jewish immigrants for their daughters inspired aspirations that left the dream of a house in the suburbs far behind.

Source: Herman Wouk, *Marjorie Morningstar* (New York: Doubleday, 1955).

Background: http://www.jewishmediafund.org/courses/course_notes/mtc_web/MTC_AVery.pdf.

Bibliography

Eder, Bruce. "Herman Wouk Details." All Movie Guide. http://movies.amctv.com/person/182786/Herman-Wouk/details.

Erens, Patricia. *The Jew in American Cinema.* Bloomington: Indiana University Press, 1984.

Heifetz, Laurie. "Scarlett's Falling Morningstar." *Jewish Daily Forward*, May 11, 2007. http://www.forward.com/articles/10677/.

Hutner, Gordon. "The Meaning of Marjorie Morningstar." In *Key Texts in American Jewish Culture*, edited by Jack Kugelmass, 46–56. New Brunswick, NJ: Rutgers University Press, 2003.

Lipsitz, George. "The Meaning of Memory: Family, Class and Ethnicity in Early Network Television." *Collective Memory and American Popular Culture*, Minneapolis: University of Minnesota Press 1990. 39–76

May, Elaine Tyler. *Homeward Bound: American Families in the Cold War.* New York: Basic, 1988.

Moffitt, Jack. "Marjorie Morningstar." *Hollywood Reporter*, March 11, 1958.

Newhouse, Alana. "*Marjorie Morningstar*: The Conservative Novel that Liberal Feminists Love. *Slate Magazine* September 14, 2005. http://www.slate.com/id/2126022/.

Prell, Riv-Ellen. *Fighting to Become Americans: Jews, Gender and the Anxiety of Assimilation.* Boston: Beacon, 1999.

Smith, Judith E. *Visions of Belonging: Family Stories, Popular Culture, and Postwar Democracy, 1940–1960,* New York: Columbia University Press, 2004.

Wouk, Herman. "My Search for Marjorie." *American Weekly*, May 11, 1958,

37. Of Lox and Columbus

Jewish and American Themes in *Goodbye, Columbus*

JOELLYN WALLEN ZOLLMAN

Goodbye Columbus, directed by
Larry Peerce [A]
United States, 1969

"First of all, no matter what anyone says, this is not a Jewish movie," insisted Stanley Jaffe, the producer of *Goodbye, Columbus*, during a production interview with the *New York Times* in September 1968 (Jonas 1968). "The only thing that's Jewish about the movie is that the characters in it happen to be Jewish," he explained. Larry Peerce, the film's director, agreed. In the same article, Peerce stated: "What we're doing is telling the story of the upper middle class of America. But the story takes place in the Jewish world, and we portray that world honestly." Jewish characters, playing out a Jewish story, in a Jewish world—that sounds like a formula for a Jewish film. Add to that the fact that the novella on which the film is based, Philip Roth's *Goodbye, Columbus*, won the Jewish Book Council of America Award in 1960, and it seems that these filmmakers doth protest too much.

Why would the director and producer be so concerned that their movie not be marketed or received as a "Jewish" film? In part, their concern was probably tied to the economic success of the film—a picture pigeonholed as "ethnic" was often doomed to lackluster box office returns. If the movie were too particularistic, it would not appeal to a general audience. Peerce and Jaffe's insistence on the universal appeal of the film was meant to reassure potential filmgoers that there

was something for everyone in this story. And they're not wrong. *Goodbye Columbus* is at once a quintessentially Jewish and an undeniably American story. In their defense of the film, Peerce and Jaffe hit on the combination that allowed *Goodbye, Columbus* contemporaneous and continued success: the novella and the film use the particular realities of the postwar American Jewish experience to illuminate universal American themes.

Philip Roth's *Goodbye, Columbus and Five Short Stories* was published to critical acclaim in 1959. In addition to the Jewish Book Council of America Award, Roth's collection won the National Book Award in 1960. *Goodbye, Columbus*, the novella that opens the collection, is the story of a summer romance between two American Jews from different economic backgrounds. The protagonist, Neil Klugman, has recently returned from a stint in the army. A graduate of Rutgers College, he is working as a librarian and living with his overbearing Aunt Gladys and Uncle Max in a working-class Jewish neighborhood in Newark. Neil meets and falls in love with Brenda Patimkin, who is home from Radcliffe for the summer, living with her parents in suburban opulence in Short Hills, New Jersey. They meet at Brenda's suburban Jewish country club, where Neil, as a guest of his cousin for the day, holds her glasses while she swims. Neil continues to test the role of guest in Brenda's life as he pursues a romantic relationship with her.

Like Columbus, Neil is on a journey of discovery. He sets out to explore the postwar American Jewish suburban experience, a terrain markedly different from his own urban, working-class Jewish reality. Neil maps the physical differences between city and suburb: "Once I'd driven out of Newark, past Irvington and the packed in

Jack Klugman (as Ben Patimkin) assures his daughter Ali MacGraw (as Brenda Patimkin) that he'll always provide for her. From *Goodbye, Columbus* (1969), directed by Larry Peerce.
PARAMOUNT/PHOTOFEST

tangle of railroad crossings, switchmen shacks, lumberyards, Dairy Queens, and used car lots, the night grew cooler. It was, in fact, as though the hundred and eighty feet that the suburbs rose in altitude above Newark brought one closer to heaven, for the sun itself became bigger, lower, and rounder, and soon I was driving past long lawns which seemed to be twirling water on themselves, and past houses where no one sat on stoops, where lights were on but no windows open, for those inside, refusing to share the very texture of their life with those of us outside" (Roth 1959, 8).

Brenda brings Neil, the outsider, into her life.

Will he remain a guest or become a permanent resident? The novella traces his journey.

Paramount Pictures released the film *Goodbye, Columbus* in 1969. The movie was directed by Peerce, produced by Jaffe, and featured an Oscar-nominated screenplay by Arnold Shulman that stuck very closely to Roth's novella, repeating whole pages of dialogue verbatim. Richard Benjamin, best known at the time for his starring role in the TV series *He and She*, portrayed Neil Klugman. Benjamin would go on to play Roth's most infamous Jewish character, Alexander Portnoy, in *Portnoy's Complaint* (1972). Ali MacGraw, a model turned actress, had her film debut as Brenda Patimkin. On the choice of MacGraw to play Brenda, Peerce explained: "American Jews are like the American-Irish or American-Italian, their great desire—despite the fact that they deny it—is to become part of the great amorphous fog-bank of American middle-class life. Ali's looks represent the ideal that they're aiming for" (Jonas 1968). Other notable members of the cast include Jack Klugman as Mr. Patimkin and Nan Martin as Mrs. Patimkin.

Goodbye, Columbus faithfully translates Roth's story to the screen. There's a change in venue: Newark and Short Hills, New Jersey, become the Bronx and Westchester, New York, respectively. Still, all of the elements of Roth's story come to life, and the audience is treated to a rendering of the postwar American Jewish experience including suburbanization, economic mobility, and the changing image of American Jewish women.

The Patimkin and Klugman families fall into typical American Jewish demographic categories. The Patimkins are transplants from the city to the suburbs. Their move mirrors the experience of the majority of American Jews in the postwar period. Although suburbanization was a postwar trend nationally, American Jews moved to the suburbs at a rate almost four times that of their non-Jewish neighbors. This Jewish exodus to the suburbs was fueled, in part, by their movement, en masse, into the middle class. This was certainly the case for the Patimkin family. The success of the Patimkin family business, Patimkin Kitchen and Bathroom Sinks (Patimkin Plumbing Supply in the film), allowed the family to move to the suburbs when Brenda was a child. (Presumably, the very existence of the suburbs allowed for the continued success of Patimkin sinks—the housing boom feeding the demand for the Patimkin product.)

The Klugmans represent another stratum of postwar American Jewish life. Neil's parents have retired to Arizona. American Jews moved in significant numbers to sunbelt cities after World War II. Drawn by good weather and increased economic opportunity, many American Jews relocated to places like Miami and Los Angeles. Neil's parents' move, fueled by health concerns, reflects this trend. Neil's Aunt Gladys and Uncle Max still live in an apartment in an urban Jewish neighborhood. They haven't had the economic success that would allow them to move to the more expensive suburbs. Aunt Gladys and Uncle Max personify the old neighborhood, the rapidly fading urban, ethnic, working-class Jewish experience. Neil is the next generation, full of potential, and at the brink of adulthood. He has attended college, the first steppingstone to upward mobility. Now he must choose his next step. Should he continue along the typical American Jewish pathway to success, or reject suburbanization and upward mobility and create his own version of the Jewish American dream?

Neil explores the suburban, upper-class Jewish experience through his relationship with Brenda and her family. From the beginning, Neil is both drawn to and discomfited by the Patim-kins' lifestyle. Roth portrays the suburbs as a sort of Garden of Eden, fraught with poisonous temptations. The filmmakers depict the allure and danger of the suburbs in a variety of ways. The opening scene features a bevy of beautiful young women tanning and swimming at a posh suburban country club. Neil is relaxing on a lounge chair, enjoying the view, when the scene shifts. Suddenly, instead of bikini-clad beauties, we see middle-aged women, wrinkly and jiggly mothers and grandmothers gossiping with their friends and fighting with their children. The message is clear: Neil can ogle attractive young women, but he shouldn't forget what they are destined to become.

Similarly, the Patimkins' suburban residence both invites and disturbs the viewer. On the outside, it's a massive white colonial house with an endless green lawn and shade trees, perfect for family time and recreation. The film shows the youngest Patimkin, Julie, playing basketball and golfing with her father on the lawn; Neil and Brenda picnicking under a tree; the family having dessert on the porch. But inside the house, and the Patimkin family, there is discontent and drama. Mrs. Patimkin is shrill and snobbish; Mr. Patimkin unashamed in his indulgence of his children's whims and desires. When Neil first meets the Patimkins at a family dinner, this interplay between beauty and ugliness is evident. The family dining room is lavishly decorated, but the family dinner table is silent, devoid of meaningful conversation. When the family does interact, it's to condescend, tease, or otherwise display poor manners.

Roth delights in revealing the unappealing flip side of suburban allure. His penchant for dichotomy—inside/outside, surface/interior—translates well into the visual mode of film. This is particularly true in the case of Brenda's body/self. Neil is clearly attracted to Brenda. From their first meeting at the pool, he finds her beautiful. On their first date, he learns that she has had her nose "fixed." Neil teases her relentlessly throughout the movie about other potential fixes: why don't you fix your eyes (instead of wearing contact lenses or glasses); can't you fix your "funny knuckles"? Neil is bothered by the materialism inherent in this surgical solution, the idea that there is a monetary fix to every problem. Yet he is also raising a deeper philosophical question. What does one have to change in order to fit into this world? Specifically, what would he need to change or fix in order to live there? In an image that makes more of an impression on the screen than in the novella, Neil's cousin Doris sits at the country club, peeling her sunburned skin. Her family recently moved to the suburbs, and she is symbolically shedding her old skin.

Although Brenda's surface, her physical appearance, may be characterized by deception, she is undeniably beautiful. Defending her nose job, Brenda explains, "I was pretty, and now I'm prettier." Roth describes Brenda as physically attractive, and the filmmakers portray her that way. "Even when seen under 16 successive layers of makeup, the nose of Ali MacGraw is a thing of beauty—a flawless masterpiece that Brenda Patimkin's plastic surgeon would have been proud to take credit for," noted the *New York Times* (Jonas 1968).

Brenda's exterior is nearly flawless, but her interior is less than perfect: her personality is deeply unattractive. Neil presents an interesting contrast. He's not obviously attractive. ("Richard Benjamin's nose is his own," quipped the *New York Times* critic Paul Wilkes [1969].) He's snarky, awkward, and often unkind. Yet whereas Neil is described by critics as a "decent, edgy" guy, Brenda elicits a different reaction. "In her first movie, Ali MacGraw comes on as a class A, number one,

American bitch," wrote Wilkes. Brenda Patimkin is often credited with the dubious honor of being one of the first Jewish American Princesses (JAPs). Along with her counterpart in print and film, Marjorie Morningstar, Brenda is considered a prototype for the spoiled, aggressive, beautiful, manipulative Jewish daughter who would become a mainstay stereotype in American popular culture.

The character of Brenda Patimkin was recognizable to audiences. Benjamin recalled dating a number of "Brendas." MacGraw noted, in an interview: "I kept saying to myself as I approached the part of Brenda that we had nothing in common.... Only when I discovered there's a little of Brenda in every honest woman could I even start to play her. You know what I mean: that certain arrogance, a high-handedness that makes you feel good while others have to crawl, the cruel flirtiness, that certain tease, tease, tease and then stop" (Wilkes 1969). Roth is tapping into and contributing to a negative shift in the perception of American Jewish daughters.

Goodbye, Columbus is not a celebration of American Jewish women. The film is replete with unappealing female images, from the neurotic Aunt Gladys to the snobbish Mrs. Patimkin, and the whiny little sister, Julie, to the daft new sister-in-law, Harriet. The character of Brenda represents a new package of negative traits. Riv-Ellen Prell argues that the JAP stereotype, as personified by Brenda, was created by Jewish men as a representation of their own anxieties about adulthood. In other words, Brenda was born from Neil's (Roth's) anxiety about the death of his dreams in the face of postwar expectations regarding family, faith, and work. *Goodbye, Columbus* certainly suggests that by marrying Brenda, Neil would marry into a very specific future.

Neil and Brenda's summer ends with a wedding, though not their own. Brenda's brother, Ron Patimkin, marries Harriet, his college sweetheart, in a lavish ceremony. The wedding is the clearest depiction of religion in the movie, and the scene critics frequently deemed antisemitic. From the standpoint of character and plot development, the wedding suggests a possible ending for Neil and Brenda. They are told "you're next" several times during the reception. Yet the wedding contains the beginning of the end of Neil and Brenda's relationship. Mr. Patimkin's heartfelt conversation with Brenda about trust and morality sets the stage for the couple's eventual breakup.

As a portrayal of American Jews, the wedding satirizes a postwar penchant for extravagant celebrations of rites of passage. Roth grounds his story in historical reality. American Jewish upward economic and social mobility led to an increasingly opulent lifestyle, in which ostentation prevailed over religion. The Patimkin wedding was filmed at the Delmonico Hotel on New York's Park Avenue. The setting is elegant; the guests are well dressed, and the ceremony features identifiable Jewish markers, including a rabbi chanting in Hebrew, a *huppah* [wedding canopy], the breaking of the glass, and the shouts of "*Mazel tov*!"

The wedding reception, however, contains the unattractive flip side of the elegant ceremony. The guests attack the buffet. Mr. Patimkin beheads a chicken sculpted out of chopped liver, smooshes some on a cracker and proceeds, with his mouth full, to compliment his own party as "the classiest buffet of the year." Children and adults shove their way to the front of the table, and the camera focuses on arms and mouths, grabbing and devouring various foods. The film cuts back to the buffet table several times during the reception, reminding the audience of the

pushiness, the crassness, the uncivilized manners of these seemingly elegant guests. Peerce scoffed at the charge that the scene was antisemitic and cited honesty as a motivating factor. "The middle class are the loudest yellers of all. Have you been to a Jewish wedding?" he asked in an interview (Jonas 1968). "No one in the movie has a Yiddish accent," said Jaffe, defending the film. "*That* would be vulgar." Antisemitic, honest, funny, glamorous or crass, the Patimkin wedding is rich in religious and ethnic imagery.

Neil's journey is characterized by particular Jewish situations that are played out on the landscape of American history. In this sense, Neil is a sort of ethnic Everyman, whose experiences resonate with those of other American ethnic and minority groups. Neil is an immigrant. He leaves the old world (the old Jewish neighborhood in the Bronx) and contemplates settling in the new (rich, suburban Westchester). His is a one-way journey. We don't see Brenda schlepping to the Bronx because she is not considering resettlement. Neil's exploration touches on themes familiar to all immigrant tales, including culture shock, intergenerational conflict, and the question of how to maintain one's identity while acculturating into new surroundings.

Mr. Patimkin's speech to Neil is a perfect example of the universal characteristics of intergenerational conflict: "You kids. The way you look at us while we're out here batting our brains out trying to make a living, like we're a bunch of freaks and you're something special." The tense relationship between Mrs. Patimkin and Brenda is motivated by issues that ring true to female audiences, especially the difference in opportunity afforded to the younger generation. There is nothing particularly Jewish about these exchanges—they are recognizable to audiences because they represent conversations and issues that could have occurred between parents and their almost-adult children in any American household.

Neil is a hyphenated American, and when considering his future, he must navigate both sides of the hyphen. Navigating the hyphen is practically an American pastime. African Americans, Italian Americans, Irish Americans, Mexican Americans, Chinese Americans, Arab Americans, and other minority groups have struggled with balancing both portions of their identity; Neil's interactions with a young African American boy at the library point to the common challenges faced by members of minority groups. The boy is fascinated by a book of Paul Gauguin's Polynesian paintings. He returns daily to gaze at Gauguin's portraits of natives in the lush, tropical landscape. (Like Neil, Gauguin was bothered by societal standards of success. He moved to Tahiti to escape everything that was artificial and commercial about European society.) The African American boy feels out of his element at the library, a feeling heightened by many of the employees, who suspect that he won't behave properly. They treat him like an outsider. But he is drawn to Gauguin's pictures of paradise, where black people bathe in sun and sand. Neil is fiercely protective of the boy and his book because Neil is also an outsider gazing on a potential paradise. The young Gauguin fan gives voice to their shared predicament. As the scene fades from the library and the Patimkin property comes into view, he says, "Man, ain't that the life."

At its core, *Goodbye, Columbus* is a story about the American dream, with all of its prizes and pitfalls. The Patimkin family appears to have achieved the American dream. They have achieved material success, bought the huge house in the suburbs, and plan to transfer their wealth to the next generation. But scratch the shiny and beautiful surface, and all kinds of ugliness and dysfunctionality are revealed, including snobbery, stupidity, and manipulative behavior. Neil rejects this version of success and happiness, while Brenda clings to it. "They're my parents. They've given me everything I've ever wanted. How could I not go home? I have to go home," cries Brenda at the end of the film. Neil neither understands nor appreciates the appeal of Brenda's home. He leaves, breaking up with Brenda and her version of the American dream. In the spirit of rugged individualism, he will chart his own course and realize his own version of the American dream.

Finally, *Goodbye, Columbus* is a laugh-out-loud example of American ethnic humor. Ethnic humor is a mainstay of American culture, and often a critical part of Americanization. Although the process of becoming American poses serious challenges, it has often been lightened by exploring the comic potential inherent in cultural adjustment and change. *Goodbye, Columbus* contains situational and dialogue-based comedy that is both funny and familiar to viewers. The scenes between Neil and his Aunt Gladys represent classic intergenerational comedy characterized by cultural misunderstanding and confusion. He thinks she is exasperatingly old-fashioned and overbearing; she can't imagine the motivations for his behavior. Conflicts over what to eat, what to wear, and how to behave are recurring features of American ethnic comedies. The witty dialogue between Brenda and Neil represents another aspect of American ethnic humor—namely, the use of comedy as a cushion to soften the tense insider/outsider situation. In one such scene, when Brenda questions Neil about his future, he explains: "You want to know want my plans are for the future. I'm not planning anything. Besides,

I'm not a planner, I'm a liver." Brenda responds, "I'm a pancreas!" Here Brenda uses wordplay—a mainstay in ethnic comedy—to diffuse a stressful situation.

The act of saying goodbye suggests movement. *Goodbye, Columbus* portrays a variety of defining Jewish movements: a young Jewish man on a voyage of discovery regarding his future; an American Jewish community in transition from poor immigrants to affluent suburban citizens; and the creation of the image of the Jewish American Princess, a character inextricably tied to the anxieties of postwar American Jewish life.

The film also moves the audience to contemplate several larger American themes, including immigration, assimilation, consumerism, and the American dream. Rich in imagery and symbolism, *Goodbye, Columbus* is thus not a true goodbye, but rather the beginning of a conversation about race, religion, class, and gender in America.

Source: Philip Roth, *Goodbye, Columbus and Five Short Stories* (Boston: Houghton-Mifflin, 1959).

Background: http://www.myjewishlearning.com/history/Modern_History/1948–1980/America/Suburbanization/Jewish_Women_and_Suburbanization.shtml.

Bibliography

Canby, Vincent. "Screen: A Vivid 'Goodbye, Columbus.'" *New York Times*, August 4, 1969.

Cooper, Philip. *Philip Roth and the Jews*. Albany: State University Press of New York, 1996.

Erens, Patricia. *The Jew in American Cinema*. Bloomington: Indiana University Press, 1984.

Hoberman, J. "Flaunting It: The Rise and Fall of Hollywood's 'Nice' Jewish (Bad) Boys." In *Entertaining America: Jews, Movies, and Broadcasting*, edited by J. Hoberman and Jeffrey Shandler, 220–43. Princeton, NJ: Princeton University Press, 2003.

Jonas, Gerald. "Hello Again to 'Goodbye, Columbus.'" *New York Times*, September 8, 1968.

Prell, Riv-Ellen. "Why Jewish Princesses Don't Sweat: Desire and Consumption in Postwar American Jewish Culture." In *People of the Body: Jews and Judaism from an Embodied Perspective*, edited by Howard Eilberg-Schwartz, 329–60. Albany: State University Press of New York, 1992.

Rabin, Jessica G. "Still (Resonant, Relevant and) Crazy after All These Years: *Goodbye Columbus and Five Short Stories*." In *Philip Roth: New Perspectives on an American Author*, edited by Derek Parker Royal, 9–23. Westport, CT: Praeger, 2005.

Rosenblum, Ralph, and Robert Karen. *When the Shooting Stops, the Cutting Begins: A Film Editor's Story*. New York: Da Capo, 1986.

Roth, Philip. *Reading Myself and Others*. New York: Farrar, Straus and Giroux, 1975.

Wilkes, Paul. "Goodbye Columbus, Hello Ali." *New York Times*, May 18, 1969.

38. A Serious Film

NORBERT SAMUELSON

A Serious Man, directed by Ethan and Joel Coen [A]
France, United States, United Kingdom, 2009

The first shot of *A Serious Man* is a quotation attributed to the medieval commentator Rashi that says, "Receive simply everything that happens to you." This lesson is a dominant theme in the film. The quotation is followed by a prologue that is seemingly independent of anything else that happens in the film. Commenting on this separate story, Joel Coen likens it to the cartoons or shorts that used to play before the main feature in the movie theaters of his youth. The Coens frame all of their work in terms of allusions to film history. But just because the Coens say this is why the short subject was made does not mean that they are telling the truth here about their intentions. This Eastern European Jewish preface closely parallels—in content, form, and literary setting—the opening three chapters of the Book of Job. However, a film, like any other kind of story, can have more than one level of meaning and of literary allusion.

The introductory scene is a traditional nineteenth-century Jewish fantasy, set on a cold winter night during a blizzard in an Eastern European village near Lublin. Returning to his modest home, Velvel (Allen Lewish Rickman) tells his wife, Dora (Yelena Schmulenson), that he helped someone on the road who said he was an old friend of Dora and identified himself as Reb Treitle Groshkover (Fyvush Finkel). Velvel says the man is a scholar of the Mishnah (that is, of Jewish law) and the Zohar (that is, of Jewish mysticism). Dora's expression shows that the information clearly upsets her. She says that "God has cursed us," because Treitle died three years earlier and has become a dybbuk—a man whose soul cannot leave his body because it is not yet clear whether it should be admitted into heaven or assigned to hell. The wife's reference to a curse parallels the curse of Job's wife in Job 2:9, which introduces a second theme of *A Serious Man* because the hero of the main story is himself a kind of dybbuk—a kind of living dead, like a zombie.

Velvel has invited the stranger to their cabin for a bowl of soup. Reb Groshkover knocks at the door and enters. When offered the soup he turns it down. Dora says that is because dybbuks don't eat. Velvel responds, "I don't believe in such things; I'm a rational man," but to prove her point Dora stabs an ice pick through Reb Groshkover's heart. The dybbuk, proven to be a dybbuk because he doesn't bleed and doesn't die, laughs and leaves, after which Dora says, "Blessed be the Lord; good riddance to evil," which parallels the

two lines given to the wife in the Book of Job: "You still keep your integrity! Blaspheme God and die!" (Job 2:9). Job responds (paralleling the supposed Rashi quotation), "Naked I came out of my mother's womb, and naked shall I return there; the Lord has given, and the Lord has taken away; blessed be the name of the Lord" (Job 1:21).

The main story of the film opens with Danny (Aaron Wolf), the son of Larry and Judith Gopnik (Michael Stuhlberg and Sari Lennick), wearing headphones in his synagogue Hebrew class, listening to "Don't You Need Somebody to Love" on his portable tape recorder, as the teacher, ignored by the entire class (an interesting critique of American Jewish education), conjugates the Hebrew sentence, *ani halach baita* (I am going home). Home, or the yearning to be able to go home, has already been introduced in the opening short subject. That marriage fails to provide a home is another theme I subsume under the category of "family."

While his son Danny is failing in Hebrew school, we see a brief flash of Danny's father failing a medical test at his doctor's office. He sits nervously, wearing only white underwear and high black socks as the doctor examines his ears and eyes. In terms of the Hebrew scriptures, he has eyes with which to see and ears with which to hear, but he neither hears nor sees anything happening in his life. The direct reference is Jeremiah 5:21, "Hear this, O foolish people, Devoid of intelligence, that have eyes but can't see, that have ears but can't hear!" But the theme of lacking hearing ears and seeing eyes occurs frequently in the prophetic writings with reference to both idols and idolaters. The Coens transform this statement about idolatry into a statement of the human condition that applies to the faithful no less than to the sinners.

The movie flashes back to Danny in Hebrew

school, placing a $20 bill in his tape recorder case to pass over to the next student, Fagle. The teacher confiscates the recorder as the class laughs. Fagle is the school's local drug dealer, and Danny owes him $20 for some pot. Danny stole the $20 from his sister Sarah (Jessica McManus), who stole it from her father's wallet. Now, however, the money is buried, undetected in the cassette player's case. The search to get back the lost money is a major story line, and the idea that unintentional actions bring unintended consequences is a major theme of the film.

Larry's physician offers Larry a cigarette while telling him "You're in good health." This is another joke, but it is also a good example of the long-term, ultimately disastrous, consequences of unintended (and therefore accidental) human actions on human lives. Thereafter we see Larry lecturing at the university where he teachers. He has filled a two-tiered blackboard with algebraic equations that express Werner Heisenberg's uncertainty principle, which Larry illustrates by relating Erwin Schrödinger's paradox of the cat in the box. That the audience recognizes the paradox and the equation, though both are unexplained in the film, is taken for granted. The students are asked, "Is the cat dead or is the cat alive?" Neither we nor the students nor Larry know the answer. As becomes clear through Judith's bungled attempt to divorce Larry, Larry is oblivious to what is happening around him outside of the physics classroom. Larry's physics students are as clueless and uninterested as Danny and his classmates in Hebrew school. At both levels of education, no one listens and understands. Both Larry and Schrödinger's cat are, like the dybbuk, neither alive nor dead.

Then we are introduced to a South Korean physics student, Clive Park (David Kang), who has come to Larry's office to complain about a grade he received on the test on the Heisenberg principle. Clive says that he understood the physics but not the math. Since he didn't know that the exam would be based on the math, he requests to retake the exam or to have his grade raised. Larry says no to both options because it wouldn't "be fair" to the other students, observing that "You can't understand the physics if you don't understand the math." Larry says that physics is just "stories" or "fables" (like the dybbuk story). It is the math, not the stories, that reveals reality. He tells Clive: "The stories I give you in class are just fables. The math tells you how it works." After Clive leaves the office in silence, Larry notices an envelope filled with money on his desk. Larry runs out of the office to catch Clive. When Clive left, Larry had been distracted by a phone call from the current nemesis of his life, his wife's lover and his university colleague, Sy Ableman (Fred Melamed).

It is in keeping with the Jobian fatalism of the film that Larry, like Job, does not do anything that matters in the plot. Both men are subject to horrendous accidents that change their lives, but they have not caused the events or directed their outcomes. Instead both Job and Larry must either reject their fate (curse God and die) or accept their fate (and live). Many unnamed people are God's agents in bringing about Job's fate, but they have no idea what or why they are doing. Larry's fate is affected by the actions of people who are unaware of what they are doing, including his wife, her lover, and Larry's children.

In the next scene we observe an American Jewish breakfast at the Gopnik home. Clearly the Gopniks are a dysfunctional family. Sarah is always angry. Her uncle, Larry's brother Arthur (Richard Kind), is barricaded in the bathroom, draining a sebaceous cyst growing on the back of his neck. In their bathroom confrontation, both

Arthur and Sarah are struggling over futile passions—Arthur's to remove the cyst that will not go away, and Sarah's to wash her hair, which she thinks will make her beautiful. At one point in the film, Larry quips that Sarah chose not to study for a bat mitzvah because washing her hair took all of her time.

The children leave their horrendous family to join their horrendous classmates on the school bus (where we learn why Fagle is always chasing Danny to get paid his dope money), which is seen from their colorless, ugly neighborhood comprised of mass-produced houses built after World War II. It is a world utterly lacking in value or meaning. Inside their house, Larry sits grading exams when his wife tells him that she wants a divorce and that she and Sy "are very close." Presumably they are having sex, but both are so manipulative and pathetic in their own ways—Sy pretends to be feeling and sensitive and is obviously neither, and Judith pretends to care about the welfare of her family but cares only about herself—that it is possible that they don't have sex, or that if they do, it's not very good sex. We learn later that Larry's tenure committee has been receiving anonymous letters written by Sy, accusing Larry of immorality. The Gopniks and the Ablemans have been neighbors for fifteen years. Esther, Sy's wife, died three years ago, but Judith tells Larry that their life together "was a loveless marriage." Undoubtedly it was loveless, but everything we learn about their characters tells us that a marriage of Sy and Judith would be no less loveless than the Ableman and Gopnik marriages. At this point we know only that Sy is the only one of these four Jews who is religiously observant. He insists that Larry give Judith a *get* (a writ of divorce that the husband transmits to the wife through a rabbi) so that Judith will not become an *agunah* (a woman who cannot remarry for lack of a *get* or proof that her husband is dead). Sy seems to be the only one who knows what a *get* (let alone an *agunah*) is, including the rabbis.

Sy comes to the door bearing a (Trojan?) gift, a bottle of wine, but the gift is more an attack than a genuine gift, since he goes on and on about how this is "a real wine" and nothing like the sweet Jewish wine that Larry drinks at Jewish family liturgical functions, like weddings and bar mitzvahs. The gift is followed by a smothering hug that is no less manipulative than the gift. Those in the film who talk most about being sensitive seem to be least sensitive, especially when they try to be sensitive. This, of course, is another joke, as the Coen brothers put down the expertise of professors, rabbis, and therapists.

The manipulative Sy and Judith take Larry out to dinner to convince him that it would be better for all concerned if Larry would move out of his house (rather than having Judith move into Sy's house) and take a room for himself and his brother at a nearby hotel. That Larry actually agrees to this without resistance is astounding. His passivity reinforces the identity of Larry as the hero who is admonished at the very opening of the film with Rashi's advice, "Receive simply everything that happens to you." In addition, Larry's acceptance of this demand contributes to his success at the end of the film. Because of this arrangement Sy drives daily, at the very time that Larry drives to the university, from Judith's house to play golf. Pulling out of the driveway, Sy is hit by another car coming around a blind corner and killed. Ableman's death and funeral are the first steps in the Book of Job's theme of reestablishing divine order in this little universe, for with the death of Sy, the villain, the Gopnik family is seemingly reunited, whether for good or for bad.

At this point the film returns to the subplot of the confrontation between Larry and his South

Korean student. Clive denies that he left the money. Larry says, "Actions always have consequences" to which Clive responds, "Yes, often." In turn, Larry angrily replies, "No, in this office always." Actually the scene is a lovely little joke about the new physics, in which the student demonstrates that he understands the lesson of Heisenberg and Schrödinger better than his teacher, at least as they may be applicable to the laws of morality. In Larry's world the universe is Newtonian—that is, it follows strict laws of cause-and-effect determinism. What Larry eventually learns is that what is true of quantum mechanics—or at least quantum mechanics as the Coen brothers understand it—is true of life as well: nothing is determined. For all our wisdom, we don't know anything.

Later Clive's father, Steven Park, visits Larry and complicates this subplot further. He gives Larry a choice between raising Clive's grade or being sued for defamation of Clive's character. Larry points out the logical inconsistency of the father's offer. He can't have it both ways. The threat to sue Larry for defamation presupposes that there was no real threat, but the use of extortion to raise the grade proves that there was a threat, and therefore the charge Larry leveled is true. But logic is of no avail. Clive's father calmly responds, "Accept the mystery." In both life and physics the real teachers are Clive and his father, while the professor is the slow learner.

In the next scene we see Danny studying for his bar mitzvah by memorizing the Hebrew text and chanting on a cassette provided by his school. It is apparent that whatever Danny is learning from Hebrew school, it is neither how to read nor how to chant Hebrew. Danny is stuck on the first half of the first verse of his portion, *vayomer adonai el moshe lamor* (and the Lord spoke to Moses, saying). God said something to Moses, but neither we nor Danny has any idea what it was. Similarly, Larry seeks advice from three rabbis (as Job constantly asks his three so-called friends), asking what he is supposed to learn from his seemingly meaningless suffering, but neither Larry nor Job ever gets an answer to the question.

Danny is just as shallow as his hair-washing, religiously uneducated sister. Danny is obsessed with adjusting the rooftop antenna of the family TV so he can watch the program *F Troop*. Danny even calls his father at the office of his divorce lawyer to tell him to come home and fix the antenna. When Larry comes home, Danny asks him if he has fixed the antenna, and Judith asks if he has seen a divorce lawyer. Posed sequentially, these two questions seem equally significant. In other words, the wife's demand for a divorce is just as shallow and just as much a vain pursuit of hedonism as is the son's demand to watch *F Troop*. Larry screams, "What's going on?" For the first time, he recognizes that there is something wrong with his life, that it lacks the meaning that any life should have.

The life of Larry's brother, Arthur, now moves to the center of the plot. Arthur's life, while superficially being very different, closely parallels Larry's. Arthur was born with the same native ability of his brother to think complex thoughts in mathematical language, and Arthur used his talent to develop something called a pentaculus. We see what it is in a notebook that Arthur always carries with him, and we realize that it is his academically untrained counterpart to Heisenberg's principle. However, its purpose is not to solve the mysteries of the universe. Rather, it has the more limited function of providing a system for success in gambling with the small-time local gentile gamblers in the Gopniks' Minnesota town.

At this point we are introduced to the only non-Jews in this secular American Jewish biblical commentary on the problem of divine justice in nature. They are Larry's neighbors, Mr. Brandt (Peter Breitmayer) and his son, Mitch (Brent Braunschweig), who are constantly together (unlike Larry and his children), seemingly enjoying a physical life of playing baseball and hunting deer. The roles of the non-Jewish neighbors are minor; their only plot function seems to be to highlight what we will see as the Jewish community story develops: that whatever happiness there is to discover in life, the Jewish family (contrary to popular Jewish belief) is in no favored position over its gentile neighbors.

Now the plot refocuses on the main characters, the Jewish community and its rabbis, in Larry's quest for meaning. Judith, the Jewish wife, empties Larry's bank account even though she continues to send him the bills for both Sy's funeral and Danny's bar mitzvah. Larry finally goes to see an attorney (Adam Arkin), who advises Larry to go see their synagogue's elderly retired rabbi, Rabbi Marshak (Alan Mandell), whom Larry's secular Jewish lawyer calls "a very wise man." Larry never gets to talk to him. The elderly and presumably wise Marshak talks only to bar mitzvah boys on the day of their bar mitzvah and, as we shall see with Danny, he doesn't really tell them anything (maybe).

At a Hillel picnic (presumably a singles mixer), Larry discusses the meaning of his life with a female friend in leg braces. He says to her, "What does that mean: that everything that I thought was one way was another?" For all his wisdom about how the universe runs, he knows nothing about his own life. The woman says: "Then it's an opportunity to learn the way things really are. It's not easy deciphering what God is trying to tell you. . . . And that's something you'll have to figure out all by yourself. We Jews, we have that well of tradition to draw on to help us understand.

When we are puzzled, we have the stories handed down by people who have had the same problems." We in the audience know enough to tell that the synagogue, the rabbis, and their messages to their congregation, are Conservative, not Orthodox, because they do heterodox things like having mixed seating in services, and not Reform, because they are far too liturgically traditional. Therefore what is passed on from Judaism as religious thought are stories—not creeds, not theology, and not philosophy. The crippled female friend's advice to Larry to make sense out of his life is to see the rabbi and to listen to his stories.

Requesting to see the congregation's active senior rabbi, Rabbi Nachtner (George Wyner), Larry is instead given an appointment with the junior rabbi, Rabbi Scott (Simon Helberg). Meeting with the junior rabbi signifies the low esteem that his congregation has for Larry. Whereas Rabbi Nachtner dresses in a suit, Rabbi Scott appears in a short-sleeved shirt and tie. Larry tells his story, but after asking what a *get* is (as did Larry's lawyer), Rabbi Scott drops Larry's story altogether and preaches a sermon about God's existence. He says, "If you can see Ha-Shem [God] in the world, things aren't so bad; look at the parking lot." There seems to be no obvious connections between the parking lot and God's existence; it seems to be merely a stream of consciousness (and therefore accidental association) because while talking. Scott has totally lost any focus on Larry and looked out the window at the lot. What the camera shows is an ugly gravel expanse, which quickly fades into the street on which Larry lives. There is a connection between Larry's lot and the parking lot. Both are ugly, as ugly as Larry's life seems to be, and this ugliness presumably is the world that God created.

Larry meets with Rabbi Nachtner and again tells his story. At first the rabbi listens and asks if

Larry would want everything to go back to the way it was. Larry admits that he would, but as a rational scientist, he knows that it cannot. He asks the concrete Jobian questions: "What was my life before? . . . What does it all mean? What is Ha-Shem trying to tell me?" The rabbi, like Job's so-called friends, cannot give an answer. Job's friends covered up their ignorance with orthodox theological clichés. Rabbi Nachtner covers up his ignorance with his stock story about "The Goy's Teeth."

The story parallels the opening tale about the dybbuk. It illustrates how traditional Judaism adjusts to new circumstances, transposing itself from the premodern mystical world of the Eastern European *shtetl* (small village) to the modern, secularized capitalist world. The film often plays in the background a Yiddish song about the demise of the *shtetl*. In the present, some Jews learn Heisenberg rather than Rashi, and work as professionals or professors in gentile universities rather than as Jewish peddlers. The mystery of the dybbuk is transformed into the miracle of the engraved dentures. A Jewish orthodontist, working on the teeth of a goy (a non-Jew), discovers the Hebrew word *hoshiy'ani*, which means "save me," engraved on the inside of his lower incisors. He interprets the numerical value of the seven Hebrew letters to be "8,454,473," which turns out to be the telephone number of a grocery store in Bloomington, Indiana. The dentist goes there, but finds nothing. For a while the dentist vainly looks at the incisors of other gentiles to find engraved Hebrew messages. Eventually he stops looking.

This event was, in the language of physics, a singularity, as was God's creation of the world of endless, ugly, seemingly meaningless parking lots and suburban neighborhoods. But this is not what Rabbi Nachtner sees in the story. In-

stead, he preaches: "What does it mean? Is the answer in Torah? In Kabbalah [Jewish mysticism]? Or is there even a question?" The rabbi, like Job's friends and even God, offers no answer. Instead, he questions the question, saying "Ha-Shem doesn't owe us the answer." But the Jobian Larry protests, "Why does He [God] make us feel the questions if He's not going to give the answers?" The rabbi responds with a big smile and a typical Coen brothers' joke: "He hasn't told me." Larry seems to care more about the personal than the abstract. "What happened to the goy?" he demands, and the rabbi responds, "The goy? Who cares?" What the rabbi says about his story in the name of Judaism, Larry subsequently says about the equations he has written on the blackboard. After he finishes writing them, Larry, this spokesman for modern science, declares, "It proves we can't ever really know what's going on." Science and the rabbi agree. Larry adds, "But you'll still be responsible for it on the midterm." Even though we can't understand what the principle says, we are nonetheless responsible for what it means; similarly, we—like Larry—cannot understand what life means, but nonetheless we remain responsible for our lives.

Rabbi Nachtner is not one to care about real people. We see that clearly at Sy Ableman's funeral, where the rabbi's eulogy has nothing to do with the real Sy. First the rabbi calls Sy a *lamed vav-nik* (that is, one of the thirty-six righteous people in each generation for whose sake God endures the evil world and allows it to continue to survive), which Sy clearly was not. Then the rabbi drops even the pretense of talking about the deceased to preach about redemption in the world to come. As it turns out, Larry must pay for Sy's funeral because Sy's estate is in probate.

Meanwhile, Arthur is picked up by the police and charged with sodomy. Larry is given hints by the head of his tenure committee, Arlen Finkle (Ari Hoptman), that the anonymous letters charging Larry with improper moral behavior have placed his otherwise certain tenure in doubt. Larry cries out in protest: "I'm not an evil man. I haven't done anything" (although he does confess that he hasn't published anything, either).

Larry's cry of despair is matched and raised by the despair of his brother. Arthur lies awake at night and cries: "God hasn't given me shit. Now I can't even play cards." Arthur played to find companionship. For him, devising the pentaculus facilitated his playing and winning. He gave the money he won to Danny, to pay off his debt to Fagle. In the end Larry saves his brother's life. He drives Arthur to a lake on the Canadian border and sends him off in a canoe to start a new life. As he paddles away, Arthur calls out to his brother, "Larry, I'm sorry what I said last night." Arthur's life is not empty of meaning. It is saved by the love of his brother. Love is another frequent theme in the Coen brothers' movies, which usually depict love between human beings, especially within families, as the answer to the meaninglessness of life.

Danny has his bar mitzvah. Despite being stoned on grass and blanking out at first, he performs successfully. His success motivates Larry and Judith to reconnect in their marriage. Larry gets a notice telling him that he was awarded tenure, implicitly because the accidental death of Sy prevented him from writing any more anonymous letters to the tenure committee.

Near the end of the film, paralleling the opening scene in Eastern Europe, Danny meets with Rabbi Marshak. The rabbi gives Danny the following words of wisdom: "When the truth is found to be lies and all hope within you dies, then what?" Expressing a central theme of the story, the words have been taken from the rock song by the Jefferson Airplane, which Danny played at the beginning of the movie. The old world rabbi had been holding Danny's tape recorder and had listened to the music on the tape left in it. He then returns the recorder to Danny and tells him, his final words of wisdom, "Be a good boy!"

All seems resolved in this happy ending. However, the Coen brothers do not end anything on such an upbeat note. Beyond every salvation lies another catastrophe. Dr. Len Shapiro (Raye Birk) calls Larry to tell him that his most recent x-rays seem problematic, and Danny and Fagle look beyond the schoolyard at an approaching tornado. The latter alludes to the "mighty wind" that destroys the home of Job's brother and kills Job's children (Job 1:19).

Although truth may not be their prime concern, the Coen brothers are very much interested in studying community, and sometimes the community studied is Jewish. Three communal institutions are commonly critiqued in their films—law enforcement, education, and family.

The preemancipation experience of hostility between Jewish communities and their antisemitic host societies left a legacy of distrust between law enforcement and Jews after their immigration to the United States. That hostility probably was a factor not only in the involvement of some first-generation Jewish immigrants in organized crime, but also in the kinds of slapstick jokes used by early film heroes and policemen, from police chases in silent film comedies to Woody Allen's hysterical way of handling a policeman's traffic ticket in *Annie Hall*. The Coens employ this treatment of the police from earlier Jewish comedies not so much as a social commentary on the police, but as a humorous invocation of a common film stereotype. We see this in the two clearly non-Jewish cops who harass Larry's brother, Arthur.

Education earns only slightly more respect as

a community institution. Most Coen films find fault with all kinds of education, from the secular university to the synagogue and Hebrew school. The misuse of Heisenberg's uncertainty principle in *A Serious Man* has direct precedence in *The Man Who Wasn't There*. For example, Doris's skilled defense lawyer bases her defense on Heisenberg's principle. You can't convict a person of murder, he argues, if you have a reasonable doubt, and modern science teaches that everything is in doubt.

More sacred for the Coens than the schools is the family, but it is far from being a spiritually, intellectually, or morally healthy institution. Larry's son can think only about watching *F Troop*, and his daughter's only thoughts are about washing her hair. Larry's marriage to Judith was apparently loveless. Larry cheats on Judith with Mrs. Samsky, his sexually liberated neighbor, whose husband always seems to be away. All of this illustrates how flawed the institution of marriage is in our modern world. Marriage may be a reasonable way of achieving financial security, but it is a bad way to try to find happiness. Whatever the value of the family, clearly in many of their films, the Coens believe that human beings need love. In *A Serious Man* the verse from the Jefferson Airplane is often repeated: "Don't you need somebody to love?" Larry's support of his brother, despite the charges lodged against him, constitutes sincere concern.

Clearly, the Coens' most consistent theme is what I characterize as a Jobian belief in cosmic chance coupled with considerable skepticism about the efficacy of human choice. This theme is the most pertinent one to the Jewish theology of their films. Before turning to cosmic determinism, I want to highlight what they say about dreams, Judaism, and the Jewish people. In the Hebrew scriptures, most transmissions of divine revelation through spiritual people like the prophets occur by means of dreams. Generally, dreams are the mechanism that the Coen brothers employ to provide footnotes to their plots. In other films they considered returning home as a form of salvation. The Hebrew lesson in *A Serious Man* teaches the sentence *ani halach baita* (I am going home). Larry longs to return home from the hotel room where he has been banished during his pending divorce from Judith.

Clearly *A Serious Man* is the most overtly Jewish film of all the Coen brothers' works. For the Coens, American antisemitism seems to be more a humorous than a serious problem. The police in *A Serious Man* are ignorant of who or what Jews are, and are ostensibly antisemitic only out of ignorance. Yet anxiety about the potential danger of antisemitism is real, as evidenced by the nightmare Larry has about his gentile neighbor and the man's son shooting Arthur on one of their hunting excursions. The Coens are not antisemites. They, like Philip Roth (in fiction) and Mel Brooks (in films), are sufficiently secure and comfortable with their Jewish and American identities to satirize stereotypes that don't really fit Jewish Americans like them. To assure the audience of their comic rather than malicious intent, the final credits assert that "no Jews were harmed in the making of this film."

The Coens are aware of the importance of religious ritual in Jewish life. Communal rituals are important in their films. Danny's bar mitzvah seems to be redemptive because it stimulates the restoration of Larry and Judith's marriage, at least for the moment.

Except for the very few cases where there is real marital love, most of life, according to Joel and Ethan Coen, happens without any discernible meaning. There does not seem to be anything you can do about it. This is one possible way of reading the lesson of the opening and concluding narrative of the Book of Job. What happens to Job is not because of what he did but because of a cosmic gamble between God and Satan. In the end, after Job's book-length search for (in the words of Larry in *A Serious Man*) "what it all means," he is only told to stop asking and just accept, which he does. "I have heard you with my ears, but now I see you with my eyes; therefore I recant and relent [still without an explanation], being but dust and ashes" (Job 42:5–6). It echoes the quotation from Rashi with which *A Serious Man* began, "Receive simply everything that happens to you."

All quotations from the Hebrew scriptures are taken from the English translation in *JPS Hebrew-English Tanakh: The Traditional Hebrew Text and the New* JPS Translation, 2nd ed. (Philadelphia: Jewish Publication Society, 1999).

Source: Ethan and Joel Coen, *A Serious Man*, (London: Faber and Faber, 2009).

Background: http://www.fordham.edu/halsall/ancient/job-rsv.html.

Bibliography

Allen, William Rodney, ed. *The Coen Brothers: Interviews*. Jackson: University Press of Mississippi, 2006.

Bergan, Ronald. *The Coen Brothers*. New York: Thunder's Mouth, 2000.

Conrad, Mark T. *The Philosophy of the Coen Brothers*. Lexington: University of Kentucky Press, 2009.

Doom, Ryan F. *The Brothers Coen: Unique Characters of Violence*. Santa Barbara, CA: Praeger, 2009.

Falsani, Cathleen. *The Dude Abides: The Gospel According to the Coen Brothers*. Grand Rapids, MI: Zondervan, 2009.

Levine, Josh. *The Coen Brothers: The Story of Two American Filmmakers*. Toronto: Ecco, 2000.

Rowell, Erica. *The Brothers Coen: The Films of Ethan and Joel Coen*. Lanham, MD: Scarecrow, 2007.

39. When Chippewa Falls Meets Manhattan

SYLVIA BARACK FISHMAN

Annie Hall, directed by Woody Allen [A]
United States, 1977

During the 1960s and 1970s, American culture percolated with unrest produced by the Vietnam War and its protesters, civil rights activists, second-wave feminism, and diverse ethnic pride movements. Spurred by a new fascination both with ethnic roots and with the differing ways males and females experience ethnicity, commercial American films began to feature colorful characters and situations exploring the intersection between Jewishness and gender. These films marked a dramatic change from American films of the 1930s and 1940s, when ethnic material had been largely suppressed, and the years immediately after World War II, when portrayals of Jews tended to be pleas for tolerance (*Gentleman's Agreement*, 1947) earnest evocations of suffering (*The Pawnbroker*, 1965), or both (*The Diary of Anne Frank*, 1959). The emerging film style also diverged from the heroic (*Exodus*, 1960) or nostalgic (*Fiddler on the Roof*, 1971) tones of Technicolor celebrations of Jewishness.

Replacing these kinds of portrayals of Jews, a plethora of satiric cinematic images of Jewish women and men began to fill the screen. The Jewish male as hustler or anxious worrier, and the Jewish female as overbearing mother or spoiled and demanding princess, rapidly became dominant stereotypes. To be fair, these images were not entirely unprecedented. Yiddish literature, theater, and film had certainly included portrayals of dishonest, entrepreneurial men, ineffectual

Shown from left: Opposites attract temporarily as Woody Allen (as Alvy Singer) and Diane Keaton (as Annie Hall) stroll through Central Park. From *Annie Hall* (1977), directed by Woody Allen. UNITED ARTISTS/PHOTOFEST

wimps, schlemazels and schlemiels, and loud-mouthed or shrewish women, along with para-gons of male piety and female competence. Simi-lar stereotypes were common in nineteenth-century antisemitic writings. But the attention to Jewishness, together with the portrayal of Ameri-can Jewish hybridity that contextualized satiric depictions of Jews in American Jewish films in the 1960s and 1970s, was arguably unprecedented in history. These films, and the novels on which many of them were based, were important antece-dents to the emergence of Woody Allen as the iconic cinematic voice of American Jewishness.

At the hands of a prolific flock of Jewish filmmakers, Jews were pictured as exemplars of middle-class mores—and the butt of cinematic critiques of consumerism. Directors like Paul Mazursky made fun of pretentious middle-class Jews preoccupied by their possessions, devoted to self-gratification, and oblivious to the suffering of others and to deeper concerns in life. In cinematic renditions of the works of novelists Jerome Weid-man and Canada's Mordecai Richler, to cite two of many examples, Jewish men are depicted as ruthlessly ambitious and immoral businessmen. A more frequent caricature of Jewish men in American media, however, was the overly intel-lectual, fearful, and not very virile cautious man.

Liberated by the rise of multiculturalism rather than the melting pot, humorist filmmakers such as Mel Brooks and stand-up comics like Alan King, Jackie Mason, Joan Rivers, and others found that overtly (and sometimes abrasive) Jewish humor was immensely salable and began including Jewish materials in their language, plots, and references in their comic routines. Jewish men as the hustler and the wimp were unforgettably brought to the screen in Mel Brooks's original comedy, *The Producers* (1968), starring the comic geniuses Zero Mostel and Gene Wilder. Indeed, the transition from Zero Mostel's ethnically unidentified performance in the musical comedy *A Funny Thing Happened on the Way to the Forum* (1966), only two years earlier, to the edgy, transgressive Jewish humor of *The Producers* hilariously illustrates the shift in cultural paradigms.

Liberated to satirize and hyperbolize Jewish foibles, Jewish writers and moviemakers frequently took an intensively gendered approach. Jewish men were often portrayed as sensitive, responsible—if overly anxious—souls, but Jewish women characters were more savagely satirized. Together, the novelists Herman Wouk and Philip Roth launched in the public imagination negative stereotypical images of Jewish women. In his 1955 novel, *Marjorie Morningstar*, Wouk introduced readers to the Jewish daughter known as the "Shirley"—the ultimate bourgeois consumer who wants a "big diamond engagement ring, house in a good neighborhood, furniture, children, well-made clothes, furs," and so on. A year after the film version of *Marjorie Morningstar* (1958), Philip Roth's novella *Goodbye, Columbus* created an even less likable version of the kind of woman who came to be known as the Jewish American Princess, or JAP: the coolly controlling Brenda Patimkin, heiress to a Jewish plumbing fortune.

One of the primary characteristics of these upper-middle-class young Jewish women was their skill in using sexual favors to manipulate would-be suitors.

A decade later, Roth contributed the domineering Jewish mother Sophie Portnoy, who pointed a bread knife at Alex, her son, to eliminate his resistance to dinner. Understandably neurotic and sexually obsessed, Roth's protagonist poured his heart out to his psychiatrist for nearly 300 pages, graphically detailing his yearning to have sexual relationships with blond American women, both out of lust for the American way of life and aggressive sexualized hatred for its insipid bourgeois stupidity. Portnoy condemned not only his parents, but Jewish religious culture as well, requiring a "kosher and bloodless" existence, "self-control, sobriety, sanctions—this is the key to human life, saith all those endless dietary laws" (*Portnoy's Complaint*, 80–81). In a double whammy to the image of the Jewish woman, within months of the publication of *Portnoy's Complaint* (1967), the film version of *Goodbye, Columbus* brought to the screen the first extended ostentatious, food-obsessed Jewish wedding scene, with aging, sequined Jewish matrons dripping their sagging décolletage over platters of chopped liver.

While these negative, satirical images were becoming stereotypes on the American screen in the 1960s, Woody Allen, a voracious consumer of film and literature and a prolific writer of humorous and sometimes thoughtful explorations of cinematic and literary themes, was producing comic films that included few if any overtly Jewish materials. By the late 1970s, however, Allen turned his cinematic focus to satirical analysis of the identifying characteristics of Jewish—and non-Jewish—families.

By the time that Allen was creating *Annie Hall* (1977), cinematic portrayals of hustling or wimpish Jewish men, and especially of loud, manipulative Jewish mothers and high-maintenance, petulant Jewish daughters had been burned into the public consciousness. The gendered manifestations of Jewish assimilation had also been laid out on the American screen. In *Annie Hall*, Allen brilliantly reworks, unpacks, and analyzes those stereotypes.

Woody Allen directed *Annie Hall*, which he wrote with Marshall Brickman, and stars as the film's protagonist, Alvy Singer. With one deft touch after another, the film captures the quixotic nature of sexual attraction between men and women of different ethnic, religious, and cultural backgrounds. Alvy Singer, a scrawny, intellectual, thin-skinned, and nervous Jewish male, recalls that his first wife, Allison Porchnik, was ideal for him in every way: she was "beautiful, willing, and intelligent." However, Carol Kane's ironic, frizzy-maned Allison is luminously Jewish in every way. The two meet at an Adlai Stevenson campaign rally, and Alvy declares on first meeting her that she is clearly the product of a New York Jewish environment, socialist summer camps, Jewish artistic sensibilities, and Brandeis University. "I love being reduced to a cultural stereotype," Allison shoots back, thereby invoking yet another Jewish woman stereotype: the big mouth. The two share political attitudes, intellectual consciousness, social concerns, and artistic tendencies. Their verbal battles ring incessantly in their book-filled apartment, as Alvy uses fights about political issues as a way of avoiding sex as their marriage falls apart. Their marriage fails, Alvy muses, because Alison is Jewish, and thus not sufficiently exotic and inaccessible—neither one of them represents middle America.

Diane Keaton's Annie Hall, on the other hand, is a gentile female-female in the tradition of the "dizzy dames" of 1930s and 1940s romantic comedies. Tall, long-legged, willowy, and born with straight, fair hair, she can eat lobsters even though they scuttle across the kitchen floor like monstrous black roaches. Unlike the clever, articulate, politically active, and self-confident Jewish Allison, Annie has little self-confidence, knows less of the world, and can hardly string two words together coherently: "Ah, well, lah de dah, lah de dah," is her idea of a conversation. Alvy Singer is bewitched by her utter unlikeness to any woman he has ever known, and he falls head over heels in love.

The contrast between New York Jewish and Midwestern non-Jewish families is rendered in stunning chiaroscuro when Alvy and Annie fly out to Wisconsin to have Easter dinner with Annie Hall's bland, blond American family. There, in a clean, open dining room flooded with Midwestern brightness, Alvy describes his fifteen-year psychiatric treatment to Annie's tall, beautiful mother and father, who sip endless alcoholic drinks in calm bewilderment at his every ironic quip. In his head, at least, every stereotype Alvy holds about Christian antisemitism is upheld in the chilly Hall household, where people talk of perfectly cooked hams, boats, and swap meets. Mrs. Hall complains that Randolph Hunt got drunk. "You remember Randy Hunk, Annie," she says, parodying Jewish perceptions of gentile names. Alvy imagines that Grammy—"a classic Jew hater"—sees him as an alien, red-bearded Hasid.

Woody Allen uses a split-screen technique to juxtapose Alvy Singer's family—talking incessantly (and simultaneously) about death and disease, wolfing huge quantities of food down in a dark, crowded dining room in their house underneath an amusement park ride in Coney Island—with the Halls. While Annie's Grammy says that "Jews just make money," and gives her darling granddaughter charming gifts, Alvy responds morosely: "My granny never gave gifts. She was too busy being raped by Cossacks." These people are nothing like his family, Alvy observes. "They look very American and very healthy, like they never get sick." But the scene indicates that under the vapid veneer of normalcy, bourgeois white America may hide festering ills: Annie's father says he can't drive to the airport because he hasn't finished his drink. And Alvy may be neurotic, but Annie's strong, handsome brother is revealed to be a delusional psychotic who yearns to crash his car into oncoming traffic as he drives them to the airport in blinding rain.

When Alvy "gets" Annie—at least for a portion of the picture—Woody Allen is turning a long-standing romantic film convention on its head. Prior to *Annie Hall*, the male lead was almost never identified as belonging to a minority group. Although Jewish actors with non-Jewish names sometimes starred in romantic films, their film personas were usually deracinated and they were not identified as minorities. Roles for identified Jewish men—like roles for African American men—were auxiliary slots, included in order to carry a subtext of importance to the film, or to provide a comic foil. (This is, of course, a convention that has changed dramatically in recent decades.)

Thus, when Woody Allen introduced Alvy Singer as a clearly and stereotypically ethnic Jewish male lead who pursues, tries to save, but ultimately rejects the eroticized Annie Hall, the brilliance of the film arises partially from the ways in which Allen subverts the Hollywood formula. Allen seems to be "passing" as a romantic lead, despite his hyperbolic Jewishness. But in the film's memorable Easter dinner in Chippewa Falls, discussed above, Grammy Hall is symbolically "outing" the Jew who dares to stand in narrative shoes that should be occupied by a real American. Woody Allen—like Philip Roth and others who ushered in a wave of novels, films, and television programs in which an overtly Jewish male embraces an eroticized perfect woman who is a sweet and cool and bland as "custard," in Roth's words (*Portnoy's Complaint*, p. 151)—portrayed a brave new Hollywood in which a Jewish man's "nose" and "name" have "become as nothing," because "for every Eddie [Cantor] yearning for a Debbie, there is a Debbie yearning for an Eddie" (*Portnoy's Complaint*, p. 152). For the Allison Porchniks of American film, the next step would be fading into near-oblivion, as subsequent cinematic and television portrayals of Jews focus almost exclusively on men, with only the ubiquitous (and usually unpleasant) "Jewish mother" character incorporated to establish the hero's Jewish bona fides.

Encapsulated in scenes that are sometimes just a few minutes long, *Annie Hall* glosses the social psychology and politics of differing types of American Jews. Alvy Singer's excruciatingly sensitive social conscience, for example, is more than a personal quirk—it is also Woody Allen's take on the American Jewish sensibility. The African American woman who cleans Alvy Singer's parents' lower-middle-class apartment weekly is allowed to steal from them because, as Alvy's father says, "she suffered enough," and "from whom else should she steal?" Sociological measurements show that American Jews as a group continue to be far more liberal than other Americans who enjoy similar levels of educational, occupational, financial, and social success. In election after election, Jews in the middle and upper middle classes vote more like blacks, Hispanics, and unemployed people than like other affluent white Americans. Even after the pain of being eased out of leadership positions in the civil rights movement, American Jews continued to identify with those they perceived as downtrodden, in a kind of continuity with the idealistic political consciousness and activism that stretches back in some families to the socialist and union activities of the immigrant generation. The Singer family's political liberalism is thus a social characteristic, as well as a comic motif.

Annie Hall also captures the typical American Jewish lack of depth in matters religious and spiritual: the family fasts in celebration of Yom Kippur "to atone for our sins," for example, but confesses they don't know what sins they have committed, or why they have to fast for them. Religion, per se, is not a subject that Allen is particularly attentive to in this particular film (although he certainly explores religiosity in subsequent films). In contrast to the shallowness of his religious reflections, Alvy Singer's awareness of and sensitivity to antisemitism is developed to the edge of paranoia. Obsessed by antisemitism and the Holocaust, Alvy feels that he is the butt of constant antisemitic remarks. "The rest of the country thinks that we [New Yorkers] are left-wing Communist Jewish homosexual pornographers," he complains. "I live here and I think of us sometimes like that." Alvy hears anti-Jewish slurs everywhere. In one memorable scene, a seemingly empty New York sidewalk and street fills the screen, stretching into the urban horizon. The viewer hears a conversation between Woody Allen and Tony Roberts, but doesn't see them. As the conversation proceeds, two tiny people emerge, entering the frame of the screen from the back, walking up the street toward the front of the frame and the camera. By the time the viewer can see who these two men are, the subject of their conversation has already been revealed: ubiquitous antisemitism. "Did you hear what he said to me?" Alvy

demands incredulously of his tall, savvy friend, "He said, 'Jew eat.' Not 'did you eat'—Jew eat! Jew eat!'"

Alvy wants to be fully aware in every encounter, partially because he is terrified of what may happen if he is not always, and fully, attentive and in charge, and partially because that kind of alertness is a particular New York style. Annie, on the other hand, frequently seeks substances that will blur life's troubling edges. When Alvy insists that she have sex with him without first relaxing through marijuana, Annie is so removed from their sexual encounter that she leaves her prone body lying on the bed with Alvy, while her ghostlike consciousness walks around the room, commenting on various topics.

Not only Alvy and Annie but also all the other characters serve as foils for each other, especially the relationship between Allen and Roberts, who eventually moves to California, home of sunshine, casual clothing, and the phoniness of the Hollywood movie set. The West Coast is presented as cultural anathema to the born-and-bred New Yorker, just as fully as Midwestern Christendom is anathema to the New York Jew. Los Angeles show-business entrepreneur Tony Lacey, played with delicious sleaze by Paul Simon, convinces Annie Hall that her future lies in California sunshine, opportunity, and happiness, rather than in Alvy Singer's edgy, suspicious New York.

Ultimately, Alvy's relationship with Annie is doomed, in part because of the binary outlook with which he sees the Jewish and non-Jewish worlds that he and she represent, respectively, but also because of his preoccupation with antisemitism and his squeamish revulsion with the imperfections of the world. "I'm obsessed with death," Alvy admits. "I think life is divided into two categories—the horrible and the miserable." He takes dates and ex-wives to see long documentary films about the victims of the Nazis. He knows that "if one guy is starving somewhere it puts a crimp in my evening," and that "I don't respond well to mellow."

When Alvy Singer and Annie Hall break up, the room in which they divide their household goods features a prominent Christmas tree studded with ornaments, and a lonely pair of Sabbath candlesticks on the mantelpiece. "You think I'm not smart enough for you," Annie accuses Alvy, repeatedly and accurately. Annie also accuses Alvy of acting as though he and, by implication, other Jews—while not necessarily physically robust—are intellectually and morally superior to non-Jews like her.

Sociological studies reveal the kernels of truth in Woody Allen's manipulation of familial and ethnic stereotypes. Families were in transition in the 1970s and seemed to be fighting for survival even in their most limited nuclear incarnation, with larger percentages of the population delaying or avoiding marriage, and increasing numbers of romantic liaisons and marriage ending in separation or divorce. Intermarriage rates grew among every population, as images of the warm, controlling, irritating extended ethnic family gave way to a new model: the multicultural household. American Jews who were simultaneously proud of and embarrassed about—and very defensive of—their Jewishness became romantically involved with non-Jews at increasing rates as the decades passed. For some Jews, gentile mates seemed healthier, less neurotic, and certainly less obsessed with historical and contemporary catastrophes. However, as films such as *Annie Hall* suggest, some Jews were both drawn to and repelled by the innate moral innocence of their lovers, for whom historical evil did not seem to be quite real. This in-

nocence sometimes seemed to provide the gentile partner with protection against evil itself. The ebb and flow of sexual activity among Alvy and his friends; their relationships with their therapists; Alvy's continuing dislike of authority figures, including teachers; and the repeated evidence of his anxiety about cosmic issues all provide the film with important clues about what motivates this particular type of character. Alvy Singer is the definitive figure of the secular, urban Jewish male of his generation, who acknowledged his debt to Groucho Marx when he revealed, "I would never join a club that would admit me."

Woody Allen's *Annie Hall* explores ethnicity and gendered relationships by using deliberate hyperbole and satire, while at the same time exercising rigorous artistic control over the whole project. The subject matter and characters in this film are typically over the top, while cinematically, scenes are cut with exquisite precision, juxtaposed with breathtaking perfection, never a second too long. The effect was exhilarating, fresh, and startling when it first appeared. *Annie Hall* won an Oscar for best picture, unusual for a comedy. Today, most younger American Jews see themselves very differently than the way Woody Allen and his generation saw themselves. His division of the world into "us" and "them," for example, has all but disappeared among American Jews in their twenties and thirties. The concerns about assimilation that dominated his generation have been replaced by pluralism and multicultural fusion, bringing Jewish cultural motifs together with global flavors. Nevertheless, unlike some other comedies that have aged poorly, *Annie Hall* continues to engage new generations of viewers. Woody Allen's playing with stereotypes that were already established when he created the film yields a fresh, powerful, and unforgettable masterpiece that still leaves new and veteran viewers gasping with painful laughter.

Background: http://www.myjewishlearning.com/culture/2/Film/American_and_European/Hollywood_and_Judaism/Woody_Allen.shtml.

Bibliography

Antler, Joyce, ed. *Talking Back: Images of Jewish Women in American Popular Culture*. Waltham, MA: Brandeis University Press, 1998.

Bernheimer, Kathryn. *The 50 Greatest Jewish Movies: A Critic's Ranking of the Very Best*. Secaucus, NJ: Birch Lane, 1998.

Desser, David, and Lester D. Friedman. *American Jewish Filmmakers* 2nd ed. Urbana: University of Illinois Press, 2004.

Fishman, Sylvia Barack. *Double or Nothing? Jewish Families and Mixed Marriage*. Waltham, MA: Brandeis University Press, 2004.

Gilman, Sander L. *The Jew's Body*. New York: Routledge, 1991.

Goldman, Eric A. *The American Jewish Experience through the Lens of Cinema: Film History as Haggadah*. New York: American Jewish Committee, 2008.

Hyman, Paula. *Gender and Assimilation in Modern Jewish History: The Roles and Representations of Women*. Seattle: University of Washington Press, 1995.

Lax, Eric. *Woody Allen*. New York: Knopf, 1991.

Roth, Philip. *Portnoy's Complaint*. New York: Random House, 1967.

Whitfield, Stephen J. *In Search of American Jewish Culture*. Waltham, MA: Brandeis University Press, 1999.

PART EIGHT

A Diverse Diaspora

40. *Like a Bride*

The Chicken and the Egg

ELISSA RASHKIN

Like a Bride (*Novia que te Vea*), directed by
Guita Schyfter [A]
Mexico, 1993

In the beginning of her autobiography, *Las genea-logías* (The Family Tree), Margo Glantz lists a number of items that she, a second-generation Mexican and a secular Jew, has in her home: a shofar and some inherited candelabras rest next to images of Catholic saints, Christ, and pre-Hispanic deities, a juxtaposition that causes a cousin to comment that she does not seem Jewish, "because we Jews, like our first cousins the Arabs, have a horror of images." She, however, concludes otherwise: that "all of it is mine and isn't, and I seem Jewish and don't, and for this reason I write—these—my genealogies."

The mixture of religious traditions on Glantz's altar partly reflects the cultural phenomena that perhaps most deeply characterize the Americas: *mestizaje*, hybridity, syncretism. The fusion of in-digenous and Catholic beliefs is at the heart of Mexican religious practice; the Jewish elements, however, disturb this otherwise common mix-ture. While the veneration of holy objects is seem-ingly universal, Glantz explains only the signifi-

cance of the shofar and candelabras, presuming her readers' unfamiliarity; moreover, the Jewish "horror of images" indicates a basic incompatibil-ity between the traditions. To be Mexican and Jewish, Glantz seems to say, requires an embrace of contradiction that is potentially threatening to guardians of tradition on either side.

This embrace is the theme of Guita Schyfter's first feature film, *Novia que te vea* (*Like a Bride*), based on Rosa Nissán's novel by the same name. Nissán's semi-autobiographical narrative tells of growing up in Mexico City's Jewish community, building on Glantz's work of a decade earlier. Schyfter, a Costa Rican–born Jew of Polish/Ukrainian descent, adapted the novel in 1992, bringing one of the first representations of Jew-ish experience to the Mexican screen. The film, which encompasses gender and generational con-flict as well as religious-cultural difference, raises questions about Mexican national identity: spe-cifically, about the myth of a "*mestizo* nation" and the patriarchal understanding of the nation as a single "family."

As the film indicates, the history of Jews in the Americas is linked with that of the conquest of these continents; 1492, the year of Columbus's first voyage, is also the year that the Jews were expelled from Spain. The Inquisition followed them to Mexico; its first trial, on February 28, 1574, targeted Jews along with other heretics. Many were burned to death in the public square, yet many survived, and more recent immigration has added to the Jewish minority. Yet in spite of its deep roots, Mexico's Jewish population has been largely invisible, and excluded from the foundational ideology of Mexico as a *mestizo* nation, part indigenous and part Spanish. Ilan Stavans understands the notion of *mestizaje* as one that fails to include the waves of immigrants, Jewish and otherwise, that over 500 years have "created a mosaic of racial multiplicity." He describes Mexican Jews as "some 50,000 frontier dwellers and hyphen people like Dr. Jekyll and Mr. Hyde, a sum of sums of parts, a multiplicity of multiplicities."

The sense of marginality and exclusion Stavans describes is echoed by Schyfter, who says of her childhood: "When I was a little girl and studied the history of Costa Rica, and they said, 'Then the Spanish came' and then 'He was our president . . .' I never felt that had anything to do with me. So I became an observer." As a documentary filmmaker in Mexico, she read an interview with the renowned Yiddish writer Isaac Bashevis Singer in which he encouraged writers to look into their roots. This advice inspired her to develop *Like a Bride*. With the backing of the Mexican Film Institute, she was able to make a film that addressed her own experience of outsiderness and exclusion, as well as the history of Mexican Jews as a whole.

That Schyfter's reexamination of being Mexican through Jewish eyes came to the screen in the 1990s has much to do with larger changes taking place during this period. The collapse of myths of national unity in the wake of successive economic and political crises, and the emergence of alternative discourses such as feminism, gay and lesbian movements, and indigenous activism, have had direct and indirect consequences for national filmmaking. Classical Mexican cinema had de-

fined "Mexican" in terms that implied limited constructs of gender, race, class, and ethnic identity. Charles Ramírez Berg documents how political and economic disruptions undercut the viability of those constructs; but if, as he argues, "by 1969, the problems of the dominant ideology overwhelmed the classical narrative's ability to contain them," that breakdown also opened the way for new, potentially oppositional projects. As the foundational ideologies of the nation continued to collapse, it is not surprising that new voices, such as those of women, gays, and Jews, began to emerge in the cinema.

What is profound about *Like a Bride* is not so much its making visible a cultural minority, but rather the challenge that it poses to the dominant construct of Mexican identity. Its reexamination of Mexican history goes beyond Stavans's plea for acknowledgment of difference, while its analysis of gender divisions within the communities it portrays complicates its position still further. Rather than substituting one tradition for another at the center of cinematic representation, it calls all hegemonic tradition into question.

Like a Bride's opening sequence situates the film within the tradition, affirmed each year at Passover, that links all Jewish stories to the Exodus. In this prologue the protagonists, Oshinica Mataraso (Claudette Maille) and Rifke Groman (Maya Mishalska), look at Oshi's family album showing her family's arrival in Mexico and her own childhood, which the film will dramatize. In a voice-over, Oshi comments that the photos of her ancestors once seemed to her to be "illustrations of the Bible." What ensues is thus located in a history that transcends its time and setting, even as it details the particular experiences of two young Jewish women in Mexico.

The film's chronological editing, framed within an extended flashback, attests to Schyfter's documentary background. Black-and-white footage at the beginning tells the story of Oshi's family's arrival in Mexico in the early 1920s. Vignettes of Oshi's and Rifke's childhoods then show what it was like to grow up Jewish in Mexico City: speaking Ladino [a Jewish version of Spanish] or Yiddish at home; being teased by other children; playing in the Lagunilla marketplace; hearing debates over politics, Israel, and socialism; the fear and fascination of Catholicism; in short, childhoods both typically Mexican and constantly marked by difference.

In *Genealogías*, Glantz mentions feeling deprived at being excluded from celebrations like the Día de los Reyes, when the children around her all received gifts; Jewish rituals could not compensate for that feeling of loss. In *Like a Bride*, Oshi too remembers having "a foot in both worlds": "I used to cross myself, just in case." Early on she is shown visiting a church with her nanny; she is amazed by the plaster Christ's wounds, and begs the nanny not to tell anyone that she is Jewish. Rifke, the daughter of liberal Ashkenazim, also exhibits longing toward Catholic culture; her pride in her heritage does not fully compensate for a desire to erase the feeling of difference that the dominant culture imposes on her. Looking back as an adult, she recalls: "I wanted to belong. To say 'we' this, 'we' that, 'we.' I believed that you had to choose between Jewishness and the rest, but you can't choose. You stay in limbo. You're not here, you're not there, you're *not*, period." Because much of her family was killed in Europe, Rifke believed "I had no history, that I had sprung from nothing, like a mushroom." Her family's complex internal differences regarding the Holocaust, Israel, and their adopted country motivate her to forge her own identity out of the confusing material of the Jewish Diaspora.

Oshi, for her part, feels torn less between two cultural worlds than between the requirements of her upbringing and her own desire to be an artist. While seemingly accepting her preordained trajectory toward marriage and domesticity, she struggles to convince her parents to let her study painting, an undertaking they find unsuitable for a daughter. In her family, a young woman's only thoughts should be of her wedding, as the compliment "*novia que te vea* [I hope to see you a bride]" implies. Scenes in her home depict the embroidering of her trousseau amid gossip about the weddings and engagements of others, a feminine sphere whose only objective is its own survival and reproduction—and thereby that of the Sephardim as a whole.

But Oshi's rebellious spirit is inflamed by her contact with Ashkenazi Zionist and leftist youth, who in the early 1960s were influenced not only by the political currents informing Mexican youth culture in general, but also by the promise of the Israeli kibbutzim. Interestingly, while Nissán's novel ends in 1957, Schyfter sets the bulk of the film in the late 1950s and early 1960s, contemporaneous with the first years of the Cuban Revolution and the growth of an anti-imperialist Left whose political critique would bring it into conflict with the Mexican government. Although anti-Communist repression appears in the film, the fact that *Like a Bride* unfolds prior to the massacre of 1968—in which soldiers opened fire on student demonstrators in Mexico City, killing many and crippling the student movement—allows it to depict its characters' ideals without bitterness, as wellsprings of hope and personal empowerment. The young Jews' idealization of Israel becomes a variant of this, a Jewish "translation" (to use Stavans's term) of Che Guevara's dream of the "new man." The influence of such thinking extends beyond activist circles; in the context of the new ideas espoused by Rifke, Shomer leader Ari (Daniel Gruener), and their Communist friends, Oshi finds the support she needs to fight for her own self-determination.

Like a Bride's characters grow up in the central city, among the living remnants of a culture that places them at a paradoxical distance. Scenes of Rifke painting pro-Cuba banners, restoring Mesoamerican artifacts, and flirting with Saavedra (Ernesto Laguardia) in the cobblestone streets around the National Preparatory School recall Glantz's reminiscences: "At one time I was a Zionist. And it was during my best years, the ones I spent in San Ildefonso, beside the frescos of José Clemente Orozco."

The Orozco murals to which she refers, which also appear in *Like a Bride*, portray harsh scenes drawn from national history. But Glantz's identification is not with this history per se, but rather with the "pitiless women" who appear in the frescos. Moreover, the murals are associated in Glantz's memory with Zionism. Through a complex series of associations, Glantz appropriates symbols of local and national identity, making them the natural terrain of Jewish women.

Like a Bride makes similar appropriations, particularly through the character of Rifke, but also in Oshi's attempt to mediate between her family's traditionalism and the modern environment in which she finds herself. In this respect, Oshi's choice of vocation is significant. The visual arts in Mexico are rooted in indigenous traditions of pictorial language and decoration; in the colonial era, the fusion of Catholic and indigenous styles produced elaborate, baroque religious art; and in the 1920s and 1930s, the muralist movement secularized the form and made it the privileged public expression of the modern nation. In Jewish tradition, in contrast, visual images are prohibited in religious contexts, and thus not es-

pecially privileged in the secular realm. Yet it seems almost inevitable that the Jewish presence in Mexico would give birth to new syncretisms. Indeed, Arnold Belkin's painting of a mural in the city's first synagogue took place under the vigilance of a rabbi, a community leader, and the poet Jacobo Glantz, who calmed the painter's fears of controversy by telling him "paint whatever you feel like painting." In both Belkin's mural and that painted by Fanny Rabell at the Jewish Sports Center during the 1950s, the influence of the muralists meets Jewish subject matter, creating art that is unique to its cultural context. Oshi's art can be seen as one of the film's tropes of fusion and syncretism, identifying her with a generation that does not reject the past so much as it embraces a more encompassing vision of identity.

It is with Rifke's immersion in anthropology, however, that the film moves farthest beyond a narrative representation of Jewish history and toward an analysis of the consequences of that history for Mexican identity. Her study of the indigenous peoples of Mexico is used to revise the role of Jews in the cultural construct of the nation, which at midcentury was often referred to as the "great Mexican family." At the university, Rifke learns of Mexico's settlement by tribes from the north, ending with the Aztecs in 1325. Rifke's professor explains: "The brilliant Tenochtitlan was the product of successive migrations. . . . Culture after culture imposed itself on and merged with earlier cultures."

The emphasis on migration helps the film relocate the Jewish Diaspora within canonical notions of Mexican nationhood. The dominant view of Mexican origins stresses the originality of indigenous peoples and the transgressor/invader status of Europeans, and culminates in the fusion of the two via the creation of a "cosmic" race. Delving into the region's pre-Cortesian history sets the stage for conceptualizing Mexico as an immigrant nation. The synthesis that underlies the concept of the *mestizo* race is found to be inadequate, not only for describing Mexico's sizable indigenous population, but also in accounting for the nation that continues to evolve after 1521 and that includes blacks, Germans, successive waves of Spaniards, and many other immigrants, including Jews.

Rifke's studies reinforce her Mexican identity and help her locate the Jewish experience within the construct of the nation. In a campfire discussion during a Shomer outing, Oshi and Ari remark that although their parents are from Turkey and Poland, they themselves feel no connection with those countries. Rifke, whom we have seen frequently upset at being treated as a foreigner by non-Jews, joins the conversation: "I was born in Mexico. I study archaeology and I'm learning Nahuatl." Later she visits her boyfriend Saavedra's family home, where she confronts the exclusionary views held by segments of the Mexican bourgeoisie. Saavedra's father is a government official, and their other guest is a conservative journalist. Pleased by Rifke's response to a point of contention between his son and himself, Saavedra Sr. comments that he has some close friends who are "Israelis." This disclosure of Rifke's Jewishness provokes hostility from the journalist, who asks how many Jews there are in Mexico (about 40,000, she responds) and comments, "Is that all? Are you sure? I thought there were about two million. . . . They seem like a lot because they're everywhere, but they don't integrate."

The camera, framing Saavedra and Rifke as the reverse shot of the close-up of the journalist, emphasizes their unity, and it is Saavedra who responds: "Integrate into what? The 'great Mexican family'?" He then lashes out at that concept: "There are few ideas that disgust me as much as

that of the 'great Mexican family.' Because it presumes that we all want the same thing, and it's not true. Some want to exploit, others want not to be exploited." Here the leftist thought of the 1960s, condemning myths of national unity based on shared patrimony, provides an opening for the embrace of diversity as well. But the politics of cultural identity are not those of class struggle, and the journalist insists: "In this class society, where are the Jews? Among the exploited?" Saavedra's mother attempts to keep the peace by naming examples of Jewish achievement: Einstein, Freud, Marx. But Rifke, exasperated by references to her people as other, again invokes pro-indigenous discourse, arguing that "the great Mexican family also has its cultural minorities: the Otomí, the Cora, the Tarahumara, the Huichol, the Nahua . . . the Jews."

As the party falls into a stalemate and the two older men excuse themselves, the scene is resolved in an interesting way. Saavedra, trying to smooth over Rifke's indignation, tells her that his mother was a teacher during the 1930s and knows the "Internationale." A common ground emerges that transcends the divisions imposed by the two conservative men: Rifke, previously seated next to Saavedra, steps out of the frame and reappears in the reverse shot with his mother, singing and embracing. In this moment, the bitterness provoked by the journalist's anti-Semitism gives way to a vision of progressive idealism as the leveler of differences.

Such a vision informs Rifke's entire relationship with Saavedra. Their politics bring them together in ways that would not happen otherwise, given both the latent anti-Semitism of the dominant culture and the separatism of the city's Jewish community. Although at first Rifke is defensive, she comes to trust and respect him, just as he comes to accept that her participation in the

Communist Party will always be secondary to her Zionist activities. Although Rifke defies her family by falling in love with a gentile, she never compromises her Jewishness, but rather demonstrates that it is possible to live the hybrid reality that is, after all, the reality of the Americas even though (she says) "they always want to make you choose."

Schyfter uses several striking visual devices to place the couple within a larger context of historical representation. Much of their courtship takes place in and around the National Preparatory School, whose stairwells display the Orozco frescos mentioned earlier. Prominent among these is his *Cortés and Malinche*, which depicts the conqueror and his indigenous translator, adviser and companion as Adam and Eve. The painting is notably ambivalent; the couple is naked, connoting innocence, yet at their feet is an amorphous body, and Cortés's arm stretches out in a gesture of restraint, holding Malinche back from some ambiguous movement. Although its details are not visible, it is an image that many spectators would recognize when Saavedra pauses underneath it, watching Rifke walk away after refusing another of his invitations. Later they walk down the stairwell together, displacing the images of conqueror and conquered with the alliance of Jew and gentile on their way to protest Yankee imperialism.

In this and other scenes, the film graphically evokes the utopian possibilities unleashed by the progressive movement of the 1960s and its rejection of patriarchal notions of national identity. Politics are a catalyst for romance, and both are set against a historical narrative going back hundreds of years, which both the leftists and Jews must claim in order to achieve their own empowerment. Importantly, Rifke's journey of self-discovery is balanced by Saavedra's acceptance of their differences. Through Rifke and Saavedra,

the dialectical concept of *mestizaje* gives way to a celebration of diversity and multiplicity.

Although the film affirms Jewish culture and history as part of the nation, the institutions of Mexican Jewry did not necessarily welcome its message. When Nissán's novel was published, her brother, a prominent community leader, objected to its semi-autobiographical representation and spoke out against it. His opinion influenced Jewish organizations not to support the film, which went into production almost simultaneously with the novel's publication. Schyfter was refused permission to film at the old synagogue and the Jewish cemetery, on the grounds that the film included an intermarriage—thus replicating the very conflict portrayed in the film. Other segments of the community, however, have become more open to change. Jewish investors helped to finance the film, and more broadly, the success of Jewish-themed works by writers and artists like Glantz, Nissán, Schyfter, and Sabina Berman indicates that many Jews are questioning aspects of the tradition without abandoning their Jewish identity. Rifke and Oshi may be threatening to some guardians of orthodoxy, but the choices they make in the film echo those made by many contemporary men and women.

In public discussions of *Like a Bride*, Schyfter revealed the difficulties she confronted in adapting the novel, since Nissán's Sephardic culture was unfamiliar to the director. Nissán, a photographer, wrote her novel in a workshop led by Elena Poniatowska, who recommended it to Schyfter; Nissán, Schyfter, and playwright Hugo Hiriart then forged the script. The collaboration resulted in a synthesis that is rich and multilayered, characters were added, dropped, and modified; the setting was moved to the early 1960s; and the social conflicts of that period were made central rather than peripheral. The film thus combines the story of Oshi's coming of age with other aspects of the panorama of Jewish experience. What remains of Nissán's novel is a deep questioning of gender roles, from a perspective that is both specific to the Sephardic community and familiar to feminists everywhere, who cannot but empathize with Oshi's struggle to determine her own destiny as a human being.

"I was born to marry," Oshi explains to Rifke, "and according to custom, the sooner the better." The model of femininity imposed on Oshi involves running the household, gossiping and playing cards with other women, and replicating this model in the next generation. Education for girls is not valued, and Oshi's activities are permitted only to the extent that they enhance her marriageability. Yet early in the film, Oshi's grandmother teaches her a lesson that, according to the logic of the narrative, will have repercussions later. The grandmother, a sympathetic woman who teaches in the Jewish tradition, "by telling stories," puts Oshi to bed one night with the story of a Jewish girl who married a rich king and went away from her homeland to live in luxury. Once there, she realized that she couldn't adapt to her new country, nor did it accept her. "She thought she had found a treasure," explains the grandmother, "but it was a poisoned treasure." She cautions Oshi that, if the poisoned treasure should appear, she should "let it go."

Like many parables, the grandmother's story is ambiguous. On the one hand, it can be read as a cautionary tale against straying from one's own clan, and thus as an endorsement of the prohibition on intermarriage. Yet because the key to knowing if the treasure is poisoned or not is looking into one's own heart, the story is also an indictment of marriage for external material reasons, and a validation of the individual's right to free choice and the pursuit of happiness. It is the latter lesson that Oshi ultimately absorbs, though not without struggle.

When Oshi meets a medical student at a dance, her fate is sealed; her enthusiastic mother sets the wedding date almost before Oshi has a chance to realize what is happening. Soon she realizes that she will never be happy married to Leon Levy, whose jokes, mustache, and patriarchal arrogance she comes to despise, and who shows no signs of supporting her effort to become an artist. Troubled, Oshi nevertheless goes along with the wedding plans. But when her mother makes her stop taking art classes, Oshi realizes that her dreams are more important than her family's wishes and breaks the engagement. She confesses her feelings to her father, who seems sympathetic yet unable to conceive of breaking so abruptly with custom. He tells her that love comes later, that no one is in love when s/he marries. His counsel has the opposite of the intended effect. When Rifke leaves town to escape the crisis triggered by Saavedra's arrest, Oshi decides to accompany her.

The two women must separate themselves from their families and communities in order to achieve their own liberation; however, the journey is brief, easily achieving a resolution of both women's conflicts. They go to the home of Oshi's grandmother, whose "poisoned treasure" parable years earlier foreshadowed Oshi's dilemma. In Oshi's absence, Leon so irritates her father that he throws him out of the house, effectively breaking the engagement. Meanwhile, Saavedra's pursuit of Rifke cements their union and convinces Rifke that she cannot leave him.

The film proposes that Rifke's and Oshi's choices are linked to the larger force of destiny, a notion that draws on the melodramatic convention of romance across social boundaries, and invokes the Talmudic teaching that human destiny is written at the moment of creation, but that it is nevertheless up to the individual to make moral choices. When we return to the adult Oshi and Rifke, they have each found ways to integrate the different sides of their lives into a harmonious whole. Oshi has married Ari, has children, and paints. Rifke has continued her scholarship, writing about Aztec and Mexican Jewish history. With her son raised as a Jew and her husband in Congress, her break with convention seems to have resulted in a comfortable outcome. The protagonists, it seems, live happily ever after; more importantly, what had seemed to be profound cultural conflicts are resolved, and the notion of a conciliatory Jewish *mexicanidad* is affirmed.

The didactic elements in *Like a Bride* invite an analysis of the film as a commentary on the role of Jews in Mexico, yet equally significant is the film's use of melodramatic conventions. Ana López, among others, has noted the privileged place of melodrama in Mexican culture, citing its intersections with the "three master narratives of Mexican society: religion, nationalism, and modernization." Rendering social issues as personal moral conflicts, melodramatic films defined models of femininity that were—or were not—compatible with the national project. These models often involved self-sacrifice, with the subduing of the melodramatic heroine's will typically becoming the key to her own happiness. In *Like a Bride*, the union between Saavedra and Rifke is a choice for which the heroine has struggled, and that has implications beyond the personal. The placement of a bedroom scene just after Saavedra's appeal to universal history suggests their sexual union is itself a historically significant act with the potential to replace the heritage of the Conquest with a Mexican identity based on acceptance rather than violence.

Like a Bride does not question the institution of marriage as such, but rather the injunction to marry for reasons other than love. Its protagonists escape the confines of patriarchal tradition *and* end up with men who help them realize their personal dreams. Leftist politics are linked to both personal freedom and narrative romance: the first linkage implies that men as well as women will be free when oppressive traditions are overturned, while the second implies that the fairy-tale scenarios of popular melodrama need not be completely rejected by feminists.

The film's association with melodrama is reinforced by one of its ads, which shows Oshi in close-up with her eyes aimed at the film's title above her head. In the title *Novia que te vea*, the *u* of "que" stretches to form a menorah whose candles are red, white, and green, the colors of the Mexican flag. The copy reads: "Oshinica is at the age to discover everything. Only one thing stands in the way . . . being a Mexican Jewish woman in the turbulent 1960s." Ironically, this assertion epitomizes rather than explicates the problematic of the film, and more broadly, of gendered Jewish identity in Mexico. For the "one thing" standing in the way of Oshi's "discovery" is a compound of several factors: being Jewish *and* Mexican *and* female *and* in the turbulent 1960s. Yet the preferred reading, reinforced by the menorah in Oshinica's gaze, points to "Jewish" as the obstacle, since it is being Jewish that constitutes the film's singularity.

But what is it that Oshi would "discover" if she were not Jewish? Viewing the film does not yield an answer, but both novel and film make it clear that her overprotected upbringing results from a specifically Sephardic tradition and, within that, from the values of her family. In the novel, the permissive upbringing of Oshi's future sisters-in-law contrasts with that of Oshi herself, who is so sheltered that she is shocked the first time she realizes that there are stars in the sky. Other Jewish characters in the novel and film enjoy varying degrees of freedom from and within their families. In this respect, the characterization of Oshi as held back by her Jewishness is misleading; whereas the ad poses her minority status as an obstacle, the film itself argues for the adaptability of the "Mexican family" to include a "multiplicity of multiplicities." Moreover, the displacement of social concerns onto the characters' personal circumstances is only partial; although the film works within the conventions of a coming-of-age melodrama, the discovering of Mexico's multifaceted Jewish culture ultimately takes precedence over the individual dilemma stressed in the advertisement.

The word "discovery," however, is particularly interesting in this context. In the writings of Jews on Mexico, the "discovery" or conquest of the Americas is a recurring theme, and one that is addressed in unique ways. In texts from Jacobo Glantz's *Colón* to Ilan Stavans's *Imagining Columbus*, the voyages that historically led to the devastation of a continent instead become voyages of the imagination and of the imaginary. These are touched by the horror of the Inquisition and the recurrent Exodus; the dream of a promised land, the Jerusalem still to be found; and the chronic state of homelessness that is the Jewish condition.

This motif occurs repeatedly in *Genealogías*; it is, moreover, personalized, gendered, feminized. "All women have something of Columbus (or a lot) in us," Glantz writes. "We've all dealt with the egg; all of us, before Columbus, have tried to resolve the famous placentary enigma. All of us have had, if not in the head then somewhere else, to resolve the dichotomy in practice and have joined the chicken and the egg even in our writing." She argues that women are compelled to explore the world and acquire knowledge, not for gold or material gain but because it has been denied to them for so long. But associating women's liberation with the conquistadors displaces history and substitutes a utopian vision in which women, and Jews, can conquer the world from inside themselves, and in which power need not negatively determine human relations. In this sense, Oshi and Rifke's "discovery" of the world in *Like a Bride* is not a discovery, much less a conquest, but a creation or remaking: a promised land.

What distinguishes this act of imagination/creation from the usual ending of film melodrama is that in it, contradictions are embraced rather than resolved. In one of the film's most salient moments, the Groman family tests out their new record player with Bach's "Concerto for Two Violins." Rifke comments in a voice-over: "It was a puzzle I could never forget. How could Heifetz play the two violins at the same time?" This, though, is just what Rifke will go on to do: juggle identities, worlds, desires, traditions. Like Glantz's reconciliation of the chicken and the egg, *Like a Bride* asserts that one *can* be Jewish, Mexican, and female and still discover everything, *especially* if it is the "turbulent 1960s." For in that decade, canonical notions of national identity and gender boundaries began to break down, allowing the emergence of new social formations and new subject positions. The cinematic interventions made in the 1980s and 1990s by women like Schyfter are both a result and a continuation of this dissolution. If their films retain many conventions of mainstream cinema, they also use those conventions to further a feminist agenda, in which the trope of feminine sacrifice, for the greater good of the nation as well as the patriarchal family, is replaced with an inclusive vision that affirms rather than eradicates women's capacity for self-determination.

Abridged from: Elissa Rashkin, *Women Filmmakers in Mexico: The Country of Which We Dream* (Austin: University of Texas Press, 2001).

Source: Rosa Nissán, *Like a Bride, and Like a Mother*, translated by Dick Gerdes (Albuquerque: University of New Mexico Press, 2002).

Background: http://insidemex.com/people/lifestyle/out-of-sight?page=0%2C5.

Bibliography

Alfero-Velcamp, Theresa. " 'Reelizing' Arab and Jewish Ethnicity in Mexican Film." *Americas* 63, no. 2 (2006): 261–80.

Cimet, Adina. *Askenazi Jews in Mexico: Ideologies in the Structuring of a Community.* Albany: State University of New York Press, 1997.

Glantz, Margo. *The Family Tree.* Translated by Susan Bassnett. London: Serpent's Tail, 1991.

Goldman, Ilene S. "Mexican Women, Jewish Women: *Novia que te vea*; From Book to Screen and Back Again." In *Latin American Jewish Cultural Production*, edited by David William Foster, 157–77. Nashville: Vanderbilt University Press, 2009.

Lerner, Ira T. *Mexican Jewry in the Land of the Aztecs: A Guide.* 6th ed. Edited by Saul Lokier. Mexico: Costa-Amic, 1973.

López, Ana M. "Tears and Desire: Women and Melodrama in the 'Old' Mexican Cinema." In *Mediating Two Worlds: Cinematic Encounters in the Americas*, edited by John King, Ana M. López, and Manuel Alvarado, 147–63. London: BFI, 1993.

Presner, Kathryn. "Guita Schyfter: Insights from an Outsider." *Angles* 2, no. 3 (1994): 12–13.

Ramírez Berg, Charles. *Cinema of Solitude: A Critical Study of Mexican Film, 1967–1983.* Austin: University of Texas Press, 1992.

Stavans, Ilan. "Lost in Translation." *Massachusetts Review* 34 (Winter 1993–94): 489–502.

——, ed. *Tropical Synagogues: Short Stories by Jewish-Latin American Writers.* New York: Holmes and Meier, 1994.

41. The American Dream on St. Urbain Street

Richler's Duddy Kravitz and Canadian Cinema

SCOTT HENDERSON

The Apprenticeship of Duddy Kravitz, directed by Ted Kotcheff [A]
Canada, 1974

With the 2010 release of Richard Lewis's *Barney's Version*, the relation of Mordecai Richler to Canadian cinema has drawn renewed attention. While *Barney's Version* had been eagerly anticipated, it is unlikely that it will match the significance of Ted Kotcheff's *The Apprenticeship of Duddy Kravitz*. Indeed, it is the fond remembrance of the earlier film's success, combined with a national affection for the late Richler, that had inspired such expectations for the newer film. *Barney's Version* also belongs to a different era of filmmaking, in which, outside of Hollywood, international coproduction has become the norm, and the boundaries that once defined any sense of national cinema are being eroded.

While *Barney's Version* is a Canadian/Italian coproduction, the stature of Richler as one of Canada's best-known writers, and its setting within his familiar milieu of Montreal's Jewish community, places the film distinctly within Canadian cinema. Nonetheless, the national cinema landscape differs markedly from that of the 1970s, when *The Apprenticeship of Duddy Kravitz* was made. This earlier film has an interesting if accidental metaphoric value: it was a critical success in an era when Canadian filmmaking was at a low ebb. As a character, Duddy Kravitz could easily have been a "player" in the Canadian film

Richard Dreyfuss (as Duddy) and Micheline Lanctôt (as Yvette) go on a picnic in the Laurentian Mountains. From *The Apprenticeship of Duddy Kravitz* (1974), directed by Ted Kotcheff. PARAMOUNT PICTURES/PHOTOFEST

industry of the 1970s. Under the tax-shelter rules brought in during that decade, money invested in Canadian film could be recouped 100 percent against taxes. This encouraged the shooting of numerous films in this era, and the hatching of numerous get-rich-quick schemes. Rarely did these films reach cinema screens. The casting of American stars, usually in need of a career boost, and the reliance on hackneyed genre plots lured investors, but not necessarily spectators or exhibitors. The entire operation sounds reminiscent of one of Duddy's schemes, the irony being that this particular film was a critical and commercial success, and its American star was not washed up but, rather, the up-and-coming Richard Dreyfuss. The film thus stands as a model of what Canadian cinema could have been in the tax-shelter era.

That it was based on Richler's screenplay, which remained faithful to his popular 1959 novel, no doubt contributed to the film's success. The film, like the novel, follows the rise of a ruthless young Jewish go-getter from Montreal's St. Urbain Street, the locale for many of Richler's stories. Not only does the film capture the particular cultural history of the era in which it is set, postwar 1948, but it also represents, in the time it was made, the end of another cultural era. Less than two years after the film was released, Quebec elected its first separatist Parti Québécois government, and the English exodus from Montreal began in earnest.

Like so many Canadian films, *The Apprenticeship of Duddy Kravitz* is a film about identity, both personal and cultural, as Duddy comes to understand his place as a working-class Jew in a Francophone city. In his attempt to become "somebody," Duddy must give up his sense of self, as financial success brings about ethical destruction, a notion that could also be used to describe the tax-shelter era. Initially the film was accused of being anti-Semitic. As Daniel Golden has observed, it exposed "Duddy and the Jewish subculture in Montreal as harshly venal, crass, and materialistic." Yet it was giving voice to the realities of the culture in which Richler had lived. Indeed, in a tribute written shortly after Richler's death, Anthony Wilson-Smith referred to the author as an "equal opportunity offender" for his mocking of the idiosyncrasies of the various cultures that comprised and influenced Montreal. Stuck between the French culture and the WASP aristocracy of Montreal, the Jewish subculture around St. Urbain Street struggled to avoid cultural assimilation. By the end of the film, Duddy has passed his apprenticeship into the adult world but has lost the love of his girl and the respect of his grandfather. Ultimately, Daniel Golden finds that *The Apprenticeship of Duddy Kravitz* "demonstrates the perversion of the American dream, Canadian-style."

Canadian filmmaking in the 1970s itself represented an era that might be described as a "perversion of the American dream." With a film industry that was largely controlled by American interests and dominated by American films, Canada had long struggled to find ways to compete. As a result of the Canadian Co-operation Project (coincidentally adopted in 1948, the same year in which *The Apprenticeship of Duddy Kravitz* is set), the post–World War II era had been essentially conceded to American films. The agreement stipulated that the Canadian government refrain from subsidizing the production of domestic feature films in exchange for Hollywood's promise to

refer to Canada favorably and occasionally film in Canadian settings. What this led to was a dearth of English-Canadian feature films. While the French-Canadian industry continued to address the popular audience in Quebec, in English Canada it was Hollywood films and their depiction of the American dream that dominated movie screens. Finally, in 1967, after much lobbying, and following the critical success of small features like Don Owen's *Nobody Waved Goodbye*, the government began to support private-sector feature-film production through the Canadian Film Development Corporation (later renamed Telefilm Canada). In an effort to increase private-sector funding and production, the government permitted tax write-offs for any films that the government could deem "certifiably Canadian,' a process referred to as the Capital Cost Allowance. As already noted, the idea eventually resembled the sort of scheme in which Duddy became involved. To stimulate further investment, the government raised the ceiling until it was offering a 100 percent write-off by 1974. The resulting rise in production levels (from three features annually prior to 1974 up to sixty-six in 1979) has been described by Geoff Pevere as generating "countless films made for precisely the wrong reasons and (it was loudly suggested) by precisely the wrong people," films that were "substandard knock-offs of American commercial fodder." Consequently, tax-shelter movies began to dominate the industry, pushing aside more-established Canadian filmmakers.

Amid this mess, quality Canadian films that addressed national concerns were still made. In 1984, when the Capital Cost Allowance came to an end, the Toronto Film Festival presented a retrospective of Canadian cinema. It compiled a "ten best" list based on a poll of various critics, film professors, and industry professionals, both from Canada and worldwide. A surprising result of the poll was that while the largely mediocre tax-shelter films had dominated production in the preceding era, critics still recognized the notable Canadian films that had emerged, including *The Apprenticeship of Duddy Kravitz*, which placed fourth on the list. Even more notable is that on a subsequent list in 1993, while four of the original ten had been supplanted, *Duddy Kravitz* remained in seventh place. Clearly the film's themes resonated with Canadian critics and audiences.

Director Ted Kotcheff's trajectory parallels the history of English-Canadian feature film. Given the dire state of the Canadian film industry in the 1950s and 1960s, Kotcheff headed to England, where he worked in television and directed two feature films. He returned to Canada to direct *Duddy Kravitz* before heading to Hollywood, where he has directed films in a wide variety of genres. His work includes the first Rambo film, *First Blood* (1982), as well as the comedy *Weekend at Bernie's* (1989). More recently he has worked in television, having directed episodes in the popular *Law and Order* series. Kotcheff's career seems almost a Canadian version of the American dream.

While an element of the American dream exists in Duddy's ambitions, it is given a distinctly Canadian inflection in terms of his goals and the ways in which his success is measured. Beginning with the more obvious aspects of the latter, while Duddy does achieve material success, it is a rather hollow victory. The film's ending would seem, at first glance, to valorize Duddy's success, but a more careful consideration points to ways in which the accolades from his father, Max (Jack Warden), tarnish our view of both Duddy and his neighborhood. While Duddy receives an approving "thumbs up" from his father after be-

ing granted credit at the elder Kravitz's favourite restaurant/bar, this resulted from Duddy's having cheated those close to him. As a consequence of his deceptive actions, Duddy is rejected by the girl he loves, Yvette (Micheline Lanctôt), and his friend Virgil (Randy Quaid), who is paralyzed and confined to a wheelchair as a direct result of Duddy's hubris. That success comes at such a high price flies in the face of Hollywood conventions of the American dream, where success in life goes hand in hand with success in love. As the credits come up, Duddy's father is heard in a voice-over extolling the virtues of the son he now claims he always knew would make it, despite the doubts he has voiced throughout the film—like when he encouraged Duddy to emulate his brother, Lenny (Alan Rosenthal), and study to become a doctor. Rather than plaudits, Max's parting words function more as a form of self-reassurance. There is a note of uncertainty in what Max says, for Duddy may have achieved the dreams cherished in his neighborhood, but the reality of those dreams, and their inappropriateness to the Canadian environment, have also been made increasingly clear. The film may function more as a critique, not only of the aspirations of those in Montreal's Jewish community, but also of the forces that conspire to keep them there, and that shape such problematic aspirations.

One of the inspirations for Duddy's efforts is an old friend of his father's, Jerry Dingleman (Henry Ramer), known colloquially as "the boy wonder." Early in the film, when the audience is first introduced to Max, he is relating the story of "the boy wonder," who left St. Urbain Street penniless, but through a Horatio Algeresque combination of pluck and luck returned from the United States a rich man. Yet when we finally see "the boy wonder" he is, in Daniel Golden's words, "a cheap hood who built his fortune on heroin and prostitution, and is fat and crippled in his middle age." If this is the ideal to which Duddy is expected to aspire, the costs of such achievement will clearly be personal. Dingleman comes across as a bitter, angry man, hardly somebody who has been able to enjoy his success. With Duddy's securing the land for "Kravitzville" at the expense of Dingleman, we might surmise that Duddy faces a similar future. Again, as Golden puts it, "Duddy thus also becomes a 'somebody,' but at the cost of the family love and unity he has so desperately sought, and he pays the price in isolation and degradation." As an ideal, the American dream falls short when translated into the environment of St. Urbain Street and, more widely, into the Canadian milieu.

A primary force in instilling these dreams was the Hollywood film industry. Yet the dreams it offered were not truly suited to the mean inner-city streets of Montreal. They offered promises that cultural and social circumstances, particularly those related to race and religion, would deny. When Duddy sets up a company to film bar mitzvahs and weddings, he hires a drunken and blacklisted film director, John Friar (Denholm Elliott), whose lecture he has attended. The resulting film is itself a response to the ideals espoused by "classical Hollywood." Rather than being about the bar mitzvah, the film captures, according to Friar, aspects of ritual and tradition. The montage of primitive tribal rituals with shots from the actual bar mitzvah leaves the audience at the film's initial screening baffled. Yet when the rabbi (Jonathan Robinson) declares the film "a work of art," it is given a rapturous reception. The bar mitzvah film may be a parody of the excesses of the avant-garde, but it also serves as a reminder of the existence of film sensibilities distinct from Hollywood tradition. That the rabbi is able to see art in the film, and that Friar has been able to capture the essence of this ritual, illustrates that there are other modes of giving voice to people via film. The essence of the bar mitzvah is presumably captured in Friar's film, without resorting to the formulaic language and aspirations of Hollywood.

Yet it is not only American culture that holds down the Jewish residents of St. Urbain Street, but also the Anglophone elite of Westmount who prey on the aspirations of its downtrodden Jewish, as well as French, inhabitants, as is so often pointed out in Richler's work. This elitism is evident in the way in which his fellow waiters at the summer resort initially treat Duddy. Lacking their upbringing and education, Duddy is looked down upon and frequently ridiculed. Nonetheless, in the end, his cunning and street smarts bring him success, first at roulette and then, when that ultimately fails, through the patronage of Bernie Farber (Joe Silver), who admires Duddy's attitude. It is Farber who allows Duddy and Friar to film his son's bar mitzvah, the first venture of Duddy Kane Enterprises (a name that obviously offers an allusion to the rags-to-riches story of *Citizen Kane*). Later, it is Lenny who suffers at the hands of the Westmount gentiles, who have manipulated him into performing an illegal abortion. Distressed at how easily he has been misled, and fearful of the shame he may bring to his family, Lenny has fled to Toronto. Duddy brings him back and then proceeds to charm the father of the girl who had the abortion. Duddy, who initially becomes friendly with the Westmount gentile, soon recognizes that he is being as manipulated as his brother was, and that, despite being allowed into the Westmount home and being allowed to play snooker, he will only be seen as the Jew from St. Urbain Street.

A great deal has been made of Richler's attachment to his neighborhood, and that remains conspicuous in his adaptation of the novel to the screen and in Kotcheff's visualization of it. Much of the reminiscing following Richler's death from cancer in 2001 centered on his ties to Montreal in general, and to the St. Urbain Street neighborhood in particular. Richler understood the social causes of the ghettoization of the Jews there. As Wilson-Smith has observed, "He grew up in an era when Montreal's McGill University had quotas on the number of Jews it admitted, and when Francophones and Jews fought each other in the inner-city mean streets of St. Urbain, or sometimes made common cause against the Anglo elite that kept them stuck there." Aware of the cultural position he held as a Jew in Montreal, Richler had been a member of a religious and ethnic minority in an English-dominated city, while later he became a linguistic minority as a unilingual Anglophone in a now French-dominated city. In remembering Richler, Benoît Aubin notes that "when Richler was a kid, his Mile-End enclave—a now-gentrified neighborhood—was a ghetto where one could thrive and succeed speaking only Yiddish," but that "seventy years later, Yiddish had all but vanished here, and French is the lingua franca in the province. Language was not a central element of Jewish identity. It is for Quebec Francophones."

The film marks these shifts. While it may be set in 1948 and the novel published in 1959, the film in 1974 displays an awareness of the changes that Montreal and, more widely, Quebec, were undergoing. It would be hard to conceive of a Montreal-set film in 1974 that could not evoke recollections of the October Crisis and the resulting War Measures Act of 1970, and the corresponding rise in Quebec separatist sentiment. A series of bombings throughout the 1960s escalated to the kidnapping of two government officials, one of whom was killed by his captors. These actions by members of the Front de libera-

tion du Québec (FLQ) had taken Quebec's supposed "quiet revolution" of the 1960s in a violent new direction. Prime Minister Pierre Trudeau's imposition of the War Measures Act, which saw Canadian troops patrolling Quebec streets, led to a shift away from terror tactics, and toward political means of achieving Quebec's separation. With the violent acts of the FLQ, the images of troops in the streets still so fresh in Canadian minds, and separatist political fortunes on the rise, a Montreal-set film could not avoid these associations, even if it was set over twenty-five years earlier.

The cinematic qualities that evocatively capture a sense of Montreal in 1948, in terms of setting as well as the film style, allow the film to function ostensibly as a nostalgia piece. Golden notes that Kotcheff "captures a sense of post–World War II filmmaking in his grainy, high-contrast color photography. This in turn lends a naturalistic flavor to many of the external shots of St. Urbain Street." This is evident in the film's opening, as the camera follows a group of army cadets, Duddy included, as they march through the streets. Kotcheff's camera captures the sights and sounds of Montreal in 1948 while also revealing themes central to the film. The cadets encounter a group of Francophone children who berate and harass them. While the band performs "When the Saints Go Marching In," and the flags of Canada and the United Kingdom are carried at the front of the procession, led by the visibly older Anglo squadron leader, Duddy is seen breaking from this group. He becomes a constant visual and physical disruption of this Anglo demonstration through the city streets. He sneaks away from the band to purchase and consume bagels, inflates a condom that is then bounced among the marchers, and finally hides inside a parked delivery van before sneaking off to join his father and his father's friend at a local restaurant. Just like the French children who pester the marchers, Duddy is not truly part of this Anglo culture. The same squadron subsequently passes Duddy. Their influence and visual presence have waned, and Duddy is no longer part of the traditions they uphold.

The aforementioned critiques of Duddy's adherence to notions of the American dream undercut any nostalgic sentiment that this opening may provide. In fact, the film's nostalgia is almost misleading and serves more as a reminder of Montreal's past in relation to 1974 than it does as a positive evocation of days gone by. With the clashes between Anglophones and Francophones of the 1970s fresh in mind, the film seems to address the roots of some of these problems. The Montreal represented in the film is not a unified, homogeneous city; it is, rather, one that is beset by factions—Jewish, French, Anglo, working-class, upper-class, and so forth. At one point during the opening march, a horse-drawn wagon belonging to a French business stops in front of the parade and the horse defecates. The squadron leader, determined not to alter his sense of right of way, treads through the horse manure, while his younger and more flexible charges step around it: perhaps a sign of their being more willing to share the street, and hence the city. That these antagonisms and splits would proliferate seems, by 1974, a foregone conclusion, and the election of the separatist government in 1976 not so much a beginning as a culmination of events.

The film does not idealize Richler's era on St. Urbain Street. Shots of the Kravitzes' cramped apartment, where Duddy, Lenny, and their father are forced to maneuver carefully around each other, point to the economic disparity that inspires much of Duddy's desperate scheming. These conditions contrast with the ambitions Duddy has of developing Kravitzville on land in the Laurentian Mountain region. Yet it is not initially greed that brings him to this space, but Yvette, wanting to show him the pastoral landscape that she loves. While Duddy may see development potential, it is still a potential tied to the ideals of the land that gives his goals a stereotypically Canadian inflection. The city is seen as stifling, and certainly, given the control of the Anglo elite, not a space of opportunity for Duddy, as affectionate as Richler may be toward Montreal. Instead, it is land that drives this Canadian version of the American dream. Duddy's grandfather (Zvee Scooler), whose words provide inspiration to Duddy, claims that "a man without land is a nobody."

As it is Duddy's stated desire to become a "somebody," he must obtain land. He seeks to have a voice and importance in a society where so often Duddy has seen fellow Jews manipulated and left weak, much like his own father. These ties to land also serve to bind Duddy's aspirations to the sorts of notions of a Canadian imagination described by Peter Harcourt, where "an almost mystical concern for the land dominates a great deal of our writing, painting and filmmaking." Yvette's reaction to the beauty she finds in the landscape aligns with Harcourt's observations that "there is a yearning for the pastoral, which seems incongruously inappropriate both for the severity of our climate and for the harshness of our terrain." What is beautiful to Yvette becomes merely another commodity to Duddy, further underlining the inappropriateness of his American ideals. At the same time, it is the beauty of the landscape that both initially inspires him and leaves the film's ending so problematic.

The last shot of Yvette, after her final rejection of Duddy, is framed by a sunset with the rolling Laurentians in the background. This is a beautiful shot—which is immediately followed by a tight one of Duddy placing his order in his father's favorite restaurant. After the brief exchange between father and son, Duddy emerges onto the street, a concrete, urban landscape that, as the film closes with a crane shot, seems to swallow him up. Duddy may have "made it," but as he disappears into the streetscape, he seems somehow anonymous, and even his father's voice-over accolades are not enough to erase this anonymity.

In effect, Duddy has sold his soul, and his soul is linked to the quintessentially Canadian landscape he has purchased and plans to develop. In his quest to become somebody and express himself, Duddy has appropriated a voice that is not his own. It is one that will leave him as isolated and "crippled" as "the boy wonder." As a result the film remains a resolutely Canadian film. It is one that takes its very specific Canadian voice, a voice peculiar not only to a Jewish perspective but also to one rooted in a particular time and place, and employs that voice to work against the dominant American myths. Given the dominance of American media in Canada, these myths undoubtedly have a hold over many Canadians. *The Apprenticeship of Duddy Kravitz* reveals that a Canadian perspective—and more directly a particular local perspective, that of the Jewish community residing around St. Urbain Street—can deflate those myths and illustrate how problematic and destructive their repetition in a Canadian environment can be.

Republished from: Scott Henderson, "Ted Kotcheff: *The Apprenticeship of Duddy Kravitz*," in *Where Are the Voices Coming From? Canadian Culture and the Legacies of History*, edited by Coral Ann Howells, 247–58 (New York: Rodopi, 2004). Revised by the author, 2010.

Source: Mordecai Richler, *The Apprenticeship of Duddy Kravitz* (London: Andre Deutsch, 1959).

Bibliography

Aubin, Benoît. "Mordecai Was Here." *Maclean's*, July 16, 2001, 20–21.

Gittings, Christopher E. *Canadian National Cinema.* New York: Routledge, 2002.

Golden, Daniel. "What Makes Duddy Run." In *Canadian Film Reader*, edited by Seth Feldman and Joyce Nelson, 258–62. Toronto: Peter Martin Associates, 1977.

Handling, Piers. "Canada's Ten Best." *Postscript* 15, no. 1 (1995): 6–8.

Harcourt, Peter. "The Canadian Nation—An Unfinished Text." *Canadian Journal of Film Studies* 2, nos. 2–3 (1993): 5–26.

Leach, Jim. *Film in Canada.* New York: Oxford University Press, 2006.

McSorley, Tom. "The Apprenticeship of Duddy Kravitz or The Anxiety of Influence." In *Canada's Best Features: Critical Essays on 15 Canadian Films*, edited by Gene Walz, 53–71. New York: Rodopi, 2002.

Melnyk, George. *One Hundred Years of Canadian Cinema.* Toronto: University of Toronto Press, 2004.

Pevere, Geoff. "Middle of Nowhere: Ontario Movies after 1980." *Postscript* 15, no. 1 (1995): 9–22.

Wilson-Smith, Anthony. "Richler Remembered." *Maclean's* July 16, 2001, 18.

42. Jewish Assimilation in Hungary, the Holocaust, and Epic Film

Reflections on Szabó's *Sunshine*

SUSAN RUBIN SULEIMAN

Sunshine, directed by István Szabó [A]
Austria, Canada, Germany, and Hungary, 1999

Sunshine sums up the history of Jews in modern Hungary by telling the story of a single family over four generations. Emmanuel Sonnenschein, while still a boy, leaves the village where his father, the local tavern keeper, has been killed by an explosion in his distillery, and makes his way to Budapest. This evidently occurs in the mid-nineteenth century, after the Revolution of 1848 and just before establishment of the Dual Austro-Hungarian Monarchy (1867–1918). Emmanuel, a poor devout Jew, takes with him the precious black notebook that contains his father's secret recipe. By the time Ralph Fiennes makes his appearance as Emmanuel's young adult son, the Sonnenscheins have become rich through Emmanuel's distillery, which fabricates the tonic he calls "a Taste of Sunshine."

The voice-over narration by the last male descendant of Emmanuel Sonnenschein, his great-grandson Ivan (spoken by Ralph Fiennes, playing all three roles of son, grandson, and great-grandson) opens and closes the film, and intervenes at various moments throughout. These interventions indicate that the story is recounted by a specific individual, not an omniscient narrator. This point has not been sufficiently taken into account in critical responses to the film. After the prologue, the story divides neatly into three historical periods mirroring the meteorological metaphor suggested by the film's title: the "sunlit age," roughly 1890–1914; the "stormy age," roughly 1914–44; and the "overcast age," 1945 to our day.

When Emmanuel's two sons, Ignatz and Gustave, reach young manhood in the 1890s, the era of Hungarian prosperity and cultural achievement is at its height, and Jews play a prominent role in it. Historians have often described the "assimilationist contract" that linked the liberal nobility to Jewish industry and finance in this period. The liberals, inspired by the Enlightenment and Magyar patriotism, sought to modernize a backward, quasi-feudal country and to create a unified nation despite the number of minority ethnic groups scattered over its large territory.

The "assimilationist contract" gave Jews, especially those living in Budapest, an opportunity to participate fully in modernization and the creation of a modern Hungarian identity and culture. In return, as historian András Kovács explains, "Hungarian Jews were expected to demonstrate total loyalty to the Hungarian state, to accept the political hegemony of the nobility, and to strive for complete assimilation within the Hungarian community."

Ignatz Sonnenschein becomes a jurist and is quickly promoted to the high position of a Central Court judge; but since, as his liberal Christian patron tells him, "a Central Court judge cannot have a name like Sonnenschein," he changes his name to the more Magyar Sors, which means fate. His brother Gustave, a doctor, does likewise, and so does his adopted sister, Valerie, who soon becomes his wife. Drafted into the officer corps as a military judge during World War I, Ignatz remains a lifelong loyalist to Emperor Franz Joseph. Gustave follows a more radical route, joining the Socialist Party and later the revolutionary government of Béla Kun (1919). After the fall of the Kun regime, he is forced to leave Hungary.

"Magyarizing" one's name before World War I did not have the same anxious connotation (hiding one's Jewishness for fear of persecution) it would acquire during the 1930s. It was practiced not only by Jews but by other ethnic minorities in Hungary—Slovaks, Croats, Germans—who wanted to affirm their loyalty. For Jews, who had acquired Germanic names in the eighteenth century under the Habsburg Emperor Joseph II, Magyarizing was a sign of patriotism as well as of belief in the promises of assimilation. It did not necessarily imply a renunciation of Jewish self-identification or of Jewish practice, although assimilated Jews in Budapest generally practiced a Reform brand of Judaism in opposition to the

Orthodox practice of most Jews in the provinces. By changing their name when they do, Ignatz, Gustave, and Valerie are not giving up their Jewishness, but rather affirming their Hungarianness.

The vexing question asked by this film is whether one can be both Jewish and Hungarian after the Holocaust. The "assimilationist contract" proved more fragile than it seemed to Ignatz and Gustave Sonnenschein/Sors's generation. The contract could not withstand the economic crisis and the aggravated nationalism that followed the dismemberment of the Habsburg Empire after World War I, when Hungary lost two-thirds of its territory. Nor did it foresee the Communist upheavals in Russia and Hungary (where the short-lived Kun regime, dominated by assimilated Jews, was brutally put down by the authoritarian regime of Miklós Horthy), or the rise of Nazism and radical anti-Semitism in Germany. Many Jews, seeing the handwriting on the wall, emigrated from Hungary in the early years of the Horthy regime and in the 1930s. Those who stayed faced increasing hostility and state persecution, culminating in the Jewish laws of 1938 and 1939, which excluded Jews from Hungarian economic, cultural, and political life.

Ignatz Sors does not live to see that day, for he dies shortly after World War I; but his two sons, István and Adam, experience virulent anti-Semitism while they are still teenagers. Adam, who takes up fencing after being attacked by his own schoolmates, becomes a national and Olympic champion, and an ardent patriot. By that time, however, Jewishness and Hungarian patriotism coexist only in a highly problematic fashion. When Adam is told he must convert to Catholicism to join the officers' fencing club, he does so, accompanied by his brother and by the women they will marry. In the character of Adam, Szabó explores the psychology of the "par-iah" parvenu, who, once he is accepted by a group or an institution, becomes overly loyal to it, losing all ability to judge his situation and getting destroyed in the process, morally and physically. This psychology is epitomized by Adam. At the 1936 Berlin Olympics, he is oblivious to everything other than winning for Hungary—oblivious to the swastika banners, the crowds in uniform, the disquieting atmosphere, none of which escape his Christian trainer. Married to a Jewish woman, the trainer soon emigrates from Hungary; upon hearing of this, Adam calls him a traitor. The rigidity of Adam is beautifully captured by Fiennes's performance.

In 1941, the Hungarian government, an ally of Nazi Germany, conscripted most Jewish men into forced labor service, where they were subjected to treatment that ranged from harsh to homicidal. Adam is tortured to death in a work camp by Hungarian gendarmes, when he insists on wearing a white armband signaling he is a convert and on identifying himself as "Adam Sors, an officer in the Hungarian army and Olympic gold-medal winner." Adam is modeled on the Hungarian fencing champion Attila Petschauer, a Jewish convert to Catholicism who was beaten to death in a forced labor camp. Adam's teenage son, Ivan (our narrator) watches helplessly as his father is stripped naked, beaten, strung up on a tree, and doused with cold water, slowly turning him into an ice statue for refusing to call himself a Jew.

In March 1944, the Germans invaded Hungary and started deporting Jews from the provinces, an operation administered by Hungarian officials and enforced by Hungarian police. Two-thirds of Hungary's Jews, close to half a million people, perished through deportation and other forms of murder. The deportations never reached Budapest, which accounts for the relatively large number of Jews who remained in Hungary after the war. However, in the last winter of the war, Budapest Jews were hounded by Hungarian Nazis, the Arrow Cross, led by Ferenc Szálasi, who replaced Horthy in October 1944. Adam Sors's family is murdered by Hungarian Nazis in Budapest; the only survivor, besides Ivan, is his grandmother Valerie, who returns to an empty apartment in 1945. To signal the end of the war, Szabó inserts archival footage of bombed-out buildings and dead horses on the street, which people cut up for food.

Ivan's story brings us up to the present. Like many young Jews after the war, Ivan becomes an ardent Communist. He works for the dreaded secret police, the AVO, until his boss and friend Andor Knorr (played by William Hurt), a survivor of Auschwitz, is arrested on trumped-up charges of "Zionist conspiracy" and tortured to death by the Communist regime. We are in 1952, just as the anti-Jewish Slansky Trial is starting in Czechoslovakia and Stalin's repression of the alleged Jewish "doctor's plot" to kill him is about to be launched in the Soviet Union. Ivan quits the police, eventually becomes a leader of the failed 1956 revolution, and spends several years in prison. In the 1960s, after Valerie's death, he finds a letter addressed by his great-grandfather Emmanuel to his son Ignatz, advising him to stay true to himself and his origins. Taking this letter to heart, Ivan changes his name back to Sonnenschein—and for the first time in his life, he announces in a final voice-over, he "breathes freely" in the streets of Budapest. In a huge temporal leap, the film's last sequence is of Ivan walking with the crowds in present-day Budapest, on a recently created pedestrian street. As the final credits roll, the camera slowly and lovingly pans over the city, with its river and bridges and the hills of Buda.

Inevitably, Szabó relies on a certain simplification, if for no other reason than the huge temporal sweep of the narrative. Characters function as types, rather than as fully developed figures; plot and narration are linear, avoiding flashbacks, dream sequences, and other disruptive techniques. The narrative relies on repetition and parallelism as its most important tropes. These tropes occur not only on the level of plot and characters, but in the mise-en-scène as a whole, including décor, lighting, and music. The family's apartment and the building in which it is located are one major repeated element, used to great effect: the physical deterioration of these spaces tracks both the family's and Hungary's decline. The visual evolution from the comfortable, replete bourgeois interior of the Habsburg years (with shiny furniture, cluttered walls, expensive silver and china) to the threadbare dinginess of the communal apartment in the Stalinist years communicates a huge amount of historical information in cinematic terms. Similarly, colors mark the film's movement from sunshine to darkness and back to at least a partial sunshine. The film opens with a blue sky studded with white clouds; at the end, the sky is light but overcast. In the middle, when the family listens to the announcement of the Jewish Law on the radio, the screen is almost black and they are barely visible in the darkened room.

The musical score (by Maurice Jarre, who composed the music for *Lawrence of Arabia*) is also highly patterned, with the leitmotif borrowed from Schubert's Fantasia in F Minor for Two Pianos accompanying the family's evolution. Played by Valerie and Ignatz as young lovers, the Schubert piece becomes the Sonnenschein theme music, sometimes fully orchestrated, at other times reduced to a single piano. In the sequence of Adam's murder, there is no music at all; in the concluding sequence, when the Sonnenschein name is revived, the Schubert melody swells again to full orchestration. Szabó uses other musical motifs as well; the Hungarian folk song "Spring Wind," which is played at Valerie and Ignatz's wedding and recurs often, underlines the family's love of Hungary and its deep sense of "Hungarianness," according to Szabó.

On the level of plot and characters, repetition and parallelism ensure narrative cohesion and underline the film's major themes. The choice of a single actor to play the three generations of protagonists is the most obvious example, emphasizing the similarities in character and situation, as well as the physical resemblance of the three men. However, it also highlights the pitfalls of repetition as a thematic trope. A number of reviewers in England and North America criticized the film for being too repetitive and found particular fault with the recurrence of Ralph Fiennes. In the final sequence, when Ivan reads his great-grandfather's letter, we see the latter's face and then two faces of Ralph Fiennes as Ignatz and Adam, mouthing the words while the third Fiennes holds the letter. The transmission of the letter's "message" from generation to generation could have been achieved without such visual redundancy, especially since Ignatz and Adam have been shown not to follow it ("Know yourself; don't abandon your religion").

In other instances, however, repetition effectively communicates a meaning cinematically that is not stated verbally. For example, we see Ignatz dressed in military uniform, approaching a palace that the voice-over tells us is that of the Emperor Franz Joseph: it is World War I, and Ignatz, a military judge, is going to have a private audience with the Emperor. The meeting lasts only a minute and is perfunctory, but Ignatz is deeply moved: afterward, approaching the staircase, he touches his shoulder where the Emperor briefly placed his hand.

The palace scene is crucial to the film's theme of assimilation/accommodation, and is repeated with variations in Adam's and Ivan's stories. Adam, after his Olympic victory, enters a grand building, dressed in uniform, and receives a military decoration; afterward, he stiffly descends the staircase, moved beyond words. Ironically, it is this same military stiffness and loyalty to the "homeland" that get him killed a few scenes later: he is singled out by the camp guard while wearing his Army coat. Adam's decoration "repeats" his father's meeting with the Emperor and foreshadows his own death, developing the theme of assimilation. Ignatz's understandable loyalty to Hungary becomes a tragic blindness in his son, who remains loyal to a system that seeks his destruction.

There is yet a third decoration scene, which pushes the accommodation theme even further: Ivan, on Stalin's birthday, is decorated along with other police officers in a public ceremony in the Opera House (another grand building), and is chosen to give the formal speech of thanks. Standing on the stage in his uniform before a large crowd, Ivan shouts: "Comrade Stalin has shown us the way!" His eyes stare ahead, oddly recalling the boy's stare at his father being tortured. Afterward, he descends a grand staircase—but there is no pride in his face, only his usual pained look. This sequence "repeats" the two earlier ones, but turns the wheel once more: whereas his father and grandfather were men of will and power, Ivan is an automaton. His face constantly frozen into an anxious mask, he is the embodiment of trauma.

In *Sunshine*, sexual transgression is repeated from generation to generation: Ignatz marries his first cousin and adopted sister, Valerie, against his parents' wishes; Adam, the proper patriot, engages in an adulterous love affair with his brother's wife. True, it is she who pursues him and he hates himself for yielding to her; but it is significant that their first sexual encounter takes place immediately after he descends the grand staircase with his decoration, as if to "correct" his rigid conformism and propriety. Similarly, it is while descending the staircase after his Stalin speech that Ivan has his first encounter with Carol, the married blond policewoman who teases him about his anxious look. In the next scene in his office, they make breathless love on his desk.

Transgressive sexuality presents itself as the subversive counterpart to "good boy" integration into the system, a possibility of self-affirmation outside institutional or political norms. Women function as outsiders to authority, possible vehicles of freedom—but by the same token, they are outside the political realm and history. Szabó has stated: "[Women] are much closer to nature, to every part of nature, including blood, than men. For that very reason, they are less likely to fall prey to the attractions of ideologies and of history; they are more able to safeguard their identity than men." A compliment, but also a sexist stereotype.

Furthermore, the women in *Sunshine* are not only outside politics but appear to be outside ordinary ethical standards as well. Adultery is not only a societal transgression; it is also a personal betrayal, and the women in *Sunshine* become increasingly crass. The progression is downward as the generations advance. Valerie, who leaves Ignatz for another man after World War I, declaring him too much of a conformist to the Empire, returns to him when he becomes an outcast during the Kun regime; Adam's sister-in-law, by contrast, never regrets betraying her husband with his own brother. As for Carol, she betrays not only her husband but her lover, Ivan: despite their passionate lovemaking, she drops him im-

mediately when he falls from official grace; and when they meet by chance on the subway years later, she escapes, refusing to have any contact with him.

Perhaps in keeping with his theory about women's firmer grasp of reality, Szabó makes the old Valerie (beautifully played by Rosemary Harris) into the moral center of the film. Enduring through all four generations (the young Valerie is played by Harris's daughter, Jennifer Ehle), Valerie expresses the ethical norms of the film when she tells Ivan that politics and history are not the important things in life; what really matters is the appreciation of life's beauty. If there is a "message" in the film, this affirmation of individualist values—and of art, for Valerie is for a time a professional photographer—may well sum it up.

Why is the ending of *Sunshine*, Ivan's giving up his Magyarized name, so shocking to Hungarian viewers? That question leads us into the very center of Jewish identity and its dilemmas in contemporary Hungary, and probably in Central Europe—with this difference that most Jews have disappeared from Poland and other Central European countries, whereas the Jewish population of Hungary is still large, usually estimated at around 100,000. Szabó himself has offered interpretations of his ending in interviews. For him, the film's real theme is that of personal identity: by taking back his Jewish-sounding name, Ivan breaks the pattern of accommodation to authority, with its alienation of self, begun by his grandfather: "The protagonist finally understands who he is, and assumes that identity. That is much more important than the change of name. Ivan realizes that in order to be part of society, he does not have to renounce his self." In another interview Szabó generalized this theme to other ethnic minorities, not only Jews, and not only in Hungary: "The film is about an identity crisis. . . . This is not only a Jewish problem. Millions of people suffer from the same question."

Yet Szabó well knows that the Jews in Hungary are not really comparable to Turkish "guest workers" in Germany, or to Asian immigrants in England. Until the Holocaust, Hungarian Jews *felt* Hungarian: they were not exiles, Hungary was their home. Furthermore, they played an important historical role in the modernization of Hungary and in the creation of modern Hungarian identity. Jewish intellectuals—writers, journalists, publishers—played major roles in Hungarian cultural life, and at times constituted more than 50 percent of the liberal professions. The Jewish Laws of the late 1930s were designed precisely to do away with this Jewish "domination." They suddenly informed the Jews, even upper-class, assimilated, or converted Jews like Adam Sors, that they were not true Magyars; that in true Magyar eyes, they were pariahs.

For over forty years after World War II, the Jews who had survived and had decided to remain in Hungary persuaded themselves that anti-Semitism was a thing of the past: Jewishness was irrelevant in Communist Hungary. Many Jews born after the war didn't even realize until much later that their family was Jewish. "How I learned that I was a Jew" practically became a subgenre of autobiography in the early 1990s. During the Communist period, the word "Jew" could hardly be printed in the newspaper, nor were overtly anti-Semitic writings publishable. It's true that the official anti-Zionist discourse of the Soviet bloc, starting in 1949 and revived periodically afterward, was often a convenient cover for anti-Semitism, in Hungary and elsewhere. Still, Hungarian nationalism and the anti-Semitism that traditionally had accompanied it were not overtly endorsed by the Communist regime.

After the collapse of Communism in 1989 and the lifting of official censorship of the press and book publishing, traditional anti-Semitic discourse once again became possible and actual. The MDF, the center-right party that came to power in the 1990 elections, tolerated an extreme xenophobic and nationalist wing that eventually formed its own party, the "Magyar Truth and Justice Party" (MIEP), led by the writer István Csurka. Csurka edits the party's weekly newspaper, which is unabashedly and explicitly anti-Semitic. Evicted in the 1994 elections, the MIEP bounced back in 1998 and became quite close to the governing party, the once liberal but now conservative "Young Democrats" (FIDESZ), led by Viktor Orbán. In 1999, for the first time in fifty years, a member of the government referred to the "Jewish question" in Hungary. This provoked some indignation, whereupon a government spokesman denied that the Minister meant anything anti-Semitic. The "Young Democrats" were ousted by the Socialists in 2002, but were elected again with an overwhelming majority in 2010; and Csurka's party has been succeeded by a quasi-military formation of right-wing "patriots," who managed to receive enough votes in 2010 to enter the Parliament.

Despite these troubling manifestations, however, it would be a mistake to compare today's Hungary to the 1930s, let alone the 1940s. The majority of Hungarians does not appear to be in favor of anti-Semitism. The Jews of Hungary have reacted vigorously, on the whole, to the re-emergence of anti-Semitism. Many assimilated Jewish intellectuals who had never spoken, or probably ever thought, much about their Jewish ancestry have in recent years begun writing or speaking about it. Aside from assimilated Jews, there is a thriving Jewish community in today's Hungary, almost all in Budapest, with synagogues, Jewish schools, and Jewish cultural journals. One does not have the feeling in Hungary, as in bordering countries, that only a few old people know anything about Judaism and Jewish practice.

Szabó's film is neither about these self-identified Hungarian Jews nor is it chiefly addressed to them. Rather, it is aimed at assimilated Jews who, like Szabó himself, have only recently begun avowing their Jewish ancestry. The critics who most passionately attacked *Sunshine* in Hungary belong precisely to this group. "I left the movie sad and puzzled," wrote one well-known liberal journalist. According to her, Szabó's "answer" to the search for identity is the "worst possible" one, for it supports those (that is, the anti-Semites) who "contest our inherited Hungarianness." If Ivan Sors can find his true identity only by becoming Sonnenschein, why shouldn't all the Kovács and Kis (common Hungarian names, meaning "Smith" and "Little") whose families changed their name generations ago take back their Kohn name? In fact, the extreme right-wing press has taken recently to "outing" assimilated Jews by digging up their family's original Germanic name.

Péter György criticizes Szabó for bowing to global market pressures in producing a film chiefly for an "American" audience. He charges that Szabó has simplified Hungarian reality and presented a negative view of Hungary by not showing any "decent," ordinary non-Jewish Hungarians, nor any extraordinary ones who sheltered Jews during the war. This is the image "the world will have of our Hungarian history, and this one-sidedness pains me," writes György. But his biggest worry is that Jewish and gentile Hungarians will be driven apart by the "example" proposed in the film's ending with Ivan's change of name.

Although its anxious critics read Szabó's ending as pessimistic ("assimilation has failed; there is no way for a Jew to be just Hungarian"), the film seems to offer a more optimistic possibility. To be "outed" as a Jew is humiliating, but to come out of the closet—to take back one's Jewish name willingly—is liberating. Ivan breathes freely in Budapest as Sonnenschein; he does not leave Hungary but makes his life there. The film's final panorama of Budapest, beneath a muted sky, suggests that the beauty of the city so closely identified with the Sonnenscheins' history may console Ivan for the losses and humiliations his family has suffered.

To an American viewer, even a Jewish American born in Hungary, this ending seems quite plausible: one can be Hungarian with a Jewish name; pluralistic democracy can work in Hungary. I for one applaud this multicultural dream. For reasons quite different from those of the Hungarian critics, however, I am a bit troubled by it, too: the dream is tenuous, even as a dream. The change of name is secondary, Szabó has stated; what matters is the recovery of roots and of a suppressed identity. But at the end of this film, Ivan has *nothing but* the name to tie him to Jewishness or to his family's past: he is the baptized son of two Catholic converts, and he has thrown out all traces that might constitute a cultural archive. Photographs, letters, papers carefully saved by the Catholic family servant during the war, even the famous black notebook that was at the origin of the family fortune—Ivan discards them all. The notebook falls to the ground, unseen and unrecognized by him, then joins the rest of the archive in the garbage van. Nor does Ivan have progeny; he is the last of the Sonnenscheins, alone in the city crowds.

Yet the ending of the film is clearly meant to be upbeat: the pan over Budapest, the swelling music, Ivan's final voice-over announcing that he feels free indicate a hopeful mood. Is this a triumph of individualism and an affirmation of the individual artist? What if, instead of reading the final images of *Sunshine* as a promise, we were to read it as ironic: not Szabó's dream, but a delusion of his traumatized hero? Like the Danube that flows in Budapest, beautiful but full of Jewish ghosts, *Sunshine* is a deeply moving and troubling film.

Abridged from: Susan Rubin Suleiman, "Jewish Assimilation in Hungary, the Holocaust, and Epic Film: Reflections on István Szabü's *Sunshine*," *Yale Journal of Criticsm* 14, no. 1 (2001): 232–52; updated by the author.
    Background: http://www.porges.net/JewishHistory OfHungary.html.

Bibliography

Braham, Randolph L. *The Politics of Genocide: The Holocaust in Hungary.* Detroit: Wayne State University Press, 2000.

Cunningham, John. *Hungarian Cinema: From Coffee House to Multiplex.* London: Wallflower, 2004.

Déak, István. "Strangers at Home." *New York Review of Books*, July 20, 2000, 30–32.

Kaufman, Jonathan. *A Hole in the Heart of the World: Being Jewish in Eastern Europe after World War II.* New York: Viking, 1997.

Kovács, András. "Jewish Groups and Identity Strategies in Post-Communist Hungary." In *New Jewish Identities: Contemporary Europe and Beyond*, edited by Zvi Gitelman, Barry Kosmin, and András Kovács. New York: Central European University Press, 2002. 211–42.

McCagg, William O., Jr. *A History of the Hapsburg Jews, 1670–1918.* Bloomington: Indiana University Press, 1992.

Patai, Raphael. *The Jews of Hungary: History, Culture, Psychology.* Detroit: Wayne State University Press, 1996.

43. Burman's Ode to El Once Neighborhood

The Lost Embrace

TAMARA L. FALICOV

Lost Embrace (*El abrazo partido*), directed by Daniel Burman [A]
Argentina, France, Italy, and Spain, 2003

In the mid-1990s, young directors such as Daniel Burman began making films about ethnic identities and multiple subjectivities in Argentina. Because these filmmakers relied more on personal stories than on overtly political or historical issues, they paved the way for various ethnic communities to be the focus of Argentine films. Although there is a history of Jewish-themed films in Argentine cinema, there have been few Jewish directors who told these tales from a personal, semi-autobiographical standpoint. In previous decades, the few films that represented narratives of Argentine Jews included Juan José Jusid's *The Jewish Gauchos* (1974); Beda Docampo Feijóo's World War II drama, *Beneath the World* (1987); Raúl de la Torre's *Poor Butterfly* (1986); and Eduardo Mignogna's *Autumn Sun* (1996). The directors themselves, with the exception of Feijóo, were not of Jewish origin, but they made thoughtful films with wide-ranging and nuanced depictions of Jews in Argentina.

    Currently, Daniel Burman and his contemporaries are making films that expand the traditional notion of what it means to be Argentine, thus including characters who have traditionally been invisible or excluded from Argentine screens. Moreover, many in this newer group of filmmakers do not identify with a European-influenced culture. Rather, they identify with

From left to right, Daniel Hendler (as Ariel), Adriana Aizenberg (as Sonia), and Jorge D'Elia (as Elias), at the family shop in the Once. From *Lost Embrace* (2003), directed by Daniel Burman. NEW YORKER FILMS/PHOTOFEST

ethnic minorities and working-class people living and working in urban areas such as Buenos Aires. One of their aims is to project a more varied and heterogeneous face of national identity in Argentina. Along with Burman, the filmmakers Ariel Winograd (*Cheesehead* aka *My First Ghetto* [2006]) and Gabriel Lichtmann (*Jews in Space, or Why Is This Night Different from All Other Nights?* [2005]) are shedding a more youthful light on the Jewish community in Buenos Aires. Told from a twenty-something perspective, peppered with a lot of bittersweet and self-effacing humor, these movies recall early Woody Allen films.

One might call Daniel Burman the godfather of the new Argentine-Jewish cinema. In fact Burman has become one of the most important Argentine filmmakers to come on the scene in the

1990s as the auteur par excellence of the Argentine Jewish community. Director of ten films, he is best known for his trilogy dealing with Jewish identity: *Waiting for the Messiah* (2000), *Lost Embrace* (2004), and *Family Law* (2006). His first feature film, *A Chrysanthemum Bursts in Cinco-esquinas* (1998), features an Orthodox Jewish man in a supporting role. His documentary *Seven Days in Once* (2001) profiles Jewish community members of Once, a historic Jewish neighborhood and in the garment district that forms the backdrop for all of Burman's Jewish-themed films. His most recent documentary, *36 Righteous Men* (2011), follows Orthodox Jews on an annual pilgrimage to the tombs of *tzaddikim* [righteous men] in Russia, Ukraine, and Poland, culminating at the tomb of the seventeenth-century founder of Hasidism, the Baal Shem Tov.

With the current Jewish population estimated at roughly 250,000 inhabitants, Argentina's Jewish community is the largest in Latin America. Historically, the Jewish community settled in two Jewish neighborhoods in Buenos Aires; the aforementioned Once and Villa Crespo. The principal setting and actions in *Lost Embrace* are the daily goings-on in a galleria in Once—a mall-like arcade, with all of the shopkeepers' daily lives keeping the story abuzz with the various business transactions and social interactions that form daily life in the barrio. The protagonist of *Lost Embrace*, Ariel Makaroff, is our tour guide, taking the viewer into the labyrinthine passageways of the galleria, where he and his mother, Sonia, work at the family-owned lingerie shop. In a quirky, sputtering, voice-over narration, Ariel introduces us to the multicultural scene that is the galleria, with members of Italian, Korean, Jewish, and other ethnic groups selling their wares and eking out a living during a difficult economic downturn. Ariel informs us that while they may not be earth-shattering stories, each store owner or worker has stories to tell. These are personal, sometimes humorous, pieces describing average people in a small, intertwined world that they inhabit—something akin to what a modern-day Isaac Bashevis Singer might produce. Rather than a typical omniscient narrator, Ariel resembles a native informant interested in exposing those who may not be familiar with them to the local cultural codes transmitted in this spirited and busy workplace.

For example, when the audience is introduced to the Saligani family, the Italians who own the radio repair shop and the beauty salon, Ariel says that they are known to speak loudly or shout, but that although the viewer might think they are angry people, for them, culturally, "yelling is their way of communicating." He goes on to show other tenants in the galleria, such as the Korean couple who own the feng shui shop, the cousins—not brothers—who own the Levin Brothers fabric shop, and other characters, like Ariel's brother, Joseph, who would have liked to be a rabbi but instead sells cheap imported tchotchkes (knickknacks) from an upstairs office.

Critics have noted that the galleria is a microcosm for life in Buenos Aires reflecting the period after the economic crisis that befell the country in 2001 (Lerer). What was once a Jewish neighborhood has been transformed by Koreans, Peruvians, Armenians, and Italians. According to Burman, they work in this multicultural milieu "without any problems of intolerance." (Burman quoted in Feinstein) Burman's "Ariel" trilogy (all three films have a protagonist with the same first name, although they have different surnames) are all semi-autobiographical films, with Daniel Hendler, a Uruguayan Jewish actor, as the lead and Burman's alter ego in all three films. The script of *Lost Embrace* was written with Marcelo Birmajer, an Argentine Jewish novelist who also writes on urban themes. Moreover, César Lerner, who composed the original score, and Alejandro Brodersohn, the film's editor, are also Argentine Jews.

Because Burman grew up in Once, his objective is to tell everyday stories characteristic of the area. To add verisimilitude to the project, Burman rented an abandoned shopping mall two blocks from where he grew up and created a movie set there. The film's documentary feel is accentuated when scenes take place out on neighborhood streets amid the traffic and the noise—for instance, on Tucumán and J. E. Uriburu streets, near the Argentine Israeli Mutual Association (AMIA)—and in interior spaces such as the Jewish club Hacoaj, where Burman spent much of his childhood.

Carolina Rocha (344) notes how the film uses

the formalist qualities of documentary filmmaking, such as the use of the zoom lens, the constant reframing of the image, and the hand-held camera. Burman noted his reason for using these techniques: he "needed the immediacy of contact with the characters, which explains why [he] chose this [form of filming] device." (Metzger quoted in Rocha) In the "Making of *Lost Embrace*," a feature on the DVD of the film, Burman states: "I think that El Once is very ugly, and it is always a challenge to find the beauty among such ugliness. All of that noise and chaos makes it impossible to believe that in every moment and every frame of that chaos, there are a ton of stories that one wouldn't know about otherwise . . . a person carrying rolls of fabric, a person screaming on his cellphone arguing about the price per meter of fabric."

Despite the neighborhood's depiction as a densely inhabited space—with people from all walks of life milling about, carrying out their business—it is also seen as a space of danger. Burman alludes to security concerns in the earlier *Waiting for the Messiah*, when the viewer sees orange safety pylons outside of synagogues and Jewish community centers. This brief mention in the opening of the film refers to a horrific attack on the Jewish community (and the community at large) on July 18, 1994, when a car bomb exploded in front of the AMIA building, leaving 85 people dead and wounding 300 others. It was the biggest attack on Argentine soil since World War II.

In *Lost Embrace*, Ariel Makaroff often seems confused, inarticulate, and neurotic. He frequently wishes to escape his comfortable, insular surroundings (which he calls "the bubble") in pursuit of something "out there"—whether that be a better life in Europe, or an illicit relationship with an older, leggy, blond, non-Jewish woman who runs an Internet café (and who invariably disappoints his mother). Traumatized by his father's abandonment and the breakup of the family, Ariel later learns that his father did not leave Argentina for Israel in pursuit of the Zionist ideal, as Ariel had thought. Rather, he wanted to escape the infidelity of his wife with the shopkeeper next door. Instead of confronting the situation, the father left. Like his father, Ariel prefers to run away in times of crisis.

As Pablo Suárez (59) rightly observes, Burman's preferred camerawork has been characterized as "frenetic handheld movement, jump cuts, and maddening rhythms," clearly influenced by the French New Wave. Burman uses this camera technique to emphasize Ariel's inability to articulate his feelings and thoughts. For example, in one scene between Ariel and his grandmother, a Holocaust survivor from Poland, Ariel asks for her Polish citizenship papers so that he can apply for Polish citizenship and move to Europe in search of better economic prospects. Ariel arrives at her apartment, and the camera focuses on him asking for the papers. He asks for them in fits and starts; there are rapid, jerky editing movements demonstrating how difficult it is for him to ask her for the documents. The audience can infer that he is aware of her discomfort at the request. She loathes the experiences she witnessed in Poland, and he worries that she will not want to talk about them and probably does not approve of his plan to gain Polish citizenship, a country where her people were annihilated.

The grandmother acts as a repository of cultural memory. She once lived a blissful life as a young Jewish girl in Poland. She grew up to love singing in Yiddish, her mother tongue, until her husband forbade it, perhaps because Yiddish was a marker of difference. Ariel, in contrast, tries to skirt the issue of what gaining Polish citizenship for a Jewish person might imply. It is one of the many personal issues that he has yet to confront, but in this particular instance he does not engage in an interior monologue about the conflict between his Jewish identity and his desire to leave Argentina.

His decision might also be a product of the times. During that period, after the 2001 economic crisis, many Argentines tried to secure citizenship papers from the Old Country—that is, from their grandparents who had immigrated from Italy, Spain, or Eastern Europe. Thus, in a reversal of their journeys to Argentina to *hacer la América* [to have the American dream], the immigrants' grandchildren were heading back to Europe in search of greater economic opportunity. Indeed, even the sage rabbi who gives Ariel advice decides to leave for greener pastures in Miami Beach, to serve the Latino Jewish community there. And Daniel Burman in real life used his Polish ancestry to move temporarily to Poland during an especially severe economic downturn in Argentina. In the end of the scene, Ariel's grandmother relents and gives him her papers, but not without fulfilling her wish to burn her Polish passport. Ariel offers to witness and assist her in this cathartic act.

In addition to his difficulties dealing with an older generation, Ariel also has trouble relating to Jewish women. The film demonstrates that he cannot sustain a long-term relationship with his girlfriend, Estela, who is now pregnant and has moved on with her life. Meanwhile, Ariel, always in a holding pattern, has a vapid fling with the manager of the Internet café. This tension of not rushing to marry the "nice Jewish girl" next door in spite of family expectations to do so is a narrative thread that runs through both *Lost Embrace* and *Waiting for the Messiah*. Burman himself faced that dilemma and has been quoted in an interview as saying that there was needless pres-

sure for him to marry within the faith, and that in his opinion, there was no such thing as a "Jewish-ometer" that calibrated if one was a "good enough" Jew (Quoted in Falicov 136).

In essence, then, Burman's films explore questions of Jewish identity in the context of a largely Catholic country. Although these films treat the Argentine-Jewish experience in specific ways (from the perspective of a bewildered, bumbling, youthful, and naive male, peppered with a lot of humor), they attempt to grapple with age-old questions that plague all minority communities: about continuing the legacy of traditions, intermarriage, getting along with one's elders, and how to interact with members of the dominant culture and one's own community.

In the "The Making of *Lost Embrace*," Burman explains that for him, the most important facet of the film is the relationship between father and son. He is interested in the construction of paternity and how Elias, the father, abandons his sons and how this shapes young Ariel's worldview. This focus becomes more pronounced with the revelation that the father left for Israel to "pursue his ideals" the day after Ariel's ritual circumcision, which occurs eight days after birth. His father's departure affects Ariel's whole life, and, as Burman points out, "the father's absence has a more profound effect on him than if he were present" ("The Making of Lost Embrace," DVD). In essence, Elias assumes mythical proportions in Ariel's mind. Any memory, story, or rumor about Elias is seized on by his impressionable son, who has no personal memory of Elias. Ariel seems to always be waiting for his father, despite resenting him for leaving without any explanation. Norberto Padilla (300) points out that it is no coincidence that the name Elias in Spanish is Elijah in Hebrew. Perhaps the waiting for and the return of Elias has resonance for those who await the ghost of Elijah, the prophet who heralds the coming of the Messiah each year during the Passover seder.

Lost Embrace met with much critical acclaim when it was released, winning two awards at the Berlin Film Festival: the Grand Jury Prize and a Silver Bear for best actor (Daniel Hendler). The film went on to be Argentina's nomination for best foreign film in the 2004 Academy Awards.

Background: http://www.jewishvirtuallibrary.org/jsource/vjw/Argentina.html.

Bibliography

Falicov, Tamara L. *The Cinematic Tango: Contemporary Argentine Film*. London: Wallflower, 2007.

Feinstein, Howard. "The Moral Dilemma of Burman's *Lost Embrace*." indieWire (Feb. 5, 2005), http://www.indiewire.com/article/the_moral_dilemma_of_burmans_lost_embrace/.

Foster, David William. *Perspectives on the City and Cultural Production*. Gainsville: University Press of Florida, 1998.

Lerer, Diego. "Tiempos Polacos" *Clarín*, March 25, 2004, 4.

Padilla, Norberto."Dos miradas sobre el judaismo argentino" [Two views on Argentine Judaism]." *Criterio 6*, no. 2294 (2004), 299–301.

Rein, Ranaan. *Argentine Jews or Jewish Argentines?* Leiden, the Netherlands: Brill, 2010.

Rocha, Carolina. "The Many Faces of Buenos Aires: Migrants, Foreigners, and Immigrants in Contemporary Argentine Cinema (1996–2008)." In *Visual Communication: Urban Representations in Latin America*, edited by David Foster and Denise Correa Araujo, 110–38. Porto Alegre, Brazil: EditoraPlus, 2008. http://www.siue.edu/crocha/files/visual.pdf.

Suárez, Pablo. "The Burman Identity: Who Is Argentine Director Daniel Burman? And Why Can't His Characters Get It Together?" *Film Comment* 42, no. 3 (2006): 54–59.

44. Sexuality, Orthodoxy, and Modernity in France

North African Jewish Immigrants in Karin Albou's *La Petite Jérusalem*

ALYSSA GOLDSTEIN SEPINWALL

Little Jerusalem (*La Petite Jérusalem*), directed by Karin Albou [A]
France, 2005

Philosophy won't fulfill you! Philosophy won't give you children!

—Laura's mother

La Petite Jérusalem is a deceptively simple film. On one level, it is a classic French coming-of-age story. But this rich film has multiple dimensions. It offers a glimpse into several important themes in modern Jewish and French history: the tensions between tradition and modernity, the place of women in Orthodox Judaism, the migration of North African Jews to France, intergroup relations in France, and the future of Jews in contemporary Europe. The film's reception also reveals much about modern French ambivalence toward cultural diversity.

Jews have lived in France for centuries. Large Ashkenazi populations have historically lived in Alsace and Lorraine, with a sizable Sephardic community (refugees from Spain and Portugal during the Inquisition) in the region of Bordeaux. France's history with regard to the Jews has had multiple outcomes. On the one hand, some of the most prominent nineteenth-century antisemites were French, and the country also gave birth to World War II's collaborationist Vichy regime. On the other hand, France has launched some of the most tolerant ideals in

modern history. The birthplace of Enlightenment ideals of equality, France was the first modern nation-state to grant equal citizenship to its
Jewish population, doing so during the French
Revolution (the United States granted equality
to Jews in 1789, but only at the federal level; restrictions continued in some states). Since then,
with the notable exception of the Vichy period,
French Jews have enjoyed greater acceptance and
social integration than Jews nearly anywhere else
in the world. Americans have yet to have even a
Jewish vice president, but France has had five
Jewish prime ministers (three with two Jewish
parents, and two with Jewish fathers). Outside of
politics, French Jews have found success in numerous fields, and they have created a full range
of Jewish communal organizations.

French Jews have benefited from France's distinctive model of dealing with diversity—known
as republican universalism—in which all citizens
are presumed to be equal and indistinguishable.
This means that, at least in the public realm, their
differences are seen as irrelevant; all French citizens are considered to be exactly the same. What
the French call American-style "communitarization"—where members of a particular group act
as a bloc in public life, rather than as individuals—
has remained suspect in the French republican
system, where people are supposed to speak in
politics only as individuals and without reference
to their "private" differences. Related to this is the
French model of *laïcité* (secularism). This model
stems from the French Revolution's efforts to
break the control of the Roman Catholic Church
(long an economic powerhouse in the country as
well as the dominant religion); it still governs the
way most French people think about church and
state today. Whatever their religion, French people are expected to keep their practices private; in
the public realm, they are to act only as French

individuals, not as Catholics, Protestants, or Jews.
French Jews, grateful for their emancipation, long
embraced this model; although not pluralist in
the American style, it has led to a relatively safe
and well-integrated existence that was the envy of
Jews in other parts of Europe (and often attracted
Jewish immigrants from other countries).

After the Holocaust, French Jews' perceptions
changed. Reacting to the horrific separating out
of Jews from other French citizens, many Jews
began to chafe at "assimilationism"; they became
more assertive about their Jewishness. The immigration of large numbers of North African Jews
to France in the 1960s changed this status quo
even further. Morocco, Tunisia, and Algeria had
been colonized by France in the nineteenth century. Their Jewish inhabitants had been granted
special privileges, distinguished legally from their
Muslim neighbors (something at odds with the
universalism practiced in metropolitan France).
This practice stemmed both from a classic colonial
strategy of favoring certain groups over others to
gain local allies and from lobbying by French Jews
in favor of their fellow Jews overseas. When the
colonies became independent in the 1950s and
1960s, a large portion of their Jewish populations,
along with French white settlers, left to live in
France. Jewish emigration to France was spurred
further by ongoing tension in Arab countries after
the creation of the state of Israel.

Having lived under French rule for a century
or more, North African Jews who immigrated to
France shared many commonalities with native-
born French Jews. Many had eagerly embraced
French culture under colonization, attending
French schools and making French their daily
language. Frenchification was particularly strong
among Algerian Jews, as Algeria had become an
actual French department, the equivalent of
statehood in the United States.

Still, these new arrivals differed from metropolitan French Jews in a number of ways. Although they are sometimes called Sephardim, many of the immigrants did not descend from Spanish Jews but were indigenous to North Africa. Their mother tongue was Judeo-Arabic, although younger urban Jews in North Africa had begun to use French instead. Another difference between these Jews and their metropolitan counterparts was economic. Although Jews in North Africa had had a variety of socioeconomic statuses—some had been wealthy merchants and civil servants; others had been artisans—they arrived poorer than most French Jews because they had to leave most of their possessions behind. Moreover, the metropolitan economy often forced them to work in lower-status jobs than they had previously held. Many settled in the housing projects built for postcolonial refugees just outside Paris. (French urban geography is different from that in the United States, with French inner-city districts being wealthier, and the suburbs containing more lower-income and multiethnic communities.)

A more fundamental difference has come from the immigrants' conception of Judaism's place in society. They thought of themselves as Jews first; they did not feel called to hide their religion in public. Tunisians and Moroccans in particular also tended to be more religiously observant than many Ashkenazim (on other differences among North African Jews, see Sussman, as well as Simon, Laskier, and Reguer). Their "cultural self-confidence as Jews," in Shmuel Trigano's words (185), added a new element to French Jewry. As Sarah Sussman has noted, metropolitan Jews eagerly welcomed the new arrivals in the hope that they could inject new life into what had become a depleted community in the wake of the Holocaust. The new immigrants did revive France's

Jewish community, and spurred the creation of myriad community organizations.

La Petite Jérusalem introduces us to the North African Jewish community in France by focusing on one Tunisian-born family. Laura, the main character, immigrated as a young child from Djerba, one of Tunisia's more traditional Jewish communities. Her family consists of her pious older sister, Mathilde; Mathilde's husband, Ariel, an Orthodox man of Ashkenazi descent; Mathilde and Ariel's four young children; and Laura and Mathilde's mother. They live together in a small apartment in the high-rise housing projects of Sarcelles (a heavily Jewish area nicknamed "Little Jerusalem"), just north of Paris. Laura follows religious rules scrupulously, yet as an eighteen-year-old philosophy student at the University of Paris, she has begun questioning her faith.

Given that the film's writer and director, Karin Albou, is Jewish and of Algerian descent, one might guess that the film reflects her own autobiographical struggles. The reality is more complex, however. Although Albou's father is a Jew born in Algeria, her mother is a French non-Jew; other relatives through marriage are from the Caribbean. Albou married an Israeli and converted to Judaism as an adult. Never Orthodox herself, she befriended many Orthodox people while growing up, and the story line reflects her imaginings about their struggles. She nevertheless has conceded that she sees a lot of her eighteen-year-old self in Laura.

Albou has suggested that the film's central tension is between law and freedom (interview with Albou on DVD). The film begins by showing Laura deeply imbedded in her Orthodox community; she is studying the Torah as she gets dressed for Tashlich, a service held on Rosh Hashanah. However, Laura leaves the community's confines frequently to go to central Paris, where she is studying Enlightenment philosophy. Her professor poses a question: "Is freedom won by obeying the law or by breaking it?" Laura is the only one in the class to support the former proposition; even as she questions her faith, she still believes that law and ritual provide an essential structure for living. She begins substituting Kantian rituals (including a promenade at exactly the same hour each night) for halakhic ones, before abandoning both as she gives in to her passions. In an interview on the DVD of the film, Albou says she wants viewers to debate what freedom means to them after viewing it.

Though the law-freedom dialectic is certainly an important one, the film contains many other themes as well, which are perhaps of greater significance for viewers interested in the modern Jewish historical experience. In its basic story line, *La Petite Jérusalem* parallels other French coming-of-age films. A young woman who has no experience of love finds herself attracted to a stranger. After trying to repress her thoughts of him, she succumbs to passion. In explicit scenes certain to unsettle any Orthodox viewers, the film traces Laura's discovery of her sexuality and her delight in erotic pleasures.

In contrast to other French coming-of-age films, there are some significant twists. First, since Laura's family is Orthodox, sexuality has a different meaning than in general French culture; the coming-of-age story turns into a conflict between traditional and modern values. In a classic French girl's coming-of-age film like *36 Fillette* (directed by Catherine Breillat; 1989), such an affair appears as a natural and necessary rite of passage. However, since Orthodox Judaism permits sex only within marriage, and in some interpretations prohibits any physical contact between an unmarried man and woman, a young woman's

sexual explorations are unacceptable transgressions. Interestingly, in contrast to how the film's characters regard Laura's actions, the filmmaker treats Laura's affair in a more classic French style; it marks her transition to being a fully mature adult, capable of making her own decisions about sexuality. As Albou states in her interview on the DVD, Laura's character is built around her fear of her desires; when she develops a real attraction to a man, her preconceptions about love collapse.

The conflict between traditional and modern values with respect to women and sexuality can also be seen through the experiences of Laura's sister, Mathilde. Though Mathilde has borne four children, she remains profoundly uncomfortable with her own sexuality. She deeply loves her husband, but when she discovers that he is having an affair (signaled by her finding blond hairs on his black suit), she is forced to realize that her understanding of Judaism has made her sexually repressed. To Mathilde, modesty is the quality most required for Orthodox women; Ariel's claim that he had the affair because he "respected" her and did not want to "ask her to do things only I like" at first sounds extremely disingenuous. Yet Mathilde eventually reveals that her conception of modesty has prohibited her from even touching her husband's genitals, let alone initiating or taking pleasure in their sexual encounters. Since she desperately wants to preserve her marriage, the film shows her seeking marital advice from a woman who works at the mikvah [the ritual bath], and eventually deciding (after much reluctance) that she can explore her sexuality with her husband while retaining her modesty. Albou has said that this story line was informed by an Orthodox friend's account of the differences between French Orthodox and their counterparts abroad: "They [French Orthodox] are Orthodox for all other issues, and their rabbi said that for sexuality they were liberated. He said the most important thing is to save the marriage" (quoted in Hiller). Here, the film's message seems to be that general French attitudes about sexuality are more natural than those of many Orthodox, and that maturity requires exploring sexual desire instead of being overly constrained by religious law.

In addition to these Orthodox twists on the coming-of-age tale, *La Petite Jérusalem* offers a second surprise: the man with whom Laura has her sexual awakening is an Algerian Muslim (named Djamel). This plot device adds dramatic tension to the film. From a historical perspective, it also allows viewers to see that there are more similarities between North African Jews and Muslims in France than they might imagine. Both Laura's family and Djamel's are of modest means; they live in the same projects in Sarcelles. Both Laura and Djamel work as custodians at a preschool. Both are intellectuals. Djamel was journalist in Algeria and wrote a book about a female mystic. Both are seeking to break away from parts of their religion that they find restrictive. Both were born in North Africa and speak Arabic.

Yet the film also shows that, despite these similarities, traditional taboos remain strong. Even in the modern era, individuals do not have complete autonomy but often find themselves bound by the ties of community. Djamel brings Laura home to meet his relatives, hoping that they will embrace her. His hopes are disappointed, however. As an undocumented immigrant, he is dependent on them; when they declare that they cannot accept Laura unless she converts to Islam, Djamel breaks off the affair to avoid being ejected from their home. Laura's desire for Djamel is so strong that she would have risked estrangement from her family to be with him; she is heartbroken and attempts suicide. Here, the possibility

of a Muslim-Jewish romance appears as a mirage. In Alan Astro's view, the film differs from *Romeo and Juliet* or *West Side Story*; in *La Petite Jérusalem*, opposition to intergroup romances appears not only inevitable but also not unreasonable, given social realities.

The film shows still more serious signs of fissure between Muslims and Jews in France. The reemergence of antisemitism there since 2000 is signaled by two incidents: one in which the synagogue is set ablaze, and another in which masked men brutally attack a group of men and boys wearing yarmulkes as they play soccer. These scenes reflect the rise in violence against Jews in France and elsewhere in Europe since the outbreak of the second intifada in the West Bank and Gaza. Although overt antisemitism largely disappeared in France after the Holocaust, as the French confronted the horror of what had happened to their Jewish fellow citizens, it has reappeared among many young Muslims in the suburbs, who themselves feel ill accepted in French society and are increasingly falling prey to new kinds of antisemitism.

Finally, the film offers insights into other dimensions of North African Jewish acculturation in France. Laura's mother still practices the folk Judaism common among rural North African women. However, she will be the last in her family to do so. Her daughters are both acculturating to French norms, if in different ways. Mathilde has adopted Ariel's Ashkenazi Orthodoxy and now practices a text-based Hasidic-style Judaism that would be unfamiliar to her ancestors. Laura has acculturated to French society in another manner. Equally disinclined toward her mother's belief in spells and her sister's Orthodoxy, she is more attracted to Enlightenment conceptions of freedom.

When it was released in 2005, *La Petite Jéru-*

salem received an unusually enthusiastic reception. With a few notable exceptions (like Mathieu Kassovitz's 1995 film *La Haine* and the 2006 Algerian-French production *Les Indigènes*), mainstream French films have generally shied away from portraying multicultural communities. Albou has stated that it is hard to make a film in France on North African subjects, that raising money for *La Petite Jérusalem* was difficult, and that many potential producers were frightened off by its subject matter (Albou's comments in Bouchardeau). Yet, in contrast to the obscurity of many other films on multicultural topics, Albou's film became a sensation, winning awards at the Cannes and Deauville film festivals and from the French Film Critics Association, and two nominations for the Césars, the French equivalent of the Oscars. Fanny Valette, who plays Laura, also won several awards. The film reached a much wider viewership than most independent films, as it was shown several times on major television channels and designated as a "film of the week" in the newspaper *Le Monde*.

Why did this film capture attention in a way that other French films on multicultural themes had not? Albou believes that it was her focus on issues with universal appeal like love and family. The film's dramatic tension and its believable dialogue no doubt helped, as did the strong acting of Valette and the rest of the cast. Albou's erotic treatment of the material likewise attracted attention to the film; many critics hailed her feminine sensibility in an industry dominated by masculine perspectives on sexuality.

However, the film scholar Carrie Tarr has argued that the film's success has more to do with how it plays into French ambivalence about cultural difference. First, Tarr (82) contends, Albou's film has been popular because it offers the "exotic spectacle for non-Jewish audiences" of Orthodox Jewish rituals, even though this may not have been Albou's intention. More fundamentally, Tarr (79) maintains, *La Petite Jérusalem*'s "vision of the minority community as inward-looking, rigid and constrained works to justify dominant negative perceptions of communitarianism." The influx of North Africans to France, combined with an increased cultural confidence among other French ethnic groups, has spurred an anxiety that the model of republican universalism is breaking down, that immigrants' desire to preserve their cultural particularities has created a self-segregating "communitarization" that threatens national unity. Tarr (78) notes that some less popular films about postcolonial migrants in France, such as *Rue des Figuiers* (directed by Yasmina Yahiaoui; 2005) have challenged these concerns by portraying the "hybrid, multicultural nature of postcolonial French society" as something positive. Albou, in contrast, allows Laura a choice between two alternatives: accept community strictures and remain isolated, or abandon her family and assimilate into the mass of French society.

Tarr's comments raise the issue of the ending of the film, in which Laura's family members decide that France is no longer their home and prepare to move to Israel. Their choice is not an isolated one; Carl Hoffman (80) has estimated that 11,148 French Jews made aliyah from 2000 to 2005 as antisemitic attacks on identifiably Orthodox Jews increased. Yet Albou permits Laura, who follows the more traditional Franco-Jewish path of adopting secular French values instead of exclusively Jewish ones, to remain in France. The film ends with Laura, alone but more enlightened, ready to start a new life on her own in Paris.

Albou has said that she did not mean to suggest that Orthodox Jews have no future in France. In an interview with Jordan Hiller, she insisted,

"French orthodoxy has a future. It better have one. That is my home." Viewers may feel, however, that the film's ending undermines this position. As Tarr (84) notes, the film "offers the prospect of integration only to the individual who chooses to abandon both family and community." Alan Astro (78) has argued that Laura can stay only because she has become a "latter-day maskilah" (a Jewish Enlightenment figure).

Tarr's critique of the film seems valid, based on the reactions of many non-Jewish French viewers. In the film journal *Positif*, Matthieu Darras, an important figure in European cinema, argued that the film revealed a "terrible collective failure, a France where the transmission of [national] values no longer works, where different communities do not succeed in cohabitating in the midst of the national community." He charged that the film shows only "too well the rise in communitarianism." Other critics have echoed this view, describing Laura as "stifled by her Orthodox Jewish family" before finally "opening herself to the world" ("Les Autres"). *Les Echos* noted archly that "the communitarianism sketched out here is not that of imams, but of rabbis" ("Entre Kant et la Torah").

Still, it would be unjust to see the film as one that depicts Jews only in a negative manner. Albou portrays a little-understood community in a way that might invite voyeurism, but she also invites empathy with her characters. Sometimes they make choices or have beliefs that the audience might not share or might even disdain (such as Laura's mother's criticism of Laura's secular studies, or Ariel's cheating on his wife). Yet they are complex characters who are portrayed sympathetically in other ways (as when Laura's mother sells her ring so that Laura can start afresh in Paris, or when Ariel patiently recommits himself to a wife who has been unable to show passion). Indeed, while many critics have focused on the "communitarian" aspects of the film, others have dwelt on its less political themes: the family dynamics, the law-freedom question, or the "beautiful revelation" that is Valette. The review in *La Tribune* ("Les Autres"), for instance, argued that the film transcends clichés about the suburbs. It is also worth noting how Albou underscores for non-Jewish audiences—who are sometimes told that antisemitic violence reflects fighting between French Jews and Muslims over Middle Eastern politics—that recent antisemitism has been unprovoked, and directed even at children.

The film's portrayal of Judaism is also more complex than Tarr's otherwise insightful critique allows. Albou (quoted in Hiller) has claimed that she tried to make Judaism appealing in the film. Jewish holidays pervade *La Petite Jérusalem*, signaling the passage of time. Albou told Hiller that she aimed to show the joy even of minor holidays: "I wanted to show things positively with a Shabbat meal where people are laughing and singing. I wanted to show Simchat Torah because . . . it's so special." These wonderful moments of community, which we see Laura fully enjoying, make her choice more wrenching than if Orthodox Judaism were portrayed only in a negative fashion.

Still, Albou's ambivalent feelings emerge when she states in her DVD interview that Judaism is a "nice religion" but that "when it is lived in an Orthodox way, it is very suffocating." Both because of its ambiguities and the breadth of the subjects it covers, *La Petite Jérusalem* remains a fascinating film. While it may reinforce certain French anxieties about cultural difference, it also humanizes North African Jews and sheds light on numerous aspects of contemporary French Jewish life. The film shows the enduring relevance of tensions between tradition and modernity, while also raising questions about Jews' future in contemporary Europe.

Background: http://sefarad.org/publication/lm/045/8.html; http://www.ifcj.org/site/News2?page=NewsArticle&id=12593.

Bibliography

Astro, Alan. "The Phenomenology of Francophonia in Three Philosophers and a Historian: Memmi, Derrida, Ben Aych, and Bénabou." *Jewish Social Studies*, n.s., 14, no. 3 (2008): 60–84.

Bouchardeau, Hélène. "L'Europe multiculturelle a-t-elle besoin du cinéma pour exister?" http://www.paris-europe.eu/IMG/pdf/MDE_06_synthese_cinema_et_multiculturalisme.pdf

Darras, Matthieu. "La Petite Jérusalem: Laura au pays des communautarismes." *Positif* 538 (December 2005): 28.

"Entre Kant et la Torah." *Les Echos,* December 14, 2005.

Hiller, Jordan. "Movies That Bang: La Petit Jerusalem [*sic*]." http://www.bangitout.com/reviews119.html.

"Jerusalem/s," *Le monde télévision*. April 12, 2009.

"Les autres films de la semaine." *La tribune*, December 14, 2005.

Schnapper, Dominique. *Jewish Identities in France*. Translated by Arthur Goldhammer. Chicago: University of Chicago Press, 1983.

Simon, Reeva S., Michael M. Laskier, and Sara Reguer, eds. *The Jews of the Middle East and North Africa in Modern Times*. New York: Columbia University Press, 2003.

Sussman, Sarah Beth. "Changing Lands, Changing Identities: The Migration of Algerian Jewry to France, 1954–1967." PhD diss., Stanford University, 2002.

Tarr, Carrie. "Community, Identity and the Dynamics of Borders in Yasmina Yahiaoui's *Rue des Figuiers* (2005) and Karin Albou's *La Petite Jérusalem* (2006) [*sic*]." *International Journal of Francophone Studies* 12, no. 1 (2009): 77–90.

Trigano, Shmuel. "The Notion of a 'Jewish Community' in France: A Special Case of Jewish Identity." In Jonathan Webber, ed., 179–88, *Jewish Identities in the New Europe*. Washington: Littman Library of Jewish Civilization, 1994.

PART NINE

Contemporary Israeli Experiences

45. *Munich*
A Bitter Fruit on the Olive Branch

NIGEL MORRIS

Munich, directed by Steven Spielberg [A]
Canada, France, and the United States, 2005

Days after *War of the Worlds* successfully opened, a terse statement announced Spielberg had started a film based on the massacre of eleven Israeli athletes during the 1972 Olympics. It premiered in the United States less than six months later, after low-key marketing—a review, background feature, and interview with the director in *Time* magazine, but no test, press, or industry screenings—and elsewhere fairly quietly in ensuing weeks.

Time's cover featured the director, solemn in a black polo neck, minus baseball cap, and the headline "Spielberg's Secret Masterpiece." This implied a revelatory dimension and claimed high-cultural auteur status. Spielberg declared profit was not his object. Following a blockbuster with a personal venture, he presented *Munich* as his "prayer for peace." The cover flagged "Spielberg on why his movies have changed," oblivious to the confirmation of *Jurassic Park 4* and *Indiana Jones 4* shortly after.

The initial announcement provoked controversy. *Munich*'s long-contested source book, George Jonas's *Vengeance*, reappeared with a fore-word by Avner Kaufman, purportedly its Mossad assassin. The filmmakers reportedly spoke to Avner "at great length" while shielding his identity. Aaron Klein, a *Time* journalist who also happens to be an Israeli intelligence officer, published simultaneously with the film's release a book claiming access to secret documents and interviews with Mossad agents and high-ranking officials. He appeared in two television documentaries timed to coincide with *Munich*'s release. Klein offered a different account from Jonas's regarding the Mossad's motivation and strategy, thereby reviving questions about Avner's credibility. Yossi Melman and Steven Hartov claimed to have evidence that Avner "never served in Mossad, or any Israeli intelligence organisation," but did not share it. Given the premise of *Vengeance* and *Munich* that Avner officially never existed, and the journalists' unlikely credentials—specializing in "intelligence affairs" and editing *Special Operations Report*—it hardly takes a conspiracy theorist to sense a smoke screen."Leaked" reports that Spielberg, afraid of condoning or condemning Israel's action, had consulted former President Clinton over the script, and enlisted some of his top aides to influence Jewish American and Israeli opinion over the movie's reception, reinforced the cachet of a significant cultural and political event. When Jonas lambasted Spielberg for "humanizing" Palestinian "demons," more publicity followed surrounding the movie and the book.

Shown (*from left*): Eric Bana (as Avner Kauffman) is briefed about his mission by Geoffrey Rush (as Ephraim, a Mossad case officer). From *Munich* (2005), directed by Steven Spielberg. UNIVERSAL STUDIOS/PHOTOFEST

Munich's release coincided with a political crisis instigated by the serious illness of Israeli Prime Minister Ariel Sharon, whose military tactic of *ex talionis* (an eye for an eye, a tooth for a tooth) had "become a guiding principle and tool of the Israeli army." Simultaneously militant Islamists won the Palestinian Authority election without a majority. Meanwhile hullabaloo raged over "extraordinary renditions" abroad of American-held prisoners for torture. This again questioned what "civilized" conduct is. As Golda Meir argues in the film: "Every civilization finds it necessary to negotiate compromises with its own values." Middle-East politics and American policy made the film a timely intervention.

Pundits who had not seen the film determined its reception. A Jewish pressure group demanded a boycott well in advance. Whereas DreamWorks solicitously screened it to relatives of the murdered athletes, who praised its treatment and intent, right-wing pro-Israelis initiated virulent opposition predicated less on historical accuracy than political presuppositions. One e-mail urged readers to shun "this Nazi propaganda movie made by Steven Spielberg in support of Arab murderers." In a rare interview Spielberg insisted "this film was not in any way, shape or form going to be an attack on Israel." After all, this was the filmmaker vilified by some for Zionist leanings in *Schindler's List*. Conversely, Abu-Daoud, who admitted masterminding Munich, objected to Spielberg's screenings for Israeli widows while neglecting the families of Palestinian victims.

Avner's relationship with father figures elaborates a recurrent Spielberg theme. Carl, the secret agent from *Catch Me If You Can*, returns as Carl the burly Mossad agent, similarly seen in phone booths wearing a porkpie hat, distinctive glasses, and tightly buttoned suits. Avner's actual father remains unseen in the movie. The grotesque Papa, an international Godfather selling names, services, and weapons to the highest bidder, becomes his surrogate. Other symbolic fathers, such as Mossad and several assassination targets, involve Avner in Oedipal conflicts in which good father and obscene father become indistinguishable, while Avner's doubts grow with his emergence into paternity and eventual need to protect his family from forces he has served.

Munich equally foregrounds motherhood. Avner's wife's pregnancy, mothers and grandmothers on both sides watching the Munich atrocity on television, and the centrality of Golda Meir, as Avner's dispatcher, and of his mother, whose convictions contrast with his nightmares, evoke associations with the nation and family he initially reveres, that then loom close to the monstrous feminine archetype.

Unlike *Schindler's List*, precise facts cannot be corroborated. Covert operations are by definition unverifiable. Intelligence organizations deceive as a matter of policy. That reportedly internecine executions within Arab factions might have been Mossad missions complicates *Munich*'s story, while the Mossad was prepared to take credit for assassinations performed by others. Klein's book informs readers that for "dramatic effect, minor details of certain instances have been changed, in keeping with the known habits and demeanour of participants." The documentary, *Munich: Mossad's Revenge*, aired before *Munich*'s UK release, features interviews with agents whose "appearance has been changed and their words spoken by actors."

Munich's creators called it "historical fiction" to recognize that it is clearly a cinematic thriller. The Oscar-winning documentary, *One Day in September*, had already pieced together the known facts about the massacre. Spielberg concentrated on its human and ethical cost, using thriller conventions to reach a mainstream audience. Most reviewers recognized this ambivalence. Andrew Anthony defined it as "an action thriller that is also something of a morality tale." Weaving "ethical drama into a jet-setting spy thriller," *Munich*, Michele Goldberg noted, explored how "vengeance and violence corrupt both their victims and their perpetrators."

Philip French dismissed the protagonists' guilt over "the way they're being morally corrupted by the incessant killing" as "pure Hollywood." Yet the film faithfully reproduces this from Jonas. Given that in the heat of the Beirut machine-gunning, executioners shine torches onto photographs to verify the victims' identities, it is inconceivable none experienced misgivings. Peter Bradshaw questioned the "attempts to insulate Avner's men from the mucky business of doing business with ideologues and political agencies by having them get all their information from an apolitical French mafia capo: a deeply unlikely invention which is frankly an insult to the intelligence." But Jonas plausibly accounts for Papa's organization. Amid proliferating militancy, Papa promotes a free market in terror, reasoning that most causes are ultimately just and that if factions are going to kill each other, they might as well get on with it, destabilizing governments that Papa mistrusts. This, after all, is not unlike the amorality of international arms trading, legitimate or otherwise.

Munich, then, as Richard Schickel insists, "is, morally speaking, infinitely more complex than the action films it superficially resembles." With little agreement over the Israeli-Palestinian conflict, *Munich* is a productively ambiguous offering. As a thriller it resembles Jonas's use of focalization on Avner's story overlaid with his own point of view. This dual focalization disquiets those expecting certainty through unproblematic identification, comforting fiction, undisputed evidence, or overt ideological statement. After the prologue the status of the Munich reconstructions become ambiguous. Are they subjective flashbacks, as the editing suggests—except Avner was not there—or "objective" drama-documentary?

While *Munich* deals with the Mossad myth that no antagonist was safe from reach, Melman and Hartov considered it disturbing "that it is substantially a fiction—which, given Hollywood's influence, may soon be regarded as a definitive account." They evoke the gullible spectator, unable to distinguish Hollywood thriller from documentary. They date these events thirty years in the past though Klein recounts assassinations into the 1990s. They claim that Spielberg could have phoned former Mossad and Black September heads for the facts. Conversely, Neil Ascherson insists that "the Israeli authorities remain unwilling to discuss the operation," and Klein notes that the agents who took part in it "led secret lives even within the Mossad."

Debates around *Munich* and Spielberg concern the film less than preexisting discourses about contentious issues: Middle East politics and docudramas for dramatizing factual material. A key moment is Avner's conversation with Ali, the gunman killed when guarding the team's next victim, about Palestinian aspirations. Critics considered it contrived that Avner's team found themselves sharing a safe house with Palestine Liberation Organization members. "Without that exchange, I would have been making a Charles Bronson movie—good guys vs. bad guys

and Jews killing Arabs without any context," Spielberg argued. To some the discussion treats both sides as morally equivalent, which does not fit their politics. To others, that it never really happened compromises whatever truth the movie might claim. Docudrama is "problematical," as Derek Paget explains, because like *Munich*'s initial caption, "it openly proclaims both a documentary and a dramatic provenance. This 'both/and' claim is often met with a critical refusal, an 'either/or' counter-claim that ends up treating it as 'bad documentary, bad drama, or both.'"

As a thriller, it replicates Johan's use of focalization on Avner's story overlaid with a more detached point of view. *Munich: Mossad's Revenge* contains interviews with sources, strident voice-over narration, thriller-style reconstructions, documentary news clips and stills, and dramatic music, structured sensationally with climaxes around commercial breaks. *Munich* similarly includes documentary clips. Rather than edited seamlessly into the film, they appear within the film's story line, or in close-up so that television scanning lines are prominent. Actual documentary material provides exposition and authenticates the narrative without disrupting its flow and anchors the action in time and place. Close-ups of poor-quality documentary footage, Paget argues, "suture" the framing narrative into reality. *Munich* not only includes broadcast television images, sometimes as a backdrop to staged interactions, but reconstructs the reporters' stakeouts from where they filmed.

Munich neither claims to be factual journalism nor insists that everything onscreen must have documentation. It does, however, as Paget puts it, try "to make a difference in the historical and political world . . . by going to places that are originally denied to the camera." One recurrent problem with docudrama, to which *Munich* is subject, is that personalization of issues, inherent in naturalistic drama, militates against objectivity and detachment in relation to moral and ethical predicaments. *Munich* deals, however, with the human implications of policies and prejudices, rather than questioning the rightness of positions, to draw viewers into the public debate about them.

Whereas classical narrative cinema promotes audience identification and catharsis, documentary addresses a distant and dispassionate observer. The mixing of forms in *Munich* occasions either suspicion and rejection or productive tension. The viewer seeks to confirm emotionally what he or she already knows intellectually. The spectator may possibly be drawn in by voyeuristic pleasure and accept that events might have looked and sounded as depicted. Crucially, the partly detached spectator can wonder if *Munich*'s meaning would differ if the documented and (speculated) events did not look and sound precisely like their screen enactments.

Julia Hallam discerns a "critically contentious trend" whereby Hollywood movies exploring political and social concerns utilize documentary footage to advance truth claims. This courts accusations of confusing "fact and fiction, official history and popular memory." She identifies three variants, each discernible in *Munich*: locations that are or appear to be where events actually occurred; period referencing that appropriates an era's stylistic techniques (*Munich* frequently adopts a 1970s style uncharacteristic of Spielberg, utilizing zooms in conjunction with pans, tilts, and racking focus, and panning and tracking to link parts of a location); and intertextual referencing that incorporates other films as "reference points." *Munich*'s television footage—much of it recognized from *One Day in September* and, for older spectators, from firsthand

memory—affords Spielberg's reconstruction an authenticating iconography. *Munich* features moments of double separation: when optimism expressed on television screens filters through the irony of knowing the outcome or when a roll call of dead athletes accompanies their living, smiling images in flickering monochrome on an oblique screen, intercut with Mossad's assembling of photographs of its intended targets.

Spielberg references other films to convey *Munich*'s themes. The subtle allusion to *Dr. Strangelove*, a satire on nuclear Mutually Assured Destruction, evoked by the Mossad war room with its suspended strip lights, may for some spur questioning of the utility and morality of retribution. The milk blending with blood and wine following the first assassination recalls Frankenheimer's *The Manchurian Candidate*, a paranoid thriller about shady governmental operations. The final sex scene, intercut with the Munich slayings, makes sense intellectually when recognized as an *homage* to Coppola's *The Godfather*, in which a christening alternates with a killing spree. The closing of Coppola's *The Conversation*, when espionage rebounds on its perpetrators, is recalled when Avner's activities return to haunt him and he slashes apart his mattress and dismantles his phone and television in search of explosives. Spielberg cites scenes from his own films, such as the severed forearm hanging from a fan after the hotel bombing, graphically similar to a horrific moment in *Jurassic Park*.

Whereas in *Munich* the protagonists' identities are unknown, Golda Meir and several Mossad targets resemble their historical counterparts. The casting also involved celebrity associations to imply how to view Daniel Craig (Steve), who already had been announced to play the next James Bond, appropriately for a spy thriller. Mathieu Kassovitz (Robert) had appeared in many successful French films; Ciaran Hinds (Carl) had been long associated with docudrama; Hans Zischler, a German, and Australians Eric Bana and Geoffrey Rush complete the ensemble, stressing the international composition of Israeli Jewry and increasing the movie's multinational appeal.

"With drama-documentary," a television executive told Paget, "there's always somebody who doesn't want it made." Since Klein confirmed a CIA and PLO link alleged in the film, efforts to undermine *Munich*'s credibility are unsurprising. *Walk the Line*, a contemporaneous release that claimed to be "inspired by real events," did not provoke debates about accuracy. Authenticity is questioned only when texts challenge common assumptions.

Self-reflexivity underscores *Munich*'s dialogic relationship with history and fiction. "They're movie stars," one of Avner's team complains when the freed Munich terrorists appear on television. Exposition of the kidnapping and several later events, such as the Lufthansa hijacking and a letter bomb campaign against Israeli embassies, occur on television screens in Israeli and Palestinian homes and cafés, on monitors in a broadcast control room, and viewfinders of news teams' cameras. The Munich outrage, the defining moment of modern-day terrorism, was deliberately a media event to spotlight the Palestinian issue. Over 900 million watched, including the captors themselves, who became aware of police approaching from live coverage of the intended rescue. Spielberg reinforces the point by juxtaposing within a single shot the iconic image of a ski-masked terrorist stepping onto the balcony on a black-and-white television with his identical action in color, seen from indoors in a simultaneous reconstruction.

Sexualization of their violence pathologizes the Mossad killers. It remains unclear whether they are sadistic as a result of previous trauma (arising from the shared experience of Jewish history) or become warped by their actions. The Dutch woman's horrible death indicates their depravity in concurrence with Robert's declining the unauthorized mission on grounds of wanting to remain righteous. Their actions degrade them as much as their victims, to whose level retribution sinks them. Hans drunkenly laments, "I wish I had let you close up her housecoat." Ascherson considers this execution "humiliating for the watcher." One may object to the scene, which is not real but a reconstruction, yet accept the deed and even desire it, proportional to identification with the killers. It does not indicate general misogyny on their part or the film's. They hate her personally because they are seeking vengeance.

Munich contains Spielberg's usual inscriptions of cinematic technology and institutions. Robert's toy Ferris wheel (recall the full-size versions in *1941* and *A. I.*) resembles a movie reel. There is a close up on it, accompanied by projector-like whirring, immediately before his life ends violently, if inadvertently, by his own hand. Golda Meir in her cabinet room sits in a projected beam, as does Papa during his last phone call to Avner. A flashback to Munich materializes on a DreamWorks cloudscape, Avner's projection on the rectangular surface of the airliner porthole as he flies to his mission in Geneva. The horrors that materialize seem very immediate in comparison with the news coverage shown. Ambient sounds fade to silence at key moments, as in *Saving Private Ryan*, enhancing psychological realism and emphasizing textuality. Papa's household, traversed by light shafts when Avner meets him, is followed by Avner looking back through the car window at an unattainable father since he, who as a child was sent to a kibbutz, is "excluded" by Papa: "We'll do business. But you aren't family."

Docudrama often exists precisely to reopen unresolved issues and hence does not rule out progressive potential. *Munich's* final shot, for example, showing the World Trade Center, evokes the photo effect; it therefore declares artifice and with it confronts the spectator, leaving unanswered questions about the point of including it.

Spielberg's archetypes—the Lacanian Imaginary, restoration of the family, Oedipal conflict—reappear curiously. Since Avner was "abandoned" in a kibbutz, his wife suggests: "Now you think Israel is your mother."' Meir, a wise, sensitive matriarch, tough and determined yet small and vulnerable, knows Avner's mother, emphasizing Israel's closeness and symbolic status as "motherland." His mother personifies Zionism when she tells Avner proudly he is what she and other Holocaust survivors "prayed for." Future Israeli Prime Minister Ehud Barak's participation wearing drag during the Beirut killings (a well-documented fact) bizarrely convolutes the state/mother conflation.

Like *Schindler's List, Munich* does not treat Jews as a homogeneous community. Relationships between family, nation, state, ethnicity, politics, and identity are complicated when Avner is described not simply as an Israeli but a *Yekke*, of assimilated Western European roots—an "outsider"—as opposed to Galicianers originally from Eastern European ghettos. The multinationalism of Avner's team—German, Belgian, South African, and Ukrainian—which permits them to operate discreetly in Europe, underlines the point.

The only families seen, other than distraught relatives of both the Israeli athletes and the Black September terrorists, are those Avner destroys (the second target, with his wife and daughter in Paris; a wife who is killed with the targets in Beirut); subsequently Avner with his, although he misses his daughter's infancy; and Papa's extended household. That Avner moves his family and eventually himself from Israel to New York sits uneasily with Zionism's agenda of establishing a Jewish homeland. His Mossad case officer—Ephraim, an older paternal authority who substitutes for Avner's absent father—refuses to accept Avner's traditional Jewish offer of hospitality and repudiates Avner and his qualms. Meanwhile, Avner's alternative to his horrific mission—he told his wife in the maternity room: "You're the only home I have"—represented in the kitchen showroom, is quashed when she says of their New York apartment: "The kitchen's too big."

Avner cooking gourmet meals at the head of his team, a virtual family, clearly parallels Papa. Noticing Avner's "butcher's hands," like his own, Papa claims these signify "gentle souls," an affinity between them. Family and home equate with closeness to the land. "Papa was a rolling stone," sings Steve nervously before one bombing, "wherever he went there was his home"—a detail that recalls Jewish statelessness before Israel. Ali's declaration, "We want to be nations—home is everything," follows Avner asking whether he misses his father's olive trees. Papa's garden parallels the good life, the Promised Land, for which Avner is fighting. Like Israel, guards patrol it. It is a corruption, an abomination. To do business, Avner negotiates compromise with his principles. If ethnicity rooted in religion is the basis of Israel's nationhood, strategic abandonment of its principles is no light matter. Meir's speech about negotiating compromise renders her either sinister or indeed compromised, hence essentially good, as the soft focus on her suggests. However, a photograph of her with Richard Nixon associates her with another leader whose compromising of the highest values was his downfall.

Munich offers not an "anything goes" of emptied signifiers, nor propaganda for a fixed position, but a post-9/11 engagement with real uncertainties. Objections to the film's politics express made-up minds and impose fixed agendas. As *Munich* enters the most intractable conflict in the world, this is unremarkable. Nevertheless, some of those views require consideration to demonstrate how *Munich* parleys them.

Schindler's List ended with allegedly pro-Zionist sentiment; it stressed continuity between surviving Jews and contemporary Israel. *Munich* seriously questions Israeli policies. Spielberg was criticized for recognizing that some Mossad victims were, as he put it, even if living double lives, "reasonable and civilized too." Conversely, Joseph Massad, a professor of Arab politics, unequivocally labels Avner's team a "terrorist cell" and protests that Spielberg "humanizes them." The movie's core is the dawning recognition of the ambiguity of "counterterrorism." The phrase equally implies *action against* terrorism and an opposing force that *uses* terrorism.

The world would be simpler if terrorists were not human. But the accusation that Spielberg "humanizes" any demon misses the point that humans are irredeemably flawed. Whatever one thinks of Mossad's executions, to deny humanity in those who perpetrate them and those targeted would diminish the enormity of events portrayed. Some operatives are doggedly persistent for personal reasons. Their mission combines prevention, deterrence, and revenge. In *Munich* the defence chiefs' first meeting makes clear that already sixty Arabs have died in retaliatory attacks.

Munich strives to maintain detached, challenging the viewer to reach a conclusion. Expectations of Hollywood heroism and villainy cause critics to detect unacceptable bias. Arabic dialogue subtitled into English in *Munich* makes Black September seem foreign—but then so does the Hebrew spoken at Mossad headquarters during the same sequence. Avner's conversation with an imminent target on a hotel balcony emphasizes common humanity and the possibility of dialogue. This actually occurs in the safe house, when Ali states the PLO position—"We want to be nations. Home is everything"—and in the compromise over music playing on the radio.

From a pro-Israeli position, Jonas distinguished the mission's "rightness" from its "usefulness" and the utility of counterterrorism generally. The debate surrounding morality in the film was already waged in its source book over twenty years ago, as was the question of the narrative's veracity. Klein too proclaims "utility" while ducking the issue of "justness" as "well beyond the scope" of his account." Yet these are precisely issues that the film raises emotionally and intellectually without offering answers.

When Spielberg shows Avner in a low-angle telephoto shot on the hotel balcony, the composition unmistakably recalls the famous Associated Press photograph of a hooded Munich terrorist. This does not *assert* moral equivalence but invites consideration of the possibility. Similarly, Israeli commandos changing clothes after landing in the Lebanon raid parallels the Munich terrorists after traversing the gates at the start. Jonas does not liken the assassins to terrorists, but reports them debating the distinction, with some of them indifferent to it. This preempts the criticism of highly placed Israelis and friends of Israel who accused *Munich* of "incorrect moral equation." The film stresses the team's efforts to protect innocents such as Hamshari's daughter.

Debates about distortion and bias could continue endlessly, missing the points that no representation is neutral and that *Munich* is not concerned with supporting one side or the other, but with exposing an endless cycle of violence. Ascherson objects that, although some Palestinians are presented sympathetically and given a brief voice, "apart from some shots of families watching television as the Munich tragedy unfolds, the Palestinians we see are almost exclusively terrorists." But other than Avner's wife and child and the Munich victims, almost every Israeli shown is either an assassin or a supporter of the policy. Hamshari and his French wife passionately argue the PLO case to Robert, posing as a journalist, and cite recent bloodshed at the hands of Israel. Klein shows Israel in a far worse light than Spielberg, whose film is about eleven lives for eleven lives, by observing that in the two-day attack on south Lebanon after Munich, "None of those killed [forty-five alleged terrorists] or captured [sixteen Palestinians] had any covert or operational affiliation with Black September." Revenge was less discriminating than the film suggests because it aimed at creating "a sense of permanent threat in the minds of Palestinian operatives and potential inductees."

Steve's conclusion, "The only blood that counts for me is Jewish blood"—a hard-line position uncomfortably mirroring that which spawned the Holocaust—is one position in a debate, not that of all Israelis. "By revealing Israel's internal dissent," Jonathan Freedland argues, pro-Israeli artists like Spielberg show the nation "in its best light." Israel has never officially accepted responsibility for assassinating PLO members blamed for Munich. Reflection on past deeds must be a prerequisite for progress.

Klein argues that Israel considered the assassinations effective in reducing attacks on Israeli targets abroad. Ephraim unsurprisingly makes the Israeli case when he tells Avner: "If these guys live, Israelis die. Whatever doubts you have." In *Munich: Mossad's Revenge*, Barak, who led the Beirut raid, states that some younger officers had voiced doubts. Ankie Spitzer, a Munich victim's widow, expresses her lack of sympathy with the killings

and poses the question Avner asks, why the alleged perpetrators could not be captured and tried. The contradictions *Munich* embodies have less to do with the film and more to do with the paradox it dramatizes, nowhere more apparent than in Meir's speech to a special gathering of the Israeli parliament one week after the atrocity: "From the blood-drenched history of the Jewish nation, we learn that violence which begins with the murder of Jews, ends with the spread of violence and danger to all people, in all nations, . . . We have no choice but to strike at terrorist organizations wherever we can reach them."

When Avner's team foresees the rise of more ruthless forms of terrorism, Avner concludes, "There's no peace at the end of this."

The myth of Mossad's effectiveness and tenacity equally suits Israel and Palestinian organizations involved in infighting. Truth is unlikely ever to emerge concerning the film's authenticity. Whether Avner really existed is beside the point. Events outside his direct experience are already public knowledge. Divergences from competing accounts are minimal (whether a bomb was inside a telephone or the table underneath) and alternative versions provide no higher degree of certainty. *Munich* acknowledges arguments and facts on both sides and tries to be balanced in its presentation of them. Without proposing an alternative or seriously questioning the necessity of Avner's team's actions (although certainly their effectiveness), *Munich* highlights the human and moral cost of such operations carried out, not only by Israel, in the name of freedom and civilization. It is important that the horror of both sides' activities is brought home in the aftermath of the hotel bombing, machine-gun executions in Beirut, and spurting bullet holes in the Dutch assassin's naked body, as well as in the Munich atrocity. Avner's mother, who stated earlier, "I look at you and I know everything you do," does not want to discuss his activities, declaring herself just thankful for "a place on earth." She and Papa represent every comfortable, "apolitical" individual who inhabits an economy heavily reliant on arms dealing or who would rather not know what violence governments perpetrate in the name of freedom.

Abridged from: Nigel Morris, *The Cinema of Steven Spielberg: Empire of Light* (London: Wallflower, 2007).

Source: George Jonas, *Vengeance: The True Story of an Israel Counter-Terrorism Team* (New York: Simon and Schuster, 1984).

Background: http://en.wikipedia.org/wiki/Operation _Wrath_of_God.

Bibliography

Ensaleco. Mark. *Middle Eastern Terrorism: From Black September to September 11*. Philadelphia: University of Pennsylvania Press, 2007.

Foy, Joseph J. "Terrorism, Counterterrorism, and the 'The Story of What Happens Next' in *Munich*." In *Steven Spielberg and Philosophy: We're Gonna Need a Bigger Book*, ed. Dean A. Kowalski, 170–87. Lexington: University of Kentucky Press, 2008.

Hallam, Julia, and Margaret Marshment. *Realism and Popular Cinema*. Manchester, UK: Manchester University Press, 2000.

Klein, Aaron J. *Striking Back: The 1972 Munich Olympics Massacre and Israel's Deadly Response*. New York: Random House, 2006.

Massad, Joseph. "The Moral Dilemma of Fighting Fire with Fire." *Times Higher Education Supplement*, January 27, 2006, 15.

Melman, Yossi, and Steven Hartov. "*Munich*: Fact and Fantasy." *Guardian*, January 17, 2006.

Paget, Derek. *No Other Way to Tell It: Dramadoc/Docudrama on Television*. Manchester, UK: Manchester University Press, 1998.

Reeve, Simon. *One Day in September: The Full Story of the 1972 Olympics Massacre and the Israeli Revenge Operation "Wrath of God."* New York: Arcade, 2000.

Schamus, James. "Next Year in Munich: Zionism, Masculinity, and Diaspora in Spielberg's Epic." *Representations* 100 (Fall 2007): 53–66.

Waltzer, Kenneth. "Spielberg's *Munich*, Ethics, and Israel." *Israel Studies* 11, no. 2 (2006): 168–71.

46. Dancing Solo in the Lebanese Mud

ILAN AVISAR

Waltz with Bashir (*Vals Im Bashir*), directed by Ari Folman [A]
Israel, France, and Germany, 2008

Israeli cinema is in search of itself—a surprising fact, considering how far it has come. Indeed, in many ways, the trajectory of Israeli cinema coincides with the history of the Jewish national movement. Back when it was a mere gleam in Herzl's eye, the father of modern Zionism considered producing a film to further interest in his cause. Later, foreign crews and local photographers alike captured images from the first decades of Jewish settlement in the land of Israel. Jewish entrepreneurs with vision established film companies in the 1930s, which went on to become Geva and Carmel Studios, the country's leading producers of newsreels two decades later. But Israeli cinema truly came of age only in the 1960s, on account of the efforts of prominent filmmakers Uri Zohar, Menahem Golan, and Ephraim Kishon. The three withdrew from the local cinema industry at the end of the 1970s, however, with Kishon's move to Switzerland, Golan's to Hollywood, and Zohar's turn to Orthodox Judaism. Then, in 1979, the Israel Film Fund was established, which went on to shape local cinema in the decades to come. To this day, the vast majority of Israeli films are produced under its auspices. Since the fund appoints referees to select which films are worthy of production, the public's taste is rarely taken into consideration. Not surprisingly, then, most Israeli films are noticeably noncommercial and marked by a highly personal—and frequently political—tone.

Whether in spite of these conditions or because of them, Israeli cinema must constantly battle for both status and survival. For three decades it has failed to turn out renowned filmmakers on even a local scale; so, too, has it failed to produce any films that might be considered true assets to Israeli culture. To be sure, in recent years Israel has seen its share of breakout films, relatively modest productions that have garnered significant attention abroad, even winning prizes at international film festivals—undoubtedly due, in large part, to their provocative political message. Yet it seems that Israeli cinema, hampered by a significant lack of funding, has difficulty aspiring to more than this, and perhaps for good reason: in the age of globalization, it faces stiff competition, not only from the Hollywood goliath, but also from the film industries of countries such as Japan, France, Italy, Russia, Germany, and China, all of which boast their own proud cinematic traditions.

Against this backdrop, it is clear why *Waltz with Bashir*, the 2008 animated documentary, caused such a stir at home. And not only here. After winning the 2008 Ophir Prize from the Israeli Academy for Film and Television, it went on to win both a Golden Globe and a César Award for best foreign film, along with numerous other awards and honorable mentions at international film festivals, making it the most celebrated Israeli film of all time. Nevertheless, Israelis will remember the film not only for its wins, but also for its losses. Although it was the front-runner at Cannes for the Golden Palm award for best film, *Waltz with Bashir* lost out to the French film *The Class*; likewise, while it was favored to win at the Oscars, it lost out once again, this time to the Japanese film *Departures*.

Ari Folman, *Waltz with Bashir*'s writer, director, and producer, belongs to the generation of Israeli filmmakers born in the 1960s. His first film, the documentary *Comfortably Numb* (1991), dealt with the effects of the Gulf War on a group of people from Tel Aviv. Here, Folman focused on the myriad and mundane details of everyday life disrupted by war. The end result is an ironic—and almost comical—portrayal of a society that yearns for normalcy even as it accustoms itself to life under fire. In 1996, Folman's first feature film, *Saint Clara*, opened to both critical acclaim and financial success. A teen drama based on the novel by Czech writer Pavel Kohout, the film's central character is a thirteen-year-old girl who acquires supernatural powers leading to catastrophic consequences. In *Made in Israel* (2001), Folman turned his attention once again to the malaise of Israeli reality, and dealt with sensitive issues of security, peace, and Holocaust remembrance. The story of the extradition of the last Nazi on earth from Syria to Israel on the eve of the signing of a peace treaty between the two countries, *Made in Israel* quickly descends into an over-the-top comedy as two criminals attempt to intercept the Nazi en route. They are charged with bringing him home to their Israeli boss, who seeks to kill him with his bare hands in revenge for the horrors suffered by his father during the Holocaust. Although it boasts impressive visuals and a number of profoundly moving scenes, *Made in Israel* is ultimately a cynical film, one that aspires to dismiss the notion that some topics are off-limits to criticism, and some cultural values above ridicule.

In *Waltz with Bashir*, Folman continues his journey into Israel's heart of darkness. That he does so by means of his own personal experience does not preclude the film's larger political significance; this journey, after all, also takes place in the nation's collective memory. And yet it is precisely his politics that Folman has refused to concede openly, preferring instead to let his film make implicit, evasive statements for him. By focusing on his own subjective point of view and sense of alienation, Folman would have us believe that *Waltz with Bashir* is free of ideological baggage and overt moral didacticism. This oblique approach makes the film a cinematic work deserving of careful examination—and, as it turns out, serious criticism as well.

The hero of *Waltz with Bashir* is Ari Folman himself, who seeks to remember his experience as a young soldier in the First Lebanon War (1982). Following his discharge from service, Folman made a clean break with his military past. Not only did he sever relationships with his fellow soldiers, but he also succeeded in suppressing all memories of his time in the army. *Waltz with Bashir*, therefore, turns this very process on its head. Now, Folman the director seeks to revisit the past and determine what traumas lie there. The psychological turmoil from which he suffers is made manifest by a string of remarkable images, beginning with the film's opening gambit: a pack of crazed, snarling dogs surge down an urban street, chasing after an invisible man. This, we learn, is the recurring nightmare that befalls an old army buddy with whom he meets up one night in a Tel Aviv bar after more than twenty years. During the war, the friend explains, he was charged with killing local dogs, whose barks might disclose the approach of Israeli soldiers on their way to carry out missions in Lebanese villages. The number of dogs he killed was twenty-

six—the same number that makes up the pack in his dreams.

It is this meeting that provides the catalyst for Folman's journey into the past. This kind of journey, which invariably leads back to some formative event, is a common narrative device in war films; usually, the result is a dreaded confrontation with the painful experience that continues to haunt the characters in question until the present day. Among the more famous films that utilize this device are *Hiroshima Mon Amour*, *The Manchurian Candidate*, *The Deer Hunter*, *Flags of Our Fathers*, and *In the Valley of Elah*, to name just a few. As in these films, *Waltz with Bashir* deals with issues of increasing importance in today's cultural discourse, such as testimony, memory, and persistent trauma.

As if to stake out its place among the heirs of a certain cinematic legacy, the film makes numerous referential nods to many of its well-known predecessors, primarily those depicting the Vietnam War. The song "Good Morning, Lebanon," for example, recalls the film *Good Morning, Vietnam*, and the image of an injured soldier sprawled in the center of an open plaza, sharpshooters waiting to pick off anyone who tries to pull him to safety, is reminiscent of a powerful scene from Stanley Kubrick's *Full Metal Jacket*. A nod to *Apocalypse Now* is also felt in the bombardment scenes, which streak the skyline with rising flames; in the battle montages to rock-music accompaniment; in the absurd juxtaposition of soldiers surfing while helicopters pound Beirut in the background; and finally, in the central image of the film, and the only one the hero remembers—three figures emerging naked from the ocean onto the shores of Beirut, a clear reference to the famous scene from *Apocalypse Now* in which the hero emerges from a jungle swamp to carry out one last murderous assignment. This imagery has been used—and abused—repeatedly in popular action films starring Sylvester Stallone (*Rambo*) and Chuck Norris (*Missing in Action*) and stirs, not coincidentally, associations with the great amphibious landings of World War II. Loaded with mythological and symbolic meaning, the motif draws its power from the obvious contrast between the purity of the water and the horrors of the battlefield, as well as from the metaphor of birth, the shock of moving from the innocence and security of the womb to the brutal and bloody world of reality. The same motif is also clearly visible in the dream of one of the film's soldiers, who sees himself jumping into water with a giant woman, and curling up on her stomach in a fetal position (the inspiration for which is the famous "penetration" scene in Pedro Almodúvar's *Talk to Her*).

But *Waltz with Bashir* is not a run-of-the-mill war film. It is also a documentary, and—perhaps its most innovative aspect—animated. The documentary aspect of the film comprises a series of interviews that Folman conducts with men who fought and served in Lebanon. While all but two interviewees speak in their own voices, the scenes in which they participate are converted into animation. Although at first glance, this technique appears a bit awkward, it allows the film to jump easily between different states of consciousness: testimonies, memories, hallucinations, and dreams. The dominant shades of gray and yellow also intensify the sense of an imminent apocalypse, and the characters are portrayed as though floating through a fluid reality in which real horrors and nightmares comingle with ease. Deadened, emotionless faces elicit a strong expressionist effect and convey mental states of detachment and horror. Usually identified with children's tales, animation is here employed in the service of sophisticated (mature) art, and pro-vides an unexpected means of coping with extreme psychological situations.

The oxymoron of documentary animation is a brilliant contribution by Ari Folman to the genre of war films in particular and the language of cinema in general. It also makes great practical sense. It permits Folman to present complex visual imagery that Israeli cinema, with its limited resources, would otherwise be unable to produce. Nevertheless, even the film's $1.3 million budget required numerous sources of foreign funding. In addition to four different Israeli production companies, *Waltz with Bashir* was produced with the help of two French companies, two German companies, and a British and American one. This level of foreign involvement in Israeli filmmaking usually has clear political implications. As we shall see, *Waltz with Bashir* is no exception.

Of the Israeli films produced with European funding in the 1980s and 1990s, many were what are known as "protest films," dealing with the Palestinian problem from a radical-left viewpoint. Then as now, a sizable number of Israelis were uneasy about this support; they believe, and frequently with good reason, that it is motivated by the anti-Zionist agenda of certain groups on the European Left. They also suspect that portraying Israelis as occupiers and war criminals helps the Europeans to salve their guilty consciences for the mass murder of Jews that took place on their continent a mere generation ago. Indeed, most of the political films produced in Israel with foreign support have portrayed Israeli society as both harshly militaristic and steeped in nationalist and fascist fervor. These films' protagonists are usually sensitive, artistic types—often, as in the case of *Waltz with Bashir*, fashioned in the image of the filmmaker himself—who are profoundly troubled by the nature and deeds of their country.

Folman thus travels along a well-trodden path. And yet, in public appearances, he has insisted that the message of *Waltz with Bashir* is not political, but rather simply "antiwar." Now either Folman is being extremely naive, or else he is putting us on. The glowing reception the film has received both at home and abroad was hardly on account of its "apolitical" stance. *New York Times* film critic A. O. Scott, for example, implied that the movie completes the findings of the Kahan Commission, which placed indirect blame for the 1982 Sabra and Shatila massacre of Palestinians, carried out by Lebanese Christian Phalangists, on the occupying Israeli military command. "What no commission of inquiry can precisely define is the responsibility of the ordinary soldiers, who were nearby, witnessing the slaughter and allowing it to continue," wrote Scott. "And this ethical question becomes more and more urgent as Mr. Folman's patient probing brings him closer to the awful facts his mind had suppressed for so long." In a similar vein, John Anderson argued in the *Washington Post* that the film reflects "an entire nation's guilt complex," and Peter Bradshaw commented in *The Guardian* that in *Waltz with Bashir*, "Folman submits his very own (Viet) Nam flashback: a memory of how the Israel Defense forces, of which he was a part, effectively presided over mass murder."

For a film that professes to explore and document the Lebanon War, *Waltz with Bashir* nonetheless smacks of a clear bias. It contains no reference to the circumstances leading up to the war, its goals, the situation in and politics of Lebanon at the time, or the threats it posed to Israel. As a result, the Israeli invasion comes off as a heedlessly violent, destructive, and ultimately pointless campaign. Moreover, the conduct of IDF [Israeli Defense Forces] soldiers, if we are to go by the depiction provided in the film, was al-

most always atrocious. The first "combat" scene, for instance, shows frenzied IDF soldiers firing at a passing car, killing the unsuspecting Lebanese family inside. Israeli tanks advance single-mindedly through the narrow streets, crushing parked cars with apathetic brutality. Military leaders display shockingly inhumane attitudes toward the wounded and the dead, as evidenced by the scene in which Ari is commanded to pile dead bodies onto a helicopter landing pad like so much refuse. Moreover, the only enemy combatant in the film shown aiming at Israeli soldiers is a young boy, who is summarily mowed down by intense IDF fire. Noticeably absent is even *one* instance of bravery, sacrifice, camaraderie, or devotion to the cause among Israeli soldiers—motifs that appear even in films that purport to be antiwar. Indeed, *Waltz with Bashir* grants the IDF not even a single, perfunctory iota of approbation.

Folman seems to believe that he can skirt the larger issues surrounding the First Lebanon War by means of the film's central, deliberately narrow question: "Where was I during the Sabra and Shatila massacre?" Yet the very choice to treat the infamous bloodbath, committed by Christian militias, as a formative event in *Israel's* collective memory is itself of deep political significance. Yes, Ari's attempt to recall where he was during the massacre forms the film's motivation. Yet by its end, the hero's personal story is dwarfed by the accumulation of testimonials about what occurred in the camps and what *all* the IDF soldiers present or nearby did or did not see.

Furthermore, it is impossible not be vexed by the director's decision to assign Holocaust imagery to the events surrounding Sabra and Shatila. In one scene, Israeli journalist Ron Ben-Yishai, one of the film's real-life characters, recalls a picture of Palestinian women and children that reminded him of the famous photograph of the young boy with his arms raised in the Warsaw Ghetto. Another character notes that the trauma of the massacre is most likely connected to Ari's own family legacy, since both his parents are Auschwitz survivors. Finally, Ari himself wonders out loud what exactly Israeli soldiers in the refugee camps know about the "genocide" that took place there.

Does the film strike this particular historical nerve in order to test the moral and emotional strength of a post-traumatic society? Or is Folman indeed trying to portray Israelis as the new Nazis? According to Ari's friend, who tells him, "You have been forcibly cast in the role of Nazi," the answer is far from ambiguous. Had any doubts remained, we need only look to the film's final scene: as an IDF officer announces an end to the war's operations, a group of Palestinian women and children are instructed to return to the camps. The viewer's perspective follows the miserable women as they return to their homes, the site of the massacre. The "camera," or point of view, trails them from behind and zooms in on the direction they are headed. At the end of the street, they come face to face with Ari, whose terrified countenance fills the screen. At this point in the film, Folman cuts to actual archival images of Palestinian women in mourning, pointing to the rubble of their destroyed homes. The use of Folman's point-of-view shot, together with the real documentary footage, reveals that *this* is the picture missing from Ari's memory, the images that triggered the personal journey the film describes. The shift from animation to real photos is clearly intended to shock the audience, and to make a statement about the immense gap separating the animated, personal accounts of the Israeli characters and the real tragedy of the massacre's victims. And in this, it succeeds.

Yet, despite the undeniably one-sided picture that the film offers, Ari Folman refuses to carry the flag of political protest. He refuses to play the role of preacher, of the artist crying out to the world to save Israel from itself (and the Palestinians from Israel, as did filmmaker Keren Yedaya upon acceptance of a 2004 Cannes award for her film *Or*). It is doubtful that this decision stems from a kind of reflexive, ingrained patriotism; more likely, it is connected to the general mood of the film: alienated individualism, devoid of any feelings of belonging or any kind of ideological commitment.

Indeed, it is difficult to ignore the narcissistic aspect of Folman's film, which ultimately boils down to the story of one man's intense self-involvement. The narcissism is most readily apparent in Folman's choice of himself to play the film's hero, but is also revealed in more subtle fashion through the sense of both social and psychological detachment that permeates the film. The visual style of the dialogue scenes, for example, emphasizes the estrangement between Ari and the characters with whom he converses, and while the feeble conversation he has with his friend Uri Sivan sets the plot in motion, there is no hint of emotional reciprocity, and certainly not of real friendship. Throughout *Waltz with Bashir*, Ari gives nothing to his fellow man; he has no "comrades in arms," nor does he identify in any way with the Israeli side in the war. For Ari, this journey into memory is no waltz. He dances solo.

It is, perhaps, on account of this display of blatant individualism, this focus on personal redemption through excessive self-examination, that the film angered the "hardcore" Israeli Left. While the Right protested the negative depiction of Israeli soldiers, the Left's radical fringe condemned *Waltz with Bashir* as a demonstration of futile hypocrisy lacking any substantive criticism of Israeli aggression. Israeli journalist Gideon Levy, for example, that weariless provocateur, went so far as to call the film, in an article in *Haaretz*, "an act of fraud and deceit, intended to allow us to pat ourselves on the back and to tell us and the world how lovely we are." Likewise, on the popular news show, *London and Kirschenbaum*, the Israel Prize–winning director Yehuda "Judd" Ne'eman, a staunch anti-Zionist, accused the film of attempting to cover up Israel's responsibility for Sabra and Shatila. In both cases, these radical leftists were incensed by what appeared to them as an offensive attempt at catharsis and a shameful effort to bring the circle of historic guilt to a close.

Nevertheless, the majority of Israelis appears to have received the film positively. Its success at international festivals, culminating in its candidacy for an Oscar, generated immense enthusiasm, and even—somewhat ironically—an eruption of patriotism at home. Indeed it seemed at times that the Israeli media, so desperate for Folman to "bring home" the gold statuette, had forgotten that they were dealing with a film—especially one consumed with self-criticism—and not with a national soccer team heading off to a prestigious international tournament. Certainly, Folman himself—a sincere man with a pleasant sense of humor and an unassuming personality—has aroused nothing but empathy. In countless interviews he has repeatedly expressed his most fervent hope that his own children will not have to undergo the same experiences that he did—and who would argue with that? What Israeli *wouldn't* identify with such a noble aspiration, even one so patently banal?

But *Waltz with Bashir*, it must be said, is not a banal film. It is an important artistic creation that conveys a harsh and serious statement. As a cinematic work, it is deserving of all the praise it has received, and it may rightly be considered a breakthrough of a sort. As a political text, however, it is both problematic and dangerously manipulative. Our appreciation of the former should not distract us from our recognition of the latter.

Republished from: Avisar, Ilan, "Dancing Solo in the Lebanese Mud," *Azure* 36 (Spring 2009): 107–15.

Source: Ari Folman and David Polonsky, *Waltz with Bashir: A Lebanon War Story*. New York: Metropolitan, 2009.

Background: http://www.thedavidproject.org/index.php?option=com_content&view=article&id=429:analysis&catid=102:1982-first-lebanon-war-&Itemid=141.

Bibliography

Avisar, Ilan. "The National and the Popular in Israeli Cinema." *Shofar* 24, no. 1 (2005): 125–43.

The Beirut Massacre: The Complete Kahan Commission Report. Princeton, NJ: Karz-Cohl, 1983.

Friedman, Thomas L. *From Beirut to Jerusalem*. New York: Farrar, Straus, Giroux, 1989.

Kronish, Amy, and Costel Safirman. *Israeli Film: A Reference Guide*. Westport, CT: Praeger, 2003.

Linn, Ruth. *Conscience at War: The Israeli Soldier as a Moral Critic*. Albany: State University of New York, 1996.

Rabinovich, Itamar. *The War for Lebanon, 1970–1983*. Ithaca, NY: Cornell University Press, 1984.

Schiff, Ze'ev, and Ehud Ya'ari. *Israel's Lebanon War*. Translated by Ina Friedman. New York: Simon and Schuster, 1985.

Yosef, Raz. *The Politics of Loss and Trauma in Contemporary Israeli Cinema*. New York: Routledge, 2011.

47. Beta Israel in the State of Israel

LAWRENCE BARON

Live and Become (*Va, vis et deviens*), directed by
Radu Mihaileanu [A]
Belgium, France, Israel, and Italy, 2005

Between late November 1984 and late January
1985, the Israeli government airlifted to Israel
some 8,000 Ethiopian Jews who had trekked on
foot with other African refugees to camps in
Sudan to escape discrimination, famine, and the
violence of civil wars in their native countries.
Four thousand more Ethiopian Jews died from
attacks by bandits, illnesses, starvation, and thirst
during the arduous journey. Named Operation
Moses to evoke the ancient Exodus from Egypt,
this mass rescue effort of the Beta Israel (House
of Israel), as the Ethiopian Jews call themselves,
fulfilled a basic tenet of Zionism that Israel was a
haven for oppressed Jews from the Diaspora and
followed the precedents of missions that Israel
had conducted to save Jewish populations in
Arab nations, where they faced persecution after
the creation of Israel. Operation Moses also anticipated Operation Solomon of 1991, in which
Israeli jetliners and military transport planes
evacuated the 14,000 Jews who had remained in
Ethiopia.

According to Zionist ideology, the return of
the Jews to their biblical homeland, and the establishment of a sovereign state there, ultimately
would transcend the ethnic, linguistic, racial, and
religious differences they had acquired in the Diaspora. Under the Law of Return promulgated in
1950 and amended in 1970, any person who had
converted to Judaism under Orthodox auspices

or whose mother was Jewish was entitled to Israeli citizenship, as were his or her grandparents,
spouses, and children, who were also considered
Jews. The government policy of *mizug galuyot*
(the mixing of the exiles) promoted the rapid and
thorough absorption of newcomers into the Hebrew culture, modern economy, and secular lifestyle of the Askenazi elites who dominated the
Zionist movement and the government, after
statehood was achieved. Nevertheless, cultural,
ethnic, linguistic, and religious differences have
persisted in Israeli society.

Whereas the vast majority of Israelis are descended from Middle Eastern Semites who continued to reside in the region or migrated to Asia,
Europe, or North Africa, the Beta Israel are indigenous African blacks who trace their lineage
back to the liaison between King Solomon and
the queen of Sheba dating to approximately 900
BCE. In Ethiopian Jewish scripture, the son born
of this union, King Menelik I, grew up in Jerusalem and brought the tablets of the Ten Commandments, stolen by his entourage of temple
priests, to Ethiopia when he returned to ascend to
the throne. The Hebrew Bible and Books of the
Prophets refer to Jews residing beyond the Nile
River or in the land of Cush, which encompasses
modern-day Ethiopia and Sudan. Modern scholars hypothesize either that the Beta Israel originated as native Ethiopians who converted to Judaism or intermarried with Jews from nearby
Yemen, which had a thriving Jewish community
and had once been ruled by Ethiopia, or that
they represented a schism from the Orthodox
Christian Church of Ethiopia that accentuated
the latter's reverence for biblical Judaism, but
renounced its Christian theology. Whatever their
origins, Ethiopian Jews remained isolated from
the development of rabbinic Judaism and its

codification in the Talmud. Their Orit (equivalent of the Torah) was written in the indigenous Ethiopian languages of Ge'ez and Amharic, and not in Hebrew. Though observing Jewish holidays of biblical provenance, Ethiopian Jews never celebrated postexilic holidays like Hanukah and Purim, or rituals like the bar mitzvah. Although some of their customs and holidays were unique, others were antiquated practices from the First and Second Temple periods—like animal sacrifices—that were no longer sanctioned by Jewish law.

The voice-over narrator of Radu Mihaileanu's *Live and Become* briefly chronicles the history of the "forgotten Jews" who lived on the mountaintops near the ancient Ethiopian imperial capital of Gondar. As black-and-white documentary photographs of the "Falashas"—an epithet used by Christian Ethiopians to describe the Jewish "strangers" who were forbidden to own land—and of their perilous trek to Sudan flash on the screen, he recounts their genealogy as the heirs of Solomon and Sheba who yearned over the millennia to return to the land of their biblical ancestors. A wide-angle shot of a camp in the Sudanese desert where distant figures of refugees congregate zooms to a close-up of a mother's face (Mimi Abonesh Kebede) as she learns from a doctor that the emaciated infant she cradles in her arms is dead. That evening the child is buried in the sand as the kaddish is chanted by the mourners. A Christian woman (Meskie Shibru Sivan) watches a convoy of trucks drive up to ferry Jewish refugees to the airliners that will fly them to Israel. She awakens her son, points at the queue of Jews waiting to climb on the trucks, and orders him to go. He cannot fathom why he should leave her, but she sternly commands him "to live and become!" He hesitantly walks up to Hana, the woman whose infant died, and grasps her hand.

When her identity is checked before boarding the truck, she claims the boy is her son, and the doctor confirms this. On the ride to the planes, a Jewish boy wonders if they will turn white when they get to the Holy Land. His mother assures him it is a paradise "flowing with milk and honey."

On landing in Israel, the Ethiopian Jews encounter Israeli personnel who benignly seek to make their transition to Israel a smooth one, but who patronizingly strip them of their Ethiopian identities in the process. On the bus trip from the airport, Qes Amhra—a *qes* is a religious leader equivalent to a rabbi—played by Yitzhak Edgar, is bluntly told, "In Israel all Jews are white." At the absorption center, the Ethiopians are outwardly transformed into Israelis. They clumsily put on socks and shoes instead of going barefoot. They surrender their robes for Western-style dresses, pants, and shirts. The staff of the facility burns the old garments from Ethiopia in a bonfire as if they were contaminated. An official interrogates the immigrants to ascertain if they really are Jews and then arbitrarily assigns them new names. Adisalem becomes Eddy; and Hana's son, whom she called Solomon, is dubbed Schlomo. Soon he is orphaned a second time, when Hana dies. Schlomo, played by Moshe Agazai, manifests his anger over the loss of both his birth and adoptive mothers and his resistance to the lifestyle being imposed on him by fighting with classmates, refusing to eat, sleeping on the floor instead of in a bed, and sneaking away from the boarding school barefoot and draped with a sheet in a futile attempt to walk back to Ethiopia.

Although adopted by a loving couple, Yael (Yaël Abecassis) and Yoram (Roschdy Zem), Schlomo has difficulty adjusting to his new family. To dispel negative stereotypes of Israelis, Mihaileanu and his cowriter Alain-Michel Blanc depict Yael and Yoram as secular, left-wing Israelis involved in the movement to negotiate peace with the Palestinians. Both bear the stamp of the Diasporic origins of their parents. Yoram's father Papy (Rami Danon) hails from Egypt, and Yoram's face, hair, and skin color are distinctly Middle Eastern. Yael's family came from France, and she speaks French when conversing with Yoram and her mother. With the addition of Schlomo, the family is an ethnic and racial composite of Israeli Jewry. Schlomo's adoptive brother, Dany, and sister, Tali, try to make him feel comfortable, but Dany has a knack of asking questions that exacerbate Schlomo's sense of alienation and loss. Schlomo continues to sleep on the floor and not eat meals. Yet he quickly masters French and Hebrew, reads the Bible, and yearns to become a real Jew who speaks Yiddish like the elderly Jewish woman Yael and he regularly visit. Papy demonstrates his acceptance of his grandson by recounting the illustrious genealogy of the Beta Israel and giving Schlomo an Amharic book as an incentive to learn his mother tongue.

At school, however, Schlomo encounters racial prejudice. On his first day of classes, a girl curiously touches his skin, expecting its pigmentation to stain her hand. Subsequently, the principal informs Yael that his classmates' parents are threatening to withdraw their children from the school if Schlomo does not transfer to another institution. They fear he will bring down the educational standards of the school and infect their children with "African diseases." Indeed, this latter issue sparked a controversy in the 1990s, when it was disclosed that Israeli hospitals were discarding blood donated by Ethiopian Jews on the grounds that it had a higher likelihood of being tainted with the HIV virus. Yael angrily defends her son's intelligence and health and licks his face, to prove she is not afraid of catching anything from him. As he gains trust in her, she recipro-

cates by not walking him to school. Nevertheless, she follows him and discovers that he relaxes on his way home from school by taking off his shoes and socks to feel the grass and soil beneath his bare feet, as he did when he lived in Ethiopia.

The personal affronts that Schlomo endures at school foreshadow a more serious challenge to the Beta Israel's legitimacy as Jews. In the 1970s the chief rabbis of Israel recognized the authenticity of the group's Jewish origins with the proviso that its members undergo a conversion immersion in a mikvah (ritual bath) and a symbolic circumcision of taking a drop of blood from the penis of males to eliminate doubts about their claims of being Jewish. The Orthodox rabbinate suspected that many Ethiopian Jews were the offspring of intermarriages in which the mother was not Jewish, and that those who had converted to Judaism had not done so under Orthodox supervision. Whether Ethiopian Jews knowingly agreed to these stipulations or unwittingly signed such pledges to gain entry to Israel remains an open question.

Live and Become reenacts a real incident in which Ethiopian Jews, including Schlomo, report for mandated medical exams, only to discover this is a pretext to have them immersed in a mikvah or symbolically circumcised. Once this becomes apparent, the Ethiopian Jews panic and flee. That evening Schlomo and his family watch the television coverage of the event. An Orthodox rabbi explains that the members of the Beta Israel are not fully Jewish because they are descendants of the queen of Sheba, and Judaic law determines ancestry through the mother. He assures the Ethiopians, "This is not about purifying blood; it's about purifying doubt." Qes Amhra addresses a protest rally against the humiliating procedures and notes the irony that his brethren had been persecuted as Jews and witches in Ethiopia and now are reviled as gentile *"kushim"* (people from Cush) and "niggers" in Israel. As if speaking directly to Schlomo, he points out that, "children are living alone in Israel, while their parents are still in Africa." On hearing this, Schlomo resolves to meet Amhra and eventually hires him to write letters in Amharic to his birth mother in Ethiopia. After soliciting the advice of an Ethiopian healer to cure her son's despondency, Yael intuitively knows where he has gone and does not reveal his secret to Yoram. It is only then that Schlomo consumes the food that Yael serves him.

The film segues into Schlomo's adolescence when he, now played by the older Moshe Abebe, convincingly demonstrates to the audience if not to himself that being Jewish and Israeli are identities that are cultivated rather than inherited. At his bar mitzvah he recites the blessings over the Torah, earning an approving pat on the shoulder from his rabbi. This signifies more than a token gesture because the rabbi had surmised but never disclosed that Schlomo was raised as a Christian ever since as a new student he had blurted out in class that he considered Jesus the founder of Judaism. At the bar mitzvah reception, Israeli dance and music alternate with their Ethiopian counterparts. Gyrating shoulders Ethiopian style, Schlomo dances with the *qes* and then Yael. Considering Schlomo a starving Ethiopian Christian who lied about being Jewish to feed off Israel's bounty, the Orthodox father of Sarah, a girl from Schlomo's school, forbids him to attend her birthday party. Sarah (Roni Hadar), significantly bearing the name of the wife of the first Jew, Abraham, has a crush on Schlomo and drops by his home to apologize and flirt with him. When the synagogue stages a Torah debate, Schlomo seizes the opportunity to impress Sarah's father, who is one of the judges, with his command of Hebrew scripture. The question under deliberation is

"What color was Adam?" Schlomo's opponent contends Adam was white, and that Cush, the eldest son of Ham, who migrated to Africa, was condemned along with his progeny to be blacks and slaves. Schlomo counters that Adam was red because God fashioned him from red clay. The Hebrew words for Adam, clay, and red, he argues, share the same etymological root. The Beta Israel see themselves as red, though in the movie it is Sarah who declares that Schlomo is red. Schlomo wins the debate, but not the acceptance of Sarah's father. Out of despair, Schlomo goes to the police and admits he entered the country under false pretenses. Sympathizing with the plight of the Ethiopian Jews in Israel, the officer responds: "Even you're starting to believe it. You're as Jewish as we are, more than us! Don't you understand, more faithful to the Torah? It's shameful the way they treat you."

Shortly thereafter, Schlomo has his political awakening as an Israeli. Having quarreled with Yoram following his release by the police, Schlomo is sent to work on a kibbutz to let time heal the rift that has developed between the two. On his arrival there, he proudly reads the inscription under a photograph of Papy displayed at the entrance, lauding him as a founder of the kibbutz and a hero of Israel. Tilling the soil and feeding the cows as both Papy and Yoram had done when they lived on the kibbutz deepens Schlomo's attachment to his second homeland. During a visit from Papy, a conversation crystallizes Schlomo's commitment to Israel and peace. Reacting to headlines about Arabs killed in reprisals for a terrorist attack on a bus, Schlomo asks Papy whether the Jews should give back land that belonged to their ancestors and gave them hope during their lengthy exile. Papy recalls that he had planted the tree whose shade they are enjoying, but that a nearby tree was there before the kibbutz was established fifty years ago. Therefore, he concludes, "I think we should share the land, like the sun and the shade, so others can know love too." Like a typical Israeli hawk, Schlomo exclaims, "Even if we risk being pushed into the sea and dying?" Papy responds: "Love doesn't come without risks. And it's difficult to decide how others should love." His wisdom applies not only to the conflict between the Israelis and the Palestinians, but to that within Schomo's family.

From this point on, the Arab-Israeli conflict increasingly intrudes into the film's plotline. Scud missile attacks launched by Iraq against Israel during the first Gulf War in 1991 force Qes Amhra and Schlomo to scramble into a crowded bomb shelter. Amid rows of people wearing gas masks—Saddam Hussein was believed to have equipped the rockets with biological and chemical warheads—the *qes* helps Schlomo put on his mask so he can survive and one day find his mother. For Yael, the air raids portend future wars in which her sons will have to serve as soldiers. She proposes to Yoram that they move to Canada or France to prevent this from ever happening. He refuses to abandon Israel to the "right-wing fools who want war," reminding her that this is his country too. In the next scene, Schlomo participates with his family and the *qes* in a peace demonstration in 1993, shouting in unison with the marchers: "Yes to peace! No to the occupation!" The television broadcast of President Clinton, flanked by the PLO leader Yassir Arafat and Israeli Prime Minister Yitzhak Rabin shaking hands, in the same year seems to be a harbinger that "things will get better." Two years after, in a scene that comes while Schlomo is studying in France to be a doctor, he hears a radio bulletin announcing that Rabin has been assassinated, and the voice-over of Yael plaintively asks, "Why did they kill him?"

As these momentous events unfold, Schlomo becomes more aware of the legacy he carries as an Ethiopian Israeli. Sarah pressures him to make a commitment to their relationship, but Schlomo hesitates because even if she is colorblind, the rest of Israeli society is not. Moved by television footage of the suffering of Ethiopians in refugee camps in Sudan, he tells the *qes* he plans to return there. The *qes* warns him that this could be dangerous and recollects witnessing his son's murder and daughter-in-law's rape by the guides the family had hired to lead them to the Sudan. In the wake of such loss, he believes the only option "is to serve those who survived" and shows Schlomo the Orit he smuggled out of Ethiopia. Confused about his future, Schlomo gets drunk at a discotheque, where he is propositioned by an Ethiopian prostitute. He reveals to her that he is not Jewish, but that he feels he is. His confession is wasted, since she lures him into her room so her brothers can beat him and steal his money. Battered and distraught, Schlomo throws stones at the *qes*'s house and yells, "We were simply extras in Operation Moses." The police respond to the disturbance and handcuff Schlomo, but the *qes* prevents him from being arrested by claiming to be his father. Having calmed down, Schlomo reveals his true religious identity and traumatic past to his mentor. In the camp, Schlomo's mother had sent him to purchase water from a gang that controlled the well. They took his money but withheld the water. A fight between onlookers who sided with Schlomo and the gang erupted, in the course of which his older brother was killed. Schlomo felt guilty for his death—as intimated earlier in the film, when he took his first shower at the absorption center and desperately tried to stop the water from running into the drain. The *qes* brings Schlomo to the same doctor who had treated Hana's baby. The *qes* knew the doctor from the camp and had officiated at the burial of Hana's infant, and then arranged for Schlomo to pretend to be her son. Schlomo decides to become a doctor before going into the Israeli army. Though Yoram views this as an evasion of military service, Schlomo feels destined to be a healer and cannot contemplate ever killing anyone.

In the remainder of the film, the adult Schlomo, played by Sirak Sabahat, comes to terms with the divided loyalties that have pulled him in opposite directions throughout his life. He attends medical school in Paris, where people express astonishment that he could be both Jewish and black. In a phone call, the *qes* advises him to stay in France to avoid being swept up in deportation proceedings that have been initiated against other Ethiopian and Russian Christians who had posed as Jews to immigrate to Israel. While serving as a field doctor in the Occupied Territories, Schlomo stops to care for a wounded Palestinian boy, whose victimization reminds him of his own childhood. The boy's embittered father draws a gun on Schlomo and orders him not to touch the child, cursing at him: "You'll end up in the sea, in hell, kike!" Schlomo's commanding officer, an Israeli mirror image of the irate father, rebukes Schlomo for assisting a Palestinian: "Our men first! Understand, kushee?" Literally and figuratively caught in the crossfire, Schlomo is hit by a bullet and collapses. Sarah visits him at the hospital, and Yael jokingly threatens to kill him if he doesn't marry Sarah.

Schlomo's rehabilitation commences with his marriage to Sarah, his "beautiful Polish bride." The joyous wedding reception is marred by her parents' absence. Deeming Schlomo a gentile, her father has pronounced Sarah dead. Learning that she is pregnant, Schlomo musters up the courage to share his secret with her. Enraged more by his failure to confide in her than by his Christian origins, she leaves him until Yael, at his request, pleads with her to stay with him by contextualizing his mentality: "Try to imagine Schlomo's trauma: a mother who loves him so desperately, she's willing to send him away and never see him again, ready to lose him to save him, and a man who loves his wife so much that he does not tell his secret for fear of losing her." Sarah returns to Schlomo, but she makes him promise that he will volunteer to be a doctor in the refugee camps in Sudan, to achieve some closure on that tragic part of his life.

In a camp resembling the one from the opening scene of the movie, he receives a cellphone call from Sarah and hears his baby son say "daddy" for the first time. In the distance he glimpses a crouching woman, her weathered face veiled from nose to neck, and recognizes it is his mother. He embraces her and she emits a mournful piercing cry. The camera draws back to a bird's-eye view of the camp and the otherwise anonymous silhouettes inhabiting it. Each has a story that merits a closer focus.

To be sure, this ending can be faulted for being too contrived and emotionally manipulative. The plot device of Schlomo's adoption by a middle-class Israeli family spares the audience from dealing with the disorientation and all-too-frequent disintegration of Ethiopian families coping with a radically different economic system, generational and gender roles, and secular values than they were accustomed to in Ethiopia. Ultimately, however, the film's message is that people are infinitely adaptable. They can learn to embrace a country, culture, family, race, and religion other than the ones they were born into. They can "become" members of adoptive families without forgetting their birth parents, patriotic without being chauvinistic, and pious without being intolerant. Summarizing the film's message, Radu Mihaileanu asserted, "All the stupidity we live through today, fighting over religion and differences of skin color, is absurd. We can see that human beings are close to each other, despite our surface differences" (Mihaileanu, n.d.).

Background: http://en.wikipedia.org/wiki/Ethiopian_Jews_in_Israel.

Bibliography:

Ashkenazi, Michael, and Alex Weingrod, eds, *Ethiopian Jews and Israel*. New Brunswick, NJ: Transaction, 1987.

Bard, Mitchell. *From Tragedy to Triumph: The Politics behind the Rescue of Ethiopian Jewry*. Westport, CT: Prager, 2002.

Ben-Ezer, Gadi. *The Migration Journey: The Ethiopian Jewish Exodus*. New Brunswick, NJ: Transaction, 2005.

Ben-Porat, Guy, et al. *Israel since 1980*. New York: Cambridge University Press, 2008.

Kaplan, Steven. *The Beta Israel (Falasha) in Ethiopia: From Earliest Times to the Twentieth Century*. New York: New York University Press, 1992.

Mihaileanu, Radu. "We Become What We Become, To Live: The Roots of My Film." *LandmarkTheatres.com*, n.d. http://www.landmarktheatres.com/mn/liveandbecome.html.

Schwartz, Tanya. *Ethiopian Jewish Immigrants in Israel: The Homeland Postponed*. Richmond, UK: Curzon, 2001.

Spector, Stephen. *Operation Solomon: The Daring Rescue of Ethiopian Jews*. New York: Oxford University Press, 2005.

Wagaw, Teshome. *For Our Soul: Ethiopian Jews in Israel*. Detroit: Wayne State University Press, 1993.

Westheimer, Ruth, and Steven Kaplan. *Surviving Salvation: The Ethiopian Jewish Family in Transition*. New York: New York University Press, 1992.

48. Love in Search of Belief, Belief in Search of Love

SHAI GINSBURG

Kadosh, directed by Amos Gitai [A]
France and Israel, 1999
Ushpizin (*Ha-Ushpizin*), directed by
Gidi Dar [A]
Israel, 2004

Until the 1990s, the ultra-Orthodox religious experience rarely entered the purview of Israeli films. This should not surprise us, for Israeli cinema, both as an establishment and in its themes, tended to celebrate a seemingly secular Israel. It perceived religion as a mark of an ethnic nationality rather than a true framework for everyday life. From the late 1990s on, however, the religious experience has moved ever more into the center of the stage of Israeli cinema. Two films in particular, Amos Gitai's *Kadosh* (Sacred) and Gidi Dar's *Ushpizin* (Holy Guests), marked this new interest and helped set the coordinates within which other Israeli films have since imagined the ultra-Orthodox experience.

Kadosh portrays the Orthodox world from the perspective of a presumably "enlightened" and "liberated" secular world. From this perspective, a binary opposition is set between religious narrow-mindedness and secular liberalism; Jewish Law—the *Halacha*—as the form of Jewish religious life, is perceived as nothing but oppressive and repressive, and the only possibility open to characters who wish to be true to themselves and realize their aspirations is to shed its yoke altogether. *Ushpizin* explicitly counters Gitai's harsh critique. The film is the joint creation of director Dar and the film's main actor, Shuli Rand, who recently reembraced

Orthodox Judaism after a hiatus of a number of years in the secular world, and so depicts the Orthodox world as nourishing and supportive. Though *Kadosh* and *Ushpizin* focus on different ultra-Orthodox communities, neither stresses the great diversity of that world and each presents itself as the embodiment of its spirit or essence.

At the center of *Ushpizin* lies the question of faith: What does it mean to believe? How does faith shape our life? What sacrifices does it force us to make? The film tells the story of Moshe and Malli Bellanga, a couple of *Ba'alei Teshuvah*, "Born Again Jews," who join the Breslau community in Jerusalem. On the eve of *Sukkot*—the Feast of Tabernacles—the two find themselves too poor to build a *sukkah* [a temporary hut with three walls and a roof that permits people inside to see the sky] and buy the four species that are central to the holiday ritual. In their distress they beseech God. When a local charity leaves a thousand dollars on their doorstep, they take it to be a miracle in answer to their prayers. The miracle appears complete when Moshe learns of an apparently abandoned *sukkah* the couple can use. With the prospects of finally being able to celebrate the holiday in a becoming manner in his mind, Moshe rushes out to buy the most beautiful and expensive *etrog*, a species of citron required for the celebration of *Sukkot*. In the meantime, two of Moshe's former associates escape from prison and come looking for him. Since it is also customary during the feast to invite guests (called *Ushpizin)* to one's *sukkah*, Moshe and Malli warmly welcome them. Unfortunately, the two fugitives take advantage of the couple's hospitality: they drink, smoke, and play loud music, mocking their hosts' Orthodox lifestyle, and questioning Moshe's newfound faith. Could Moshe, a previously violent and angry individual, truly have become someone whose life centers upon the love of God?

The havoc created by the guests brings to the fore the main issue that confounds Moshe and Malli's relationship: despite their best efforts to live a devout lifestyle and after five years of marriage, the couple still does not have a child. Moshe and Malli now face a difficult question. Should they maintain their relationship despite the fact that they cannot conceive, or should Moshe, to comply with the commandment to "be fruitful and multiply and replenish the earth" (Gen. 1:28), one of the most important edicts of religious life, divorce Malli, and look for a new wife with whom to try to have children?

Ushpizin endeavors to address the critique articulated by Amos Gitai *in Kadosh,* which likewise explores the distress of ultra-Orthodox childless couples. Set in an ultra-Orthodox neighborhood of Jerusalem, that film tells the story of Meir and Rivka, who have been married for ten years without giving birth to a child. Despite their love for each other, his father, who leads the community as its rabbi, reminds Meir of the importance of the commandment and pressures him to divorce Rivka so he can remarry and uphold the commandment. *Kadosh* interweaves Meir and Rivka's emotional struggle with the travails of Malka, Rivka's sister. While Malka is in love with Ya'akov, who has left the Orthodox world for secular Jerusalem, the rabbi decrees that she should marry his disciple, Yossef. Malka now has to choose between her love and her loyalty to her family and community.

Ushpizin portrays a world that revels in the presence of God in everyday life, a God who works in mysterious ways to reward the faithful and answer the prayers of those who are firm in their belief. It is a world made and ruled by love: the love of God for human beings, and the love between men and women. In their love for each other, Moshe and Malli reinforce each other's love for God, and their love helps them to overcome the obstacles life puts in their way. *Kadosh*, on the other hand, portrays a world without grace, a world in which the edicts of the *Halacha*, Jewish law, are a synonym for paternalistic chauvinism used to control and subordinate women. Indeed, the film suggests that men's meticulous adherence to *Halachic* rituals, an adherence upon which ultra-Orthodox communities pride themselves, obstructs the ability of men and women alike to realize their love for each other. Ultimately faith brings havoc to the household of Meir and Rivka, ironically undermining the only sacred space available to them.

Consider, for instance, the role that the rabbi plays in each film. In both, he serves as a father figure, literally and/or metaphorically, a stand-in for the Law and for God in the community. But in *Kadosh*, the rabbi is also the spokesperson for a militant brand of misogyny. Pressuring Meir to divorce Rivka, he describes women as shapeless matter that receives its true form from men. Moreover, the rabbi asserts, a barren woman is not a woman: a Jewish woman's only *raison d'être* is to bear and raise Jewish children and serve her husband so as to enable him to study Torah. Only in these does she find her true joy and happiness. The rabbi's chauvinist discourse, however, does not only mark the coercion of women, but also that of men. For the Orthodox community, so the rabbi insists, is engaged in a war with the secular state in the name of its faith; its main weapon in this war is its birth rate, which far surpasses that of the secular sectors. Men and women alike must sacrifice their personal happiness, and no concessions can be made for human frailty. The rabbi's misogynistic discourse serves as the cornerstone of an instrumentalist morality (or, from the director's perspective, lack thereof), where religion does not serve the believer, to address his or her emotional needs and anxieties, but rather the other way round, the believer is to serve religion at whatever cost to him- or herself.

By contrast, *Ushpizin* portrays the rabbi as a loving father. A radiant figure with a pale face, long white beard, white skullcap, and white gown, Dar's rabbi appears as a holy man who turns nights into days immersed in study and prayer, conversing with God, and imparting His love to the community. A far cry from Gitai's domineering and warlike rabbi, Dar's does not privilege the learned over the simpleton, or man over woman, but welcomes all benevolently and compassionately, and speaks to each in his or her own tongue. Despite the fact that Moshe and Malli are childless, the rabbi neither condemns their marriage nor attempts to undo it. On the contrary, he serves as a marriage counselor, working to strengthen the bond between them, reassuring the couple of their love of God and of each other. God ultimately will answer their prayers and bless them with a child.

The rationale of faith as the rabbi expounds it contrasts sharply with the rationale that informs the world of faith in *Kadosh*. "A thing of wonder," as the rabbi calls it, it validates human bewilderment and even misery in the face of God's mysterious ways, linking worldly trials and spiritual elevation. To elevate oneself to the next spiritual level, one has to rupture something within oneself. Commonly, one then comes to believe that one could rest, but it is precisely at this point that God summons one with an even harder test. "There is no rest in this world," the rabbi concludes. Rather than dismissing human distress as inconsequential, the rabbi underscores its centrality to an experience of faith that places human beings—he does not distinguish between men and women—in direct relationship with God, not as an instrument of a divine plan but as a responsible, responsive subject to God's presence. Consequently, *Ushpizin* paints a picture of a community whose faith in God can bring about a true realization of love, both religious and humane.

Kadosh, on the other hand, depicts a community that, in its struggle with a liberated secular world and under the weight of its rituals and laws, forsakes both its search for the divine and for the emotional well-being of its members. This double failure is most clearly embodied in Yossef, the rabbi's favorite disciple. Early in the film, Meir and Yossef are at the yeshiva [religious college]. Yossef is praying, crying out loud to God to open his heart to love Him and to sanctify His name, while the others present study quietly at their desks, insensible to his outburst. Meir then turns to Yossef with a Talmudic question: How should one make tea on the Sabbath? Should one put the sugar in first, or pour water into the cup first and only then add the sugar? The ensuing lengthy, intricate, and legalistic debate over seemingly immaterial minutiae seeks, no doubt, to impart the level of regulation of life under the regime of Orthodox faith. It also appears to embody the traditional hostile characterization of Talmudic Judaism put forward by secular Jews, which often resembles Christian anti-Jewish discourse. Yossef's insistence that "the learned should duly be as stringent as the stringent" serves to put into relief his religious intransigent fervor.

Moreover, Yossef's zeal is not merely theoretical, for it manifests itself in violence, whose victim is Malka, Yossef's new wife. Thus, on their wedding night, Yossef is more preoccupied with the commandment to procreate than with the well-being of his wife. The sexual act between the two, which begins as Yossef mechanically declaims—as is proscribed—a few words of love and proceeds when Yossef "arranges" Malka's body to suit the act, turns abusive as he futilely attempts to pene-

trate her body. His failure to show love—emotionally and physically—exposes the violence inherent in his strident outcry for God. The more he seeks to love God, the less he is able to love another human being.

Ushpizin's Moshe Bellanga, on the other hand, builds on the Hasidic belief in an immediate, intimate interaction between the faithful and God. In his hours of need, Moshe seeks a secluded space, often in the forest, where he can address God in private. In these intimate conversations, Moshe expresses profound agitation and anxiety that inform not only his words, but also the very language of his body. At stake for him are not the intricacies of a Talmudic discussion but, rather, the truly fundamental question of his faith: why does he encounter so many obstacles in his attempt to maintain basic religious obligations, not as a "show off" of his piety, but as a testimony of his love for God? Exasperated by the behavior of his two guests, Moshe runs to the forest and earnestly implores God. "I do not understand," he howls, "I do not understand, have mercy on me." Ultimately, he fears, his guests would unleash his anger of old and, with it, violence. *Ushpizin* thus conflates the secular world—embodied in the characters of the two guests—with unchecked desires and aggressions that are celebrated for their own sake and threaten to rob one of the presence of God. Indeed, faith is the unending endeavor to overcome these for the sake of the love of God.

The Law in Dar's film is therefore not the "learned" legal one, but the Law of Love. The love between a husband and a wife is but a reflection of their love for God. The one permeates the other and turns their home into a space where they jointly deliberate on matters of faith, religion, emotional needs, and material needs and on the relationship between these four. To divert Malli's attention from their material needs, from the fact that his Yeshiva would not provide for them this month because Moshe does not attend lessons regularly as well as from their inability to conceive a child, Moshe tells Malli of a nice thing he heard that day: "Wherever something is lacking, I know that either it wasn't prayed for, or that it wasn't prayed for enough." In reaction, and despite his protests—he would have liked to rest—Malli sends him off to pray. Moshe obliges, walks through the busy streets, and ends up on a bench overlooking a makeshift playground, where he confesses his misery to God. If not for his own sake, Moshe reasons, the couple should be blessed with a child for the sake of his wife and her great love for God. Dar then repeatedly intercuts between Moshe's free discourse; Malli, sitting by the kitchen table and reading from *Psalms*, likewise praying for a miracle; and two collectors of a charity fund, rushing to allocate all alms before the holiday. Left with some money, the two look for someone to whom they could give it. As the collectors begin to go over the lists of those in need, the cuts between the three locations become ever more rapid, and Moshe and Malli's plea appears to take over their whole bodies: as they shake, clap their hands, and ultimately shout. The scene builds toward an emotional (and theological) climax when the collectors pick Moshe's name from their list. Then one of them hurries to deliver the money. God indeed works a miracle in response to Moshe and Malli's forthright, candid faith and love, for Him as well as for each other. The end of the film shows that faith, religion, emotional needs, and material needs are truly one and the same, and all can be addressed through love.

Gitai argues differently. Adherence to the letter of the Jewish Law, *Kadosh* suggests, produces alienation between men and women. Despite their great love and respect for each other, Meir and Rivka face the same predicament, as the very

first scene of the film visually makes clear. The scene is set in Meir and Rivka's dark bedroom, as they lie asleep in their separate beds. The early morning light that penetrates the windows wakes Meir, and as he rubs his face, rises from his bed, washes his hands, dresses, and puts on the prayer shawl, he recites the pertinent Morning Blessings. The single, long take lasts more than seven and a half minutes, and the minimal use of pans and zooms helps to accent Meir's motions and lends gravity to the minutiae of the rituals. Louis Sclavis's melancholic clarinet piece *"Mariage"*—a clear reference to the East European Jewish musical tradition—accompanies the first part of the scene. When it stops after about three minutes, Meir's recitation, "Blessed are you, Lord, our God, ruler of the universe who has not created me a woman," is clearly heard. As Meir continues to put on the tefillin, his muffled words, hissed breath, and the rustles of his movements are audible. For the better part of the scene, Meir is alone within the frame, his white shirt and prayer shawl brightly illuminated against the darkened background. Only when the last of the Morning Blessings is recited does he approach the beds again, and as the camera follows him, Rivka enters the frame. Meir gently wakes her up to say that it is time for him to leave for prayer. Their interaction, though affectionate and tender, is brief, and they are co-present within the frame for just over a minute. Bracketed within the demands of a male-chauvinist religious ritual that by and large takes Meir away from the home, little time is left for shared intimacy.

Not surprisingly, the two films treat their female characters in contrasting ways. In *Kadosh*, women are second-class citizens in the Orthodox community. They can only save themselves if they escape its oppressive authority and move to the secular world, as Malka does, when she finally leaves her husband to join Ya'akov. No wonder, then, that the rabbi conceives of secular society to be so threatening. Rivka, on the other hand, is trapped. Despite the fact that after a visit to a gynecologist Rivka learns that she is fertile, she remains unable to raise the issue. To be sure, both Meir and Rivka suffer emotionally because of the rabbi's edict; yet it is Rivka who pays the price. Stigmatized as a divorcee and as barren, unable to overcome her love for Meir, she is doomed to a life of solitude, while Meir retains his position within the community. In *Ushpizin* husband and wife fulfill their designated roles with love and respect for each other. In fact, Moshe depends on his wife as much as, if not more than, she depends on him. Following yet another mishap with their guests, she finally leaves him, insisting that he should find another wife with whom he could have children. Ignoring Moshe's protests—"only with you, only with you"—Malli departs, while Moshe becomes helpless, unable to maintain his life. The unity and the love of family are at the center of his faith. It is this love that ultimately provides the substrate upon which God's miracles work, showing His love for the world.

Notwithstanding their profound visual and ideological differences, however, both *Ushpizin* and *Kadosh* struggle with the seeming irreconcilability of piety and interpersonal love. Indeed, over and against Gitai's unsympathetic portrayal of alienation and loneliness set in a harsh urban reality, Dar posits a fairy tale–like world of faith and miracle that overcomes all obstacles. Yet even *Ushpizin*'s fairy tale–like world—where miracles really do come true and childless couples are welcome—is still informed by the allegedly oppressive traits of the Orthodox tradition and the havoc they wreck on the lives of those who choose to commit themselves to God. Whereas on one hand *Ushpizin* aims to be a celebration of candid faith and divine intervention; on the other hand it appears to be an admission that the contradictions that beleaguer believers can only be resolved in the realm of an escapist fairy tale. Ultimately, then, both *Ushpizin* and *Kadosh* leave unanswered the question whether a true life of faith necessarily entails forsaking human love.

Expanded version of: Shai Ginsburg, "Love in Search of Belief, Belief in Search of Love," *Tikkun* 21, no. 3 (2006): 75–76.

Background: http://en.wikipedia.org/wiki/Haredi_Judaism.

Bibliography

Biale, David. "Israeli Secularists' Revenge." *Tikkun* 15, no. 4 (2000): 69–71.

Franke, Anselm, Antje Ehmann, and Katharina Fichtner, eds. *Amos Gitai: News from Home*. Cologne, Germany: Walter König, 2006.

Gitai, Amos. "In a Search Light." In *The Religion and Film Reader*, edited by Jolyon Mitchell and S. Brent Plate, 82–86. New York: Routledge, 2007.

Gold, Michael. *And Hannah Wept: Infertility, Adoption, and the Jewish Couple*. Philadelphia: Jewish Publication Society of America, 1993.

Heilman, Samuel. *Defenders of the Faith: Inside Ultra-Orthodox Jewry*. Berkeley: University of California Press, 1999.

Kauffmann, Stanley. "Actualities and Miracles." *New Republic*, November 7, 2005, 24–25.

Stadler, Nurit. *Yeshiva Fundamentalism: Piety, Gender, and Resistance in the Ultra-Orthodox World*. New York: New York University Press, 2009.

Stein, Rebecca L. "The Oslo Process, Israeli Popular Culture, and the Remaking of National Space." In *The Struggle for Sovereignty: Palestine and Israel, 1993–2005*, edited by Joel Beinin and Rebecca L. Stein, 231–36. Stanford, CA: Stanford University Press, 2006.

49. The Arrangement

Time of Favor

YVONNE KOZLOVSKY GOLAN

Time of Favor (*Ha Hesder*), directed by Joseph
Cedar [A]
Israel, 2000

Mandatory national service is required of most
Israeli citizens. When an Israeli reaches the age of
eighteen, he or she must go to the induction office
closest to home, be tested, and be assigned to a
job according to the needs of the Israel Defense
Forces (IDF). Men serve for three years, women
for two. Women—and men, in some cases—can
substitute community service for military service.
Exempted from the draft are members of minority groups—including Muslims, Christians, and
Armenians—and the heredim, ultra-Orthodox
Jews who consider their full-time engagement in
Talmudic studies to be their profession.

The ultra-Orthodox are exempted from service in the IDF under an agreement made in 1948
between David Ben-Gurion's government and
the remnant of the scholars studying in yeshivas—
schools devoted to learning and interpreting Jewish religious texts—who arrived in the new state
from Europe when the embers of the Holocaust
were still smoking. To continue this tradition of
religious education after so many Jewish scholars
had been murdered in the Holocaust, the yeshiva
scholars were exempted from military duty. It
would have been difficult for them to adjust
to army life, which was so different from the
closed communities in which they lived. Moreover, many were physically not able to meet the
army's requirements. Despite the government's
gesture toward the ultra-Orthodox, the extreme

heredim honor only Jewish Law—Halakha—and
deny the sovereignty of the secular Jewish state.

Since the establishment of the state of Israel in
1948, the majority of soldiers who have served in
the IDF have been secular. They have hailed from
urban centers, agricultural collectives (kibbutzim), or private or collective farms (moshavim).
However, the IDF contains a growing group of
religious Zionists who follow the philosophy of
Rabbi Abraham Isaac Kook, who believed in inte-
grating Torah study with the building of the state.

This group is called the national religious sector. It gained tremendous momentum after the
Six Day War of 1967, when many Israelis considered their country's victory as the beginning of
the Redemption that could culminate in the coming of the Messiah. Modern religious Zionists,
loyal believers in Jewish religious law as well loyal
citizens of Israel, are found throughout all levels
of government, society, and culture. They fulfill
all of their civic responsibilities. Their traditional
political party, the Mafdal (National Religious
Party), has been represented in the Knesset, Israel's parliament, since it was founded. Members
of the national religious sector live in all types of
agricultural and urban settlements in Israel. The
young men are inducted into the IDF—usually
into combat units, some of which are coed—and
are highly motivated. Many of the national religious women opt to perform community service
in uniform, usually as teachers of new immigrant
soldiers, or as civilian tutors working with school-
children in remote Israeli towns. The members of
this sector support the "settler movement" in Judea and Samaria—which Palestinians and more
liberal and leftist Israelis call the "occupied territories," otherwise known as the West Bank and
Gaza. For the adherents of the national religious
movement, the Land of Israel is indivisible. It was

The Orthodox Israeli soldier Aki Avni (as Menachem) prays. From *Time of Favor* (2000), directed by Joseph Cedar. PHOTOFEST / KINO INTERNATIONAL

promised to the people of Israel by God, as stated in the Bible, and it must be settled in its entirety after the return of large areas of the biblical Land of Israel to Israeli sovereignty—especially the capital, Jerusalem.

There is a more strictly religious Zionist group whose members do not believe in men and women serving together. In order to recruit them, the IDF had to find a suitable solution. In the mid-1950s, the government decided to recruit national religious yeshiva students under a special *hesder* (arrangement) for five years of service, combining periods of Torah study at a yeshiva with periods of active military service, such as training, maintaining equipment, guard duty, and, if necessary, combat duty. A yeshiva for such students is called a *Hesder Yeshiva*.

The name of this film in Hebrew, *Ha Hesder*, refers to the arrangement between the government and the settler movement on army service but embodies a dilemma of loyalty. Does the religious soldier obey his IDF commander or the rabbi who is the head of his yeshiva? The tension between the two loyalties is the dramatic foundation of the film.

Written and directed by Joseph Cedar and released with the English title *Time of Favor*, the film won five Ophir prizes (the Israeli equivalent of Oscars)—for screenplay, cinematography, editing, and best male and female actors (Aki Avni and Tinkerbell, respectively). It was nominated for a Peace Award by the American Political Film Society in 2003.

Born into a religious Zionist family, Cedar defines himself as a National religious Zionist. In order to write the screenplay, he lived for two years in the Dolev community settlement on the West Bank, about six kilometers from Ramallah. (It falls under the jurisdiction of the Benjamin Local Council, named for the area allocated in the Bible to the tribe of Benjamin.) This is the first time that an observant Jew has succeeded in making a feature film of international quality about the settlements in Judea and Samaria. From inside knowledge of the National religious community, dubbed yarmulke wearers, he explains the issue of being under dual command (rabbinical and military), and the conflict of loyalty during a crisis. (In Israeli society, the type of yarmulke or skullcap—black, white, or colorful; velvet or crocheted; large or small; patterned or embroidered; and so forth—indicates a person's political and religious leanings. Those affiliated with the National religious group are usually associated with crocheted yarmulkes.) The issue of settlements in the West Bank remains an explosive issue, polarizing public opinion in Israel. Cedar's film not only accurately captured the settler's lifestyle, but it also attracted an international audience.

The film was shot at Mitzpeh Yeriho (the name literally means Jericho Overlook), in the Judean Desert. The primordial landscape of Jerusalem and the reddish Judean Hills provide the natural setting for this story. The protagonists include Rabbi Meltzer (Assi Dayan), the charismatic rabbi of a small settlement who is also the principal of a high-school yeshiva that includes a preparatory program for the IDF. This type of high school is very different from an ultra-Orthodox yeshiva, whose curriculum consists only of the Talmud, the Bible, and Jewish law—no instruction in secular studies, math, or foreign languages. The high-school yeshiva in the film integrates secular and religious studies to prepare students to enter civil society in any profession they select, while it is assumed that all will be inducted into the IDF after high school and before their university studies. The academic level is usually high, and students have the drive to excel in all their studies. The IDF preparatory component teaches leadership training and Israel's geography and political history. Graduates of this type of integrated training served as outstanding combat soldiers in the Second Lebanon War (2006) and the recent Operation Cast Lead, the war in Gaza in 2008.

Rabbi Meltzer, who runs his school and community very authoritatively, is idolized by his students, who consider him to be the "Talmudical genius of the current generation." A widower, the rabbi plans to promise his daughter, Michal (Tinkerbell), in marriage to his best student, Pinhas (Idan Alterman). Michal is in her late teens, while Pinhas, or "Pini," is in his early twenties. Thin, pale, and diabetic, he is a religious zealot.

The plot revolves around two axes: Rabbi Meltzer and his present and former students Pini—another Talmudical genius, in spite of his poor health—and Menachem, a successful combat officer (Aki Avni, a star of Israeli television who, after this film, left Israel to try his luck in Hollywood); and Itamar (Micha Selektar), now married and a father. Inspired by Meltzer, the three—who have been best friends since their student days—dream aloud of blowing up the al-Aqsa Mosque, which is situated on the Temple Mount—above the sacred Western Wall, a remnant of the Second Temple, Judaism's holiest site. This scene is an exposition of the messianic expectations of the three friends, who ardently await the building of the Third Temple, but for whom removing the al-Aqsa Mosque is only a theoretical prospect. The second axis is the relationship between the rabbi and his daughter, who rejects Pini in favor of Menachem.

The film begins with a long shot of a winding, deserted road in Judea. A soldier stands at a hitchhiking post and thumbs a ride to his settlement. (Israel has official hitchhiking stations where soldiers can stop cars for rides home on weekends, a leftover from the early days of the state when there was little public transportation and few private cars.) This shot shows the remote location of Menachem's community.

Based on their devotion to their country and religion, the Jewish settlers are committed to making this barren region bloom and to defending it at all costs. From this perspective, the view of the empty road has a symbolic significance for the future. Rabbi Meltzer dreams of establishing a renewed Kingdom of Israel and redeeming the land from its desolation. Immediately after Menachem and Michal meet hitchhiking to the settlement, the scene moves to a darkened alley where three shadows walk stealthily, fearing discovery.

They are Menachem, Pini, and Micha. The alley-way is in the Old City of Jerusalem, in an area located near the Temple Mount. After they sneak past Israeli security guards and Waqf personnel (the Waqf is the Arab religious authority in charge of Muslim holy places), they lower themselves down to bathe in the waters of the underground Gihon Spring. The underground tunnel dates back to biblical times. It was hewn into the rock to bring water to Jerusalem when the city was besieged by the Assyrians. The waters of the Gihon still flow in the same channel, and immersion in it is believed to be more spiritually enriching than purification in the water of a mikvah, or ritual bath. The channel of the Gihon is located beneath the al-Aqsa Mosque, which stands on top of the Temple Mount.

Ultra-Orthodox non-Zionist rabbis strictly prohibit stepping onto the Temple Mount, since this is the site of the destroyed First Temple, built by Solomon, and the Second Temple, built by Herod. As long as the Messiah has not yet come, and the Holy Temple has not yet been rebuilt, Jews—especially those who have not undergone religious purification—must not step onto the site. This prohibition has been breached by other rabbis (usually religious Zionists) who believe that ever since Israel regained control over the Temple Mount in the Six Day War, Jews are obligated to rebuild the Holy Temple there. For political convenience, the government of Israel adheres to the ultra-Orthodox ban and forbids Jews to climb the Temple Mount.

Thus, these three young men are violating the ban by immersing themselves in the Gihon. Their clandestine bathing in this place brings them into a world of mystery and sacred awe. Their proximity to the al-Aqsa Mosque and the possibility that dynamiting it could ignite the Middle East in a bloody jihad—a holy war waged by Muslims against "unbelievers"—arouses the young men's adrenaline and sense of religious duty.

Since 1968, the government of Israel has attempted to place a physical barrier between Jews and Arabs at the Temple Mount, realizing how important the location is to both groups. By incredible luck, an attempt to blow up the Temple Mount by a young, mentally ill Australian on August 21, 1969, was thwarted. Michael Dennis Rohan, an evangelical Christian, confessed that he was trying to accelerate the coming of the Messiah by establishing the Holy Temple on the Temple Mount. Since then, the fear of a disturbed "visionary" who might take the law into his own hands has haunted the Israeli government and its law enforcement and security agencies.

There has been a persistent fear that radical religious Zionists might take their rabbis' sermons very literally. Sermons encouraging students to purify themselves in preparation for the restoration of the Holy Temple could incite them to hasten the coming of the Messiah by destroying the al-Aqsa Mosque.

The three young men in the film discuss the establishment of a combat unit, to be made up of soldiers from their *Hesder Yeshiva*. Menachem, who is an IDF officer, will lead the unit, which Rabbi Meltzer had lobbied the IDF to create. Agencies such as the General Security Service, Israel's equivalent of the US Federal Bureau of Investigation, and the Mossad, the equivalent of the Central Intelligence Agency, worry about what would happen if the rabbi has more influence over this unit than its military commanders do. The unit might act on its religious convictions and disobey orders.

Military units made up of soldiers who are also yeshiva students have existed for decades. The film erroneously portrays the establishment of the unit as an exceptional case. Cedar consciously made this choice to highlight the rebellion that might arise if the soldiers shifted their loyalty from the IDF military commanders to religious leaders. The fear of such activities derives from incidents in the past, particularly the so-called "Jewish Underground" affair.

During the 1980s, reserve officers living in settlements in the territories took the law into their own hands and created a clandestine organization, dubbed the "Jewish Underground," that intended to attack Palestinian targets in the West Bank. They used standard IDF equipment and randomly murdered three students, wounded dozens of others, and attempted to assassinate three Palestinian mayors. Two of the mayors were seriously wounded; one had to have his legs amputated. A Border Patrol demolitions expert was blinded when he tried to dismantle an explosive device planted by the Jewish Underground. The group was also suspected of planning to blow up the Dome of the Rock and the al-Aqsa Mosque, but its members were caught while attempting to blow up five buses in eastern Jerusalem. Indictments were filed against twenty-nine people who belonged to the organization, fifteen of whom were convicted and imprisoned.

Cedar based his screenplay on this event, without knowing to what extent reality would follow his plot. In 2009, after imposing a freeze on the building of new settlements, the government of Israel announced that it would evacuate some settlers from the West Bank, as it had done in the Gaza Strip in 2005. Soldiers from a *Hesder Yeshiva* performed an act unacceptable in an army: they waved a poster during a military ceremony, announcing that their unit would not evacuate their relatives from the settlements. The army considered this open revolt; the soldiers were arrested and sent to military prison. This did not prevent the rabbis of their *Hesder Yeshiva*, Har Beracha,

from giving them and their families money and praising them as heroes. In response, the IDF, headed by Ehud Barak, the minister of defense, severed its arrangement with the yeshiva and prohibited its students from serving in the IDF.

In the film, Menachem takes command of the unit and appoints his friend Micha as second in command, to assist him. "What is the secret of their success?" asks a secular officer of his religious colleague. "It is the call to recite the *Shema* prayer [Hear O Israel, the Lord is God, the Lord is One]," responds the religious officer. "The moment that a religious soldier hears that he's fighting for God, he invests his entire self in the mission and brings about its success."

Meanwhile, Pini is invited to be a Sabbath guest at the rabbi's home, which is a great honor. The invitation denotes Rabbi Meltzer's desire to have Pini for his son-in-law. This plan runs into opposition from Michal, who refuses the arranged match. She has had her eye on Menachem for some time and encourages him to pursue her. Menachem reciprocates her affection and goes to the rabbi to express his feelings. Rabbi Meltzer insinuates that Menachem's love for Michal contains a murderous element since she is intended for Pini: it is as if Menachem has murdered Pini and taken his future bride. Menachem retreats into himself and almost stops visiting the settlement. Pini attempts repeatedly to become closer to Michal, but nothing helps. She spurns his advances. The rabbi pressures his daughter to marry Pini, but instead she leaves the settlement to live in an apartment in Jerusalem.

Pini doesn't "get the girl," but he consoles himself with the rabbi's sermons, which glorify Jerusalem as the pinnacle of the hopes and longings of the Jewish people. Rabbi Meltzer emphasizes that the Temple Mount embodies Judaism's dream of Redemption and the coming of the Messiah. Pini, the rabbi's protégé, draws the conclusion that the time for action has arrived. He incites Micha to commit a crime by telling him that the rabbi has ordered them to blow up the Temple Mount, and that Menachem is part of the plot. Micha steals explosives and ammunition from the unit's arsenal and brings them to the tunnel under the Western Wall, the same tunnel featured in the earlier scene.

Rabbinic authorization for a crime recalls an extremely traumatic event in Israeli history: the assassination of Prime Minister Yitzhak Rabin on November 4, 1995, by a radical religious Zionist who felt that he had rabbinical sanction to kill Rabin as a *moser*, someone who gives away the Land of Israel or delivers Jews into the hands of non-Jews. The Oslo Accords heralded the return of territory occupied by Israel to the Palestinians in return for a peace agreement. The Oslo Accords were intended to be the framework for future negotiations between the Israeli government and Palestinians, within which all outstanding "final status issues" between the two sides would be resolved. Some religious right-wingers considered Rabin as fitting the description of a *moser*. It is still unclear if the assassin acted alone or if some rabbis confirmed his opinion, and if so, who they were.

In the film, it is Pini who decides to bomb the holy site. He goes behind Menachem's back and deceives Micha into believing that Rabbi Meltzer had approved the plot. If Pini and Micha accomplished their goal, it would endanger state security and the well-being of all Israelis. Just before setting out on his private mission, he boasts to Michal of his plan.

Michal dutifully notifies the police and security forces. They set out to trap the attackers, without knowing where and how they intend to

strike. They suspect Menachem is implicated because he is Pini's friend and commander, and it is from his unit that the explosives were stolen. At the climax of a battle exercise, Menachem is arrested as his soldiers look on, and is brought in to be interrogated by the General Security Service. The interrogation produces no results. Menachem knows nothing and cannot reveal anything. When Michal arrives and explains, Menachem understands what has happened and sets out to stop Pini and Micha.

Menachem's character epitomizes the religious Zionist: a moral person and peerless warrior, a disciplined soldier, obeying God and the rabbis and also adhering to the civil law of the land. Menachem's reputation may be compromised by extremist religious interpretations that could destroy the delicate balance between religious and secular Zionists. The popular Israeli television star Aki Avni plays Menachem. Avni has built his career on playing many roles as the tough soldier who is nevertheless sensitive to the needs of his men, and beloved by those in his command. Rabbi Meltzer is portrayed by the noted actor Assi Dayan, son of General Moshe Dayan. Dayan served as the Israeli minister of defense during the Six Day War, granted the Waqf control over the Temple Mount, and established Israeli governance in the territories conquered in that war. It is interesting to watch Assi Dayan's performance as someone who both continues and subverts his father's legacy.

The one flaw in the film was the casting of Idan Alterman as Pini. He fails to develop his complex role as the Talmud student turned terrorist. Alterman is too well known to Israeli audiences as a gifted comedian. Most of his performances are in nonsense roles; he is short and small of stature, with a silly smile permanently on his face, like an Israeli Buster Keaton. Neither the audience nor the critics found his portrayal of Pini credible.

Cedar collaborated on the screenplay with Jackie Levy, a national religious entertainer and comedian with perceptive insights about the precarious relationship between the religious and secular sectors. The screenplay exposes the ambivalence of life in the yeshiva and in civil society: the predicament of translating a rabbi's zealous sermons into political action while still honoring the obligations of the citizen vis-à-vis secular law. Cedar and Levy propose that Israel should not point fingers at Menachem and those like him, who constitute the majority of religious Zionists, without sufficient evidence—as Israeli leftist organizations did when they cast aspersions on national religious circles for complicity in the Rabin assassination. Cedar and Levy concede that there are rogue religious Zionists like Pini in the community, but they are few in number. After all, Pini is depicted as arrogant and sickly. His diabetes may symbolize not only physical illness, but mental illness as well. Cedar is using the exceptional case to warn against one possible scenario. He lifts the veil from national religious society and does not idealize it.

Nevertheless, *Time of Favor* received critical acclaim in Israel for its pioneering glimpse into the national religious subculture. It challenged prejudices that secular Israelis often harbor toward the settler movement in general, and Orthodox soldiers in particular. Respect for state policy is exhibited in both the religious and secular sectors of Israeli society. The majority of yeshiva students object to disobeying the government. The film shows that they are not a monolithic group and emphasizes that most of them are like Menachem. They defer to their military commanders when their religious sentiments contradict their obligations as soldiers. In addition, the film gave Israeli audiences insights into the complexities of life for religious soldiers and the tensions in their communities, as exemplified in the romantic triangle between Menachem, Pini, and Michal. Mutual trust between religious and secular Zionists eroded around the time of the Rabin assassination, and when the Jewish Underground was exposed. Cedar's film aims at reestablishing that trust.

Background: http://www.jcpa.org/jpsr/s99-yc.htm; http://www.ynetnews.com/articles/0,7340,L-3819361,00.html.

Bibliography

Friedman, Robert I. *Zealots for Zion: Inside Israel's West Bank Settler Movement.* New Brunswick, NJ: Rutgers University Press, 1994.

Gorenberg, Gershom. *Fundamentalism and the Struggle for the Temple Mount.* New York: Oxford University Press, 2002.

Inbari, Motti. *Jewish Fundamentalism and the Temple Mount: Who Will Build the Third Temple?* Translated by Shaul Vardi. Albany: State University of New York Press, 2009.

Ravitzky, Aviezer. *Messianism, Zionism, and Jewish Religious Radicalism.* Translated by Michael Swirsky and Jonathan Chipman. Chicago: University of Chicago Press, 1996.

Zertal, Idith. *Lords of the Land: The War over Israel's Settlements in the Occupied Territories.* New York: Nation, 2007.

PART TEN

Contemporary American Jewish Identities

50. Jewish New York in *Crossing Delancey*

DAVID I. GROSSVOGEL

Crossing Delancey, directed by Joan Micklin Silver [A]
United States, 1988

During the seventeenth and eighteenth centuries, before it was urbanized, the Lower East Side attracted a prosperous population of landowners. Among these were the DeLanceys. The father, Stephen, was a well-known merchant and politician who sent his son James to be educated in England. James eventually became the colony's chief justice of the Supreme Court. The name of this prominent family is memorialized in the city's artery that still bears its name, Delancey Street—their farmland having been located in that area.

When Joan Micklin Silver made *Hester Street*, she narrowed her focus to a specific part of the Lower East Side at a specific moment, 1896. *Crossing Delancey* moves us into the present to examine what happened to Jewish life in Manhattan a century later. This time, the street is no longer a focal point but rather a boundary that delimits the northern edge of the Lower East Side and separates it from a world less well defined, known as uptown. It is also the boundary separating two cultures, the Jewish universe south of Delancey, from whose perspective Silver will tell her story, and what that perspective views as the diaspora beyond Delancey.

Crossing Delancey opens in that diaspora, a party at "the last real bookstore" in Manhattan, an intellectual center that has managed to survive despite the large chains (a theme Nora Ephron would pick up ten years later in *You've Got Mail*, to update her remake of Lubitsch's *Shop around the Corner*). The party celebrates the bookshop's survival and allows Joan Micklin Silver to show it as a warm and friendly place, presided over by an amiable boss. His small staff includes Isabella "Izzy" Grossman (Amy Irving), an attractive young woman, attracted in turn by one of the celebrity guest authors, the writer Anton Maes (Jeroen Krabbé).

The party also allows Silver to show that the mega-bookstores are not the only sharks in whose midst they must swim. One of the guests, an elegantly dressed woman, takes advantage of the crowd to steal a book off a shelf and slip it into her handbag. Izzy uses the cover of the same crowd to steal the book back from the woman and return it to the shelf. The book's short trajectory symbolizes the relaxed mores of this social set—an amoral freedom that extends into Izzy's own life. When she returns to her apartment, carrying under her arm the yet unread Sunday *Times*, a surrogate companion of this single woman, she is followed by one of her married friends, Nick (John Bedford Lloyd). He wants to spend the night. Izzy asks him, "Where's Katrina?" To his terse reply, "Chicago," she replies just as tersely, "O.K."

Periodically, Izzy crosses the Delancey border, leaving her uptown world in order to visit her grandmother's. Silver stresses the fact that it is another world through its first image, that of a Hasidic child, a little boy in a dark suit with skullcap and earlocks. Behind him stretches a Jewish street: the shops have Hebrew signs, the men are older versions of the little boy; women sit on street benches.

This is the world of "Bubbie" Kantor (Reizl Bozyk), who has replaced Izzy's parents, the latter having deserted Manhattan for Florida. In many ways, it is an old world. Bubbie carries her savings in a bag under her frock, believes that a dream of water is good luck, and is convinced that her granddaughter, having crossed that other fateful boundary, the age of thirty, faces a dismal future by remaining single. She has therefore engaged the services of a matchmaker, Hannah Mandelbaum (Sylvia Miles), to whom she complains that Izzy "lives alone in a room like a dog." Bubbie does this against the loud protests of her grandchild, who angrily refuses her good offices— "This is not the way I live, this is a hundred years ago"—asserting that she is a happy person, enjoying a rent-controlled apartment, and with a wonderful job. Her climactic "I don't need a man to feel complete" falls, like the rest of her tirade, on Bubbie's deaf ears.

So, in due time, Izzy is introduced by Bubbie to Sam Posner (Peter Riegert), a pickle merchant who wears a skullcap and walks to the synagogue for his ritual prayers. The arranged meeting between the two turns into an unmitigated disaster. Izzy tells Sam what she already told her grandmother, "This is not the way I live." And she adds, as incontrovertible proof, "I live uptown." The pickle man, who has accepted Hannah's services only because he has long been taken with Izzy, tells her about a man whose face was always hidden by the same cap he wore. When one day the cap was lost and he replaced it, he and his world were both changed. This parable notwithstanding, Izzy rushes back uptown in pursuit of the writer with whom she was instantly smitten at the opening party.

Still, Izzy is drawn back into the world below Delancey, presumably because her only parent [sic] in Manhattan lives there, and because some childhood friends have remained where they were when she first knew them. At a bris (circumcision ceremony) performed with mock seriousness by a comical officiant (Moishe Rosenfeld), she meets some of her old girlfriends and they talk about the availability of men. Still determined to shake Sam Posner, who, in memory of his parable, has sent her a gaucho hat as a birthday present (to which coworkers react with uptown sophistication: "Look, a reincarnation of Annie Hall"), Izzy hatches an elaborate plan to set up her friend, the desperate Marilyn Cohen (Suzzy Roche), with the pickle man. She will go on a date with Sam to a fancy restaurant where, as if by accident, Marilyn will show up and be introduced to him. But like her first meeting with Sam, this encounter turns into a fiasco, due in part to Izzy's emotional pendulum, which has swung sufficiently toward Sam for her to forget Marilyn, who is drinking herself into a giddy state at the bar.

Meanwhile uptown, Izzy is periodically confronted with the evidence of how self-centered is Anton Maes, the man on whom she has set her sights. This causes her to move toward Sam. She invites him into her uptown world for another celebrity gathering in the bookstore. Here we witness more of a milieu made up of too many thoughtless egomaniacs like Maes, who believe that their wit and reputation allows them every kind of self-indulgence, whether it be petty larceny, sex, or cattiness, flaws that the contrasting presence of straight shooter Sam makes Izzy notice, seemingly for the first time.

However, Izzy is still not ready for Sam. Instead, she responds to an invitation from Anton and stands up the pickle man. She meets the writer in his apartment. Emblematically, it is completely unfurnished but for a large bed. Only after realizing that Anton is after her body rather than her mind, and sees her as little more than one of his groupies, does Izzy finally turn to Sam, who has waited up for her, and perhaps to the world in which she is supposed to have roots.

The opening credits of the motion picture show Delancey Street at night, and the drapery of lights that are its nighttime extension—those of the Williamsburg Bridge. Silver locates it immediately in its central role as the border between two cultural worlds that are shown to be utterly dissimilar and unassimilable. But even though Delancey is a mere three blocks south and to the west of Hester Street, and though we see it in its unabashed Jewishness, the director has lost the savor that permeated her movie *Hester Street*.

Between *Hester Street* and *Crossing Delancey*, Silver expanded the themes and concerns evidenced in her first feature. Films like *Bernice Bobs Her Hair* (1976), based on an F. Scott Fitzgerald story about the metamorphosis of an ugly duckling; *Between the Lines* (1977), whose protagonist was an underground newspaper editor; or *Finnegan Begin Again* (1985), which examined the romance of two middle-aged people, were vehicles for her continued interest in the ethnic texture of our society, the avatars of women in the battle of the sexes, and comedy. But this ex-

pansion, which placed her characters in diverse locations and social strata, also weakened the deep roots that breathed life into them on Hester Street.

Crossing Delancey's Isabella Grossman, like most of the other characters in this film, suffers from a similar attenuation of roots. Her moving through Manhattan, back and forth across Delancey, mirrors the emotional pendulum that defines her. Since she appears to be rooted in neither her uptown world nor in that of her grandmother on the Lower East Side, she is unable to focus her emotional needs on a particular man.

Of the three men in her life, Anton, Sam, and Nick, Anton is clearly the one who fits best into the social and intellectual world she has created for herself after she crossed Delancey and moved northward: she gives Bubbie as evidence of her wonderful life the fact that she converses with the likes of Isaac Bashevis Singer (unfortunately, her grandmother does not seem to have heard of him, even though Izzy selected him presumably for maximum ethnic conviction. Anton, however, is so obsessively self-centered that it is difficult to understand his attractiveness.

Anton is drawn as such a superficial character that one wonders whether Izzy's problem is not actually Micklin Silver's. Requiring Izzy to be attracted to such a person intensifies Izzy's lie too much, when she asserts that she does not need a man to feel complete: we can accept that she needs men in her life, but the desperate quality of that need is overemphasized by the clichés that compose Anton, an intellectual whose veneer of sophistication is undercut by his womanizing, a macho style displayed in the titles of his books and his egoism.

Though Izzy finally leaves the writer, her reason for doing so comes so late, after so many hesitations, and in response to such blatancy, that one wonders whether she has learned anything. It is only after Anton has made it clear that he wants her as a combination sex object and flunky that she gets up from the bed onto which they had fallen. One cannot help but imagine that a phone call from Anton rectifying such a crude faux pas would cause the pendulum to swing one more time and bring her instantly back.

The role of Nick, another evidence of Izzy's poor judgment when it comes to men, seems limited to infusing her world with a bohemian tincture (uptown can afford anything, even bohemia). He is shabby in his clothing and morals, seems to have screwed up his life, and, if he affords sex for Izzy, that is the only utility we can imagine him providing her.

Sam Posner, the obvious choice from the very start, ends up being hardly more satisfactory as a character. Just as Anton was turned into too much of a caricature of the egomaniacal intellectual, Sam is located too far at the other extreme: there seems to be no reason why Izzy's two choices should be such antipodes—the literary lion and the man who sells pickles. Those dislocations serve only to exaggerate the heroine's emotional swings.

Compared to the characters of *Hester Street* (even Jake), Sam is singularly jejune. Though he courts Bubbie, who sees in him an ideal grandson-in-law, wears a dutiful skullcap, assures us that he attends the synagogue regularly, and sells (presumably kosher) pickles, he lacks any ethnic density. He is the attentive, patient, reflective, good-humored, fairly good-looking, but finally utterly generic man that any girl next door could have seen as the perfect guy next store. Izzy assures him "you're a nice guy," and that seems the extent of Sam's character.

Though firmly implanted with his pickles within the depths of the Lower East Side, Sam has

as much trouble as Izzy convincing us that he has roots. The fault is once again the picture's. It is not so much because Izzy moves back and forth between two worlds that she cannot take root; it is because she has not been given the human density that assumes such roots and feeds on them. And Sam, for all his good intentions, lacks it too.

In *Hester Street*, the Yiddish background of the character actors, and the Yiddish they speak, added to the depth of characterization. In *Crossing Delancey*, Reizl Bozyk, her Yiddish theater background notwithstanding, is little more than a dialect comedian in her role as Izzy's grandmother. She and her matchmaker partner (Sylvia Miles) are a turn straight out of the Borscht Belt. The two exist only for their one-liners, just as Sam is there to epitomize the good son and worthy marital prospect, and Anton will do little more than personify the obnoxious and self-seeking intellectual. As movie critic Roger Ebert concluded, "The people in this movie have intelligence in their eyes, but their words are defined by the requirements of formula comedy." Silver has created characters better able to sustain a humorous tone than their intended definition.

Izzy is irritated at her grandmother for believing that without a man she must be unfulfilled, and her counterarguments would seem to be valid: she has a stimulating job; she meets unusually interesting people; she is independent. We have seen, however, how her determination to pursue Anton undercuts those arguments. Her words are further subverted by the director when the film sends us a clear signal that a woman's manifest destiny is to mate, as when the sight of a girlfriend breast-feeding her child (south of Delancey; obviously this is not an uptown practice) plunges Izzy into a pensive mood.

If Izzy's arguments fail, then Bubbie is right and her wisdom confirms Silver's apparent belief that a woman alone *is* unfulfilled. But Bubbie has no more claim to wisdom than any of the others: though less heavy than Faye Lapinsky, the Jewish mother in Paul Mazursky's *Next Stop Greenwich Village* (1976), she is an ethnic caricature. And because these people can neither comment on what they are, nor demonstrate it, the spectator is asked to accept their Jewishness without proof—an especially unfortunate necessity since so much rides on whether or not they are Jewish—the answers to the big questions about a woman's life, liberty, and her pursuit of happiness being located in the Jewish enclave south of Delancey where Joan Micklin Silver has chosen to position herself.

By labeling Sam a pickle merchant, Silver deliberately decked him out in a disguise that distances him as much as possible from the intellectual world to which Izzy has escaped. The label defines him as the most ordinary of people, someone with material concerns rather than those of the mind. What the disguise hides, and what Silver presumably wants Izzy to discover, is the fact that Sam is Jewish—that is to say, informed with all the social and moral properties a woman would want in a husband. (While she must simultaneously discover that however glamorous the disguise—Anton's, for example—it can hide a wolf in cheap intellectual clothing.

Because both Sam and Anton are one-dimensional sketches that render transparent the disguises Silver has thrown over them, Izzy's (belated) discovery of their true identities makes her appear singularly obtuse to the spectator, who has had no difficulty seeing through those concealments from the start. And the sketchy dimensions of both men do not allow one to understand what Izzy might indeed find to share with Sam once she has given up the world in which she felt comfortable: if there is no more to Sam than the viewer is allowed to fathom, he can certainly not be a substitute for the stimulating world of uptown bookstores and its trove of creative and intelligent people. The answer is, of course, that she and Sam will share a common Jewishness, but that answer is not satisfactory since Izzy felt fulfilled by the world of the bookstore—a world in which the question of Jewishness never arose. Her moments of greatest friction with her beloved grandmother come when Bubbie attempts to foist Judaism on her.

The insertion of Izzy's dependency on men, even though she left home and found a way of making her life rewarding in every other respect, is one more instance of the circularity that the film's messages convey. Izzy has to be unfulfilled emotionally *in order* to return to her roots. Unfortunately, she doesn't really have any. As Roger Ebert wondered, "Is it a good idea to get married simply because the rules of plot construction call for it? In life, maybe that be OK, but it's not good enough for a movie."

The idea that people are where they live is simplistic. Curiously, Sam questions that simplicity when he asks: "Is my world so small? Does it define me?" This is a plea for Izzy to understand that the Lower East Side is not as narrow as she believes. Simply being from there should not define anyone, but in order to escape from such pat characterizations, these people would have to give the spectator more than simply an address to vouch for their credibility. Without that, viewers are left with only the geography of Manhattan to guide them.

Crossing Delancey confirms Alan Spiegel's belief that, in proportion to his ubiquity, the Jew in recent Hollywood films has lost visibility and definition. Speaking of the Jew's "vanishing act," Spiegel notes that "he seems so thoroughly swallowed by the demotic American dream of Jewish men and woman that one may legitimately ask how much of his person and manner still belong to himself?" That "swallowing" is what allows Jews to be the relatively unself-conscious objects of comedy, but that is hardly a good vehicle for analytic examination. The spectator is left more with a lighthearted primer about finding romance in Manhattan than with anything else. *Crossing Delancy* lays claim to exemplifying "Jewish New York," though its more rightful place might well be "romantic New York." But it did achieve for Joan Micklin Silver the box office success that had eluded her with *Hester Street*.

Abridged from: David I. Grossvogel, *Scenes in the City: Film Visions of Manhattan before 9/11* (New York: Peter Lang, 2003).

Background: http://en.wikipedia.org/wiki/Lower_East_Side; http://jwa.org/encyclopedia/article/silver-joan-micklin.

Bibliography

Acker, Amy. *Reel Women: Pioneers of the Cinema, 1896 to the Present*. New York: Continuum, 1991.

Bernheimer, Kathryn. *The 50 Greatest Jewish Movies: A Critic's Ranking of the Very Best*. Secaucus, NJ: Birch Lane, 1998.

Biga, Leo Adam. "Joan Micklin Silver, Shattering Cinema's Glass Ceiling." *Leo Adam Biga's Blog*, May 18, 2010 http://leoadambiga.wordpress.com/2010/05/18/shattering-cinemas-glass-ceiling/.

"Dialogue on Film: Joan Micklin Silver." *American Film* (May 1989): 22–27.

Gertel, Elliot B. *Over the Top Judaism: Precedents and Trends in the Depiction of Jewish Beliefs and Observances in Film and Television*. Lanham, MD: University Press of America, 2003.

Spiegel, Alan. "The Vanishing Act: A Typology of the Jew in Contemporary American Film." In *From Hester Street to Hollywood: The Jewish-American Stage and Screen*, edited by Sarah Blacher Cohen, 257–75. Bloomington: Indiana University Press, 1983.

51. *Torch Song Trilogy*

Gay and Jewish Foundations

JONATHAN C. FRIEDMAN

Torch Song Triology, directed by Paul Bogart
[A]
United States, 1988

In the late 1960s and early 1970s, many playwrights, screenwriters, filmmakers, and theater producers brought sex out of the unspoken world and into the forum of public discourse. The effect was almost anarchic, producing some of the most provocative representations of human sexuality even by twenty-first century standards. However, mainstream theatrical and cinematic works of the 1970s that featured gay and lesbian characters or story lines about homosexuality were often as homophobic as their predecessors, sometimes more so, rendering gay men as salacious thugs or deviant psychopaths who "deserved" to die gruesome deaths. Works that bucked this trend were few and far between, but those that did frequently had Jewish authorship. Few can dispute the foundational importance to theater and film history of works such as *Sunday Bloody Sunday*, *Bent*, *March of the Falsettos*, *If This Isn't Love*, and *Torch Song Trilogy*. In this essay, I will focus on the latter to assess its dual Jewish and gay foundations.

In the 1970s, gay life and culture evolved in complex ways politically and sexually. The Gay Liberation Front, or GLF, was formed in the wake of the Stonewall riots as an advocacy group for the gay community, but disillusionment with its tactics and philosophies led to the creation of splinter groups that were not as left-wing, such as the Gay Activists Alliance, or that represented

Anne Bancroft (as Mrs. Beckoff) asks her gay son, Harvey Fierstein (as Arnold), why he hasn't married a nice Jewish girl yet. From *Torch Song Trilogy* (1988), directed by Paul Bogart. NEW LINE CINEMA/PHOTOFEST

constituencies that the GLF ignored, such as transgendered people and people of color. In the early 1970s, the first openly gay politicians won seats in statehouses and city halls, and in 1977, Miami became the first city to pass a gay rights ordinance. In both developments, gay Jews figured prominently—Harvey Milk, as councilman in San Francisco, and Ethan Geto, as leader of the gay rights effort in Dade County, Florida. By the beginning of the 1980s, Harvey Milk was dead, assassinated along with the mayor of San Francisco, George Moscone; Anita Bryant and her antigay minions had succeeded in overturning Miami's antidiscrimination decree; and AIDS was about to become the pandemic of the decade.

It was in this tenuous environment of both increasing visibility and intolerance toward gay men that Harvey Fierstein's *Torch Song Trilogy*

emerged. Winner of the Tony Award for Best Play in 1983, the play is a compilation of three separate one-acts that appeared at the La Mama Experimental Theatre Club off-off Broadway. Act One is "The International Stud," which opened in February 1978, Act Two is "Fugue in a Nursery," and Act Three is "Widows and Children First," both of which premiered eight months apart in 1979. Although Fierstein had a difficult time finding a producer who would stage the one-acts together as a single show, he eventually found a sponsor in The Glines, one of the leading gay theater companies in New York City. The combined, four-hour-long *Torch Song* began off-off Broadway in 1981 and moved to the Little Theatre on Broadway in June 1982, where it ran for nearly three years.

The major characters in the plays are Fierstein's character, Arnold Beckoff, and his on-again, off-again bisexual lover/friend, Ed. Set in the early 1970s, "The International Stud" focuses on Arnold's life as a Jewish drag queen and the rise and fall of his relationship with Ed. In "Fugue in a Nursery," Arnold is dating Alan, played by Matthew Broderick in the 1988 movie version, and he and Arnold visit Ed and his fiancée Laurel for a weekend, during which Alan and Ed have sex. (In the play, the actors performed the entire act on a large bed.) "Widows and Children First," set in the spring of 1980, has Ed estranged from his wife and "rooming" with Arnold, who has adopted a troubled gay foster teen, David. Over the course of this sequence, it is revealed that Alan is dead, having been beaten to death by gay bashers. The 1988 film depicts the beating at the end of the second act.

For our discussion, Arnold's Jewish upbringing begins to inform the dialogue and tension more overtly in the third act of the film ("Widows and Children" in the play), as Arnold's mother, Mrs. Beckoff, comes to visit. While "Widows" is clearly structured around the trope of the Jewish mother, it is the film that adds depth to Arnold's ethnic heritage. In its second act, Arnold's father dies, and Arnold and Alan attend his funeral, during which a rabbi chants the emblematic Jewish prayer for the dead, the kaddish. After the funeral, Arnold's mother, played by Anne Bancroft, shows her two sons where she intends to be buried and where Arnold, his brother, their wives, and their children are to be buried as well. Mrs. Beckoff turns to Arnold and says, "You might meet a nice girl, someday. You never know," to which Arnold responds, "Believe me, ma, I know." Irritated, Mrs. Beckoff looks to Arnold's brother: "God doesn't know. My son knows."

The scene quickly cuts to Arnold and Alan

sitting shiva, another tradition of Jewish mourning. Alan asks, "Why are all the mirrors covered?" Arnold replies, "So we don't see the pain in our faces." Alan then asks, "And why are you sitting on boxes?" prompting Arnold to quip, "To make sure there's pain in our faces." The camera pulls back to reveal a seething Anne Bancroft, giving both Alan and Arnold the "evil eye." She snarls: "You told me he was Jewish." Arnold says that he's "outta town Jewish."

In the film's third act, mourning in a Jewish context provides the space for an argument over gay rights as Arnold and his mother return to the cemetery. When Arnold begins to recite kaddish for Alan, Mrs. Beckoff swoops in with an attack on her son's sexuality, and Arnold offers a rejoinder that cuts so negatively, it reveals both individual and group trauma. It is, more importantly, one of the most passionate pleas for gay rights ever put to film.

Mrs. Beckoff: That's it. Arnold, honestly, I've had it up to here with you. Your father left these plots to you. This is what you want to do with them? Fine. That's your business. But I will not stand here and watch you spit on your father's grave.

Arnold: What?

Mrs. Beckoff: What are you doing?

Arnold: What do you mean?

Mrs. Beckoff: What are you doing?

Arnold: I'm doing the same thing you're doing.

Mrs. Beckoff: No! I'm reciting kaddish for my husband! You're blaspheming your religion.

Arnold: Mama, you know who this is, this is my lover.

Mrs. Beckoff: Wait. Wait. You're gonna compare my marriage to you and Alan? Your father and I were married for thirty-five years. We had two children together! You dare compare yourself to that?

Arnold: I'm talking about the loss.

Mrs. Beckoff: What loss? What loss did you have? You fooled around with some boy. Huh? Where do you come to compare that with a marriage of thirty-five years? Come on, Arnold! This isn't one of your pals you're talking to.

Arnold: Mama, I lost someone I loved very much.

Mrs. Beckoff: So you felt bad, maybe you even cried a little. What would you know about what I felt? Thirty-five years I lived with this man! He got sick, I took him to the hospital. You know what they gave me? Huh? I gave them a man. They gave me a place to visit on high holy days. How could you possibly know how I felt? It took me two months before I could sleep in our bed alone, and a year! It took me a year before I could say I instead of we! Huh? And you're gonna tell me you were mourning? How dare you!

Arnold: You're right, ma. How dare I? I couldn't possibly know how it feels to take somebody's things and put 'em in plastic bags and watch garbage men take 'em away. Or how it feels when you forget and you set him a place at the table. How 'bout the food that rots in the refrigerator because you forgot how to shop for one? How dare I, right? Ma! How dare . . . believe me, you had it easy. You know what my friends said? What the fuck are you carrying on about, at least you had a lover! That's right, ma, you had it easy. You lost your husband in a nice clean hospital! You know where I lost mine? I lost mine on the street!

That's right! They killed him on the street! Twenty-seven years old, laying dead on a street killed by a bunch of kids with baseball bats! That's right, ma! Killed by children! Children taught by people like you! 'Cos everybody knows that queers don't matter! Queers don't love! And those that do deserve what they get!!!

In his commentary on the film, Fierstein called the cemetery scene a "very hard shoot," filled with emotions that few people wanted to confront, but one that was absolutely key to the growth of the characters. Although claiming that the dialogue did not have a basis in his personal past, Fierstein reveals that the entire Alan subplot grew out of anger over a gay friend whose beating went unpunished.

The cemetery scene is illustrative not only of gay identity, but also of American Jewish identity at the end of the twentieth century. Jewishness informs the generational disconnect between Arnold, whose sensibilities are basically secular and cosmopolitan, and his mother, who, while not Orthodox, still ascribes immorality to gayness based on Jewish custom and tradition. Although she reaches a point at the end where she can sympathize with Arnold's pain, she does not accept his homosexuality. The play's ragged ending, which sees Mrs. Beckoff leave without any clear resolution, conforms to Fierstein's optimistic, yet bittersweet outlook, which is itself the product of a tension between his supportive upbringing and the constant public struggle of being a minority within a minority. Fierstein has said in the past that his sense of humor has been "based on seeing the opposite—which is . . . very Jewish. . . . It's like my saying that I perceive every human being to be gay until I'm told otherwise. It's seeing everything

in the world as funny because it's all upside down."
He has also said that "every good thing you get in
this world is a gift. And all the bad stuff you deserve. I guess I'm very Jewish."

Fierstein forges the most obvious link between
gay life and Jewish history in a surprising comment by David, Arnold's foster teen. Apparently,
David did not initially understand why one of the
first bonding moments between him and Arnold
involved a visit to Alan's grave.

> *David*: Then about a week later we were
> watchin' the news on TV and there was this
> protest march; a bunch of Jews marchin'
> against Nazis. They had these signs that
> said "Never Again" and "We Remember."
> And I looked over at Arnold and he was
> like cryin' real soft, and just like that I con-
> nected. I knew why he showed me this.

The statement might just be the most important line in Fierstein's play. In the end, Arnold is
guided by collective Jewish memory—in this case,
the memory of suffering—and it is this experience
that adds context and motivation to his fight for
civil rights as a gay man.

Fierstein's "universalizing" approach and message of family, love, and acceptance did not sit well
with the more sexually free-spirited set within the
gay community who fought against the blanket
assimilation of heterosexual "norms." The mix of
tragicomedy and redemption also did not win
Torch Song the film a wide audience; it garnered
less than five million dollars at the box office. Although Fierstein admits that his narrative structure has a Jewish coloring, it is a stretch to argue
that his Jewishness propelled him toward main-
streaming. Indeed, redemption as a plotline has a
long-standing tradition on stage and screen. In-
tangible factors related to Fierstein's overall personality and values undoubtedly are relevant here

as well. And yet the words of David Shneer and
Caryn Aviv are illuminating, as they capture the
middle ground that Jews have occupied on this
issue:

> For queer Jews, creating family involves
> both adopting the dominant social paradigms
> —a monogamous couple with two kids and a
> picket fence—and moving beyond the mere
> assimilation of bourgeois definitions by under-
> mining the assumption that family is deter-
> mined solely by biology.

Despite its critical and popular shortcomings,
Torch Song Trilogy remains a groundbreaking
work of stage and cinema. The play and film may
actually be more resonant now, at the beginning
of the twenty-first century, than in the mid-to-
late 1980s, when the discourse over gay identity
was commonly fused to a discussion about AIDS.
Filtering the theme of sexuality through a distinctly Jewish prism, Fierstein appropriated, and
then reinvented, traditions from Jewish and non-
Jewish theater and film, such as the clash between
traditional and modern ways, the intergenerational conflict over family and life-cycle events,
and the timeless struggle between Jewish mother
and son. Tropes with a Jewish basis became vehicles for Fierstein's ventilation of gay issues, and
as the following quote demonstrates, Jewishness
continues to play an informative (although not
necessarily singular) role in Fierstein's mixed-bag
identity:

> I believe that democracy was conceived to
> nurture and protect diversity, and that diver-
> sity is what makes this country great. I am gay.
> I am Jewish, which makes me some other peo-
> ple's nightmare, and I am a radical. I'm proud
> to be all of them. I am also naturally gray. I
> am pro–pursuit of happiness, which means

I am pro-choice. I am also pro-family, pro-commitment, pro-marriage, pro-divorce, and pro-money. I am pro-children whether they are gay or, God forbid, straight.

Republished from: Jonathan C. Friedman, *Rainbow Jews: Jewish and Gay Identity in the Performing Arts* (Lanham, MD: Lexington Books, 2007.

    Source: Harvey Fierstein, *Torch Song Triology: Three Plays*, New York: Penguin, 1988).

    Background: http://www.myjewishlearning.com/life/Sex_and_Sexuality/Homosexuality.shtml.

Bibliography

Aviv, Caryn, and David Shneer, eds. *Queer Jews*, New York: Routledge, 2002.

Benshoff, Harry M., and Sean Griffin. *Queer Images: A History of Gay and Lesbian Film in America*. Lanham, MD: Rowman and Littlefield, 2005.

Clendinen, Dudley, and Adam Nagourney. *Out for Good: The Struggle to Build a Gay Rights Movement in America*. New York: Touchstone, 1990.

Clum, John. *Still Acting Gay: Male Homosexuality in Modern Drama*. New York: St. Martin's, 2000.

Furnish, Ben. *Nostalgia in Jewish-American Theatre and Film, 1979–2004*. New York: Peter Lang, 2005.

Gree, William. "*Torch Song Trilogy*: A Gay Comedy with a Dying Fall." *Maske und Kothurn* 30, nos. 1–2 (1984): 217–24.

Hoffman, Warren. *The Passing Game: Queering Jewish American Culture*. Syracuse, NJ: Syracuse University Press, 2009.

Kakutani, Michiko. "Fierstein and 'Torch Song:' A Daring Climb from Obscurity." *New York Times*, July 14 1982.

Plaskin, Glenn. "Harvey Fierstein." *Mandate* 9, no. 12 (1984): 14–17, 66, 81–82.

52. Against Tribalism

David Mamet's *Homicide*

PHILIP HANSON

Homicide, directed by David Mamet [A]
United States, 1991

David Mamet's 1991 film, *Homicide*, is so grounded in its historical moment that the historical moment takes over. The film represents a break with the previous boundaries of Mamet's views on ethnic identity, which emerged in his short plays immediately leading up to *Homicide*. Historically, it is not coincidental that Mamet's film appeared the same year Arthur Schlesinger's now-famous essay, "The Cult of Ethnicity, Good and Bad," appeared in *Time* magazine. Schlesinger wrote: "The United States escaped the divisiveness of a multiethnic society by a brilliant solution: the creation of a brand-new national identity. The point of America was not to preserve old cultures but to forge a new American culture." By 1991, this pressure had in many ways reversed itself; Americans were increasingly becoming divided along ethnic lines. *Homicide* examines this tension between ethnic and American identity.

On the subject of ethnic identity, sociologist Craig Calhoun suggests, "Self-knowledge is always a construction no matter how much it feels like a discovery." In *Homicide*, Mamet explores the implications of Calhoun's remark for Jewish American notions of ethnic identity in the early 1990s. Fears about the possible balkanization of America in the face of a trend to identify with one's ethnic group were emerging in various discourses. Schlesinger cautioned, "On every side today ethnicity is breaking up nations. . . . If separatist tendencies go unchecked, the result can only

Joe Mantegna (as Robert Gold) is a tough cop in search of his Jewish identity. From *Homicide* (1991), directed by David Mamet. PHOTOFEST

be the fragmentation, resegregation, and tribalization of American life." In *Homicide*, Mamet grapples with the questions of competing meanings of Jewishness in the contemporary Jewish American community to suggest the possibility of postethnicity.

Police detective Robert Gold, a nonpracticing Jew (played by Joe Mantegna), stumbles into the candy store murder of an old Jewish woman, Mrs. Klein, who was once a freedom fighter for the State of Israel. Initially, Gold believes the murder to be just a petty robbery, but Mrs. Klein's family insists the murder is the result of anti-Semitism. Gold and his partner, Tim Sullivan (played by William H. Macy), are also trying to capture Randolph, an African American drug dealer. Mamet uses these ethnic affiliations to pose questions about the meaning of group identity.

Initially, however, *Homicide* appears to be part of a subgenre in American film and literature about a Jew recognizing his neglected Jewish identity when confronted by anti-Semitism, an idea Mamet had already explored in *The Disappearance of the Jews* (1982). Instead, Mamet ends up subverting accepted notions of tribal identity. Gold finds real anti-Semitism when he joins a Jewish cabal Mrs. Klein had belonged to, only to be betrayed by his fellow Jews. The film ends with Gold's attraction to ethnic identity ruining him with the police community and getting his partner and closest friend killed.

Gold develops a new identity on the basis of past prejudice he has experienced as a Jewish police officer. His name itself suggests that his parents or ancestors severed themselves from their ethnic roots by shortening their name from Goldberg or Goldstein. Mamet uses the name Bobby Gould in his earlier *Disappearance of the Jews* to raise many of the same ethnic questions. His exposure to the Jewish underground cell involves the process Anthony J. Cascardi describes in the formation of personal identity: "The modern subject is defined by its insertion into a series of separate value spheres, each one of which tends to exclude or attempts to assert its priority over the rest." Cascardi notes that the process of identity formation creates a series of contradictions within the "subject-self." ' Such contradictions in Gold's identity are apparent from the film's outset. As Gold and Sullivan sit with other officers and listen to two men from the mayor's office discuss the need to arrest an African American drug dealer, Gold makes a casual joke. Mr. Patterson (played by Louis Murray), an African American official from the mayor's office, tells Gold, "you come out with a joke . . . it's no joke, Mister, and if it happened to a white man, then it wouldn't be a joke. . . ."

When Gold attempts to make amends with Patterson, Patterson calls him a "little kike." The tension between the African American Patterson and the Jewish Gold introduces a racial structure that connects Gold's growing interest in ethnic identity—or in arriving at a sense of identity based on tribal affiliation—to the trend for ethnic groups in the larger culture to do so. Mamet explores the difference between the construction of personal identity and the reconstruction of identity as part of an ethnic group. The implications for relations between African Americans and American Jews extend well beyond the film. The causes of Gold's uneasiness and his growing interest in tribal identification are summarized in a remark made by Vaclav Havel: "The fewer the answers the era of rational knowledge provides to the basic questions of human beings, the more

deeply it would seem people . . . cling to the ancient certainties of their tribe."

As a director, Mamet provides a recurring visual narrative of racial tensions in America. That a black man calls a Jew a kike in *Homicide* conjures up recent clashes between African Americans and Jews that arose out of perceptions of one's own ethnic identity and the ethnic identity of the other. *Homicide* provides a consistent flow of small reminders about the omnipresence of racial tension in America. Why, for example, does Gold feel compelled, against Sullivan's instinctive resistance (and against police subculture wisdom), to find Randolph? One early version of the film's response to this question materializes in the police squad room in the area of a holding cell. After Patterson's anti-Semitic remark, several officers articulate their support and affection for Gold. Sullivan is willing to fight Patterson. Detective Olcott (an African American officer played by Lionel Mark Smith) approaches Gold and remarks, "You all right, man? Fucker had no call to get on you like that." Olcott's support illustrates that for him police relations take precedence over tribal relations. Detective Frank tries to reassure Gold by commenting: "Gimme couple serious Irish cops, cigars in their mouths, go out there . . . go bring your man in." Of course, when the Irish came to dominate police forces, they did so partly because they had been excluded from other professions due to ethnic bias. But the reference reminds Gold that he is not Irish, not one of the traditional cops.

Later, in their squad car, as Gold and Sullivan head for a gym to pick up Randolph's brother, Gold remarks, "he had no fucken call to get racial on me." Sullivan responds much more casually, "So he called you one, you called him one." When Sullivan gives Gold the meat from his sandwich to put on the bump on his head, Gold responds,

"Hey, what don't you know? You are one smart Indian." Gold wants to talk about ethnicity. But what is one to make of Sullivan's casual response to ethnic slurs? The easy answer is that Sullivan is simply insensitive to minority feelings. But the film does not substantiate such an interpretation. Sullivan's interest in relationships is doggedly personal. Mamet uses Sullivan to represent for Gold a familial (as opposed to tribal) relationship, and an identity based on personal relations rather than on tribal relations. Sullivan represents one of the instances in *Homicide* where Mamet looks to postethnicity as a desired goal.

Mamet stresses the personal relationships the officers have with Gold. A couple of cops escort Grounder, a character who killed his family with a deer rifle, into a holding cell. Grounder temporarily escapes and snatches Gold's gun, breaking his holster strap and injuring him. The responses of other officers to Gold's injury are familial. Bates, Brown, and Lieutenant Senna (Vincent Guastaferro) ask Gold if he is all right. Senna asks someone to get him a glass of water. In the patrol car, Sullivan gives Gold the meat from his sandwich to put on his bump. Gold subsequently tells Sullivan, "You're like my family, Tim," to which Sullivan replies, "Bob . . . I am your family." His remark challenges traditional definitions of ethnic and familial bonds.

Gold's police family represents one of the group structures Mamet offers as a possibility for group loyalty. His partnership with Sullivan offers another, more intimate relationship. Randolph, the drug dealer (played by Ving Rhames), enjoys a similar familial relationship with his mother. The Jewish Klein family, to which Gold is attracted, exists as another version of family. A fourth family unit is that of Grounder. Grounder claims he has murdered his family "to protect them." The Jewish underground group serves as a competing alternative, a tribal structure, to which Gold is attracted. Mamet fashions these groups as potential models for Gold's collective identity. To return to Cascardi's point, the social groups in *Homicide* present Gold with a variety of values upon which to construct his identity.

Gold is introduced to the Kleins when their grandmother is murdered in a predominantly African American neighborhood, where she has run a candy store for many years. The murder appears to be a store holdup. Outside the store, an African American boy and an African American woman tell Gold the old lady was murdered for the treasure she kept in her basement. The explanation reflects the community's effort to explain why a rich old woman would remain in such a neighborhood. When the Kleins enter the store to view the old woman's body, however, they offer a different explanation for the murder. Dr. Klein (J. S. Block) remarks, "It never stops, does it?" When Gold asks the doctor's daughter (Rebecca Pidgeon), "What is it that never stops?" Miss Klein replies, "Against the Jews." Such a remark opens up one avenue of inquiry that dominates this film. The Kleins identify themselves in ethnic terms; whereas Gold, who is also Jewish, initially does not. Dr. Klein uses his influence to get Gold assigned to the murder investigation of his mother because Gold is Jewish. When Gold objects to Lieutenant Senna, Senna tells him: "The doctor's got this clout. He wants you; you were there; you're his 'people.'" Gold responds, "I'm his people? I thought I was your people, Lou." The difference in perspective reveals the multiple dimensions of identity. Later, Gold will identify himself as a Jew, an outsider to the police. Here he identifies himself as one of the police and an outsider to the Jews.

The Kleins believe in an essentialist definition of identity, a belief that their Jewish ethnicity comes out of something "natural" in an individual. Gold believes that he is Lieutenant Senna's "people" based on the history and values the police share. For holding this view, Gold is challenged by Jewish characters throughout the film. These challenges lead Gold to the conclusion that he must discover his "natural" identity. The problem Gold fails to see soon enough is described by Joane Nagel: "Ethnic identity is most closely associated with the issue of boundaries. Ethnic boundaries determine who is a member and who is not and designate which ethnic categories are available for individual identification at a particular time and place."

Gold is called to the Kleins' apartment when the Kleins believe they have heard gunfire on a roof adjacent to their building. Gold dismisses this as paranoia, to which Dr. Klein responds, "It's always a 'fantasy' isn't it? . . . When someone wants to hurt the Jews. . . . When the fantasy is true, when we've been killed, then you say 'what a coincidence.' What a coincidence. That at the same time we were being paranoid, someone was coincidentally trying to hurt us." When Gold receives a telephone call from Sullivan, he retreats to a room in the Kleins' apartment, where he delivers a series of remarks about Jews that smack of anti-Semitism and self-hatred: "I'm stuck here with my Jews. You should see this fucken room. . . . They pay-so-much-taxes . . . Not . . . my people, baby . . . there's so much anti-Semitism, last four thousand years, they must be doin something bring it about." As Gold turns around, the camera reveals that Miss Klein has overheard his conversation with Sullivan. She tells Gold, "You're a Jew. And you talk that way. In the house of the dead. Do you have any shame? . . . Do you hate yourself that

much? Do you belong nowhere?" Her questions provoke Gold to examine his ethnic identity and tap into latent feelings of wishing to belong somewhere other than with the police or Sullivan.

In America, the question of Jewish identity has been complex. In the 1930s, anti-Semitism kept Jews out of many areas of American life. According to Arthur Hertzberg, a "1988 survey of the Jewish students at Dartmouth College found not a single respondent who thought that being Jewish made any difference to his or her future." Intermarriage, the single most sensitive indicator of the Jewish community, was continuing to rise in the 1980s. In 1989, Stephen M. Cohen observed, "Israeli and American Jewry have been parting company politically, culturally, and religiously." Hertzberg remarks, "Ethnic tasks and memories, some warm and some angry, could not stop the erosion of Jewishness even at a time when Jews had become powerful and accepted." In 1983, Jonathan Woocher, "who had praised Jewish activism . . . found one astonishing result: [among establishment religious Jews] two out of three insisted that the Jews were God's 'chosen people.'" Hertzberg remarks, "An ethnic group cannot assert 'chosenness' without falling into chauvinism or worse."

Miss Klein provides the film's first example of what it means to be a Jew and raises the issue of "belonging." Gold is sensitive to this issue. He has already raised it with Randolph's mother (Mary Jefferson). The question of belonging to one's ethnic group is directly relevant to African Americans, the only ethnic group that did not come to the United States by choice. Randolph's mother puts her refusal to cooperate with the police in familial and racial terms. The police storm Randolph's mother's apartment and find he is not there. Sullivan asks Randolph's mother: "Where is he?" She responds, "I should kill my baby that I brought into this world. White folks? Why would that be?" Gold, the police negotiator, convinces Randolph's mother to cooperate. The whole situation is clearly orchestrated by the police, who smirk as Gold speaks. Gold's logic will bear directly on his own soon-to-be-divided loyalties: "Our job's to bring him down alive . . . I know that there's so much death in the world. I know that it's full of hatred, Momma. . . . Here we are; here we are; we're the garbage men. You think I don't know that? I know that. Looking for something to love? You got something to love. You got your boy. That's something. Look in my eyes. . . . I want to save your son. Before God, I want to save your boy."

Gold's appeal is to family identification. He addresses Randolph's mother as "Momma," which intensifies the irony of his own dilemma over identity, for he will have to decide whether he wants to draw his identity from his police "family" or his ethnic group. Gold's tragedy is that he, too, has something (a familial relationship with Sullivan), but he realizes it too late. He tries to determine what his essential identity is, but that identity for Gold is an ongoing construction.

As he delves deeper into the murder of Mrs. Klein, he receives more information on what it means to "be" a Jew. On the roof Gold has found a scrap of paper bearing the word GROFAZ. He asks a Jewish shoemaker what it means, and the old man tells him it is another name for Hitler. This clue plays with the audience's expectations, since so many post–World War II films and television dramas have revolved around characters who stumble onto nests of post–World War II secret Nazi organizations. One expects Gold to find and foil a Nazi organization and in the process find himself as a Jew. Gold takes the word GROFAZ to a Jewish library. There the Jewish

librarian interprets the word to be a German acronym meaning "the greatest . . . strategist of all time" and confirms the letters "refer to Hitler." Gold is shaken. The librarian asks, "Are you all right?" Gold must reconsider whether the Kleins' claims are true and not paranoid.

In the library Gold meets a Jewish scholar, who explains the significance of the police badge star and how it differs from the Star of David. The scholar concludes by pointing to some words in Hebrew from *The Book of Esther.* "Do you see?" the scholar asks Gold. Gold responds, "I can't read it." The scholar then expands upon Miss Klein's definition of Jewishness: "You say you're a Jew and you can't read Hebrew. What are you, then?" By Miss Klein's logic, Gold belongs nowhere, and by the scholar's logic, he is nothing. Gold realizes the librarian has lied in denying him material he requested when he overhears that the librarian is sending it to someone else. Gold manages to find the address where it is being sent.

The address leads Gold to an abandoned schoolhouse, where Gold finds a secret organization of Jews meeting. Some of them he recognizes as having been present at the *shiva* [a mourning gathering for the family of the deceased] for old Mrs. Klein. From the maid he learns that Mrs. Klein had been a fighter for the establishment of the Jewish state of Israel. Earlier, in Mrs. Klein's candy store, he had found a packing crate that once contained machine guns. In it he found a list that he filed as police evidence. During the meeting of the Jewish organization Gold expresses his desire to participate in the group's project, though it is not specified what it is. Rather, Gold's encounter with the group provides him with the opportunity to embrace a tribal identity. Benjamin (Adolph Mall), the apparent leader, initially welcomes Gold to the group. In the screen directions, Mamet writes, Benjamin "gestures as if to say 'As I foretold he is one of us."' He then leans over and "kisses Gold on the cheek." Benjamin recounts how Mrs. Klein had smuggled guns: "During our War of Independence. In our country, we call her a hero." Benjamin refers to the group as "Good Americans. Good Jews."

This introduces the question of national identification, which becomes important to Gold. Having learned of the list, which contains the names of other men in the city who helped run guns, Benjamin asks Gold for it, but Gold will only give him a copy, since he has logged in the original as police evidence. He informs Benjamin, "I took an oath." Benjamin writes Gold's name in Hebrew on a blackboard and asks him, "Are you a Jew?" When Gold answers affirmatively, Benjamin asserts, "Then be a Jew!" Though Benjamin insists, Gold responds, "Anything else . . ." Benjamin responds, "Where are your loyalties? You want the glory; you want the home; you are willing to do nothing." Benjamin demands that the tribal identity that attracts Gold supersede all else, regardless of other loyalties. Gold is expelled from the group and told that returning to the schoolhouse will be pointless since the group will not be there.

What exactly does Gold want from this group? Outside the schoolhouse, Gold spies Chava (Natalia Nogulich), a woman who is a member of the cabal. He insists on accompanying her on whatever mission she has been assigned, and she reluctantly allows him to go along. Chava's mission clears up a question that the film raised. Does *Homicide* insinuate that modern American Jews have been historically conditioned to see persecution where none exists? Were the Kleins paranoid? Gold takes over Chava's assignment to determine if the owner of a toy train store is actually a Nazi who has been posting circulars in the ghetto neighborhood. The circulars depict Jews as

rats who cause the ghetto. Gold finds a room full of Nazi paraphernalia, including disturbing photographs, one of which depicts a Nazi shooting a young Jewish mother and her baby. Gold detonates a bomb in the store, and he and Chava leave. *Homicide* examines the meaning of resorting to ethnic identity as a response to either being the target of prejudice (as Mrs. Klein's circle were during and after World War II) or longing for a transcendent sense of belonging to supplant one's current condition. Prior to bombing the train shop, Gold explains why he wants to be part of the group. Gold tells Chava, "What can I tell you about it? They said . . . I was a pussy all my life. They said I was a pussy because I was a Jew. Other cops, they'd say, send a Jew, might as well send a broad on the job, send a broad through the door. . . . All my goddamned life, and I listened to it . . . uh-huh . . . ? I was the donkey . . . I was the clown."

Earlier in the film, Gold joked about kissing F.B.I. agents, implying they are homosexual. When Patterson insulted Gold by calling him a kike, Sullivan responded by challenging Patterson, "Step out in the alley? You fucken faggot, I'll kill your ass right here." In a film about ethnic outsiders, Mamet shows Gold telling a woman from the group that he felt bad when others compared him to a woman. In the Nazi newspaper that Gold finds in the train shop, one of the racist outbursts against Jews reads, "the effeminate ideals and weak appearance of the Jew, proclaims to all their inferiority." The remark links the police, the Nazis, and Gold in its denigration of the feminine. Earlier, Sullivan and Gold both used gay epithets to insult others. In its interest in insiders and outsiders, *Homicide* demonstrates how often we think of someone as "other" while resisting becoming "other" ourselves. Such a concept exposes an innate problem in group identity: by constructing boundaries defining the group, one inevitably places someone else outside the defining circle (which is different from being forcibly bound by persecution).

Chava puts her finger on this point when she responds to Gold by saying, "You were the outsider." Gold then reveals the core reasons why he wants to join the organization."You have your own home," he tells Chava. "Now what can that be like?" he asks, and adds, "To have your own country?" Gold elaborates, "I sat with those guys tonight . . . with heroes . . . Jewish guys who had nothing to prove. And I felt . . . I felt, Jesus, all my life, I got to be the first one in the door . . . and . . . Huh? Not for me, all for someone else. Why? Because I was no good. Because I'm nobody. I want to be part of it, that's all."

Paradoxically, to be part of Chava's enterprise, Gold has to prove himself by bombing the train store, thereby repeating the test of being the first cop to enter in police raids. Gold is presented as unaware of the point that his contruction of the Jewish group resembles the police heroism for which he had been decorated twenty-two times. His assessment of why he has to be first on raids is challenged in the film. At Randolph's house, when Gold rushes ahead of Sullivan, Sullivan remarks, "How come you always gotta be the first one through the door?" If Gold intends to display that Jews can be brave, Sullivan doesn't perceive it this way. Gold's feelings may result from his own image of his place within the police—even while the film acknowledges that these actions occur in a world where anti-Semitism persists. To deny such a point would be anti-Semitic.

Gold's sense of attaining a tribal identity by bombing the train shop is undermined in the diner afterward. A young Jewish man from the schoolhouse and a Jewish chauffeur, also a member of the cabal, join Gold for diner. Gold tells the

chauffeur, "I want to be part of it." The chauffeur responds, "Then you are part of it. You've shown it. And now we need something from you." The chauffeur tells him they still want the original list of names. Here the cabal suspects a conspiracy to murder old Mrs. Klein and fears a reprisal. But the gun running is such an old story that Mamet presents their response as excessive. The group's members cannot believe the old lady was just killed in the robbery. Chava also asks for the list. When Gold again refuses, the young man hands an envelope to the chauffeur, who tells Gold, "The building you entered was under surveillance, here are some photographs of you entering and leaving. . . . Look at them at your leisure." The cabal is now blackmailing Gold to get the list. The betrayal provokes Gold to try to hit the chauffeur, who in turn hits Gold in the stomach. The three cabal members leave Gold, where, in the brightly lit diner, alone and doubled over in pain, his betrayal is visualized. The incident has quickly reversed Gold's supposed identity. He no longer is part of the group, but rather an enemy. Or, if one thinks in terms of his construction of tribal identity, he was a Jew, and then he was not. This repeats the question of what constitutes essential Jewish identity.

In *Homicide*, Mamet presents ethnic persecution as immoral and tribal identification as either a flawed choice or a longing for an identity that, for historical reasons, cannot be recovered. He sees the two as potentially related, which makes tribalism all the more undesirable in American society. Mamet's position engages the debates over the Melting Pot or multicultural models of ethnic assimilation or parochialism in the United States. The former believes America will eventually assimilate everyone. Jews have generally supported this position, since it has prevented the United States from becoming a country dominated by its Christian majority. Jews have succeeded to the point of becoming insiders in the American system. African Americans have sided with the multicultural camp, which sees race as too significant a barrier in America to be assimilated. They also question the value of assimilating and leaving behind their own cultural traditions. Mamet views both positions as potentially harmful. He posits relationships he considers to be natural (familial, for example), and which he believes do not force the individual to conform to the group. He can be regarded as either looking forward to postethnicity or trying to get beneath the surface of pluralist and multiculturalist ethnic categories to something organic.

Mamet's use of the family, as a magnetic attracting force, seriously challenges the logic of Gold's desire to abandon relationships he has established and the identity he has developed as a part of the police. Mamet locates the positive aspect of the Gold-Sullivan relationship partly in its having developed outside of any ethnic affiliation. He finds the police, as a subgroup, an economic necessity where organic relationships may or may not develop. This point is enforced when Grounder asks Gold if he wants to know "how to solve the problem of evil." Gold responds sarcastically, "No, man, cause if I did, then I'd be out of a job."

After Gold has been slugged in the diner, he draws the incriminating photos out of his shirt pocket. Among the photos he finds Randolph's forged passport, with which the police and Randolph's mother intend to lure Randolph into being captured. On an envelope, Gold has jotted the address and the time of the meeting with Randolph. The time is 5:00. He looks at his watch and it is 5:03. Gold races to the spot and finds the police in a shootout with Randolph's gang. Sullivan has been shot; Gold charges into the

building to look for him. Sullivan, near death, rambles incoherently. But his remarks make sense in terms of the decisions Gold has made regarding identity. Sullivan remarks: "He [the other officer with him] shot the gun dry. I said, 'Don't be doing that.' Because you move around, and there's his partner. Do you see, Bobby?" Unlike Gold, Randolph's partner was present for him. He shot Sullivan. Sullivan goes on, "Cause it, finally, doesn't make any difference. If you do or you don't. I swear to Christ I don't know what they're talking about. If you're moved, there's someone doing it."

This remark gets to the core question about identity. In Foucault's sense, we are always part of a system of representations that have preceded us. If one reformulates his or her identity, "there's always someone doing it," there is always a set of concepts originated by others that precedes self-knowledge. Finally, Sullivan's dying remark arises from his and Gold's shared experience: "Bob . . . Bob . . . Bobby . . . You remember that girl that time? Bob." Sullivan recalls a shared moment and addresses Gold with his nickname, but then returns to "Bob." Retracing Gold's letting Sullivan down by not being there to finesse Randolph's mother (who would only talk to Gold), Sullivan's address moved to the intimate and backed away from it. Gold failed to appreciate his relationship with Sullivan, which he betrayed in favor of his tribe. Gold races off to pursue Randolph. For the first time in the film, Gold racially slurs Randolph, "You shot my partner, you fucking nigger." His perception of the danger of ethnic identification turns against someone he stereotypes racially. Identifying the other in racial terms is what bigots do. It is neither fair nor rational, but psychologically Freud would call it transference.

Near the end of the film Randolph and Gold have been shot and lie bleeding together. Gold takes Randolph's hand. This scene visually shows the viewer they have something in common. They have been led into a disaster by betrayals resulting from not valuing personal relationships. The gesture moves Gold away from the racial epithet to a personal connection. Seconds before a policeman shoots Randolph, Gold has shouted out the worst thing he can think of at Randolph, "Your momma turned you over, Man." He too has let Sullivan down. He charges that Randolph's own mother has betrayed her maternal bond. Gold should know. He was part of the charade that persuaded Randolph's mother to do so. And Gold failed to understand the intimate language of personal relations he employed to persuade her.

The lesson was repeated for Gold in the Kleins' home, but he missed its significance. At the *shiva*, the close family relations and genuine feelings of grief attract Gold to wanting to share their tribal identity. But he mistakes genuine family emotions for constructed tribal relations. Drawn to Benjamin's remarks in the eulogy for Mrs. Klein, Gold asks Chava to translate. Chava translates Benjamin's remarks about Mrs. Klein being a great woman during the years of the formation of the State of Israel. But then Chava stops translating, telling him, "It's . . . you know . . . it's a jargon language, Yiddish. I don't speak Yiddish that well." She has stopped translating because Gold is still an outsider. Gold fails to see that the ethnic identity shared by the people at the *shiva* arises out of historical conditions (which occurred at a particular place during a particular period), global anti-Semitism, over which the participants had no control.

The lesson of making such a mistake is delivered by Grounder, who has murdered his family. The cabal's stated reason for underground activity is to protect Jews. Yet they wind up assaulting Gold because he will not betray the police and his oath. When Officer Brown asks Grounder why he killed his family, Grounder responds, "I did it to protect them." At the film's end, Gold has lost his partner and has been dismissed from the homicide squad. He then sees three things. First, he sees a report that demonstrates that the letters GROFAZ were torn from a flyer that read GROFAZ Pigeon Feeds. He sees the young African American boy who was present at Mrs. Klein's murder scene and had told him she was killed for her treasure. The boy killed her. Gold realizes there was no conspiracy. Sometimes a candy store murder is just a candy store murder. Finally, he sees Grounder led away in chains. Grounder has made good on his promise to show Gold the "nature of evil," whether Gold wanted to see it or not. Grounder, like Randolph's mother and like Gold, (at least in terms of responsibility), has "killed off" all of the people with whom he shared an intimate relationship.

Abridged from: Philip Hanson, "Against Tribalism: The Perils of Ethnic Identity in Mamet's Homicide." *Clio* 31, no. 3 (2002): 257–79.

Source: David Mamet, *Homicide: A Screenplay* (New York: Grove Weidenfeld, 1992).

Background: http://www.mtholyoke.edu/news/stories/4792639.

Bibliography

Breines, Paul. *Tough Jews: Political Fantasies and the Moral Dilemma of American Jewry.* New York: Basic, 1990.

Jacobson, Mathew Frye. *Roots Too: White Ethnic Revival in Post–Civil Rights America.* Cambridge: Harvard University Press, 2006.

Kane, Leslie. *Weasels and Wisemen: Ethics and Ethnicity in the Works of David Mamet.* New York: St. Martin's, 1999.

Mamet, David. *The Wicked Son: Anti-Semitism, Self-Hatred, and the Jews.* New York: Schocken, 2006.

Rosenberg, Warren. *Legacy of Rage: Jewish Masculinity, Violence, and Culture.* Amherst: University of Massachusetts Press, 2001.

Roth, Laurence. *Inspecting Jews: American Jewish Detective Stores.* New Brunswick, NJ: Rutgers University Press, 2003.

Schlesinger, Arthur, Jr. "The Cult of Ethnicity, Good and Bad." *Time,* July 8, 1991, 21.

Sherman, Ranan Omer. "The Metaphysics of Loss and Jewish Identity in David Mamet's *Homicide.*" *Modern Jewish Studies Annual* 11 (1999): 37–50.

53. Self-Criticism in Public

DAVID KRAEMER

The Believer, directed by Henry Bean [A]
United States, 2001

The Believer is a film with the power to evoke strong emotions. There is something in this story that touches a tender nerve, particularly if the viewer is a Jew. How else can we explain the condemnation of *The Believer* by one rabbi, who described it as "a primer for anti-Semitic actions," given that nothing it portrays is unavailable to the curious thug on extremist Web sites? Or the reaction of a viewer in Israel who exploded in anger, criticizing various small details in the film with an emotion totally out of proportion with the nature of the criticism? The film's main character, Danny, is unavoidably provocative. But it is not immediately obvious what about him has this power. What makes him, and the film that is his vehicle, so successfully troubling?

Undoubtedly, part of the answer is Danny's hateful brutality. From the very first scene, we know Danny as a violent bully. And his verbal bullying is often more brutal than his physical.

For some viewers, this is disturbing enough. But movies today are filled with violence, often more extreme than that depicted here. And the representation of bigoted thugs often makes us feel not troubled but smug and superior; "I could never be like that," we say to ourselves in a self-congratulatory tone. But Danny doesn't allow us to respond with such easy superiority, for it is not obvious to some of us, at least, that "we could never be like that." Or, to be more accurate, even if we couldn't imagine *doing* what Danny does, we could imagine *feeling* as he feels. It is this, I would argue, that ultimately makes his provocation so powerful.

What makes *The Believer* so compelling as narrative and important as commentary is the Danny who both hates and loves his Jewishness and provides equally good reasons for both. The underlying reasonableness of both sides of Danny's ambivalence allows his character to transcend the mundane. If Danny's affection for the tradition of his ancestors alone made sense, then this film would have been an act of pandering. It is because Danny's anger also commands consideration that the thoughtful viewer cannot repress *The Believer* from consciousness.

What is the source of Danny's venom toward Judaism and Jews? Perhaps personal motivations in his individual history turn him against the faith of his father(s). Surely we can feel frustrated, even infuriated, with the passive, pathetic figure who is Danny's father. But this is a weak, unelaborated foundation. If there is one complaint I have heard repeatedly, it is the absence of any dynamic explorations of Danny's psychology or character. The youthful Danny is already a magnificent critic of the tradition, one whose criticism borders on rage. How did he get to be this way? We have little way of knowing. Certainly, the declining father of later years cannot offer sufficient explanation. So it is not richly detailed biography that explains Danny's anger. In fact, it seems to me that Danny's anger is not personal at all. The absence of the personal suggests that what he expresses is not his own. It is, as a conceptualization of both history and theology, an expression of anger on behalf of the Jewish people as a whole. What Danny gives voice to is what any Jew might say—if he could allow himself. Consider Danny's debate with his teacher in the yeshiva classroom. The discussion focuses on the story of the binding of Isaac by his father (called the "Akedah" in Jewish tradition). Danny challenges the Torah's narrative, or at least his teacher's representation of it, in virtually every detail. To the Torah command that Abraham take his "only son," Danny responds that Abraham had another son, Ishmael. When his classmate, Avi, explains that Isaac was the only son whom Abraham loved, Danny responds sarcastically, "Oh, they only kill them when they love them?" He then characterizes the God of the story as a bully. When his teacher rebukes him for judging God, Danny responds that God gave us free will and intelligence, and our exercise of judgment must therefore be the will of God. He then heightens his protest by declaring that Abraham actually killed Isaac. Even if he didn't, Danny observes, Isaac was so traumatized by the event that he was as good as dead for the rest of his life.

In this scene, Danny is hardly the conventional pious yeshiva *bocher* (student). His angry challenge will not be turned aside. He surely goes no further than might any modern person who has read the biblical story. Who has not wondered about the nature of the God who commands Abraham to sacrifice his son? What modern Jew has not tried to rationalize or suppress the simple meaning of the Torah's starkly trou-

bling narrative? The moment one allows for critical questioning, one cannot help but observe what Danny observes. If Danny is extreme in this scene, it is only for his unwillingness to avert his critical gaze.

Consider the characterizations offered by the adult Danny to Guy, the *New York Times* reporter in the café. Explaining the perversity—sexual and otherwise—of the Jews, Danny argues that "a people—a real people—derives its genius from the land: the sun, the sea, the soil. This is how they know themselves. But the Jew doesn't have soil." Asked about the Israelis, Danny responds "those aren't real Jews. . . . They no longer need Judaism because they have the soil. The real Jew is a wanderer, a nomad. He has no roots, no attachments. So he universalizes everything." In this exchange, Danny begins as a modern romantic, espousing the ideas that energized Zionism in the nineteenth century. Is it not true that there is something abnormal about the condition of a people without a land? The leaders of Zionism over the past century certainly thought this to be so. The flip side of Danny's argument, claiming that Israelis are not "real Jews" because "real Jews" are landless and universalist, is a slightly edgy articulation of the modern Jewish philosopher Franz Rosenzweig's praise of "the people in exile." The Jewish Diaspora has not been an entirely negative legacy. Jews and Judaism have been enriched by the need to learn to live in multiple civilizations. So, is it a good thing that Jews have once again built a society on their own soil? Not a few liberal Jews have wondered about this. And is the secular "macho" Israeli really a Jew? In other words, Danny is in good modern Jewish company.

Elsewhere Danny expresses what other Jews might express if they could permit themselves. In his confrontation with the elderly Holocaust survivors, which is part of his sensitivity training, Danny's lack of sympathy (until the last moment) is appalling. But who can dismiss his questions to the man who watched the murder of his son— "What did you do while the sergeant was killing your son?" Is it not true that centuries of persecution left Jews in Europe with a legacy of passivity that was self-destructive? Has Israel not learned the lesson implicit in Danny's question and refused to let itself stand by while its children are murdered? Danny is not wrong and his anger is understandable. If he is pitiless in the way he presents his criticism, he is also too candid for the contemporary Jew not to hear the truth in what he speaks.

Of a similar quality is Danny's assertion that to destroy the Jew one must love the Jew. "The Jew wants to be hated," he suggests provocatively. "He longs for our scorn. He clings to it as if it were the very core and mystery of his being. If Hitler had not existed, the Jews would have invented him. For without such hatred, the so-called Chosen People would vanish from the earth." However perverse Danny's argument is, there is something right about his claim. How else might one explain the continued fund-raising success of the Anti-Defamation League when, by all objective accounts, anti-Semitism is at an all-time low in the United States? How can we understand the relatively high rate of affirmative answers by Jews to survey questions asking whether "anti-Semitism is a serious/very serious problem in this country"? Even Danny's claim that Jews would have invented Hitler is not entirely off base. The Jews who answer "yes" to the "serious problem" question are inventing anti-Semites in their imaginations every day. Scholars have established that Haman, in the book of Esther, is a fictional character. So if Jews did not invent Hitler, we did

invent Haman. The problem with Danny's argument is in the details.

If Danny does not always speak *the* truth, he generally speaks *a* truth that almost always has modern Jewish support. And his argument often has a pedigree that extends back into Jewish tradition. For example, his exchange with his teacher over God's command that Abraham sacrifice Isaac replicates questions that Rashi, the paramount medieval Jewish commentator, had articulated. "Take your son," says God; "I have two sons," says Rashi, putting words in Abraham's mouth. "Your only son," says God; "each is unique to his mother," says Rashi. "The one whom you love," says God; "I love both of them," says Rashi for Abraham. Danny is a genuine yeshiva *bocher*, who argues often, if not always, from within the tradition. It might outrage the modern secular Jew to learn that Abraham might in fact have killed Isaac. But the educated Danny knows that one midrashic (exegetic) tradition represents exactly that version of the story. Far better than his teacher, Danny knows there is no reason not to follow that midrash, which is recorded in the canonical tradition and therefore a legitimate view.

So what is the problem with Danny, the Talmudic critic of ancient and recent Jewish wisdom? The answer begins with the way Danny often says what he says. However acute his perceptions of Jewish flaws may be, his resentment often makes his critique too caustic. His distortions, too, make it difficult for the listener to separate the true kernel contained in his observation from the useless husk. Two other qualities also make his criticism so difficult to hear. First, Danny allows himself to say many things that many a Jew knows to be true but is afraid to admit. It is painful to face parts of reality one has worked hard to suppress, and Danny forces the viewer to do so. Second, Danny does what he does in public, on the movie screen. It is Danny the *public* critic who causes such a stir in the Jewish gut. It is here that Danny strays farthest from both ancient and modern Jewish tradition.

Jewish tradition is well known for its questioning and even critical character. One of its foundational stories has Abraham challenging God to be just with the residents of Sodom and Gomorrah. "Will the judge of all the word not do justice?" he exclaims. If there are but ten righteous residents in the cities, Abraham argues, God must save the cities on their account. God does not have the right to act arbitrarily, Abraham assumes, and he lets God know it.

The same tradition of critique carries forward into classical rabbinic culture. The most striking expression of this critical voice is found in the Talmud's representations of the death of Rabbi Aqiba at the hands of the Romans in the early second century. In one version, the deceased Moses ascends to heaven to find God placing decorative crowns on the tops of letters in the Torah scroll. Moses inquires into the purpose of these crowns and is told that in the future, Rabbi Aqiba will use them as a basis for deriving laws. Moses asks to be transported into Aqiba's school to witness his interpretive skills. Finding himself impressed, Moses questions God concerning Aqiba's future reward. God then transports Moses to witness the flesh of Aqiba, who has been tortured and murdered by the Romans, being weighed out in the marketplace. Moses protests this grisly scene by asking, "This is Torah and this its rewards?" God offers only a feeble response: "This is what it occurred to me to do."

Rooted in the history of persecutions of Jews by the Romans during the revolt led by Bar Kochba (133–35 CE), this Talmudic story bears witness to the brutality of that experience. The story's most remarkable element is the way it responds to that brutality; Moses, the giver of Torah, the great hero of rabbinic tradition, articulates the ultimate question—how can God allow one who observes God's Torah to suffer so grievously and unjustly? Yet it is Moses, or the Ministering Angels in another Talmudic version, who challenges God. It is not the evil rebel who raises this question, not the unbeliever who wonders how God can be passive in the face of such cruelty. It is the most respected figure in the tradition—indeed, the true "Believer"—who speaks the truth and protests false pieties.

Both of these stories entail the rebuke of God. In each, the hero seems to fulfill the command from Leviticus, "you shall surely rebuke your neighbor" in connection with God. That the object of each rebuke is the divine covenantal partner does not remove this model from the human realm. It merely demonstrates how deeply the obligation to offer correction is embedded in the covenantal ideal. If it is appropriate to rebuke even God for perceived injustices, how much more necessary is it to offer correction to human partners in the covenant of Israel?

But here is the rub. The command of Leviticus directs a person to offer private rebuke to his neighbor. Emphasizing the difficulty of properly fulfilling this directive, the Talmud cautions that one not rebuke another if he or she is unlikely to be able to hear it. Undoubtedly, correction offered in public is more difficult, if not impossible, to hear. Contrary to what we might assume, Moses's challenge to God is a "private" rebuke. How can this be if it is expressed in a public document? In reality, the Talmud is an insider's work, accessible, until modernity, only to scholars who had engaged in long years of specialized study. "Private" here means inside, and there is no doubt that insiders share questions and critiques that would be inappropriate if spoken in a more public domain. Even the Torah's rebuke, offered in the voice of Abraham, is less than public. It is unimaginable that the Torah originally was meant to be recited beyond the circle of Israel. Besides, Abraham's plea for justice in the story of Sodom and Gomorrah is more than offset by his silence and acceptance in the "Akedah." It is the model of this latter Abraham that has been revered most by traditional Jews and Christians.

When we return to Danny, whose critique is that of a believer in the ancient model, we must ask whether his is a rebuke offered in a manner in which it might be heard. He is obviously not speaking to insiders, as one Jew to his neighbor. He yells his critique mostly as an outsider, no matter how powerfully his emotions draw him back to the Jewish center. And his fictional voice is expressed by means of the most public of contemporary media—film. Can such a rebuke fulfill the ideal of Leviticus? Or is Danny's—and Bean's—the way of the Talmudic informer, who is hated for telling even the truth in a way that can be hurtful to his people?

Let me define the category of "informer" by relating a midrashic example. In the midrash's version of the story of Esther, the wicked Haman seeks to destroy the Jews by enticing them to participate in sin (if they sin, God will punish them). Haman persuades Mordechai to invite his Jewish subjects to an orgy, and, despite Mordechai's attempt to dissuade them, many attend. The moment they begin to participate in sinful activity, Satan arises. Informing God of their sin, Satan succeeds in persuading God to destroy them (of course, this is not the end of the story).

In this story, the informer is Satan. In other rabbinic stories, the informer might be the snake (from the Garden of Eden). Without exception, the informer is a hated or condemned figure, and

what makes him hateful is his willingness to speak against Israel, often to foreign authorities (such as the Romans), in a way that brings them harm. This is so whether or not what he says against Israel is true.

The hatred of the informer in Jewish tradition and history was extreme. The rabbis instituted a prayer to be recited three times a day to curse the informer. The Talmud insists that informers will be punished in Hell for all generations, with no hope of reprieve. In Europe in the Middle Ages—and particularly in Spain—the plague of informers was so profound that local Jewish courts sometimes condemned them to death, buying the cooperation of the authorities to carry out the court's verdict.

Why was the attitude toward informers so excessive? This obviously was because their actions potentially brought harm, whether economic or physical, to the Jewish community. During centuries when the well-being of Jews was repeatedly in jeopardy, the possible harm done by the imprudent speech of insiders could not be tolerated. When the consequences might be so grievous, the community felt it had the right to suppress the potentially damaging utterance.

Is Danny a rebuker, seeking to correct the wrongs he perceives as a sympathetic compatriot, or an informer, bringing potential harm to his former community by exposing their blemishes to the gaze of unsympathetic outsiders? Before responding too quickly, let us examine a contemporary analogy that may force us to reconsider.

Jewish organizations in the United States have repeatedly condemned the mainstream press for what they allege to be bias in reporting about Israel. They commonly insist that Israel and her policies are represented critically and unfairly in the American media. By contrast the Jewish press supposedly is more objective in its reporting. This is despite the fact that the American news media broadcast and publish a wide variety of views concerning events in the Middle East; whereas the American Jewish press tends to print a narrower range of acceptable opinions. Indeed, the Jewish press almost always will support "Israel's side" of any incident.

The habits of the American Jewish press are not replicated in Israel. Israeli newspapers print opinions from a broad range of perspectives. Whether leaning to the right or to the left, they do not hesitate to level criticism—often biting criticism—of their government, its leaders, and its policies. For example, a recent column questioned the justice of Israeli policies in the West Bank during the second intifada (Palestinian violence against the Israeli occupation following the visit of future prime minister Ariel Sharon to the Temple Mount in 2000), policies that protect the right of relatively few Jewish settlers in the West Bank to move about freely while restricting the mobility of hundreds of thousands of Palestinians. Why, the author wondered, must Israel expend its resources to protect the Jewish residents of settlements that are opposed by many Israelis? Whatever wrongs might be committed by Palestinian militants cannot erase the wrong promulgated by this Israeli policy, or so the columnist argued. I cannot remember the last time I saw such criticism of Israel expressed in the mainstream American Jewish press.

But how can we explain this dichotomy between the Israeli and American Jewish press? Why will one community permit outspoken dissent while the other will not? A sympathetic explanation would reference the "inside-outside" distinction made previously. The Israeli press is an "inside" press. In Israeli media, Israelis speak to Israelis. Therefore, commentators may feel free to express their opinions as openly as they like,

for there is no fear of doing harm when the audience is one's brothers and sisters. But the American Jewish press is an "outside" organ, for it represents Israel and the Jewish community before the American populace at large. Being too critical might do harm, for such criticism could be (mis)interpreted as evidence of absence of support for Israel. Thus, the argument goes, it is better to exclude critical opinion from the Anglo-Jewish press, even at the expense of community self-censorship.

Whatever the logic of this distinction, it is impossible to sustain in a world where the critical Israeli editorial can be accessed in English by the click of a mouse. With information technologies being what they are, there is no longer a real difference between "inside" and outside." All expression for the record is "outside." It is all public in the widest sense of the word. Moreover, Israel operates on the world stage. Her actions and policies are debated in the public forum. She has no secrets because there would be no way to keep a secret for very long. In such a world, the belief that what one says among insiders will not be heard among outsiders is simply naive. The traditional Jewish distinction between the rebuker and the informer may no longer be sustained. It is impossible to speak among insiders alone. It would be a mistake to conclude that the public nature of rebuke requires that the sharpness of the criticism be blunted. Any compromise with conscience will be a *public* compromise. A partial rebuke will be seen for what it is—that is, only a half-truth.

Though a rebuke must be expressed honestly, it must still be offered in a manner in which it might be heard. Here there is admittedly doubt whether Danny's—or shall we say Bean's—critique succeeds. Danny's violence, both physical and verbal, makes him a problematic messenger for rebuke. Moreover, the distortions that are often the vehicle for his messages make it difficult to hear what is right in what he says; some viewers will simply be too consumed in trying to correct his distortions. Perhaps these problematic qualities are in the service of dramatic characterization. Indeed Danny does demand that we sit up and take notice. Furthermore we must admit that the rebuker to whom we pay no attention is no rebuker at all. But is this justification enough to mitigate the extremism and brutality that will make some viewers so uncomfortable? Only the individual viewer can answer for him or herself.

My personal answer to this question is an unhesitating yes. It seems to me that the voice of *The Believer* is the voice of one who loves Jewish tradition, but hates its flaws. Both are spoken with total honesty, as least as the rebuker understands it. In his view, the Torah is mysterious and sacred. Its discipline provides direction and comfort, but it is also a repository of arbitrary, even cruel, laws. Its discipline often seems like an exercise in divine power for its own sake. Can one deny the wisdom of this insight?

Does the bile of the messenger diminish the profundity of his message? For me, the answer is no because his resentment and outrage are real. Who cannot feel resentment at the injustices of this, as of any, tradition? Who will deny the outrage of historical victimhood transformed into a cultural value? Moreover, for most people, including myself, it is difficult to articulate critiques of a tradition one loves. Where I might vacillate, Danny does not hesitate. In the end critiques are better expressed than suppressed. Since I am a Jew committed to the tradition of my people, I too stand among the rebuked. I am better able to hear the rebuke because it is, by virtue of its dramatic context, oblique and not direct.

The Believer offers a model of what might be described as a postmodern rebuke. In the age of potentially universal public access to information, no rebuke, however culturally specific, can be truly private. Being public, perhaps it is wisest that it be expressed indirectly through film rather than in the pious banality of a sermon. Since it is refracted through the artistic medium, the one who cannot hear it will not. He or she will turn aside or dismiss it as absurd. Still, in the distorted voice of dramatic exaggeration a truer critique might well reside, and that critique will be heard by those who are willing to listen. *The Believer* is an experiment in such a postmodern rebuke, and whether successful as rebuke or not, its intuition is brilliant.

Abridged from: David Kraemer, "Self-Criticism in Public," in *The Believer: Confronting Jewish Self-Hatred*, ed. Henry Bean, 203–18 (New York: Thunder's Mouth, 2002).

Source: Henry Bean, "The Believer: The Screenplay," in *The Believer: Confronting Jewish Self-Hatred*, ed. Henry Bean, 25–182 (New York: Thunder's Mouth, 2002).

Background: http://www.jewishvirtuallibrary.org/ jsource/judaica/ejud_0002_0018_0_17991.html.

Bibliography

Berman, Louis Arthur. *Akedah: The Binding of Isaac.* Northvale, NJ: Aronson, 1997.

Carr, Steven Alan. "L.I.E., *The Believer*, and the Sexuality of the Jewish Boy." In *Where the Boys Are: Cinemas of Masculinity and Youth*, edited by Murray Pomerance and Frances Gatewood, 316–32. Detroit: Wayne State University Press, 2005.

Delaney, Carol. *Abraham on Trial: The Social Legacy of Biblical Myth.* Princeton, NJ: Princeton University Press, 1998.

Gilman, Sander. *Jewish Self-Hatred: Anti-Semitism and the Hidden Language of the Jews.* Baltimore: Johns Hopkins University Press, 1986.

Ridgeway, James. *Blood in the Face: The Ku Klux Klan,*

Aryan Nations, Nazi Skinheads, and the Rise of a New White Culture. 2nd ed. New York: Thunder's Mouth, 1995.

Rosenthal, A.M., and Arthur Gelb. *One More Victim*. New York: New American Library, 1967.

54. *Keeping the Faith*

A Multicultural *Jazz Singer*

LAWRENCE BARON

Keeping the Faith, directed by
Edward Norton [A]
United States, 2000

Much of the popular appeal of *The Jazz Singer* (1927) emanated from its tapping into the generational conflicts that beset Jewish and other immigrant families in the 1920s. Adult Jews fleeing discrimination and persecution in Eastern Europe or seeking the greater economic opportunities afforded by the United States resided in predominantly Jewish neighborhoods as they struggled to gain a foothold in their new homeland. Their children, who either entered the country as youngsters or were born there, adapted more quickly and felt more comfortable in American society than their parents did.

From Hollywood's perspective, Americanization revolved around an assertion of individual choice of a career or a non-Jewish spouse, in defiance of parental pressure. Thus, Jakie Rabinowitz's aspiration to be a popular singer clashes with his father's demand that he continue the family tradition by becoming a cantor. Secondarily, his affection for the singer Mary Dale—who is the star of the first Broadway review in which Jakie is a performer—makes his mother worry that her son is courting a gentile woman. The problem of mixed marriages was more prominent in films like *Abie's Irish Rose* (1928), in which the coupling of a Jewish man with a non-Jewish—usually an Irish Catholic—woman conquers all, erasing differences among the new immigrants through assimilation and intermarriage. In real life, intermarriage in the 1920s was far less common that it was on the screen.

At the beginning of the twenty-first century, much has changed for American Jewry. As a group, Jewish Americans have moved from the cultural, economic, political, and social margins of American society to its mainstream. To be sure, this has been accompanied by decreasing rates of synagogue membership and increasing rates of intermarriage, both of which registered at approximately 50 percent in the *American Jewish Identity Poll 2001* (Mayer, Kosmin, Keysar 2002). Whereas antisemitic discrimination in employment, housing, and private clubs and universities posed serious problems for Jewish Americans before World War II, today the most urgent issue facing them is whether their offspring and their families will identify themselves as Jews. Paradoxically, the steady attrition of the commitment of Jewish Americans to perpetuate the legacy of their ancestors coincides with a shift away from the melting pot model of Americanization to a multicultural one that celebrates ethnic, racial, and religious pluralism.

Although a light romantic comedy, Edward Norton's directorial debut *Keeping the Faith* (2000) reverses the formulaic strategy of effacing minority differences for the sake of integration into American society and rapid upward socioeconomic mobility. Instead, Norton and the screenwriter, Stuart Blumberg, fashion the movie as a plea for respecting cultural, racial, and

Ben Stiller (as Rabbi Jake), on the left, and Edward Norton (as Father Brian) epitomize hipness as they strut down the street in their neighborhood. From *Keeping the Faith* (2000), directed by Edward Norton. BUENA VISTA PICTURES/PHOTOFEST

religious diversity. When asked about his solution to the high rate of Jewish intermarriages, Blumberg remarked, "The best way for the Jewish community to respond, in my opinion, is to make Jewish tradition and Judaism as relevant as possible and to also help those who are in interfaith marriages to be part of the Jewish community" (quoted in Friedland n.d.) The privileging of spiritual fulfillment over material success and multicultural pluralism subverts the conventional narrative of Jewish assimilation and economic achievement. Indeed, the film epitomizes a trend in recent films such as *The Hebrew Hammer* (2003), *Meet the Fockers* (2004), and *You Don't Mess with the Zohan* (2008), which accentuate the Jewish distinctiveness of their main characters.

Although Blumberg and Norton attribute *Keeping the Faith*'s love triangle scenario to *The Philadelphia Story* (1940) and *Jules and Jim* (1962), the film's narrative structure parallels that of *The Jazz Singer*, while inverting its message of attaining the American dream by abandoning familial and religious traditions. *The Jazz Singer* introduces Cantor Rabinowitz as "a chanter of hymns in the synagogue who stubbornly held to the ancient traditions of his race." His confined surroundings, Old World appearance, and parochialism contrast sharply with the exterior shots of the Lower East Side of New York, bustling with immigrant merchants and children playing on a merry-go-round topped by American flags. A few blocks away his son, Jakie, belts out a ragtime tune to an appreciative audience at a neighborhood saloon. Dressed in street clothes, he wears memo-rabilia buttons on the front of his shirt. The med-dlesome Yudelson recognizes Jakie and rushes to tell the cantor about his son's transgression. Jakie's exuberant performance, which incidentally fea-tures a shuffle-step precursor to Michael Jackson's moon walk, is abruptly halted by the cantor, who drags his son home by the scruff of his neck. De-spite his wife's admonition that "our boy does not think like we do," the cantor whips Jakie for "de-basing the voice God gave him." Jakie vows never to return home. At the Kol Nidre service, the cantor announces that he no longer has a son.

Keeping the Faith likewise flashes back to the childhood of its protagonists to contextualize the remainder of its story line. Father Brian Finn, played by Norton, traces the chain of events that contributed to his inebriated binge in the opening scene of the film. Confiding in a sympa-thetic bartender, he recalls his childhood friend-ship with Anna Riley and Jake Schram who run, skip, and take subway rides against the upscale backdrop of New York's Upper West Side. Their middle-class families clearly do not live in an impoverished immigrant enclave. When Anna's family moves away to California, where her father has been transferred, Brian and Jake gravitate to-ward their respective religions. Jake's transition from the secular to the sacred is manifested by his collecting "Heroes of the Torah" trading cards. Even as Brian and Jake initiate each other into the rituals of their religions, an innate inhibition prevents them from accurately reenacting them. Brian ends up hitting himself in the face while trying to form the Hebrew letter shin with his fingers, and Jake cannot manage to make the sign of the cross and outlines a Star of David and other symbols on his chest instead. Like Cantor Ra-binowitz, Jake's father expected his son to follow in his footsteps and become a partner in the fam-ily's investment banking firm, but Jake pursues his calling as a rabbi rather than join his father's business.

Synthesizing revelation and relevance, the newly ordained Father Brian and Rabbi Jake, played by Ben Stiller, don black leather jackets and sunglasses and stride through their neighborhood as the "God Squad," with the Latin beat of San-tana's "Smooth" playing in the background. As Jake succinctly puts it, "We're going to give them [their congregants] an Old World God with a New Age spin." Though both pepper their ser-mons with contemporary references and irre-verent humor, they ultimately preach core Chris-tian or Jewish precepts. After questioning his congregants about the meaning of Lot's protec-tion of the angels who visited his home, Jake ob-serves: "God is like Blanche DuBois [the lead character in *A Streetcar Named Desire*, by Ten-nessee Williams]. He's always relied on the kind-ness of strangers. That's really what the story's about. It's about us taking care of each other. God relies on us to take care of each other." With-out mentioning the Hebrew phrase *tikkun olam*, which translates into the "repair of the world," Jake articulates its ethic of restoring the wholeness of God's creation by exhibiting compassion to-ward others. Similarly, Brian updates the argu-ment of Blaise Pascal that, even though human beings cannot prove the existence of God, they should wager that God exists rather than bet against his existence and risk the chance of being forsaken for eternity. Brian explains to his parish-ioners: "Faith is not about having the right an-swers. Faith is a feeling, a hunch, that there is something bigger connecting it all, connecting us all together, and that feeling, that hunch, is God. And coming here on your Sunday evening to con-nect with that feeling is an act of faith." Brian's and Jake's improvisational style and ecumenical receptivity contrast sharply with Cantor Rabino-witz's ceremonialism and parochialism.

The treatment of ethnic and racial imitation in *The Jazz Singer* and *Keeping the Faith* provides another point of comparison that underscores how dramatically mainstream American attitudes toward minorities changed over the course of the twentieth century. From its opening, *The Jazz Singer* conflates jazz and Jewish liturgical music: "In every living soul, a spirit cries for expression—perhaps this plaintive, wailing song of jazz is, after all, the misunderstood utterance of a prayer." Played by the famed entertainer Al Jolson, the adult Jakie adopts the stage name of Jack Robin. Onlookers comment that he sings with a tear or a cry in his voice, implying that this stems from the Jewish experience of oppression in Europe, which parallels that of blacks in the United States. In the post–civil rights era, it is embarrassing and offensive to watch Al Jolson sing the last two songs of the film in blackface. His nappy wig, enlarged white lips, and darkened face epitomize the grotesque stereotype of African American men held by most whites in the 1920s. Although some scholars interpret Jack's visual and vocal simulation of a black jazz singer as an expression of genuine admiration of a uniquely American musical style; others perceive it as an attempt by Jewish and other immigrant performers to prove their whiteness by denigrating blacks. Blackface emblematizes the dichotomy between the Jewish Jakie and the American Jack. When his mother first sees him in his makeup, she doesn't recognize him. Looking at himself in the mirror, Jack sees the image of his father chanting "Kol Nidre." When Jack rehearses, however, his mother hears the sorrowful inflection in his voice that links the son to the father. She accepts that he is destined to share this gift with the whole world, not just Jews.

In *Keeping the Faith* Jake borrows from African American and other religious traditions to enrich the spiritual life of his congregation. Jake feels his congregation's singing of the inspirational hymn "Ein Keloheinu" (There is none like our God) is too lethargic. To model how it can be sung joyfully, he invites an African American gospel choir to perform it at a Shabbat service. Jack exploits blackface to authenticate his musical or racial credentials; Jake "outsources" a Jewish melody to African Americans because they display the fervent kavanah (heartfelt intentionality) that Jake seeks to cultivate among his staid congregants. In another scene, Jake leads a yoga circle, alternating Hebrew and Hindu terms for breathing exercises and meditation. When a boy gets discouraged because his voice breaks as he practices his Torah portion for his bar mitzvah, Jake tells him: "This is a rite of passage. This happens in all cultures. It's about you being thirteen years old. God knew your voice was going to change when you're thirteen." Thus, Jake restores a primordial meaning to what often degenerates into a perfunctory exercise in memorization. Nevertheless, the senior rabbi of the synagogue cautions Jake "to appreciate the fact that a lot of people come here for a sense of continuity. . . . Tradition is not old habit; it's comforting to people."

Norton replaces blackface with karaoke as a democratizing medium through which anyone can copy the singing style of performers from different ethnic and racial backgrounds without relinquishing his or her individual or collective identity in the process. Brian and Jake plan to open an interfaith senior center that will focus on karaoke to bring the elderly people in their diverse neighborhood together. Brian hopes it will be "a sort of *Fiddler on the Roof* meets *Lord of the Dance* meets *Buena Vista Social Club*." When Brian and Jake go to purchase a karaoke machine, they witness how ethnic ventriloquism is sometimes a response to stereotyping. They first encounter Don, played by Ken Leung, incongruously singing the lyrics of Rick Springfield's "Jesse's Girl" with a thick Korean accent. Don's exaggerated gestures and hard-sell tactics corroborate preconceptions of first-generation immigrant merchants. When his sales pitch fails to convince Brian and Jake to buy the more expensive machine he is pushing, Don causally reverts back to his real self, an everyday American guy with no accent, just trying to give his customers the best deal possible. He initially projected the image of an Asian electronics salesman that he anticipated Brian and Jake had conjured up in their minds.

Notwithstanding its appreciation of diversity, *Keeping the Faith* does not endorse the fragmentation of the United States into ethnic, racial, and religious ghettos. The bartender, Paulie, symbolizes the heterogeneity of America's population. Originally, Norton and Blumberg considered making the bartender Irish, since this was a cinematic cliché. They ultimately decided to cast the Indian actor Brian George, as a reflection of the changes over time in the ethnic groups that occupy certain niches in the job market, like bartenders or cabdrivers. In homage to the stock figure of the Irish bartender, Paulie sports a button that reads, "Kiss Me, I'm Irish," but his slight British accent and relatively dark complexion belie this stereotype. When he finally gets an opportunity to tell Brian about himself, he discloses that he is half Punjabi Sikh, one-quarter Tamil separatist, and one-quarter Irish, with Jewish in-laws. Commenting on the DVD about the thematic purpose of Paulie's complicated genealogy, Norton asserted that it showed "the idea that everybody in New York is a mutt."

Unlike the 1980 remake starring Neil Diamond, the original *Jazz Singer* subordinated its interfaith love story to Jack's struggle to establish his career as an entertainer, despite being disowned by his father and subsequently pressured by his mother to sing "Kol Nidre" on the night his Broadway review is scheduled to premier. To be sure, Jack is infatuated with Mary Dale—who, incidentally, was played by the Irish starlet of silent movies, May McAvoy. The potential for intermarriage is raised briefly when Jack's mother reads a passage in one of his letters where he raves about Mary. She worries: "Maybe he's fallen in love with a shiksa?" Yudelson calms her down by suggesting that Mary Dale may just be a stage name masking the woman's Jewish origins. Reciprocating Jack's affection, Mary realizes Jack is more devoted to his career than to her or his parents. As he anguishes over whether to sing "Kol Nidre" for his dying father or to bask in the spotlight, she reminds him, "Your career is the place God has put you," and he replies, "You're right, my career means more to me than anything else in the world." Then she asks, "More than me?" He nods yes. Though his mother implores him to substitute for his father on Yom Kippur eve, Jack overcomes his indecisiveness only after his dying father professes his love for him.

The conflicting demands of career versus love affect all three protagonists in *Keeping the Faith*. At their reunion as adults, Anna, played by Jenna Elfman, frankly admits: "I don't have time for relationships. No, I work harder than God. If He had hired me, He would have made the world by Thursday." Indeed, Anna's most intimate relationship seems to be with her cellphone, which she straps to her thigh on the vibration setting when she is too busy to take calls right away. In those moments when she leaves her Manhattan office to enjoy the company of her old pals, she starts to realize that her obsession with work has deprived her of romance and spirituality. Excited about the prospect of her love affair with Jake leading to marriage, she considers turning down a promotion to run her company from San Francisco to remain with him in New York. In doing so, she chooses not to repeat her father's choice of uprooting his family from New York by moving to California to advance his career.

Brian initially has no doubts about entering the priesthood. When Anna asks how he copes with the vow of celibacy, he explains: "I'm completely committed to what I do, to my work, to my ministering. It defines me completely. . . . That particular sacrifice is a gesture; it's a symbol of my commitment." Unaware that Anna and Jake are romantically involved, Brian begins to have sexual fantasies about her. Resolving to profess his love to her, he vacillates about whether he should wear his clerical collar or a regular shirt when he tells her. When he hears that Anna loves Jake, he is shattered and seeks the advice of his father superior, who counsels him: "If you're a priest or you marry a woman, it's the same challenge. You cannot make a real commitment unless you accept that it's a choice you keep making again and again and again."

Jake does not want to run the risk of losing the love of his mother Ruth (Anne Bancroft) or alienating his congregation by marrying outside the faith. His brother, Aaron, had married a gentile, and Ruth had boycotted their wedding. Aaron retaliated by not speaking to her. Cognizant that he serves as a role model for other Jews of marriageable age, Jake assumes his future wife must be Jewish. Of course, the women at his synagogue always want to fix him up with their daughters. This leads to one disastrous date with a stereotypical Jewish American Princess who is obsessed with her physical fitness and getting the rabbi to sleep with her. In their commentary on the DVD,

Blumberg and Norton recount how they balanced the "date from hell" by pairing Jake up with a "perfect-on-paper, amazing, gorgeous Jewess," Rachel Rose, a network television correspondent who covers the Middle East. After his lackluster date with Rachel, Jake recognizes that he is really attracted to Anna and goes to her apartment. As long as the relationship is casual, the chemistry between the two is electric and seems to have the consent of Ruth, who enjoys Anna's company. Invited to a Shabbat dinner at her flat, Ruth intuitively senses that Anna and Jake are romantically involved and pries the truth out of Anna.

In a deleted scene on the DVD, Ruth explains why she had reacted so negatively to Aaron's marriage: "I was raised by a mother who lost her entire family in Europe, and she raised me with a sense of responsibility to preserve the traditions of our faith. I raised my family with that same conviction." (The deletion is consistent with the film's avoidance of invoking either the Holocaust or support for Israel as vicarious sources of American Jewish identity.) Ruth now realizes that her insistence on a Jewish daughter-in-law has cost her a son. She tacitly gives her blessing to Anna but warns her, "As far as you and Jake are concerned, I think I'm the least of your problems." Their tearful embrace is the only part of this scene left in the film's final cut.

Back in Anna's apartment, Anna informs Jake that Ruth knows about their relationship. Jake fears the rift that it will cause between him and his mother and congregation. He acts exactly as his mother had predicted: "It might be hard for you to accept that the fact that you're not Jewish is a real problem for me." Beyond these personal complications, he suspects that his religious lifestyle is not compatible with Anna's workaholic priorities. She counters by assuring him that his "faith is a huge part" of what she loves about him and advises him to "put some faith in other people." He walks out of her door and presumably out of her life. Shortly thereafter, Ruth has a minor stroke. Like Cantor Rabinowitz's deathbed reconciliation with Jack, Ruth acknowledges she made a mistake with Aaron and encourages Jake to follow his heart.

As in *The Jazz Singer, Keeping the Faith*'s resolution coincides with Yom Kippur and its themes of atonement and forgiveness. In his sermon Jake underscores the film's multicultural message and opens up the possibility of his return to Anna: "We live in a really complex world, a world where boundaries and differences are blurring and bleeding into each other in ways that I think challenge us not just as Jews, but as human beings." Then he confesses that he has fallen in love with a non-Jewish woman. Heeding Anna's advice, he asks his congregants to forgive him for having "too little faith" that they would respond compassionately to his dilemma.

Both *The Jazz Singer* and *Keeping the Faith* conclude triumphantly. After singing "Kol Nidre," Jack returns to Broadway to sing "Mammie" to his beaming mother. His moment as a cantor was a minor detour on his road to showbiz success. Learning he has been hired to replace the retiring Rabbi Lewis, Jake gladly heeds Brian's advice to reconcile with Anna. Later that same day, the interfaith senior center has its grand opening. Brian and Don harmonize to a song that mirrors Jake's decision: Barry Manilow's "Ready to Take a Chance Again." Rachel Rose introduces her mother to the handsome black man escorting her. Judging by the surprised look on her mother's face, he probably is Rachel's fiancé. Rabbi Lewis greets Anna after she enters the center with Jake and asks why she has missed his last few classes. Since Anna had already mentioned that she was trying to reconnect with her spirituality, it is ob-

vious she has been studying Judaism with the intent to convert. Lest the film's pluralistic partisanship be lost on the audience, Jake comments how wonderful it is to see "so much interfaith dancing." And Brian adds, "It's like the end of *West Side Story.*"

In the past, the male partner in movies about Christian-Jewish romances would abandon his religion and sever his filial ties to attain material success and marital bliss. *Keeping the Faith*, however, is more attuned to the ethnic, racial, and religious influences and interactions that shape the experience of contemporary Jews. Jake finds fulfillment in his ministry as a rabbi, and his soul mate in a woman willing to convert to Judaism to be with him. The synagogue board's decision to hire him validates his modernization of liturgy and fostering of interreligious cooperation. *Keeping the Faith* delivers a timely message—namely, that ethnic or religious continuity depends more on selective adaptation and reciprocity than on the dogmatic traditionalism and self-segregation of Cantor Rabinowitz, or the secularization and potential intermarriage of Jack.

Background: http://www.simpletoremember.com/vitals/ajisbook.pdf.

Bibliography

Aviv, Caryn, and David Shneer. *New Jews: The End of the Jewish Diaspora*. New York: New York University Press, 2005.

Baskind, Samantha. "The Fockerized Jew? Questioning Jewishness as Cool in American Popular Entertainment." *Shofar* 25, no. 4 (2007): 3–17.

Biale, David, Michael Gelschinsky, and Susannah Heschel, eds. *Insider/Outsider: American Jews and Multiculturalism*. Berkeley: University of California Press, 1998.

Friedland, Ronnie. "Interview with Stuart Blumberg, Author and Co-Producer of *Keeping the Faith*."

InterfaithFamily.com, n.d. http://www.interfaithfamily
.com/arts_and_entertainment/popular_culture/
Interview_with_Stuart_Blumberg_Author_and
_Co-Producer_of_Keeping_the_Faith.shtml.

Gertel, Elliot B. *Over the Top Judaism: Precedents and
Trends in the Depiction of Jewish Beliefs and Observances in Film and Television*. Lanham, MD: University Press of America, 2003.

Itzkovitz, Daniel. "They Are All Jews." In *"You Should
See Yourself": Jewish Identity in Postmodern America*,
edited by Vincent Brook, 230–52. New Brunswick,
NJ: Rutgers University Press, 2006.

Kellerman, Henry. *Greedy, Cowardly, and Weak: Hollywood's Jewish Stereotypes*. Fort Lee, NJ: Barricade,
2009.

Mayer, Egon, Barry Kosmin, and Ariela Keysar. *American
Jewish Identity Survey 2001*. New York: Center for
Jewish Studies, Graduate Center of the City University of New York, 2002. http://www.gc.cuny.edu/
faculty/research_studies/ajis.pdf.

Taub, Michael. *Films about Jewish Life and Culture*.
Lewiston, ME: Edwin Mellen, 2005.

Appendix

Alternate Films

For additional information on each film, consult the Internet Movie Database (www.imdb.com).

Part I. Advancement and Animosity in Western Europe, 1874–1924

East and West, dir. Sidney Goldin and Ivan Abrahamson (Austria, 1923) [NCJF].

Esther Kahn, dir. Arnaud Desplechin (France and United Kingdom, 2000) [A].

Solomon and Gaenor, dir. Paul Morrison (United Kingdom, 1999) [A].

Sofie, dir. Liv Ullmann (Denmark, Norway, and Sweden, 1992) [A].

Young Dr. Freud, dir. Alex Corti (Austria and West Germany, 1976) [A]

Part II. The *Shtetl* on the Precipice: Eastern Europe, 1881–1921

Austeria, dir. Jerzy Kawalerowicz (Poland, 1982) [A].

The Death of a President, dir. Jerzy Kawalerowicz (Poland, 1977) [A].

The Fixer, dir. John Frankenheimer (United States, 1968) [VHS only].

His Excellency, dir. Girgori Roshal (Soviet Union: 1928) [NCJF].

Jewish Luck, dir. Alexander Granovsky (Soviet Union, 1925) [NCJF].

Laughter through Tears, dir. Grigori Gricher-Cherikover (Soviet Union, 1928) [NCJF].

A Letter to Mother, dir. Joseph Green and Leon Krystand (Poland, 1939) [NCJF].

Promised Land, dir. Andrzej Wajda (Poland, 1975) [A].

Part III. The Americanization of the Jewish Immigrant, 1880–1932

Avalon, dir. Barry Levinson (United States, 1990) [A].

Breaking Home Ties, dir. Frank N. Selzer and George K. Rowlands (United States: 1922) [NCJF].

Funny Girl, dir. William Wyler (United States, 1968) [A].

His People, dir. Edward Sloman (United States, 1925) [NCJF].

Once upon a Time in America, dir. Sergio Leone (Italy and United States, 1984) [A].

Street Scene, dir. King Vidor (United States, 1931) [A].

Part IV. Revolutionary Alternatives: Zionism and Communism, 1880–1932

Ben-Gurion: An Appointment with Destiny, dir. David Perlov (United States, 1968) [EM].

Benya Kirk, dir. Vladimir Vilner (Soviet Union: 1926) [NCJF].

Berlin-Jerusalem, dir. Amos Gitai (France, Israel, Italy, the Netherlands, and the United Kingdom, 1989) [A].

Rutenberg, dir. Eli Cohen (Israel, 2002) [NCJF].

Seekers of Happiness, dir. Vladimir Korsh-Sablin (Soviet Union, 1934) [NCJF].

The Unsettled Land, dir. Uri Barbash (Israel, 1987) [VHS only].

The Wandering Jew aka *The Life of Theodor Herzl*, dir. Otto Kreisler (Austria: 1921) [NCJF].

Part V. The Holocaust and Its Repercussions

Almost Peaceful, dir. Michel Deville (France, 2002) [A].

The Boat Is Full, dir. Marcus Imhoof (Austria, Germany, and Switzerland, 1981) [A].

Cabaret, dir. Bob Fosse (United States, 1972) [A].

The Counterfeiters, dir. Stefan Ruzowitzky (Austria and Germany, 2007) [A].

Defiance, dir. Edward Zwick (United States, 2007) [A].

The Diary of Anne Frank, dir. George Stevens (United States, 1959) [A].

Distant Journey, dir. Alfred Radok (Czechoslovakia, 1949) [A].

Divided We Fall, dir. Jan Hrebejk (Czech Republic, 2000) [A].

Europa, Europa, dir. Agnieszka Holland (France, Germany, and Poland, 1990) [A].

The Grey Zone, dir. Tim Blake Nelson (United States, 2001) [A].

Jew Boy Levi, dir. Didi Danquart (Austria, Germany, and Switzerland, 1999) [A]

Just beyond That Forest, dir. Jan Lomnicki (Poland, 1991) [www.polandbymail.com].

Ladies' Tailor, dir. Leonid Gorovets (Soviet Union, 1990) [NCJF].

The Last Stage, dir. Wanda Jakubowska (Poland, 1948) [www.polandbymail.com].

My Mother's Courage, dir. Michael Verhoeven (Austria, Germany, and the United Kingdom, 1995) [NCJF].

Out of the Ashes, dir. Joseph Sargent (United States, 2003) [A].

The Quarrel, dir. Eli Cohen (Canada, 1991) [NCJF].

The Revolt of Job, dir. Imre Gyöngyössy and Barna Kabay (Hungary, 1983) [www.cvmc.net].

Reunion, dir. Jerry Schatzberg (France, United Kingdom, and West Germany, 1989) [VHS only].

The Round-Up, dir. Rose Bosch (France, Germany, and Hungary, 2010) [A].

Sarah's Key, dir. Gilles Paquet-Brenner (France: 2010) [A].

A Secret, dir. Claude Miller (France, 2007) [A].

Voyage of the Damned, dir. Stuart Rosenberg (United Kingdom, 1976) [www.ccvideo.com].

Voyages, dir. Emmanuel Finkiel (Belgium, France, and Poland, 1999). [A]

The Wedding Song, dir. Karin Albou (France and Tunisia, 2008) [A].

Part VI. Israel's Heroic Years, 1947–1967

Cast a Giant Shadow, dir. Melville Shavelson (United States, 1966) [A].

Crossfire, dir. Gideon Ganani (Israel, 1989) [EM].

The House on Chelouche Street, dir. Moshe Mizrahi (Israel, 1973) [A].

The Impossible Spy, dir. Jim Goddard (United Kingdom and the United States 1987) [A].

Kippur, dir: Amos Gitai (France and Israel, 2000) [A].

The Little Traitor, dir. Lynn Roth (Israel and the United States: 2007) [A].

Noa at 17, dir. Yitzhak Yeshurun (Israel, 1982) [A, EM].

O, Jerusalem, dir. Elie Chouraqui (France, Israel, Italy, the United Kingdom, and the United States, 2006) [A].

Siege, dir. Gilberto Tofano (Israel, 1970) [EM].

The Summer of Aviya, dir. Eli Cohen (Israel, 1988) [A, EM]

Under the Donim Tree, dir. Eli Cohen (Israel, 1994) [EM].

A Woman Called Golda, dir. Alan Gibson (United States, 1982) [A].

The Wooden Gun, dir. Ilan Moshenson (Israel, 1979) [A, EM].

Part VII. Acceptance in Postwar America, 1945–1977

Biloxi Blues, dir. Mike Nichols (United States, 1988) [A].

Body and Soul, dir. Robert Rossen (United States, 1947) [A].

Citizen Cohn, dir. Frank Pierson (United States, 1992) [A].

Crossfire, dir. Edward Dmytryk (United States, 1947) [A].

Daniel, dir. Sidney Lumet (United States, 1983) [A].

The Front, dir. Martin Ritt (United States, 1976) [A].

The Heartbreak Kid, dir. Elaine May (United States, 1972) [A].

Lenny, dir. Bob Fosse (United States, 1974) [A].

Liberty Heights, dir. Barry Levinson (United States, 1999) [A].

Next Stop, Greenwich Village, dir. Paul Mazursky (United States, 1976) [A].

Quiz Show, dir. Robert Redford (United States, 1994) [A].

School Ties, dir. Robert Mandel (United States, 1992) [A].

Sweet Lorraine, dir. Steve Gomer (United States, 1987) [A].

Unstrung Heroes, dir. Diane Keaton (United States, 1995) [A].

A Walk on the Moon, dir. Tony Goldwyn (United States, 1999) [A].

The Way We Were, dir. Sydney Pollack (United States, 1973) [A].

Part VIII. A Diverse Diaspora

Autumn Sun, dir. Eduardo Mignogna (Argentina, 1996) [A].

Barney's Version, dir. Richard J. Lewis (Canada and Italy, 2010) [A].

The Concert, dir. Radu Mihaileanu (Belgium, France, Italy, Romania, and Russia, 2009) [A].

Everything Is Illuminated, dir. Liev Schreiber (United States, 2005) [A].

Father's Footsteps, dir. Marco Carmel (France and Israel, 2007) [NCJF].

Fugitive Pieces, dir. Jeremy Podeswa (Canada and Greece, 2007) [A].

Gebürtig, dir. Robert Schindel and Lukas Stepanik (Austria, Germany, and Poland, 2002).

Glamour, dir. Frigyes Gödrös (Hungary, 2000) [A].

Go for Zucker, dir. Dani Levi (Germany, 2004) [A].

Hey Hey It's Esther Blueburger, dir. Cathy Randall (Australia, 2008) [A].

The Infidel, dir. Josh Appiganesi (United Kingdom, 2010) [A].

A Kid for Two Farthings, dir. Carol Reed (United Kingdom, 2010) [www.ccvideo.com].

Left Luggage, dir. Jeroen Krabbé (Belgium, the Netherlands, the United Kingdom, and the United States, 1998) [A].

Lies My Father Told Me, dir. Ján Kadár (Canada, 1975) [EM].

My Mexican Shiva, dir. Alejandro Springall (Mexico and the United States, 2007) [A].

Nora's Will, dir. Mariana Chenillo (Mexico: 2010) [A].

One Day You'll Understand, dir. Amos Gitai (France, Germany, and Israel, 2008) [A].

The Outside Chance of Maximilian Glick, dir. Allan A. Goldstein (Canada, 1988) [www.cmvc.net].

Pillar of Salt, dir. Chaim Shiran (Israel, 1980) [NCJF].

Rosenzweig's Freedom, dir Liliane Targownik (Germany: 1998) [NCJF].

Shine, dir. Scott Hicks (Australia, 1996) [A].

Sixty Six, dir. Paul Weiland (France and the United Kingdom, 2006) [A].

A Summer of La Goulette, dir. Férid Boughedir (Belgium, France, and Tunisia, 1996) [A].

Ticket to Heaven, dir. Ralph H. Thomas (Canada, 1981) [www.ccvideo.com].

Voyages, dir. Emmanuel Finkiel (Belgium, France, and Poland, 1999). [A]

Waiting for the Messiah, dir. Daniel Burman (Argentina, Italy, and Spain, 2000) [A].

A World Apart, dir. Chris Menges (United Kingdom and Zimbabwe, 1988) [A].

Wondrous Oblivion, dir. Paul Morrison (France, Germany, and the United Kingdom, 2003) [A].

Zalman: Or, the Madness of God, dir. Peter Levin and Alan Scheider (United States, 1975) [A].

Part IX. Contemporary Israeli Experiences

The Barbecue People, dir. Yossi Madmoni and David Ofek (Israel, 2003) [A].

Beaufort, dir. Joseph Cedar (Israel, 2007) [A].

The Bubble, dir. Eytan Fox (Israel, 2006) [A].

Campfire, dir. Joseph Cedar (Israel, 2004) [A].

Close to Home, dir. Vidu Bilu and Dalia Hager (Israel, 2005) [A].

Cup Final, dir. Eran Riklis (Israel, 1992) [A].

Double Edge, dir. Amos Kollek (Israel, the United States, 1992) [A].

Fictitious Marriage, dir. Haim Bouzaglo (Israel, 1988) [EM].

Free Zone, dir. Amos Gitai (Belgium, France, Israel, and Spain, 2005) [A].

Hamsin, dir, Daniel Wachsmann (Israel, 1982) [EM].

Holy Land, dir. Eitan Gorlin (Israel, 2003) [A].

James' Journey to Jerusalem, dir. Ra'anan Alexandrowicz (Israel, 2003).

Lebanon, dir. Samuel Maoz (France, Germany, Israel, and Lebanon, 2009) [A].

The Lemon Tree, dir. Eran Riklis (France, Germany, and Israel, 2008) [A].

Life According to Agfa, dir. Assi Dayan (Israel, 1992) [A].

Metallic Blues, dir. Dan Verete (Canada, Germany, and Israel, 2004) [A].

My Father, My Lord, dir. David Volach (Israel, 2007) [A].

Nadia, dir. Amnon Rubinstein (Israel, 1986) [EM].

The Secrets, dir. Avi Nesher (France and Israel, 2007) [A].

Smile of the Lamb, dir. Shomon Dotan (Israel, 1986) [EM].

The Syrian Bride, dir. Eran Riklis (France, Germany, and Israel, 2004) [A].

Turn Left at the End of the World, dir. Avi Nesher (France and Israel, 2004) [A].

Walk on Water, dir. Eytan Fox (Israel and Sweden, 2004) [A].

Yossi and Jagger, dir. Eytan Fox (Israel, 2002) [A].

Part X. Contemporary American Jewish Identities

Amongst Friends, dir. Rob Weiss (United States, 1993) [A].

Angels in America, dir. Mike Nichols (United States, 2003) [A].

Arranged, dir. Stefan Schaefer and Diane Crespo (United States, 2007) [A].

Bee Season, dir. Scott McGehee and David Siegel (United States, 2005) [A].

Crimes and Misdemeanors, dir. Woody Allen (United States, 1989) [A].

Crown Heights, dir. Jeremy Kagan (United States, 2002) [A].

David and Layla, dir. Jan Jonroy (United States, 2002) [A].

Eyewitness, dir. Peter Yates (United States, 1981) [A].

The Hebrew Hammer, dir. Jonathan Kesselman (United States, 2003) [A].

Keeping Up with the Steins, dir. Scott Marshall (United States 2006) [A].

Kissing Jessica Stein, dir. Charles Herman-Wurmfeld (United States, 2002) [A].

Little Odessa, dir. James Gray (United States, 1994) [A].

Meet the Fockers, dir. Jay Roach (United States, 2004) [A].

The Memory Thief, dir. Gil Kofman (United States, 2007) [A].

Mendy: A Question of Faith, dir. Adam Vardy (United States, 2003) [A].

Pi, dir. Darren Aronofsky (United States, 1991) [A].

A Price above Rubies, dir. Boaz Yakin (United Kingdom and the United States, 1998) [A].

Private Benjamin, dir. Howard Zieff (United States, 1980) [A].

A Stranger among Us, dir. Sidney Lumet (United States, 1992) [A].

Then She Found Me, dir. Helen Hunt (United States, 2007) [A].

The Tollbooth, dir. Debra Kirschner (United States, 2007) [A].

Twilight of the Golds, dir. Ross Kagan Marks (United States, 1997) [www.amazon.com].

What's Cooking, dir. Gurinder Chadha (United Kingdom and the United States, 2000) [A].

You Don't Mess with the Zohan, dir. Dennis Dugan (United States, 2008) [A].

Contributor Biographies

Ilan Avisar is an associate professor in the Film and Television Department at Tel Aviv University. He is the author of several books and numerous articles, including *Screening the Holocaust: Cinema's Images of the Unimaginable*.

Lawrence Baron holds the Nasatir Chair in Modern Jewish History at San Diego State University. He authored *Projecting the Holocaust into the Present: The Changing Focus of Contemporary Holocaust Cinema*. He is the founder of the Western Jewish Studies Association.

Benjamin Ben-David teaches contemporary film theory at Tel Aviv University.

Nico Carpentier is a senior lecturer in the Department of Social Sciences, University of Loughborough, and an associate professor in the Department of Communication Studies, Vrije Universiteit Brussel. His research focuses on media, journalism, politics, and culture.

Steven Alan Carr is an associate professor and the graduate program director of communication at Indiana University–Purdue University, Fort Wayne. He authored *Hollywood and Anti-Semitism: A Cultural History up to World War II*.

Ellis Cashmore is the author of *Martin Scorsese's America*, *Tyson: Nurture of the Beast*, and *Celebrity/Culture*. He is currently a professor of culture, media, and sport at Staffordshire University.

Hasia Diner is the Steinberg Professor of American Jewish History at New York University, and she has joint appointments in the History Department and the Skirball Department of Hebrew and Judaic Studies. She is the director of the Goldstein Goren Center for American Jewish History.

Tamara L. Falicov is associate professor and department chair in Film and Media Studies at the University of Kansas, where she teaches courses about Latin American and Israeli cinema. She is the author of *The Cinematic Tango: Contemporary Argentine Film*.

Ariel L. Feldestein is an associate professor in the Culture Studies Department at Sapir College. His recent publications include *Ben-Gurion, Zionism and American Jewry* and *Pioneer, Toil, Camera: Cinema in Service of the Zionist Ideology, 1917–1939* [Hebrew].

Hannah Berliner Fischthal is an adjunct professor of English at St. John's University. She is a book review editor at *Studies in American Jewish Literature*. She is completing a book about Jews in eastern Upper Silesia during the Holocaust.

Sylvia Barack Fishman is the Foster Professor of Judaic Studies, chair of Brandeis University's Near Eastern and Judaic Studies Department, co-director of the Hadassah-Brandeis Institute, and author of *The Way into the Varieties of Jewishness*.

Jonathan C. Friedman is a professor of history and the director of the Holocaust and Genocide Studies Program at West Chester University. He is the author or editor of six books, having most recently edited *The Routledge History of the Holocaust*.

Shai Ginsburg is an assistant professor of Hebrew and Israeli studies at Duke University. He writes on Israeli literature, cinema, historiography, Zionist ideology and politics, and cultural and literary theory.

David I. Grossvogel is the Smith Professor Emeritus of Comparative Literature and Romance Studies at Cornell University. He founded the journal *Diacritics* and has authored many books, including *Scenes in the City: Film Visions of Manhattan before 9/11*.

Philip Hanson is an associate professor of interdisciplinary studies at the University of San Francisco. His first book, *This Side of Despair*, dealt with American film and literature during the Great Depression.

Scott Henderson is an associate professor of film and popular culture at Brock University. He teaches courses in British and Canadian popular culture, film, and music and in film theory.

J. Hoberman writes for *The Village Voice* and teaches cinema history at the Cooper Union for the Advancement of Science and Art. His books include the recently reissued *Bridge of Light: Yiddish Film between Two Worlds*. He is the coauthor (with Jeffrey Shandler) of *Entertaining America: Jews, Movies, and Broadcasting*.

Ruth D. Johnston is the director of the Film and Screen Studies Program and a professor of English at Pace University. She has written articles on the deconstruction of identity categories in hybrid narrative forms, including "Jewish Disappearing Acts and the Construction of Gender."

Eldad Kedem teaches Israeli cinema and contemporary American cinema at the Open University of Israel. His articles about the depiction of the kibbutz in Israeli films are available on the Internet.

Ira Konigsberg is a professor emeritus of film at the University of Michigan. He serves as the editor of *Projections: The Journal for Movies and Mind* and writes on the relationship between film and psychology.

Delia Caparoso Konzett is an assistant professor of English and of cinema, American, and women's studies at the University of New Hampshire. She is the author of *Ethnic Modernisms: Anzia Yezierska, Zora Neale Hurston, Jean Rhys, and the Aesthetics of Dislocation*.

Yvonne Kozlovsky Golan is the chair of the Graduate Program in Culture and Film Studies at the University of Haifa. She is the author of *The Death Penalty in American Cinema*.

David Kraemer is the Abbell Librarian at the Jewish Theological Seminary, where he serves as a professor of Talmud and rabbinics. He has authored many books, including *The Mind of the Talmud* and, most recently, *Jewish Eating and Identity through the Ages*.

Tony Kushner is the Marcus Sieff Professor in History and the director of the Parkes Institute for the Study of Jewish/Non-Jewish Relations at the University of Southampton. He is the author of seven monographs, the latest of which is *Anglo-Jewry since 1066*.

Giacomo Lichtner is a senior lecturer in history at Victoria University of Wellington. He is the author of *Film and the Shoah in France and Italy* and has published essays on the politics of history in European and Indian cinema.

Yosefa Loshitzky is a professor of film at the University of East London. Her books include *Screening Strangers, Identity Politics on the Israeli Screen,* and—as editor—*Spielberg's Holocaust: Critical Perspectives on Schindler's List.* Her latest book is *Screening Strangers: Migration and Diaspora in Contemporary European Cinema.*

Frank Manchel is a professor emeritus of English and film studies at the University of Vermont. He is the author of the four-volume *Film Study: An Analytical Bibliography,* as well as *Every Step a Struggle: Interviews with Seven Who Shaped the African-American Image in Movies.*

Millicent Marcus is a professor of Italian at Yale University. Her specializations include Italian cinema and medieval literature. She is the author of many books, including *After Fellini: National Cinema in the Postmodern Age* and *Italian Film in the Shadow of Auschwitz.*

Eliza R. L. McGraw is the author of *Two Covenants: Representations of Southern Jewishness.* She has contributed essays to the collections *Dixie Diaspora: An Anthology of Southern Jewish History* and *Jewish Roots in Southern Soil: A New History.*

Asher Z. Milbauer is a professor of English, the director of graduate studies in literature, and the director of the Exile Studies Program at Florida International University. He is the author of *Transcending Exile: Conrad, Nabokov, I. B. Singer* and the coeditor (with Donald G. Watson) of *Reading Philip Roth.*

Elena Monastireva-Ansdell is an assistant professor of Russian at Colby College. Her research interests include contemporary Russian cinema, Russian national mythology, and media constructions of ethnic relations.

Nigel Morris is a principal lecturer in media theory and the director of Film and Television BA at the University of Lincoln. His publications include *The Cinema of Steven Spielberg: Empire of Light.* His current research explores media representations of science and technology.

Pamela S. Nadell holds the Clendenen Chair in Women's and Gender History and is also a professor of history and Jewish studies at American University. Her books include *Women Who Would Be Rabbis: A History of Women's Ordination, 1889–1985.*

Yaron Peleg is the director of the Hebrew Program and associate professor of Hebrew literature and Israeli culture at George Washington University. He has authored three books, including *Israeli Culture between the Two Intifadas: A Brief Romance.*

Catherine Portuges is a professor of comparative literature and the director of the Interdepartmental Program in Film Studies at the University of Massachusetts, Amherst. Her most recent book is *Cinemas in Transition: Post-Communism in East-Central Europe.*

Riv-Ellen Prell is a professor of American studies at the University of Minnesota. Among her publications are *Fighting to Become Americans: Jews, Gender and the Anxiety of Assimilation* and *Women Remaking American Judaism.*

Elissa Rashkin is a researcher in cultural and communication studies at the Universidad Veracruzana and the author of *Women Filmmakers in Mexico: The Country of Which We Dream* and *The Stridentist Movement in Mexico: The Avant-Garde and Cultural Change in the 1920s.*

Alan Rosen is the author of *The Wonder of Their Voices: The 1946 Holocaust Interviews of David Boder* and *Sounds of Defiance: The Holocaust, Multilingualism, and the Problem of English.* He lectures regularly on Holocaust literature at Yad Vashem.

Joel Rosenberg is the McCollester Associate Professor of Biblical Studies and codirector of Tufts University's Program in Judaic Studies. He is the author of *King and Kin: Political Allegory in the Hebrew Bible.* He recently completed a study of Michal Waszyński's classic Yiddish film, *The Dybbuk*, and Paul Wegener's silent film, *The Golem.*

Michael W. Rubinoff teaches film and media studies along with Jewish studies at Arizona State University. His most recent publication is "Nuances and Subtleties in Jewish Film Humor," in *Jews and Humor.*

Maurice Samuels is a professor of French at Yale University. He is the author of *The Spectacular Past: Popular History and the Novel in Nineteenth-Century France* and *Inventing the Israelite: Jewish Fiction in Nineteenth-Century France.*

Norbert Samuelson holds the Harold and Jean Grossman Chair of Jewish Studies at Arizona State University. Four of his books—*The First Seven Days, Judaism and the Doctrine of Creation, Revelation and the God of Israel*, and *Jewish Faith and Modern Science*—deal with science and Judaism.

Jeffrey Saperstein is a professor of English at Radford University. He also is a poet, and his work has appeared in *The Deronda Review, The Sow's Ear Poetry Review*, and *Common Ground Review.*

Alyssa Goldstein Sepinwall is professor of history at California State University, San Marcos. She is the author of *The Abbé Grégoire and the French Revolution: The Making of Modern Universalism* and essays on French Jewry and French ideas about diversity.

Christopher Shorley was a senior lecturer in French studies at Queens University, in Belfast. His research interests included cinema, literature, and music. His last book, *A Time of Transition in the French Novel*, was published in 2006, a year before his death.

Zehavit Stern is the Idel and Isaac Haase Fellow in Eastern European Jewish Civilization at the University of Oxford. She received her Ph.D. in Jewish studies from the University of California, Berkeley, and the Graduate Theological Union.

Michael Stevenson, now retired, was a faculty member in the Film, Theatre, and Television Department of the University of Reading. He is the author of numerous articles on Polish cinema and the Holocaust.

Susan Rubin Suleiman is the Dillon Professor of the Civilization of France and a professor of comparative literature at Harvard University. Her most recent book is *Crises of Memory and the Second World War.*

Daphne Tsimhoni teaches modern Middle Eastern history at the Technion–Israel Institute of

Technology. She specializes in minorities in the modern Middle East. She has published numerous articles on the Jews of Iraq and Egypt and is the author of *Christian Communities in Jerusalem and the West Bank since 1948*.

Stephen J. Whitfield holds the Richter Chair in American Civilization at Brandeis University. He is the author of *In Search of American Jewish Culture* and seven other books, and the editor of *A Companion to Twentieth-Century America*.

Joellyn Wallen Zollman received her Ph.D. in Jewish history from Brandeis University and has taught Jewish history and religion at San Diego State University and the University of California-San Diego. She specializes in Jewish art and history and has worked with the Jewish material culture collections at the Smithsonian Institution, the Skirball Museum, and the American Jewish Historical Society.

Acknowledgments

Journals and publishers have granted permission to republish abridged or complete versions of the following articles or excerpts from the following books:

Avisar, Ilan. "Dancing Solo in the Lebanese Mud." *Azure* 36 (Spring 2009): 107–15. Published with permission as it originally appeared in *Azure*.

Baron, Lawrence. *Projecting the Holocaust into the Present: The Changing Focus of Contemporary Holocaust Cinema*. Lanham, MD: Rowman and Littlefield, 2005.

Carpentier, Nico. "From Individual Tragedy to Societal Dislocation: The Film Representation of Tragedy, Dislocation, and Cultural Trauma in the Dreyfus Affair." In *Culture, Trauma, and Conflict: Cultural Studies Perspectives on War*, edited by Nico Carpentier, 245–70. New Castle, UK: Cambridge Scholars, 2007.

Cashmore, Ellis. "*Chariots of Fire:* Bigotry, Manhood and Moral Certitude in an Age of Individualism." *Sport in Society* 11, nos. 2–3 (March–May 2008): 159–73. Permission granted by the Taylor and Francis Group.

Fischthal, Hannah Berliner. "Uncle Moses." In *When Joseph Met Molly: A Reader on Yiddish Film*, edited by Sylvia Paskin, 217–30. Nottingham, UK: Five Leaves, 1999.

Friedman, Jonathan. *Rainbow Jews: Jewish and Gay Identity in the Performing Arts*. Lanham, MD: Lexington Books, 2007.

Ginsburg, Shai. "Love in Search of Belief, Belief in Search of Love." *Tikkun* 21, no. 3 (2006): 75–76.

Grossvogel, David I. *Scenes in the City: Film Visions of Manhattan Before 9/11*. New York: Peter Lang, 2003.

Hanson, Philip. "Against Tribalism: The Perils of Ethnic Identity in Mamet's *Homicide*." *Clio* 31, no. 3 (2002): 257–79.

Henderson, Scott. "Ted Kotcheff: *The Apprenticeship of Duddy Kravitz*." In *Where Are the Voices Coming From? Canadian Culture and the Legacies of History*, edited by Coral Ann Howells, 247–58. New York: Rodopi, 2004. Revised by the author, 2010.

Hoberman, J. *Bridge of Light: Yiddish Film Between Two Worlds*. Updated and expanded ed. Hanover, NH: University Press of New England, 2010.

Johnston, Ruth D. "Ethnic and Discursive Drag in Woody Allen's *Zelig*." *Quarterly Review of Film and Video* 24, no. 3 (2007): 397–406. Taylor and Francis Group.

Konigsberg, Ira. "*Our Children* and the Limits of Cinema: Early Jewish Responses to the Holocaust." *Film Quarterly* 52, no. 1 (1998): 7–19. © Regents of the University of California. Published by the University of California Press.

Konzett, Delia Caparoso. "From Hollywood to Hester Street: Ghetto Film, Melodrama, and the Image of the Assimilated Jew in *Hungry Hearts*." *Journal of Film and Video* 50, no. 4 (1998–99): 18–34.

Kraemer, David. "Self-Criticism in Public." In Henry Bean, *The Believer: Confronting Jewish Self-Hatred*, 205–17. New York: Thunder's Mouth Press, 2002.

Kushner, Tony. "One of Us? Contesting Disraeli's Jewishness and Englishness in the Twentieth Century." In *Disraeli's Jewishness*, edited by Todd M. Endelman and Tony Kushner, 201–61. London: Vallentine Mitchell, 2002.

Lichtner, Giacomo. *Film and the Shoah in France and Italy*. London: Vallentine Mitchell, 2008.

Loshitzky, Yosefa. *Identity Politics on the Israeli Screen*. Austin: University of Texas Press, 2001. Courtesy of the University of Texas Press.

Manchel, Frank. "A Reel Witness: Steven Spielberg's Representation of the Holocaust in

Schindler's List." *Journal of Modern History* 67, no. 1 (1995): 83–100.

Marcus, Millicent. *After Fellini: National Cinema in the Postmodern Age*. Baltimore, MD: Johns Hopkins University Press, 2002. Reprinted with the permission of Johns Hopkins University Press.

McGraw, Eliza R. L. "*Driving Miss Daisy*: Southern Jewishness on the Big Screen. *Southern Cultures* 7, no. 2 (2001): 41–59. Courtesy of *Southern Cultures*: www.SouthernCultures.org.

Monastireva-Ansdell, Elena. "Redressing the Commissar: Thaw Cinema Revises Soviet Structuring Myths." *Russian Review* 65, no. 2 (2006): 230–49. John Wiley and Sons Ltd.

Morris, Nigel. *The Cinema of Steven Spielberg: Empire of Light*. London: Wallflower, 2007. Republished with permission of Wallflower Press.

Nadell, Pamela S. "Yentl: From Yeshiva Boy to Syndrome." In *New Essays in American Jewish History: Commemorating the Sixtieth Anniversary of the Founding of the American Jewish Archives*, edited by Pamela S. Nadell, Jonathan D. Sarna, and Lance J. Sussman, 467–83. Cincinnati, OH: American Jewish Archives, 2010.

Peleg, Yaron. "From Black to White: Changing Images of Mizrahim in Israeli Cinema." *Israel Studies* 12, no. 2 (2008): 122–44. Courtesy of Indiana University Press.

Rashkin, Elissa. *Women Filmmakers in Mexico: The Country of Which We Dream*. Austin: University of Texas Press, 2001.

Rosen, Alan. "Teach Me Gold: Pedagogy and Memory in *The Pawnbroker*." *Prooftexts* 22, nos. 1–2 (2002): 77–117. Courtesy of Indiana University Press.

Rosenberg, Joel. "What You Ain't Heard Yet: The Languages of *The Jazz Singer*." *Prooftexts* 22, nos. 1–2 (2002): 11–54. Courtesy of Indiana University Press.

Samuels, Maurice. "Renoir's *La Grande Illusion* and the 'Jewish Question.'" *Historical Reflections/*

Reflexions Historiques 32, no.1 (2006):165–92. Berghahn Journals.

Saperstein, Jeffrey. "'All Men Are Jews': Tragic Transcendence in Kadár's *The Shop on Main Street*." *Literature/Film Quarterly* 19, no. 4 (1991): 247–51. Reprinted with permission of *Literature/Film Quarterly*, Salisbury University, Salisbury, MD.

Shorley, Christopher. "History, Memory, and Art in Louis Malle's *Au revoir les enfants*." In *The Seeing Century: Film, Vision and Identity*, edited by Wendy Everett, 49–59. Amsterdam: Rodopi, 2000.

Stern, Zehavit. "Ghosts on the Silver Screen: The Challenge of Memory in the Film *Der Dybbuk*." In *Do Not Chase Me Away: New Studies on The Dybbuk*, edited by Shimon Levy and Dorit Yerushalmi, 98–119. Tel Aviv: Assaph Theater Studies and Safra, 2009.

Stevenson, Michael. "*The Pianist* and Its Contexts: Polanski's Narration of Holocaust Evasion and Survival." In *The Cinema of Roman Polanski: Dark Spaces of the World*, edited by John Orr and Elżbieta Ostrowska, 146–57. London: Wallflower, 2006.

Suleiman, Susan Rubin. "Jewish Assimilation in Hungary, the Holocaust, and Epic Film: Reflections on István Szabó's *Sunshine*." *Yale Journal of Criticism* 14, no.1 (2001): 232–52. © Yale University and The Johns Hopkins University Press. Reprinted with permission of The Johns Hopkins University Press.

Whifield, Stephen J. "Fiddling with Sholem Aleichem: A History of *Fiddler on the Roof*." In *Key Texts in American Jewish Culture*, edited by Jack Kugelmass, 105–25. New Brunswick, NJ: Rutgers University Press, 2003. Copyright © 2003 by Rutgers, the State University of New Jersey. Reprinted by permission of Rutgers University Press.

Index